Through a Speculum That Shines

Through a Speculum That Shines

VISION AND IMAGINATION IN MEDIEVAL JEWISH MYSTICISM

• *ELLIOT R. WOLFSON* •

PRINCETON UNIVERSITY PRESS

PRINCETON, NEW JERSEY

Published by Princeton University Press, 41 William Street, Princeton, New Jersey 08540
In the United Kingdom: Princeton University Press, Chichester, West Sussex

---

Library of Congress Cataloging-in-Publication Data

Wolfson, Elliot R.
Through a speculum that shines : vision and imagination in medieval
Jewish mysticism / Elliot R. Wolfson.
p. cm.
Includes bibliographical references and index.
ISBN 0-691-07343-0
ISBN 0-691-01722-0 (pbk.)
1. Cabala—History. 2. Mysticism—Judaism—History. 3. Visions.
4. Imagination—Religious aspects—Judaism. I. Title.
BM526.W65 1994
296.7'12'0902–dc20 94-18186 CIP

This book has been composed in Sabon Typeface

Princeton University Press books are printed on acid-free paper and meet the guidelines for permanence and durability of the Committee on Production Guidelines for Book Longevity of the Council on Library Resources

Second printing, and first paperback printing, 1997

http://pup.princeton.edu

Printed in the United States of America

3 5 7 9 10 8 6 4

• *FOR ELIZABETH* •

THE BOOK WITHIN THE BOOK

• CONTENTS •

• ACKNOWLEDGMENTS •

THE RESEARCH and writing of this book began in August 1986, when I arrived at Cornell University as a Post-Doctoral Andrew W. Mellon Fellow in the Humanities. From the beginning of my study of Jewish mystical literature I was fascinated with the emphasis on visionary experience against the backdrop of the supposedly official aniconism of Judaism. I suspected at a very early stage that one could write the history of Jewish mysticism from the particular vantage point of this problem. The theological tension between vision and invisibility provides the narrative context to articulate the esoteric dialectic of concealment and disclosure so characteristic of the various currents of Jewish mysticism. To see the God who is hidden—or, more precisely, the aspect of God that is hiddenness as such—is the destiny of the Jewish mystic, bestowed upon him by the name Israel, which, as some ancient authors playfully proposed, signifies the one who sees God. The ocularcentric preoccupation is the phenomenological expression of the dialectic that marks the way of Jewish esotericism. A true appreciation of Jewish mysticism therefore necessitated a sustained reflection on the problem of visualizing the divine in a religious culture ostensibly averse to iconic representation of the deity.

Like any scholarly endeavor, this one, too, has benefited from a community of colleagues and students, with whom I have discussed my ideas in many stimulating conversations. My colleagues in the Skirball Department of Hebrew and Judaic Studies, New York University, especially Professors Robert Chazan, Lawrence Schiffman, and Baruch Levine, have been most supportive these last seven years and to them I owe much gratitude. Research for parts of this book was funded by summer stipends from the Skirball Department in 1988 and 1989 and by a Presidential Fellowship in the spring semester of 1989 that released me from my teaching obligations.

In addition to my teaching responsibilities at New York University, I have also had the unique opportunity to teach graduate seminars in the Department of History at Columbia University and in the Jewish Theological Seminary of America. I have truly benefited from my contact with the different students, using the seminar room as a laboratory to test and refine my ideas at every opportunity. Although their names are not mentioned in the pages of this book, the many graduate students who have attended my seminars in the three institutions mentioned above have contributed greatly to the formulation of my ideas. The final draft of this work also bears the mark of my brief tenure as Regenstein Visiting Professor of Jewish Studies at the Divinity School of the University of Chicago, winter quarter 1992. I thank the faculty and students there for treating me with such warmth and for engaging me in intellectually challenging and provocative ways, always forcing me to convey the esoteric ideas of Jewish mysticism in categories pertinent to the history of religion.

The manuscript in its entirety was read by Professors Moshe Idel, of the

Hebrew University in Jerusalem, and Elliot Ginsburg, of the University of Michigan. Both made very useful comments and suggestions that have improved my work. Several other colleagues have been especially helpful and supportive these past years: Professors Marvin Fox, of Brandeis University (emeritus); Peter Schafer, of the Freie Universitat in Berlin; Ithamar Gruenwald, of Tel-Aviv University; Michael Fishbane, of the University of Chicago; Daniel Matt, of the Graduate Theological Union; Michael Stanislawski, of Columbia University; Steven Wasserstrom, of Reed College; David Stern, of University of Pennsylvania; Tsvi Blanchard, of The National Jewish Center for Learning and Leadership, New York; Michael Swartz, of Ohio State University; Arthur Green, of Brandeis University; Ronald Kiener, of Trinity College; and Hava Tirosh-Rothschild, of Indiana University. I cherish their friendship and collegiality.

A special word of thanks goes to the library staff at the Jewish Theological Seminary of America. The rich treasures of that unique institution have always been graciously put at my disposal. I have greatly benefited from having such immediate access to their wealth of manuscripts and rare books. In particular, Rabbi Jerry Schwarzbard has over the years facilitated my scholarly needs and requests, and to him I owe a special note of thanks.

I must also express a deep sense of gratitude to Ann Himmelberger Wald, the religion editor at Princeton University Press, for demonstrating a steadfast commitment to this book. Her firm but gentle editorial hand has vastly improved the manuscript. Many thanks are also due Chris Rohmann for the meticulous attention he gave this manuscript in the process of copyediting. Both style and content have been greatly enhanced by his efforts.

Parts of chapter 4 appeared in *Jewish History* 6 (1992) and the *Proceedings of the American Academy of Jewish Research* 57 (1991). Parts of chapter 5 are based on articles appearing in the proceedings of the conference "Mystik, Magie und Kabbala im Aschkenasischen Judentum" (Frankfurt 9–11 December 1991) and *The Jewish Quarterly Review* 84 (1993). Chapter 7 is a revised version of an article that appeared in *Religion* 18 (1988). I thank all the relevant publishers for permission to use this material.

This reckoning of gratitude would be incomplete if I did not mention my wife, Elizabeth, and our two children, Elijah Gabriel and Josiah Abraham. The burden of scholarship is great, but no one must bear it more stoically than the loved ones of a scholar. I am profoundly thankful for the love, devotion, understanding, and emotional support that my family has shown me, and I can only pray that this book will be received by them as a small token of my heartfelt appreciation.

Through a Speculum That Shines

"What I have received as my inheritance," he said, "is the hope for a book."
"Poisoned legacy! With each of my works, a little more of this hope fades away."

—*Edmond Jabès*

• INTRODUCTION •

"O Human Imagination O Divine Body"

—*William Blake*

JUDAISM, Christianity, and Islam, in varying degrees, have struggled with the question of the imaging of the divine, although only in the case of Christianity did such theoretical issues translate into a debate concerning actual iconic worship.[1] In traditional forms of Islam and Judaism no evidence exists for the use of icons in divine service, even if we know today that examples of representational religious art abound in both of these religions.[2] Despite overwhelming evidence for aniconism in Jewish texts and rituals, one must acknowledge, on the basis of archaeological remains from synagogues in Late Antiquity as well as illuminated manuscripts from the Middle Ages, that God was occasionally depicted in a Jewish setting. In the former instance it was in the form of a pagan deity, such as Helios, and in the latter it was in terms of a full form or isolated bodily limbs (e.g., an outstretched hand), connected to a particular biblical narrative. Still, there is no indication that these visible forms of God were used iconically as part of Jewish worship. It must be concluded, therefore, that the pictorial images of God served either a decorative or symbolic function, but not a cultic purpose. Yet, in the case of Judaism, as in Islam and Christianity to an extent, the problem of figuration or representation of God in mental images was discussed in philosophical and theological literature, more often than not couched in exegetical comments or scholastic debates concerning the proper interpretation of visions of the divine recorded in biblical prophecy. Moreover, this very problem informed the mystical literature of these different traditions, as the mystic visionary wrestled with the conflict of experiencing an almost tangible object of his or her vision, on the one hand, and with the stated normative belief that God in his true nature is incorporeal and hence invisible, on

Note: Citations of sources found in the bibliographies of primary and secondary sources are generally abbreviated, giving only the author's surname and the main title of the work. Facts of publication are given for sources not in the bibliographies.

[1] See Grabar, *Christian Iconography;* Pelikan, *Imago Dei;* Herrin, *The Formation of Christendom,* pp. 307–343. See also Barasch, *Icon.* On the centrality of visual images in religious discourse and practice, see Miles, *Image as Insight.*

[2] See Gutmann, "The 'Second Commandment' and the Image in Judaism," pp. 161–174; Prigent, *Le Judaisme et l'image;* Neusner, *Symbol and Theology in Early Judaism,* pp. 142–175; Schubert, "Jewish Pictorial Traditions in Early Christian Art," pp. 147–260; Allen, "Aniconism and Figural Representation in Islamic Art."

the other.[3] The perennial clash between the view that God is not susceptible to portrayal by images (the myth of aniconism) and the basic religious need to imagine the divine in figurative representation is captured in this statement by the art historian David Freedberg: "In order to grasp the divinity, man must figure it, and the only appropriate figure he knows is that of man himself, or a glorified image of him: enthroned, anointed, and crowned. All this, at any rate, for Greek and Judaeo-Christian culture, where man is the highest being and is himself the image of God."[4]

Precisely such a need lies at the heart of the mystical vision within the iconoclastic traditions of Judaism and Islam, and Christianity to an extent as well. If I may be allowed a generalization at the outset with respect to Judaism: the will to visualize God in images without succumbing to apophatism, on the one hand, or rejecting iconoclasm, on the other, is the ultimate challenge of the prophetic, apocalyptic, and mystical imagination as it expressed itself in a plethora of sources from Antiquity through the Middle Ages. It lies beyond the concern of this study to deal in a comprehensive manner with the issue of visualization of the divine in the biblical, apocalyptic, and rabbinic corpora, for a thorough study of any of these would require a separate volume. It is nevertheless necessary to remark at the outset that the tension between the iconic/visual and aniconic/aural representations of God found in these foundational documents of Judaism set the tone for subsequent visionary mystics. The problem of the visionary experience of God represents one of the major axes about which the wheel of Jewish mystical speculation in its various permutations turns. Indeed, literary evidence attests that the religious experience described in the different currents of Jewish mysticism from Late Antiquity through the Middle Ages is overwhelmingly visual.[5]

[3] A sensitive treatment of this problem can be found in Temple, *Icons and the Mystical Origins of Christianity.* Although I do not accept the author's theoretical framework with respect to the universal nature of mysticism within world religions, I believe his analysis of the role of icons in the formulation of Christian mysticism is persuasive.

[4] Freedberg, *The Power of Images,* p. 60.

[5] See Cohen, *The Shi'ur Qomah: Liturgy and Theurgy,* p. 105. Although the comments of Cohen only relate the biblical theophanies to the visual accounts in early Jewish mysticism, his remarks could be extended to the medieval sources as well. Interestingly enough, in that context Cohen refers to the "great mystic passages of the Bible." The use of the word "mystic" in relation to biblical texts represents a major departure from the general view taken by scholars who follow the lead of Gershom Scholem. See his *Major Trends in Jewish Mysticism,* pp. 6–7: "The fact is that nobody seriously thinks of applying the term *mysticism* to the classic manifestations of the great religions. It would be absurd to call Moses, the man of God, a mystic, or to apply this term to the Prophets, on the strength of their immediate religious experience." See also idem, *On the Kabbalah and Its Symbolism,* p. 9. For discussion of this axiom of Scholem's typological classification of Jewish mysticism, see Schweid, *Judaism and Mysticism According to Gershom Scholem,* pp. 57–58, 61–68. For an alternative approach that emphasizes the interplay of prophecy and mysticism, see Verman, *The Books of Contemplation,* pp. 5–8. Verman has likewise noted that the experiences of later Jewish mystics "were conditioned and influenced by the literary heritage" (p. 6). "So pervasive is this interfacing that it is virtually impossible to read a single page of any Jewish mystical text without coming upon a citation or allusion to a previous work, be it biblical or postbiblical" (p. 8).

While the experiences related by Jewish mystics may involve other senses, including most importantly hearing, there is little question that the sense of sight assumes a certain epistemic priority, reflecting and building on those scriptural passages that affirm the visual nature of revelatory experience.[6] Moreover, it seems clear, as will be pointed out in several places in this book, that the ocularcentrism of various Jewish mystical traditions, related to visionary passages in the Bible, is indicative of a phallomorphic culture, that is, the scopic mentality of Jewish mystics betrays an androcentric eroticism that places the externalized and representable form, the phallus, at the center of the visual encounter. Not only the object seen, however, but the eye itself corresponds to (or substitutes for) the penis. The mystic vision expressed in Jewish sources is fundamentally a phallic gaze.[7]

In order to prevent any misunderstanding on this point, let me state emphatically that I am not reducing the phenomenon of Jewish mysticism in any of its historical manifestations to the issue of visionary theophanies of God as they are expressed in the aforementioned sources. Rather, the claim being made here is that the tension of aniconism, on the one hand, and visualizing the deity, on the other, is an essential component of the relevant varieties of Jewish mystical speculation. Furthermore, these corpora provide the religious foundation for later accounts of visionary experience in Jewish philosophical and mystical texts. Whatever the "origins" of the different currents of mystical speculation in medieval Jewish society, it is self-evident that the earlier traditions colored the nature of visionary experience in the different stages of Jewish mysticism. Indeed, as I will argue at several points in the following pages, one cannot speak of mystical experience (of which vision is one specific type) divorced from some interpretative framework, and that framework is shaped by a particular religious tradition. The Jewish mystic, whether he is the anonymous *yored merkavah*, Eleazar of Worms, Abraham Abulafia, or Moses de León, sees the divine glory in a way that is distinctively Jewish and therefore not Christian, Muslim, Hindu, or Buddhist.

While I would avoid defining Jewish mysticism in any monolithic way, I would claim that my study sets out to reconfigure the physiognomy of this multidimensional and complex phenomenon: the religious texture of the var-

[6] The position I have articulated can be contrasted with that expressed by Scholem, who privileged the auditory dimension of revelation in general and the kabbalistic interpretation of revelation in particular. See Biale, *Gershom Scholem*, pp. 88, 92–94. In my view, it is the visual aspect of biblical revelation that informed subsequent mystical (including kabbalistic) hermeneutics. (See as well the viewpoint of Verman referred to in the previous note.) This is not to deny those passages in Scripture that emphasize the auditory over the visual, or even those that theoretically exclude the latter, but only to argue that it was the visionary texts that inspired later Jewish mystics and informed their own revelatory experiences.

[7] My thinking here reflects the insights and terminology of the French feminist philosopher and psychoanalyst Luce Irigaray, who has emphasized the link between ocularcentrism and phallocentrism in Western culture. See, for instance, *Speculum of the Other Woman*, pp. 47–48, 145–146, and *This Sex Which Is Not One*, pp. 25–26; also the analysis in Jay, *Downcast Eyes*, pp. 523–542. See also Eilberg-Schwartz, "The Problem of the Body for the People of the Book."

ious streams of mystical life within historical Judaism is in a central way colored by the concern of seeing the divine form as expressed in the foundational documents that make up the religious canon. Ironically enough, the lack of fixed iconic representation in ancient Israelite religion and subsequently in the diverse forms of Judaism from the period of the Second Temple onwards provided the ongoing context for visualization of divinity. Accordingly, I begin this book with a discussion of the problem of seeing God in the biblical, apocalyptic, and rabbinic sources from the classical period. My discussion is necessarily limited, and the principle of selectivity has been influenced, by my overall concern to illuminate the nature of visionary experience in various trends of medieval Jewish mysticism.

A full appreciation of the phenomenological parameters of religious experience within historical Judaism necessitates the appropriation of what the French anthropologist Gilbert Durand referred to as the "paradoxical valorization of imagination in iconoclastic Judaism." Such a paradox is clearly operative in the quest for mystical vision in the various periods of Jewish history. While a full-scale phenomenology of the imagination in the spiritual and intellectual cultures of Judaism in its various historical periods is a scholarly desideratum, my presentation here will be primarily concerned with the function of the symbolic imagination[8] as a vehicle for revelation of God and things divine in select medieval Jewish mystical texts. At the outset it should be noted that the characterization of the imagination will differ in the writers to be discussed in accordance with the different philosophic systems that influenced their respective thought. It is evident, as Hans Jonas astutely observed, that

> without an antecedent dogmatics there would be no valid mysticism. . . . Having an objective theory, the mystic goes beyond theory; he wants experience of and identity with the object; and he wants to be able to claim such an identity. Thus, in order that certain experiences may become possible and even conceivable . . . speculation must have set the framework, the way, and the goal—long before the subjectivity has learned to walk the way.[9]

That is to say, the mystic not only seeks to express his or her experience within an accepted theoretical framework, but it is the latter that informs and shapes the former. The point has been made more recently by Bernard McGinn:

> Mystical theology is not some form of epiphenomenon, a shell or covering that can be peeled off to reveal the "real" thing. The interactions between conscious acts and their symbolic and theoretical thematizations are much more complex than that. . . . Rather than being something added on to mystical experience, mystical theory in most cases precedes and guides the mystic's whole way of life. . . . Until

[8] The term is borrowed from Durand, *L'imagination symbolique.* My thinking has also been influenced by Durand's other writings, especially *Les structures anthropologiques de l'imaginaire,* as well as the work of C. G. Jung and P. Ricoeur (see discussion in chapter 3).

[9] Jonas, "Myth and Mysticism," pp. 328–329.

> recent years, overconcentration on the highly ambiguous notion of mystical experience has blocked careful analysis of the special hermeneutics of mystical texts.[10]

As a corrective to this scholarly imbalance, McGinn calls for the "recognition of the interdependence of experience and interpretation."[11] Given this dialectical relationship between theory and experience, it is impossible to apply one model to all the data and thereby reduce the different forms of mystical experience (or, more specifically, the mystical vision) to one typology. The Jewish mystics are no exception to the general hermeneutical principle that the visionary experience itself is shaped by (and not merely interpreted in light of) certain theoretical assumptions.

Even if we isolate the imagination as the instrumental faculty that facilitates the mystical vision in the case of the Jewish mystics, it is evident that the role accorded the imagination will not be the same in the different individuals or distinctive groups of mystics. For example, one mystic who will not be discussed in great detail, Abraham Abulafia, appropriated as his theoretical model the Maimonidean conception of prophecy, itself based on earlier Islamic philosophic sources (Alfarabi and Avicenna), and thus assigned a significant role to the imagination as the means by which the intellectual overflow is transformed into visual images and sounds. Although the imagination similarly plays a critical role in two other major trends of medieval Jewish mysticism that will be discussed in elaborate detail in this study—the Pietists of the Rhineland and the theosophic kabbalists of Provence and northern Spain in the twelfth and thirteenth centuries—the fact is that in these two instances the imagination assumes a different role from that found in the Abulafian tradition. The theoretical assumptions regarding the imagination in the Pietistic sources are not identical to those that inform the theosophic kabbalists. Needless to say, the imagination operative in the Hekhalot mysticism is of a different sort than any of the medieval traditions mentioned above.

Yet, in spite of the obvious differences, it is valid, in my view, to examine the varied sources from the shared vantage point of the imagination. The latter, to borrow the formulation of a recent author, is "neither an Argus of a thousand glances nor a Cyclops of one eye."[12] That is to say, the imagination is not whatever phenomenon we choose to name as such, nor is it a timeless essence that remains unchanged in various religious and cultural settings. Within the diversity of its applications there must be an "analogical relation of unity through resemblance."[13] If we do not assume unity through diversity, then the expression becomes meaningless.

My analysis of visionary experience in medieval Jewish mysticism thus ad-

[10] McGinn, *The Foundations of Mysticism*, p. xiv.

[11] Ibid.

[12] I have borrowed this formulation from Richard Kearney's description of the imagination in his *Wake of Imagination*, p. 16.

[13] Here again I have utilized Kearney's language.

heres to a contextualist approach but nonetheless assumes a foundation for the phenomenology of mystical experience that is to be located in the symbolic imagination, that is, the divine element of the soul that enables one to gain access to the realm of incorporeality by transferring or transmuting sensory data and/or rational concepts into symbols. In that regard the primary function of the imagination may be viewed as hermeneutical. Through the images within the heart, the locus of the imagination, the divine, whose pure essence is incompatible with all form, is nevertheless manifest in a form belonging to the "Imaginative Presence," to borrow a technical term employed by Henry Corbin in his description of the thirteenth-century Sufi Ibn ʿArabī.[14] The paradox that the *deus absconditus* appears to human beings in multiple forms, including, most significantly, that of an anthropos, is the enduring legacy of the prophetic tradition that has informed and challenged Judaism throughout the ages. Moreover, the role of the imaginal, to employ Corbin's terminology once again,[15] serving as a symbolic intermediary allowing for the imaging of the imageless God, is a tradition that has its roots in the biblical and rabbinic texts, although it is developed and articulated most fully in the medieval mystical literature.

The prophetic tradition, epitomized in Hosea 12:11, that God can be represented in images served as an exegetical basis for certain mythic ideas that evolved in the aggadah from the formative period of rabbinic Judaism. The most significant of these is that God assumed "incarnational forms" (the terms used in the midrashic, liturgical, and medieval philosophical and mystical texts are *demuyot, dimmuyot, dimyonot* and *dimyonim*) at critical moments in Israel's sacred history: at the splitting of the Red Sea he is said to have appeared as a young warrior and at Sinai as a merciful elder; he is sometimes further depicted as a scribe teaching Torah.

The polymorphous nature of God articulated in the aggadic tradition, which bears a striking resemblance to the docetic orientation found in several Christian Apocryphal and Gnostic texts of the third and fourth centuries,[16] is developed at length in the medieval mystical literature, enhanced by the theoretical assumptions of various authors in the tenth to twelfth centuries writing on the nature of the divine glory and prophetic-mystical revelation. The theophanic imaging of God affirmed by the German Pietists and Provençal-Spanish kabbalists should be seen as continuous both with the aggadic motifs, which are themselves exegetical elaborations of the prophetic tradition of Scripture linked specifically to visualization of divine forms, and the docetic reinterpretation of Hekhalot visions influenced in some cases by a Neoplatonic epistemology. It will also be shown, in chapter 4, that a theosophic interpretation of the double doctrine of the glory, central to German Pietism and theosophic kabbalah as they evolved in the twelfth and thirteenth centuries, was already present two centuries earlier. Particularly relevant is the thought of the tenth-century south-

[14] *Creative Imagination in the Sūfism of Ibn ʿArabī*, pp. 188, 218.

[15] Ibid., pp. 179–195, 216–220.

[16] Stroumsa, "Polymorphie divine et transformations d'un mythologème."

ern Italian philosopher and scientist Shabbetai Donnolo, who preserved a theosophic reading of the ancient work of Jewish esotericism, *Sefer Yeṣirah,* interpreting the critical term *sefirot* as a reference to the visible power of the invisible form of the divine. In this case, too, we come upon a major anticipation of a key turn in the later mystical theosophies of both the German Pietists and the Provençal-Spanish kabbalists. I have included this chapter for two reasons: first, it provides the conceptual framework most proximate to the mystical sources discussed in detail in the heart of the book (chapters 5 to 7), and, secondly, a reevaluation of these sources demonstrates how much of what was later articulated in writings characterized by scholars as mystical is already present in these works. Indeed, these philosophical sources provide the ideational basis for isolating the faculty of imagination as the locus of the mystical envisioning of the glory. The recontextualization of older prophetic and mystical traditions regarding the visualization of the divine form within the philosophic framework found in these sources provides an essential link in the development of mystical theosophies in the High Middle Ages.

This book, then, is an attempt to treat in a comprehensive manner the problem of visionary experience in some of the main texts of the classical period of medieval Jewish mysticism. I have isolated the problem of vision and visualization since this constitutes one of the essential phenomenological concerns in the various mystical corpora produced by Jewish authors throughout history. I make no claim that mysticism is identical to or collapsable into the phenomenon of vision. I do, however, maintain that the examination of this issue provides an excellent speculum through which to view the religious experience of different Jewish mystics.

While the major focus of this book, from a chronological perspective, is the High Middle Ages, principally the twelfth and thirteenth centuries (chapters 5 to 7), in chapter 3 I discuss the nature of the vision of the glory in the ancient Jewish mystical corpus known as the Hekhalot or Merkavah literature. The justification for including this chapter is both historical-textual and phenomenological. From the former standpoint, this material in all likelihood took shape in the post-talmudic (sixth-seventh century) or even Geonic (ninth-tenth century) periods, thus qualifying it as a medieval phenomenon. Although the roots of this form of mystical speculation, and indeed some components of the texts themselves, are clearly much older, perhaps stretching back into Late Antiquity, the corpus as a whole justifiably should be classified as medieval and thus ought to be treated in a study of visionary experience in medieval Jewish mysticism. (In some cases the redactional hand of later copyists, e.g., the German Pietists of the twelfth and thirteenth centuries, is clearly discernible.)

From a phenomenological perspective as well, it is obvious that the Hekhalot corpus is an intrinsic part of such a study, insofar as the vision of the glory and the chariot served as the paradigm for visionary experience in later Jewish mystics, influenced in particular, as I have already intimated, by the philosophical reinterpretations of this religious experience, as will be discussed in chapter 4. To be sure, in the twelfth and thirteenth centuries the various "trends" of Jewish mysticism took shape in such a way that the chariot vision is hermeneutically transformed. It is nevertheless the case that the major mystical ideologies of the period to be discussed in this monograph, the German Pietists and the Provencal-Spanish kabbalists of the theosophic trend, orient themselves in terms of the vision of the chariot. In that sense we can speak of these schools as hermeneutical transformations of the Hekhalot mysticism. This reorientation is true to a certain extent for the ecstatic trend of thirteenth-century kabbalah as well.

Although Abulafia is clearly an important mystic, I have chosen not to discuss him at length in this book because I wish to focus on several theosophic trends whose visionary component has been less appreciated. The omission of the prophetic-ecstatic kabbalah of Abulafia makes no statement regarding his central importance either in the history of Jewish mysticism in general or with respect to this issue in particular. It should be noted, however, that despite the presence of visual elements in Abulafia's mystical system he clearly privileged the verbal aspect of prophecy. Indeed, in one passage in his epistle to Judah Salmon, written in Sicily and sent to Barcelona in the latter part of the 1280s, he explicitly contrasts theosophic kabbalah with ecstatic kabbalah on the grounds that the prophetic experience in the former is purely visual, whereas in the latter there is both a visual and a verbal dimension. It is the verbal aspect that renders ecstatic kabbalah superior inasmuch as it leads to true prophecy.[17]

In a second text, an epistle that Abulafia sent to a certain R. Abraham (perhaps R. Abraham ben Shalom of Palermo), he specified that the "true cause" of the essence of prophecy (*mahut ha-nevu'ah*) consists of the "speech that reaches the prophets from God through the perfect language that comprises seventy languages, the holy language that alone is comprised in twenty-two holy letters."[18] This passage underscores again that for Abulafia the auditory and not the visual is the most critical epistemic mode of prophecy. I have therefore limited my discussion to the mystical theosophies that give preference to the visual pole of the experience.

Let me conclude this introduction by stating clearly that this monograph is not a textbook that seeks to provide an overview of all possible relevant material, nor does it claim to exhaust the subject of visionary experience of God in medieval Jewish mysticism. It is rather an attempt to reflect on the visionary components of certain mystical authors in order to demonstrate that this issue

[17] See Idel, *The Mystical Experience in Abraham Abulafia*, pp. 77–78, and my discussion in chapter 6. On the privileging of the auditory, see Abulafia, *Sefer ha-Ḥesheq*, MS New York–JTSA Mic. 1801, fol. 35b. Also telling in this context is the comment of Abulafia in *Sitre Torah*, MS Paris–BN 774, fol. 129b, where the Active Intellect (*sekhel ha-po'el*) is numerically equated with the expression "he sees but is not seen" (*hu ro'eh we-'eino nir'eh*), i.e., both equal 541. Inasmuch as the Active Intellect is usually the pole of the visual experience for Abulafia, personified in the form of Meṭaṭron, this statement is quite important. That is, what is generally designated as the object of vision here is especially characterized as that which is not seen. See also the fragment of Abulafia's *Sefer ha-Melammed* in MS Paris–BN 680, fol. 289a. On the identification of this text, see Idel, "The Writings of R. Abraham Abulafia and His Teaching" pp. 15–16.

[18] Jellinek, *Philosophie und Kabbala*, pp. 8–9.

lies at the phenomenological core of mystical experience in the different theosophic systems to be discussed. The last chapter of the book, and the chronological endpoint of this study, deals with the problem of vision in the major source of thirteenth-century theosophic kabbalah, the *Zohar,* an anthology of texts composed in Castile in the latter part of that century. Ending with the zoharic text is justified both historically and phenomenologically. It represents the crystallization of theosophic speculation and a concerted attempt to express the system in a normative key that would have wide appeal in the Jewish community. Secondly, the convergence of interpretation and revelation that one finds expressed in the *Zohar* brings the analysis of the symbolic imagination full circle. The imaging of the formless God in iconic forms is related in the *Zohar* to the hermeneutical act of reading. To see God is to read the sacred text of Torah, which is the embodiment of God. There is no corporeality without textuality and no textuality without corporeality. The gap between revelation and interpretation is fully closed, inasmuch as interpreting Scripture is itself a revelatory experience.

• CHAPTER ONE •

"Israel: The One Who Sees God"—Visualization of God in Biblical, Apocalyptic, and Rabbinic Sources

Auditory vs. Visual Modes

One of the seminal problems in theology and religious philosophy is the possibility of a visionary experience of God. In the case of Jewish studies an analysis of this problem gains added significance, since it has been common for scholars to characterize Hebraic thought—especially in contrast to Greek thought—as essentially auditory and nonvisual in its orientation. The classical formulation of this distinction between the visual orientation of ancient Greek (pagan) culture and the auditory orientation of ancient Israelite (monotheistic) culture was given by the German Jewish historian Heinrich Graetz in the nineteenth century.[1] This distinction has been more systematically treated in this century by Thorlief Boman[2] and has been widely repeated by many scholars from various disciplines.[3] Two of the more recent exponents of this claim are Susan Handelman and José Faur, writers who have both attempted to apply the techniques and categories of contemporary literary criticism to rabbinic thought. Handelman writes, "Whereas for Jews, God manifested Himself through words in a divine text, for the Greeks theophany was visual, not verbal—a direct, immediate experience of the gods."[4] Faur, for his part, expresses the same view as follows:

> The Hebrew and Greek types of truth correspond to two different levels of reality. The Greek truth is visual. Therefore it is related to the spatial World-Out-There. For the Hebrews the highest form of truth is perceived at the auditory level . . . . Verbal representation of God, even in anthropomorphic terms, is common both to Scripture and to the rabbis. What was offensive to the Hebrew was 'to see' God; that is, to express His reality at the visual level.[5]

[1] See Graetz, *The Structure of Jewish History,* p. 68.

[2] Boman, *Hebrew Thought Compared with Greek,* pp. 68ff. and esp. 206–207.

[3] See, e.g., Auerbach, *Mimesis,* pp. 8–9; Ong, *The Presence of the Word,* pp. 179ff.; Wilder, *Early Christian Rhetoric,* pp. 10–11; M. Buber, *Darkho shel ha-Miqra* (Jerusalem, 1978), pp. 41–58; Chidester, "Word against Light"; also the expanded discussion in idem, *Word and Light,* pp. 1–50. See also R. David ha-Cohen, *Qol ha-Nevu'ah* (Jerusalem, 1970), which is based entirely on this proposition. On the thesis of an inherent lack of visual talent amongst the Jews, see H. Howarth, "Jewish Art and the Fear of Images," *Commentary* 9 (1950): 142–150.

[4] *The Slayers of Moses,* p. 33.

[5] *Golden Doves with Silver Dots,* pp. 29–30.

There can be no doubt that the view that became normative in the history of Judaism is one that favored auditory over visual images. With very few exceptions Jews shunned the graphic representation of God, preferring language as the appropriate means to describe and characterize the divine nature. Even in the ancient world many outsiders were struck by the conspicuous fact that, especially in the area of worship, Judaism is a religion without images.[6] While the epistemic privileging of hearing over seeing in relation to God is attested in various biblical writers, including many of the classical prophets, the aversion to iconic representation of the deity can be traced most particularly to the Deuteronomist author who stressed that the essential and exclusive medium of revelation was the divine voice and not a visible form.[7] The Deuteronomist used this fact to support the commandment against making graven images,[8] a commandment found in the Decalogue[9] without any connection, however, to the theological claim that the Sinaitic theophany was strictly a matter of hearing and not seeing. Whatever the "original" rationale for the prohibition on the iconic representation of God in ancient Israelite culture, whether theological or socio-political,[10] it seems likely that the Deuteronomist restriction on the visualization of God is a later interpretation of an already existing proscription.

The underlying conceptual assumption here is clear enough: God possesses no visible form and therefore cannot be worshiped through created images. While the figural representation of the deity is deemed offensive or even blasphemous, the hearing of a voice is an acceptable form of anthropomorphic representation, for, phenomenologically speaking, the voice does not necessarily imply an externalized concrete shape that is bound by specific spatial dimensions.

The philosopher and critic Jacques Derrida has articulated, in an early work, the epistemological basis for the preference of auditory to visual forms—a preference, I might add, that represents an essential reversion of the dominant ocu-

[6] See Strabo, *Geographica* 16.2.35, in M. Stern, *Greek and Latin Authors on Jews and Judaism* (Jerusalem, 1976), 1:299–300; and see p. 305 n. 35.

[7] Cf. Deut. 4:12, 15. See also Gutmann, "Deuteronomy."

[8] Deut. 4:16–19. See the pertinent remarks of Fishbane, *Biblical Interpretation in Ancient Israel,* p. 322 n. 19.

[9] Cf. Exod. 20:4, Deut. 5:8. See also the introductory remarks in the "Book of the Covenant" in Exod. 20:19–20, where the fact that YHWH speaks from heaven is offered as a rationale for the prohibition against making gods of gold and silver. This comment does not yet advance the Deuteronomic position that clearly links the prohibition of graven images to the fact that no visible form of God was seen. On the prohibition on depicting the deity in images, see also Exod. 34:17, Deut. 27:15.

[10] See Childs, *The Book of Exodus,* pp. 405–408; Hendel, "The Social Origins of the Aniconic Tradition in Early Israel"; Barasch, *Icon,* pp. 13–22. And see Eilberg-Schwartz, "The Problem of the Body for the People of the Book," pp. 27–35; he proposes a connection between the prohibition against iconic representation of God in material or bodily form and Israel's ambivalence toward the question of the gender and sexuality of the deity. Also relevant in this connection are the observations of Luce Irigaray in "Questions to Emmanuel Levinas: On the Divinity of Love," trans. M. Whitford, in *Re-Reading Levinas,* ed. R. Bernasconi and S. Critchley (Bloomington, 1991), esp. pp. 116–117.

larcentric trend in Western thinking.[11] Derrida writes that the phonic signs, or the voices that are heard,[12] "can only be expressed in an element whose phenomenality does not have worldly form."[13] The *phōnē* has a certain primacy and immediate presence in consciousness, for that which is heard, in contrast to the nonphonic (visual) signifier, transforms "the worldly opacity of its body into pure diaphaneity. This effacement of the sensible body and its exteriority is for consciousness the very form of the immediate presence of the signified."[14] Derrida's point is that for things that are heard, the exteriority of the phenomenon, its sense of being "outside" one's consciousness in bodily form, is reduced. The voice admits no spatial reference in the external world and is therefore presumed to be immediately present. The application of Derrida's comments is very helpful in understanding the ancient preference reflected in the Deuteronomic author: it is appropriate to speak of a voice of God rather than a visible form because the former implies a sense of phenomenological immediacy without necessitating spatial or worldly exteriority. Hence, representing God anthropomorphically in auditory imagery is not theologically offensive, for that mode of representation does not violate the basic principle of God's irreducible otherness. Indeed, it is alone the speech of God that bridges the gap separating humanity and the divine. Thus one finds a verbal/auditory emphasis affirmed in many prophetic revelations that conform to the Deuteronomic restriction on iconic representation yet preserve the lived immediacy of biblical religion. The logic entailed by this line of thinking is clearly drawn by the German Jewish philosopher Franz Rosenzweig: "The ways of God are different from the ways of man, but the word of God and the word of man are the same. What man hears in his heart as his own human speech is the very word which comes out of God's mouth."[15] Only by virtue of language can one speak of any resemblance linking humanity and God, and on account of that resemblance one can continue to speak in a religiously significant and vital way of God's mouth and the word that comes therefrom. Anthropomorphic expression can be appropriated as a meaningful mode of discourse if it is circumscribed within

[11] On the ocularcentrism in Western culture, see Jonas, "The Nobility of Sight." See also the collection of essays in Levin, *Modernity and the Hegemony of Vision;* Jay, *Downcast Eyes,* pp. 21–82.

[12] The original French reads *entendus,* which implies both "heard" and "understood."

[13] *Speech and Phenomena,* p. 76.

[14] Ibid., p. 77. See, however, Chidester (*Word and Light,* pp. 12–13), who explains Derrida's insistence on difference and absence in verbal communication—spoken or written—in terms of the distinction between the immediate and continuous presence of visual communication, on one hand, and the mediate, indirect, discontinuous nature of verbal communication, on the other. As the author demonstrates, the characterization of visual perception as immediate and verbal (auditory) as mediate is quite widespread in Western philosophy; hence the approach I have taken with respect to the biblical materials represents a significant departure.

[15] *The Star of Redemption,* trans. W. W. Hallo (New York, 1970), p. 151. Cf. N. N. Glatzer, "The Concept of Language in Rosenzweig's Thought," in *The Philosophy of Franz Rosenzweig,* ed. P. Mendes-Flohr (Hanover, 1988), pp. 172–178, esp. 176; Y. Kornberg Greenberg, "A Jewish Postmodern Critique of Rosenzweig's Speech Thinking and the Conception of Revelation," *Journal of Jewish Thought and Philosophy* 2 no. 1 (1992): 63–76, esp. 68–70.

a linguistic field.[16] That one has heard the voice of God is not nearly as crude an anthropomorphism as the claim that one has seen, let alone kissed, the mouth of God.[17]

Anthropomorphism, Theomorphism, and the Visibility of God

Other biblical writers took for granted the possibility of the manifestation of God in one visible form or another, even though no archaeological evidence has surfaced to indicate that these visualizations resulted in the production of material images.[18] The personalist element in biblical thinking, as in other theistic religions, remains, as R. J. Zwi Werblowsky has aptly put it, "an irreducible anthropomorphism."[19] "The ultimate residual anthropomorphism . . . is the theistic notion of God as personal, in contrast to an impersonal conception of the divine."[20] Moreover, this conception of personhood endows the biblical God with a human form that can be, and in fact is, manifest in specifically visual terms. Indeed, it has been argued that the manifestations of God in the biblical period primarily took the form of anthropomorphic theophanies—that is, YHWH was seen almost exclusively in the form of an anthropos.[21]

[16] It must be noted that Rosenzweig accorded legitimacy to anthropomorphisms from another perspective, viz., anthropomorphic characterizations do not describe God's essence but rather the encounter or relation between God and human. Cf. Rosenzweig, *Kleinere Schriften* (Berlin, 1937), pp. 167–181, and see B. Galli, "Rosenzweig Speaking of Meetings and Monotheism in Biblical Anthropomorphisms," *Journal of Jewish Thought and Philosophy* 2 no. 2 (1993): 219–243. See also S. Mosès, *System and Revelation: The Philosophy of Franz Rosenzweig,* trans. C. Tihanyi (Detroit, 1992), pp. 283–286; Mosès notes that the need for anthropomorphism is expressed in Rosenzweig especially in relation to the vision of the divine face through a human face, an idea that resonates with classical theosophic kabbalah. For the possible affinity of Rosenzweig's approach to kabbalistic sources, see M. Idel, "Franz Rosenzweig and the Kabbalah," in *The Philosophy of Franz Rosenzweig,* pp. 162–171.

[17] One could, of course, argue, as Henri Atlan put it, that the theistic fight against idolatry entails the paradoxical situation that the only discourse about God that is not idolatrous—i.e., does not turn the divine into a fixed object—is atheistic discourse: a radical denial of all God-talk. See "Niveau de signification et athéisme de l'écriture," p. 86. This is a contemporary affirmation of the negative theology espoused by medieval thinkers such as Maimonides, for whom both language and image were idolatrous insofar as both turned God into a representable form. See recent discussion in Halbertal and Margalit, *Idolatry,* pp. 37–66.

[18] This is not to deny the evidence the Bible itself supplies (confirmed by archaeological discoveries) regarding the ritualistic use of icons in ancient Israel, whether within the spatial confines of the Jerusalem Temple or in altars outside it. These iconic images reflect the syncretism of Israelite Yahwism and Canaanite religion. There is no evidence, however, that these syncretistic practices led to the iconic representation of the God of Israel, YHWH, as part of any official cultic worship. See Fishbane, *The Garments of Torah,* pp. 49–63, esp. 55–58.

[19] "Anthropomorphism," in *Encyclopedia of Religion* (New York, 1987), 1:318.

[20] Ibid., p. 317.

[21] See Exod. 24:10; 1 Kings 22:19; Isa. 6:1; Ezek. 1:26; Dan. 7:9. See Barr, "Theophany and Anthropomorphism in the Old Testament," pp. 32–33; Cherbonnier, "The Logic of Biblical Anthropomorphism." Eichrodt, in *Theology of the Old Testament,* 1:16–22, argues that, according to the ancient Israelite view, divine manifestation primarily takes the form of either nature or

The anthropomorphic manifestation of the divine in ancient Israelite culture is connected with another major theme in the Hebrew Bible: the concern with the presence of God and his nearness.[22] This concern was expressed cultically in terms of the Temple in Jerusalem that served as the set residence of the God of Israel. Indeed, it seems that the two cherubim, carved of wood and plated with gold, that stood in the *devir* (the Holy of Holies) of Solomon's Temple served as the *cathedra,* the special throne for the invisible God,[23] as the Ark of the Covenant of the Lord (*'aron berit YHWH*), described especially in Deuteronomic and Priestly writers, itself represented the palace-shrine of YHWH. Hence we find the technical expression *yoshev ha-keruvim* (see 1 Sam. 4:4; 2 Sam. 6:2; 2 Kings 19:15; Isa. 37:16; Ps. 80:1, 99:1), clearly signifying that the deity is enthroned upon the cherubim in the Temple. That the cherubim symbolize the throne is also attested by the explicit reference to them as the chariot (see 1 Chron. 28:18; Sirach 49:8). Analogously, according to the Priestly account of the Tabernacle in the desert, there were two cherubim on the ark-cover (*kapporet*). From a comparison of the two narratives scholars have concluded that these cherubim also symbolize the throne of God.[24] Furthermore, it is assumed by scholars that the cherubim-throne is an "empty seat," for the deity is present but not visualized. The conception implied here, of an invisibly present God, is "at once both aniconic and anthropomorphic."[25] As Menahem Haran has concluded, we have here a set of symbols—throne, footstool, House of God, all rooted in pre-biblical mythological culture—combined with a concept of God that is decidedly non-mythological.[26] The fact of the matter, however, is that there is sufficient textual evidence from the biblical canon to demonstrate that the enthroned Presence of God in the Temple often took the form of visual images and was not restricted to the auditory realm.[27] Thus it was

humanity. A similar claim can be made with respect to theophanies of the ancient Greek gods; see Fox, *Pagans and Christians,* p. 106: "There was no end to the gods' human disguises, as old men and women, heralds and, frequently, young and beautiful people. . . . Essentially anthropomorphic, the gods stalked the world as mortals, disguising themselves so well that people could never be totally sure that a stranger was all that he seemed." On the phenomenon of seeing God in Hebrew Scripture, see Baudissin's comprehensive study "'Gott schauen' in der alttestamentlichen Religion." See also Terrien, *The Elusive Presence,* pp. 63–105, 227–277.

[22] The bibliography on this theme is quite extensive; I will cite only a few exemplary studies: see Haran, "The Divine Presence in the Israelite Cult and the Cultic Institutions"; Lindblom, "Theophanies in Holy Places in Hebrew Religion"; Levine, *In the Presence of the Lord;* Weinfeld, *Deuteronomy and the Deuteronomic School,* pp. 191–209.

[23] See Haran, "The Ark and the Cherubim"; idem, *Temples and Temple-Service in Ancient Israel,* pp. 247–259.

[24] See Haran, "Ark and the Cherubim," pp. 33ff.; Tarragen, "La Kapporet est-elle une fiction ou un élément du culte tardif?" and references on pp. 10–11 n. 16.

[25] Mettinger, *The Dethronement of Sabaoth,* p. 37. See also Haran's formulation in *Temples and Temple-Service,* p. 246.

[26] "Ark and the Cherubim," p. 92.

[27] See Isa. 6:1; Amos 9:1; Ps. 11:4–7, 27:4, 42:3, 63:3, 84:8; Exod. 23:17, 34:23–24; Deut. 16:16, 31:11. In the case of Ps. 42:3 it is likely that there is a change from the original *qal* form *'ereh,* "I will behold," to the masoretic vocalization in the niphal *'era'eh,* "I will be seen." See

especially in the Temple, the *hagios topos,* that one beheld God's countenance.[28]

We come, then, to the fundamental paradox: there was no fixed iconic representation of the deity upon the throne, but it was precisely this institution that provided the context for visualization of the divine Presence.[29] This basic insight was understood by the phenomenologist Gerardus van der Leeuw, who wrote, "The ark of Jahveh, for instance, was an empty throne of God. . . . This of course does not involve any 'purely spiritual' worship of God, but merely that the deity should assume his place on the empty throne at his epiphany."[30] Moreover, the cultic image of the enthroned God in the earthly Temple yielded the genre of a "throne vision" or "throne theophany" (i.e., the visionary experience of God in human form seated on the heavenly throne in the celestial Palace),[31] which became especially important in the Jewish apocalyptic[32] and

---

Gunkel, *Die Psalmen,* s.v. Ps. 42:3. It is likely, moreover, that a similar change occurred at the hand of editors in Ps. 84:8, where the first word in the masoretic reading *yera'eh 'el 'elohim be-ṣiyyon,* "appearing before God in Zion," probably was originally *yir'eh,* "seeing." See M. Buttenwieser, *The Psalms* (New York, 1969), pp. 774–776. Other verses in which a change from the active to the passive, in an effort to attentuate the possibility of seeing God, is suspected are Exod. 23:15, 17, 34:20; Deut. 31:11; 1 Sam. 1:22; Isa. 1:12. See Baudissin, "Gott schauen," pp. 181–185. See also R. Sollamo, in *Renderings of the Hebrew Semiprepositions in the Septuagint* (Helsinki, 1979), p. 118, where he suggests that the Greek translators "understood the phrase 'to see God's face' as a metaphor meaning 'to appear before God.'"

[28] See Baudissin, "Gott schauen," pp. 175–178, 202–207; G. R. Berry, "The Glory of Yahweh and the Temple," *Journal of Biblical Literature* 56 (1937): 115–117; Terrien, *Elusive Presence,* pp. 161–226, 278–349; Levenson, "The Jerusalem Temple in Devotional and Visionary Experience"; Uffenheimer, "The Religious Experience of the Psalmists and the Prophetic Mind"; Smith, "'Seeing God' in the Psalms." See, however, Gruenwald, "Priests, Prophets, Apocalyptic Visionaries, and Mystics," in his *From Apocalypticism to Gnosticism,* pp. 135–136, where he expresses the view that most of the prophets "rarely prophesied in the temple or saw visions there," a fact related to a "self-imposed separation of Prophecy from the temple." See idem, "The Impact of Priestly Traditions on the Creation of Merkabah Mysticism and the Shiur Komah," pp. 72–74. On the other hand, Gruenwald acknowledges that, especially in the Second Temple period—when prophecy no longer had an authoritative status—there evolved a cluster of traditions that attributed revelatory experiences (visual and auditory) to priests in the Temple; see *Apocalyptic and Merkavah Mysticism,* pp. 96–97; "Impact of Priestly Traditions," pp. 79–87. See Gnuse, "The Temple Experience of Jaddus in the *Antiquities* of Josephus."

[29] See Levine, *The Aramaic Version of the Bible,* pp. 47–48. On visionary experience in biblical prophecy, see Sister, "Die Typen der prophetischen Visionen in der Bibel."

[30] *Religion in Essence and Manifestation,* p. 449.

[31] The key passages in the Hebrew Bible are 1 Kings 22:19, Ezek. 1:26, and Dan. 7:9–13.

[32] See Hamerton-Kelly, "The Temple and the Origins of Jewish Apocalyptic." For a discussion of the development of the throne-vision in these passages and in the subsequent Enoch tradition, see Black, "The Throne-Theophany Prophetic Commision and the 'Son of Man.'" A critical text in this regard is Testament of Levi 5:1ff., which reports a vision of God sitting on the throne in the heavenly temple. Subsequent rabbinic interpretations of the vision in Isa. 6:1 reflect the tendency to shift the locus of the vision from the terrestrial to the celestial Temple; see Uffenheimer, "The Consecration of Isaiah in Rabbinic Exegesis," pp. 238ff. See also Himmelfarb, "From Prophecy to Apocalypse," pp. 150–151, and idem, *Ascent to Heaven in Early Judaism and Christianity,* pp. 25–46. For the view that the distancing of God from the earthly to the heavenly Temple in apocalyptic writings represents the social opposition to the Jerusalemite Temple and the priesthood, see Gruenwald, "Priests, Prophets, Apocalyptic Visionaries, and Mystics," pp. 129–130, 137–139.

mystical traditions[33] and whose influence is clearly discernible in both Christianity[34] and Islam.[35]

The visionary genre is well rooted in the earlier conception of God enthroned upon the cherubim in the Holy of Holies. This conception continued to have a decisive influence on later rabbinic authorities, as may be shown, for example, in the talmudic legend, assumed to be related to the Jewish mystical tradition,[36] concerning R. Ishmael ben Elisha having a vision of Akatriel sitting on the throne in the innermost sanctum of the Temple.[37] The Holy of Holies, in which the Ark of the Covenant was enshrined, was the seat of the divine Presence, and hence the locus for the visualization of God. Echoes of this Jewish tradition can be heard in the New Testament as well. In Acts 22:17–18 Paul reports his ecstatic vision of Jesus in the Temple: "When I had returned to Jerusalem and was praying in the Temple, I fell into a deep trance and saw him saying to me, 'Make haste and get quickly out of Jerusalem, because they will not accept your testimony about me.'"[38] In this context it is of interest to recall, as well, the record of the father of John the Baptist, Zechariah, who had a vision of Gabriel, identified as the angel of the Lord (Luke 1:8–11), who "stands in the presence

33 See Neher, "Le Voyage mystique des quatre"; Maier, *Vom Kultus zur Gnosis,* p. 106; Chernus, "The Pilgrimage to the Merkavah: An Interpretation of Early Jewish Mysticism." A similar approach has been taken with respect to the 4Q Shirot 'Olat ha-Shabbat, presumably composed by the covenantal community at Qumran: the Temple liturgy projected into the heavenly realm may have occasioned an ecstatic transport of members of the community to the celestial Temple, wherein they may have participated with the angelic priests. See Maier, pp. 133–135; Newson, *Songs of the Sabbath Sacrifice,* pp. 59–72; idem, "'He Has Established for Himself Priests,'" pp. 114–115.

34 Cf. Matt. 22:44 (cf. Mark 12:36, Luke 20:42–43) and 26:64 (cf. Mark 14:62, Luke 22:69), based on Ps. 110:1. See also Rev. 3:21, 4:2, 5:1 and passim. Cf. Hay, *Glory at the Right Hand,* pp. 52–103; Flusser, *Judaism and the Origins of Christianity,* pp. 27–28.

35 Qur'an 2:255, 7:54, 10:3. See Corbin, "Et son trône était porté sur l'eau," pp. 293ff.; Gätje, *Qur'an and Its Exegesis,* pp. 146–149.

36 See Scholem, *Jewish Gnosticism, Merkabah Mysticism, and Talmudic Tradition,* pp. 51–54.

37 B. (Babylonian Talmud) Berakhot 7a. See Gruenwald, *Apocalyptic and Merkavah Mysticism,* p. 96; idem, "Impact of Priestly Traditions," pp. 82–83; Mach, *Entwicklungsstadien des jüdischen Engelglaubens in vorrabbinischer Zeit,* pp. 205–208. Interesting in this regard is another legend, preserved in P. (Palestinian Talmud) Yoma 8:3, 42c (cf. B. Yoma 39b) concerning the high priest Simeon the Just: on every Yom Kippur, when Simeon entered the Holy of Holies, he was accompanied by an old man clad and wrapped in white. R. Abahu reportedly said that this old man was not a human being but God himself. Although this is not an enthronement vision per se, it is nevertheless significant that the vision of God in human form reportedly occurs within the spatial confines of the Temple. That the Temple was viewed by certain rabbis as the locus for other sorts of visions, including prognostications, is evident from the classical sources as well. See *Midrash Wayyikra Rabbah,* 20:4, pp. 454–455; B. Yoma 21b; Baba Batra 147a. The Temple was also viewed as a locus for auditory revelations, as is shown by legends regarding Johanan Hyrcanus the high priest and Simeon the Righteous; cf. T. (Tosefta) Soṭah 13:5–6; Josephus, *Jewish Antiquities* 13.282–283. See also Gruenwald, *Apocalyptic and Merkavah Mysticism,* p. 96; idem, "Impact of Priestly Traditions," pp. 81–82.

38 Cf. Betz, "Die Vision des Paulus im Tempel von Jerusalem," pp. 113ff. See also Heb. 6:19–20, where Jesus is described as the "high priest after the order of Melchizedek" who has entered the inner shrine behind the veil; and cf. the extended discussion of related motifs in Renwick, *Paul, the Temple, and the Presence of God.*

of God" (1:19) in the Temple.[39] Interestingly enough, according to a passage in one of the major compositions in the corpus of early Jewish mysticism, *Hekhalot Rabbati,* the third entrance of the Temple (see Jer. 38:14) is set as the scene for the disclosure of the techniques for visionary ascent transmitted by the master, R. Neḥuniah ben ha-Qanah, to the other members of the mystical fellowship, an incident that is obviously supposed to have taken place before the destruction of the Second Temple, in 70 C.E.[40] Within the context of this literature, in line with earlier apocalyptic sources, the locus of the vision is the heavenly realm and not the terrestrial Temple. Even so, it is significant that the latter is selected as the place in which the master divulges the secrets of the mystical technique required in order to ascend to heaven to have a vision of the enthroned divine Presence.[41] Following the same trajectory, in a later text, the classic of medieval Jewish mysticism, the *Zohar,* we find descriptions of ecstatic experience connected especially with the high priest's entry into the Holy of Holies on Yom Kippur.[42] As a result of the service he has performed below, he is translated to the spiritual realm of the *sefirot,* the divine emanations. While obviously different from the earlier visionary texts, there is nevertheless continuity, since the ecstatic experience is set specifically within the confines of the Temple as a result of cultic worship.

A critical factor in determining the biblical (and, by extension, subsequent Jewish) attitude toward visualization of God concerns the question of the morphological resemblance between the human body and the divine. Indeed, it

[39] See Gruenwald ("Impact of Priestly Traditions," p. 82), who cites this source and rightly notes that it reflects the influence of Zech. 3:1ff.

[40] Schäfer et al., eds., *Synopse zur Hekhalot-Literatur,* §§ 202–203. See Alexander, "The Historical Setting of the Hebrew Book of Enoch," p. 169.

[41] See Gruenwald, "Priests, Prophets, Apocalyptic Visionaries, and Mystics," p. 142.

[42] See sources cited by Scholem in *Major Trends in Jewish Mysticism,* p. 378 n. 9. It should be noted that in the case of the *Zohar* the high priest's entry into the Holy of Holies may also have erotic undertones, for the Holy of Holies symbolizes the feminine aspect of the divine and entry thereto is a form of sexual union (see esp. *Zohar* 3:296b; the symbolic connection between the inner sanctum of the Temple and the womb of God's wife is already implied in Ezek. 16 and 23; see Galambush, *Jerusalem in the Book of Ezekiel,* pp. 89–125, esp. 104). The mystical experience of the high priest, therefore, also involves the theurgical and soteriological function of *tiqqun,* i.e., uniting the male and female elements of divinity (see *Zohar* 3:66b). See Liebes, "The Messiah of the Zohar," pp. 194–195 (English trans., *Studies in the Zohar,* pp. 65–66). See also pp. 230–232 (this material was not translated in the English version), where Liebes notes an interesting parallel between the zoharic motif and a passage in the Valentinian Gnostic work *The Gospel of Philip* (69.25–30) that identifies the Holy of Holies as the bridal chamber wherein the sexes are cultically united, a process that is referred to as redemption. (See Idel, "Sexual Metaphors and Praxis in the Kabbalah," pp. 203–204.) See also "Messiah," p. 195 n. 364 (English trans., *Studies,* p. 188 n. 185), where Liebes remarks that there is no evidence that either R. Simeon bar Yoḥai or R. Moses de León was a priest. However, I have found one possible piece of such evidence. In MS New York–JTSA Mic. 1609, fol. 129b it is stated: "This is the commentary on the thirteen attributes by way of truth from the sage, R. Moses de León, the Priest." There is no doubt that this text is in fact a work of de León, but there is no way of verifying if this scribal attestation is historically accurate. It is nonetheless interesting in light of the special role accorded the high priest in the *Zohar* as a prototype of the visionary ecstatic.

seems that the problem of God's visibility is invariably linked to the question of God's corporeality, which, in turn, is bound up with the matter of human likeness to God.[43] The strictures against idol-making only attest to the basic propensity of the human spirit to figure the divine in human form.[44] Although the official cult of ancient Israelite religion prohibited the making of images or icons of God, this basic need to figure or image God in human form found expression in other ways, including the prophetic visions of God as an anthropos, as well as the basic tenet of the similitude of man and divinity.[45]

The biblical conception is such that the anthropos is as much cast in the image of God as God is cast in the image of the anthropos. This is stated in the very account of the creation of the human being in the first chapter of Genesis (attributed to P) in the claim that Adam was created in the image of God. It has been long debated by scholars how this pivotal notion should be interpreted: does the divine image involve concrete, physical resemblance, or is it rather an abstract likeness based on spirit, soul, reason, or some behavioral mode? According to some biblical scholars, in this context the words *ṣelem* (image) and *demut* (likeness) imply physical resemblance, as may be proven on the basis of ancient Near Eastern cognates,[46] whereas for others these terms suggest a behavioral or abstract spiritual resemblance[47] or simply the notion of an object consecrated by the divine spirit.[48] It can be shown from a number of passages—the majority, it would seem, of a postexilic provenance, but clearly reflecting older mythological notions—that the biblical conception is such that the human likeness to God is based on man's external form.[49]

[43] See Freedberg, *The Power of Images,* p. 60.

[44] The point is particularly relevant in the context of orthodox Christianity, where the incarnation of the Father in the flesh of the Son would seem to allow readily for the making of images of God. Nevertheless, or perhaps on account of this, the early Church showed hostility toward the making of images See Clerc, *Les théories relatives au culte des images chez les auteurs grecs du IIe siècle après J.-C.,* pp. 125–168; Bevan, *Holy Images,* pp. 84–112; Baynes, "Idolatry and the Early Church," pp. 116–143; Grabar, *Christian Iconography.* For other references, see Grigg, "Constantine the Great and the Cult without Images," pp. 3 n. 7, 24–32. See also Pelikan, *Imago Dei,* pp. 41–98; Barasch, *Icon,* pp. 95–182.

[45] See Moore, "Prophetic Iconoclasm," p. 209.

[46] See Weinfeld, "God the Creator in Gen. I and in the Prophecy of Second Isaiah," pp. 113–116; von Rad, *Genesis: A Commentary,* pp. 57–58.

[47] See N. Sarna, *Understanding Genesis* (New York, 1970), pp. 15–16; C. Westermann, *Genesis 1–11,* trans. J. J. Scullion (Minneapolis, 1984), pp. 147–150; Miller, "In the 'Image' and 'Likeness' of God"; Sawyer, "The Meaning of 'In the Image of God' in Genesis I–XI."

[48] See van Buren, "The Salmê in Mesopotamia in Art and Religion."

[49] See Barr ("Theophany and Anthropomorphism," pp. 31–38), who originally suggested that the biblical conception of the image of God presupposed a resemblance between human and divine forms. See, however, his subsequent retraction in "The Image of God in the Book of Genesis." That the words *ṣelem* and *demut* have the connotation of physical resemblance or form throughout the Bible can be shown from a careful examination of most of the relevant sources. Of the seventeen times the word *ṣelem* occurs, five are related to the problem at hand; in ten other instances the meaning is concrete or physical resemblance; in the two remaining cases (Ps. 39:7 and 73:20) the connotation seems to be dream or shadow. That *demut* likewise connotes physical likeness can be shown from its usage in the relevant biblical passages, excluding for the moment those passages

This is most evident, for example, in Ezek. 1:26, which can be viewed as the "midrashic" underpinning of Gen. 1:26,[50] that is, the fact that the glory of God appears in the form of the image of a human being grounds the assertion that the human being is made in the image of God. According to Ezekiel, the glory is the human form of God's manifestation and not a hypostasis distinct from God.[51] To be sure, in other biblical contexts the *kavod* does not necessarily imply the human form of God. The particular usage of *kevod YHWH* (Presence of the Lord) is a characteristic feature of the Priestly stratum, where it serves as a *terminus technicus* to describe God's indwelling and nearness to Israel, which is manifest as a fiery brightness, splendor, and radiance that, due to the human incapacity to bear the sight of it, is usually enveloped in a thick cloud.[52] (In the case of Ezekiel, as well, the conception of the glory as a luminous body is apparent from the description of the enthroned figure as being surrounded with splendor from the waist up and with fire from the waist down, a motif found elsewhere in the Bible, with parallels in Sumerian and Babylonian materials.[53]) That this luminous *kavod,* however, had the capacity to be visualized as an anthropos is illustrated from the case of Ezekiel. The *kavod* idea developed by the latter, although apparently based in great measure on Mesopotamian and Syrian iconography,[54] is without doubt related to older assumptions of biblical *homo religiosus* concerning the anthropomorphic form of God.[55]

---

that speak of the divine likeness. See Gen. 5:3; 2 Kings 16:10; Isa. 40:18; Ezek. 1:5, 10, 13, 16, 22, 26, 28; 10:1, 21, 22, and 23:15; 2 Chron. 4:3; Dan. 10:16. Two exceptions are Isa. 13:4 and Ps. 58:5, where *demut* is used in the sense of metaphorical resemblance. Cf. N. Porteous, "Image of God," in *The Interpreter's Dictionary of the Bible* (New York, 1962), 2:683, where he makes a distinction between *ṣelem* and *demut,* arguing that the former is concrete and the latter more abstract. See also Miller, "In the 'Image,'" p. 291. Other scholars maintain that the word *ṣelem* was employed in order to avoid the suggestion of the resemblance of the human body and God's form. Cf. Barr, "Image of God," pp. 20–24; Miller, pp. 301–302. See also Sawyer, "Meaning," p. 420. I see no philological basis for such distinctions.

[50] Some scholars maintain that Ezekiel was influenced by the Priestly account in Genesis, whereas other scholars, who follow in the Wellhausian tradition, argue that Ezekiel's vision made possible the doctrine of the image of God in P. See Weinfeld, "God the Creator," p. 113 n. 50. On the relationship of P and Ezekiel, see the recent remarks of B. A. Levine in *The JPS Torah Commentary: Leviticus* (Philadelphia, 1989), p. xxix.

[51] See Fossum, *The Name of God and the Angel of the Lord,* pp. 177–178. See, however, the remark of Segal in *Rebecca's Children: Judaism and Christianity in the Roman World,* p. 14, to the effect that Ezekiel distinguished the "essential personhood of God" from the glory in which he manifested himself as a human form. See also Everson, "Ezekiel and the Glory of the Lord Tradition."

[52] Exod. 16:10, 24:16–17, 40:34–35; Lev. 9:23–24; Num. 14:10, 16:19. See Aalen, *Die Begriffe 'Licht' und 'Finsternis' im Alten Testament,* pp. 73–86.

[53] See A. L. Oppenheim, "Akkadian pul(u)h(t)u and melammū," *Journal of the American Oriental Studies* 63 (1943): 31–34; Cassin, *La splendeur divine,* pp. 65–82; Weinfeld, "God the Creator," 131–132; N. M. Waldman, "A Note on Ezek. 1:18," *Journal of Biblical Literature* 103 (1984): 614–618.

[54] See L'Orange, *Studies on the Iconography of Cosmic Kingship in the Ancient World,* pp. 48–63; Keel, *Jahwe-Visionen und Siegelkunst;* Greenberg, "Ezekiel's Vision," pp. 163ff. See also A. Parrot, *Babylon and the Old Testament,* trans S. H. Hooke (New York, 1958), pp. 128–136; Landersdorfer, *Baal Tetramorphos und die Kerube des Ezechiel.*

[55] See Weinfeld, "God the Creator," pp. 116–120; M. Greenberg, *Ezekiel 1–20* (New York,

Sufficient textual evidence exists to demonstrate that some later rabbinic interpreters, partially under the influence of Hellenistic philosophy, understood the notion of the divine image in a decidedly nonanthropomorphic way,[56] whereas for other authorities it implied the corporealization of divinity in human form.[57] Interestingly, the anthropomorphic reading of Gen. 1:26 endured as a standard polemical stance in Christian writing from the first centuries into the Middle Ages,[58] as well as in Islamic and Karaite antirabbinic polemics.[59] The morphological resemblance between the divine and human image, rooted in biblical thinking, played a central role in the subsequent development of Jewish mysticism in all of its stages. As will become evident in the course of this study, the problem of visionary experience in Jewish mysticism cannot be treated in isolation from the question of God's form or image. The problem surrounding the claim for visionary experience invariably touches upon the larger philosophical-theological problem of God's having a visible form or body.

To be sure, the issues of visionary experience and anthropomorphism are theoretically distinct. That is, from an analytical standpoint it is possible to conceive of a divine body that is nevertheless invisible to human beings. Conversely, God may be visible, but not in human form. It is nevertheless the case that the two are often intertwined in classical theological and philosophical texts in general and in the primary sources of biblical and postbiblical Judaism in particular. The inextricable link between anthropomorphism and visionary experience from the vantage point of Judaism is brought out in a striking way in a passage in Justin Martyr's *Dialogue with Trypho,* where he reports of

---

1983), p. 51 n. 28. See, however, G. von Rad's comment in "δοξα," *Theological Dictionary of the New Testament*, ed. G. Kittel and trans. G. W. Bromiley (Grand Rapids, 1983), 2:241 (hereafter *TDNT*): "The other distinctive feature is that Ezekiel portrays the כבוד יהוה in human form, with the strongest possible emphasis on the nature of God as light." See idem, *Old Testament Theology,* 1:240 n. 119. While it is fair enough to contrast Ezekiel's depiction of the glory with that of the Priestly authorship, it seems to me that the anthropomorphic understanding of the glory is not completely innovated by Ezekiel. Indeed, the narrative in Exod. 33:18ff. already suggests such a conception. Cf. Maier, *Vom Kultus zur Gnosis,* pp. 119–120.

[56] Jervell, *Imago Dei,* pp. 71–121; Altmann, "*Homo Imago Dei* in Jewish and Christian Theology"; Barr, "Image of God," p. 13; Grözinger, "Der Mensch als Ebenbild Gottes," pp. 64–65.

[57] See, for example, Marmorstein, *The Old Rabbinic Idea of God,* pp. 50–52; Smith, "The Image of God." It would be of interest to compare this line of thinking in rabbinic sources to the statement in the Pseudo-Clementine *Homilies* 11.4, 1: "You are the image of the invisible God. . . . For the image of God is man. He who wishes to be pious towards God does good to man, because the body of man bears the image of God" (regarding this text, see n. 61, below). On the centrality of an anthropological reading of Gen. 1:26 and 2:7 in Gnostic mythology, see Filoramo, *A History of Gnosticism,* pp. 87–100.

[58] See Stroumsa, "Form(s) of God," pp. 271–272. On the other hand, there is ample evidence in Christian authors to demonstrate that a corporeal understanding of Gen. 1:26, perhaps mediated by Ezek. 1:26, influenced attitudes about Christ as the visible image of the invisible Father.

[59] See, for example, Nemoy, "Al-Qirqisani's Account of the Jewish Sects and Christianity," pp. 331, 350–351; Mann, *Texts and Studies in Jewish History and Literature,* 2:38–39, 83–86; Altmann, *Studies in Religious Philosophy and Mysticism,* p. 183; Lieberman, *Shkiin,* pp. 11–14; Sharf, *The Universe of Shabbetai Donnolo,* pp. 73–93; Orfali, "Anthropomorphism in the Christian Reproach of the Jews in Spain."

the Jews that they imagine that "the Father of all, the unbegotten God, has hands and feet, and fingers, and a soul, like a composite being; and they for this reason teach that it was the Father Himself who appeared to Abraham and to Jacob."[60]

A second, and perhaps more poignant, example of this linkage can be found in the Pseudo-Clementine *Homilies* 17, whose terminological and conceptual relationship to ancient Jewish mysticism has been noted by various scholars.[61] In this text, as well, one finds that the attribution of bodily form to God is linked directly to the issue of visionary experience: "He has the most beautiful Form for the sake of man, in order that the pure in heart shall be able to see Him, that they shall rejoice on account of whatever they have endured."[62] As Shlomo Pines has noted,[63] the last sentence is probably a commentary on the verse in the Beatitudes (Matt. 5:8): "Blessed are the pure in heart, for they shall see God."

In the case of the Jewish-Christian document, the content of the vision is specified further in terms of God's form, which, as we learn from the continuation of the text, is a shape that is limited or located in space. From the vantage point of this doctrine of Jewish Christianity, closely alligned with what we find in Jewish esotericism of Late Antiquity, God has a visible form, and, consequently, the image of God in humanity is to be found in the body.[64] There can be little question, moreover, that historically the theological discussion concerning anthropomorphism in both medieval Islamic and Jewish philosophy starts from the problem of the vision of God implied by the prophetic tradition: if God could be seen he would fall under the category of visible objects, yet only that which possesses a body is visible. Hence, to assert that God is visible is effectively to posit that God can assume corporeal form.

Denial of God's Visibility

A significant element in the biblical tradition, as we have seen in the case of the Deuteronomist, opposes physical anthropomorphism, emphasizing the verbal/auditory over the iconic/visual. Positing that God addresses human beings through speech does not affect the claim to divine transcendence, that is, the utter incomparability of God to anything created, humanity included. The most extreme formulation of such a demythologizing trend occurs in Deutero-Isaiah: "To whom, then, can you liken God, what form [*demut*] compare to Him?" (Isa. 40:18; cf. 40:25, 46:5). In this verse one can perceive, as has been

[60] In *The Ante-Nicene Fathers* (Grand Rapids, 1981), 1:256.

[61] Graetz, *Gnostizismus und Judentum,* pp. 110–115; Scholem, *Jewish Gnosticism,* p. 41; idem, *On the Kabbalah,* pp. 172–173; Pines, "Points of Similarity between the Exposition of the Doctrine of the Sefirot in the Sefer Yezira and a Text of the Pseudo-Clementine Homilies."

[62] Pines, "Points of Similarity," p. 64.

[63] Ibid., p. 102.

[64] Cf. Quispel, "The Discussion of Judaic Christianity," pp. 148, 153–154.

pointed out by Moshe Weinfeld,[65] a direct polemic against the Priestly tradition that man is created in God's image. This tradition implies two things: first, that God has an image (*demut*), and, second, that in virtue of that image in which Adam was created there is a basic similarity or likeness between human and divine. The verse in Deutero-Isaiah attacks both of these presumptions: since no image can be attributed to God it cannot be said that the human being is created in God's image. From this vantage point there is an unbridgeable and irreducible gap separating Creator and creature.

It has long been recognized by scholars that a fundamental tension emerges from the various literary units of the Bible with respect to the question of anthropomorphism and the description of God. Addressing this issue, Walther Eichrodt was led to conclude that a gradual "spiritualization of theophany" is discernible in Old Testament theology.[66] Eichrodt's position, fairly commonplace in biblical studies, assumes a chronological evolution, with the more advanced stages of spirituality marked by a concomitant rejection of iconicity and anthropomorphic representation.

The form-critical method allows us to resolve some of the more glaring textual discrepancies, at least on one level. Thus, to take an example from the Sinai pericopae, the older theophanic tradition in Exod. 19:11 that God descended on Mount Sinai before the sight of the people, implying thereby that the divine possesses or assumes a visible form, or the even more striking account in Exod. 24:10–11 in which Moses, Aaron, Nadab, Abihu, and the seventy elders saw a corporeal manifestation of God on the mountain, stand in marked contrast to Deut. 4:11, which flatly denies that anyone saw an image of God at Sinai. Appeal to the literary-critical approach can resolve these contradictory accounts of the Sinaitic theophany.

Although the chapter in Deuteronomy appears itself to be an exegetical elaboration of Exod. 19, which, in contrast to Exod. 24, highlights the auditory as opposed to the visual element of the prophetic revelation,[67] a careful reading of the two contexts shows that the Deuteronomist completely eliminated any reference or possible inference concerning God's visible form. That is, the author of Exod. 19 takes for granted that God has a visible form but that vision of that form may be harmful or injurious to the seer.[68] Hence, God commanded Moses to establish the proper barriers around the mountain (Exod. 19:12) so that no one would perish by gazing upon the Lord (19:21). On the basis of this account the Deuteronomist repeatedly affirms that at Sinai the divine voice

[65] Weinfeld, "God the Creator," pp. 124–125; see also Fishbane, *Biblical Interpretation in Ancient Israel,* pp. 325–326.

[66] Eichrodt, *Theology of the Old Testament,* 1:23ff. Cf. von Rad, *Old Testament Theology,* 1:190, 239ff.

[67] See Uffenheimer, *Prophecy in Ancient Israel,* p. 107; Nicholson, "The Interpretation of Exodus XXIV 9–11," p. 95; idem, "The Antiquity of the Tradition in Exodus XXIV 9–11," pp. 75–76.

[68] The potential harm resulting from the manifestation of a god is a common motif in pagan sources as well; see Fox, *Pagans and Christians,* p. 109.

spoke out of the fire (4:12, 15, 36; 5:4) but no shape was visible. This author, however, stresses not the potential harm of the visible image but rather the inherent impossibility of God being circumscribed in any image or form. In these instances, then, a certain chronological evolution can be charted by comparative analysis of the different texts and their contexts.

The paradox nevertheless consists of the fact that sometimes within the same source contradictory views can be discerned. Thus, for example, underlying the statement of Exod. 24:10, as we have seen, is the claim that God can manifest himself in a visible form. On the other hand, Exod. 33:20 seems to limit severely the possibility of visionary experience by stating categorically that no mortal creature, even of the stature of Moses, can see the divine face. To be sure, in that context Moses was granted a vision of the divine back (v. 23); thus, in this case, there is no absolute rejection of the claim that God has a visible form, as we find, for instance, in Deuteronomy and Deutero-Isaiah. Nevertheless, Exod. 33:20 and 23 do state that Moses could not have a vision of the divine form in its frontal aspect, implying, therefore, that he, like other mortal humans, could not see the likeness of God in its fullest manifestation.

If we assume that both Exod. 24:10 and 33:20 derive from the same literary source, as is generally claimed, appeal to the form-critical method to resolve textual discrepancies in this instance will be of no avail. This example demonstrates that the developmental hypothesis, based on a progression from pagan-mythological to monotheistic belief, does not sufficiently account for the paradoxical character within Israelite culture (as it is to be reconstructed from its literary remains) on this fundamental issue. We are dealing not with a strictly chronological sequence, but rather with one that is typological in nature. The complexity arises precisely because not every instance of textual contradiction can be resolved by appeal to the historicity of literary sources. That is to say, therefore, that the "naive" conception of the anthropomorphic manifestation of God and the more "spiritualized" conceptions must lie side by side if one is to take account faithfully of the biblical perspective. It is of interest to note in this connection that the rabbis of the second century were bothered by the apparent contradiction between Exod. 33:20 and Isa. 6:1—how could Isaiah say, "I saw my Lord seated on a high and lofty throne" when Moses himself had already said that no mortal creature could see God's face? According to the answer given in the Talmud, all the prophets, excluding Moses, perceived some form of the divine, for they saw through the speculum that does not shine; Moses, by contrast, saw no form, for he saw through a speculum that shines.[69]

[69] B. Yevamot 49b. The rabbinic distinction should be compared to the words of Paul in 1 Corinthians 13:12, "For now we see in a mirror through a riddle, but then face to face." For Paul, the vision of God in this corporeal existence is an impossibility—we see now only as if through a mirror and then only dimly—but in the world-to-come it will be possible. The view of Paul is similar to that of R. Dosa's interpretation of Exod. 33:20 cited at n. 134. To anticipate the discussion below, the impossibility of seeing God is tied to one's bodily existence; hence, after the death of the body such a vision is possible. In medieval Christendom the generally accepted view was likewise that the *visio beatifica* was possible for the blessed in Paradise. Similarly, the majority of

The rabbis are sensitive to the fact that the apparently contradictory claims in the biblical canon with respect to the issue of seeing God must be resolved typologically and not chronologically. Not every textual contradiction can be resolved by appeal to the source theory that has dominated contemporary hermeneutics of the Bible. On the contrary, we must be aware of the fact that any given culture fosters divergent views that are not always logically consistent. Indeed, different impulses can be operative within a culture at the same time without necessitating a resolution that adopts one alternative to the exclusion of the others. Hegemony may be the desire of priests or autocrats, but it is rarely the measure or mark of cultural creativity.

Moreover, a diachronic approach like that adopted by Eichrodt is a problem because in relatively late sources we find an elaborate use of anthropomorphic language in visionary contexts, precisely where one would expect to find an extreme rejection of anthropomorphism. A striking example of this can be gathered from a comparison of Exod. 33:20 and Num. 12:8. We have already noted that the former case affirms the inherent inability of Moses to see the face of God. In Num. 12:8 it is stated, by contrast, and without qualification, that Moses beheld "the likeness of the Lord" (*temunat YHWH*).[70]

In this set of contradictory verses the chronologically earlier source, Exod. 33:20, attributed to J, limits the extent of the vision, while the later source, Num. 12:8, deriving from P, does not. Significantly, the Priestly source ascribes a visible form or likeness to God (which is in keeping with what we discussed above in connection with the notion of the divine image and likeness in Gen. 1:26). Alternatively, one could argue that in the case of Exod. 33:20 the issue is not having such an experience, but surviving it.[71] That is, even according to that context, one may theoretically see God, though one could not live to tell about it. The seeing of God's face is objectionable not because it is theologically impossible but rather because of the ensuing danger that it necessarily entails.[72] The biblical God is not invisible *de jure*, but rather, as E. L. Cherbonnier put it, "as a matter of tactics. *De facto*, men seldom do see him. Upon occasion, however he does show himself."[73]

Even if we grant the veracity of this interpretation, the fact of the matter

Mutakallimun maintained that a vision of Allah was possible only in the next world. See Wensinck, *The Muslim Creed*, pp. 64–68; Altmann, *Studies*, p. 144. Finally, mention should be made of John 6:46, "No one has seen the Father except he who is from God [i.e., the Son]; he has seen the Father" (cf. 1:18). This seems to be a new interpretation of Exod. 33:20, which claimed that even Moses could not see God. The stature of Jesus is thus raised above the greatest of Old Testament prophets, Moses. See Segal, *Two Powers in Heaven*, p. 213; *The Gospel According to John I–XII*, introduction, translation, and notes by R. E. Brown (The Anchor Bible, vol. 29; Garden City, N.Y., 1966), p. 36.

70 Cf. W. Zimmerli, *Old Testament Theology* (Atlanta, 1978), p. 74.

71 This is a point often overlooked by interpreters ancient and modern, who understand the verse as asserting that theoretically no mortal can see God. The danger implicit in encountering God is also emphasized in Deut. 4:21–23. See also Judges 13:22.

72 See Marmorstein, *The Old Rabbinic Idea of God*, p. 95.

73 "The Logic of Biblical Anthropomorphism," p. 199.

remains that the later source expresses the position that seems more appropriate for the earlier one. The point is made even more poignantly by the case of the apocalyptic vision recorded in the seventh chapter of Daniel. (According to critical scholars, this belongs to the part of that book composed during the reign of Antiochus IV in the second century B.C.E., between 168 and 165.) The vision of the divine in anthropomorphic form is not a regression to some primitive modality long since overtaken by a more spiritual faith. This vision, as that which was developed in other apocalyptic writings, reestablishes an older Israelite tradition regarding the visible form of God as an anthropos.

The apparently contradictory beliefs about God's visibility (and hence corporeality) in the Bible should be viewed typologically and not chronologically. Indeed, even with respect to those examples of textual discrepancies to which the source method applies, if one adopts a more organic approach, viewing the Bible hermeneutically from the perspective of the canon in its completed form, the problem is raised to a secondary level: Given the final redaction of the sources, how can the two be reconciled? How can both assertions be simultaneously maintained? How can the two statements inhabit the same corpus? Yet it is precisely because both points of view, so strikingly different, inhabit the same corpus that the history of Jewish attitudes toward the visual imaging of God unfolded in the dialectical way it did.

Vision of God in Jewish Apocalyptic

While it clearly lies beyond the scope of this chapter to present an exhaustive treatment of the problem of visionary experience in apocalyptic literature, it would be inexcusable to ignore the issue entirely, especially in light of the widely accepted view that the early Jewish mystical texts, known as the Hekhalot, preserve elements of the older Jewish apocalypses.[74] The apocalyptic writings—in reality an eclectic group of texts that share some basic literary and theological traits but are not reducible in any essentialist way—are characterized by a number of distinctive features. One feature is that the recorded visions of the enthroned form of God's presence (or glory) and/or the angelic hosts in the heavenly realm result from otherworldly journeys that, one may presume, were induced by specific visionary practices, though the records of these visions were often expressed in conventional imagery drawn from the theophanic traditions in Hebrew Scripture.[75] The apocalyptic orientation is manifest in some Jewish and Christian texts from Late Antiquity, written dur-

[74] This, of course, is the basic assumption of Scholem; see *Major Trends,* p. 43, and the fuller working out of this hypothesis in Gruenwald, *Apocalyptic and Merkavah Mysticism.* See also Maier, "Das Gefährdungsmotiv bei der Himmelsreise in der jüdischen Apokalyptik und Gnosis"; and the more recent discussions by Halperin, *The Faces of the Chariot,* pp. 63–114; Himmelfarb, "Heavenly Ascent and the Relationship of the Apocalypses and the *Hekhalot* Literature"; Morray-Jones, "Transformational Mysticism in the Apocalyptic-Merkabah Tradition."

[75] See Merkur, "The Visionary Practices of Jewish Apocalyptists."

ing the period of roughly 250 B.C.E. to 250 C.E. The attempts to define the genre of apocalyptic are manifold and universal consensus is still lacking.[76] I am not here concerned with providing a precise taxonomy of apocalyptic writings, but wish only to cast a glance in the direction of one central issue: the visual encounter with the divine.[77] It is evident that such visions, in the framework of apocalypticism, are part of the much larger phenomenon regarding the disclosure of divine secrets.[78] That is, apocalyptic is the revelation of divine mysteries through the agency of visions, dreams, and other paranormal states of consciousness. Needless to say, the context of these visions varies considerably in the range of texts grouped together under the genus apocalyptic. Again, my focus is necessarily limited, as I am concerned exclusively with visions of God.

The narrowness of my concern is doubly clear when it is realized that I am interested only in Jewish apocalyptic, leaving aside, therefore, the genre of Christian apocalyptic.[79] A sense of uneasiness arises from this distinction for two reasons. First, many of the relevant texts have undergone such a complicated redactional process that it is not always easy to disentangle the historical threads of the Jewish text and Christian interpolations. Second, from a phenomenological perspective many of the themes central to Jewish apocalypticism are shared by Christian sources. It may even be suggested that one of the main components of the socio-religious matrix Christianity derived from was the apocalyptic tendency in later Hellenistic Judaism within Palestine.[80] This being the case, it is somewhat arbitrary to ignore Christian apocalypticism in a discussion of Jewish apocalyptic. Yet every portrait is limited by the boundaries of its canvas, and my canvas has been determined in such a way that a journey into the Christian sources would take us too far from the main focus of this chapter.

That vision of the divine form is central to apocalyptic writings in Judaism is evident from the one apocalypse included in the Hebrew biblical canon, the Book of Daniel. As I have already noted, in the seventh chapter of that work there is found an explicit and relatively elaborate description of the vision of the

[76] Collins, "Introduction: Towards the Morphology of a Genre." See also Gruenwald, "Jewish Apocalyptic Literature," esp. pp. 103–107; Hartman, "Survey of the Problem of Apocalyptic Genre," pp. 329–343; Sanders, "The Genre of Palestinian Jewish Apocalypses," pp. 447–460; Collins, "The Genre Apocalypse in Hellenistic Judaism," pp. 531–548.

[77] This theme has been discussed in many scholarly works. See, for example, Stone, "Lists of Revealed Things in the Apocalyptic Literature"; Rowland, "The Visions of God in Apocalyptic Literature"; idem, *The Open Heaven*, pp. 78–123, 358–402; Niditch, "The Visionary."

[78] Cf. G. Bornkamm, "μυστηριον," *TDNT* 4:815. See also D. Flusser, "Apocalypses," in *Encyclopaedia Judaica* 3: col. 179; Russell, *The Method and Message of Jewish Apocalyptic*, pp. 107–118; Rowland, *The Open Heaven*, pp. 9–32; and the section on "Pseudepigraphy, Inspiration, and Esotericism" in Stone, "Apocalyptic Literature," pp. 427–433.

[79] On the nature of Christian apocalyptic as a distinctive type, see Schüssler Fiorenza, "The Phenomenon of Early Christian Apocalyptic."

[80] See Koester, *Introduction to the New Testament*, 1:230, 239; 2:56, 71–72, 148–149, 242–261. See also E. Käsemann, "The Beginnings of Christian Theology," *Journal for Theology and the Church* 6 (1969): 40: "Apocalyptic was the mother of Christian theology."

Ancient of Days, obviously a technical reference to the enthroned divine form. Quite a bit of information is supplied concerning this form; in fact, there is no discernible effort on the part of the author to qualify the vision in any way. It is simply assumed that the apocalyptic visionary (Daniel) has seen the divine in this manner. From still other Jewish apocalyptic sources it is clear that the vision of God represents the climax of a heavenly ascent (often enough, later accounts draw upon Daniel 7,[81] as well as other biblical texts, most notably, Isa. 6:1–3 and Ezek. 1:26–27), although the clarity or accessibility of that vision is not left unchallenged by the widely accepted belief that no creature, angelic or human, can behold the luminous Presence of God. For example, in the theophany recorded in 1 Enoch 14:8–25—part of the "Book of Watchers" (1 Enoch 1–36), which we now know from the Aramaic fragments of 1 Enoch from Qumran (including the "Book of the Heavenly Luminaries," 1 Enoch 72–82) is the earliest extant apocalypse, predating even the canonized book of Daniel,[82]—the apocalypticist unreservedly describes the enthroned form of God but at the same time emphasizes the inherent invisibility of that form:

> And I observed and saw inside it a lofty throne—its appearance was like crystal and its wheels like the shining sun. . . . It was difficult to look at it. And the Great Glory was sitting upon it—as for his gown, which was shining more brightly than the sun, it was whiter than snow. None of the angels was able to come in and see the face of the Excellent and Glorious One; and no one of the flesh can see him—the flaming fire was round about him, and a great fire stood before him. No one could come near unto him from among those that surrounded the tens of millions (that stood) before him. . . . Until then I was prostrate on my face covered and trembling. And the Lord called me with his own mouth and said to me, "Come near to me, Enoch, and to my holy Word." And he lifted me up and brought me near to the gate, but I (continued) to look down with my face. (14:19–25)[83]

The author of this text sees a luminous figure on the throne in the shape of an anthropos (the divine glory, *dòxa*), and despite his claim that neither angel nor mortal can behold the enthroned glory, that is precisely what he is able to accomplish.[84] In a second passage in 1 Enoch 71 (the last chapter of the so-called "Similitudes of Enoch") there is another elaborate description of the vision of God, as well as of the four archangels (Michael, Raphael, Gabriel, and Phanuel) and numerous other angels who surround the throne of glory. The actual description of the enthroned form of God is based on the language of Daniel's epiphany: "With them is the Antecedent of Time [*ʿatiq yomin*]: His

[81] See Beale, *The Use of Daniel in Jewish Apocalyptic Literature and in the Revelation of St. John.*

[82] See Milik, *The Books of Enoch;* Stone, "The Book of Enoch and Judaism in the Third Century, B.C.E."; Nickelsburg, "Enoch, Levi, and Peter."

[83] Translated by E. Isaac in *The Old Testament Pseudepigrapha,* ed. J. H. Charlesworth (Garden City, N.Y., 1983), 1:21 (hereafter *TOTP*).

[84] See Rowland, *Open Heaven,* p. 222. On the centrality of light imagery in the description of the divine glory in apocalyptic literature, see Aalen, *Die Begriffe 'Licht' und 'Finsternis,'* pp. 195–202.

head is white and pure like wool and his garment is indescribable. I fell on my face, my whole body mollified and my spirit transformed" (71:10–11).[85] Here, too, one can discern the clash between the vision of the enthroned form (thus allowing for the description of his hair and the mentioning of his garment) and the overwhelming sense that such a vision is impossible (thus the visionary falls to the ground). It is of interest to note that Christopher Rowland cites the beginning of this chapter of 1 Enoch, "And I saw two streams of fire, and the light of that fire shone like hyacinth, and I fell on my face before the Lord of spirits," as evidence of the tendency in apocalyptic theophanies to move "away from the direct description of God and his throne."[86] While this opening statement may indicate a reluctance to speak of God's form, it is nevertheless the case that the continuation of this passage, cited above, is quite explicit in its description of that form, a description presumably resulting from a direct visual encounter.

In 2 Enoch one finds various references to the visionary experience of the divine form. In one context there is a brief allusion to the vision of the enthroned glory and the attending angels in the seventh heaven: "And they showed me from a distance the Lord, sitting in his throne. And all the heavenly armies assembled, according to their rank, advancing and doing obeisance to the Lord" (20:3).[87] In a subsequent chapter the vision is again mentioned: "I saw the Lord. His face was strong and very glorious and terrible. Who (is) to give an account of the dimensions of the being of the face of the Lord, strong and very terrible? . . . And I fell down flat and did obeisance to the Lord" (22:1–4).[88] The longer version of this text is even more elaborate in its detail of Enoch's visual encounter with the enthroned form of God:

> And on the tenth heaven, Aravoth, I saw the view of the face of the Lord, like iron made burning hot in a fire and brought out, and it emits sparks and is incandescent. Thus even I saw the face of the Lord. But the face of the Lord is not to be talked about, it is so very marvelous and supremely awesome and supremely frightening. And who am I to give an account of the incomprehensible being of the Lord, and of his face, so extremely strange and indescribable? . . . Who can give an account of his beautiful appearance, never changing and indescribable, and his great glory? And I fell down flat and did obeisance to the Lord. (22:1–4)[89]

One senses in this passage, especially in the longer recension but in the shorter one as well, the tension of the moment: standing before the face of God, yet being unable to describe or fathom it. The visionary falls down to worship God, but in the continuation we are told that he was summoned by God to rise and stand before the divine face; this is followed by an account of his transmutation into an angelic being. The reluctance here to speak of the form on the

[85] Rowland *Open Heaven*, p. 50.
[86] Ibid., p. 87.
[87] Translated by F. I. Andersen in *TOTP* 1:135.
[88] Ibid., p. 137.
[89] Ibid., p. 136.

throne of glory shows the basic tension between the stated goal of the visionary, on the one hand, and the belief that such a vision is implicitly dangerous and therefore best avoided, on the other. What the apocalyptist assumes, however, is that there is a divine form with dimensions that are nevertheless too great for a human to measure. Thus in a third passage Enoch refers to his vision of God in even more graphic detail:

> As for you, you hear my words, out of my lips, a human being created equal to yourselves; but I, I have heard the words from the fiery lips of the Lord. For the lips of the Lord are a furnace of fire, and his words are the fiery flames which come out. You my children, you see my face, a human being created just like yourselves; I, I am one who has seen the face of the Lord, like iron made burning hot by a fire, emitting sparks. For you gaze into my eyes, a human being created just like yourselves; but I have gazed into the eyes of the Lord, like rays of the shining sun and terrifying the eyes of a human being. You my children, you see my right hand beckoning you, a human being created identical to yourselves; but I, I have seen the right hand of the Lord, beckoning me, who fills heaven. You, you see the extent of my body, the same as your own; but I, I have seen the extent of the Lord, without measure and without analogy, who has no end. (39:1–6)[90]

Other apocalyptic texts attest to the tension outlined above. One text worthy of particular comment is in chapters 18–19 of the Apocalypse of Abraham, wherein there is a reworking of Ezekiel's chariot vision. Interestingly enough, in this context the anthropomorphic imagery is displaced from the visual to the auditory realm:

> And while I was standing and watching, I saw behind the living creatures a chariot with fiery wheels. Each wheel was full of eyes round about. And above the wheels was the throne I had seen. And it was covered with fire and the fire encircled it round about, and an indescribable light surrounded the fiery crowd. And I heard the voice of their sanctification like the voice of a single man. And a voice came to me out of the midst of the fire. (18:12–19:1)[91]

A careful examination of each of the relevant passages in the respective literary contexts would demonstrate that there is reflected in the apocalyptic literature the basic tension that we have seen emerge from the various strata of the Hebrew Scriptures. On the one hand, there is a record of visions of the divine form; on the other, a significant effort is made to qualify, if not challenge entirely, just such a possibility. The issue here is not one of inconsistent or even contradictory thinking, nor is it a matter of textual discrepancies that reflect diverse hands over an extended and varied redactional process. It is rather the curious paradox central to the prophetic, apocalyptic, and, as will be seen in more detail below, mystical visionary texts: a God invisible renders himself

[90] Ibid., p. 163. See Rowland, (*Open Heaven*, p. 85), who concludes that "this text comes closest to the extravagant descriptions of the limbs of God, the *shiʿur qomah* speculation" of later Jewish mystics.

[91] Translated by R. Rubinkiewicz in *TOTP* 1:698.

visible to select individuals. The one and the same divine reality who is not seen under ordinary circumstances can be seen by distinct persons in given moments of history.

Visibility and Invisibility of God in Rabbinic Sources

Theophanic Forms of God

A careful scrutiny of the voluminous corpus of rabbinic writings from the classical period (roughly 200–600 C.E.) indicates that the rabbis developed their own theophanic traditions, based to a degree on the relevant biblical texts but in some cases going beyond them in their morphological detail. In this section I would like to discuss several key traditions that, in my view, represent the most important claims for the imaging of God in human form in the rabbinic sources. Let me state emphatically that I make no pretense in the following of exhausting the relevant comments in the many rabbinic documents at our disposal, nor do I claim any sweeping generalizations about the rabbinic sources. There is no attempt here to present a comprehensive review of such a vast corpus. Rather, I have isolated various tradition-complexes that span several centuries of redacted rabbinic texts. Despite the fact that some of the midrashic texts to be discussed are relatively late—that is, from the post-classical period—it is evident that there is a discernible trajectory connected with the traditions that I have isolated regarding the visual imagining of God in iconic form. Precisely such traditions, moreover, were reshaped and reformulated by later Jewish mystics. My principle of selection has therefore been determined by a foreward glance into the mystical literature. I am interested in highlighting the rabbinic passages that provided the grist for the mill of subsequent interpreters.

The explicit preference accorded the visual/iconic element of revelation over the auditory/verbal is expressed succinctly in the midrashic compilation *Mekhilta de-Rabbi Ishmael*, generally considered to contain traditions of tannaitic authorities from the first and second centuries C.E., on the book of Exodus: "[The Israelites] said [to Moses]: It is our desire to see our king, for the one who hears cannot be compared to one who sees."[92] That some of the rabbinic authorities assumed that the anthropomorphic manifestation of God in concrete, visible forms was a basic part of biblical faith is especially highlighted in another passage from the same midrashic collection, where one finds a discussion concerning various epiphanies and their respective axiological frame of reference:

> "The Lord is a man of war" (Exod. 15:3). Why is this said? For at the sea He appeared as a warrior doing battle, as it says, "The Lord is a man of war." At Sinai

[92] *Mekhilta de-Rabbi Ishmael*, Baḥodesh, 2, pp. 210–211. For other sources that utilize the proverb "hearing is not like seeing," see Ginzberg, *The Legends of the Jews*, 6:33 n. 191.

He appeared as an old man full of mercy, as it says, "And they saw the God of Israel etc." (ibid., 24:10). And when they were redeemed what does it say? "Like the very sky for purity" (ibid.). And it says, "As I looked on, thrones were set in place, and the Ancient of Days took his seat" (Dan. 7:9); but it also says, "A river of fire [streamed forth before Him] etc." (ibid., 10). In order to give no opportunity to the nations of the world to say, "There are two powers," Scripture reads: "The Lord is a man of war, the Lord is his name."[93]

As several scholars have noted,[94] the exegetical problem here is the repetition of the divine name, YHWH, in Exod. 15:3. This can be understood in clearer fashion from a parallel text in a second tannaitic collection of scriptural exegeses on Exodus, the *Mekhilta de-Rabbi Shimʿon bar Yoḥai:*

Another interpretation: "YHWH is a man of war, YHWH is His name." Because when the Holy One, blessed be He, was revealed at the sea He appeared as a young man making war. "YHWH is His name." He appeared to them at Sinai like an old man full of mercy. "As I looked on, thrones were set in place" (Dan. 7:9). So as not to give an opportunity [for one] to say, "There are two powers in heaven," [it is written] rather "YHWH is a man of war."[95]

The real issue underlying these comments is a polemic against the belief in two powers, a phrase that the rabbis employed to name various heresies ranging from Christianity to Gnosticism. As Alan Segal has suggested in connection with the midrashic passages cited above,[96] the root heresy involved in this context seems to have been the belief in two complementary divine powers exegetically derived from the repetition of the divine name in Exod. 15:3. The point of this midrashic statement is that the repetition attests to the fact that there is only one God, who reveals himself under various guises, a notion further supported by Exod. 24:10 and Dan. 7:9–10. The multiple manifestation of God in the Bible is only a literary technique—in fact, a heuristic device—and should not be construed as a description of more than one divine being.

The last point is further substantiated by a comparison of Exod. 15:3 and 24:10: in the former case, the miracle at the sea, God appeared as a young man at war, whereas in the latter case, the theophany at Sinai, God appeared as an old man full of mercy. The stark anthropomorphism of the biblical theophanies, according to the midrashic reading, both in the core tradition and in the later accretions, is treated in light of the manifestation of God's attributes of justice and mercy. The anthropomorphism and visionary elements are thus subsumed under the normative categories of ethical behavior as applied to God. What was experienced at the Red Sea and at Sinai was nothing other than the God of Israel expressing himself in terms of two attributes, judgment and

[93] *Mekhilta de-Rabbi Ishmael,* Shirata, 4, p. 129. See Urbach, *The Sages,* p. 399.

[94] E.g., Goldin, *The Song at the Sea,* p. 126; Segal, *Two Powers in Heaven,* p. 36.

[95] *Mekhilta de-Rabbi Shimʿon bar Yoḥai,* p. 81.

[96] *Two Powers in Heaven,* pp. 33–57.

mercy, respectively personified as a warrior doing battle and as an old man full of mercy.

This midrashic view is further expanded in a later collection of rabbinic homilies, *Pesiqta de-Rav Kahana,* but in this context the connection between the divine manifestations and the specific moral attributes is weakened. In contrast to the *Mekhilta,* in the relevant passage here the different manifestations of God are presented as a known tradition without any exegetical grounding in the relevant texts.[97] It is simply stated as common knowledge that the God of the Jewish people assumed the corporeal form of a heroic warrior at the Red Sea, a scribe at Sinai, an old teacher in the days of Daniel, and a youthful lover in the time of Solomon. While clearly drawing on the earlier midrashic tradition, the author of this statement has gone substantially further in his understanding of the visible incarnation of God in the different theophanic forms (*dimmuyot*).[98] It is this later development of the earlier formulation that is most essential to our analysis, for the further expansion of the incarnational forms of God affirmed in the various mystical theosophies of the High Middle Ages is based most precisely on these aggadic sources.

The idea of the polymorphous nature of God is expressed exegetically in an anonymous comment contained in *Shir ha-Shirim Rabbah* on the verse "My beloved is like a gazelle" (Cant. 2:9): the different manifestations of the divine at the critical points in ancient Israelite history are compared to the leaping motion of the gazelle.[99] Similarly, in a liturgical poem by R. Yannai that is essentially a midrashic gloss in poetic form on Canticles, we read, "'[My beloved] is like [a gazelle]'—He thrived and prospered in several images [*demuyot*]."[100] The poet links the biblical expression *domeh* to the aggadic term *demuyot,* a *terminus technicus* for the theophanic forms through which God is revealed to the Jewish people.[101] We find similar evidence for this tradi-

[97] *Pesiqta de-Rav Kahana,* ed. Mandelbaum, 12:24, p. 223.

[98] For a recent treatment of this topic, see Neusner, *The Incarnation of God;* and see my review of Neusner's book in *Jewish Quarterly Review* 81 (1990–91): 219–222. See also Stern in "Imitatio Hominis," where he approaches the anthropomorphic statements of the rabbis in a literary, figurative manner to determine what the rabbis believed not about the nature or being of God but about his character. It is my contention that the rabbinic notion of theophanic forms is based on an ontological assumption regarding the possibility of God assuming a visible shape. The nature of the vision, therefore, is not mental or spiritual, as in the Platonic tradition, but rather is a corporeal seeing. See Boyarin, "The Eye in the Torah"; idem, "'This We Know to Be the Carnal Israel,'" pp. 497–500.

[99] *Midrash Rabbah Shir ha-Shirim* 2:20, pp. 66–67. See the targumic rendering of "My beloved is like a gazelle" (Cant. 2:9): "When the glory of the Lord appeared in Egypt on the night of Passover and he killed all the firstborn, he was riding upon a swift cloud [cf. Isa. 19:1], running as a deer and a young gazelle, and he protected the houses where we were."

[100] *The Liturgical Poems of Rabbi Yannai according to the Triennial Cycle of the Pentateuch and the Holidays* (in Hebrew), ed. Z. M. Rabinovitz (Jerusalem, 1985–87), 2:277.

[101] This usage is evident particularly in the *piyyuṭ* literature. Thus, e.g., see the poem of Eleazar Qallir in *Jubelschrift zum neunzigsten Geburtstag des Dr. L. Zunz* (Berlin, 1884), p. 204: להבת כנראת ארבע דמיונות. Cf. *The Liturgical Poems of Rabbi Yannai* 2:277: דומה לכמה דמויות. See also

tion in a poem composed by the sixth-century Palestinian poet Eleazar Qallir. The poet describes God's appearance at Sinai thus: "He appeared [*nidmeh*] to them as the Ancient of Days and luminous."[102] Qallir combined the midrashic tradition and the verses Daniel 7:9 and Canticles 5:10 in order to depict the manner of God's manifestation at the Sinaitic theophany.

The polymorphous nature of the divine expressed in the aggadic and poetic sources, which bears a striking resemblance to several Christian Apocryphal and Gnostic texts of the third and fourth centuries,[103] may properly speaking be referred to as a docetic orientation,[104] since the forms by which God is perceived, the theophanic images, are mental constructs or phantasma—although, as I will suggest below, these forms are not considered by the Jewish sages to have been shaped exclusively in accordance with individual human capacity. The notion of divine accommodation is found in midrashic sources with respect to the problem of hearing God's word,[105] but in the case of this aggadic tradition concerning God's multiple manifestations the primary issue is the imaginative seeing of the theophanic forms (*dimmuyot*) that accommodate

---

Y. David, "Yotzer for Passover by Abraham 'Ezrah' bar Matityahu from Rome" (in Hebrew), in *Papers on Medieval Hebrew Literature Presented to A. M. Habermann on the Occasion of His Seventy-fifth Birthday,* ed. Z. Malachi (Jerusalem, 1977), p. 98, where the celestial beasts (*ḥayyot*) seen by Ezekiel are referred to as the four images (*demuyot*). For the same usage, see Ṭobiah bar Eliezer, *Midrash Leqaḥ Ṭov* 8a: היכון כסא כבודו על ארבעה דמויות הללו; commentary on the *piyyuṭ* by Eleazar Qallir, *we-ḥayyot 'asher hennah merubba'ot kisse'*, in a collection by Aaron ben Ḥayyim ha-Kohen (MS Oxford-Bodleian 1206, fol. 146b): וכן לד' ריבעיהם יש להם דמויות הללו; A. M. Habermann, *Piyyuṭe R. 'Efrayim mi-Bonn* (Jerusalem, 1969), no. 27, p. 76: עלו דמויות אשר לחיות. See also no. 10, p. 22, where the word *dimyonim* is employed as a synonym for the image (*demut*) of God in which humanity is said to have been created. On the technical use of the word *dimyon* in the sense of image or appearance in the poetry of Yannai and in some later sources, see M. Zulai, "Studies in the Language of the Poems of Yannai" (in Hebrew), in *Studies of the Research Institute for Hebrew Poetry in Jerusalem* (Jerusalem, 1945), 6:183–184; for a similar usage in some other medieval sources, see Ta-Shema, "On the Commentary on the Aramaic Piyyutim in the Mahzor Vitry." In this context mention should also be made of the occurrence of the word *dimyonim* in *Megilloth Midbar Yehuda: The Scrolls from the Judean Desert,* ed. A. M. Habermann (Tel-Aviv, 1959), p. 100: ולכול מראי דמיונים.

102 The citation is from Qallir's liturgical poem *'Eleh ha-'edut we-ha-ḥuqqim 'asher nittenu le-'am ḥashuqim,* which is part of his larger composition *'Ereṣ maṭah we-ra'ashah*. The poem has been frequently printed in traditional prayer books for Pentecost. For a relatively recent edition see *Maḥzor Sha'ar 'Efrayim la-Shavu'ot* (Jerusalem, 1989), p. 199. For a recent study of Qallir's intricate use of midrashic material, see M. Schmelzer, "Some Examples of Poetic Reformulations of Biblical and Midrashic Passages in Liturgy and Piyyut," in *Porat Yosef: Studies Presented to Rabbi Dr. Joseph Safran,* ed. B. Safran and E. Safran (Hoboken, N.J., 1991), pp. 217–224, especially 219–223.

103 See Stroumsa, "Polymorphie divine et transformations d'un mythologème." On revelatory visions in Gnosticism, see E. Pagels, "Visions, Appearances, and Apostolic Authority: Gnostic and Orthodox Traditions," in *Gnosis: Festschrift für Hans Jonas,* ed. U. Bianchi, M. Krause, J. Robinson and G. Widengren (Göttingen, 1978), pp. 415–430; Filoramo, *A History of Gnosticism,* pp. 153–176; Merkur, *Gnosis,* pp. 129–146.

104 See Davies, "The Origins of Docetism"; Bianchi, "Docetism."

105 See Benin, "The Mutability of an Immutable God," p. 71, and the author's fuller treatment of the problem in his monograph *The Footprints of God.*

humanity's limited capacity to apprehend the divine. The conceptual principle underlying this motif is articulated in other passages within the rabbinic aggadah, and most importantly in a statement attributed in the majority of sources to R. Yudan. In this context I will cite the relevant lemma from *Pesiqta de-Rav Kahana:*

> "A man's wisdom lights up his face" (Eccles. 8:1). R. Yudan said: Great is the power of the prophets who compare the image of the Dynamis above to a human image. "I heard a human voice from the middle of Ulai calling out" (Dan. 8:16). R. Judah ben R. Simeon [said]: There is another verse that is clearer than this: "and on top, upon this semblance of a throne, there was the semblance of a human form" (Ezek. 1:26). "And the strength of his face will change" (Eccles. 8:1). He changes from the attribute of justice to that of mercy with respect to Israel.[106]

It is generally assumed by modern scholars, reflecting the interpretation of various medieval exegetes, that the point of the statement attributed to R. Yudan is that the prophets had the capacity to speak of God in figurative or allegorical terms.[107] This is taken to be the import of the claim that the prophets compare (*medamim*) the image of the glory above to a human image. The fact of the matter, however, is that the context does not warrant or support such an interpretation. The point of R. Yudan's teaching is that the prophets were able to imagine the divine in human terms, with respect to both auditory and visual revelations, attested by the respective proof-texts from Daniel and Ezekiel. The issue at hand is the figural corporealization of God, that is, the imagining of God as human form in the sense of an actualized ontic presence, and not merely the linguistic representation of God. The point is reinforced by the end of the passage, which emphasizes that God changes his hypostatic form from one attribute to another, a change that occurs as a result of or in response to Israel's activities below.[108] The issue, again, is not merely one of how the prophets spoke about God, but rather the way in which the divine is manifest. One must, therefore, be careful to distinguish between rhetoric and religious experience: the prophets, according to the sages, did not only speak of God in figurative

[106] *Pesiqta de-Rav Kahana* 4:4, pp. 65–66; *Pesiqta Rabbati* 14, 61b; *Bemidbar Rabbah* 19:4; *Midrash ha-Gadol on Leviticus*, p. 582. Cf. *Qohelet Rabbah* 8:1; *Yalqut Shim'oni*, pt. 2, § 977, where the reading is: "Great is the power of the prophets who compare the form to its Creator." See also *Bereshit Rabbah* 27:1.

[107] An important exception is Fishbane, "Some Forms of Divine Appearance in Ancient Jewish Thought." Fishbane understands the dictum attributed to R. Yudan as underscoring the daring of the prophets to compare the divine hypostasis, which is an anthropomorphic form (*ṣurah*), to the Creator (*yoṣer*), who is an invisible, transcendent being. My interpretation is nuanced in a slightly different way. See also Aaron, "Polemics and Mythology," pp. 369–377, whose reading of this midrashic text is similar to my own.

[108] The notion that righteous action can effect a change in God's manifestation from justice to mercy and, conversely, that the wicked can cause a change from mercy to justice is a commonplace in rabbinic texts. Cf. *Bereshit Rabbah* 33:3, p. 308; *Wayyikra Rabbah* 29:3–4, pp. 674–675; *Pesiqta de-Rav Kahana* 23:3, pp. 336–337; *Midrash Tehillim* 47:2, 137b; B. Berakhot 7a; Sukkah 14a.

language; they heard and saw him in the shape of an anthropos. My reading is clearly substantiated by an examination of the relevant verses cited in the continuation of the passage, the one verse indicating a prophet's capacity to hear God as a human voice and the other emphasizing the capacity to visualize the divine glory as a human form seated upon the sapphire throne. The force of this aggadic tradition, then, is the figuring of the deity in imaginative terms, the very issue that underlies the texts that discuss God's appearance at the Red Sea and Sinai.

The implication of R. Yudan's teaching is drawn explicitly in a textual witness from a later source: "R. Yudan said: Great is the power of the prophets who compare the form to its Creator, as it says, 'I heard a human voice' (Dan. 8:16), and it is written, 'Upon this semblance of a throne, there was the semblance of a human form' (Ezek. 1:26) for [God] appears to them in many images (*dimyonot*), as it says, 'and through the prophets I was imaged' (Hosea 12:11)."[109] A link is thus forged between the comment of R. Yudan and the verse in Hosea, an understanding of the verse that is attested in the LXX and is reflected in later Jewish exegesis as well, for example, the eleventh-century commentary of R. Solomon ben Isaac of Troyes (Rashi): "Through the prophets I was imagined, that is, I appeared to them in several forms (*demuyot*)." This interpretation of Hosea 12:11 is implied as well in the following passage from *Pesiqta Rabbati,* commenting on Lam. 2:13, "what can I liken to You" (*mah 'adammeh lakh*):

> I appeared to them in several images (*demuyot*). At the sea I appeared to them as a warrior doing battle, as it is written, "The Lord, the Warrior" (Exod. 15:3). And at Sinai I appeared as an elder teaching Torah. . . . At the Tabernacle I appeared to them as a bridegroom entering his chamber. This is [the meaning of] "what can I liken to You." The Holy One, blessed be He, said to Israel: Did I not appear to the prophets in many images . . . as it is written, "I multiplied great visions and through the prophets I was imaged."[110]

This formulation influenced another relatively late midrashic collection, *'Aggadat Bereshit,* a passage from which reads as follows:

> The Holy One, blessed be He, said: Certainly "I spoke to the prophets," but "I multiplied visions," for the prophecy of one was not like that of another. Amos saw Me standing . . . Isaiah saw Me sitting . . . Moses saw Me as a warrior . . . Daniel saw Me as an elder. . . . Therefore it says, "through the prophets I was imaged."[111]

The docetic interpretation of divine manifestation is expressed in other midrashic texts as well. For example, in *Midrash Shir ha-Shirim Zuṭa,* the following interpretation of the verse "I have likened you, my darling" (Cant. 1:9) is offered: "The expression 'I have likened you' (*dimmitikha*) connotes images (*demuyot*). This teaches that through an image (*dimyon*) God was revealed to

[109] *Midrash Zuṭa* on Eccl. 8:1, ed. Buber, p. 117.
[110] *Pesiqta Rabbati* 33, 155b.
[111] *'Aggadat Bereshit,* 14, p. 30.

Israel; as a person who sees his friend and says, This is the one, so Israel looked upon the Holy One, blessed be He, and imagined (*medamim*) Him."[112]

The inherent docetism of the aggadic tradition, as I will argue in a later chapter, is greatly extended and elaborated on in medieval Jewish mystical texts, partially due to the influence of philosophical interpretations of prophetology. In this context it is important to note, however, that in the case of the midrashic pericopae it appears that the visible images through which God is manifest are not entirely dependent on the imaginative constitution of prophetic consciousness. The community of vision is established by reference to the external object that assumes its visible form in accordance not with individual imagination but with the received tradition each member of the faith community participates in by virtue of belonging to that community. In the final analysis, it is the divine will that determines the specific theophanic forms through which God is manifest at certain junctures in the historical process. Close in spirit to the rabbinic view, as I have delineated it, is the following account of the vision of the triune Saviour—Father, Mother, and Son—in the Gnostic *Apocryphon of John* 2:4–8: "[I] saw within the light a child standing before me. When I saw . . . like an elderly person. And it changes [its] manner of appearance to be like a young person . . . in my presence. And within the light there was a multiform image. . . . And the [manners of appearance] were appearing through one another. [And] the [manner of appearance] had three forms."[113] The forms of appearance are not simply images in the mind of the recipient of the vision, but reflect the inherent nature of that which is visualized. The forms, then, are ontological realities that have the capacity of being seen within the imagination of the visionary.

That this formulation applies to the conception expressed in the rabbinic sources is supported by the following passage in *Pesiqta Rabbati:*

> Another interpretation: "Face to face [the Lord spoke to you]" (Deut. 5:4). R. Levi said: In many images (*demuyot*) He appeared to them. To one He appeared standing, to another sitting; to one He appeared as a youth, to another as an old man. How is this? When the Holy One, blessed be He, was revealed at the Red Sea to do battle for His children and to punish the Egyptians, He appeared as a youth. . . . When the Holy One, blessed be He, was revealed on Mount Sinai to give the Torah to Israel, He appeared as an elder. . . . And similarly Daniel said, "As I looked on, thrones were set in place, and the Ancient of Days took His seat" (Dan. 7:9). R. Ḥiyya bar Abba said: If the son of a whore should say to you, "There are two gods," say to him: "I am He at the Sea, I am He at Sinai."[114]

As several scholars have already noted, the anti-Christian polemic is quite obvious at the end of this passage.[115] The bone of contention, however, is not

[112] *Midrash Zuṭa,* p. 13.

[113] B. Layton, *The Gnostic Scriptures* (New York, 1987), p. 29. See Stroumsa, "Polymorphie divine," pp. 413–414.

[114] *Pesiqta Rabbati* 21, 100b–101a.

[115] See the comment of Friedmann in his edition of the *Pesiqta Rabbati* 101a n. 31; R. T. Herford, *Christianity in Talmud and Midrash* (London, 1903), pp. 304–306; Green, "The Children in Egypt and the Theophany at the Sea," pp. 455–456.

the possibility of God assuming various corporeal forms, but only the hypostatization of these images into distinct divine entities, as is posited in classical Christian doctrine. Within the rabbinic setting the different appearances of God are understood as multiple theophanic manifestations of the singular God that are not reducible to mere images in the mind of the visionary. The word *dimmuyot,* which I have translated as "images" but may be best rendered with the Latin term *figurae,* does not here denote purely subjective forms within the imagination; the theophanic forms by which the divine is manifest are ontic paradigms. Thus, the terminology is employed in a second passage from the same midrashic collection:

> "What can I liken (*'adammeh*) to you" (Lam. 2:13)? [I have appeared] to you in several forms (*demuyot*). At the sea I appeared to you as a warrior engaged in war. . . . At Sinai I appeared as an elder teaching Torah. . . . At the Tabernacle I appeared as a bridegroom entering his nuptial chamber.[116]

Further confirmation of this interpretation can be found in another tradition, attributed to R. Eliezer in the *Mekhilta,* concerning the lowly maidservant at the Red Sea who "saw that which Isaiah and Ezekiel did not see"—a clear and direct vision of God.[117] Clearly, the implication of this text is not that only the maidservant was privileged to have such a vision, but rather that of all Israel who were present, even the maidservant had this experience. The plausibility of this interpretation is borne out by a passage in the *Mekhilta de-Rabbi Shimʿon bar Yoḥai,* where R. Eliezer's teaching is removed from its context as a midrash on the crossing of the Red Sea and applied to the Sinaitic epiphany: " 'And the people saw it' (Exod. 20:15). What did they see? They saw the great glory (*kavod gadol*). R. Eliezer said: Whence do we know that the Israelite maidservant saw that which the greatest of prophets did not see? It is written, 'And the people saw it.' What did they see? They saw the great glory."[118]

From this passage it is obvious that R. Eliezer's laudatory observation regarding the maidservant is meant to be inclusive rather than exclusive: it applies to all of Israel, including even one at the bottom of the socio-economic scale. This is confirmed by another variant on the theme of the vision of God at Sinai in the *Mekhilta de-Rabbi Ishmael:* " '[For on the third day the Lord will come down upon Mount Sinai] in the sight of all the people' (Exod. 19:11). This teaches that in that moment they [the Israelites] saw what Ezekiel and Isaiah never saw, as it says, 'and [I] spoke parables through the prophets' (Hosea 12:11)."[119] Moreover, it is of interest to note that in the passage from *Mekhilta de-Rabbi Shimʿon bar Yoḥai,* Israel's experience at Sinai is expressed in terms of seeing the "great glory" (*kavod gadol*), an expression that, as Scholem

[116] *Pesiqta Rabbati* 33, 155b.

[117] *Mekhilta de-Rabbi Ishmael,* Beshallaḥ, 3, pp. 126–127; *Mekhilta de-Rabbi Shimʿon bar Yoḥai,* p. 78 (the attribution there is to R. Eleazar, but see the critical apparatus ad loc.).

[118] *Mekhilta de-Rabbi Shimʿon bar Yoḥai,* pp. 154–155. On the inclusiveness of the theophany at the Red Sea, see P. Soṭah 5:6, 16c.

[119] *Mekhilta de-Rabbi Ishmael,* Baḥodesh, 3, p. 212. Cf. *Devarim Rabbah* 7:8.

has shown on the basis of Greek and Aramaic parallels in apocalyptic and mystical sources, was used as a *terminus technicus* to name the glory enthroned on the chariot.[120] On philological as well as conceptual grounds, therefore, there is good reason to place this passage within the context of Jewish esotericism: according to this midrashist, the people of Israel beheld the theophanic form of God at Sinai, a theme, as we shall presently see, affirmed in a host of aggadic and midrashic sources.[121] What is critical from my vantage point is that these statements further strengthen the view that, according to rabbinic authorities, the object of vision at the Red Sea or Sinai was not constituted by each one's intentionality, but by the collective consciousness of the people.

The latter point is also brought out in a midrashic interpretation, attributed to R. Aqiva, of the verse "I have likened you, my darling, to a mare in Pharaoh's chariots" (Cant. 1:9):

> Pharaoh rode on a male horse, and the Holy One, blessed be He, as it were, was revealed on a male horse, as it is written, "He mounted a cherub and flew" (Ps. 18:11). Pharaoh said, This male horse will kill its master in war so I will ride on a female horse, as it is written, "to a mare in Pharaoh's chariot." Pharaoh then rode on a red horse, followed by a white horse and then black. The Holy One, blessed be He, as it were, was revealed on a red horse, a white horse, and then a black, as it says, "You will make your steeds tread through the sea" (Hab. 3:15), steeds that change one after the other.[122]

The midrashic pericope continues with several other images, but it is sufficient for my purposes to comment on the part of the text translated above. Clearly, the lover in the verse functions as an allegorical depiction of God, who is thus being compared to the horse in Pharaoh's chariot. Read midrashically, the verse indicates that the forms in which God appeared at the Red Sea correspond to the modes of Pharaoh's own appearance. These forms are not simply mental constructs but are rather the external shapes that God assumes in the moment of revelation. Of course, these forms are perceived by the mind, as are all sensory phenomena, yet they are characterized as well by an element of transcendence outside the mind.

Shekhinah as the Locus of Vision

Other examples from the rabbinic corpus that emphasize the seeing of God could be easily adduced, but especially relevant is the idea of seeing the divine Presence (*Shekhinah*) which is emphasized in a host of rabbinic texts in connection with various normative modes of behavior, for example, studying Torah

[120] See Scholem, *Jewish Gnosticism*, pp. 68, 133.

[121] See Chernus, *Mysticism in Rabbinic Judaism*, pp. 14, 21.

[122] *Shir ha-Shirim Rabbah* 1:48. I have followed the division of the text according to Dunaski's edition of *Midrash Rabbah Shir ha-Shirim*. Cf. *'Avot de-Rabbi Natan*, version A, chap. 27; *Midrash Tehillim* 18:14, 71b–72b; *Yalqut Shim'oni*, pt. 2, §§ 167, 565. Cf. the *qerovah* for Passover in *Liturgical Poems of Rabbi Yannai* 2:273: לסוסתי טרם בים אראה בעב קל בצוען אראה.

and liturgical worship.[123] For the most part it appears that seeing the *Shekhinah* is not a purely mental vision, but involves some corporeal shape or tangible form—if only in the imagination—usually described as luminous in nature, as is attested, for example, by the idiom used in several contexts, "to receive the countenance of the Presence" (*lehaqbil pene ha-shekhinah*),[124] or by the expressions "to be nourished by the splendor of the Presence" (*lazun mi-ziw ha-shekhinah*) and "to derive pleasure[125] from the splendor of the Presence" (*lehanot mi-ziw ha-shekhinah*).[126] It is important to note, moreover, that in some of the sources wherein these idiomatic expressions occur the vision of the divine Presence involves an intensely erotic encounter. Consider, for example, the following midrashic interpretation of Exod. 24:11, "They saw God, and ate and drank," reflecting on the death of Aaron's sons, Nadab and Abihu (cf. Lev. 16:1ff.):

> R. Tanḥuma said: This teaches that they loosened [the covering of] their heads, their hearts became haughty, and their eyes feasted upon the Presence (*we-zanu ʿeinehem min ha-shekhinah*). R. Joshua of Sikhnin said in the name of R. Levi: Moses did not feast his eyes upon the Presence, yet he derived pleasure from the Presence (*neheneh min ha-shekhinah*). He did not feast his eyes upon the Presence, as it says, "And Moses hid his face" (Exod. 3:6). Yet he derived pleasure from the Presence, as it says, "Moses was not aware that the skin of his face was radiant" (ibid., 34:30).[127]

[123] See, e.g., B. Berakhot 6a, 64a; Moʿed Qaṭan 29a; *Midrash Tehillim* 69:1, 161a; 105:1, 224b; 149:1, 270a. See Marmorstein, *The Old Rabbinic Idea of God,* pp. 94–106; Aalen, *Die Begriffe 'Licht' und 'Finsternis',* pp. 272–282; Kadushin, *The Rabbinic Mind,* pp. 223ff.; Urbach, *The Sages,* pp. 37–65; Goldberg, *Untersuchungen über die Vorstellung von der Schekhinah in der frühen rabbinischen Literatur,* pp. 513–515.

[124] See Abelson, *The Immanence of God in Rabbinical Literature,* pp. 98–103; Goldin, *Studies in Midrash and Related Literature,* pp. 329–330.

[125] I have followed conventional usage here and translated the expression *lehanot* as derive pleasure. See, however, Chernus (*Mysticism in Rabbinic Judaism,* p. 79 n. 34), who suggests that in these contexts the expression may best be translated as "to feed upon." I agree with Chernus that the verb *lehanot* in this context has the connotation of "to consume," rather than simply "to enjoy," but in my opinion the implicit meaning may involve a form of religious ecstasy comparable to sexual pleasure that parallels eating and drinking in the mundane sphere. See Boyarin, *Carnal Israel,* pp. 70–75, 116–117, 123.

[126] For discussion of the relevant references, see Chernus, *Mysticism in Rabbinic Judaism,* pp. 74–87.

[127] *Wayyikra Rabbah* 20:10, p. 466, and parallels cited in n. 3 ad loc. Cf. *Bemidbar Rabbah* 5:9: "R. Judah ha-Levi the son of Shalom said: If you want to learn about the reason for the death of the sons of Kohat, go and learn from this verse, '[But let them not go inside] and look at the sacred objects even for a moment, lest they die' (Num. 4:20). When they came to carry the ark they would rend the curtain from before it, and they would feast their eyes upon the ark (*hayu zanim ʿeinehem min ha-'aron*). Therefore they were destroyed, as it says, 'no man shall see me and live' (Exod. 33:20)." Cf. M. Middot 4:5, where we read that precautions were taken when the Temple was built so that the eyes of the workmen would not be nourished by the Holy of Holies; cf. P. Bikkurim 2:1, 64c; B. Pesaḥim 26a. See also *Sifre on Deuteronomy* 355, pp. 422–423; see discussion of this midrashic source in Fishbane, "The 'Measures' of God's Glory in the Ancient Midrash," p. 61. The

It is likely that in this context the head or face functions as a displacement for the phallus and the uncovering of the head symbolizes the disclosure of the male organ, perhaps in an ejaculatory state.[128] The sexual promiscuity or brazenness of the sons of Aaron (signified by the loosening of the head cover[129]) that led to their sexual arousal (implied by the act of feasting their eyes upon the Presence) is contrasted with the modesty of Moses, who hid his face when he encountered the Presence—that is, sublimated his sexual arousal vis-à-vis the divine.[130] It is important to bear in mind the prooftext that serves as the basis for the teachings of R. Tanḥuma and R. Joshua of Sikhnin: "They saw God, and ate and drank" (Exod. 24:11). It may very well be the case that the verbs "eating" and "drinking" assume here a sexual connotation, a strategy not uncommon in religious literature in general[131] and in rabbinic literature in particular.[132] Feasting one's eyes upon the splendor of the Presence involves a visual experience whose intimacy and pleasure is best characterized in terms of metaphors related to the function of eating and drinking.

The rabbinic characterization of the divine Presence (*Shekhinah*) as light is based, of course, on similar descriptions of the glory (*kavod*) in biblical and apocalyptic sources. This motif reaches its most explicit formulation in the

---

idiom to be sustained by the splendor of the Presence (*nizonim mi-ziw ha-shekhinah*) is also applied more specifically to the spiritual state of the angels, who do not eat or drink in a physical sense. Cf. *Pesiqta Rabbati* 16, 80a; *Pesiqta de-Rav Kahana* 6:1, p. 110.

128 It should be noted that the expression *gilluy panim*—literally, the disclosure of the face—is used in rabbinic literature as a technical term for impudence; cf. B. ʿEruvin 69a, Soṭah 42b.

129 In Hellenistic Judaism, reflecting older ancient Near East customs, the uncovered head is associated with masculinity, whereas the veil is an emblem of modesty or shame that is associated with women as a sign of their social inferiority and subordination to men. See MacDonald, "Corinthian Veils and Gnostic Androgynes," and references to other relevant studies on pp. 280 n. 17, 281 n. 20. See also Zimmer, "Men's Headcovering."

130 Cf. *Wayyikra Rabbah* 23:13, p. 548 (for parallels see n. 6 ad loc.), where the idiom *lehaqbil pene ha-shekhinah*, to receive the face of the Presence, is presented as the reward of one who sees an obscene matter (*devar ʿervah*) and does not feast his eyes upon it, i.e., does not become sexually aroused or excited. Given the logic of the midrashic presentation, one must assume that the reward is commensurate with the act: seeing the Presence takes the place of looking at the erotic scene. On the sexual nuance of looking with one's eyes, see *Esther Rabbah* 3:14. It is likely that the erotic understanding of visionary experience also underlies the midrashic traditions that locate the recitation of Canticles, an overtly erotic poem, at either the splitting of the Red Sea or the giving of the Decalogue at Sinai, two essential theophanic moments in Israelite history; see Lieberman, "Mishnath Shir ha-Shirim," pp. 118–126. Finally, mention should be made of a passage attributed to Judah bar Ilai in *Shir ha-Shirim Rabbah* 3:15 (interpreting Cant. 3:9), in which the visual encounter between God and Israel is couched in implicitly sexual terms. Before the king's daughter (Israel) reaches puberty (receives the Torah), the king (God) can see and converse with her in public. Once she reaches puberty, however, the king must meet her in a pavillion (tabernacle). If one does not assume an erotic dimension here, the force of the parable is lost. The issue is not simply proper social etiquette (see Green, "Bride, Spouse, Daughter," pp. 251–253), but rather the sexual nature of the visual encounter that becomes inappropriate at a certain juncture. Cultural maturation necessitates the enclosing of the visual encounter between God and Israel so that the erotic embrace will be concealed from the view of others.

131 See chapter 6 n. 90.

132 See Boyarin, *Carnal Israel*, pp. 70–75, 116–117, 123.

statement attributed to Ḥanina ben Hama: "The Holy One, blessed be He, is entirely light."[133] The depiction of God as light in the rabbinic material is not meant as a merely theological axiom, devoid of any experiential component. On the contrary, the Presence is so characterized because it is through the phenomenon of light that the divine is rendered accessible to human experience. However, according to certain rabbinic authorities, the seeing of the Presence was restricted to a postmortem experience. The *locus classicus* for such a view is the interpretation of Exod. 33:20 attributed in some sources to R. Dosa: "'A man shall not see me and live': when they are alive they do not see, but in the time of their deaths they see."[134] A careful investigation of the contexts in which this statement occurs indicates that the issue at hand is not the denial of God's visibility, but rather the claim that the human being in a bodily state cannot endure such an experience.

Thus, for example, in the *Sifra* on Leviticus the immediate discussion concerns the locus of the appearance of God in the Tent of Meeting. R. Simeon ben Azzai reportedly makes a statement that the appearance of the glory between the cherubim, which are above the *kapporet,* is a sign of God's great love for Israel, since another verse (Jer. 23:24) explicitly states that the glory fills all heaven and earth and therefore cannot be contained in one limited place. After this statement the interpretation of three rabbis of the expression *wa-ḥai* in Exod. 33:20, "man may not see Me and live," is reported: (1) R. Dosa suggests this implies that only upon death can one see the Presence, a theme recurring in a significant number of midrashic sources;[135] (2) R. Aqiva interprets the verse to mean that even the *ḥayyot,* the celestial beasts who bear the throne, cannot see the glory; and (3) R. Simeon ben Azzai remarks that the verse implies that the ministering angels who are eternal cannot see the glory. The editor/redactor of the midrashic pericope conflated two distinct traditions regarding the seeing of the divine Presence. The former view, placed in the mouth of R. Simeon ben Azzai, emphasizes the fact that the glory was indeed seen from between cherubim in the Tent of Meeting. The later view offers three different explanations, one attributed to R. Simeon ben Azzai, which limit the vision of the Presence. The interpretation here attributed to R. Dosa explicitly affirms the visibility of the Presence, although it is restricted to an experience after the death of the body. The views of R. Aqiva and R. Simeon—in essence one opinion with slightly different nuances—more severely limit the vision of the Presence, yet even in those cases there is no explicit statement to the effect that God is by nature invisible or that he possesses no image or form.

Let us compare the text of the *Sifra* to a parallel passage in the *Sifre.* The immediate exegetical context of the latter is an interpretation of the verse "When a prophet of the Lord arises among you, I make Myself known to him in a vision, I speak with him in a dream" (Num. 12:6). More specifically, the

[133] *Midrash Tanḥuma,* ed. Buber, Behaʿalotekha, 7, 24b; *Bemidbar Rabbah* 15:7. See also *Midrash Tehillim* 22:11, 93b. And see Abelson, *Immanence of God,* pp. 82–97.

[134] *Sifra on Leviticus* 2:18.

[135] See, for example, *Sifre on Deuteronomy* 357, p. 431; *Midrash Tehillim* 22:32, 99a.

exegesis turns on the precise intent of the expression "in a vision" (*ba-mar'ah*): "This is a vision of speech (*mar'eh dibbur*). You say this is a vision of speech, but perhaps it is a vision of the Presence (*mar'eh shekhinah*)? The text, however, reads, 'He said, you cannot see My face, for man may not see Me and live' (Exod. 33:20)."[136]

This comment is followed by three interpretations of the expression "and live" (*wa-ḥai*) in the verse from Exodus: (1) the view attributed to R. Aqiva that this word refers to the ministering angels; (2) R. Simeon ha-Timni's assertion that the word alludes to the fact that neither the beasts nor the ministering angels see the Presence; and (3) the view of R. Eleazar ben Jose that this signifies that only at the hour of death does one see the Presence. In addition to the obvious fact that the traditions reported in this case do not correspond to the ones in the *Sifra* text, the other striking difference lies in the fact that the opening comment in the *Sifre* is meant to limit further the possibility of the vision of the Presence by emphasizing that all prophets, with the exception of Moses, beheld God in a vision of speech that is contrasted with a vision of the Presence proper. Scripture explicitly states that God makes himself known to the prophets in a vision, which presumably entails some visionary experience of the divine. The anonymous voice of the midrash, by contrast, places a more exacting limit on the vision by emphasizing that it is a vision of the divine speech[137] rather than a vision of the Presence itself.

Other comments in later midrashic or aggadic literature that betray clear intertextual links to the passages discussed above support the position that the rabbinic restriction on seeing the divine Presence involves the potential harm that might accrue to one who undergoes such an experience. For example, in one of the recensions of the *Midrash Tanḥuma* the following passage appears:

> Thus you find that the whole tribe of Levi is very sparse. Why were they so few in number? For they looked upon the Presence. . . . The Holy One, blessed be He, said: In this world they vanished on account of the fact that they looked at My glory, as it says, "man may not see Me and live." However, in the world-to-come, when I return My Presence to Zion, I will be revealed in My glory to all of Israel, and they will see Me and will live eternally.[138]

The impending danger consequent to a vision of the Presence, as opposed to a blatant denial of such a vision on theoretical grounds, is evident as well in the tradition recorded in the *Pirqe Rabbi 'Eli'ezer:*

136 *Sifre on Numbers* 103, p. 101. Cf. *Bemidbar Rabbah* 14:22.

137 Perhaps this comment should be viewed in relation to the description of the *dibbur* as a luminous presence in *Shir ha-Shirim Rabbah* 1:13. See also Targum Pseudo-Jonathan to Num. 12:6, where the biblical idiom "I make myself known to him in a vision," is rendered as "the word of God in a vision is revealed to them." This passage thus provides one example wherein the targumic *memra* is virtually interchangeable with the visible presence of God, the *Shekhinah*. On this whole topic, see Hayward, *Divine Name and Presence*, pp. 15–37, esp. 32–33, and 106–107. It may be the case, therefore, that the midrashic expression "vision of speech" (*mar'eh dibbur*) signifies an intermediary akin to the targumic conception of the word of God.

138 *Midrash Tanḥuma*, ed. Buber, Bemidbar, 20.

R. Simeon said: When Isaac was bound to the altar he lifted his eyes and saw the Presence. But it is written, "man may not see Me and live." In lieu of death his eyes dimmed when he got older, as it says, "When Isaac was old and his eyes were too dim to see" (Gen. 27:1). From here you learn that[139] blindness is considered as death.[140]

Isaac's blindness is thus explained in terms of his gazing upon the Presence, an idea reflected as well in the Targum Pseudo-Jonathan to Gen. 27:1, where it is stated in a midrashic gloss that Isaac's eyes dimmed when he got older "because he looked at the throne of glory when his father bound him." Blindness is a substitute for death, the latter being the appropriate consequence of having seen the divine Presence.[141]

It is clear from this, as well as other rabbinic sources that cannot be cited here, that the Presence becomes the locus of visionary experience. In this context I would like to mention one other midrashic tradition, already noted above, regarding the Sinaitic theophany that, in open contradiction to the Deuteronomist, emphasizes the supremacy of the visual over the auditory as an epistemic mode: "They [the Israelites] said: Our wish is to see our king; one who hears is not comparable to one who sees.[142] God said to him [Moses]: Give them what they have requested, 'For on the third day the Lord will descend in the sight of all the people upon Mount Sinai' (Exod. 19:11)."[143]

A parallel to this comment in another midrashic source is attributed to R. Simeon bar Yoḥai who taught, "This is what they [the Israelites] demanded. They said: Our wish is to see the glory of our king."[144] It is noteworthy that the statement attributed to R. Simeon, in contrast to the anonymous assertion, employs the term "glory." Two possible explanations for this may be suggested. First, it may be proposed that perhaps what is intended is an attempt to qualify the vision of God by inserting the word "glory," a tactic that we find, for example, in the various Targumim on key passages in Scripture that affirm some sort of visionary experience of the divine.[145] One could argue, then, that by means of the insertion of the word "glory" in the statement attributed to Simeon bar Yoḥai, the contrast between the midrashist's view and that of the Deuteronomist is somewhat mitigated. Hence, in a later reflection of R. Simeon's view, attributed to R. Levi, scriptural support for the affirmation of the vision of God's glory at Sinai is actually derived from a verse in Deuteronomy: "R. Levi

[139] Cf. B. Nedarim 64b.

[140] *Pirqe Rabbi 'Eliʿezer,* 32, 73b. See also *Devarim Rabbah* 11:3.

[141] Cf. *Pirqe Rabbi 'Eliʿezer* 46, 111b–112a.

[142] Cf. the statement of Eusebius in the *Ecclesiastical History* X.iv.44: "the witness of the eyes leaves no place for the instruction that comes through the ears." See n. 92, above.

[143] *Mekhilta de-Rabbi Ishmael,* Baḥodesh, 2, p. 211.

[144] *Shir ha-Shirim Rabbah* 1:14.

[145] See the respective Targumim on Exod. 24:10; Num. 12:8; Isa. 6:1, 66:1; Jer. 23:24; Ezek. 1:1, 28, 43:7; Amos 9:1; Hab. 3:4. See Ginsburger, *Die Anthropomorphismen in den Thargumim;* Moore, "Intermediaries in Jewish Theology," pp. 55–59; McNamara, *Targum and Testament,* pp. 74, 98–99; Levine, *The Aramaic Version of the Bible,* p. 59.

said: Israel asked two things of the Holy One, blessed be He—that they might see His glory (*kevodo*) and hear His voice. And they did see His glory and hear His voice, as it is written, 'The Lord our God has just shown us His majestic Presence, and we have heard His voice out of the fire' (Deut. 5:21)."[146] R. Levi, like R. Simeon, asserts that the glory of God was visible to the Israelites who stood at Sinai, and support for his claim, in contrast to the anonymous view reported in the *Mekhilta,* is derived from a verse in Deuteronomy, not Exodus.

An alternative interpretation for the insertion of the word "glory" in the respective statements of R. Simeon and R. Levi is possible and, in my view, preferrable. The use of this term may reflect an esoteric tradition concerning the corporeal manifestation of the divine on the throne. Rather than seeking to attenuate the biblical anthropomorphism, these midrashists sought to highlight it. Support for this contention is to be found in yet another tradition, attributed to R. Pineḥas ben Ḥama, where the view of R. Levi is preserved with some important terminological modifications: "R. Pineḥas ben Ḥama said: Israel asked two things of the Holy One, blessed be He—that they might see His image (*demuto*) and hear the [ten] commandments from His mouth, as it is written, 'Let him give me of the kisses of his mouth' (Cant. 1:2)."[147]

For our purposes it is necessary to focus only on the first part of the passage. Here, instead of the glory it is the vision of God's very likeness (*demuto*) that is sought. It is certain, however, that in this case the word "likeness" (*demut*) is interchangeable with "form,"[148] and is thus identical with the word "glory" (*kavod*). It is of interest to note that the same semantic equivalence between *demut* and *kavod* is detectable in some of the Hekhalot texts of ancient Jewish mysticism, for both words likewise refer to the divine form upon the throne.[149] It is plausible, then, that the midrashic view is rooted in or, at the very least, parallels the esoteric tradition. Hence, what the Israelites requested, according to R. Simeon, R. Levi, and R. Pineḥas ben Ḥama, was to see the visible form of God on the throne. Although the nature of that likeness or form is not specified in the midrash, it stands to reason, as it appears to be the case from the mystical texts, that it involved the anthropomorphic manifestation of the divine.

This interpretation should be applied to another critical passage in the midrashic collection, *Shemot Rabbah,* where mention is again made of seeing the divine image:

[146] *Shemot Rabbah* 29:3.

[147] *Shemot Rabbah* 41:3. The second part of this passage reflects the view attributed elsewhere to the rabbis who, in opposition to R. Yoḥanan, derive from this verse in Canticles that the Israelites heard the commandments directly from God; cf. *Shir ha-Shirim Rabbah* 1:13. For a discussion of this matter, see Urbach, "The Homiletical Interpretations of the Sages and the Expositions of Origen on Canticles, and the Jewish-Christian Disputation," pp. 253–256.

[148] See Fossum, *Name of God,* pp. 269–270. See also Scholem's remarks in *On the Mystical Shape of the Godhead,* p. 29, concerning the probable use of the word μορφή to refer to physical stature in 2 Enoch 13. For a study on the anthropomorphic connotation of the word μορφή in early Christian and Gnostic texts, in some cases reflecting Jewish attitudes, see Stroumsa, "Form(s) of God," and B. Behm, "μορφή," *TDNT* 4:746–748.

[149] Cf. *Synopse,* §§ 7, 183, 581, 813.

> R. Berechiah said: Observe the greatness of those who went down to the sea. How much did Moses have to beg and prostrate himself before God before he saw the [divine] image (*ha-demut*), as it says, "Let me behold Your glory" (Exod. 33:18). The Holy One, blessed be He, said to him, "You cannot see My face" (ibid., 20). In the end God showed him a token of it, as it says, "as My glory passes by" (ibid., 22). The beasts who carry the throne do not recognize the [divine] image. When the time comes for them to sing their praises, they say: Where is He? We do not know if He is here or somewhere else. Yet, wherever He may be, "blessed be the glory of the Lord from His place" (Ezek. 3:12). Each and every one of those who came up from the sea could point with his finger and say: "This is my God, and I will glorify Him" (Exod. 15:2).[150]

In this passage the midrashist extols the praise of the Israelites at the sea by putting them on a higher level than Moses or the celestial beasts that bear the throne. Moses had a partial vision of the divine image, whereas the beasts have none. Those who went down to and came up from the sea, however, witness God in such a pure form that they had the clearest and most certain vision. What is of especial interest is the technical use of the term "likeness" (*demut*) used interchangeably with *kavod,* for a theophanic image of God that, I submit, should be further construed anthropomorphically. Perhaps the same connotation of the word *demut* is implied in the following interpretation of the verse "He beholds the likeness of the Lord" (Num. 12:8), describing Mosaic prophecy in contrast to that of all other prophets: "R. Simeon said that he saw the image immediately."[151] It is instructive that the biblical expression *temunat YHWH,* the likeness of the Lord, is rendered in the rabbinic gloss as *ha-demut,* the image. Although no further specification of the *demut* is given in this context, it seems reasonable to suggest on the basis of other texts that this word denotes the visible form apprehended in the shape of an anthropos.[152]

In claiming that at Sinai the Israelites actively sought a vision of God, or the divine glory, these rabbis were following the lead of R. Aqiva, as may be gathered from several of the statements of the latter as well as from those attributed to some of his other students, most notably Judah bar Ilai.[153] Some scholars have even claimed that Aqiva's teaching regarding the vision of the glory at Sinai must be understood in the context of the Jewish esoteric tradition concerning the appearance of the bodily form of God on the chariot-throne.[154]

[150] *Shemot Rabbah* 23:15.

[151] *Sifre Zuṭa* to Num. 12:8, ed. Horovitz, p. 276.

[152] The anthropomorphic interpretation of the word *demut* in what appears to be a decidedly mystical sense is substantiated further by several other rabbinic texts; two of the more salient examples are *Pesiqta de-Rav Kahana* 4:4, p. 65, and *'Avot de-Rabbi Natan,* version A, chap. 39, p. 116. See also J. Goldin, *The Fathers According to R. Nathan* (New York, 1955), p. 216 n. 6; Lieberman, "How Much Greek in Jewish Palestine?," p. 141; Mopsik, *Le livre hébreu d'hénoch ou livre des palais,* p. 223.

[153] Cf. *Shir ha-Shirim Rabbah* 3:15.

[154] See Lieberman, "Mishnath Shir ha-Shirim," pp. 119–121; Chernus, *Mysticism in Rabbinic Judaism,* pp. 3–5 passim.

That is, Aqiva's understanding of the Sinaitic event reflects the mystical tradition concerning the visual appearance of God—referred to by the technical expression *kavod*[155]—on the chariot. While this may indeed be the case, it is necessary to bear in mind that these affirmations of the vision of God at Sinai are, at least in part, midrashic elaborations of biblical statements that do emphasize that the Israelites saw God at Sinai. One might even venture to say that the esoteric tradition itself has been fostered by these same theophanic statements in the Bible, especially the narrative in Exod. 24:10, which affirms a vision of God sitting on his throne in connection with the Sinaitic revelation.[156]

Whatever the influence might have been between the exoteric midrashic traditions regarding the Sinaitic revelation and the esoteric chariot traditions—a correlation institutionalized by the liturgical practice of reading the vision of Ezekiel 1 as the *hafṭarah* portion on Pentecost in conjunction with the narrative of the Sinai revelation in Exodus[157]—what is clear is that the visionary element in the biblical narrative was not entirely obscured in the rabbinic academies, and this despite the inherent reservations of the Deuteronomist. Suffice it to say, from the examples that I have noted, that at least some of the rabbis understood full well that biblical faith demanded a view of God who appeared to human beings in various visible forms. The anthropomorphism of the Bible is inseparable from the problem of visionary experience.

It lies beyond the scope of this study to present a comprehensive survey of the manifold opinions found in Jewish texts regarding the problem of seeing the divine. Such an ambitious undertaking will have to await a later date. Suffice it to say that one can find in a whole spectrum of literature from the formative period of rabbinic Judaism some exegetical strategy that attempts to remove the Godhead from visual experience but at the same time uphold the scriptural

[155] On the technical use of *kavod* in Hekhalot mysticism see Scholem, *Major Trends,* pp. 46, 66, 358 n. 16; idem, *Jewish Gnosticism,* pp. 67–68; Elior in *Hekhalot Zuṭarti,* p. 65 nn. 97–99; idem, "The Concept of God in Hekhalot Mysticism," pp. 34–35 (English translation, pp. 101–102). Elior correctly points out that the word "glory" is used in the Hekhalot texts to refer to all the spiritual entities that fill the divine pleroma, not only the divine form on the throne. For the terminological equivalence of the word "glory," *kavod,* and the expression "account of the chariot," *maʿaseh merkavah,* see the remarks of S. Lieberman in *Tosefta Ki-Fshutah, Order Moʿed* (New York, 1962), p. 1288 n. 10.

[156] Sinai as a locus of a throne-vision appears in the *Exagoge,* a drama composed in the second century B.C.E. in Alexandria, attributed to Ezekiel the Tragedian, as cited by Eusebius, *Praeparatio Evangelica* IX, 29:5. See Jacobson, *The Exagoge of Ezekiel,* p. 199 n. 2; Wacholder and Bowman, "Ezechielus the Dramatist and Ezekiel the Prophet," p. 274 n. 64 (I thank S. Bowman for calling my attention to this reference); Jacobson, "Mysticism and Apocalyptic in Ezekiel the Tragedian," p. 276; Gruenwald, *Apocalyptic,* pp. 128–129. This theme was later expanded, often using Ps. 68:18 as the exegetical axis, in both tannaitic and amoraic midrashim, where the experience of Israel at Sinai is described in terms analogous to the experience of the Merkavah visionaries. See references to studies of Lieberman and Chernus in n. 154. On the coupling of the Sinaitic revelation and exposition on the vision of the chariot in later rabbinic sources, see Urbach, "The Traditions about Merkabah Mysticism in the Tannaitic Period," pp. 8–9; Goldberg, "Rabban Yoḥanans Traum"; Halperin, *The Merkabah in Rabbinic Literature,* pp. 128–133, 184; idem, *Faces of the Chariot,* pp. 17–23, 141–149, 289–322.

[157] See Halperin, *Faces of the Chariot,* pp. 17–19.

claims that God appeared both to individual prophets and to the nation at large. There have thus been many efforts in the vast corpus of rabbinic writings to preserve the invisible transcendence of God without entirely doing away with the visual dimension that is so important to Jewish belief. The commonplace characterization of Jewish thought with which I began this chapter, as auditory, as opposed to the Greek, which is visual, is a gross oversimplification. In striking contrast to the characterizations of Jewish faith as exclusively auditory, one would do well to consider the etymology of the word "Israel" as "one who sees God," preserved in Philo and, following him, many writers, including both Christian and Gnostic authors.[158]

To be sure, the Philonic conception, whether referring specifically to the nation of Israel or to the generic class of humanity called by the name Israel involves an intellectual vision of God (*theoria,* contemplation), perhaps of a mystical sort,[159] and not the physical sense of sight. Nevertheless, it is instructive that Philo singled out vision of God as the distinguishing mark of the Israelite. Lest one hasten to argue that the example of Philo proves the correctness of the distinction that I am contesting between Greek and Jew, inasmuch as the Philonic emphasis on vision is best understood in light of its Platonic background, it should be borne in mind that Philo's view is also grounded in the theophanic traditions of the Bible. The emphasis on vision, it can be argued, is indigenous to the religious mentality of the ancient Near East and can be explained, therefore, without difficulties on the basis of its native "Jewish" roots. The etymology of "Israel" as "one who sees God" is posited by Philo in such a way that some scholars have concluded that he did not invent this Hebrew *jeu de mots* but rather accepted an already established tradition. Moreover, this etymology is found in other writings, such as the *Prayer of Joseph*[160] and the relatively late midrashic collection *Seder 'Eliyahu Rabbah,*[161] without any obvious connection to a Greek ideal of *vita contemplativa*. Even more interesting is the use of this etymology in the Gnostic text from Nag Hammadi, *On the Origin of the World,* where it is applied to the firstborn of the angels in the eighth heaven, the locus of the divine chariot, which is described in terms that bear a striking resemblance to Jewish esotericism.[162]

In sum, it may be said that the patrimony of the biblical prophetic tradition in subsequent stages of Jewish religious history has made it impossible for the visionary dimension to be entirely neglected. The distinction between the visual and auditory orientation with respect to the divine does not signify a clash between Athens and Jerusalem. Rather, both epistemic modes are part of the

[158] The numerous places in the Philonic corpus where this etymology occurs have been conveniently listed by Smith, "The Prayer of Joseph," p. 266 n. 1. See also Delling, "The 'One Who Sees God' in Philo."

[159] See Winston, "Was Philo a Mystic?"; idem, *Logos and Mystical Theology in Philo of Alexandria,* esp. pp. 43–58.

[160] Smith, "Prayer of Joseph," pp. 265–268.

[161] *Seder 'Eliyahu Rabbah* 27, pp. 138–139.

[162] See *The Nag Hammadi Library in English,* ed. J. M. Robinson (San Francisco, 1988), p. 176.

biblical legacy. An approach more congruous with biblical, apocalyptic, rabbinic, and medieval mystical sources is one that aims at maintaining the concomitant affirmation and denial of the visualization of God. The cultural tension and the need to preserve both perspectives discussed above, without negating one or the other, is well reflected in the following comment in the midrashic collection *Tanḥuma:*

> Why is it written, "Seek out His countenance continually" (1 Chron. 16:11)? This is to teach that the Holy One, blessed be He, at times is seen and at times not seen, at times hears and at times does not want to hear, at times responds and at times does not want to respond, at times can be sought and at times cannot be sought, at times is found and at times not found, at times is close and at times not close. How is this? He was seen by Moses, as it says, "The Lord spoke to Moses [face to face as one speaks to another]" (Exod. 33:11). Afterwards He was hidden from him, as it says, "Show me Your glory" (ibid., 18). And similarly He was seen by Israel at Sinai, as it says, "And they saw the God of Israel" (ibid., 24:10), and it says, "Now the Presence of the Lord appeared [in the sight of the Israelites as a consuming fire on the top of the mountain]" (ibid., 17). Afterwards He was hidden from them, as it says, "For you have seen no image" (Deut. 4:15), and it says, "You heard the sound of the words [but perceived no shape, nothing but a voice]" (ibid., 12).[163]

From one perspective it is clearly impossible to speak of seeing God, since it is axiomatic that God does not possess a material form; yet from another it is precisely such a claim to visionary experience that must be upheld if one is to make sense out of a substantial part of the biblical text. Jewish exegesis has been driven by these apparently contradictory claims.[164] As I will demonstrate, in the classical texts of medieval Jewish mysticism these two poles are clearly discernible as well.

[163] *Midrash Tanḥuma,* Ha'azinu, 4. Cf. *Pesiqta de-Rav Kahana,* p. 471, where a version of this text has been copied.

[164] In this connection it is of interest to note the argument set forth by Gershenzon and Slomovic in "A Second Century Jewish-Gnostic Debate," pp. 12–18, that in some comments of R. Jose to the matrona recorded in aggadic literature he is responding to the Gnostic view that posits a dualism of the supreme God and the demiurge on the basis that the spatially manifest deity cannot be the highest God. The rabbinic view represented by R. Jose is precisely the opposite, viz., the God of Judaism is both transcendent and immanent.

• CHAPTER TWO •

Vision of God in Mystical Sources: A Typological Analysis

Contextualism and the Phenomenological Foundation of Mystical Experience

The problem of attaining a vision of God is particularly significant when assessing the mystical traditions of any given religion. Scholars who have attempted to delineate the phenomenological parameters of mysticism have duly noted the centrality of vision, particularly the *visio beatifica,* to the mystic experience.[1] Before proceeding to an examination of the theme of visionary experience in specifically Jewish texts, it is necessary to make a brief programmatic observation on the nature of mystical vision in general. Let me preface this by saying that I do not wish to ignore or take issue with a growing consensus among scholars that the mystical experience is itself conditioned by and rooted in the cultural-religious situation of the mystic.[2] On the contrary, I subscribe to the view that mystical experience, like experience more generally, is contextual.

The contextualist position in its strongest version, especially as it has been formulated by Steven Katz, has been criticized on the grounds that it is a form of "hyper-Kantianism."[3] Yet it seems to me correct to assess mystical experience in terms of human experience in general. The notion of an originary, first-hand, unmediated experience—a pure-givenness-in-consciousness-itself implied by the so-called "doctrine of unanimity," which posits a cross-cultural, universal mystical experience—is problematic. What experience can claim for itself the efficacy of a presuppositionless, immediately grounded datum given in consciousness? That which is experienced by the mystic is mediated by meanings that accrue from a perception and reception of the world informed by the religious and cultural affiliation of the particular mystic.[4] Indeed, as a variety of

[1] Some representative studies include: Herman, *The Meaning and Value of Mysticism,* pp. 45–68; Underhill, *Mysticism,* pp. 279–297; Kirk, *The Vision of God;* K. Rahner, *Visions and Prophecies* (London, 1963); Benz, *Die Vision Erfahrungsformen und Bilderwelt.* See also Moore, "Mystical Experience, Mystical Doctrine, Mystical Technique," pp. 119–120.

[2] See Coe, "The Sources of the Mystical Revelation," pp. 362–363, 367; Baruzi, "Introduction à des recherches sur le langage mystique," pp. 71–72; Arbman, *Ecstasy or Religious Trance* 1:347; Garside, "Language and the Interpretation of Mystical Experience"; Katz, "Language, Epistemology, and Mysticism"; idem, "Models, Modeling, and Mystical Training"; idem, "The Conservative Character of Mystical Experience"; Almond, *Mystical Experience and Religious Doctrine.*

[3] Forgie, "Hyper-Kantianism in Recent Discussions of Mystical Experience"; and see the more recent critique by Evans, "Can Philosophers Limit What Mystics Can Do?"

[4] See Finke, "Mystical Bodies and the Dialogics of Vision," p. 441.

scholars have recognized, mysticism is always part of a larger whole, which is the concrete religion of a given mystic.[5] It follows that the mystic's religious tradition provides an interpretative framework that is a constitutive factor of the mystical experience itself. The nature of mystical experience is such that it is difficult, if not impossible, to isolate an "essence" of the vision—an unchanging phenomenological core, as it were—that can be specified independently of the representational modes in the mystic's consciousness, modes that are informed by the mystic's own tradition. Put another way, one can distinguish but cannot ultimately separate the act of visual experience from interpretation. In a very fundamental sense perception is a hermeneutical act,[6] for we cannot "see" a thing without interpreting it in terms of practical interests and linguistic structures that shape the event of being.[7] In normal, everyday modes of perception the process of representation or interpretation is itself part of experience, for one does not merely see two- or three-dimensional colored shapes, but rather objects that represent the world as being (as Wittgenstein insisted, following a Kantian line[8]); so, too, in the realm of mystical experience.

Mystics' experiences are not isolated phenomena, but are rather links in a continuous chain of tradition. Hence, each mystic receives something from his or her predecessor, but that legacy is enriched by personal experiences. The biographical data of individual mystics must be viewed in a historical perspective.[9] It is the case, nevertheless, that the sense of immediacy experienced within the mediation constitutes the hallmark of mystical vision, which, in turn, helps to inform the tradition that gave it context and shape. Thus a dialectical relationship ensues between past visions recorded in literary texts and the present visionary experience, making the new experience, in effect, the reenvisioning of an original event. Furthermore, insofar as the visionary experience is hermeneutically related to the text, it may be said that the way of seeing is simultaneously a way of reading. In that regard, as Michael Lieb recently expressed it, one can speak of a "visionary hermeneutics that is both self-perpetuating and self-authorizing. . . . [F]or in the act of reenvisioning, that is, in writing the

[5] See, e.g., the classic study by Baron F. von Hügel, *The Mystical Element of Religion as Studied in Saint Catherine of Genoa and Her Friends*. Von Hügel's conclusion is developed in McGinn, *Foundations of Mysticism*, pp. xvi, 296.

[6] I have borrowed this locution from Heelan, "Perception as a Hermeneutical Act."

[7] See Nicholson, "Seeing and Reading: Aspects of Their Connection," pp. 34–42, and the more extended discussion in idem, *Seeing and Reading*. See also Yarian, "In the Eye of the Beholder," pp. 72–85. In the technical language of philosophical phenomenology, all being is phenomenal, but the phenomenality of being is constituted by the intentionality of transcendental subjectivity. Hence, while it is the primary task of the phenomenological reduction to attain a "pure seeing" that consists of grasping the "absolute self-givenness" of the phenomenal datum, the secondary stage of phenomenological analysis requires reflection on the intentional structure of consciousness. I share with phenomenologists such as Edmund Husserl, Martin Heidegger, and Maurice Merleau-Ponty the assumption that "things" seen are constituted in consciousness. From the vantage point of the phenomenal seeing, therefore, there is no distinction between an experienced and an imagined object.

[8] See M. Budd, "Wittgenstein On Seeing Aspects," *Mind* 96 (1987): 1–18, esp. 13–17.

[9] Lagorio, "The Medieval Continental Women Mystics," p. 161.

vision anew, the hermeneut is able to claim an interpretive authority tantamount to that which promulgated the visionary experience at its most primal level."[10] As I will argue in the concluding section of the next chapter, the whole distinction between experience and interpretation from the vantage point of the mystical sources within Judaism cannot be upheld.

The starting point of this analysis is a recognition of multiplicity in mystical traditions. But it seems to me a legitimate enterprise (as Katz denied) to probe the extant visionary accounts in search of a "foundation for a phenomenology of mysticism." In other words, there still can be a "typology of comparative mystical experience"[11] even if we grant that the experience, and not merely the postexperiential interpretation, is shaped by preexperiential beliefs that are, in some measure, unique to each mystic. Indeed, without that typology how could one account for, or even chart, the differences? In this respect I find myself in agreement with the structuralist view espoused by Mircea Eliade with regard to the specific issue of heavenly ascent: "In the history of religions, as in other mental disciplines, it is knowledge of structure which makes it possible to understand meanings. It is only after we have clarified, as a whole, the structure of the symbolism of the flight that we can arrive at its first meaning; the way is then open for us to understand each case separately."[12] If we substitute the word "vision" for "flight," then Eliade's statement is an entirely correct and succinct formulation of a theoretical principle to which I adhere in my analysis of mystical vision in Judaism. One can avoid the extremes of relativism or nominalism (hyper-Kantianism) and absolutism or essentialism (the doctrine of unanimity) by positing an intermediate position that seeks to determine the common structures underlying the manifold appearances of the phenomenon. By determining those structures we can appreciate the unique status of mystical vision in the different religious traditions. Within the diversity of manifestations of mystical visions in different cultural and religious contexts there must be some unity of resemblance, for without such unity through diversity the expression becomes meaningless, referring to everything and nothing.

The modified contextualism that I am advocating in light of a structuralist assumption regarding the nature of mystical experience—or more specifically, mystical vision—implies neither that all mystical experiences are the same and the descriptions of those experiences vary in accord with the different cultural-religious settings, nor that all mystical experience can be divided into "types" that cut across cultural boundaries and differ only in terms of the language used to describe them.[13] To reiterate my epistemological assumption noted above, the interpretative framework of a mystic's particular religion shapes his or her experience at the phenomenal level and not merely in the description or narrative account of the experience. This does not, however, logically preclude the

[10] Lieb, *The Visionary Mode,* p. 8.

[11] Katz, "Language, Epistemology, and Mysticism," p. 56.

[12] Eliade, *Myths, Dreams, and Mysteries,* p. 110.

[13] These are the second and third schema delineated by Katz in "Language, Epistemology, and Mysticism," p. 24.

possibility of underlying patterns of experience or deep structures that may be illuminated through a comparative study of various mystical traditions.[14] These patterns or structures are not the same as phenomenological typologies that presume some element of cross-cultural universality.

Here it would be worthwhile to recall a passage from Gershom Scholem, in which he reflects on the nature of the general phenomenon of mysticism:

> [T]here is no such thing as mysticism in the abstract, that is to say, a phenomenon or experience which has no particular relation to other religious phenomena. There is no mysticism as such, there is only the mysticism of a particular religious system, Christian, Islamic, Jewish mysticism and so on. That there remains a common characteristic it would be absurd to deny, and it is this element which is brought out in the comparative analysis of particular mystical experiences.[15]

The mystic attempts to transform the God of his or her particular religion in light of the immediate experience of the divine Presence that is characteristic of mysticism as an historical phenomenon. The parameters of the experience are therefore shaped by the given ideology of the mystic's religious affiliation. "It should now be clear," writes Scholem, "why the outward forms of mystical religion within the orbit of a given religion are to a large extent shaped by the positive content and values recognized and glorified in that religion. We cannot, therefore, expect the physiognomy of Jewish mysticism to be the same as that of Catholic mysticism, Anabaptism or Moslem Sufism."[16] It is axiomatic for Scholem that the mystic quest takes place exclusively within a prescribed tradi-

[14] The comparitivist perspective underlies Eliade's methodology in the history of religions, a methodology he calls "creative hermeneutics" which requires one to leave the familiarity of one's own cultural upbringing to explore and encounter with openness the other of archaic cultures. The hermeneut constructs the same only by discovering the other. See Yarian, "Mircea Eliade," pp. 57–71. In a fundamental sense this resonates with Scholem's claim that a comparative analysis of different mystical traditions will yield common phenomenological characteristics. The appreciation of what is shared comes only from treating a given mystical tradition as an autonomous historical reality. In yet another way the hermeneutical phenomenology of Eliade is similar to the methodology of Scholem, for a basic premise of the former is that the phenomenon of religion is not to be reduced to any other category of human experience but must be confronted on its own terms. Scholem would have readily assented to this nonreductionist approach. Moreover, while Eliade focuses on the timeless structures of religious experience, he maintains that these structures can only be studied as they manifest themselves in historical context. See *The Two and the One,* pp. 191–192: "The historian of religions in the strictest sense can never renounce his concern with the historically concrete. . . . Every expression or conceptual formulation of a given experience lies in a historical context." I think with respect to this balance between phenomenology and history there is again accord between the orientation of Eliade and that of Scholem. For a more critical approach to the noncontextualism of Eliade's comparitivist perspective, see Idel, *Kabbalah: New Perspectives,* pp. 11, 24–25, and Crapanzano, *Hermes' Dilemma and Hamlet's Desire,* pp. 219–228. See also n. 21, below.

[15] *Major Trends,* pp. 5–6.

[16] Ibid., p. 10. Scholem's more contextually-oriented approach has to be seen historically as a reaction to those scholars—including, most importantly, the early Buber—who would posit a common basis to mystical experience irrespective of differences of clime or creed, to use the description of William James. See Biale, *Gershom Scholem,* p. 89.

tion informed by religious institutions and authority.[17] Although Scholem denies the existence of mysticism as such—as an abstract mystical religion—he qualifies his contextualism as he readily admits a "common characteristic" of the mystical experience that would be clarified through a comparative analysis. Indeed, Scholem speaks of an omnipresent "essence of mystical experience" that consists of an ecstatic encounter with God.[18]

In another essay Scholem comments that "mystical experience as such is formless," for the reality toward which that experience progresses is "ultimate formlessness."[19] Elaborating on this, Scholem observes that

> the mystic's experience is by its very nature indistinct and inarticulate. . . . Indeed, it is precisely the indefinable, incommunicable character of mystical experience that is the greatest barrier to our understanding of it. It cannot be simply and totally translated into sharp images or concepts, and often it defies any attempt to supply it—even afterward—with positive content. Though many mystics have attempted such "translation," have tried to lend their experience form and body, the center of what a mystic has to say always remains a shapeless experience, regardless of whether we choose to interpret it as *unio mystica* or as "mere" communion with the divine. But it is precisely the shapeless core of his experience which spurs the mystic to his understanding of his religious world and its values, and it is this dialectic which determines his relation to the religious authority and lends it meaning.[20]

Scholem further relates the "formlessness of the original experience" to the possibility that the mystic may nihilistically reject all forms of expression, including, most significantly, the institutionalized forms of the mystic's given religion. Thus Scholem links what he considers to be the phenomenological core of mystical experience to the inherent "revolutionary" or antinomian element of mysticism. This pole is balanced by the "conservative" one that is associated with the need to lend structure and form to the inherently amorphous experience. In this secondary stage, therefore, one retrieves the contextualist orientation informed by a structuralist attitude regarding the universal formal elements present in different forms of mysticism.[21] What may be called the

[17] See *On the Kabbalah*, pp. 5–6.

[18] *Major Trends*, p. 15. See Schweid, *Judaism and Mysticism*, pp. 23–27, 53–56.

[19] *On the Kabbalah*, p. 8.

[20] Ibid., pp. 10–11.

[21] See ibid., p. 8 n. 1, where Scholem refers explicitly to one of the studies of Mircea Eliade in order to validate this point. Scholem's positive utilization of Eliade's study raises some question about Joseph Dan's generalization regarding Scholem's rejection of universal symbols and archetypal images. See Dan's foreword to Scholem, *On the Mystical Shape*, pp. 6–7. It is certainly the case that Scholem did seek the "dialectics of a dynamic historical development," as Dan puts it, and thus rejected the use of Jungian archetypes in his study of Jewish mysticism. On the other hand, it is obvious that Scholem was interested in structures of religious thought (frequently embracing the domain of symbol and myth) that must be sought in the textual remains of any community. In view of that, one can understand his explicit affirmation of the presence of "universal formal elements" in different mystical traditions that express themselves in symbolic structures such as light and

transition from experiential formlessness to narrative form is facilitated by the structures of the particular religious culture. In Scholem's own words,

> The symbols of the traditional religious authority play a prominent part in such structures. Only the most universal formal elements are the same in different forms of mysticism. For light and sound and even the name of God are merely symbolic representations of an ultimate reality which is unformed, amorphous. But these structures which are alternately broken down and built up in the course of the mystic's development also reflect certain assumptions concerning the nature of reality, which originated in, and derived their authority from, philosophical traditions, and then suprisingly (or perhaps not so suprisingly) found confirmation in mystical experience.[22]

Using Scholem's model, one could provide an antidote for the extremes of universalism and contextualism. I would not consent to Scholem's characterization

---

sound. Scholem's avoidance of Jungian archetypes must be understood in a more nuanced way as an opposition to the notion of an abstract, timeless archetype, and not to the presence of archetypal structures in lived religious cultures in general. To cite Scholem's own words: "Even though I should have had a strong affinity to Jung's concepts, which were close to religious concepts, I refrained from using them. . . . I particularly avoided the theory of archetypes." See Scholem, *On Jews and Judaism in Crisis,* p. 29, and the more balanced analysis of Scholem's relationship to Jung in Biale, *Gershom Scholem,* pp. 145–147. It should be noted that in one place Scholem actually proposes that a "peculiar mythical motif" connected to the idea of the righteous soul contains "something truly archetypal, in the Jungian sense" (*On the Mystical Shape,* p. 289 n. 58.) See also the veiled reference to the Jungian symbol of the "Great Mother" (developed by Erich Neumann), p. 161. This reference was already noted by Hava Tirosh-Rothschild in "Continuity and Revision in the Study of Kabbalah," *Association for Jewish Studies Review* 16 (1991): 183, and see n. 29 ad loc. Finally, it should be noted that in *Origins of the Kabbalah,* p. 162, Scholem uses the word "archetypes" to refer to images of the feminine in *Sefer ha-Bahir.* These examples alone suffice at least to raise doubt regarding Dan's approach. It would be absurd to deny that Scholem avoided Jungian archetypes, as he himself expressed this explicitly, but it would be equally misguided not to see that in some basic ways Scholem's phenomenological sensibility is predicated on the assumption that there are irreducible religious structures, linked to specific philological anchors, that are transmitted by oral or literary means in any given culture, although the possibility always exists that a given structure will pass from one tradition to another. I would suggest that Scholem's orientation is a kind of contextual archetypalism, a term that applies as well to Henry Corbin, another member of the Eranos Society in Scholem's time. The historical-philological method that Scholem adopted was clearly intended to provide a critical means by which the religious phenomena operative in Jewish mysticism could be evaluated and appreciated. See Scholem's letter to S. Z. Schocken, dated 29 October 1937, published in Scholem's *Explications and Implications,* pp. 29–31 (in Hebrew; original German version of the letter and English trans. in Biale, *Gershom Scholem,* pp. 74–76); and in the same volume, "Ten Unhistorical Propositions about the Kabbalah," pp. 32–38. Regarding the latter work, see Rosenstreich, "Symbolism and Transcendence"; Biale, "Gershom Scholem's Ten Unhistorical Aphorisms on Kabbalah"; Bloom, "Scholem: Unhistorical or Jewish Gnosticism," pp. 207–220; Dan, "Beyond the Kabbalistic Symbol." Underlying Dan's observations is his understanding of Scholem as historian, which he has enunciated in any number of publications, e.g., "Gershom Scholem: Between History and Historiosophy," esp. pp. 220–225. This orientation also marks the way of inquiry in Dan's *Gershom Scholem: The Mystical Dimension of Jewish History.*

22 *On the Kabbalah,* p. 8.

of the core mystical experience as being formless (inasmuch as I contend that all human consciousness is shaped by some interpretative framework,[23] and is thus symbolic in its eidetic structure), but I, too, accept a modified form of the contextualist approach along structuralist lines. It seems to me, therefore, appropriate and desirable to proceed with a methodological observation about the nature of the visionary experience of God, although I am further limiting myself to mystics working within theistic religious traditions.

Typologies of Mystical Vision: Introvertive and Cognitive

As a generalization it is reasonable to say that what is almost always intended by the mystic is a vision that is contemplative[24] or spiritual in nature rather than an actual physical vision of some aspect or entity within the spatial-temporal world. Yet it is possible to make a distinction between two types of contemplative vision in the history of Western mysticism. The first typology is that which characterizes the introvertive mystics, influenced primarily by the Neoplatonic idea of a transcendent One beyond all image and form. For such mystics the beatific vision is described as an "imageless vision" of the unity beyond differentiation and distinction. These mystics characteristically reject the senses and sensual imagery as adequate to the mystical vision. The approach to God rather is a *via negativa,* a gradual stripping away of sense experiences and rational concepts from one's mind.[25] To be sure, proponents of the mysticism of introversion will, in the end, insist that things invisible must be pursued through visible reality, particularly through the agency of the imagination.[26] For example, St. Augustine, one of the early proponents of a *via negativa,* identified "spiritual vision" (*visio spiritualis*)[27] as that which mediates

[23] It is for this reason that I also would not accept Scholem's theory of symbol as the expression of the inexpressible, a view clearly connected to his phenomenological assumptions regarding the essential formlessness of mystical experience that needs to be constantly (and ultimately inadequately) expressed. See Biale, *Gershom Scholem,* pp. 89–92; Handelman, *Fragments of Redemption,* pp. 104–109. For a critique of Scholem's theory of symbol in kabbalistic literature, see Idel, *Kabbalah: New Perspectives,* pp. 231–232, and Wolfson, "By Way of Truth," pp. 116–117 n. 43.

[24] It is of interest to note in this connection that in the Latin Church the term used to name the phenomenon we call mysticism was "contemplation." See Butler, *Western Mysticism,* pp. 4, 135.

[25] See Stace, *Mysticism and Philosophy,* pp. 111–123; Sells, "Apophasis in Plotinus." A recent, useful summary of the affirmation and negation of images in early Christian mysticism, influenced by Neoplatonism, is found in Cocking, *Imagination,* pp. 69–89. A classic example of a mystic in the Christian tradition who shunned visions as an appropriate medium for mystical experience was St. John of the Cross. See Werblowsky, "On the Mystical Rejection of Mystical Illumination."

[26] See C. Williams, *The Descent of the Dove* (Michigan, 1939), pp. 57–58; Grant, *Literature of Mysticism in Western Tradition,* pp. 25–38.

[27] See Bubacz, *St. Augustine's Theory of Knowledge,* pp. 99–103, 105–107; he notes that *visio spiritualis* is actually used in two different ways by Augustine: (1) "animal insight," which involves an outer faculty that deals with reports made by the bodily senses, and (2) "spiritual vision" proper, which is the mental capacity to form images based on what is perceived by bodily senses. Only human beings possess the capacity for *visio spiritualis* in the second sense.

between the corporeal and intellectual and which, in our terminology, corresponds to the imagination.[28] Augustine thus draws a technical distinction between "spiritual" and "intellectual" visions—the former, unlike the latter, relying on visual imagery that is perceived by the faculty of internal vision, the eye of the mind (*acies animi*).[29] Typical of this position is Augustine's explanation that the vision of the lamb in John 1:29 (cf. Apocalypse of John 5:6) involved "spiritual images of bodily figures" (*spiritualis imagines corporum*) or, alternatively, "spiritual visions of bodily images" (*spiritualibus visis imagium corporalium*).[30] For Augustine himself there is a definite hierarchy, in which intellectual vision (*intellectualis visio*) is the highest mode of seeing, surpassing corporeal and spiritual vision (*corporalis et spiritualis visio*), which correspond to sense and imagination, respectively. The capacity of intellectual vision transcends the imagination, for no images are involved.[31] For example, in one passage Augustine reflects on the scriptural claim that Moses beheld God face-to-face (Num. 12:8) and notes that this is the highest form of vision in which God is seen, for it involves neither carnal sense nor spiritual vision, but is rather a purely intellectual or rational conception.[32]

In line with this Augustinian tradition, despite the positive role accorded to images, the claim of the introvertive mystics is still that the mystical seeing in its most pristine state is without visual imagery, an intellectual vision devoid of percept or concept. Even though the introvertive mystics inevitably characterize the ultimate experience in terms derived from the phenomenal realm, such as dazzling light, darkness, or silence, it may be argued that these terms function as symbols for the unitive experience and thus transcend their primary meanings as sensible images. For the mystics especially influenced by Neoplatonism, mystical experience is an immediate or intellectual intuition, thereby bypassing the senses and the imagination. Logically, this approach should culminate in an apophatic theology that assumes that statements about what God is not have more truth value than statements about what God is. God's presence is experienced as absence, that is, consciousness of God as negation is the core of the mystical experience. "Leave aside this everywhere and this everything," wrote the anonymous author of *The Cloud of Unknowing,* "in exchange for this nowhere and this nothing. . . . A man's affection is remarkably changed in the spiritual experience of this nothing when it is achieved nowhere."[33] Imagelessness thus overcomes image in the *visio mystica,* yielding the paradoxical situation that sensible or imaginative seeing is spiritual blindness.

There is, in addition, a second typology of mystical vision well attested in the

[28] On the complex issue of imagination in Augustine, see Bundy, "The Theory of Imagination in Classical and Mediaeval Thought," pp. 153–172.

[29] Augustine, *De Genesi ad Litteram* 12.6–7, 11, 14. See also other sources discussed in Bundy, "Theory of Imagination," pp. 163–164, 167–168.

[30] *De Trinitate* II, 6:11, in *Patralogiae Latina,* 42: col. 852.

[31] See Bundy, "Theory of Imagination," pp. 167–168.

[32] *De Genesi ad Litteram* 12.27, in *Patralogiae Latina* 34: col. 477. Cf. Bundy, "Theory of Imagination," p. 171.

[33] *The Cloud of Unknowing,* ed. J. Walsh (New York, 1981), pp. 252–253.

various religions of the West and ultimately rooted in the prophetic and apocalyptic traditions.[34] This is the typology of "cognitive" mysticism, which affirms that supernatural or spiritual knowledge comes by way of revelation, intuition, or illumination. The culminating stage on the *via mystica* is not an eradication of all percepts and concepts, a stripping away of all sensational and representational form, but rather the beholding of the ultimate form—a vision of God in "gleams of ecstatic vision."[35] Although in this case as well, the mystical experience is "contemplative" and not "physical," it is inevitable that the mystical vision is experienced within the phenomenological parameters of human experience as such. Moreover, the object of that vision is form in its ultimate sense, that which renders all other forms of human experience pale reflections of the one true reality.

Scholars who deal with this kind of vision have traditionally explained it as the translation of an ineffable experience into communicable form, that is, images and metaphors used by mystics to convey the visual experience are extracted from the sensible world. (In this respect the scholars have, perhaps unwittingly, adopted the Augustinian perspective on spiritual visions in order to explain the necessary use of perceptual images by mystics.) A recent account of this process by Elizabeth Howe may be considered a rather typical approach adopted by scholars in the past: "Despite the essential incommunicability of the mystical experience, the mystics do attempt to put in writing what they have encountered in union. . . . All mystics, therefore, have recourse to images and symbols drawn from the sensible world to speak analogously of the spiritual."[36] Another rather typical account of this is found in the words of Helen Rolfson, though her focus is exclusively on mystics within the Christian tradition: "Christian mystics have always contended that their experience transcended human capacity for expression; nonetheless, images, however faltering, always played a part in their attempt to verbalize their experience of God. At the same time, that imagery told of the mystics' perception of God's relationship to them."[37] Rolfson is thus aware of the centrality of images to Christian mystics, but she insists that this imaging reflects the desire of the mystics to translate an ineffable experience of God into words for the benefit of others. The use of images on the part of mystics betrays, therefore, a need and longing to bridge the ontic chasm that separates God and human.

What scholars have not always duly noted is that recourse to sensible images and symbols is part of the mystical experience itself and is not restricted to the description of an ineffable experience in oral or written communication. Mysti-

[34] It is significant that McGinn begins his comprehensive study of Western Christian mysticism (see *Foundations of Mysticism*, pp. 9–22) with a discussion of "The Jewish Matrix," which includes more specifically the elements found in the apocalypses of the late Second Temple period that helped lay the foundation for the growth of mysticism in rabbinic Judaism and early Christianity.

[35] Underhill, *Mysticism*, p. 226.

[36] *Mystical Imagery*, pp. 44–45.

[37] "Images of God in the Mystics," p. 123.

cal vision is such that the suprasensible world is experienced in sensory imagery and not simply described in terms of the sensible.[38] The point is well made in a description of contemplation in the Christian tradition given by Margaret Miles: "*Theoria*—contemplation in which one is lifted out of one's familiar world and into the living presences of the spiritual world—begins with physical vision, with a trained and concentrated seeing that overcomes conceptual barriers between the visible and the spiritual worlds."[39] This overcoming of the boundary between spiritual and physical does not imply, in the moment of visualization, a negation or transcendence of the concrete image. In traversing the barrier between visible and spiritual worlds, the mystic experiences the latter in terms of the modalities of the former. There is no passage in which the cognitive and epistemological categories of the sensory world are consumed by the fires of spiritual reality. On the contrary, those very conditions are upheld, for they allow for an experience of the divine matters that figure prominently in the mystical vision.

To underscore the position I have adopted, let me contrast it with the view expressed by Scholem regarding the three stages of consciousness in the mystical experience. The first consists of a tendency to describe the experience in "forms drawn from the world of perception"; the second involves the replacement of these "natural forms" by "specifically mystical structures"; the third stage is the dissolution of all structures as the mystic's experience "progresses toward the ultimate formlessness."[40] Scholem's remarks betray the influence of the introvertive typology, inasmuch as the culminating phase of the mystical experience entails a formlessness that overcomes all forms. According to the cognitive typology, by contrast, that third stage is not an essential component of the mystical experience. The "specifically mystical structures" Scholem identifies as the intermediate stage between natural forms and formlessness consist, according to the alternative typology I am suggesting, of the sensible images drawn from the phenomenal world of perception. That is, I see no reason to contrast the first and second stages, insofar as the phenomenological (leaving aside the ontological) character of the latter is indistinguishable from the former. To be sure, the mystic has been psychically transported and his or her field of vision is not the sensible realm of everyday experience. Yet what is seen by the mystic are forms of experience whose phenomenality is characterized by a tangibility appropriate to sense data.

In specific, the agency for this psychical transport is the imaginative faculty by means of which the mystic envisions transcendent realities (in and of themselves not available to sense perception or intellection) as concrete and tangible symbols. Through the agency of the imagination one enters the *ʿālam al-mithāl*

[38] My argument accords with the position articulated by Chidester (*Word and Light,* pp. 1–24) to the effect that religious symbolism is grounded in sensory perception. The power of the symbol, therefore, lies in its ability to affect the whole being, including sensory experiences, and not simply theological doctrines.

[39] *Image as Insight,* pp. 150–151.

[40] *On the Kabbalah,* p. 8.

(*mundus imaginalis*), in Henry Corbin's telling phrase,[41] which is not the imaginary world of subjective fantasy or psychotic hallucination, but is instead a realm where invisible realities become visible and corporeal entities are spiritualized.[42] The world of the imaginal is an intermediary realm wherein the imaginative forms (or archetypal images) symbolize the intelligible in terms of the sensory.[43] The primary function of the imagination is hermeneutical: rather than recalling past sense data or combining these data in some innovative and, technically speaking, unexperienced way,[44] the imagination produces symbols of the spiritual entities that act as interpretative filtering screens through which these entities appear in human consciousness. In that respect one can speak of the "symbolizing power of imagination," for the images produced by the imagination are symbolic representations; imagination, therefore, is essentially a dimension of language and its most basic structural feature is semantic innovation.[45]

The function of the imagination is to say one thing in terms of another and thereby conjoin that which is inarticulate and that which is verbally circumscribed within a semantic field. Imagination is the faculty through which one opens the boundaries of the phenomenological horizon by producing symbols that express the inexpressible in such ways that there is perfect agreement between the symbol and what is symbolized. The image is a diaphanous symbol through which the opaque reality shines. Hence it is appropriate to characterize the imagination hermeneutically, as it is first and foremost an agent of

[41] *Creative Imagination in the Sūfism of Ibn ʿArabī,* pp. 189, 217.

[42] See Chittick, *The Sufi Path of Knowledge,* p. ix; idem, *The Sufi Path of Love,* pp. 248–267.

[43] See Corbin, *Spiritual Body and Celestial Earth,* pp. 76–77; Chittick, *Faith and Practice of Islam,* pp. 190–191.

[44] These are the two standard activities associated with the imagination in medieval psychology, based largely on an Aristotelian model. For a succinct formulation of the two senses of imagination—the reproductive, which retraces past sense experiences, and the productive, which combines those sense data in new and unexpected ways—see Derrida, *The Archeology of the Frivolous,* pp. 71–87.

[45] See Ricoeur, "L'imagination dans le discours et dans l'action," pp. 215–216; idem, *Hermeneutics and Human Sciences,* p. 181. See also Durand, *Les structures anthropologiques de l'imaginaire,* pp. 348, 506; Dubois, *L'imaginaire de la renaissance,* pp. 17–48; Caponigri, "Icon and Theon," pp. 29–51. On the hermeneutical function of imagination as the cognitive faculty that bestows meaning, see also Dufrene, *In the Presence of the Sensuous,* pp. 27–37. It is important to note that for Jung there is an intrinsic connection between the images conjured by the active imagination from the emotive contents of the unconscious and archetypal symbols. See, for example, *The Symbolic Life: Miscellaneous Writings,* trans. R. F. C. Hull (Princeton, 1980), p. 171: "Active imagination, as the term denotes, means that the images have a life of their own and that the symbolic events develop according to their own logic—that is, of course, if your conscious reason does not interfere." Two representative studies of Jungian active imagination are: M. L. von Franz, *Alchemical Active Imagination* (Dallas, 1979), and B. Hannah, *Encounters with the Soul: Active Imagination as Developed by C. G. Jung* (Boston, 1981). See also Casey, *Imagining,* pp. 212–217. Finally, let me note that in his study *Gnosis,* Dan Merkur has also employed the Jungian model of the active imagination to understand the dynamics of visionary experience in several traditions, including that of ancient and medieval Jewish mysticism (see pp. 155–180).

meaning in the production of symbols.[46] Not only is the imagination not to be seen as subordinate to reason, as the medieval Aristotelians would have it, but it is elevated to a position of utmost supremacy; it is, in effect, the divine element of the soul that enables one to gain access to the realm of incorporeality through a process of symbolization, that is, a process of understanding that transcends—by hermeneutically transmuting—sensory data and rational concepts. Through the iconic representation of the imagination the divine, whose pure essence is incompatible with all form, is nevertheless manifested in a symbolic form belonging to the "Imaginative Presence," to borrow another technical term employed by Corbin in his description of the Spanish Sufi Muḥyī d-Dīn Muḥammad ibn ʿAli ibn al-ʿArabī (1165–1240).[47]

The symbolic representation in the mystical vision may be compared to the production of the verbal metaphor by the poetic imagination. Thus, the visual model of the image is to be combined with the verbal. The latter is not to be privileged over the former, but rather a synchronicity must be posited, such that the seeing of a mental image is at the same time a construction of a symbol that reconciles dissimilar meanings. The religious symbol, particularly prominent in mystical literature, is a fusion of binary oppositions held together in the sensible experience of transcendence that the symbol elicits.

A striking example of this process in Jewish mysticism can be found in an esoteric doctrine concerning the secret of the garment (*sod ha-malbush*) alluded to by Moses ben Naḥman, known as Naḥmanides (1194–1270). In a separate study[48] I have discussed at length the likely meaning of this doctrine; here I will only take note of the points relevant to the present discussion. In the context of criticizing Maimonides' theory of prophecy, which linked prophetic visions with the angels, viewed as separate intellects, Naḥmanides asserts that in those cases where Scripture mentions angels as human beings, this involves the "created glory in [the form of] the angels, referred to by those who know as the garment, which is apprehended by eyes of the flesh of the pure of heart, as the pious and the sons of the prophets, but I cannot explain."[49]

In my opinion, Naḥmanides here alludes to the capacity of the divine Presence, designated as the "created glory," to assume an anthropomorphic shape that is visible to the pure of heart—the pious and sons of the prophets. The glory has the capacity to appear to certain human beings in human form, and when it does so it is an angelic state. What needs to be emphasized here is that Naḥmanides states unequivocally that the incarnate form of the glory—the garment—is seen by the physical eye. Although Naḥmanides carefully qualifies

[46] My discussion here has been influenced by Kearney's analysis of Ricoeur and Bachelard in *Poetics of Imagining,* pp. 134–169. See also Bruns, "The Problem of Figuration in Antiquity," pp. 147–164.

[47] *Creative Imagination,* p. 218.

[48] See Wolfson, "The Secret of the Garment in Naḥmanides." The symbolic portrayal of God's assuming manifest form in history in terms of donning garments is expressed in earlier rabbinic sources, in part reflecting the biblical idiom in verses such as Ps. 93:1 and 104:1.

[49] Naḥmanides' commentary to Gen. 18:1, ed. Chavel, 1:106.

his statement by claiming that this garment is seen only by the eye of the spiritually superior individual,[50] the fact is that it is seen as if it were a tangible form and its presence is such that it imprints itself on the mind of the visionary as if it were an image of sensible reality. From another comment of Naḥmanides it is clear that he maintains the possibility of the splendor of the Presence being concretized in some bodily form (the verb used in that context is *mitgashem*), as was the case with the generation of Israelites who left Egypt, for they apprehended the splendor of the Presence at the Red Sea in an anthropomorphic shape.[51] The image seen is no "subjective" phantasm in the mind, but the ontically real form assumed by the supernal light in the theophanic moment.

I will cite one example of this kind of illumination in the rich and extensive visionary literature of medieval Christian mysticism. The illustration I have selected is the celebrated description of visions given by St. Hildegard of Bingen (1098–1179) in her epistle to Guibert of Gembloux:

> In this vision my soul, as God would have it, rises up high into the vault of heaven and into the changing sky and spreads itself out among different peoples, although they are far away from me in distant lands and places. And because I see them this way in my soul, I observe them in accord with the shifting of clouds and other created things. I do not hear them with my outward ears, nor do I perceive them by the thoughts of my own heart or any combination of my five senses, but in my soul alone, while my outward eyes are open. So I have never fallen prey to ecstasy in the visions, but I see them wide awake, day and night. . . . The light that I see this is not spatial, but it is far, far brighter than a cloud that carries the sun. I can measure neither height, nor length, nor breadth in it; and I call it "the reflection of the living Light." . . . Moreover, I can no more recognize the form of this light than I can gaze directly on the sphere of the sun. Sometimes—but not often—I see within this light another light, which I call "the living Light." And I cannot describe when and how I see it, but while I see it all sorrow and anguish leave me, so that I feel like a simple girl instead of an old woman.[52]

It is evident from this account that the locus of spiritual vision is the soul rather than the physical senses or the mind. Hildegard thus explicitly rejects reducing her vision either to normal modes of sense perception or to some psychological state of altered consciousness: "I do not hear them with my outward ears, nor do I perceive them by the thoughts of my own heart or any combination of my five senses, but in my soul alone." What she "sees" or "hears" is seen or heard in the soul, which is the divine faculty by means of

[50] The idea that a vision can be seen only by an individual even though other people are present at the moment of the experience is affirmed in midrashic precedents. See, e.g., *Shemot Rabbah* 2:5.

[51] See Naḥmanides' commentary to Exod. 16:6, ed. Chavel, 1:365. For an extraordinary affirmation of an incarnational approach in a kabbalistic text, see Joseph of Hamadan, *Sefer Tashak*, ed. Zwelling, p. 13: "Therefore the Holy One, blessed be He, said to Moses our master, peace be upon him, 'Tell the Israelite people to bring me [gifts]' (Exod. 25:2), they should make a body and soul for [their] God and I will take bodily form (*'etgashem*) in it." According to this text, the Tabernacle functioned as the sacred space in which the divine assumed a bodily or concrete form.

[52] *Hildegard of Bingen. Scivias*, trans. Mother Columbia Hart and J. Bishop (New York, 1990), pp. 18–19.

which things divine are revealed. On the other hand, Hildegard emphasizes that the vision occurs "while my outward eyes are open." She insists that the visions do not result from a state of ecstasy into which she may have fallen, but rather "I see them wide awake, day and night." The content of the vision is a luminosity she calls "the reflection of the living Light," although at times she even beholds "the living Light" itself, which appears to be the luminous divine Presence.[53] Still, the reader is told that the objects of spiritual vision are observed "in accord with the shifting of clouds and other created things." That is, the vision consists of beholding a variety of figures, in terms of objects taken from the physical realm, within the light, which is not spatial or measurable.

A perusal of Hildegard's visions confirms that her visionary experiences entail intricate details drawn from the normal phenomenal field, with the light metaphors especially dominating these visual accounts. The vision, therefore, is a symbolic presentation of spiritual (luminous) realities in corporeal (phenomenal) forms. This precise correspondence is reflected in the thirty-five miniatures that accompanied the earliest manuscript of Hildegard's *Scito vias Domini* (known by its short title *Scivias*), prepared around 1165, apparently under the author's supervision. As Barbara Newman has observed, the illustrative prints draw the viewer into the numinous world of the visionary's own experience and thus resemble the didactic and meditative diagrams found in the works of Hugh of St. Victor.[54] The iconographic representations of the visions can provide a means for the reader to enter the spiritual world of the visionary, for the visionary herself has experienced matters of the spirit in iconic forms.[55]

In the descriptions of Hildegard's visions there is a natural progression from the sight of the soul—the mystical vision that exceeds the normal range of physical perception—to the sense of the object's immediacy, such that the mystic thought the object of her vision was a man of flesh and blood. In the mystical vision spirit and matter coalesce, and the thing most abstract is felt as most concrete; the experience itself can never be absolutely devoid of form and figure. Put differently, the vision is always experienced, and not merely described, in essentially symbolic terms. This, it seems, is the "sublime melancholy"[56] of the mystic visionary: human experience is such that the noetic content of consciousness is always tied to image and form—even if the goal is to experience (or not experience) the imageless and formless.[57] It is thus possible to distin-

[53] Ibid., p. 11.

[54] Ibid.

[55] For another illustration of this phenomenon in Christian visionary literature, see *The Book of Margery Kempe,* ed. and trans. W. Butler-Bowdon (New York, 1944), pp. 59, 190. Cf. Atkinson, *Mystic and Pilgrim,* pp. 41–48, p. 46. See also Pespres, "Franciscan Spirituality," pp. 12–13.

[56] I have utilized Martin Buber's telling expression from quite a different context; see Buber, *I and Thou,* trans. W. Kaufmann (New York, 1970), p. 69, and discussion in Wolfson, "The Problem of Unity in the Thought of Martin Buber," p. 438.

[57] This can be expressed in terms of the Aristotelian axiom "Nihil est in intellectu quod prius non fuerit in sensu." In the history of medieval Christian mysticism a tension arose between the Augustinian introvertive approach and Aristotelian epistemology, especially as it was expressed by Thomas Aquinas. See Mallory, *Christian Mysticism,* pp. 142–149.

guish between the contemplative vision in Jewish, Christian, and Islamic authors and the purely Neoplatonic vision on precisely the grounds that in the case of the former the vision is not entirely free of concrete and sensible images, which are supplied, at least in part, by the specific representational modes of the given religious tradition. Hence, a twelfth-century Franciscan did not envision God as an elderly sage studying Torah, nor did the thirteenth-century kabbalist see God as the Saviour nailed to the cross. Seeing God—like seeing anything—is seeing God as something, that is, under certain aspects that are informed by some prior interpretative framework. The imaging of the divine, therefore, does not simply result from the mystic's desire to translate the ineffable experience into a communicable form, but is an intrinsic part of the experience itself. That is, for the theistic mystic the vision is filtered through a religious imagination informed by a nexus of social, cultural, and historical realia. From that perspective it is form, not formlessness, that is essential to the mystical vision, even though it may be presumed that a mystic in any of these three religious traditions—especially in the High Middle Ages, the period of most intense mystical activity—would readily acknowledge that God's essential being is formless, invisible, beyond image.[58]

According to the second typology, then, the mystical vision, and not merely the postexperiential account or description of it, is at the core metaphorical or analogical, for it seeks to make the spiritual world "perceptible" to the material by relating an object from the latter to the former.[59] The symbolic vision bridges the gap between the invisible and the visible, the spiritual and the corporeal, by lending approximate expression to the transcendental truth. In that sense the dynamics of visionary experience can be compared to those of a dream, although, as we shall see, the mystics themselves upheld a distinction between dreams and mystical visions. That is, just as a dream, understood in psychoanalytic terms, is the pictorial representation of one's thoughts, impulses, or fantasies woven from the symbolic fabric of the unconscious, so the mystical vision is formed by the visionary on the basis of the symbolic network provided by his or her given religious tradition. In moments of mystical experience, that tradition functions as the unconscious repository of images and forms.

This structure, in my view, is particularly apt for describing the dynamic of the mystical vision: the image of the visible form of the invisible reality conjured in the imagination of the mystic visionary is a symbolic event informed by a series of assumptions received from the mystic's religious tradition rather than self-created. The psychic image-symbols are not derived from a Jungian collective unconscious, a common substratum that transcends all differences in culture and consciousness, but rather from the particular tradition of a given

[58] The point is made clearly within the Christian mystical tradition in a comparison of Rusybroeck's cataphatic theology and Meister Eckhart's apophatic negative theology. See Dupré, *The Common Life,* pp. 26–27; Lichtmann, "Complete Mysticism."

[59] See MacKinnon, "Some Epistemological Reflections on Mystical Experience," p. 132; Howe, *Mystical Imagery,* p. 49.

mystic. The most basic structural feature of the imagining process is that the imagination produces symbols, but the symbols that it produces conform to—indeed, are shaped by—specific religious and cultural assumptions rather than universal archetypes.

Symbolic Vision in Jewish Mysticism and the Role of the Imagination

When we come specifically to the different varieties or trends of Jewish mysticism, it is the typology of cognitive mysticism that is critical, though the *via negativa* is not entirely lacking in medieval kabbalistic sources.[60] The vision attested in Jewish mystical sources, beginning with the Hekhalot texts and continuing in the major documents of German Pietism and of ecstatic and theosophical kabbalah of the High Middle Ages, likewise reflects the coalescence of spirit and matter, which, in my terminology, renders the experience in and of itself symbolic. Although this point seems obvious enough, the failure of scholars working in the area of Jewish mysticism to articulate matters in this way has led to some confusion regarding the nature of mystical experience in these sources. By bearing in mind the basic fact that the mystical vision is characterized by this symbolic coalescence and is therefore always hermeneutical, one can answer some of the still unresolved questions with respect to the problem of visionary experience in the different phases of Jewish mysticism. The corporealization of the divine image, so central to visionary experience in the various historical stages of Jewish mystical speculation, must be seen in light of the analogical function of symbols outlined above. The symbolic form through which God is apprehended, the *protos anthropos,* both generates and is generated by the mystical consciousness within Judaism.

Mystical vision in the Jewish sources is not concerned with the unnameable, ineffable, faceless ground of being, but rather with the personal God visualized in concrete and at times intensely mythical terms. The noetic content of the

60 The negative path would be especially appropriate for the highest aspects of the Godhead, either the Infinite itself (*Ein-Sof*) or the first of the gradations (*Keter,* identified as Thought or Will). See Scholem, "Schöpfung aus Nichts und Selbstverschränkung Gottes"; idem, *Origins of the Kabbalah,* pp. 420–425, 430–443; idem, *Kabbalah,* pp. 88–96; idem, "La Lutte entre le Dieu de Plotin et la Bible dans la Kabbale ancienne"; Matt, "Ayin." See, however, Idel, "Jewish Kabbalah and Platonism in the Middle Ages and Renaissance," pp. 338–343, where he argues that the influence of a Neoplatonic negative theology is marginal in the early kabbalah, where esoteric doctrines concerning the positive and even anthropomorphic nature of the Infinite were cultivated. Interestingly, Idel singles out Ismāʿīlī thought as a possible conduit by means of which a more strictly negative theology passed into theosophic kabbalah. On the notion of a positive Infinite with anthropomorphic implications in kabbalistic sources, see Idel, "The Image of Adam above the Sefirot"; idem, "The Sefirot above the Sefirot"; idem, "Kabbalistic Material from the School of R. David ben Judah he-Ḥasid," p. 173. See also Wolfson, "Negative Theology and Positive Assertion in the Early Kabbalah".

vision, intentionally constituted within the mystic's imaginal consciousness,[61] is the luminous form of God (denoted by various terms including, most frequently, *demut, ṣurah,* and *kavod*) that is capable of appearing in a variety of forms but generally assumes the figure or shape of an anthropos. The anthropomorphic form of God is central to both the theosophical component and the ecstatic experience that characterize the diverse forms of Jewish mysticism. I do not mean to suggest that there has been universal agreement among Jewish mystics in all periods regarding the form of God. On the contrary, it is evident that the specification of this form varies widely from one historical period to another and, in some cases, from one mystic to another living at the same time and in geographical proximity. I am, however, suggesting that the very notion of a divine form or image provides us with an underlying phenomenological construct that has informed the Jewish esoteric tradition in its multiple expressions.

Jewish mystics at each stage apply their respective theosophical or theological systems to characterize in positive terms the nature of God's form. Expressed in exegetical terms, one of the critical links in Jewish mysticism is the juxtaposition of Gen. 1:26 and Ezek. 1:26. That the anthropos is made in God's image implies that God is in the image of the anthropos. Yet in the Jewish sources the divine form is never concretized in a specific human being of flesh and blood. The appearance of God as human is an imaginative process that in my understanding is essentially hermeneutical—a symbolic representation of the dissimilar. Such an understanding is implied in Ezekiel's vision of the chariot, which culminates with the following description:

> Above the firmament upon their heads was the appearance of sapphire stone, the likeness of a throne (*demut kisse'*), and upon the likeness of the throne was the

[61] I am here influenced by the claim of phenomenologists regarding the intentional structure of all imaginative experience, i.e., that intentionality is basic to the imagination and all processes of imaging. In that sense one cannot speak of an intentional object that is imaged without an intentional act of imaging, just as one cannot speak of the act without the object. See the lucid analysis in Casey, *Imagining,* pp. 38–60. By employing phenomenological categories one may avoid the pitfalls of distinguishing between "real" and "unreal" when analyzing an imagined form of consciousness. When evaluated within the phenomenological bracket, the Husserlian *epoche,* there is no objective difference in transcendental consciousness between the "real," whether perceptual or conceptual, and "imaginary" object. Consider in particular the description of the phenomenological method in Husserl, *Ideas Pertaining to a Pure Phenomenology and to a Phenomenological Philosophy, Second Book,* p. 97: "Hence the task is 'to draw out of experience' the authentic concept of the psychic. But obviously here, as elsewhere in phenomenology, this does not mean to engage straightforwardly in actual experiences, i.e., to proceed empirically, as if the empirical thesis, which binds itself to contingent facts, would be pertinent. The task is rather to examine, *in eidetic intuition, the essence of the experienced in general and as such,* precisely as it is made explicit in any experience, whether carried out actually or imaginatively (by means of a fictional transfer of oneself into a possible experience) in order to grasp intuitively, in the unfolding of the intentions essentially involved in such an experience, the sense of the experienced as such—the sense of the relevant class of regional objectivities—and to express this sense in rigorous analysis and description" (emphasis in original). See also idem, *The Idea of Phenomenology,* pp. 23–24: "I can, moreover, represent to myself in imagination or memory a perception and survey it as so given

> likeness of the appearance of a man (*demut ke-mar'eh 'adam*). And I saw the likeness of the *ḥashmal,* as the appearance of fire surrounding it, from the appearance of his loins upward, and from the appearance of his loins downward I saw the appearance of fire and splendor surrounding him. Like the appearance of a bow that is in a cloud on a rainy day, so is the appearance of the splendor surrounding him, this was the appearance of the likeness of the glory of God (*mar'eh demut kevod YHWH*).[62]

I will have occasion to discuss this vision in more detail at the end of the next chapter, but let me dwell briefly in this context on the terms used by the prophet to describe the glory that he has seen: likeness (*demut*) and appearance (*mar'eh*). The word *demut,* likeness, is derived from the verb *damah,* to be like, to resemble; the word *mar'eh,* appearance, is from the verb *ra'ah,* to see. These two words relate to two aspects of the imagination: one component of the imaginative process produces an image or copy of something, a likeness of that which is represented, whereas the image produced allows the phenomenon to appear, to take shape, to be manifest.[63] Hence the text speaks of "the likeness of the appearance of a man" (*demut ke-mar'eh 'adam*) and of "the appearance of the likeness of the glory of God" (*mar'eh demut kevod YHWH*). The combination of *demut* and *mar'eh* suggests to me that this vision is an imaginative one, for the form in which the glory is manifested on the chariot is constituted in the prophet's imagination. This is not to say that what Ezekiel saw was a hallucination or fantasy, reflecting the modern sense of the word "imagination." Rather, we see an effort to locate phenomenologically the nature of this experience: the morphology of the divine glory is here linked to the words *demut* and *mar'eh,* and these indicate that we are dealing with imagined forms. In that sense we can speak of the convergence of anthropomorphism and theomorphism in the visionary experience: to attribute human form to God is to attribute divine form to humans.

At the core of the mystical vision attested in the Jewish material to be discussed in the remainder of this book one finds the same convergence. As I noted in the introduction, the phenomenological basis for this convergence, the figural corporealization of God within the human imagination, is provided by Hosea 12:11, which describes the prophetic process, "I have multiplied visions and in the hands of the prophets I was imaged." The exegetical recasting of this verse, particularly the second clause, indicates the central role accorded the

---

to imagination. . . . perception itself stands open to my inspection as actually or imaginatively given to me."

[62] Ezek. 1:26–28.

[63] A similar philological pattern is discernible in Greek, for the term εικασια, "imagination," is derived from ἐίκω, "to be like" or "capable of being compared," and from ἐίκω derives the noun ἐίκων, i.e., an image, copy, or likeness. The other Greek term for imagination, φαντᾶσία, derives from φαίνω, "to appear," "to be apparent," "to come to light." From φαίνω developed φαντάζω, "to take shape," "to take a definite appearance," whence derived the noun φαντᾶσία, i.e., appearance or the mental state of imaging an appearance. See Bundy, "Theory of the Imagination," pp. 11–12.

imagination in the mystical consciousness within historical Judaism. The visionary realm of the imagination becomes, in the Jewish mystical tradition, the locus of God's self-revelation. This, it seems to me, is already implied in one of the most ancient books of Jewish esotericism, *Sefer Yeṣirah* ("Book of Formation").[64]

In the form in which the book has come down to us, the principles of creation are thirty-two paths of wondrous or secret wisdom denominated by the twenty-two Hebrew letters and ten entities designated by the neologism *sefirot belimah*. It is generally assumed by scholars that this term refers in this context to primordial numbers that serve, in Scholem's locution, as metaphysical principles or stages of the creation of the world.[65] It is evident, however, that in *Sefer Yeṣirah* itself the *sefirot* assume a variety of characteristics reflecting different approaches that have been welded together through a process of redaction.[66] In this context I would like to isolate for a close reading the very first textual unit, which attempts to explain the nature of the *sefirot:*

> Ten *sefirot belimah:* The number of the ten fingers, five corresponding to five. The covenant of unity is set in the middle, in the circumcision of the tongue and mouth and the circumcision of the foreskin.
>
> Ten *sefirot belimah:* Ten and not nine, ten and not eleven. Understand in wisdom and be wise in understanding, examine and investigate them. Know, contemplate, and imagine, establish the matter clearly, and set the Creator in His place (*mekhono*).[67] Their measure is ten without end.
>
> Ten *sefirot belimah:* Stop your heart from thinking and your mouth from speaking. If your heart runs, return to the place whence you came, and remember that it thus

[64] For a relatively early date for *Sefer Yeṣirah,* between the third and sixth centuries, see Scholem, *Major Trends,* p. 75; see also article of S. Pines cited in chapter 1, n. 61; and Liebes, *The Sin of Elisha,* pp. 101–103. For a review of different scholarly opinions regarding the date of this work, see Allony, "The Time of Composition of *Sefer Yeṣirah,*" pp. 44–45. Allony himself inclines toward a later dating. See also the provocative study by Wasserstrom, "*Sefer Yeṣira* and Early Islam," where he reexamines the hypothesis set forth by Louis Massignon, Paul Kraus, and Henry Corbin that *Sefer Yeṣirah* was redacted in a ninth-century Islamic milieu.

[65] See Scholem, *Major Trends,* pp. 76–77; idem, *Origins,* pp. 26–27; Gruenwald, "Some Critical Notes on the First Part of *Sefer Yeẓira,*" p. 484. For a convenient list of other scholars who accepted the mathematical approach, see Castelli, *Il commento di Sabbatai Donnolo,* p. 22. See also Dan, *Three Types of Ancient Jewish Mysticism,* pp. 20–23; idem, "The Religious Experience of the *Merkavah,*" pp. 302–304; idem, *The Ancient Jewish Mysticism* pp. 146–152.

[66] See Hayman, "Sefer Yeṣirah and the Hekhalot Literature." An attempt to reconstruct the "original" version and demarcate later redactional accretions may be found in Weinstock, "A Clarification of the Version of *Sefer Yeṣirah.*"

[67] Idel, in *Golem,* pp. 14–15, renders this word "His throne," thereby understanding the passage in a theurgical way: by certain types of contemplation of the *sefirot* one has an influence on God that is expressed in terms of setting the Creator on His throne. While my interpretation of the whole context is slightly different from Idel's, I believe his philological analysis of *mekhono* enhances my own reading.

says: "The beasts run to and fro" (Ezek. 1:14). Concerning this the covenant was made.[68]

A detailed commentary on these passages lies beyond our immediate concern. I will present here only the essential features relevant to the imaginative visualization of the divine form. In the first passage the ten *sefirot* are described in terms of anthropomorphic imagery. It does not appear to me that this imagery indicates a simple rhetorical analogy, that is, that to comprehend the numerical sum of the ten *sefirot* one should think of the ten fingers on one's hands. The reference to the covenant of unity or oneness (*berit yiḥud*) set in the middle, corresponding to the tongue and phallus, indicates that we are dealing with a full human form. With this in mind one can appreciate the mandate to know, contemplate, and imagine[69] the *sefirot:* one gains gnosis of these *sefirot* through a process of visual contemplation by forming an image in the mind.

But what precise image is thus formed? It seems that the first passage provides the answer, namely, the anthropomorphic shape assumed by these entities. The reference here is not simply to the form of the mortal human, for if that were the case the consequent statement, that by means of this contemplation one can "establish the matter clearly, and set the Creator in His place," would make little sense. If, on the other hand, the anthropomorphic imagery is applied to the *sefirot,* and the latter are presumed to refer to the divine realm, then this statement is completely intelligible.[70] In this redactional stratum of

[68] I have translated from the text established by Gruenwald, "A Preliminary Critical Edition of *Sefer Yezira,*" pp. 141–142. For an alternative attempt to reconstruct the "original" text, see Weinstock, "Clarification," pp. 36–37, and the relevant notes. The passages that serve as a key to my argument are judged by Weinstock to be later additions rather than part of the original text. See discussion of Weinstock's reconstruction in Séd, "Le Sefer Yeṣira," pp. 519–522.

[69] The word I have rendered as "imagine" is *ṣur,* which is from a root that means to give form or an image to something. Gruenwald, in "Some Critical Notes," p. 488, translates this word as "form in your mind," precisely the translation adopted by Saadiah Gaon in his commentary on *Sefer Yeṣirah,* ed. J. Kafiḥ, pp. 67 and 69. On this reading see also Allony, "The Anagramic Orientation of the Hebrew Lexicography in *Sefer Yeṣirah,*" p. 81 n. 120. As Gruenwald remarks in "Some Critical Notes," p. 489, the meaning of the term in the context of *Sefer Yeṣirah,* in the sense of forming a mental image, reflects the medieval Hebrew usage *ṣiyyur,* derived from the Arabic *taṣawwur.* For the philological history of this philosophical term, see Wolfson, *Studies in the History of Philosophy and Religion,* 1:478–492. My understanding reflects this usage as well, and I have thus translated the term as "imagine." In this connection mention should be made of a passage extant in several midrashic collections that contrasts the creative power of a human being to that of God. See *Mekhilta de-Rabbi Ishmael,* Beshallaḥ, 8, p. 144; *Mekhilta de-Rabbi Shimʿon bar Yoḥai,* pp. 93–94; *Midrash Tehillim* 18:26, 77b–78a; *Midrash Samuel* 5:6, 30a–b; Urbach, *The Sages,* p. 232. The key expression used in that context to designate the creative act is *laṣur ṣurah,* which has the double connotation of forming a representational figure (when applied to human creativity) or creating an actual form (when applied to God). The process of forming a mental image or creating an iconic form (such as a picture or statue) thus parallels the divine act of creating an external shape. I have assumed a similar connotation for this term in *Sefer Yeṣirah,* where the specific issue is mentally imagining the divine form in an anthropomorphic shape.

[70] My explanation departs from the standard scholarly view, epitomized, for instance, by Scholem, *Origins,* p. 139. Scholem emphatically states that the anthropomorphic speculation of the

Sefer Yeṣirah the philological connotation of the term *sefirot* is enumerations, that is, these are the potencies that represent the counting and delineation of God's measures apprehended through mystical contemplation.[71] The *sefirot,* therefore, are both the ontic realities that constitute the divine realm and the psychological paradigms by means of which the mystic visualizes these realities.[72]

Support for this reading may be gathered from the last passage in *Sefer Yeṣirah,* which may be a later addition but nevertheless reflects a proper understanding of the mystical task of visually contemplating the *sefirot* set out in the opening section of the first part of the book:[73] "When Abraham, our ancestor, peace be upon him, contemplated and looked, saw and investigated, understood and engraved, extracted and combined, formed and succeeded, the Master of everything, blessed be He, was revealed to him, and He placed him on His lap and kissed him upon his head, and called him My beloved[74] and made him a son."[75] It is evident that conveyed here is the notion that Abraham emulates the divine through such linguistic activities as engraving, extracting, and combining letters;[76] on the other hand, the imperative to contemplate, look, understand, and form clearly brings to mind the language applied to the *sefirot* cited above.[77] Specifically, the verb *we-ṣur* does not have the connotation of creating something by means of letter-combination, as has been suggested,[78] but rather involves the process of conjuring a mental image of the sefirotic entities in an anthropomorphic shape.

---

older sources, connected either to Ezekiel 1:126 or Canticles 5:10–16, was in no way related to the ten *sefirot* of *Sefer Yeṣirah* (or the ten *logoi* by means of which God created the world, according to some standard rabbinic texts). See also *Origins,* p. 81.

71 Support for my interpretation is found in the use of the expression *sefer midotekha,* the enumeration of God's attributes, in a poem by Eleazar Qallir, as well as the expression *middot sefurot* used by Qallir in another poem. For references, see Wolfson, "The Theosophy of Shabbetai Donnolo," p. 308 n. 67. Various scholars have noted the resemblance of a passage in one of Qallir's poems and *Sefer Yeṣirah.* See Séd, "Le Sefer Yeṣira," p. 526, and references to other scholars cited in n. 26 ad loc.

72 Liebes, in *Sin of Elisha,* p. 103 n. 31, similarly notes that the *sefirot* in the first part of *Sefer Yeṣirah* are described in a twofold manner, as instruments in the hand of the Creator and in the hand of the mystic. My approach would differ from Liebes's (as expressed in the aforementioned source) insofar as I have accepted a theosophic reading of the *sefirot,* at least in the first section of the first part, i.e., that these entities are not merely instruments in the hands of God but constitute the very form of the divine as imagined by human consciousness.

73 The intrinsic connection between the first and last passages in *Sefer Yeṣirah* has been noted by Liebes, *Sin of Elisha,* p. 102; see also Idel, *Golem,* p. 14.

74 Cf. Isa. 41:8.

75 *Sefer Yeṣirah,* ed. Gruenwald, p. 174; see Scholem, *On the Kabbalah,* pp. 169–170.

76 As emphasized by Scholem; see previous note.

77 See Idel, *Golem,* p. 14.

78 See, for example, Scholem, *On the Kabbalah,* p. 169 n. 3, where he asserts that the verb *we-ṣar* in *Sefer Yeṣirah* "is used throughout in connection with the creation of individual things and has the meaning of 'created.'" The immediate focus of Scholem's remark is the last passage in the book which attributes various actions to Abraham, including the act of forming, which Scholem thus understands as an act of creating that mimics the divine.

Yet there is an inherent danger in this process of visualization, especially if it is communicated in a public forum; hence the continuation of the text warns one to stop one's heart from meditating on, and to close one's mouth from speaking about, the *sefirot*. If one's heart runs, that is, if one gets carried away, one must return to one's point of departure, just as the celestial beasts run to and from the realm of the chariot. It is thus the process of forming an image of the *sefirot* that allows one to gain gnosis of the divine anthropos, but that process must be carefully monitored. The way is marked by a double movement of advance and retreat, the iconic imaging of the divine anthropos and the resting in the repose of imageless thought.

In the final analysis, this imaginative capacity is the distinctive quality not only of the mystic visionary but of human beings in general, at least when judged from the religious standpoint. The point is underscored in the comment of the Hasidic master Simḥah Bunem of Przysucha (1765–1827) on the verse "God said, Let us make man in our image, after our likeness" (Gen. 1:26):

> [The word] *'adam* (man) is derived from *'adammeh* [i.e., I will imagine].[79] After God made everything beautiful and glorious He wanted to display His actions so that one would see everything. But those who exist, apart from human beings, do not comprehend anything but themselves. God created man and he is the power that is comprised of the upper and lower realities, which all can be imagined in the soul of a person. This is the essence of man that he sees, comprehends, and imagines, like no one else. This is [the import of] "Let us make man in our image, after our likeness (*ki–demutenu*)," by the power of imagination (*kaf ha-dimyon*).[80]

The divine image in the human being is tied to the faculty of the imagination, for of all mortal beings the human alone can comprehend all that has been created—the celestial as well as terrestrial realms. The visionary is further distinguished by the fact that he exercises the imaginative faculty to visualize the divine form. The remainder of this study seeks to articulate the various ways in which this imaging of God as corporeal form occurs in the imagination of Jewish mystics.

[79] Cf. Abraham Abulafia, *Sitre Torah,* MS Paris–BN 774, fol. 135b: "The name Adam is derived from *'adammeh,* and according to this secret it is said 'in the hands of the prophets I was imaged' (Hosea 12:11)." See also Abulafia, *Ḥayye ha-Nefesh,* MS Munich 408, fol. 5b, where he makes a connection between *demut* (likeness) and *dimyon* (imagination), on the one hand, and *ṣelem* (image) and *sekhel* (intellect), on the other. On the supposed philological link connecting the name Adam and the words *demut* (image) and *dimyon* (imagination), see the comment in Eleazar of Worms, *Sefer ha-Ḥokhmah,* printed in *Perush ha-Roqeaḥ 'al ha-Torah* 1:18.

[80] *Qol Simḥah* to Gen. 1:26 (Jerusalem, 1992), p. 3. Interestingly, a similar point based on the same play of words is found in Naḥman of Bratslav, *Liqquṭe MoHaRaN* (Jerusalem, 1972), II, 5:9, 9b; see also II, 8:7, 17b–c. For discussion of these sources, see Green, *Tormented Master,* pp. 341–342.

• CHAPTER THREE •

Visionary Ascent and Enthronement in the Hekhalot Literature

Literary and Historical Background

In this chapter I will reflect on the role of the vision of God in what is generally accepted to be the earliest form of Jewish mysticism, the Merkavah (chariot) or Hekhalot (palace) speculation. There is still no consensus on the part of scholars as to the precise historical or sociological background of the material that comprises the main corpus of this literature. Although the authorities mentioned in the relevant compositions are all of tannaitic origin, it is generally assumed that these attributions are pseudepigraphic and thus do not reflect accurately any historical situation.[1] It is thus from a purely literary and conceptual vantage point that we are able to speak of a distinct body known as *sifrut ha-hekhalot,* the Hekhalot literature. This title has been chosen because in the relevant texts the mystic is said to pass through the seven heavenly palaces or halls (*hekhalot*) in order to reach the throne of glory (*kisse*' *ha-kavod*) or chariot (*merkavah*). While the precise nature of the description of the journey through the heavenly chambers varies from text to text, it is this structure that allows one to speak of a common literary heritage.

The question of the provenance of much of this material has not been definitively settled. In his effort to combat the views of nineteenth-century German scholars, most notably Heinrich Graetz and Philipp Bloch,[2] that the Merkavah mystics were active in the Geonic period and were influenced by Islamic mystics, Gershom Scholem advocated the view that the origins of the Hekhalot texts should be sought in Palestine as early as the first and second centuries C.E.[3] It must be noted, however, that Scholem admitted the complexity of the literary nature of these texts, allowing for later additions and accretions in the final stages of redaction, which probably occurred in the Geonic period and in the Muslim East. "As a matter of ascertained fact, however, we only know of their existence in Babylonia, from where practically all mystical tracts of this particular variety made their way to Italy and Germany; it is these tracts that

[1] For a summary account of this issue, see Cohen, *The Shi'ur Qomah: Liturgy and Theurgy,* pp. 82–87.

[2] Graetz, "Die mystische Literatur in der gaonischen Epoche"; Bloch, "Die *Yorde Merkavah,* die Mystiker der Gaonenzeit und ihr Einfluss auf die Liturgie."

[3] Scholem, *Jewish Gnosticism,* p. 8. In his earlier presentation of this material in *Major Trends,* p. 47, Scholem suggested that the oldest of the Hekhalot texts derived from the late Talmudic period, i.e., fourth or fifth centuries. See also the philological study of Levy, "Remainders of Greek Phrases and Nouns in 'Hechaloth Rabbati.'"

have come down to us in the form of manuscripts written in the late Middle Ages."[4] He was insistent, however, that Merkavah mysticism represented in the Hekhalot was a phenomenon that first appeared during the formative stages of the rabbinic period. Some of the more recent scholarship has challenged Scholem's early dating and returned in some measure to the position of nineteenth-century scholars that the material should be dated later.[5]

As to the identity of these mystics and their precise relationship to the emerging rabbinic establishment, it must be noted that Scholem's views underwent an interesting development. In the early formulation in *Major Trends in Jewish Mysticism,* Scholem's analysis is at once deliberately vague and perceptively nuanced. He maintains that the *yorde merkavah* (a term that will be discussed below) were a distinct "school of mystics" who were not prepared to reveal their secret gnosis, for their mystical speculation was "based on private religious experience" that might "come into conflict with that 'rabbinical' Judaism which was rapidly crystallizing during the same epoch."[6] In addition, Scholem remarks that if the roots of Jewish Merkavah mysticism go far back, they did not necessarily originate with the rabbinic teachers of the Mishnaic period. Rather, clear lines can be drawn connecting these later mystics and the groups that produced a large proportion of the pseudepigrapha and apocalypses of the first century before and after Christ. Moreover, this "unrecognized tradition" made its way to later generations independent of the official schools and academies of the Talmudic teachers.[7] On the other hand, focusing particularly on *Hekhalot Rabbati,* Scholem concludes that the anonymous authors of these texts "were anxious to develop their 'Gnosis' within the frame-work of Halakhic Judaism, notwithstanding its partial incompatibility with the new religious spirit."[8] There is thus a basic paradox in Scholem's analysis: the original religious impulses active in mystical circles derived from sources quite different from those of orthodox Judaism, yet an attempt is made to express the mystical experience and beliefs in a traditional framework. In a later work, *Jewish Gnosticism, Merkabah Mysticism, and Talmudic Tradition,* Scholem sought to emphasize in sharper terms the extent to which the Hekhalot writings were compatible with rabbinic Judaism:

> The texts of Merkabah mysticism that have so far come to our knowledge also display what I have called an orthodox Jewish tendency, and are in no way hereti-

[4] *Major Trends,* p. 47.

[5] See Cohen, *Shi'ur Qomah,* pp. 51–71; see also comments of Greenfield in his Prolegomenon to *3 Enoch,* ed. Odeberg, pp. xxiv–xxv; Swartz, *Mystical Prayer in Ancient Judaism,* pp. 11, 220.

[6] *Major Trends,* p. 47. I note, parenthetically, that this statement reflects a repeated pattern in Scholem's thinking wherein mystical experience–in different historical contexts–is treated as essentially private and potentially at odds with traditional authority; I will discuss this matter in more detail in chapter 6.

[7] *Major Trends,* p. 42. See, by contrast, Scholem's formulation in *Kabbalah,* p. 16: "We should not dismiss the possibility of a continuous flow of specific ideas from the Qumran sect to the Merkabah mystics and rabbinic circles in the case of the *Shi'ur Komah* as well as in other fields."

[8] *Major Trends,* p. 47.

> cal. . . . If what these texts present is Gnosticism—and their essentially Gnostic character cannot in my opinion be disputed—it is truly rabbinic Gnosis, and the illuminations and revelations granted to the adepts are such as conform to the Jewish vision of the hierarchy of beings. Indeed, all these texts go to great lengths to stress their strict conformity, even in the most minute detail, to halakhic Judaism and its prescriptions.[9]

In his last review of the historical development of early Jewish mysticism, in an entry he wrote for the *Encyclopaedia Judaica* (published separately in the volume called *Kabbalah*), Scholem again reiterated his opinion that speculation on the chariot as well as on the visionary ascent to the chariot emerged in the center and not on the margins of rabbinic circles. Basing his argument on the talmudic legends concerning the homiletical exposition of the divine chariot by Yoḥanan ben Zakkai and his disciples, Scholem concludes that this is proof that an esoteric tradition arose in the center of the evolving rabbinic establishment. Despite fundamental differences in approach, the Merkavah mysticism supposedly found in the rabbinic circles "constitutes an inner Jewish concomitant to Gnosis, and it may be termed 'Jewish and rabbinic Gnosticism.'"[10]

Scholem's views (as expressed in the later works) regarding the relation of Hekhalot mystics to rabbinic Judaism has been basically accepted by some scholars, including Saul Lieberman, who has discussed the issue purely from the vantage point of these mystics' knowledge of the intricacies of rabbinic law (*halakhah*),[11] and Ithamar Gruenwald, who has dealt with the problem from a variety of perspectives relevant to the history of religions. For Gruenwald it is not only the case that the Hekhalot mystics were not opposed to rabbinic Judaism,[12] but that rabbinic Judaism itself provided the social-religious matrix that produced this historical and literary phenomenon.[13] This is not to say that Gruenwald uncritically accepts the attribution of these texts to the tannaitic figures mentioned in the literary testimonies. To the contrary, in one place he refers to the fact that in the Merkavah literature the "pseudepigraphic heroes are images taken from the world of the Tannaim."[14] Still, the essentially rabbinic character of these literary units is not in question. On the other hand, Gruenwald has also noted the significance of both the apocalyptic and priestly backgrounds of this material.[15] Moreover, Gruenwald has distinguished more

9 *Jewish Gnosticism,* p. 10.

10 *Kabbalah,* pp. 12–13.

11 See Lieberman's appendix in Gruenwald, *Apocalyptic,* pp. 241–244. One of the key passages discussed by Lieberman is the description in *Hekhalot Rabbati* of R. Neḥuniah ben ha-Qanah's recall from mystical ecstasy. Concerning this episode, see also Scholem, *Jewish Gnosticism,* pp. 10–12; Schiffman, "The Recall of Rabbi Neḥuniah ben ha-Qanah from Ecstasy in the Hekhalot Rabbati"; Schülter, "Die Erzählung von der Rückholung des R. Neḥunya ben Haqana."

12 *Apocalyptic,* pp. 107–108. See below, n. 14.

13 Gruenwald, "Priests, Prophets, Apocalyptic Visionaries, and Mystics," in *From Apocalypticism to Gnosticism,* p. 143.

14 Gruenwald, "The Impact of Priestly Traditions," p. 77. See also *Apocalyptic,* p. 127.

15 See references to Gruenwald's articles in nn. 13–14, above, as well as his monograph *Apocalyptic and Merkavah Mysticism.*

carefully between the chariot mysticism of the Hekhalot literature and the rabbinic Merkavah speculations, although he maintains that the latter, too, betray ecstatic experiences.[16] However, in contrast to Scholem, Gruenwald is less convinced of the appropriateness of referring to the Jewish mystical texts as a concomitant to Gnosticism. Gruenwald readily acknowledges and documents the possible influence of Gnostic motifs in Merkavah texts, as well as the influence of Jewish motifs, including mystical ideas, on Gnostic sources, but he is hesitant to refer to the Jewish esotericism and mysticism on this basis as a concomitant to Gnosticism.[17]

In a similar vein, P. S. Alexander accepts the basic contention of Scholem regarding the "orthodox" character of the Hekhalot literature—emphasizing both the close relationship of that literature to the esoteric tradition referred to in the Talmuds and that Merkavah mysticism itself emanated from rabbinic circles—but challenges the accuracy of calling this speculation Gnostic. Moreover, Alexander notes some striking differences between the Hekhalot compositions and rabbinic texts, and even assumes the possibility that there was a less "orthodox" form of Merkavah mysticism that may have been a genuine concomitant to Gnosticism, against which some members of the rabbinic establishment reacted.[18]

Other recent scholars have been even less sympathetic to Scholem's attempt to emphasize the connections between apocalyptic, rabbinic Merkavah and Hekhalot texts. A major dissenter from the Scholemian view is Peter Schäfer, who lucidly delineates some major differences in orientation between the two bodies of literature.[19] While Schäfer does not commit himself absolutely to a time and date of the authorship of the Hekhalot, he does provide a possible character-sketch by assuming that this literature was an expression of an "elite post-Rabbinic group of scholars" who sought to approach God directly through heavenly ascent or to force God down to earth through magical adjuration.[20] In a recent study, Schäfer draws the contrast between the Merkavah mystics and members of the rabbinic establishment more sharply. After summarizing the basic rabbinic attitude toward God and the Torah, Schäfer observes,

> The authors and redactors of the Hekhalot literature rebel against this traditional conception of the world, which was brought forth by a grandiose literary effort. They were not unaware of the merits of prayer and the Torah, of course. . . . Nevertheless, the traditional repertoire is no longer sufficient for them. They no longer

[16] See Gruenwald, "'Knowledge' and 'Vision': Towards a Clarification of Two 'Gnostic' Concepts in Light of Their Alleged Origins," in *From Apocalypticism to Gnosticism,* p. 101. See below, n. 26.

[17] *Apocalyptic,* pp. 110–118; "'Knowledge' and 'Vision'," pp. 98–123, and in the same volume (see above), "Jewish Merkavah Mysticism and Gnosticism," pp. 191-205.

[18] Alexander, "The Historical Setting of the Hebrew Book of Enoch."

[19] Schäfer, "The Aim and Purpose of Early Jewish Mysticism," in his *Hekhalot-Studien,* pp. 289–295.

[20] Ibid., pp. 294–295.

> are satisfied with gaining access to God solely through the Torah. In the truest sense of the word, they storm heaven and force direct access to God.[21]

Schäfer thus speaks of a "revolutionary transformation" in the Hekhalot sources of the worldview expressed in classical rabbinic literature.[22] Nevertheless, he still entertains the possibility that this comprehensive transformation, or what one might better call transvaluation, was a "postrabbinic phenomenon."[23] In the final analysis, Schäfer's important textual contributions to the study of this corpus (which will be discussed further below) have not yielded any definitive historical or geographical reconstructions. On the contrary, although his textual methodology has cleared away previous assumptions regarding this corpus, we are presently in a state of uncertainty. As Schäfer himself willingly admits,

> The result thus (temporarily?) can only be a very modest one. We do not know who the authors and redactors of the Hekhalot literature were. If they belonged to rabbinic times (which has yet to be proven) then they could just as well have formed a group inside as outside the class of the rabbis; if they belonged to post-talmudic times, then the question concerning their affiliation to the rabbis is irrelevant and their social location even more difficult to determine. The same reservations finally also must be upheld concerning the question of the geographic location. . . . This question, too, cannot be answered exclusively in one or the other direction. One will have to reckon more strongly with Babylonian elements and, furthermore, both from a geographic and temporal point of view, assume a longer germination process whose decipherment will depend on the progress of the critical literary, redactional, and traditional analysis.[24]

Another outspoken critic of Scholem's attempts to locate the phenomenon of Hekhalot mysticism within the rabbinic academies of Palestine is David Halperin. In his early work *The Merkabah in Rabbinic Literature,* Halperin, following the lead of Ephraim E. Urbach,[25] sought to undermine the cornerstone of Scholem's argument for the early dating of Hekhalot mysticism, that the rabbinic *maʿaseh merkavah* is the intervening link connecting the pre-Christian apocalypses and the Hekhalot texts. Halperin argues that the earliest form of

[21] Schäfer, *The Hidden and Manifest God,* p. 161.

[22] Ibid., p. 159. Schäfer's general approach has been applied by Michael Swartz to the particular redactional unit, *Maʿaseh Merkavah.* According to Swartz (*Mystical Prayer,* p. 223), the composers of this text lived three to five hundred years after the destruction of the Temple (between the fourth and sixth centuries) and were "evidently not content to sublimate their longing for the direct presence of God" in the manner suggested in the "normative" rabbinic corpus of the Mishnah and Talmud—i.e., through liturgical worship, Torah-study, and a pious life dictated by the strictures of halakhah; they sought rather "to experience the heavenly worship directly. To this purpose they marshalled the affective powers of prayer and incantation." One may conclude, therefore, that these authors broke away from the main rabbinic groups, even though their poetics was indebted to rabbinic poetry and prayer doxologies. See ibid., pp. 12–13, 194–198.

[23] *Hidden and Manifest God,* p. 159.

[24] Ibid., pp. 160–161. See also Schäfer, "Research on Hekhalot Literature," pp. 231–232.

[25] Urbach, "The Traditions about Merkabah Mysticism in the Tannaitic Period."

rabbinic *ma'aseh merkavah,* referred to in the tannaitic materials, is exegetical in character; by contrast, the Hekhalot writings, which include mystical practices to induce heavenly ascents, belong to late amoraic Babylonia and not to tannaitic Palestine.[26] These views are reiterated in Halperin's second monograph, *The Faces of the Chariot,*[27] but there he provides a novel, and quite unexpected, explanation for the composition and provenance of the Hekhalot literature: the Hekhalot are the work of the *'am ha-'areṣ*—the common folk unschooled in rabbinic learning, "who had every reason to detest the rabbis." Consequently, the Hekhalot "are directed in large measure against the rabbis' status."[28] The enmity between the angels and humans depicted in the Hekhalot is understood by Halperin as a literary presentation of the social conflict between these two groups, the angels representing the rabbinic authorities and the ascent to heaven constituting a "rebellion against the rabbis."[29] Halperin is well aware that he is claiming that the composition of the Hekhalot was inspired by rabbinic haggadot concerning Moses' ascension at Sinai,[30] even though the authors of these texts were bitter enemies of the rabbis. Halperin accounts for this by explaining that the Hekhalot writers, though opposed to the rabbis, "took their inspiration from rabbinic lore, as transmitted by the synagogue preachers. Only in the synagogue could they gain the knowledge that would give shape to their longings, context and purpose to their magical formulae and rituals."[31] I have had occasion to discuss Halperin's daring thesis elsewhere,[32] and thus will not go over the same ground again. Suffice it here to say that this conjecture stands diametrically opposed to the orientation of Scholem, who sees the Hekhalot within the framework of normative rabbinic circles, if not simply an outgrowth of those circles.

Whatever the precise date and provenance attributed to these texts, it is widely accepted that this corpus took shape as a result of a long and complicated redactional process, with Babylonia as the likely region where the most concentrated effort at redaction occurred.[33] The study of the literary nature of

[26] Halperin, *Merkabah in Rabbinic Literature,* pp. 183–184. A similar position is adopted by Dan in "The Religious Experience of the *Merkavah,*" pp. 289–312. A middle position is taken by Gruenwald in "'Knowledge' and 'Vision'," p. 101, where he acknowledges the distinction between the exegetical emphasis of the rabbinic speculation on the chariot and the mystical nature of the Hekhalot texts focused on heavenly ascensions. He rightly notes, however, that the rabbinic Merkavah material is not devoid of ecstatic experiences.

[27] Halperin, *Faces of the Chariot,* pp. 11-37, 359–446, esp. 362.

[28] Ibid., p. 442.

[29] Ibid., p. 443.

[30] See ibid., pp. 141–149, 289–322, and esp. 450: "Moses' ascent to heaven and struggle with the angels over the Torah . . . inspired a body of literature which we may regard as an offshoot of the synagogue *merkabah* exegesis: the *Hekhalot.* Thus, we find the ascension of Moses transformed in the *Hekhalot* into the ascension materials. His seizure of the Torah is transformed into the *Sar Torah* materials."

[31] Ibid., p. 443.

[32] See my review of Halperin's *Faces of the Chariot, Jewish Quarterly Review* 81 (1990–91): 496–500. See also Schäfer's critique in *Hidden and Manifest God,* pp. 157–159.

[33] See Scholem, *Major Trends,* p. 47; Gruenwald, "New Passages from Hekhalot Literature,"

the Hekhalot corpus has been greatly enhanced by the publication by Peter Schäfer and his colleagues of the main writings, in the *Synopse zur Hekhalot-Literatur* and the *Geniza-Fragmente zur Hekhalot-Literatur.* The most important result of Schäfer's presentation of the material in synoptic form is the undermining of the view that this corpus is made up of distinct and clearly defined textual units with impermeable boundaries. The synoptic comparison of the manuscripts shows that there are enough substantial differences in the organization of material as well as within textual units included in a specific work to render it virtually impossible to establish, restore, or demarcate an Ur-text of any given composition within this corpus. It is thus a false presupposition, from Schäfer's vantage point, to reconstruct individual works of Hekhalot literature, inasmuch as the redactional identity of any given work varies in accord with the different manuscripts that were written at different times and places.

To be sure, there are discrete "texts" in the corpus, but the manuscript evidence, viewed in synoptic form, indicates that the boundaries of the texts are fluid and have been crystallized over time in what Schäfer calls "macroforms." These macroforms are superimposed literary units that were arranged into clearly defined works or texts at a certain stage in the redactional process. Within the larger macroforms are also discernible smaller literary units, "microforms," which may indeed comprise autonomous traditions that were woven into the fabric of the macroforms and thence became part of a literary tradition of a distinct textual unit.[34] It may be the case that these units were in a fluid state as late as the period in which they were being copied, either in the Orient (attested by the Genizah fragments) or in the Occident (mainly in the German manuscripts or Italian copies of them). Here it is particularly significant to note the role of the medieval German Pietists, who may have had a great hand in shaping these texts. The Pietists were not merely passive copyists; they were committed ideologues who, as various scholars have argued, adopted an aggressive attitude to this material.[35]

---

p. 355; *Re'uyot Yeḥezqel,* ed. Gruenwald, p. 106, comment to lines 19–21; idem, "Angelic Songs, the Qedushah, and the Problem of the Origin of the Hekhalot Literature," in *From Apocalypticism to Gnosticism,* pp. 145–174; Alexander, "Historical Setting," p. 165; Schäfer, *Hidden and Manifest God,* pp. 160–161; and the references to Halperin's work in nn. 26–27, above. The denial of any historical context with respect to at least one relevant text has been made by Janowitz in *The Poetics of Ascent,* p. 13. For a different approach to this text that takes into account historical context uncovered by a form-critical analysis, see Swartz, *Mystical Prayer,* esp. pp. 10, 32–34.

[34] See Schäfer, "Tradition and Redaction in Hekhalot Literature," in *Hekhalot-Studien,* pp. 8–16. In the same volume, see also "Prolegomena zu einer kritischen Edition und Analyse der *Merkava Rabba,*" pp. 17–49; "Aufbau und redaktionelle Identität der *Hekhalot Zuṭarti,*" pp. 50–62; "Zum Problem der redaktonelle Identität von *Hekhalot Rabbati,*" pp. 63–74; "Handschriften zur Hekhalot-Literatur," pp. 154–233. See also idem, "The Problem of the Redactionist Identity of 'Hekhalot Rabbati.'" For a critical evaluation of Schäfer's methodology, see Gruenwald, "Literary and Redactional Issues in the Study of the Hekhalot Literature," in *From Apocalypticism to Gnosticism,* pp. 175–189.

[35] See Gruenwald, *Apocalyptic,* pp. 210, 214 n. 9; Ta-Shema, "The Library of the Ashkenazi Sages in the Eleventh and Twelfth Centuries," p. 309; Farber, "The Concept of the Merkabah in Thirteenth-Century Jewish Esotericism," pp. 13, 88, 204 n. 9, 479–483 n. 132; P. Schäfer in

The determination of which macroforms—literary units made up of individual tradition-complexes or microforms—belong to the Hekhalot literature presupposes, of course, some working understanding of the essential conceptual features that give shape to a corpus. Here we come again to the critical question of determining the taxonomy of Hekhalot mysticism and what position these traditions assume within the larger landscape of normative rabbinic Judaism. The latter question is especially relevant to the task of ascertaining who these mystics were in terms of social and cultural identification. As I stated previously, to a great extent these questions are still unanswered. What is clear, however, is that certain motifs do recur in these different traditions, which allow us to refer to them as part of a distinctive phenomenon in the history of Judaism. To be sure, one must avoid adopting an uncritical phenomenological approach, studying the Hekhalot literature as a whole without paying attention to the various redactional layers of the different writings that make up this corpus, itself a matter of scholarly judgment. Given the complex redactional nature of these texts, with multiple layers within individual macroforms, it is impossible to explain this literature in any singular or monolithic manner. Schäfer's warning that the "Hekhalot literature is not a unity and, therefore, cannot be explained uniformly"[36] must be appropriated as a guiding light for anyone who walks on this path. Still, as a result of a more sophisticated phenomenology conditioned by a rigorous redactional analysis or form-critical approach, we can isolate themes that present themselves in the different literary settings and stages. One of the motifs that surely suggests itself as a determinative factor is that of the visionary ascent. While several scholars have lately criticized Scholem's identification of this factor as the essential feature of the Hekhalot, it nevertheless remains the case that in a significant body of texts included within this corpus the visionary component assumes a central position and functions as the organizing literary principle.

In the following section I will explore in some detail the role accorded visionary experience in some of the main units of this corpus, emphasizing especially certain aspects that have not received sufficient notice in previous scholarship. I wish to examine some neglected aspects of the vision of the glory in these literary units without entering into the question of whether the mystical emphasis or the magical adjuration is the primary element in the Hekhalot sources. For the purposes of this study this question may be bracketed. Moreover, my attempt to discuss the issue of vision on broader phenomenological grounds does not come at the expense of ignoring the sound text-critical approach of Schäfer. On the contrary, I will incorporate that approach in my own reflections, but at the same time will seek to determine something of a "core" experience that may underlie a significant portion of the tradition-complexes that helped give shape to more distinctive redactional units.

Übersetzung der Hekhalot-Literatur III, pp. xxxiii–xxxiv; idem, *Hidden and Manifest God*, p. 161; idem, "The Ideal of Piety of the Ashkenazi Hasidim and Its Roots in Jewish Tradition"; idem, "Research on Hekhalot Literature," pp. 231, 235.

36 Schäfer, *Hidden and Manifest God*, p. 152.

Vision of God in the Hekhalot Corpus

Yeridah la-Merkavah: Entry before the Chariot

As I have already intimated, it is possible to distinguish two central elements in the redactional units that make up the Hekhalot: the mystical ascent culminating in a visionary experience and the adjuration of angels, connected especially with the magical study of Torah without any effort, as it is related in the *Sar Torah* passages that appear in some of the relevant manuscripts, especially the *Hekhalot Rabbati* (the "Greater Hekhalot"), *Merkavah Rabbah* (the "Great Chariot"), and the text published by Scholem under the title *Maʿaseh Merkavah* (the "Account of the Chariot"). The focus of the mystical praxis of the adepts—technically named in some of the key documents in this corpus, principally in the *Hekhalot Rabbati*[37] as well as in a fragment from the Cairo Genizah, which a copyist has conveniently named *Ḥotam ha-Merkavah* (the "Seal of the Chariot"), but which scholars call the Ozhayah text,[38] *yorde merkavah,*—was an ascent through the seven celestial palaces located in the seventh heaven.[39] It appears from the extant documents that the ascent culminated in an entry into the throne room, resulting in a vision of the glory of God, referred to in one text as the body of the Presence (*guf ha-shekhinah*),[40] seated upon the throne in the seventh palace.

In a separate study I have argued, on the basis of a careful analysis of the relevant passages from the aforementioned sources, that the expression *yeridah la-merkavah* does not always refer to the entire ascent or outward journey (thus

[37] Cf. Schäfer et al., eds., *Synopse,* §§ 106, 163, 169, 172, 199, 203, 204, 216, 218, 224, 225, 228, 232, 234, 236, 247, 258, 260. The locution occurs in one passage in *Hekhalot Zuṭarti,* § 407, although in this unit the ascent is generally referred to by the more conventional term *ʿalah.*

[38] Schäfer, ed., *Geniza-Fragmente zur Hekhalot-Literatur,* p. 105.

[39] On the expression *yorde merkavah,* to name those who experience a visionary ascent to the chariot, see Bloch, "Die *Yorde Merkavah,*" p. 25; Scholem, *Major Trends,* p. 47; idem, *Jewish Gnosticism,* p. 20 n. 1, where Scholem suggests that the expression "to descend to the chariot" (*yored la-merkavah*) may have been influenced by the liturgical phrase *yored lifne ha-teivah.* See Chernus, "Pilgrimage to the Merkavah," p. 5; Schäfer, "Aim and Purpose," p. 281 n. 17; idem, *Hidden and Manifest God,* pp. 2–3 n. 4; Smith, "Observations on Hekhalot Rabbati," p. 150; idem, "Ascent to the Heavens and the Beginning of Christianity," p. 412 n. 29; Gruenwald, *Apocalyptic,* p. 145 n. 15; idem, "Angelic Songs," pp. 170–173. Kuyt, in "Once Again," agrees with Scholem that the term *yarad* in this context denotes an outward journey to the *merkavah,* but disagrees with Scholem by arguing that this usage was in fact the more original one, which was at some point changed to *ʿalah,* "ascend." For an alternative way to explain the derivation of this term, see Dan, *Three Types of Ancient Jewish Mysticism,* p. 34 n. 29; idem, *Ancient Jewish Mysticism,* p. 60. See also G. Stroumsa's review of Gruenwald's *Apocalyptic and Merkavah Mysticism* in *Numen* 28 (1981): 108–109, where he suggests that this expression is a linguistic cognate to *katabasis* in Greek magical papyri, which designates the preparatory rite for a mystical vision (see Betz, "Fragments from a Catabasis Ritual in a Greek Magical Papyrus"). For yet another explanation see Halperin, *Faces of the Chariot,* pp. 226–227.

[40] Cf. *Masekhet Hekhalot,* MS Parma-Palatina 3531, fol. 2a: *guf shekhinat kevodo;* MS Oxford-Bodleian Opp. Add. 4° 183, fol. 3b: *gufo demut ha-shekhinah.* See also formulation in *Synopse,* § 185, and comment in Schäfer, *Hidden and Manifest God,* p. 20 n. 35.

rendering its usage paradoxical, as is commonly held by scholars), but does on occasion refer to the last stage in the ascent, which involves entering before the chariot or throne. At the time of entry the mystic initially stands before the glory to utter the appropriate praises together with the angelic hosts and afterwards is placed either on the throne of glory or on a seat alongside it in order to have a vision of the glory.[41] Inasmuch as in the Hekhalot material and related texts sitting most properly characterizes God, or in some cases the highest angel, who is the vicegerent of God, it follows that the seating of the mystic in the throne-world symbolically depicts the narrowing of the gap that separates the divine and human nature.

It thus makes perfect sense that at some stage in the literary development of Hekhalot mysticism a book such as *3 Enoch* would have been composed, in which Enoch, the prototype of the Merkavah mystic, is transformed into Meṭaṭron, the very angel who occupies a throne alongside that of God. Here the apocalyptic tradition of the apotheosis of Enoch reaches its fullest expression.[42] In the other Hekhalot writings this last step is not taken. Not only is the distinction between God and human never fully blurred, as Scholem observed,[43] but no attempt is made to obscure the ontological distinction between man and angel in the way that is presupposed in the legend regarding the translation and transformation of the mortal Enoch into the angelic Meṭaṭron.

It is nevertheless evident that in some of the key Hekhalot macroforms one of the results of the entry to the chariot is the mystic's being seated upon a throne.[44] This in turn signifies his elevation not just to the status of angel, but the highest angel, who alone, apart from God, occupies a throne in the seventh palace of the seventh heaven. The extent to which this aspect of the mystical experience expressed in the Hekhalot literature was neglected by Scholem can be gauged from the comment that comes right after his oft-cited and influential observation that in ancient Jewish throne mysticism there is no trace of a mystical union between the human soul and God: "The mystic who in his ecstasy has passed through all the gates, braved all the dangers, now stands before the throne; he sees and hears—but that is all."[45] Well, not exactly; Scholem forgets

[41] Wolfson, "Yeridah la-Merkavah."

[42] See Black, "The Throne-Theophany, Prophetic Commission and the 'Son of Man.'"

[43] *Major Trends*, pp. 55–56. The view of Scholem is adopted by Gruenwald who comments on the nature of the heavenly ascension as described in the Hekhalot literature: "It is a mystical experience, though it never reaches the mystical climax known from pagan and Christian mysticism, that is, the sacred marriage between the mystic and the divinity, the *Hieros Gamos*" ("'Knowledge' and 'Vision'," p. 108). Gruenwald further distinguishes the ascension in the Hekhalot literature from that of Gnosticism, inasmuch as the latter is predicated on an ascent that culminates in a "virtual reunification of the soul with its divine origin" (p. 109), an idea that resonates with the description of the ascent of the soul in Plotinus.

[44] Cf. *Synopse*, §§ 227, 233, 236, 411; *Geniza-Fragmente*, p. 105. On the motif of enthronement in the Hekhalot, see Tabor, *Things Unutterable*, pp. 88–89, and my own "Yeridah la-Merkavah," where I explore this dimension more fully. The possibility of heavenly enthronement in a Qumran text has been proposed by Smith, "Ascent to the Heavens and Deification in 4QM." See idem, "Two Ascended to Heaven."

[45] *Major Trends*, p. 56.

one small item. According to the major textual units in this corpus that describe the heavenly ascent, the mystic is said to be seated in the seventh palace before the throne of glory. Scholem's emphasis on the standing position of the mystic is revealing of what is here disregarded. Essentially, Scholem has ignored the most important detail of the religious experience reported in these sources—indeed, the detail that in my opinion most precisely qualifies these texts as mystical.[46] The vision of the glory and the divine attributes normally withheld from both angelic and human creatures results from the enthronement of the mystic. In that sense, I submit, the enthronement of the mystic should be understood as a form of quasi-deification[47] or angelification, in line with the older tradition expressed in apocalyptic literature concerning the

[46] The appropriateness of the term "mystical" applied to the Hekhalot literature, according to Scholem, relates specifically to the visionary encounter between human and divine. It is evident that for Scholem the ecstatic vision of the glory replaces the ideal of union as the peak mystical experience. Thus, in *Major Trends,* p. 5, immediately after delineating the "fundamental experience" in the general history of religion known as *unio mystica,* Scholem remarks that many Jewish and non-Jewish mystics have not represented their ecstatic experiences as a union with God. One such example offered by Scholem is the ancient Jewish mystics who "speak of the ascent of the soul to the Celestial Throne where it obtains an ecstatic view of the majesty of God and the secrets of His realm." The extent to which the model of *unio mystica* had an impact on Scholem's general understanding of mystical experience can be gauged by the fact that in the very context of describing the mystical vision of the enthroned glory in Hekhalot literature Scholem feels the need to remark that there is no union in these sources; that is, the visionary experience is somewhat qualified. It will be recalled that according to Scholem's tripartite typological classification of religious experience mysticism represents the third stage, which is the romantic restoration of the broken unity of mythic consciousness. Hence, according to his own typology, union figures prominently as the key feature of the mystical experience. As is known, Scholem expressed doubt regarding the place of mystical union in the various historical manifestations of Jewish mysticism (see discussion of Scholem's view and alternative approach in Idel, *Kabbalah: New Perspectives,* pp. 59–73). The logical implication of this is that from Scholem's own standpoint the vast majority of Jewish mystical sources fall somewhat short of the ideal that he himself set up, which involves unitive experience. It is certainly the case that in the Hekhalot sources there is no union of man and God in the way Scholem described it. It may be suggested, however, that this typology of unitive experience has its intellectual roots in the idea of *henosis* in Neoplatonism, the return of the soul to its ontic source in the One. (See remark of Gruenwald in n. 43, above, which to a degree exposes the intellectual milieu of this ideal of union.) If one applies the Neoplatonic idea of union to the Hekhalot, it is obvious that one will not succeed in finding any passage to confirm such an ideal. But this model may be completely irrelevant to the corpus of Hekhalot mysticism. I submit that there is another model of mystical experience that is germane to Jewish and later Christian apocalyptic as well as to the Hekhalot sources, a model that from its own vantage point involves the narrowing of the gap between human and divine. The model to which I refer, rooted in ancient Near Eastern and Mesopotamian mythology rather than Neoplatonic ontology and epistemology, is that of the ascension to heaven and transformation into an angelic being who occupies a throne alongside the throne of glory. For a slightly different formulation of this issue, but one that equally recognizes the need to distinguish the mystical form of Hekhalot literature rooted in Yahwistic dualism (God and man-world differentiated) from that of Hellenistic mystery religions that developed from a Canaanite monism (gods-man-world as undifferentiated), see Fishbane, *Garments of Torah,* pp. 61–62.

[47] The quasi-divinization of the *yored merkavah* is also evident from the description in *Hekhalot Rabbati* of the knowledge granted to such a person as a result of the mystical experience; see *Synopse,* §§ 81–86; and discussion in Dan, *Ancient Jewish Mysticism,* pp. 64–66.

transformation of individuals into angelic beings. While the vision of the divine glory does not make the mystic divine or equal to the glory, as is implied, for instance, in 1 John 3:2[48] and several Gnostic texts,[49] the entry to the chariot does culminate in what may be called a deifying vision. At the very least, it is by virtue of the enthronement that the mystic can see that which is ordinarily concealed from both mortal and angelic eyes. The unique position of the *yored merkavah* is expressed principally in terms of his attainment of a visual experience of the glory denied even to the angels who bear the throne.

Unveiling the Veiled: The Paradox of Seeing the Hidden God

One finds repeatedly in some of the units included in this literature (*Hekhalot Rabbati, Hekhalot Zuṭarti,* the Ozhayah fragment) that the heavenly voyager is characterized as one who is worthy to enter the inner chamber and "behold the King in His beauty,"[50] a locution that is based on Isa. 33:17. It appears that in

[48] Quispel, "Judaism, Judaic Christianity, and Gnosis," pp. 53–54, and other examples of deification through vision, pp. 55–58.

[49] To give three examples: *Trimorphic Protennoia* 45:13, in *The Gnostic Scriptures,* ed. B. Layton (New York, 1987), p. 97: "When you enter it [the superior, perfect light] you will be glorified by the glorifiers; the enthroners will give you thrones; you will be given robes by the enrobers, and the baptists will baptize you; so that along with glories you become the glory in which you existed, luminous, in the beginning." *Zostrianos* 15–20, in *The Nag Hammadi Library in English,* ed. J. M. Robinson (San Francisco, 1988), p. 405: "I received the image of the glories there. I became like one of them. . . . Then they [revealed] themselves to me and wrote me in glory. I was sealed by those who are on these powers. . . . I became a root-seeing angel and stood upon the first aeon, which is the fourth." *The Gospel of Philip* 20–35, in *Nag Hammadi Library,* pp. 146–147: "It is not possible for anyone to see anything of the things that actually exist unless he becomes like them. This is not the way with man in the world: he sees the sun without being a sun; and he sees the heaven and the earth and all other things, but he is not these things. . . . But you saw something of that place, and you became those things. You saw the spirit, you became spirit. You saw Christ, you became Christ. You saw [the father, you] shall become father." See also ibid., p. 155.

[50] Cf. *Synopse,* §§ 159, 198, 248, 259, 407, 408, 409, 411, 412; *Geniza-Fragmente,* pp. 103, 105; Schäfer, *Hidden and Manifest God,* pp. 16 n. 20, 57. For a comprehensive analysis of this and related expressions, see Elior, "Concept of God," pp. 27–31 (English trans., pp. 106–108). See also Leiter, "Worthiness, Acclamation, and Appointment," pp. 143–145. The biblical expression "to behold the beauty of the king" (Isa. 33:17) is applied to the seeing of the divine Presence in midrashic literature as well, without the eschatological connotation implied by the original context; see, e.g., *Wayyikra Rabbah* 23:13. It is of interest to note that in that midrashic context the verse "When your eyes behold a king in his beauty" (Isa. 33:17) is contrasted with "Shut his eyes against looking at evil" (ibid., 15). These two verses serve respectively as prooftexts for the vision of the face of the *Shekhinah* and looking at something obscene or lewd, that is, the nakedness of the genitals exposed during a sexual act. In this midrashic passage, then, the seeing of God's Presence is presented as the reward for refraining from the temptation of voyeurism. In line with my previous remarks regarding this passage (see chapter 1, n. 130), one must wonder if the biblical idiom of beholding the king in his beauty does not imply a vision of the sexual organ of the divine, alternatively designated as the face of the Presence (*pene ha-shekhinah*). (By contrast, see P. Sanhedrin, 9:6, 20c, where Isa. 33:17 is related exegetically to the law that the king of Israel should not be seen in his nakedness, either when he cuts his hair or when he is in the bathhouse.) If my reading is correct, then in this context the word *yofi* is interpreted more specifically as a reference to the

the Hekhalot material the expression "beauty" (*yofi*) has a more specific theophanic connotation: the luminous presence of the enthroned form.[51] Insofar as this term is applied to the enthroned form of the glory, it connotes at once corporeality and luminosity; indeed, the one is expressed through the other. The ultimate particle of being in this realm is light. Hence, in *Hekhalot Rabbati* we find the combination *ziw yofi to'ar,* the "radiance of the beauty of the form,"[52] and in one of the *Shi*ʿ*ur Qomah* texts, as well as in a passage in *Merkavah Rabbah,* there appears the formulation *to'ar yofyo we-hadro,* the "form of His beauty and splendor,"[53] which captures the convergence of light symbolism and anthropomorphic imagery. To behold the splendid beauty of the glory is to gaze upon the luminous shape of the glorious body.

The realm of the chariot—including the glory, the throne, different groups of angels, and the mystic himself who participates in this realm—is essentially made of light that can be symbolized (within the human imagination) by images from the corporeal world. While we must assume this to be the case of the glory itself, it should be emphasized that the visual accounts in the various macroforms of the Hekhalot literature, including *Hekhalot Rabbati* and *Hekhalot Zuṭarti,* do not opt for the extreme anthropomorphic characterizations found in the *Shi*ʿ*ur Qomah* recensions.[54] From a redactional standpoint it is evident that one cannot entirely separate these two traditions.[55] Yet it is only

membrum virile. The phallic connotation of *yofi* seems to be implied as well in *Midrash Tanḥuma,* Wayeshev, 5: "Our rabbis, blessed be their memory, said: Once the Egyptian women assembled and they came to see the beauty of Joseph (*yofyo shel yosef*). What did the wife of Potiphar do? She took and distributed citron to each and every one of them, and she gave a knife to each and every one of them. She called Joseph and placed him before them. When they looked at the beauty of Joseph they cut their hands." See also *Midrash Tehillim* 7:14, 35b. Consider also M. Sukkah 4:4 where the word *yofi* is applied to the Tabernacle at the conclusion of the ritual of going around it seven times during the seventh day of the holiday of Sukkot. In latter kabbalistic literature, as I will show in chapter 7 specifically in the case of the *Zohar,* the term *yofi* symbolically designates the divine phallus. The extent to which the medieval kabbalists were articulating explicitly what is already implicit in the earlier sources, both mystical and midrashic, is an important question that demands further investigation.

51 See *Synopse,* §§ 41, 699; cf. § 159, where *panim shel yofi* (countenance of beauty) parallels *panim shel lehavah* (countenance of flame).

52 Ibid., § 189; for the occurrence of the expression *yofi to'ar,* see also §§ 18, 251, 260, 974.

53 Cf. *Synopse,* §§ 481, 699, 949. Consider the statement describing the Sinaitic theophany in *Pesiqta Rabbati* 20, 98b: "The Holy One, blessed be He, opened the seven heavens and was revealed to them eye to eye in His beauty (*be-yofyo*), in His glory (*bi-khevodo*), in his form (*be-to'aro*), in His crown and His throne of glory." On the possible relation of this aggadic passage to Merkavah mysticism, see Scholem, *Jewish Gnosticism,* p. 68 n. 12. On the connection between the word "beauty" (*yofi*) and "the splendor of the Presence" (*ziw ha-shekhinah*), see also *Pesiqta de-Rav Kahana* 4:4, p. 67.

54 See Cohen, *Shi*ʿ*ur Qomah,* pp. 167–185. Cohen's statement (p. 171) that one passage in *Hekhalot Rabbati* (*Synopse* § 167) "is derived" from the *Shi*ʿ*ur Qomah* needs to be corrected, inasmuch as it is obviously a later interpolation, as noted by Schäfer, *Hidden and Manifest God,* p. 16 n. 19. The other proofs that Cohen adduces for the relationship of the two traditions are not convincing. It seems that the relationship results from a particular stage in the redactional process.

55 See Schäfer, *Hidden and Manifest God,* pp. 15–16, 60, 99–102, 141.

in the case of *Merkavah Rabbah* that the gross measurements of the limbs of the divine are mentioned in the context of a macroform of Hekhalot literature. It is significant that the descriptions of the visible form of the glory in most of the relevant macroforms do not draw on or parallel the extreme anthropomorphism of the *Shiʿur Qomah*. Let us consider a statement of Martin Cohen, who compared in particular *Hekhalot Rabbati* and the *Shiʿur Qomah:* "Both authors experienced the mystic union/communion with the God of Israel, but whereas the author of the *Shiʿur Qomah* was overcome by the divine *gedullah* [greatness], the author of the *Hekhalot Rabbati* chose to develop the equally authentic theme of beauty."[56]

Phenomenologically speaking, I am not certain that the difference between greatness and beauty is so insignificant; on the contrary, it is extremely relevant that for one tradition the primary structure that informs the experience is luminous form and for the other it is an anthropomorphic shape that is assigned gross dimensions. Still, it must be conceded that the experience related in the *Shiʿur Qomah* as that of the Hekhalot is presented in an almost exclusively visionary framework. The nature of the revelation is almost exclusively visual. Moreover, the description in the relevant macroforms of Hekhalot literature of the divine glory as a luminous form is predicated as well on the attribution of an anthropomorphic shape to that form, even though that anthropomorphism pales in comparison to the elaborate and exaggerated descriptions of the *Shiʿur Qomah* material. To behold the King in his beauty is the stated goal of the *yored merkavah* who enters before the throne of glory.

On the other hand, one also finds in these very same literary sources statements to the effect that no mortal, including the celestial journeyer, can see God, nor even his throne, cloak, or sword. Scholem noted this tension when he observed that for the Merkavah visionaries the enthroned glory is "at once visible and yet, by virtue of His transcendent nature, incapable of being visualized."[57] This apparent contradiction has led scholars to differing views regarding the possibility of visionary experience in Merkavah mysticism. Scholem's own attempted resolution was to contrast the transcendent, invisible God and his corporeal—hence measurable and visible—appearance. "The ascent of *Merkavah* mystics to heaven or, in a different version, to the heavenly paradise, was considered successful if it not only led the mystic to the divine throne but also brought them a revelation of the image of the Godhead, the 'Creator of the Universe' seated on the throne. This form was that of the divine *Kavod* . . . that aspect of God that is revealed and manifest; the more invisible God becomes for the Jewish consciousness, the more problematical the meaning of this vision of the divine *Kavod*."[58] In one context Scholem even went so far as to speak of the "formulae of Merkabah mysticism" as coming close to "postulating a discrepancy between the *deus absconditus* and the appearance

[56] Cohen, *Shiʿur Qomah,* pp. 173–174.

[57] Scholem, *Major Trends,* p. 66. See idem, *Origins,* p. 164; idem, *Kabbalah,* p. 17.

[58] *On the Mystical Shape,* pp. 20–21.

of God the King-Creator on his celestial throne."[59] From this passage one could conclude that for Scholem it is proper to speak only of a vision of the corporeal appearance of God, not the substance of divinity.

In his *Apocalyptic and Merkavah Mysticism*, Gruenwald, apparently following the lead of Scholem, argues that the idea that God cannot be seen is the prevalent view of the Merkavah mystics. He writes, "As a matter of fact, the idea that the mystics and the angels cannot see God is also stressed several times in *Hekhalot* literature. Despite the daring modes of expression one can find in that literature about the contents of the mystical experience, the possibility of a direct visual encounter with God is generally ruled out."[60] Gruenwald goes on to admit that "a visual encounter with God is presupposed by the *Shiʿur Qomah* speculations, that is, the speculations concerning the corporeal appearance of God and its definition in terms of length and mystical names."[61] By contrast, Ira Chernus has argued that the relevant passages in the Hekhalot texts prove that most of the Merkavah mystics thought it possible to see God. Indeed, the vision of God represented the culmination of their visionary experiences.[62] Gruenwald himself, it should be noted, has in his more recent work modified his earlier formulation, even acknowledging in one case the correctness of Chernus's critique,[63] and accorded a greater significance and priority to the vision of the glory in these sources. In fact, in one essay he flatly states, "The main aim of Merkavah mysticism still seems to me to be the vision of God."[64]

Although there is some question as to whether the being on the throne is identical with the Godhead or is rather to be conceived of as a theophanic image of God, the distinction made by Scholem in the passage cited above does not really answer the theoretical problem of the visibility, not to mention the measurability, of God, on the one hand, and the invisible and immeasurable transcendence, on the other. What does it mean in this context to contrast the invisible substance of divinity and its visible corporeal appearance? How, after all, are these two aspects related within the divine nature? Are they distinct hypostases, or one reality? If the latter, then it is not possible to say one aspect is by nature visible and the other invisible, because the two share in one nature.

The effort to keep God in his essence free from anthropomorphism is doomed to failure unless one posits a hypostatic theology akin to that of Philo or Christianity in its classical formulation. It is not at all clear to me, however, that such a formulation can be found in the majority of the extant Hekhalot texts.[65] On the contrary, it would appear from the major sources themselves that in most cases there is no justification to make a distinction between the corporeal appearance of the divine and the transcendent God.[66] Indeed, in one

[59] *Major Trends,* p. 111.
[60] *Apocalyptic,* p. 94.
[61] Ibid.
[62] "Visions of God in Merkabah Literature," p. 146.
[63] "The Impact of Priestly Traditions," p. 105 n. 7.
[64] "Literary and Redactional Issues," p. 184. See "'Knowledge' and 'Vision'," pp. 108–109.
[65] An interesting exception is found in *Synopse,* § 597, discussed in chapter 5 n. 315.
[66] See Morray-Jones, "Transformational Mysticism," p. 2.

essay Scholem himself emphatically affirms just such a view. Reflecting on the *Shiʿur Qomah* material, he observes,

> The gnosis we are dealing with here is a strictly orthodox Jewish one. The subject of these speculations and visions—*Yotser Bereshith,* the God of Creation—is not some lowly figure such as those found in some heretical sects, similar to the Demiurge of many Gnostic doctrines, which drew a contrast between the true God and the God of Creation. In the view of the *Shiʿur Komah,* the Creator God is identical with the authentic God of monotheism, in His mystical form; there is no possibility here of dualism. . . . We likewise cannot ignore the possibility that the pronounced usage of the term *Yotser Bereshith* (Demiurge) in those fragments (the oldest of which probably go back to the second or third century) might have been introduced in order to indicate the monotheistic alternative to the position of these sectarians—in other words, with a polemical aim against certain Gnostic groups in Judaism who had been exposed to the influence of dualistic ideas, which they tried to apply in heretical, Gnostic interpretations of the Bible.[67]

The divine monarch apprehended on the throne is the creator and master of the universe, that is, the traditional God of Judaism. For example, in a passage from *Maʿaseh Merkavah,* partially indebted to the formulation of the theophany recorded in Isa. 6:1, one reads, "R. Ishmael said: When R. Neḥuniah ben ha-Qanah declared to me the mystery of the chambers of the palace ⟨and the palace⟩ of the chariot and also of the Torah—I did not forget any chamber of them—I saw the king of the universe sitting on the high and exalted throne, and all the orders of the holiness of His name and His might sanctifying His name in His praise, as it is said, 'And one would call to the other, Holy, holy, holy! The Lord of Hosts! His glory fills all the earth' (Isa. 6:3)."[68] In other passages from that macroform it is simply stated that by uttering a prayer one sees the Presence,[69] without any qualification that would entitle one to assume a hypostatic distinction between a transcendent God and his enthroned form. Similarly, in some passages of the *Shiʿur Qomah* material the vision ascribed to R. Ishmael is reported in language based on Michiah's description of his vision of God in 1 Kings 22:19 (see also 2 Chron. 18:18) and Isaiah's vision recorded in Isa. 6:1: "I saw the King of the kings of kings, blessed be He, sitting on the high and exalted throne, and His troops were standing before Him on the right and the left."[70] While I do not subscribe to the view that the Hekhalot and *Shiʿur Qomah* should be treated as one block of tradition, I think it is instructive that the narrative of the latter is framed in terms of the biblical text that describes a prophetic vision of God. With respect to this issue, at least, there is something common to the two sources: the vision of the enthroned glory, how-

[67] *On the Mystical Shape,* pp. 34–35. My thanks to Nathaniel Deutsch, who reminded me of this important passage.

[68] *Synopse,* § 556.

[69] See ibid., § 592.

[70] *Synopse,* § 947 (= *Geniza-Fragmente,* p. 101); cf. §§ 655, 688, 691, 821. See also Cohen, *Shiʿur Qomah: Texts and Recensions,* pp. 42–43, 54, 86–87, 134.

ever one is to understand it, is a vision of the God of Israel that is hidden.[71] The ontic distinction between an invisible God and the corporeal image seems unwarranted. From a phenomenological point of view the ancient Jewish mystics lived with the paradox of assuming the visibility of the essentially invisible God.[72] Here again, a comment in one of the recensions of the *Shi'ur Qomah* text is instructive:

> How much is the measure of the stature of the Holy One, blessed be He, who is concealed from all creatures? . . . The appearance of His face and the appearance of His cheeks are like the image of the spirit and the form of the soul, for no creature can recognize Him. His body is like beryl, His splendor is luminous and glows from within the darkness, and the cloud and thick darkness surround Him. . . . There is no measurement in our hands but only the names are revealed to us.[73]

In this passage one encounters an obvious paradox: on the one hand, it is stated that God is concealed from all creatures,[74] yet, on the other, a detailed specification of God's measurements is given. Moreover, it is emphasized that no creature can recognize God, while specific characteristics are in fact delineated. Even the last statement which, prima facie, would seem to limit the anthropomorphism by claiming that no measurement of the divine limbs is given but only the names of those limbs, is immediately contradicted by the continuation of the text, which elaborates on the measurements (and not merely the names) of certain limbs of God's body. These contradictions are not to be resolved by an appeal to the poor state of manuscript transmission or to later interpolations by scribes who imputed to the base text an idea not necessarily germane to the source. Nor, in my view, should one consider this passage an illustration of a spiritualization of the typically more corporeal and grossly anthropomorphic conception of the divine in these texts. It is the case, rather, that the authorship of the *Shi'ur Qomah* (if we are indeed able to speak of authors of these texts in any precise manner) reflected an inner struggle between the assumed concealment and hence immeasurability of the divine form and the central claim that this form is visible and measurable.[75] The acceptance of the paradoxical situation that God is both revealed and hidden is a far more

[71] See Schäfer, *Hidden and Manifest God,* p. 162.

[72] See Elior, "Concept of God," pp. 31–34 (English trans., pp. 108–110); Schäfer, *Hidden and Manifest God,* pp. 148–150, where he speaks of this paradox in terms of transcendence and immanence, and pp. 162–163, where he elaborates on the fact that in "the Hekhalot literature God is now, *at present,* at the same time both hidden *and* revealed" (emphasis in original).

[73] *Synopse,* §§ 948–949 (= *Geniza-Fragmente,* p. 115); cf. §§ 356, 699; Cohen, *Shi'ur Qomah: Texts and Recensions,* pp. 47, 65–66, 90–91, 141–142.

[74] On the description of God as *mekhusseh mi-kol ha-beriyyot,* see *Synopse,* §§ 484, 692, 710, 952; Cohen, *Shi'ur Qomah,* p. 87. The expression *melekh mekhusseh,* "concealed king," appears in one isolated hymn in *Synopse,* § 379.

[75] The position I have taken resonates with that expressed by other scholars. See, for example, Elior, "Concept of God," pp. 24–25 (English trans., pp. 105–106); Schäfer, *Hidden and Manifest God,* p. 162.

sophisticated and nuanced approach than viewing the enormous measurements disclosed in the text as a reductio ad absurdum of the anthropomorphic speculation on God.[76] It is necessary to embrace the paradox in its full dialectic: the divine form is conceivable in its imperceptibility, revealed in its hiddenness.

From a careful examination of the relevant material in the Hekhalot sources it can be concluded that a similar tension is operative in these compositional units as well. It follows that the restriction on vision is not due to the inherent invisibility of God, as posited by Scholem, but results, as Chernus argued,[77] from the acute awareness that such a vision may—most likely will—eventuate in the destruction of the visionary.[78] Thus in one passage, from a titleless unit dealing with the divine names, it states that if the adept "raises his eyes heavenward and beholds the countenance of the Presence he will die; if he casts his eyes to the ground, he will live."[79] The danger in seeing God implied in this passage only serves to prove that such a vision was indeed possible. In succinct fashion this passage captures what seems to me to be the overriding assumption of these visionaries or mystics, that there is a visible divine form that, if seen, can be lethal.

The point is made even more clearly in the units contained in the macroform *Hekhalot Rabbati*. The very opening passage, which sets the narrative frame for this collection of tradition-complexes, underscores the centrality of the mystical vision: R. Ishmael inquires about the means necessary for one who desires "to gaze upon the appearance of the chariot" (*lehistakkel bi-ṣefiyyat ha-merkavah*).[80] Admittedly, no direct mention is made here of seeing the glory or Presence, yet a perusal of the various contexts in which the expression *ṣefiyyat ha-merkavah* is used indicates that some such vision is implied.[81] The word "chariot" (*merkavah*) functions here metonymically for the glory (*kavod*) to which it is related. The linguistic justification here is obvious enough: the glory is the central entity on the chariot, and therefore it is sensible to refer to the former by means of the latter. The phrase *lehistakkel bi-ṣefiyyat ha-merkavah* is immediately followed by the expression *lered be-shalom we-laʿalot be-shalom*, which should be rendered "to enter in peace and to depart in peace."[82] According to my interpretation of the term *yarad* in this context, to which I have alluded above, the reference here is not to the heavenly journey in its entirety but only to its final stage at the seventh palace, which involves an entry to the throne followed by an exit therefrom. The redactor placed this comment at the beginning of the text, for that is precisely the concern of the protagonist,

[76] See *Major Trends*, p. 64; *On the Mystical Shape*, pp. 24–25; see also Dan, "The Concept of Knowledge in the *Shiʿur Qomah*," p. 69.

[77] "Visions of God," pp. 129–130.

[78] Cf. *Synopse*, §§ 102, 229.

[79] Ibid., § 489.

[80] Ibid., § 81.

[81] See, e.g., ibid., §§ 93, 403, 557, 579.

[82] The one exception is the reading preserved in MS Vatican 228, where the ascent precedes the descent.

R. Ishmael, as it is for any student receiving this tradition from a teacher or for anyone reading this text: how does one safely reach the throne to behold the glory?

Despite the stated goal of the *yored merkavah* in *Hekhalot Rabbati* to behold the King in his beauty, the fact is that on various occasions within this macroform the point is made that no creature, angelic or human, can gaze upon the enthroned form of the glory. In one microform such a limitation of vision is even applied to the robe or cloak (*ḥaluq*) of God:

> Measure of holiness, measure of might,
> an awesome and terrifying measure.
> Measure of trembling, measure of shaking,
> measure of terror, measure of panic,
> of the garment of Zoharariel, the Lord of hosts, God of Israel,
> [with which] He is wrapped when He comes to sit upon the throne of His glory.
> And all over it is inscribed, outside and inside, YHWH YHWH.
> The eyes of no creature can behold it,
> neither the eyes of any being of flesh and blood nor the eyes of His servants.
> The one who looks upon it, or glimpses or sees it,
> his eyeballs are seized by pulsations,
> and his eyeballs emit and send forth flames of fire,
> and they kindle him and burn him up.
> The fire that comes out of the man who looks kindles him and burns him.
> Why?
> Because of the appearance of the eyes of the garment of Zoharariel YHWH, God of Israel,
> who is wrapped when He comes [to sit] on the throne of His glory.
> Pleasant and sweet is His beauty,
> like the appearance of the beauty of the splendor of the glory of the eyes of the holy beasts, as it is said, "Holy, holy, holy,
> the Lord of Hosts."[83]

The essential message of this passage is the potential harm that may accrue from looking upon the garment in which God is wrapped in the moment of enthronement. On the other hand, the concluding part of this microform does indeed underscore the luminous nature (signified by the technical term "beauty") that the Presence assumes when it comes upon the throne. The claim that no eye can behold the garment does not imply the inherent invisibility of either the garment or the glory, but relates rather to the potential harm that

[83] *Synopse*, § 102. This translation, like virtually all translations of passages from *Hekhalot Rabbati* contained in this chapter, is based on the translation of Morton Smith placed in my hands by Ithamar Gruenwald. I am presently preparing an annotated translation of *Hekhalot Rabbati*, to be published in the "Classics of Western Spirituality" series, Paulist Press, ed. B. McGinn, together with my own introduction and a preface by Gruenwald. I have altered Smith's translation considerably, but his work did serve as a basis for my own.

would result from such a vision. It is likely that underlying this poetic depiction of the cloak of the glory is the dynamics of a sexual myth connected to the moment of enthronement. Significantly, the glory is said to be wrapped in this garment only when it sits upon the throne. In an obvious reversal of human sexuality, it is not nakedness but the donning of a cloak that symbolizes the sexual play of the divine glory vis-à-vis the throne.[84] The erotic dimension of gazing upon the cloak is especially underscored by the description of the eyes of the divine garment. I would suggest that the eyes function in this context as phallic symbols and that the danger of beholding the garment is related to a taboo of seeing the divine phallus.[85] The phallic symbolism of the eye also underlies the description of the ocular gyrations and fiery discharges from the eye of one who does gaze upon the cloak of the glory. The phallic understanding of the eye and the erotic aspect of the divine garment are evident in another passage from the same redactional unit:

> The diadem of His head sends forth and radiates sun and moon,
> Pleiades and Orion and Mercury and Venus,
> constellations and stars and planets
> flow and emerge from His garment [with which]
> He is wrapped when He sits on the throne of His glory.
> And He sends forth a great light from between His eyes.
> King of miracles, king of mighty acts,
> king of wonders and a king of otherness is He,
> as it is said, "Holy, holy, holy, the Lord of Hosts."[86]

[84] It should be recalled that in several biblical texts the act of a man spreading a garment over a woman's nakedness symbolizes espousal. See Lev. 18:8, 20:11; Deut. 23:1; Ezek. 16:8; Ruth 3:9. Interestingly enough, according to one aggadic tradition, God dons ten garments (*levushin*) corresponding to the ten places in Scripture where Israel is referred to as a bride. Cf. *Pesiqta de-Rav Kahana* 22:5, pp. 329–330; *Shir ha-Shirim Rabbah* 4:10; *Midrash ha-Gadol on Genesis*, p. 60; *Yalqut Shimʿoni* 2:506, 988. According to the formulation in *Devarim Rabbah* 2:37, Israel is said to crown God with ten garments corresponding to the ten times that God refers to Israel as a bride. Cf. the poetic reworking of this aggadic motif in the *yoṣer* for Rosh ha-Shanah, attributed to Qallir, *melekh ʾazur gevurah*, in *Maḥzor la-Yamim Noraʾim*, ed. E. D. Goldschmidt (Jerusalem, 1970), 1:44: *melekh ba-ʿasarah levushim hitʾazzar bi-qedoshim*. Does the fact that the donning of the ten garments on the part of God is related specifically to scriptural references in which Israel is depicted as a bride suggest that in the aggadic tradition as well, the garment implies a sexual element? It is certainly the case that in later kabbalistic literature the image of putting on a garment is used euphemistically to refer to divine sexuality and, more specifically, the erection and penetration of the penis. It would seem that with respect to this symbol there is continuity from the earlier to the later sources.

[85] In a variety of texts, from the talmudic and medieval periods, the eye is correlated with the penis, a theme that I have developed in my study "Weeping, Death, and Spiritual Ascent in Sixteenth-Century Jewish Mysticism." See also my "Beautiful Maiden without Eyes," pp. 169–170, 185–186. Specific mention should be made of a tradition cited in the name of the "masters of the chariot" (*baʿale merkavah*) in MS Oxford-Bodleian 1610, fol. 46a, to the effect that God is filled with eyes from inside and outside. This is obviously a transference of the description of the ophanim of the chariot (see Ezek. 1:18, 10:12) to God, but it seems to me that the implicit meaning here may also involve the phallic symbolism of the eye.

[86] *Synopse*, § 105. On the image of God's eyes in relation to the angelic beings beneath the throne, see § 152.

For the authorship of *Hekhalot Rabbati,* therefore, at least as may be gathered from the units I have cited, the problem is the implicit danger of seeing God rather than the intrinsic impossibility of such a vision. That this is the correct interpretation is supported by yet another passage:

> Comely countenance, glorious countenance,
> countenance of beauty, countenance of flames.
> These are the faces of YHWH, God of Israel, when He sits on the throne of His glory. . . .
> The one who looks at Him is immediately torn asunder,
> and the one who gazes upon His beauty is immediately poured out as if from a pitcher.[87]

In this text the fact that God possesses a visible face, described in multiple ways, is not called into question; nevertheless, it is said explicitly that one who looks at or contemplates the face of God will suffer tragic consequences. Schäfer has recently suggested[88] that the content of this passage is made clear only from the continuation, wherein it is stated unequivocally that those who serve God, that is, the angels, cannot observe God's beauty without perishing: "Those who serve Him today do not serve Him tomorrow, and those who serve Him tomorrow shall not serve Him again, for their strength grows weak and their faces black, and their hearts wander and their eyes darken because of the glorious splendor of the beauty of their King."[89]

This latter theme, reflected in classical rabbinic texts as well, is emphasized elsewhere in *Hekhalot Rabbati* and in other macroforms within the Hekhalot literature.[90] It is, however, unclear if, in fact, this is the only or the best explanation for the comment that the one who looks at God will immediately be torn apart. It seems to me that incorporated in this text is the restriction on the possibility of seeing God on the grounds that such a visual experience is in principle—for everyone, mortal and angel—unbearable. The redactional order of placing the text about the angels after this text results in the impression articulated by Schäfer. It may be suggested, however, that the end of the passage concerning the inevitable demise of the angels who serve God strengthens the

[87] Ibid., § 159. On the expression "to be poured out as if from a pitcher" to denote emotional and/or physical harm, see also §§ 104, 481 (= 949), 699; *Geniza-Fragmente,* p. 115. The expression is used in standard rabbinic sources as well. See, e.g., B. Shabbat 62b.

[88] *Hidden and Manifest God,* p. 17.

[89] *Synopse,* § 159. In rabbinic sources as well, one finds the idea—exegetically linked to Lam. 3:23—that angels are created each day to utter songs before God and after completing their mission they perish. Cf. *Bereshit Rabbah* 78:1, pp. 916–917; B. Ḥagigah 14a; *Midrash Eikhah Rabbah* 3:23, p. 132; Gruenwald, *Re'uyot Yeḥezqel,* pp. 125–126; Ginzberg, *Legends* 5:25–26 n. 70. The thematic link of the passage in *Hekhalot Rabbati* and this aggadic motif has previously been noted by Gruenwald in "Angelic Songs," in *From Apocalypticism to Gnosticism,* p. 160 n. 71.

[90] See, e.g., *Masekhet Hekhalot,* chap. 3, in Jellinek, ed., *Bet ha-Midrash,* 2:41. Some exceptions are, of course, found as well. See, e.g., *Synopse,* § 581, where the angel of the countenance is described as "seeing the image of Zoharariel, YHWH, God of Israel."

more general claim that anyone who looks at the beauty of the glorious King will perish. The tension between visualization of the divine beauty and the unbearability of such a vision is not to be resolved or harmonized in some exegetical manner, but rather should stand as it is, for this is, as Schäfer himself at one point acknowledges, "one of the fundamental statements of *Hekhalot Rabbati* and the Hekhalot literature as a whole (at least on the level of the Ashkenazi redaction as represented by the extensive manuscripts)."[91] Indeed, in the continuation of the very section of *Hekhalot Rabbati* cited above, the attendant angels are described in some detail. The text concludes: "Praiseworthy is the King, for these are His servants, and praiseworthy are the servants, for this is their King. Praiseworthy is the eye that is nourished and gazes upon this marvellous light, a marvellous and exceedingly strange vision."[92]

In another passage from *Hekhalot Rabbati* the tension between the special visible accessibility to the mystic of the divine countenances and the general invisibility of God emerges with utmost clarity:

> A heavenly decree will be against you,
> those who enter the chariot,
> if you do not report and tell what you have heard,
> and if you do not bear witness to what you have seen on the faces—exalted faces,
> and strength of pride and glorification. . . .
> No person knows and recognizes them,
> as it says, "Holy, holy, holy."[93]

According to this text, the *yored merkavah* not only has as his goal the seeing of the divine countenance in its multiple manifestations thrice daily—no doubt corresponding to the three liturgical moments according to normative rabbinic Judaism—but he has a mandate to narrate or discourse about that experience. The *yored merkavah* thus sees that which no other being, angelic or human, is privileged to see. The force of the text, then, would be to highlight and heighten the exceptional character of the mystic's gaze, inasmuch as he beholds that which no angel or other human being can behold. In a sense, however, the implicit danger of the vision is always lurking in the background, even for the *yored merkavah,* and hence the real tension between the act of seeing God and the harm that may ensue is not fully resolved.

On this score, it seems to me, the texts from *Hekhalot Rabbati* are in accord with early apocalyptic sources that, as I indicated briefly in the first chapter, likewise emphasize the fiery visions of God while concomitantly noting the impossibility of beholding the divine form. Here, too, any apparent contradiction is mitigated by the fact that the assumption is not that God is invisible *de jure,* but only *de facto*. This is expressed paradoxically in an oft-cited passage from *Hekhalot Zuṭarti,* in which the theoretical problem of positing a vision of

[91] Schäfer, *Hidden and Manifest God,* p. 20.
[92] *Synopse,* § 160.
[93] Ibid., § 169.

God is confronted directly, albeit in an exegetical rather than discursive manner:

> Who is able to explain? who is able to see?
> Firstly, it is written,[94] "for no man shall see Me and live."
> Secondly, it is written,[95] "man may live though God has spoken to him."
> Thirdly, it is written,[96] "I saw the Lord sitting upon the throne."[97]

As Schäfer has pointed out,[98] the three verses no doubt stand for three distinct positions related to the theoretical issue at hand—is God visible? The first verse categorically rejects the possibility of such an experience; the second verse emphasizes that a person can at least speak with God and survive; the third verse states that a visionary, unlike other mortal creatures, does indeed behold the divine upon the throne. I surmise, moreover, that the prophet here stands for the Merkavah mystic, and the locus of the enthroned glory must be transfered from the earthly Temple to the celestial throne-chamber in the seventh palace. The mystic can see precisely what others, both human and angelic creatures, cannot see. This is expressed in the continuation of the text, after an interpolation of a short passage in the vein of the *Shiʿur Qomah* material dealing with the mystical names of the Godhead: "R. Aqiva said: He is, as it were, like us, but He is greater than everything. This is His glory that is hidden from us."[99]

The glory that is hidden is said to be like the human being, albeit much greater in size; insofar as the anthropomorphic form is imputed to the glory in the first statement attributed to R. Aqiva, the second statement cannot be understood as asserting that it is inherently invisible. On the contrary, it is hidden, I suggest, precisely because it is potentially visible, that is, inasmuch as the vision of the glory can prove fatal to any mortal, it must be hidden from sight. Yet for the one who has undertaken the heavenly ascent it is precisely such a vision that is assumed to be possible. The point is made unambiguously in a second passage from the same work: "The great, mighty, awesome, glorious and strong God is hidden from the eyes of all the creatures, and concealed from the ministering angels, but He revealed himself to R. Aqiva in the account of the chariot in order to do His will."[100]

[94] Exod. 33:20.
[95] Deut. 5:21.
[96] Isa. 6:1.
[97] *Synopse,* § 350.
[98] *Übersetzung der Hekhalot Literatur,* III, p. 20 n. 1; *Hidden and Manifest God,* p. 58.
[99] *Synopse,* § 352. It is possible that this passage—the only one in the Hekhalot corpus wherein the term *nistar* occurs together with *kavod*—represents an interpolation on the part of medieval Ashkenazi scribes who introduced the element of the hiddenness of the glory. (In private conversation Michael Swartz expressed to me that he has similar suspicions regarding this text.) In a later stage of the development of German Pietistic theology there emerges a clear distinction between the inner or hidden and outer or visible glories. See chapter 5 for an elaborate discussion of this topic. See, by contrast, Scholem, *On the Mystical Shape,* p. 21; Schäfer, *Hidden and Manifest God,* pp. 58–59.
[100] *Synopse,* § 421.

The same concern is reflected in a passage from the unit *Ma'aseh Merkavah*, in a dialogue between R. Ishmael and R. Neḥuniah ben ha-Qanah:

> I said again to R. Neḥuniah ben ha-Qanah: When [one] recites the twelve things, how can one gaze upon the radiance of the Presence (*ziw ha-shekhinah*)? He answered me: He should say a prayer with all his might and he is beloved of the Presence (*shekhinah 'ahuvah lo*).[101]

It is fair to assume that the locution *ziw ha-shekhinah*, reflecting a more traditional rabbinic idiom, functions as a semantic equivalent to the term *yofi* in other Hekhalot texts, or even closer to the phrase *ziw yofi to'ar*, mentioned above. The identical expression appears in a second passage of the same macroform, where it is again stressed that if one prays a certain prayer with all his might "he can see the radiance of the Presence and he is the beloved of the Presence."[102] The import of this claim is to emphasize the theurgic efficacy of the mystic's prayer, for by reciting the appropriate prayer he will be beloved of the Presence and thus will be granted a vision without any risk of danger. The implication is drawn out in one manuscript, which concludes the passage as follows: " . . . and [God] grants him permission to see and he is not harmed."[103] In a subsequent passage, at the conclusion of a unit dealing with an enumeration of five prayers taught by R. Neḥuniah to R. Ishmael, the image is repeated in one manuscript recension and echoed in another:[104] "R. Ishmael said: R. Neḥuniah ben ha-Qanah said to me: Whoever says this prayer with all his might can gaze at the radiance of the Presence, and he will be beloved of the Presence."[105]

Even if we are to assume that the placing of the prayers into the narrative account of the visionary ascent to the chariot represents a later redactional stage in the transmission of this text,[106] and if we are further to assume that in the case of *Ma'aseh Merkavah* the text does not reflect an "active praxis" of ascent but rather a literary construct by means of which the separate prayers are organized into some discernible form,[107] the fact is that given the final

[101] Ibid., § 570.

[102] Ibid., § 591.

[103] Ibid., § 570 (MS New York–JTSA Mic. 8128). According to a passage in *3 Enoch* 5:3 (ibid., § 7) Adam and his generation were granted the possibility of gazing on "the image of the form of the radiance of the Presence" (*lehistakkel bi-demut to'aro shel ziw ha-shekhinah*) without any harm. Indeed, in that context it is emphasized that the vision of the radiance of the Presence functions apotropaically to ward off the potential harm of flies, gnats, sickness, pain, demons, or the angels. On the *Shekhinah* as an apotropaic protection against demons, see also *Bemidbar Rabbah* 12:3 (already noted by Alexander in his translation of *3 Enoch*, ed. Charlesworth, p. 259, n. 5c).

[104] MS New York–JTSA Mic. 8128; MS Oxford-Bodleian 1531.

[105] *Synopse*, § 591 (MS New York–JTSA Mic. 8128). On the redactional issues regarding this section, see Swartz, *Mystical Prayer*, p. 22.

[106] Swartz, *Mystical Prayer*, pp. 7, 11, 211–223. See also Schäfer, *Übersetzung der Hekhalot Literatur*, III, pp. xxx–xxxiv.

[107] Swartz, *Mystical Prayer*, pp. 21, 214–215.

stages of redaction (to be understood in a heuristic sense[108]) the assumption put forth by those responsible for the compilation of the text is that the visionary can see the glory. That this is the underlying assumption of this text in its redactional form is evident from one of the opening passages: "R. Aqiva said: When I ascended and gazed upon the Dynamis, I saw all the creatures that are in the pathways of the heaven, their length above and their width below, their width below and their length above."[109]

The theurgical significance of prayer, according to this text, is evident from various passages that emphasize that prayer alone facilitates the visionary experience, which otherwise would have been impossible.[110] Thus, the text begins with R. Ishmael asking R. Aqiva for the prayer that one must recite when one ascends to the chariot along with the praise of RWZYH, YHWH, God of Israel. Knowing the praise of God refers to the appropriate prayer or hymn that has the specific function of allowing for a visionary experience. To cite one other text from this literary unit: "R. Aqiva said: When I prayed this prayer I saw 6,400,000,000 ministering angels of glory standing opposite the throne of glory. And I saw the knot of the phylacteries of GRWYY, YHWH, God of Israel, and I offered praise with all my limbs."[111] Here the vision of the enthroned glory is somewhat mitigated by referring to the knot of the phylacteries, which, according to a statement found in the Babylonian Talmud,[112] is associated with the divine back mentioned in Exod. 33:23. It cannot be concluded definitively that such an interpretation is implied here as well. What is clear, however, is the fact that in this text the mystic visionary claims to see what others cannot. As I argued at some length in chapter 1, a similar theoretical posture may be assumed to be operative in the biblical sources themselves: God, though not intrinsically invisible, is for the most part invisible except when he occasionally chooses to manifest his presence. The ocular gaze is focused on that which is hidden from sight. A line of continuity can thus be drawn from the prophetic traditions of the Bible to the circles of apocalyptists and throne-mystics.

The Eroticism of the Divine Enthronement

The moment of the enthronement of the divine glory in the extant Hekhalot sources is characterized as one of illumination that is too powerful for anyone to behold. I would like to suggest, moreover, that underlying this enthronement is a profound sexual myth, as I have already intimated above. In several passages in *Hekhalot Rabbati* the enthronement is described in erotic terminology,

[108] Cf. Schäfer, *Übersetzung der Hekhalot Literatur,* III, pp. xxxii–xxxiv; Swartz, *Mystical Prayer,* p. 220.

[109] *Synopse,* § 545.

[110] See Gruenwald, *Apocalyptic,* pp. 182–184, and the study of Swartz cited above.

[111] *Synopse,* § 550.

[112] B. Berakhot 7a and Menaḥot 35b.

the throne serving as the feminine element in relation to the masculine glory.[113] The terminology employed suggests more than a mere figurative or metaphorical account; indeed, the throne is hypostasized as an autonomous entity in the pleroma of the chariot, closer to the glory than all the classes of angelic beings, prostrating itself in a liturgical posture and speaking directly to the divine form that sits upon it.[114] Furthermore, in some passages the throne is depicted as the object of the mystic's vision together with the divine King.[115]

Speculating on this literary phenomenon, Schäfer suggested the following explanation: "The throne perhaps became the object of the vision and speculation out of the desire to avoid the danger of a broader visualization of the enthroned divinity."[116] I do not think it is necessary to adopt such a view, for the extant sources indicate that the throne was an object of vision together with the enthroned glory and not a substitute for it, that is, the mystic visionary beholds the glory in an enthroned posture, which implies that both the glory and the throne upon which it sits are seen by the mystic. The respective gender characteristics attributed to the glory and the throne mitigate against viewing the visualization of the throne as a substitute for the vision of the glory. That is, the significance of seeing the throne lies in the fact that it is the feminine potency upon which the masculine glory resides.

According to *Hekhalot Rabbati,* the enthronement is a form of *hieros gamos,* and thus the connotation of the description of the *yored merkavah* as one who is worthy to see the King and his throne is that he witnesses the union above. Against this background one can appreciate the dramatic description of the throne's addressing the divine glory:

[113] My approach here represents a significant departure from the conventional view expressed by scholars who have written on this subject; e.g., Gruenwald, "'Knowledge' and 'Vision'," p. 109: "Jewish mysticism as it is found in the *Hekhalot* literature, never glides into the erotic type of mystical language." Gruenwald contrasts this "erotic" language, which he does not specify in any detail, with the visual or auditory character expressed in the Hekhalot literature. By contrast, I have suggested that it is precisely the visual encounter that smacks of eroticism. Two important exceptions to the general scholarly neglect of the sexual aspects in Hekhalot literature are Moshe Idel (see below, n. 120) and David Halperin (see below, n. 134).

[114] See Schäfer, *Hidden and Manifest God,* pp. 12–14. The description of the throne is found in other macroforms as well; see *Synopse,* § 418. For an alternative approach to the personification of the throne in *Hekhalot Rabbati,* see the comments of Olyan, *A Thousand Thousands Served Him,* p. 39 n. 37. Olyan's claim that the personification of the throne—especially in the description of the throne singing hymns before the glory—is not necessarily an indication that the throne is an angel cannot, in my opinion, be upheld in light of the obvious sexual imagery associated with the throne and the moment of enthronement.

[115] See *Synopse,* §§ 198, 229, 259. See also § 152 where Suriya, the Prince of the Countenance (*sar ha-panim*), instructs R. Ishmael about the "glory of the King and His throne." The word translated in this passage as "glory" is *shevaḥ,* which in addition to its usual meanings of "praise" and "hymn," can designate the splendid beauty of physical appearance, and thus refers to the anthropomorphic image of God on the throne. See Cohen, *Shi'ur Qomah: Liturgy and Theurgy,* pp. 221–222 n. 5.

[116] Schäfer, *Hidden and Manifest God,* p. 14 n. 11.

R. Ishmael said:
What is the recitation of the songs that a person must sing
when he enters the chariot?
He begins by reciting the introductory song:
Beginning of praise and the first song,
beginning of rejoicing and the first exultation,
the archons, who serve each day, sing
before YHWH, the God of Israel,
they exalt the wheel of His throne of glory, (singing):
Rejoice, rejoice, throne of glory!
Exult, exult, supernal dwelling!
Shout, shout for joy, precious vessel[117]
Made marvelously, and a marvel!
Gladden the King who (sits) upon you,
As the joy of the bridegroom[118] in his nuptial chamber.[119]
Let all the descendants of Jacob rejoice and exult
when they come to take refuge under your wings,
like the joy of a heart that rejoices in you.
For your conversation is with the conversation of your King,
and with your Creator do you speak,
as it is said, 'Holy, holy, holy (is the Lord of hosts,
all the earth is filled with His glory)' (Isa. 6:3).[120]

In a second passage the throne of glory is described as prostrating itself thrice daily before the glory and uttering, "Zoharariel, YHWH, God of Israel, glorify Yourself,[121] and sit down upon me, magnificent King, for Your burden is dear

[117] Cf. *Synopse,* §§ 154, 257, 686–687, where the biblical idiom *keli ḥemdah* is likewise applied to the throne. Schäfer (*Hidden and Manifest God,* p. 13 n. 7) compares the use of this expression in Hekhalot literature with standard rabbinic sources in which it generally denotes the Torah. There seems to be an interesting pattern in this text whereby images associated with the Torah in other sources are transferred to the throne. See n. 120, below.

[118] MS Vatican 228 here adds "and bride."

[119] Mention should be made of the image of the bridal chamber in certain Gnostic texts as a symbol for the pleroma. See Grant, "The Mystery of Marriage in the Gospel of Philip"; Sevrin, "Les noces spirituelles dans l'Evangile selon Philippe"; Marcovich, "The Wedding Hymn of Acta Thomae." On the association of the bridal chamber and the Torah, see the text that I translate and discuss in "Female Imaging of the Torah," pp. 282–283.

[120] *Synopse,* § 94. Cf. §§ 154, 687; *Geniza-Fragmente,* p. 185. See below, n. 123. On the feminine quality of the throne see Wolfson, "Circumcision and the Divine Name," p. 95 n. 93 (in that context I neglected to mention the important comments of Farber, "Concept of the Merkabah," pp. 116–117, 617–627, who suggested that in the writings of the German Pietists, especially Eleazar of Worms, the circular shape of the throne, symbolized by the letter *kaf,* alludes to its feminine character; see also pp. 571–574); Wolfson, "Female Imaging of the Torah," p. 283 n. 43; Idel, "Métaphores et pratiques sexuelles dans la cabale" (translation of "Sexual Metaphors and Praxis in the Kabbalah"), p. 340 n. 35 (the relevant material has been left out of the corresponding note in the English version); idem, "Additional Fragments from the Writings of R. Joseph of Hamadan," p. 49 n. 16.

[121] MS Vatican 228 reads, "I will glorify myself."

to me, and is not heavy."[122] One may assume that implicit in these remarks is an erotic relationship between the throne and the glory, and that the glory's sitting upon the throne is a metaphor for a sacred union of the masculine and feminine aspects of the divine.[123]

An aspect of the eroticism of the enthronement may also be implied in another passage from *Hekhalot Rabbati,* which describes a curious dynamic in the throne realm when the Jews below utter the Sanctus. The divine voice implores the mystics who entered before the throne to declare what they have seen:

> Bear witness to them[124]
> of the testimony you see in Me
> regarding what I do to the visage of Jacob, your father,
> which[125] is engraved[126] upon My throne of glory,[127]
> for when you say before Me, Holy,
> I bend down over it,[128] clasp it, embrace it, and kiss it,
> and My hands are on its arms,[129]
> thrice daily,
> for you say before Me Holy,
> as it says, "Holy, holy, holy."[130]

122 *Synopse,* § 99.

123 The decidedly feminine character of the throne is confirmed in another textual unit wherein the angel MYHShGH is said to adorn "TRPZWHYW the king and all the attributes of his throne like a bride for her bridal chamber." Cf. *Geniza-Fragmente,* p. 105.

124 According to MSS Vatican 228 and Budapest-Kaufmann 238. MSS Munich 40 and Philadelphia-Dropsie 436 preserve two readings: "Bear witness to him," and "to them"; MSS New York–JTSA Mic. 8128 and Oxford-Bodleian 1531 read, "Bear witness to Me"; MS Munich 22 has "Establish for them."

125 Five of the manuscripts here employ the third person feminine pronoun, שהיא. One manuscript (Munich 22) uses the third person masculine, שהוא. MS Vatican 228 has no pronoun here. The perplexing grammatical point is that the subject of the sentence, *qelaster panav,* requires a masculine form. See nn. 120 and 123, above.

126 Again the feminine form (*ḥaquqah*) is employed.

127 This aggadic motif has been discussed by various scholars, of whom I will here mention only some representative examples: Ginzberg, *Legends,* 5:290 n. 134; Smith, "Prayer of Joseph," pp. 284–286; Altmann, *Essays in Jewish Intellectual History,* p. 18; Halperin, *Faces of the Chariot,* p. 121; Kugel, *In Potiphar's House,* pp. 112–120; and Stern, *Parables in Midrash,* pp. 110–113. See also my own study "The Image of Jacob Engraved upon the Throne."

128 Here, too, the feminine form is employed, עליה, which should be rendered "over her."

129 Following the reading of MSS Vatican 228 and Munich 22, presumably referring to the throne on which is engraved the visage of Jacob. See Schäfer, *Hidden and Manifest God,* pp. 46, 119. According to MSS New York–JTSA Mic. 8128, Oxford-Bodleian 1531, Munich 40, Philadelphia-Dropsie 436, and Budapest-Kaufmann 238, the reading is "on My arms," thus conveying the image of God's full embrace of the throne with his hands wrapped around his arms.

130 *Synopse,* § 164. Cf. the passage from *Hekhalot Zuṭarti,* § 411: "R. Akiva said: Thus the light of the face of Jacob, our patriarch, shone before Adiriyon, YHWH, the God of Israel." The connection between this text and the passage from *Hekhalot Rabbati* about the visage of Jacob has been noted by Elior, in *Hekhalot Zuṭarti,* p. 73 n. 317.

Whatever the precise meaning of this text, it is evident that some expression of passionate embrace between God and the visage of Jacob (which may be the celestial representative of Israel[131]) is intended, a dynamic set in motion by Israel's utterance of the Sanctus below. Interestingly, the visage of Jacob assumes female qualities vis-à-vis the glory, for it is engraved on the throne, which is viewed in feminine terms.

The feminine nature of the throne illuminates the paradoxical issue of the invisibility of the visible glory at the moment of enthronement. That is, when the glory sits upon the throne there is a sacred union above, and the angelic beasts surrounding the throne must block out the vision of the glory, which is precisely what the mystic sees and about which he must bear witness.[132] This reading is confirmed by another passage from *Hekhalot Rabbati,* which employs the interplay of uncovering and covering the face in an overtly erotic manner:

> Each day when the time for the afternoon prayer arrives,
> the glorious King sits and extols the beasts.
> Before the words are out of His mouth
> the holy beasts come out from beneath the throne of glory,
> their mouths full of exultation,
> their wings full of rejubilation,
> their hands beating (time),
> their feet dancing.
> They encircle and surround their King,
> one on His right and another on His left,
> one before Him and another behind Him.
> They embrace Him and kiss Him,
> and uncover their faces.
> They uncover and the King of glory covers His face.
> Then the firmament, Aravot,
> breaks open like a sieve
> because of the glorious King,
> the splendor of the beauty
> of the form
> of the loveliness
> of the grace
> of the effulgence
> of the radiance
> of the likeness

[131] As suggested by Schäfer, *Hidden and Manifest God,* p. 46 n. 149.

[132] Cf. *Synopse,* § 169, where the *yorde merkavah* are obligated by a heavenly decree to report what they have heard above and to give testimony about what they have seen regarding the divine countenance. See also § 216, where mention is also made of the testimony of the mystics regarding their visionary experience. For discussion of this text see Wolfson, "Yeridah la-Merkavah," pp. 16–17.

of the appearance
of their faces,
as it is said, "Holy, holy, holy."[133]

The erotic ecstasy here is underscored by the description of the angelic beasts hugging, kissing, dancing, and encircling the enthroned King, a sequence of activities that is certainly intended to convey sexual drama. The sexual overtones of this passage have been duly noted by Halperin, who remarks, inter alia, that the reference to the beasts' uncovering of their faces (*mefareʿot penehem*) suggests the uncovering of the corona during circumcision (*periʿah*).[134] According to Halperin, moreover, the image of the splitting of the heaven like a sieve is a metaphor for the opening of the female genitalia (the sieve functioning as a symbol for the vagina in other rabbinic sources).

What particularly interests me in this context is the dynamic of the beasts' uncovering of their faces and the glory's covering of his face. It is noteworthy that the uncovering of the beasts' faces occurs after they have already embraced and kissed the glory; as they disclose their faces the glory conceals his own. It is possible that in this context the face metaphorically displaces the phallus that must be concomitantly revealed and veiled in this erotic play of gazing and hiding.[135] The critical question to be asked at this juncture is this: Does the

[133] *Synopse,* § 189. For a different rendering of this passage, see Halperin, "A Sexual Image in Hekhalot Rabbati and Its Implications," p. 119.

[134] Halperin, "Sexual Image," p. 120. In that context Halperin also mentions that the uncovering of the faces suggests a person's uncovering to defecate. I am less convinced of the relevance of this connotation in the present context. See the more cautious remark regarding this passage by Schäfer (*Hidden and Manifest God,* p. 24): "Even if one does not wish to go as far as D. Halperin, who presumes massive sexual implications here and in similar passages, one must admit that we are dealing with a very intimate scene."

[135] My comments here reflect the suggestive remarks of Eilberg-Schwartz in "People of the Body," pp. 30–33, with respect to Moses' request to see the divine face and the permission granted him to see the divine back (Exod. 33:17–23), which is connected with the narrative concerning Noah's drunkenness (Gen. 9:20–27). It would be fruitful to apply such a reading to the verse "Seraphs stood in attendance on Him. Each of them had six wings: with two he covered his face, with two he covered his legs, and with two he would fly" (Isa. 6:2). Cf. *Wayyikra Rabbah* 27:3, p. 626; *Pirqe Rabbi 'Eliʿezer* 4, 11a; *Midrash Tanḥuma,* 'Emor, 8; Ṣav, 13; *Pesiqta de-Rav Kahana* 9:3, p. 151; *Yalqut Shimʿoni* 1:642. The covering of the face is to prevent the seraphim from seeing the Presence and the covering of the feet is to prevent the Presence from seeing part of the anatomy of the seraphim. Although in some of the midrashic sources just mentioned the angelic feet are associated with calves' feet (based on Ezek. 1:7), and by further association with the feet of the golden calf, it seems to me that this may represent a secondary midrashic interpretation and that in the primary stage the covering of the feet had nothing to do with the shame of the golden calf. It is possible that the feet here function euphemistically for the phallus and that the covering of the feet represents the proper modesty required by the angelic beings when they stand near the divine glory. See Wolfson, "Images of God's Feet," pp. 145–146. Consider especially the language of the midrashic text *Ke-Tapuaḥ be-ʿAṣe ha-Yaʿar,* published from a Yemenite manuscript by Wertheimer in *Batte Midrashot,* 1:280: "He saw the angels who stood before the Holy One, blessed be He, and each one had six wings, with two wings each covered its face, with two each covered its feet, and with two each flew. With two each covered its face in order not to see the face of the Presence, and with two they covered their bodies, and with two they flew and served before the Holy One, blessed

mystic's vision of the enthroned glory also involve some kind of sexual dynamic? Does the *ṣefiyyah ba-merkavah* (gazing at the chariot) or *histakkelut ba-kavod* (contemplation of the glory) entail, as modern feminist theory would express it, a phallic gaze, the eye substituting for the penis and the object of vision signifying the externalized, representable form of the phallus?

It is difficult to ascertain from the extant Hekhalot sources whether or not the visionary experience of the Merkavah mystic himself involves the eroticized character of veiling and unveiling that I described above with respect to the angels. I note in passing, however, that such a notion of seeing the divine Presence is clearly implied in standard midrashic works,[136] as I have argued particularly with respect to the motif of the correlation of circumcision and visionary experience: the rite of circumcision serves as an initiation that results in the specularization of God, the penis functioning as the organ that facilitates vision.[137]

Other texts could be cited as proof of a phallomorphic understanding of vision in rabbinic sources, including, for instance, the traditional expression "to feast one's eyes upon the Presence,"[138] but it must be admitted that the literary evidence is insufficient to conclude decisively with respect to the mystical texts. My own predilection is to assume that it is likely that the mystic's vision of the Presence does entail an erotic relationship between seer and seen, especially given the overtly sexual quality of the passages I have discussed above.[139] To cite one other example that supports my interpretative stance:

> (I swear) by heaven and earth you will be blessed,
> those who enter the chariot,
> if you will say and declare to My children

---

be He." Hence, the biblical description of covering the feet (cf. Isa. 6:2) here becomes covering the bodies. The word used in the midrashic text to render the word *regel* (foot) of Scripture is *gewiyyah,* a term that has the connotation of "body" but can also refer to the male or female genitals. If in this context *gewiyyah* indeed refers to the *membrum virile,* then here is another instance in rabbinic literature wherein the foot functions as a euphemism for the phallus (see my study cited above). The angels' covering of the feet with two wings thus represents an act of modesty before the face of the Presence. On the locution "they covered their bodies" (*mekhasot gewiyyotehen*), based on Ezek. 1:23, see the passage in *Hekhalot Zuṭarti* in *Synopse,* § 370. Finally, it should be noted that the face-to-face encounter does assume sexual implications in the talmudic description of the cherubim (see B. Baba Batra 99a; Yoma 54a) and in later kabbalistic literature; see, e.g., *Zohar* 2:99a, 176b (*Sifra di-Ṣeniʿuta*); 3:16b, 59b, 74a, 296a (*Idra Zuṭa*); *Zohar Ḥadash* 62c; see also Liebes, "Messiah," pp. 164 n. 273, 191, 200–201 (English trans., pp. 63, 68–70).

[136] See Idel, "Sexual Metaphors and Praxis," pp. 202–203.

[137] Wolfson, "Circumcision, Vision of God, and Textual Interpretation," pp. 189–215; and see Boyarin, "'This We Know to Be the Carnal Israel'," pp. 491–497.

[138] See chapter 1, n. 126.

[139] It is noteworthy that in *Maʿaseh Merkavah* (*Synopse,* § 570) the mystic is referred to as the beloved of the divine Presence. See also *Hekhalot Rabbati* (*Synopse,* § 96), where the mystic is called "the beloved." Contrary to Scholem's generalization that there is no love between God and the Merkavah mystic (see *Major Trends,* p. 55), it is possible that the very moment of visual encounter is an erotic experience. The sexual component may be implied in the terminology "beloved" employed to refer to the mystic.

what I do in morning prayer,
and in afternoon and evening prayer,
every single day and every single hour,
when Israel says before Me, "Holy."
Teach them and say to them: Lift up your eyes to heaven,
which corresponds to your house of prayer,
when you say before Me, "Holy."
For nothing else in all My world which I created
gives Me such pleasure as that time
when your eyes are lifted toward My eyes,
and My eyes look into your eyes,
at the time when you say before Me, "Holy."
For the sound that issues from your mouth
at that time flows and rises before Me like a pleasant scent.[140]

At the time that the Jews utter the Sanctus below, they are given the opportunity of visually connecting with the divine glory, apparently without any praxis of ascent to the heavenly abode of the throne. Nothing gives the glory as much pleasure as the moment when the divine eyes gaze into the eyes of Israel engaged in prayer, which rises like a pleasant scent—according to the biblical account, like the smoke of the burnt offering. It seems hardly a coincidence that this passage is followed by one of the most erotic texts in all of Hekhalot literature, the text discussed above, describing the relationship of the glory and the image of Jacob engraved upon the throne.

Iconic Symbolization of the Divine Anthropos as Light and Name

As I noted above, it is necessary from a form-critical standpoint to distinguish the nature of the enthroned form of God depicted in the extant macroforms that constitute the Hekhalot literature, on the one hand, and the object described in the graphically anthropomorphic and corporeal terms of *Shi'ur Qomah* traditions, on the other, even though in some cases, most notably *Merkavah Rabbah,* the two strands have been woven together through the redactional process. Nevertheless, it may be surmised from the relevant sources that the vision of the glory on the throne in the Hekhalot corpus is likewise predicated on the acceptance of an anthropomorphic representation of God as a visible form, a *topos* that is, of course, rooted in the biblical theophanic tradition.[141]

[140] *Synopse,* § 163. It is noteworthy that this passage was used by later Ashkenazi authorities to support the custom of lifting the eyes heavenward when the *qedushah* is recited. See Abraham bar Azriel, *'Arugat ha-Bosem,* 1:214–215, and other references cited there, p. 215 nn. 1 and 4; Zimmer, "Poses and Postures during Prayer," pp. 94–95. See also Marcus's study referred to in chapter 5 n. 53.

[141] This is not to deny the obvious difference between the biblical sources, on one hand, and the apocalyptic and mystical sources, on the other: in the case of the latter the setting of the theophany

Despite the widespread recognition on the part of scholars of this feature of Hekhalot mysticism, little attempt has been made to discuss the issue of the iconic depiction of the divine in phenomenological terms. The weight of the scholarly treatment has been tilted in the direction of historical, textual, and philological analyses, with minimal attention paid to the experiential underpinnings of imaging God iconically. To evaluate properly the role of anthropomorphic imagery one must locate the Merkavah vision within the larger context of the phenomenology of mystical experience. When that is done it can be seen that, like other mystics in theistic traditions, the Merkavah initiates experienced (and not merely described) their field of vision in physical terms, even though the vision was clearly not of objects in the spatio-temporal world perceived by normal modes of sense perception.

In addition to the anthropomorphic imagery, the glory, throne, and attendant angels are described in the Jewish mystical literature, as they are in the apocalypses, primarily by images of light or fire culled from sensory experience; but they are clearly not corporeal entities seen by the physical eye. As noted above, one of the key technical terms used to designate the mystical vision in some of the redactional units included in this literature is "to look upon the beauty (*yofi*) of the King." A proper philological understanding of this expression as used in these contexts enables one to grasp the phenomenological import of the mystical vision. The term *yofi* denotes the luminous presence of God in the moment of enthronement; it refers, therefore, to a radiant splendor that assumes the shape of a human form for the visionary.[142] In a fundamental sense there is a blending of anthropomorphic and light imagery.[143]

The mystic visionary, after ascending to the seventh palace in the seventh heaven and entering before the throne, beholds this divine form with a vision that is neither corporeal nor purely mental. The mystical vision at once em-

---

is in the mundane world, whereas in the former the focus is turned to the celestial realm. See Elior, "Concept of God," p. 15 (English translation, p. 99). My remarks concern the issue of the nature of the theophanous object, not the means by which the theophany occurs.

142 In various Hekhalot texts the term *to'ar* functions as a synonym for *yofi,* i.e., both refer to the luminous form of the divine appearance. See *Synopse,* §§ 11, 12, 18, 189, 199, 251, 253, 481. This usage is reflected in the description of Adam in a poem of Amittai ben Shefaṭiyah published in *Megillat 'Aḥima'aṣ,* p. 68: *te'ar golem be-yofyo.* The notion that Adam was created from the primordial light is expressed in aggadic texts that may reflect Gnostic motifs. See Altmann, "Gnostic Themes in Rabbinic Cosmology," pp. 31–32.

143 It is particularly instructive to compare the usage of the word *yofi* in the Hekhalot to denote the luminosity of God's body with a similar expression, *kallos,* used to characterize the form of the divine body in the Pseudo-Clementine *Homilies* 17, a text that has been compared by several scholars, most recently Shlomo Pines, to another ancient Jewish mystical tract, *Sefer Yeṣirah.* For references, see chapter 1 n. 61, above. The critical passage reads, "For He [God] has a Form (*morphe*) for the sake of [His] first and unique beauty (*kallos*), and all the limbs . . . [for] He, as far as His body is concerned, is brighter beyond compare than the visual spirit in us and more brilliant than any light—compared to Him, the light of the sun would be held as darkness." See Pines, "Points of Similarity," p. 64, also pp. 100–101. On the use of the word "beauty" in the Pseudo-Clementine text and its possible relationship to the *Shi'ur Qomah* tradition, see Scholem, *Jewish Gnosticism,* p. 41; idem, *On the Mystical Shape,* p. 30.

braces the two realms, corporeal and spiritual. The seeing (*ṣefiyyah*) or contemplation (*histakkelut*) of the chariot overcomes the barriers between the visible and the spiritual worlds. The supersensory entities are experienced concretely as sentient realities. When matters are seen in this light the problem of positing an anthropomorphic form of the divine disappears, for the locus of the iconization is in the imagination of the visionary; in the beholding, the luminous assumes the shape of an anthropos. Within the imaginal consciousness of the mystic that form is real, indeed real as imagined. The issue of divine tangibility is a phenomenological and not a theological one. Furthermore, at the moment of ecstasy, when the mystic is before the chariot and beholds the glory, any distinction between the transcendent God and his visible appearance seems to vanish. In the moment of mystical vision *deus absconditus* and *deus revelatus* are indistinguishable. When the contours of the vision are viewed in this way it becomes difficult to distinguish between God in his transcendence and the manifest form of God, as if the latter were some secondary hypostasis. The full force of the paradox is appreciated when one acknowledges that the God seen by the mystic is the invisible God.

Another aspect of the Merkavah vision from the perspective of religious phenomenology is worth pursuing. In some of the macroforms contained in this corpus, particularly *Hekhalot Zuṭarti, Maʿaseh Merkavah,* and *Merkavah Rabbah,* the form of God is subsumed under the names of God, such that knowledge of the name replaces the vision of the glory as the goal of the mystic path. Alternatively expressed, in these redactional units there is developed the idea that the name of God is to be treated hypostatically as the luminous glory.[144] Hence, to behold the King in his beauty—to gaze upon the enthroned form of God—is effectively to have a vision of the letters of the divine names. This is in part, no doubt, suggested by the substitution of the name for the luminous glory in some biblical texts, particularly the Deuteronomist stratum.[145] To be sure, the biblical idiom of causing the name to dwell in the place of worship (the Temple) signifies no hypostatic theology, but rather the presence of God in a particular locality.

That the name of God substitutes for the glory or Presence is related to the more general conception of the name attested in the Bible, as in scriptures of other ancient Near Eastern cultures, wherein the name represents the power,

[144] Cf. *Synopse,* §§ 555, 556–557, 568, 588, 594, 596, 655. See Scholem, *On the Mystical Shape,* p. 28. On the ideology of the name in *Maʿaseh Merkabah,* see Janowitz, *Poetics of Ascent,* pp. 25–28, 83–99. The function of the name in *Hekhalot Zuṭarti* is treated by Elior in her critical edition of that text, p. 5. See also idem, "Concept of God," pp. 17–18, 20–24 (English trans., pp. 100, 103–105). On the magical-theurgical significance of the divine names in Hekhalot literature, see also Scholem, *Major Trends,* p. 56; idem, *Jewish Gnosticism,* pp. 54–55, 75–83; Gruenwald, *Apocalyptic,* pp. 104–107; Grözinger, "The Names of God and the Celestial Powers."

[145] See Deut. 12:11; 14:23; 16:2, 6, 11; 26:2. Cf. Jer. 7:12, Neh. 1:9. On the figurative treatment of the divine face/presence (*panim*) and the name (*shem*) or image (*ṣelem*) in biblical and ancient Near Eastern epigraphic sources, see Olyan, *A Thousand Thousands Served Him,* pp. 105–107.

being, personality, and substance of that which is named. It is evident, therefore, that in the relevant Hekhalot compositions there is a shift from the metaphoric to symbolic use of this term, a process attested as well in early Christian, Jewish Christian, Gnostic, Samaritan, and rabbinic literature. Yet what is found in these sources, as well as in later mystical literature, may be considered a hermeneutical elaboration of the biblical motif. The name assumes a hypostatic dimension as it is described as a luminous substance like the glory. Analogously, the anthropomorphism operative in the *Shiʿur Qomah* is attenuated somewhat in one stratum of the text by the conception of the limbs as made up of letters.[146] The linguistic conception of the divine body present in *Shiʿur Qomah* is shared, as several scholars have duly noted, by various Gnostic sources in both Christianity (e.g., the third-century Marcos)[147] and Islam (e.g., the eighth-century Mughīra ibn Saʿīd).[148]

The description of God as *lumen substantiae* is also, of course, not unique to Jewish mysticism but is found in a variety of religious and cultural traditions from diverse historical periods and geographical areas. The significant factor in the case of these Jewish mystical texts (judged from the redactional perspective) is, however, the coalescence of the anthropomorphism, light imagery, and linguistic mysticism. The body attributed by the Merkavah mystics to God—the divine image, form, or beauty—is constituted either by light or by letters. From the vantage point of the phenomenology of perception, attested here is an example in the history of religions of the interpenetration of visual and verbal symbolism, for the names of God—composed of letters that are principally auditory elements—have been identified as light. In the symbolic universe of some of the ancient Jewish throne mystics not only is the linguistic symbolism associated with light symbolism, but the former is subsumed under the latter. It is thus evident that what we confront in these texts is no ordinary conception of corporeality, but rather what I (following the work of Corbin) would call the imaginal body, i.e., the luminous form of the divine body is constituted by and within the symbolic imagination.

Ascent to the Throne: Imagined or Real?

Bearing the inherently symbolic nature of the visionary experience in mind, we can now set out to answer another question that has been posed by scholars with regard to the visionary component of this literature. Did the Merkavah mystics actually ascend to the celestial realm and did they see something "out

[146] See Scholem, *On the Mystical Shape*, p. 236; Gruenwald, *Apocalyptic*, p. 215. For the development of this motif in later kabbalistic literature, especially from an anthropological perspective, see Wolfson, "Anthropomorphic Imagery and Letter Symbolism in the Zohar."

[147] See Gaster, "Das Schiur Komah," 2:1343–1345; Scholem, *On the Mystical Shape*, pp. 25–28, 49.

[148] See Dornseiff, *Das Alphabet in Mystic und Magie*, p. 122; Idel, "The Concept of Torah in Hekhalot Literature," p. 67 n. 168; Wasserstrom, "The Moving Finger Writes," p. 12.

there," or should these visions be read as psychological accounts of what may be considered in Freudian language a type of self-hypnosis? Or, to suggest yet a third alternative, would it perhaps be most accurate to describe the heavenly journey in Jungian terms, as a descent into and discovery of the archetypal self?[149]

From a straightforward reading of the extant sources it would appear that some texts assume a bodily ascent, a translation into the heavenly realm of the whole person with all the sensory faculties intact, whereas others assume an ascent of the soul or mind separated from the body as the result of a paranormal experience such as a trance-induced state.[150] But even in the case of the latter explanation, typified most strikingly in *Hekhalot Rabbati* in the story concerning the recall of R. Neḥuniah ben ha-Qanah from his ecstatic trance, it is evident that the psychical states are experienced in terms of tactile and kinesthetic gestures and functions appropriate to the body,[151] such as the fiery gyrations of the eyeballs, ascending and descending, entering and exiting, standing and sitting, singing and uttering hymns, looking and hearing.

The intensity of the moment can only be expressed in bodily terms. Thus, in one passage in *Maʿaseh Merkavah* R. Aqiva reports that "in the seventh palace I stood with all my strength and shook with all my limbs."[152] The transformation of Enoch into the angelic Meṭaṭron, as described in *3 Enoch,* seems to be predicated on a physical translation into the celestial realm. Thus the enlargement of the transformed Enoch into the demiurgical angel is expressed in these terms:

> R. Ishmael said: Meṭaṭron, Prince of the Divine Presence, said to me: In addition to all these qualities, the Holy One, blessed be He, laid his hand on me and blessed me with 1,365,000 blessings. I was enlarged and increased in size till I matched the world in length and breadth. He made to grow on me seventy-two wings, thirty-six on one side and thirty-six on the other, and each single wing covered the entire world. He fixed in me 365,000 eyes and each eye was like the Great Light. There was no sort of splendor, brilliance, brightness, or beauty in the luminaries of the world that he failed to fix in me.[153]

I would propose that from a phenomenological perspective the question of whether the heavenly ascent is "in body" or "out of body" is misguided, for it leads to a false dichotomy between "actual" and "imagined," "real" and "hal-

[149] Such an interpretation of the ascent to the throne is found in Sufi literature. See Sells, "Bewildered Tongue."

[150] See Idel, *Kabbalah: New Perspectives,* pp. 88–89. In some of the Gnostic texts preference seems to be given to an ascent of the mind separated from the body. Cf. in *The Nag Hammadi Library: The Apocryphon of James* 15:25 (p. 36); *The Paraphrase of Shem* 1:5–10 (p. 341); *Zostrianos* 4:20–5:10 (p. 405).

[151] On the description of the ascent of the soul in bodily terms, see Hunt, *Images of Flight,* pp. 136–137. For a wide-ranging discussion of ascents of the soul, see Culianu, *Psychanodia I;* idem, *Expériences de l'extase;* idem, *Out of This World.*

[152] *Synopse,* § 558.

[153] *3 Enoch* 9:1–5, ed. Charlesworth, p. 263.

lucinatory." A more sophisticated approach to the celestial voyage as religious experience would obviate such dichotomous thinking. Before articulating more fully the mechanics of this approach, I will explore in some detail what may be called a rationalistic or psychologistic orientation to the ascent experience in Merkavah mysticism, which one finds in both classical commentaries and modern scholarship. The merit of such a discussion lies in the fact that it provides a model against which my own phenomenological method can be evaluated.

There is textual evidence from a relatively early period of a rationalistic approach that treated the mystical vision of the chariot as an intellectual vision of some inner form.[154] Such a psychological or introvertive interpretation, which effaced the ecstatic aspects of the Hekhalot experiences, is most clearly evident in the explanation of Hai Gaon and the subsequent elaboration by Nathan ben Yeḥiel of Rome, which will be discussed in detail in the next chapter. At this juncture it may be stated briefly that for Hai the ascent to the chariot is interpreted allegorically, as contemplation of the inner chambers of one's own consciousness.[155] Interestingly enough, in a passing comment regarding the term *yorde merkavah,* Scholem seems to be advocating a psychological approach similar in orientation to the one attributed to Hai Gaon according to the interpretation I have accepted, even though Scholem himself offered a different explanation of Hai's position. That is, Scholem suggests that this expression may designate "those who reach down into themselves in order to perceive the chariot."[156] It must be noted, however, that for the most part Scholem adopted a veridical approach with respect to the heavenly journey of the Hekhalot mystic.

The psychologistic interpretation of visionary ascent had a lasting effect on the subsequent history of Jewish exegesis of the chariot-vision in both philo-

[154] An interesting example of this approach, as noted already by Halperin in *Merkabah in Rabbinic Literature,* pp. 174–175 n. 136, is found in Origen's *First Homily on Ezekiel* (*PG,* XIII [Paris, 1857], col. 675), where the exiles are said "to have contemplated with the eyes of the heart" (*cordis oculis*) that which the prophet "observed with the eyes of the flesh" (*oculis carnis*). For the possible Jewish background of this passage, which may provide evidence for a psychological interpretation of the chariot vision in ancient Judaism, see Halperin, "Origen, Ezekiel's Merkabah, and the Ascension of Moses," pp. 273–274; idem, *Faces of the Chariot,* p. 335. See also Idel, *Kabbalah: New Perspectives,* pp. 90–91, and the relevant notes. It is also of interest to note in this connection that in a Christian interpretation of the first chapter of Ezekiel, composed in Armenian, one finds a similar expression used to characterize the prophetic vision of the chariot (quoted in Stone, "The Armenian Vision of Ezekiel," p. 263): "Such a marvelous vision is not to be found in all the prophets and it is the perception of the mind." For the possible background of this expression, see ibid., p. 267. In a similar vein, on various occasions in the *Corpus Hermeticum* mention is made of gazing upon the likeness of God with eyes of the heart or mind. See *Hermetica,* ed. and trans. W. Scott (Boulder, 1982), 1:157, 159, 173, 189.

[155] See Idel, *Kabbalah: New Perspectives,* p. 90. For a different interpretation of Hai Gaon, one that emphasizes an ecstatic ascent to the supernal palaces, see Scholem, *Major Trends,* pp. 49–50; Halperin, *Merkabah in Rabbinic Literature,* pp. 3, 89, 177. See, however, Halperin's formulation in *Faces of the Chariot,* pp. 32, 359, which attributes to Hai a more psychologically oriented reading.

[156] Scholem, *Kabbalah,* p. 6. This explanation for the expression *yeridah la-merkavah* has been virtually neglected by almost all scholars writing on the topic. One exception is Schäfer, *Hidden and Manifest God,* p. 3 n. 4.

sophical and mystical literature, as will be explored in more detail in the next chapter. It is nevertheless the case that a more literal understanding of the ascent was not entirely rejected. In this context I will mention only two examples. In the first instance one thinks of the assertion of the eleventh-century French exegete and talmudic commentator, R. Solomon ben Isaac of Troyes (Rashi), who commented thus on the legend, in B. Ḥagigah 14b, of the four rabbis who entered the mystical orchard (*pardes*): "They ascended to heaven by means of a name." In the opinion of this medieval commentator, then, the Hekhalot praxis, which in his view underlies the talmudic story, involved an actual ascension to heaven by means of uttering a divine name. Reacting to this interpretation the Tosafot writers, following the Geonic position as transmitted in Nathan of Rome's lexicon *Sefer he-ʿArukh,* note: "They did not actually ascend upward but it appeared to them that they ascended."

My second example is taken from *Sefer Levush Malkhut,* a text composed in 1566 by Obadiah Hamon, a kabbalist living in Safed. The author cites the views of Rashi, Hai, Nathan ben Yeḥiel, and the kabbalist Meir ibn Gabbai, who followed the line of Hai, on the interpretation of the aforementioned talmudic legend and concludes:

> Thus it seems that they did not ascend in body or soul, God forbid. Rather, when they were below in their habitations, within the thoughts of their hearts (*morashe levavam*),[157] which is Pardes, they imagined in their minds divine matters until it seemed to them as if all these things were revealed before their eyes so that they saw them with their eyes. Each one in accord with the greatness of his intellect and the breadth of his heart comprehended what he comprehended concerning what is good and what is evil.[158]

This can be taken as a fairly typical approach that is found in later medieval Jewish literature: the contemplative interpretation tends to minimize the supernatural aspect of the chariot vision. Indeed, an important source for Hamon was Judah Ḥayyat, who in his commentary on the kabbalistic composition *Maʿarekhet ha-ʾElohut* cites a long disputation of Menaḥem Recanaṭi, found in his *Commentary on the Torah,*[159] on the secret of death by a kiss, which is, in turn, based on passage from Ezra or Azriel of Gerona explaining the nature of prophecy resulting from the contemplative union of the soul with the Supernal Soul.[160] After citing Recanaṭi's text *in extenso* Ḥayyat observes, "I say this may be the matter of the four who entered Pardes. Even though Rashi, blessed be his memory, explained this literally, for they ascended heavenward by the power of the name that they mentioned, according to my humble

[157] Cf. Job 17:11.

[158] MS Oxford-Bodleian 1597, fols. 93a–b. For discussion of Obadiah Hamon and his sources, see Idel, "R. Yehudah Hallewa and His 'Ẓafenat Paʿaneaḥ,'" pp. 139–145.

[159] Recanaṭi, *Perush ʿal ha-Torah* 37d–38b.

[160] See Idel, *Mystical Experience,* p. 147 n. 29. For a fuller discussion of the kabbalistic notions implied here, see the section entitled "Prophecy, Mystical Vision, and Contemplation" in chapter 6 of the present work.

opinion Pardes is the thoughts of their hearts, for they imagined in their minds divine matters until it seemed to them that all these things were revealed before their eyes so that they saw them with their eyes."[161] It is evident, therefore, that Ḥayyat's contemplative interpretation is the immediate source for the author of *Sefer Levush Malkhut,* as the text of Ḥayyat is copied verbatim, although no name is mentioned. Yet is it instructive to consider the continuation of the later work. After asserting the commonplace view regarding the contemplative nature of the ascent, the author expresses some hesitation: "After all this in my search for truth in books I found some things that contradict what is written above. For a person can ascend in body and soul to heaven, from sphere to sphere until the throne of Aravot. This is written according to the Angel the Maggid, whose name is Azriel."[162] The author goes on to specify the name of this text as *Ha-Mar'ot la-Maggid*—"Visions of the Celestial Angel"—a reference to *Sefer ha-Meshiv,* an anonymous text that contains important divine and angelic revelations.[163] The text cited informs the reader of the techniques necessary to ascend heavenward in order to have a vision of the chariot. "The question as to whether the vision of the chariot entails a bodily ascent or is purely mental," concludes the author, "will remain in doubt until the Teacher of Righteousness [i.e., the Messiah] comes and will instruct us about the truth of this matter."[164]

This text, though relatively late, is revealing, in that it reflects a basic struggle that is present in the Jewish mystical tradition, perhaps from its earliest stages. The nature of the ascent is relevant in determining the status of the visible object and hence, by extension, the more general character of visionary experience. For those who assume an "actual" ascent to a heavenly realm, the visible object presumably lies outside the mind, whereas for those who consider the ascent purely mental in orientation, the object may be considered an inner light configured in terms of the images that are projected outward. Our discussion of visionary experience in the German Pietistic and Spanish-Provençal kabbalistic literature will revolve about these two poles. If we can accept my own analysis of the mystical vision in the Hekhalot, that the role of the imagination is critical in shaping the vision of the luminous forms in terms of corporeal substance, then the whole inside/outside dichotomy is overcome.[165] The image that is seen is indeed a form "outside" the mind, but the shape of that form is constituted by the images "inside" the imagination of the mystic visionary.

A modern advocate of the psychological interpretation is David Halperin. He has challenged several scholars, including Scholem, Johannes Lindblom, and

[161] *Minḥat Yehudah,* commentary to *Maʿarekhet ha-'Elohut,* 96b.

[162] MS Oxford-Bodleian 1597, fol. 94a. The text has been printed and discussed by Idel in "Inquiries into the Doctrine of *Sefer ha-Meshiv,*" p. 189.

[163] See Idel, "Inquiries," pp. 194–195.

[164] MS Oxford-Bodleian 1597, fol. 94a.

[165] A similar position is articulated by Merkur in *Gnosis,* p. 169: "The motifs of the merkabah . . . were considered imaginal. . . . [T]hey were both internal and external, both subjectively achieved and objectively merited."

Martin Cohen, on precisely this point. According to Halperin, these scholars naively assumed that mystical visions—in the case of Scholem, the chariot visions of the Hekhalot mystics; in the case of Lindblom, the vision of John of Patmos in chapter 12 of the Book of Revelation; and in the case of Cohen, the visions and revelations of Meṭaṭron to the author of *Shiʿur Qomah*—are of something ontically real outside the imagination of the visionary. The mark of the authenticity of the vision is the sense that there is really something "out there" that is seen.[166]

According to Halperin, these visions are hallucinatory, by which he means the imaginary construction of an experience in one's unconscious that is then taken by the one who constructs it to be something real coming from the outside.[167] When we speak of apocalypticists or throne mystics as having visions, therefore, we mean that they entered a psychological state in which fantasies are indistinguishable from sense experience. In this state the fantasy (a product of the imagination) becomes hallucination. There is no question regarding the ontic status of the contents of the vision, for they must always be explained in terms of the visionary's own psychological experiences and needs.[168] Moreover, Halperin suggests the possibility that embedded within the trance-induced hallucinations that make up the ecstatic journey to the throne in the Hekhalot literature may be some primitive sexual fantasies, which were thought to have been alleviated by means of the ecstatic techniques employed in the ascent.[169] These unconscious sexual fears, according to Halperin, "were shaped into a mythology of celestial dangers, ultimately recorded in the *Hekhalot*."[170]

Halperin suggests a more comprehensive myth underlying the heavenly ascensions of the Hekhalot that comprises the sexual fantasies and fears discussed above: the myth of the endlessly repeating struggle of the younger generation against the old. The most important thing about the ascension is not the ecstatic mystical experience, but rather the psychological assault on or invasion of the heavenly powers and ultimately God. Halperin goes so far as to propose that it is this myth of generational conflict, and not a continuous ascension tradition rooted in an ecstatic mystical practice, that links together the apoca-

166 For a classical statement of this approach, see H. M. M. Fortmann, *Als ziende de Onzienlijke* (Antwerp, 1964–68), 2:255ff., and discussion of his theory in Mallory, *Christian Mysticism*, pp. 152–157. Fortmann tries to distinguish authentic religious experience and delusion on the basis of a distinction between perception and projection: whereas perception always involves participation with an object, projection does not. However, a more sophisticated phenomenological approach to the constitution of perceptual objects might show that what Fortmann calls perception involves factors not unrelated to psychological processes like projection or sublimation.

167 Halperin, "Heavenly Ascension," p. 222. See also Smith, "Ascent to the Heavens and the Beginning," pp. 403 and 410, where heavenly ascent in Greco-Roman sources is characterized as hallucinatory. And see Schäfer, "Aim and Purpose," p. 295, where the author refers to the "fantasy of the heavenly journey" on the part of the Merkavah mystics.

168 *Faces of the Chariot,* p. 68; see also pp. 441 and 451.

169 Halperin, "Heavenly Ascension," pp. 227–229; idem, *Faces of the Chariot,* pp. 399–401.

170 "Heavenly Ascension," p. 229.

lypses and Hekhalot.[171] Thus, for Halperin it would appear that the Merkavah experience arises merely from projection, with no perceptual basis in reality. The mystic interprets reality in light of his own feelings, tendencies, and impulses, which are then projected onto reality in the form of the mythical landscape upon which the drama of the heavenly ascent and vision of the chariot unfolds.

While Halperin's analysis is at times suggestive and provocative, it seems to me that the main issue he raises, that of whether the vision is real or not, can be resolved only on the basis of a more thorough phenomenological understanding of the critical phase in this visionary experience—indeed, the very thing that makes the ascent mystical—the ecstatic seeing of God or God's glory upon the throne. It is curious that Halperin does not even mention the vision of God in his study of the heavenly ascent in Hekhalot mysticism. In his copious monograph on early Jewish responses to Ezekiel's vision of the chariot Halperin again diminishes the significance of the vision itself by stating flatly that it is not the purpose of the heavenly journey.[172] As I have already pointed out, for Halperin the ecstatic-mystical dimension of the chariot experience becomes secondary to a psychological concern for control and dominance. Thus he is quick to point out that the real reason for the ascent is theurgical or magical, that is, the visionary wishes to see God primarily to gain power over others.[173] In other words, for Halperin even the magical component of the Hekhalot material must be understood as a tool employed in the struggle for power, the struggle Halperin refers to as the eternal conflict of generations. The radical reduction —almost obliteration—of the significance of the vision of God that emerges from Halperin's analysis is troublesome. This vision is, after all, the culmination of the ascent and therefore, in my opinion, properly deserves a more prominent place in the study of the heavenly journey.

In fairness to Halperin it must be stated that he is not the only scholar of note to criticize Scholem's view that the ascent to the throne forms the center of interest of the Hekhalot authors. In a lecture originally published in 1986, Peter Schäfer likewise took issue with Scholem's thesis, arguing that the real aim of this literature is a "reverse heavenly journey," that is, to bring the angel down to earth by means of adjurations in order to carry out the mystic's wishes. The purpose of these adjurations, which consist of mentioning the divine names and displaying the magical seals (which are composed of names), is to obtain "comprehensive knowledge of the Torah" and "to be protected conclusively and forever from forgetting the Torah."[174] Schäfer's proposal as expressed in that lecture represents a radical reversal of Scholem's understanding: The prominent concern of the Hekhalot literature is not ascent of the mystic to heaven, but rather the descent of the angel to earth. It is not the heavenly journey, but rather

[171] *Faces of the Chariot,* pp. 451–452. See idem, "Ascension or Invasion."
[172] *Faces of the Chariot,* p. 370.
[173] Ibid., pp. 372–375.
[174] Schäfer, "Aim and Purpose," p. 282.

the magical adjuration ritual that lies at the center of Merkavah mysticism. It follows, moreover, from Schäfer's approach that some of our assumptions about the literary character of these texts must be altered. Thus, for instance, the literary unit that Scholem considered of secondary importance, the *Sar Torah* section "appended" to *Hekhalot Rabbati*, now assumes center position, for this text presents in elaborate detail an example of the angelic adjuration described above. For Schäfer, then, Scholem's assessment of Merkavah mysticism is too one-sided, for he overemphasizes the heavenly journey. Moreover, even a careful scrutiny of the ascent passages demonstrates that the journey ends not with the mystic's vision of God but rather with his participation in the angelic liturgy.[175] The emphasis on visionary experience of God as the central component of the Hekhalot literature is thus wrong on two counts, according to Schäfer: first, magical adjuration and not ecstatic ascent is the primary concern of these texts, and second, the purpose of the ascent itself is not a mystical vision but a liturgical act. In another context Schäfer supports the view that the aim of the heavenly journey was not the vision of God on the throne but rather participation in the angelic doxology when he notes that the object of the mystic's vision consisted of the "overwhelming event of the cosmic liturgy and the change it produces in God."[176] It must be noted, however, that while Schäfer acknowledges the preponderate presence of the magical-theurgic element in the macroforms that comprise this corpus, he still maintains (contra Halperin) the need to keep the visionary element focused on the heavenly ascent as a distinct phenomenon. He thus challenges the privileging of either the ecstatic heavenly journey or the magical-theurgic adjuration; on the contrary, Hekhalot literature is seen to move between these two poles.[177]

At this stage of research it would be premature to assign priority or originality to one of these elements over the other. Schäfer judiciously concludes that in the absence of a more critical literary and redactional deciphering of the macroforms included in the Hekhalot literature one must refrain from passing judgment on the question of the precise temporal relation between the heavenly journey and the magical-theurgic adjuration. The two must be set beside one another without any claims to chronological priority or succession.[178] Notwithstanding this sound methodological caution, Schäfer remains skeptical about the heavenly journey and the consequent visionary experience. He insists, rather, that the extant macroforms provide no information on how the

[175] Ibid., pp. 285–286.

[176] *Hidden and Manifest God*, p. 164. In the same work Schäfer is critical of Halperin's attempt to subsume the heavenly journey under the category of the *Sar Torah* tradition. "The *yored merkavah* beholds God's countenance—the fact that we are told almost nothing about the contents of what he sees does not mean that he sees nothing and instead receives the Torah. The type of heavenly journey represented (mainly) by *Hekhalot Rabbati* must remain a peculiar and legitimate offspring of the Hekhalot literature alongside the (surely overwhelming) unit of the magical-theurgic adjuration" (p. 153).

[177] Ibid., p. 150.

[178] Ibid., pp. 156–157.

journey was actually carried out or if it was indeed practiced as an ecstatic experience. Moreover, in the textual instances wherein the heavenly journey and the adjuration are connected, the magical-theurgical element is so dominant that doubts may be raised concerning a practice of a mystical heavenly journey.[179] In the final analysis, Schäfer repeats his earlier contention that the *Sitz im Leben* of the heavenly journey and the magical adjuration is liturgical. In the case of the heavenly journey man meets God in heaven, whereas in the case of the magical adjuration man meets God on earth. The common element in both, however, is the use of magical devices to insure the encounter of human and divine. Both, therefore, can be understood as ritual-liturgical actions.[180]

There is no justification to consider, as Scholem apparently did, the growth of the magical elements in the Hekhalot literature as a degeneration of ecstatic-visionary mysticism. On the other hand, one must not overlook or severely minimize the vision of God attested in these texts. It is undeniably true, as Scholem himself would have readily admitted, that in texts like *Sar Torah* the main concern is adjuration of the angel to impart knowledge of Torah by magical means, and not ecstatic ascent to see the enthroned glory. Yet, if one looks carefully at the text that Schäfer himself cites in support of his view,[181] one can see that the visionary component is not entirely lacking. That is, the specification of the types of Torah that the conjurer will master consists of Bible, Mishnah, Talmud, and vision of the chariot. Although there is no mention of an actual vision of God, nor any indication of an ecstatic ascent, I would assume that a vision of the chariot in this context implies both of these elements. Similarly, in *Maʿaseh Merkavah,* in the context of the section on the *Sar Torah* praxis, there appears the inquiry of R. Ishmael to R. Neḥuniah ben ha-Qanah referred to above, concerning gazing at the splendor of the Presence (*leṣapot beziw ha-shekhinah*).[182] That the visionary aspect is a component of the theurgical praxis of the *Sar Torah* is stated explicitly in another passage, where R. Ishmael says, "When I heard this teaching from R. Neḥuniah ben ha-Qanah I stood on my feet, and I asked him all the names of the ministers of wisdom (*sare ḥokhmah*). As a result of the question that I asked, I saw in my heart light [as bright as] the days of the heavens."[183]

If one were to argue that in neither case are we justified in assuming an ascent, that in these contexts the illuminative experience is a vision of the divine splendor that eventuates from the knowledge imparted by the *Sar Torah* rather than the consequence of a heavenly voyage to the throne, the fact remains that within its redactional setting the compilers of this text understood the visionary element as connected with heavenly ascent. Thus in the continuation R. Ishmael says, "When I stood on my feet and I saw that my face was shining from

[179] Ibid., p. 155.

[180] Ibid., pp. 155–156.

[181] "Aim and Purpose," p. 283; the text is found in *Synopse,* § 303.

[182] *Synopse,* § 570. See Chernus, *Mysticism in Rabbinic Judaism,* p. 75; and the reference to Idel above, n. 136.

[183] *Synopse,* § 580.

my wisdom I began to specify the names of the angels in each and every palace."[184] One is to infer that the illumination here does involve visionary ascent—thus R. Ishmael's gnosis includes the ability to name all the celestial archons—and Gruenwald is therefore correct when he notes that in these passages there is a reversal of the process "from Sar-Torah theurgy to the Merkavah vision."[185] Moreover, it is true that the text from *Hekhalot Zuṭarti,* which Schäfer quotes,[186] implies that the heavenly journey culminates in an adjuration. Still, in other parts of this very text, including a passage immediately following the one mentioned by Schäfer,[187] it is stated in very direct and unequivocal terms that the mystic (R. Aqiva) has a vision of God upon the throne.[188] That the experience of magical study is phenomenologically on a par with the ascent to heaven is stated explicitly in *Merkavah Rabbah:* "R. Ishmael said: When my ears heard this great mystery the world was transformed to purity for me, and my heart was as when I came new to the world, and each day it seemed to me as if my soul stood before the throne of glory."[189]

While the viewpoint of Halperin and Schäfer (bracketing the differences between them) that the importance of magical adjuration in the spectrum of Hekhalot literature should not be neglected is well taken, one should not in the process denigrate or obfuscate the role of the ecstatic ascent and the consequent vision of the divine. In the course of criticizing Scholem's view on the centrality of the visionary experience, Schäfer marvels at the fact that the ascent accounts say almost nothing about what the mystic actually sees when he arrives at the throne of glory. It is wrong to deduce from this, however, that the vision is not part of the culminating stage in the ascent. I think Schäfer is absolutely right in pointing out that a prime reason for the ascent is the participation of the adept in the liturgy of the heavenly court. Indeed, the *yeridah la-merkavah* (entry to the chariot) that follows the ascent to the seventh palace is fundamentally a liturgical act. But—and here is the critical point—participation in the angelic choir arises precisely in virtue of the mystic's entry to the realm of the chariot and consequent vision of the enthroned glory. One cannot separate in an absolute way the visionary and liturgical aspects of this experience; indeed, it might be said that in order to praise God one must see God.[190] The magical and liturgical elements are a legitimate part of the diverse textual units that make up this corpus, but they should not overshadow the position assumed by the ecstatic vision.

[184] Ibid., § 581.

[185] *Apocalyptic,* p. 187.

[186] "Aim and Purpose," p. 285; cf. *Synopse,* §§ 417–419; Halperin, *Faces of the Chariot,* pp. 372–375.

[187] *Synopse,* § 421.

[188] See Ibid., § 412.

[189] Ibid., § 680.

[190] See Leiter, "Worthiness, Acclamation, and Appointment," pp. 141–148. To a degree Schäfer himself acknowledges this in his most recent writing on the subject. Consider *Hidden and Manifest God,* p. 153 n. 19: "Vision and liturgy obviously belong close together, and it thus would be wrong to ignore the visual element in the Hekhalot literature; it is equally wrong, however, to portray the vision of God as the apparent main goal of the Merkavah mystic, as opposed to the liturgy."

Let us return to the problem concerning the nature of that vision. The content of the chariot vision is neither a positivistic datum—something objectively real in a tangible sense that can be empirically verified—nor a psychic hallucination disguising some primitive sexual fantasy or adolescent conflict. It may very well be that the account of the ecstatic journeys preserve such impulses, but in the final analysis it is the mystical valence of these journeys that is critical. To be sure, mystical experience, like religious experience more generally, belongs to the domain of psychology, as many scholars, following the pioneering work of William James, have well understood. In this regard mysticism is not unique: religion is a matter of the human psyche and therefore should be studied as an integral part of psychology.

Nevertheless, one must be careful to avoid the lure of psychoanalytic reductionism if one is to grasp the phenomenology of religious experience in general and that of mysticism in particular. It is necessary, as various historians of religion have maintained, to treat the religious phenomenon as it is without reducing it to something else. Other factors—psychology, anthropology, sociology, politics, or economics—are all significant elements in understanding the particular setting within which the religious experience expresses itself, but none of them, individually or collectively, account for what Eliade called the hierophany, the appearance of the sacred.

The texture of the religious experience expressed in the macroforms of the Hekhalot literature is not exceptional in this regard, and it is precisely such a dimension of the irreducible holiness that Scholem had in mind when he chose to refer to the hymns in Hekhalot literature by Rudolf Otto's term "numinous"—the irrational *mysterium tremendum* that the mystic attempts to reproduce in words. Although I would challenge the depiction of the numinous as irrational and essentially beyond linguistic articulation, the element of irreducibility seems to me incontestable. In the different macroforms included in the corpus of Hekhalot literature that irreducible element still seems to me to be the mystical vision of the divine King in his beauty: the splendor of the enthroned Presence who is designated by a host of often mysterious-sounding names, the *nomina barbara*.

bingo!

The Merkavah experience seeks to express the *numen praesens* in terms of commonly held cosmological and theological imagery. Let me begin with the problem of cosmology. Whether or not we moderns can believe in an ascent through seven heavens is beside the point. There is enough evidence from Late Antiquity to show that this was one, although not the only, possible way to comprehend the physical structure of the heavens. The correlation of the heavenly journey and mythical cosmologies in the Hellenistic world is a well-attested fact.[191] The Hekhalot texts do not represent a major exception to this orientation and they should not be examined in isolation from other relevant documents in the period.

191 See Segal, "Heavenly Ascent in Hellenistic Judaism, Early Christianity, and Their Environment," pp. 1341–1342.

With respect to the theological imagery, there is no question that the vision of the glory in the Hekhalot is rooted in earlier Jewish conceptions of the divine glory upon the throne. The content of the vision is thus informed in great measure by received traditions concerning the figuration of the divine in anthropomorphic or luminous form. The theophanic shape of God contemplated by these visionaries is the symbolic expression of the divine Presence realized in the imagination of the given mystic. Different visions may therefore include elements that can only be explained by peculiar psychological profiles; from that perspective it is plausible and fruitful to compare the dynamics of the vision in the Hekhalot to a dream state. Moreover, as I stated in the concluding section of the previous chapter, the comparison of mystical visions to dreams can shed light on the symbolic process of the creative imagination operating in the formation of the dream or vision. In evaluating the vision phenomenologically, however, one must consider seriously the intentionality of the mystic with respect to the object of the vision. It is with regard to this intentionality, it seems to me, that a distinction between mystical visions and dream states can and should be upheld by scholars evaluating the historical phenomena.

Several of the medieval kabbalists distinguished their own prophetology from that of the philosophers on the grounds that (according to the philosophic understanding espoused by some adherents of medieval Aristotelianism, already criticized by Judah Halevi[192]) the prophetic state is reduced to a dream vision with no objective correlate corresponding to the data of the experience.[193] Prophecy, like a dream, is not an experience of something "real" but is only imagined. For the kabbalists, by contrast, there is an objective correlate to the prophetic vision: the divine gradations or emanations that are configured within the active imagination of the mystic. The imagination is thus the organ that puts one in contact with spiritual realities that are perceptible to each individual according to the dominant images of one's religious and cultural affiliation. I will return to this issue in more detail in a subsequent chapter. Here it is critical only to reiterate that for the Merkavah visionaries (or the authors of the visionary texts), whatever their particular psychological propensity, the overriding goal was to behold the glory that is imagined in terms of particular forms distinctive to Judaism. This goal thus represents a shared theological posture—indeed, the one that most likely facilitated the eventual meshing of the Hekhalot with more normative haggadic and midrashic traditions.

Interpretation, Revelation, Tradition

At this juncture it would be beneficial to elaborate on a point made by Halperin concerning the distinction between vision and interpretation. Halperin is cor-

[192] See Davidson, "The Active Intellect in the Cuzari and Hallevi's Theory of Causality," p. 389.

[193] See Walzer, "Al-Farabi's Theory of Prophecy and Divination," pp. 206–219; Rahman, *Prophecy in Islam*, pp. 30–91; Sirat, *Les théories des visions surnaturelles dans la pensée juive du moyen âge*, pp. 141–143.

rect, in my opinion, when he questions those who would make a radical division between these two processes. The vision is itself informed by extant literary and oral traditions; thus, the interpretative process is already operative at the level of experience. Naturally, there can be postexperiential interpretation of the contents of the vision that deviate from the actual revelation; however, in the shaping of the vision itself there is clear evidence of interpretation of earlier visions recorded in authoritative documents. The dichotomy between revelation and interpretation is a false one. It seems to me, therefore, that it is of little value to distinguish between one text that assumes a "real" ascent and another that is merely a "literary" report of an ascent. Such a distinction is predicated on the ability to isolate phenomenologically an experience separated from its literary context—a questionable presumption, inasmuch as all such experiences occur within a literary framework. I do not intend to reduce the experiential dimension of these experiences by claiming that they are pure literary constructions. I simply raise the issue of mutual interdependence of the experience and its report to challenge those who would view some later texts as pure literary constructions, as opposed to the earlier texts that report actual experiences.

The pitfalls of such a dichotomy are especially evident in a study by Daniel Block, published after Halperin's essay. Although the material discussed in this study is the inaugural vision of Ezekiel and not a Hekhalot text per se, the comments made by the author are particularly helpful for highlighting the shortcomings of radically distinguishing revelation and interpretation in the Hekhalot literature as well. Block, reflecting on the language of analogy employed by Ezekiel with terms like *demut* or *marʾeh,* observes that "although Ezekiel has a clear view of what he is seeing, he is at a loss to find words which will describe the vision adequately."[194] Block has assumed something for which there is no precise evidence in the text of Ezekiel: a distinction between the vision and its interpretation. Thus he can write that Ezekiel had a clear vision but had difficulty expressing himself. This particular understanding of Ezekiel is related to a more general epistemological orientation: the content of the vision transcends the bounds of normal human experience; hence, there is a necessary discrepancy between the vision and the narrative recounting of it. The attitude toward the vision of Ezekiel implied in Block's analysis shares a hermeneutical assumption with many writers who examine the mystical phenomenon, namely, that there is an inevitable gap separating experience and description.

I would argue, by contrast, that the shaping of the text by the experience, which is itself informed by previous textual traditions, in fact precludes any dichotomization of revelation and interpretation. There is no reason to assume any radical divergence between the vision and the prophet's communication of it. The prophet Ezekiel reports what he experienced without reservation or qualification. The point of the analogical terms *ke-marʾeh, ke-ʿen,* and *demut* is to underscore the fact that there is a basic similarity between the object and its

[194] Block, "Text and Emotion," p. 429.

mode of representation. To use the language I employed in the last chapter, it is characteristic of the symbolic image that it allows the expression of something in terms of something else. What the prophet reports, he has assuredly seen. To drive the point home, let us reflect on the targumic rendering of Ezek. 1:27: "I saw something like the *ḥashmal,* like the appearance of fire from the midst of it round about, an appearance of glory that the eye is unable to see, so that it is impossible to look at it and downward."[195] The Targum has gone out of its way to emphasize the intrinsic invisibility of the divine glory, a theme unattested in the biblical account. The issue for the prophet is not the invisibility of God but the necessarily symbolic character of the images that inhere in the imagination.

This example is illustrative of the larger question. The dichotomy posited by many scholars between exegesis and experience, interpretation and revelation, seems to me to be problematic.[196] On the contrary, the connection between the process of textual interpretation (*midrash*) and prophetic states of consciousness or visionary experience—what one might call "inspired exegesis" or "pneumatic interpretation"—is found already in Ps. 119:18[197] and becomes pronounced in apocalyptic texts,[198] the Qumran scrolls,[199] and early Jewish mysticism.[200] Specifically, in the case of the Merkavah vision, the seeing of the throne-world and the glory is to be understood as an interpretative process conditioned by religious traditions and the study of Scripture. The experience does not come to the Jewish mystic ab ovo; it is shaped and cultivated by a series of cultural-religious factors. There is thus an essential convergence of tradition, revelation, and interpretation that is characteristic of the visionary experience in apocalyptic and Hekhalot literature; these are not distinct categories in religious phenomenology.

To be sure, some of the ancient rabbis ostensibly distinguished between those "who expound the chariot," referring to Ezekiel's chariot vision, and those "who see the chariot," thus implying that exposition does not amount to experience.[201] It is nonetheless clear that these domains were not, and cannot be, held in absolute distinction. Underlying the rabbinic restriction on public exposition of Ezekiel's chariot vision may have been a fear of arousing interest in the throne-world, thereby creating a context for increased visionary or ecstatic ex-

[195] "The Targum of Ezekiel," trans. S. H. Levey, in *The Aramaic Bible* (Wilmington, 1987), 13:22.

[196] See, e.g., Halivni, *Midrash, Mishna, Gemara,* p. 16; Bloch, "Midrash," p. 31; Porton, "Midrash," pp. 111–112.

[197] See Fishbane, *Biblical Interpretation,* pp. 539–543.

[198] See Gruenwald, "'Knowledge' and 'Vision'," pp. 72–73, 80–82, 104; Russell, *Method and Message,* pp. 117, 119–20, 183ff.; Collins, *The Apocalyptic Vision of the Book of Daniel,* pp. 74–78; Niditch, "The Visionary."

[199] See Schiffman, *Sectarian Law in the Dead Sea Scroll,* pp. 15–16.

[200] See Idel, "Concept of Torah," pp. 35–36, esp. 36 nn. 38–39; idem, "Infinities of Torah in Kabbalah," pp. 141–144.

[201] See T. Megillah 3:28; B. Megillah 24b. For a discussion of this text, see van Uchelen, "Tosephta Megillah III, 28."

* one must stay on the path to fly off the path

periences. This seems to be borne out by many of the legends regarding rabbinic figures who expounded the chariot, especially Yoḥanan ben Zakkai and his disciples,[202] that is, as a result of their exegetical activity they experienced paranormal states of religious inspiration frequently involving the phenomenon of fire. Even though the experiences related in the rabbinic sources typically do not involve a heavenly journey or consequent vision of the enthroned glory, the fact that exposition of the biblical text occasions a mystical state is significant. Especially interesting is a narrative unit cited in B. Ḥagigah 13a in conjunction with various traditions connected with the explanation (or lack of explanation) of the mysterious *ḥashmal* mentioned in Ezek. 1:27:

> Our rabbis taught: There was an incident with a young child who was studying the book of Ezekiel in the schoolhouse of his teacher. He understood the [matter of the] *ḥashmal* and a fire went out from the *ḥashmal* and burned him. They desired to hide the book of Ezekiel. Ḥananyah ben Ḥizqiyah said to them: If this one was wise, is everyone wise?

The implication of the ironic concluding statement is that the book of Ezekiel is not dangerous and does not have to be hidden, for the child prodigy was consumed by the fire of the *ḥashmal* when he comprehended the meaning of the text concerning the *ḥashmal* because he was exceptionally wise. The issue of hiding the book of Ezekiel is set in different literary settings and thus is given various reasons in talmudic literature,[203] but in this particular context it is clear that it is related to the potential danger from exegesis of the chariot vision. This narrative thus lends support to my general claim that the restriction on study may have been related to a fear that exegesis provides the occasion for ecstatic experiences that may be harmful or even lethal. The heavenly ascent related in the Hekhalot compositions represents one type of ecstatic experience that may have resulted from exposition of the biblical text.

It seems to me that the effort on the part of some modern scholars to distinguish sharply between an "exegetical mysticism" and an "experiential mysticism" in early Jewish Merkavah speculation is to a degree overstated. While such a position has been affirmed by a variety of scholars, perhaps the most extreme formulation is that of Halperin who, in the footsteps of Urbach, proposes against Scholem that it is necessary to segregate the Hekhalot entirely from the rabbinic Merkavah traditions. In response to this position it must be noted that the very act of interpreting Ezekiel's chariot, as is attested by some of the legendary accounts of rabbinic authorities engaged in homiletic speculation on the Merkavah, was capable of producing states through which the historic event of revelation was relived. Indeed, as Halperin himself and other scholars have duly noted, there is a clear thematic connection in rabbinic homiletical literature linking the Sinaitic revelation and Ezekiel's chariot theophany.

[202] See Neusner, "The Development of the Merkavah Tradition"; Séd, "Les traditions secrètes et les disciples de Rabbanan Yoḥanan ben Zakkai"; Halperin, *Merkabah in Rabbinic Literature,* pp. 107–140.

[203] See B. Shabbat 13b; Menaḥot 45a; Ḥagigah 13a.

I do not mean to suggest that we ought to ignore the important differences between the experiences related in the rabbinic narratives and those described in the Hekhalot texts. The former do not yet amount to a mystical praxis, at least not as defined as the ascent to the chariot. Study of Ezekiel's vision, then, does not in and of itself constitute an ecstatic vision of the chariot. Yet, given the literary and conceptual continuity linking apocalyptic and Hekhalot, it is difficult to maintain that the rabbis who lived in the period of the Mishnah were not cognizant of heavenly ascensions to the throne when they spoke of expounding the chariot.

On the other hand, the experience of ascending to and beholding the divine chariot, reported in great detail in the extra-talmudic texts that make up the Hekhalot corpus, is based at least partially on a careful and sustained reading and interpretation of prior literary accounts of the chariot vision, culled from the book of Ezekiel as well as other apocalyptic texts, just as these texts themselves are closely based on scriptural precedents. While Scholem's observation that the Hekhalot texts are not midrashic expositions of biblical passages is basically correct, his further claim that these texts are descriptions of a religious experience for which no sanction is sought in the Bible is questionable.[204] To be sure, elements of the visionary ascent—indeed, the very possibility of and techniques for achieving such an ecstatic experience—cannot be found in biblical texts, but still on the whole one is left with the distinct impression that the mystic visionaries seek to reexperience what is recorded in previous documents. Scholem acknowledges this himself when he notes that the mystic's vision of the celestial realm proceeds from an attempt to transform biblical allusions into direct personal experience. Indeed, the very description of the chariot is based on the biblical source. Nevertheless, Scholem insists that the mystical texts represent a novel and autonomous religious mentality that is not connected with an exegetical mode; on the contrary, the turn to exegesis is a sign of decline.

The theoretical assumption underlying Scholem's claim is a distinction between exegesis and inspiration—between interpretation and revelation—that may, in fact, be difficult to maintain in light of the fact that the visionary is, first and foremost, an exegete, whose visions are primarily, not secondarily, informed by visionary accounts in canonical texts. The point is well documented in Christopher Rowland's study of the vision of God in apocalyptic literature. Summing up his view of the use of Ezekiel's vision in apocalyptic, Rowland astutely observes that the differences that emerge from the various apocalypses are indicative of an ongoing speculative interest in the biblical text. The study of Ezekiel's account of the chariot involved a "free meditation" that resulted in the visionary's "seeing again" the vision of the prophet, informed by other scriptural passages as well as the unique exigencies of the particular individual.[205]

The "seeing again" is thus generated by meditation on the biblical text.

[204] *Major Trends,* p. 46.

[205] See Rowland, "Visions of God," pp. 152–153; idem, *Open Heaven,* pp. 226–227.

Study should not be reduced to mere exegesis devoid of any experiential component; on the contrary, one must assume that the visions and revelatory experiences recorded in the apocalypses are not simply literary forms but reflect actual experiences deriving from divine inspiration. It can be assumed, therefore, that at least some of the apocalyptic visions arose from reflection on Scripture: exegesis of recorded visions leads to revelation of God.[206] That a similar claim can be made about the chariot mystical texts should be self-evident.[207] The experience of seeing the chariot cannot be isolated absolutely from the interpretative framework, and while one must distinguish the theoretical-exegetical and practical-ecstatic approaches to the chariot vision, one shapes the other.

In charting the different uses of Ezekiel's chariot vision in rabbinic and mystical circles, it is necessary to distinguish between exegesis and praxis, especially if the latter is defined principally in terms of heavenly ascent. However, what I have argued here is that one would be well advised, on the one hand, not to characterize rabbinic exegesis of the chariot as fundamentally nonmystical—in Dan's terms, as "passive homiletical speculation"[208]—and, on the other, to recognize the midrashic underpinning of ecstatic visions. When the scholar begins to appreciate the active mystical nature of exegesis in general, and exegesis on the chariot vision of Ezekiel in particular, then, I think, the gap between interpretation and mystical technique will be somewhat narrowed. The midrashic recasting of visions recorded in literary documents into new visions is, as I will suggest in a later chapter, the underlying mechanism of visionary experience in the zoharic anthology, the central text of medieval theosophic kabbalah.

[206] See Patte, *Early Jewish Hermeneutic in Palestine,* pp. 181–199.

[207] See Alexander, "Historical Setting," p. 173; Halperin, *Faces of the Chariot,* p. 362; and the perceptive comment of Fishbane in *Garments of Torah,* p. 60, that the ascent of the ancient Jewish mystics to the throne of glory was achieved through "spiritual exercises and pneumatic exegesis."

[208] Dan, "Religious Experience," p. 292.

• CHAPTER FOUR •

Theories of the Glory and Visionary Experience in Pre-Kabbalistic Sources

IN ORDER to appreciate more fully the nature of visionary experience in the medieval kabbalistic sources, it is necessary to examine the treatment of visions and prophetic experience in some of the philosophical and mystical writers in the centuries (principally the tenth to twelfth) preceeding the literary emergence of kabbalistic teachings. In this chapter I have selected those authors who seemingly had the most important influence on the Jewish mystics with respect to the issue at hand: Saadiah ben Joseph Gaon (882–942), Shabbetai ben Abraham Donnolo (913–ca. 982), Hai Gaon (939–1038), Ḥananel ben Ḥushiel (d. 1055/56), Nathan ben Yeḥiel of Rome (1035–ca. 1110), Judah ben Barzillai al-Barceloni (late eleventh–early twelfth century), Abraham ibn Ezra (ca. 1092–1167) and Judah Halevi (ca. 1075–1141). The intellectual portrait that emerges from these sources provides the background required for an understanding of the mechanics of vision for a Jewish mystic living in the golden period of the literary flourishing of Pietism in northern France and Germany as well as of theosophic and ecstatic kabbalah in Provence and northern Spain. Whatever the distinctive nature of mystical experience, set apart from other forms of religious experience, as human experience it is inescapably historical and cultural. As such, an investigation of the cultural assumptions that arise within historical frameworks will help us probe the phenomenological parameters of mystical vision for medieval Pietists and kabbalists.

In this chapter I will set out to show how four distinct approaches to explaining prophetic visions—and, by extension, the larger problem of visionary experience—are to be found in this pre-kabbalistic literature: (1) the allegorical interpretation of prophetic visions, which considers the visionary details as figurative representations of discursive truth; (2) the psychological interpretation, which attributes to the visionary data the status of mental images rather than veridical reality; (3) the realist view, which stresses the objective and external character of these visions but also emphasizes that the object of the visions is a created entity and not the Godhead; (4) the emanationist approach, which maintains, like the third opinion, the veridical character of prophetic visions but which, in contrast to that view, posits that the object of vision is not a created light but an aspect of God that has the capacity to appear in tangible or sensible form to select human beings. The intellectual profile of the mystical literature of medieval Jewry must be seen as wavering between these four approaches. In some cases the second led to a position that may be properly labeled docetic in its orientation.

Saadiah Gaon

The first medieval Jewish philosopher to respond to the problem of vision and anthropomorphism in any systematic way was Saadiah Gaon. Saadiah's theory of revelation has been amply discussed in scholarly literature and it is not my intention to review this entire issue comprehensively. Suffice it here to note briefly that for Saadiah, God is not the object of prophetic or mystical visions, for God is not a body and thus is not visible. What, then, is the object of vision? As Alexander Altmann has shown, Saadiah himself oscillates between two positions: on one hand, the allegorical method (*ta'wīl*) of the rationalist theologians of Islam, the Muʿtazilites,[1] and on the other, the doctrine of the created glory, *kavod nivra'*.[2] In his major philosophical treatise, *Kitāb al-Amānāt wa'l-Iʿtiqādāt* (*Sefer ha-'Emunot we-ha-Deʿot,* "Book of Beliefs and Opinions"), Saadiah readily applies the method of *ta'wīl* to explain biblical anthropomorphisms, but in order to explain anthropomorphisms specifically connected with theophanies he offers a second approach, one that Altmann argues represents his more original and authentic position and that, in part, is rooted in the ancient Jewish chariot mysticism.[3] While Altmann may be right that Saadiah's doctrine of the glory is derived partially from older Jewish mystical sources of which he was surely cognizant, it must be pointed out that a tendency to transform earlier mystical ideas in a philosophical or scientific vein can also be detected in Saadiah's writings, as has been shown, for instance, with regard to his commentary on *Sefer Yeṣirah, Tafsir Kitāb al-Mabādi'*, written several years before the *Kitāb al-Amānāt wa'l-Iʿtiqādāt.*[4] As far as I can gather, there is no evidence that in the ancient Jewish mystical texts themselves the glory is treated as a created entity, whatever position we may assume with respect to the nature of this enthroned glory vis-à-vis the Godhead. Hence, minimally, it seems likely that Saadiah has introduced a novel approach when he asserts that this entity is created. It must also be noted that according to another scholarly view Saadiah's notion of the created glory may reflect Sufi notions of the preexistent light that functions as the medium of prophecy.[5]

The glory, Saadiah maintains, is a created light that is akin, but not identical, to the angels. According to Saadiah's theory of prophetic revelation, this created light is manifest to prophets and in the process can assume various forms, including, most prominently, that of an anthropos.[6] This created light is also

[1] This method was employed as well by Saadiah's older colleague, Isaac Israeli. See Altmann and Stern, *Isaac Israeli,* pp. 139–140, 216.

[2] Altmann, *Studies,* pp. 145–147.

[3] Ibid., pp. 153–154.

[4] See Ben-Shammai, "Saadya's Goal in his *Commentary on Sefer Yeẓira.*" On the philosophical orientation of Saadiah's commentary see also Vajda, "Saʿadya commentateur du 'Livre de la Création,'" p. 5 (reprint, p. 39); Jospe, "Early Philosophical Commentaries on the Sefer Yeẓirah," pp. 372–381.

[5] See Efros, "Saʿadia's General Ethical Theory and Its Relation to Sufism," p. 175 n. 26.

[6] Cf. *Sefer ha-'Emunot we-ha-Deʿot* II:10, ed. J. Kafiḥ, pp. 103–104; *Perushe Rabbenu Seʿadyah*

identified with the rabbinic *Shekhinah,* the divine Presence. In a responsum of Saadiah to a certain anonymous heretic, preserved in Hebrew translation in Judah ben Barzillai's *Commentary on Sefer Yeṣirah,* he further characterizes this created glory, without using the technical term, as the first of the created entities, the "great light" (*'or gadol*), the "light of the glory" (*'or ha-kavod*), the "resplendent light" (*'or ha-bahir*), also identified as the "God of Israel" seen by Moses, Aaron, Nadab, Abihu and the seventy elders (see Exod. 24:10ff.) and as Akatriel, who, according to a talmudic legend (see B. Berakhot 7a), was seen by R. Ishmael ben Elisha sitting on a throne in the Holy of Holies. In that context Saadiah also remarks that the object of the mystical speculation in the *Shiʿur Qomah* tradition refers to another created light that is apprehended only by the angels.[7] In yet a third work, his commentary on *Sefer Yeṣirah,* Saadiah identifies the glory, *Shekhinah,* and Holy Spirit (*ruaḥ ha-qodesh*), as well as the throne of glory (*kisse' ha-kavod*), with the subtle and rarefied substance he calls the "second air" from which all things emanated. It is from this second air, moreover, that the various visual and audible forms apprehended in prophetic experience derive.[8] It may be concluded, therefore, that Saadiah's response to the challenge of anthropomorphism avoids the extremes of allegorism and psychologism, for he flatly denies that prophetic or mystical visions are of God, yet at the same time they are not simply psychic phenomena or inner perceptions. Prophetic and mystical visions lie within the sphere of outer perception, for in both cases a real, luminous form, albeit created and therefore ontologically distinct from God, is apprehended, in the former case by human beings and in the latter by angels.

Shabbetai Donnolo

An alternative approach to that of Saadiah may be detected in a work composed at roughly the same time by the Byzantine writer Shabbetai Donnolo, which was also influenced to a degree by earlier Jewish mysticism but stemming from an entirely different cultural milieu.[9] In the first part of his commen-

---

Ga'on ʿal ha-Torah, p. 70 n. 7. See analysis of Saadiah's views in Sirat, *Les théories des vision surnaturelles dans la pensée juive du moyen-âge,* pp. 17–33.

[7] In Judah ben Barzillai, *Perush Sefer Yeṣirah,* ed. Halberstam, pp. 20–21.

[8] Saadiah's commentary on *Sefer Yeṣirah,* pp. 108–109. See also Altmann, *Studies,* pp. 159–160; Sirat, *Théories,* pp. 22–23.

[9] See Scholem, *Kabbalah,* pp. 33–34. Scholem's unsupported claim that Donnolo's commentary on *Sefer Yeṣirah* "was indisputably influenced by the commentary of Saadiah b. Joseph Gaon to the same work" must be corrected. See, by contrast, the more nuanced remarks of Sharf, *The Universe of Shabbetai Donnolo,* pp. 6, 127; and Pines, "Points of Similarity," p. 82 n. 156. See also the entry on Donnolo in the *Encyclopaedia Judaica* (6:169), where Dan concludes that there "is no evidence that Donnolo knew Saadiah Gaon's works" even though "there are some close parallels between the theology of Donnolo and that of Saadiah." Séd, in "Le Sefer Yeṣira," p. 515, contrasts the three tenth-century commentaries on *Sefer Yeṣirah* by calling Saadiah a theologian, Dunash a grammarian, and Donnolo a doctor and astrologer. On Donnolo as an important link in the chain of

tary on *Sefer Yeṣirah, Sefer Ḥakhmoni,* Donnolo categorically rejects the anthropomorphic interpretation of Gen. 1:26 that implies that God possesses a corporeal form in whose image and likeness Adam was created. According to Donnolo, the plural form of "Let us make man in our image, after our likeness" refers to the Creator addressing the world, a process here understood as an allegorical depiction of the fact that the human being is a microcosm reflecting the shape and structure of the macrocosm. Hence, the critical words *ṣelem* (image) and *demut* (likeness) should not be rendered in terms of physical likeness but rather as a comparison of function or activity.[10] Moreover, it has been argued by David Castelli that Donnolo, like Saadiah in his time and later Maimonides (1135–1204), sought to combat the "monstrous and invasive anthropomorphism" of the aggadic passages in the talmudic and midrashic literature.[11] Following this line of interpretation, Andrew Sharf adds that Donnolo's detailed anatomical interpretation of this verse is related to his rejection of anthropomorphism, which may have been derived in part from ancient Jewish mystical or Gnostic doctrines current in southern Italy in his time. Sharf flatly states that while Donnolo may have had knowledge of the Gnostic doctrines, transmitted either through the Jewish mystical sources such as the Hekhalot or *Shiʿur Qomah* or through Christian Gnostic texts, "There is no doubt that he implicitly rejects their fundamental assumption. . . . He looks at the nature of man as he looks at the nature of God in a way which, while not reaching the level of rational analysis by Saʿadiah or by the Rambam in their fight against superstition, is still a breeze of fresh common sense in a jungle of myth and fantasy. . . . There could be no sharper contrast between his matter of fact, exact descriptions and the emotional ambiguities of the mystics, whether Jewish, Christian or Hellenist, whether the writers of the Gnostic texts or of the *Shiʿur Komah.*"[12]

The picture, however, is a bit more complex. It can be shown that Donnolo proposed a theosophic understanding of the *sefirot,* which, while not overtly mythical, is nonetheless closer in spirit to the speculation found in the Gnostic texts or the Jewish mystical sources than it is to the rational orientation of Saadiah or Maimonides. Donnolo, as will be seen in detail below, espouses a theosophy that posits the existence of a form or image of God (*demut ha-ʾelohim*) identical with the glory (*kavod*) and composed of multiple powers (*sefirot*) that collectively make up the divine unity (*yiḥud ha-ʾel*). It is true that Donnolo employs the macrocosmic-microcosmic motif as a tool of exegesis in order to undermine the view that God has a physical likeness (*demut*) or image

---

transmission of ancient mystical traditions, see also Sirat, *Théories,* p. 89; Wolfson, "The Theosophy of Shabbetai Donnolo" (the present section is based on that study).

[10] *Sefer Ḥakhmoni,* in Castelli, *Il Commento di Sabbatai Donnolo sul Libro della Creazione,* pp. 15–16.

[11] Castelli, *Commento,* pp. 39–40 (introduction).

[12] Sharf, *Universe of Shabbetai Donnolo,* pp. 77–87, 86–87. The anti-mystical tendency of Donnolo, especially in reference to his interpretation of Gen. 1:26, is also emphasized by Sharf in his essay "Shabbetai Donnolo's Idea of the Microcosm."

(*ṣelem*) in which Adam was created. This does not, however, imply that he agreed with the claim made by many medieval Jewish philosophers that God has no *demut* at all. Indeed, given Donnolo's unambiguous rejection of a corporeal understanding of the divine image and the concomitant assertion that all anthropomorphic and anthropopathic expressions are to be treated allegorically,[13] it is all the more striking that in his treatment of prophetic visions he does not challenge the notion that God has an image, a *demut,* in a way analogous to the challenge posed by Saadiah and others in the rationalist tradition. Following earlier midrashic traditions, which seem to have connections with the mystical literature as well, Donnolo speaks of the image of God, though he fundamentally changes the term's meaning with respect to its ontological referent. It is certain that in the relevant midrashic texts the word *demut,* likeness, is interchangeable with the words *ṣurah,* form, and *kavod,* glory.[14] More specifically, as may be gathered from the various sources, the word *demut* signifies the visible form of God that is the hypostatic likeness of an anthropos. In some examples the anthropomorphic image of the divine is associated with God's activity as creator of the universe,[15] whereas in others the context is the epiphany of God at the Red Sea and at Sinai.[16] Although the nature of that likeness or form is not specified in the midrashic pericopae dealing with the appearance of God, it stands to reason that it involved an anthropomorphic manifestation. Indeed, it is plausible that even these passages are rooted in some esoteric tradition, for what the Israelites requested was to see the visible form of God on the throne at each of these critical moments in Israel's *Heilsgeschichte.* Thus in parallel texts (*Shemot Rabbah* 29:3; *Shir ha-Shirim Rabbah* 1:14) the word *kavod* is used in place of *demut,* again suggesting that the latter term, like the former, is employed in a technical way to name the enthroned anthropomorphic figure. The same semantic equivalence between *demut* and *kavod* is detectable in the Hekhalot texts, for both words refer to the divine form upon the throne.

Donnolo's language regarding the image of God draws on this earlier literature, yet for him *demut* denotes not the visible likeness of God, anthropomorphic or otherwise, but rather the aspect of God that is invisible because

[13] *Sefer Ḥakhmoni,* pp. 14–15: "Concerning that which is written, the 'eyes of God,' the 'face of God,' 'His footstool,' the 'hand of God,' the 'right of God,' 'His heart was saddened' (Gen. 6:6), all this is in accordance with human speech."

[14] See references given in chapter 1, n. 152. In this connection mention should be made of the poem "On an Image of the Archangel Michael," written by the sixth-century poet Agathias, published in B. Baldwin, *An Anthology of Byzantine Poetry* (Amsterdam, 1985), p. 67, which begins: Ασκοπον ἀγγελίαρχον, ἀσωματον ἑίδει μορφῆs. For the technical use of the term *ṣurah* in later kabbalistic literature and its philological affinity with earlier sources, see Idel, *Kabbalah: New Perspectives,* pp. 122–128.

[15] Cf. *Pesiqta de-Rav Kahana* 4:4, p. 65; *'Avot de-Rabbi Natan,* version A, chap. 39, p. 116. See also the passage published by E. E. Urbach, "Fragments of *Tanḥuma-Yelammedenu*" (in Hebrew), *Qoveṣ 'al Yad* 6 (1966): 24. See Lieberman, "How Much Greek in Jewish Palestine," p. 141; Fishbane, "Some Forms," pp. 266–267.

[16] See, e.g., *Shemot Rabbah* 23:15, 41:3.

of the inherent limitations of created beings, both angelic and human. Donnolo thus notes in one place that God did not appear to the Patriarchs, Moses, or the other ancestors who stood at Sinai "in any image" (i.e., in any fixed image), so that "Israel would not err and say 'This is His image,' resulting in their making an image of God and bowing down to it. Therefore He appeared on one occasion in fire and on another through a cloud."[17] Although the theme of God's invisibility is well known from midrashic and even some mystical texts, as I indicated in the previous chapter, it seems to me that Donnolo's insistence on God's not appearing in a specific image (*demut*) so that Israel would not err and make an icon of that image and worship it reflects the debate that raged in Byzantine Christianity between the iconoclasts and iconodules. To be sure, the roots of iconomachy in Judaism can be traced to much earlier sources incorporated in the biblical canon.[18] Nevertheless, it is possible that Donnolo's interest in this problem, and the particular way he articulates it, may best be understood in light of trends of thinking current in his Byzantine environment.[19] It should be noted, moreover, that parallels to the use of the word *demut* to refer to the invisible image of God can be found in religious poetry originating in Donnolo's milieu, or one that shares the same cultural matrix.[20] Just as we find that various poets speak of the divine image that cannot be seen by angelic beings, much less by humans, so, too, does Donnolo. Let me cite the relevant text from *Sefer Ḥakhmoni* in full:

[17] *Sefer Ḥakhmoni,* p. 9.

[18] See Isa. 40:18, 25; 46:5. This view expressed in Deutero-Isaiah must be seen as a direct polemic against the Priestly tradition that man is created in God's image. See Weinfeld, "God the Creator in Gen. I," pp. 124–125; Fishbane, *Biblical Interpretation,* pp. 325–326.

[19] For an example of such epigrams written in praise of icons, probably composed around 900 in southern Italy, see R. Browning, "An Unpublished Corpus of Byzantine Poems," *Byzantium* 33 (1963): 289–316, and the more recent discussion in B. Baldwin. "The Language and Style of Some Anonymous Byzantine Epigrams," *Byzantium* 52 (1982): 5–23. On the involvement of Jews in the iconoclast controversy, see Grabar, *L'iconoclasme byzantine,* pp. 99–103, 135–136; Sharf, *Byzantine Jewry from Justinian to the Fourth Crusade,* pp. 61–81.

[20] Consider, e.g., the words of the ninth-century Italian poet Amittai ben Shefaṭyah, in *Megillat 'Aḥima'aṣ,* p. 82: "The angels and seraphs are each covered with six wings, hiding their bodies, the image [of God] they do not see." A similar formulation is found in the liturgical poem *'Imru le'lohim 'emet we-yosher pa'alo* (attributed to Yoḥanan ben Yehoshua ha-Kohen, who apparently lived in Palestine sometime in the ninth or tenth century), in *Maḥzor la-Yamim ha-Nora'im,* ed. E. D. Goldschmidt, vol. 2, *Yom Kippur* (Jerusalem, 1970), p. 368: "His image [the angels] do not see." These poetic formulations, and others that could be cited, are based on much earlier material, including liturgical poems written in Palestine that have conceptual and terminological affinities with ancient Jewish esotericism. See, e.g., *The Liturgical Poems of Rabbi Yannai,* 1:118: "Your form is not visible" (צורתך אין לצור). The possibility that the statement of Yannai reflects the theology of the ancient Jewish esoteric *Shi'ur Qomah* speculation has already been noted by Idel in "Concept of Torah," p. 41 n. 51. Finally, it should be noted that occasionally, even in the poetry written by medieval poets influenced by philosophical rationalism, something of the older notion concerning God's image is preserved. See, e.g., *The Liturgical Poetry of Rabbi Solomon ibn Gabirol,* 2:478 (poem no. 154): "His image is far from them [the angels], and there is none who sees Him" (ודמותו מהם רחוק ואין מי יראנו).

"The secret of the Lord is for those who fear Him; to them He makes known His covenant" (Ps. 25:14). It is written, "O Lord, there is none like You! You are great and Your name is great in power" (Jer. 10:6), and it is written, "Who can tell the mighty acts of the Lord" (Ps. 106:2). Who is capable of thinking the slightest bit about the great, mighty, and awesome God, to comprehend His image (*demuto*), for even the beasts under the throne of glory and the seraphs above it, the ministering angels, the [angels called] *'er'ellim,*[21] and all the host of heaven cannot comprehend His image. . . . Even the holy ones on earth, the prophets and seers with whom He has spoken, did not comprehend or see His image as it is. Moses our master, who was the chief prophet and who spoke to Him mouth to mouth, requested to see the image of His face, but He did not heed him. As it is written, "Show me Your glory" (Exod. 33:18), and [God][22] responded to him, "You cannot see My face" (ibid., 20), and it says, "And the Lord said, 'See, there is a place near Me. Station yourself on the rock, and, as My glory passes by, etc.'" (ibid., 21). . . . From these verses we understand that Moses, may he rest in peace, requested from God only to see the image of His face as it is, but his prayer in this regard was not heard. Concerning that which the prophet Isaiah, may he rest in peace, said, "I beheld the Lord seated on a high and lofty throne [and the skirts of His robe filled the Temple], seraphs stood above Him, etc., and one would call to the other, etc." (Isa. 6:1–3), even though it says "I beheld the Lord," he did not see the image of His face but he saw the throne. He did not see the glory of the Lord upon the throne but rather the skirts [of His robe] like the skirts of a coat. Thus we have learned that Moses saw the glory of His back standing and Isaiah saw in a vision His glory seated on a throne. From the vision of the throne and the seraphs standing above Him, he understood that [the throne] was that of God. He saw, however, the glory of His skirts, which is the glory under His feet. When [the glory] was seen by Moses, Aaron, Nadab, and Abihu, and the seventy elders of Israel, [even though it is written, "And they saw the God of Israel,"] they saw only His glory that is under His feet by means of a sign and symbol (*be-'ot we-siman*), as it says, "And under His feet was the likeness of a pavement of sapphire" (Exod. 24:10). With respect to Ezekiel the prophet, even though he saw in his vision the beasts and the ophanim that were above the heads of the beasts . . . the image of God did not appear to him as it is, "for man may not see Him and live" (Exod. 33:20). [God] did not want to show him [the glory] except in the image of man, in an image which he was accustomed to seeing, so that he would not be frightened and startled from the appearance of His image, resulting in his sudden death. Thus [the glory] appeared to Adam, Cain, Abel, Enoch, Noah, the three Patriarchs, and to prophets and seers in the image of man. . . . And to Daniel [the glory] appeared in the vision of the night in the image of man, as it is written, "As I looked on

[21] Cf. Isa. 33:7.

[22] The words in brackets, which are lacking in Castelli's text, have been added according to the following manuscripts: Florence Medicea-Laurenziana, Plut. 44.16, fol. 91a; Paris–BN 767, fol. 1a; Paris–BN 770, fol. 47b; Parma-Palatina 2425 (De Rossi 417), fol. 95b; New York–JTSA Mic. 2141, fol. 2a.

> thrones were set in place, and the Ancient of Days was sitting, etc. A river of fire, etc." (Dan. 7:9–10). From all these proofs we know in truth that there is no creature in heaven or earth who can contemplate in its mind the divine image (*demut ha-'elohim*).[23]

The purpose of this elaborate discourse is to reach the conclusion that an anthropomorphic interpretation of Gen. 1:26 is simply inadequate since the image of God is not something available to human comprehension. Significantly, what Donnolo does not reject is the very claim that God has a *demut*—an image or form. On the contrary, he accepts this notion without qualification; thus at the end of the passage he refers to the *demut ha-'elohim,* even though no created being can know or comprehend that very image. Indeed, Donnolo characterizes this *demut* as the "light that has no measure or [dimension of] greatness" (*ha-'or she-'ein lo shi'ur u-gedullah*), and as "the glory that cannot be fathomed" (*ha-kavod she-'ein lo ḥeqer*).[24] In yet another context Donnolo uses similar terminology to describe the primordial light whence emerges the fire from which the spiritual entities, comprising the throne and the angels, are said to derive:

> From the radiant splendor of His great and awesome light, which cannot be fathomed and has no measure, He shines His splendor within the water. From the force of that splendor which He shone in the water a fire emerged, and from that fire He carved and hewed the throne of glory, the ophanim, the seraphs, the holy beasts, the ministering angels, and all the heavenly host.[25]

The radiant splendor (*zohar nogah*), which is an immeasurable light, also identified as the Holy Spirit (*ruaḥ ha-qodesh*), is the glory that cannot be seen, the invisible image of God.

[23] *Sefer Ḥakhmoni,* pp. 6–8.

[24] Ibid., p. 8. As Moshe Idel suggested to me, it would be fruitful to compare the views of Donnolo as I have outlined them here with ideas expressed by some of the Byzantine monks, especially St. Symeon the New Theologian (949–1022) and St. Gregory Palamas (1296–1359). On the centrality of the metaphor of light to describe the uncreated glory of God in Symeon, see, e.g., *Symeon the New Theologian: The Discourses,* trans. C. J. deCatanzaro (New York, 1980), pp. 193–197, 295–307. Gregory similarly maintained that the transcendent and incomprehensible God manifests himself in a "hyposatic" light (φος ενυποστατως), which is further described as "an illumination immaterial and divine, a grace invisibly seen and ignorantly known." See J. Meyendorff, *Grégoire Palamas: Défense des saints hésychastes* (Louvain, 1959), p. 403 (English trans. by N. Gendle in *Gregory Palamas: The Triads,* ed. J. Meyendorff [New York, 1983], p. 57). The "uncreated light" (ακτίστου φωτός) is identified as "the glory of God," which is characterized further as Christ the Lord (ʽό Θεοῦ ἐστὶ δόξα και Χριστοῦ Θεοῦ). See p. 525 (English trans., p. 67). Although Gregory insists time and again that this light is not identical with the essence of God, he emphasizes that it is the "uncreated" glory which "cannot be classified amongst the things subject to time . . . because it belongs to the divine nature in an ineffable manner." See pp. 405, 419 (English trans., pp. 57, 60). Employing the language of Pseudo-Dionysius Areopagite (*Mystical Theology* V), Gregory in one context describes this hypostatic light as the "not-being by transcendence (καθ ῆεροχὴν μὴ ον) . . . which is definitely not the divine essence, but a glory and radiance inseparable from His nature" (p. 461; English trans., p. 66).

[25] *Sefer Ḥakhmoni,* p. 40.

The divine glory assumes the image of an *anthropos* as it appears to human beings, but this is not the essential form of the glory. This point is underscored in Donnolo's interpretation of Ezek. 1:26 contained in the extended passage cited above: "[God] did not want to show him [the glory] except in the image of man, in an image he was accustomed to seeing, so that he would not be frightened and startled by the appearance of His image, resulting in his sudden death." It would seem, moreover, that Donnolo is operating with a twofold conception of the glory, a conception that is implied in Saadiah Gaon as well, though interpreted in an entirely different way, and which is developed more fully in subsequent writers, largely on the basis of a comment by Nathan ben Yeḥiel of Rome to the effect that there is a "glory above the glory." While Donnolo does not explicitly formulate such a position, it is suggested by his interpretation of Exod. 24:10 and Isa. 6:1, mentioned above—that is, that the nobles of Israel as well as Isaiah apprehended the lower glory. In the case of Isaiah this is expressed in terms of the prophet seeing the glory seated on a throne, for what he beheld was the "glory of His skirts" which is also identified as the "glory under His feet."[26] The same notion is expressed in terms of the nobles of Israel, in slightly different language: "[Even though it is written, 'And they saw the God of Israel,'] they saw only His glory that is under His feet by means of a sign and symbol (*be-'ot we-siman*), as it says, 'And under His feet was the likeness of a pavement of sapphire' (Exod. 24:10)."

The glory described as under God's feet may be equated with the anthropomorphic appearance assumed by the invisible *demut,* the unfathomable light and immeasurable glory, in the prophetic vision. This formulation is based in part on a passage attributed to R. Berechiah in *Shemot Rabbah* 23:15:

> "This is my God and I will glorify Him" (Exod. 15:2). See how great were those who went down to the sea! How much did Moses have to beg and entreat God before he saw the [divine] image (*ha-demut*), as it says, "Let me behold Your glory" (Exod. 33:18). The Holy One, blessed be He, said to him: "You cannot see My face" (ibid., 20). In the end God showed him [the *demut*] by means of a token (*be-siman*), as it says, "as My glory passes by" (ibid., 22).

A first reading of Donnolo might suggest that his position is quite similar, if not indebted, to that of Saadiah. As I discussed above, Saadiah, in his *Tafsir Kitāb al-Mabādi'*, distinguished between the "second" air, also identified as the *ruaḥ ha-qodesh,* the *kavod,* and the *Shekhinah,* and the "first" air, which permeates all reality and in which the ten *sefirot* and twenty-two letters take shape.[27] He emphasized that the "second" air is a created entity, just as in his *Kitāb al-Amānāt wa'l-I'tiqādāt* he noted that the *kavod* or *Shekhinah* is the form (*al-ṣūrah*) created from light, which can take on the shape of an anthropos seen

[26] The association of the lower glory and the feet, based on Exod. 24:10, is further developed in the theosophy of the German Pietists, especially in the writings of Eleazar of Worms. See Wolfson, "Images of God's Feet," pp. 155–160.

[27] *Sefer Yeṣirah,* ed. Kafiḥ, pp. 106–109.

by the prophets.[28] Yet on closer inspection it becomes clear that Donnolo's metaphysical assumptions are not at all comparable to Saadiah's, for Donnolo does not assert that the *ruaḥ ha-qodesh,* the light beyond measure and the incomprehensible glory, is a created form; on the contrary, for Donnolo these terms are different ways of signifying the divine likeness itself, the *demut ha-'elohim,* which is not created.[29] He makes no effort to challenge the notion that God has a *demut,* as those authors influenced by the Greek-Arabic philosophical tradition do, nor do we find Donnolo opting for the psychologistic interpretation developed by Hai Gaon and his followers Ḥananel ben Ḥushiel of Kairouan and Nathan ben Yeḥiel of Rome, according to which the locus of the visible form is solely within the mind.[30] The viewpoint adopted by Donnolo is still very much indebted to the earlier mystical and aggadic traditions that posited a divine form, a *demut,* that could assume a visible shape in relation to man.

It can be shown, moreover, that for Donnolo this *demut,* or the upper aspect of the glory, is the boundless and limitless light that contains, embraces, or encompasses the ten *sefirot.* Commenting on the passage in *Sefer Yeṣirah* 1:7,[31] "Ten *sefirot belimah,* their measure is ten without end, their end is fixed in their beginning and their beginning in their end as a flame bound to the coal," Donnolo writes, "Their beginning is God and their end is God (*teḥilatan hu' ha-'elohim we-sofan hu' ha-'elohim*), for He is the first and last.[32] He fixed these ten *sefirot belimah* in His great power (*be-khoḥo ha-gadol*) like a flame bound to the coal."[33] The first thing to note is that *koaḥ ha-gadol,* the "great power,"

[28] *Kitāb al-Amānāt wa'l-I'tiqādāt* (*Sefer ha-'Emunot we-ha-De'ot*) II:10, pp. 103–104. Dunash ibn Tamim likewise speaks of the "light of the Creator" that is distinct from God, though it is not clear if it is a created or emanated light. See *Sefer Yeṣirah with Commentary by Dunash ben Tamim,* ed. M. Grossberg, p. 31; Vajda, "Le commentaire kairouanais sur le 'Livre de la Création,'" p. 145.

[29] See the description of the *kavod* in Donnolo's thought as an "emanation from divinity" (*una emanazione della divinità*) in Castelli, *Commento,* p. 40. Dan, in *The Esoteric Theology of Ashkenazi Ḥasidism,* pp. 112–113, similarly suggests that the *kavod* in Donnolo "alludes to the actual divine glory that is not created but is closer to the nature of the divine power that emanates through the concatenation of lights in a Neoplatonic way." Dan relies on an explanation he heard orally from his teacher, Isaiah Tishby (see p. 113 n. 29; cf. p. 175 n. 9), but does not mention Castelli's earlier observation.

[30] It is of interest to note that the German Pietists had already blurred the distinction between Donnolo and the Geonic view expressed by Saadiah, Nissim ben Jacob, and Ḥananel ben Ḥushiel. In MS Parma-Palatina 2784 (De Rossi 1390), fol. 78b, and MS New York–JTSA Mic. 2411, fol. 12b (cf. Abraham bar Azriel, *'Arugat ha-Bosem,* 1:200), after the citations from Saadiah's *Sefer ha-'Emunot we-ha-De'ot* on the nature of the created glory and Ḥananel's commentary on Berakhot denying that God has an image, the author (presumably Eleazar of Worms) writes, "And so R. Nissim Gaon explained [the matter], as well as Shabbetai the doctor and sage, and I received it from my teacher, R. Judah [the Pious], who received it from our teacher, R. Samuel the Pious, his father." See below, n. 160.

[31] Following the paragraph numbering in the standard editions of the long recension. See *Sefer Yeṣirah,* ed. Gruenwald, p. 142 (par. 6).

[32] Cf. Isa. 44:6.

[33] *Sefer Ḥakhmoni,* p. 38.

is a technical term in Donnolo's *Ḥakhmoni* for the divine glory that is invisible, the *demut* that no angel or person can apprehend.[34] The expression *koaḥ ha-gadol* has already been applied to God in Scripture,[35] but its theosophical connotation as synonymous with *kavod* should be traced to the use of the Greek *dynamis* and the Hebrew *gevurah* in esoteric circles of the first or second century. As Scholem noted, we find two striking examples of this usage, both of which could very well have been known by Donnolo: the first in the Jewish apocryphon, *Vita Adae et Evae* (§ 21), where the term "great power" (*virtus magna*) is used for the divine glory, and the second in the Acts of the Apostles 8:10, where the Samaritan Simon Magus is praised as "the power of God that is called Great."[36]

Although the more common term rendered by "dynamis" is *gevurah,* one will readily see the philological connection between these expressions and the one used by Donnolo, *koaḥ ha-gadol.* While this precise formulation is not found in the extant Hekhalot texts, the word *koaḥ* itself is employed in this corpus in a technical sense as referring to the hypostatic power of God. It seems to me that this locution should be viewed in relation to another term well known from early rabbinic texts as well as the Hekhalot literature, "great glory" (*kavod gadol*). Scholem has shown on the basis of Greek and Aramaic parallels in apocalyptic and mystical sources that the expression *kavod gadol* was used as a technical term to name the glory enthroned on the chariot.[37] Scholem also suggested that the two terms "great dynamis" and "great glory" seem to have been interchangeable even in the earlier esoteric terminology. It is evident that for Donnolo this is precisely the case, for the great power of God is treated hypostatically as his glory (*kavod*) and, as will be seen below, his wisdom (*ḥokhmah*).[38] Donnolo maintains that the "great power" is not the aspect of divinity that is visible, but rather the form of God that is invisible.

Donnolo describes this "great power" in several other ways in his commentary, including God's "wonderful power," "His great and awesome light that cannot be comprehended and has no measure," the "great and powerful fire that is above the supernal heavens," the "splendor of the Holy One, blessed be He," and the "instrument" utilized by God in the act of creation.[39] It should be

[34] See ibid., p. 34. Donnolo's usage of *koaḥ ha-gadol* has a parallel in Solomon ibn Gabirol's *Keter Malkhut,* 22; cf. *Liturgical Poetry of Solomon ibn Gabirol* 1:51.

[35] Cf. Exod. 32:11; Deut. 4:37, 9:29; 2 Kings 17:36; Jer. 27:5, 32:17; Neh. 1:10. It is evident from these occurrences that the expression *koaḥ gadol* when applied to God in Scripture is used to refer exclusively to the manifestation of the divine creative (Jer. 27:5, 32:17) or redemptive (Exod. 32:11; Deut. 4:37, 9:29; 2 Kings 17:36; Neh. 1:10) power. Moreover, the term is paired frequently with other technical expressions for God's power, such as *yad ḥazaqah* (Exod. 32:11; Neh. 1:10) or *zero'a neṭuyah* (Deut. 9:29; 2 Kings 17:36; Jer. 27:5, 32:17).

[36] *Jewish Gnosticism,* p. 67.

[37] Ibid., p. 68.

[38] Donnolo may have been influenced by the apocryphal *Wisdom of Solomon* 7:25, wherein the power and glory of God are identical and wisdom is but a manifestation of that power. On the knowledge of this text by the author of *Sefer Josippon,* a work written in the same milieu and at the same time as Donnolo, see Flusser's edition, 1:144 n. 6, 2:132.

[39] *Sefer Ḥakhmoni,* pp. 28, 38, 40, 62.

noted that the expression "great light" (*'or ha-gadol*), which occurs in Isa. 9:1, appears in *Sefer Josippon,* a work written in southern Italy in the tenth century. In that context the term is used to refer to the eschatological reward of the righteous in the paradisiacal state attained after the death of the body. This usage is attested to in earlier Jewish apocalyptic writings that may have directly influenced the author of *Sefer Josippon.*[40] Yitzhak Baer has observed that the term reflects the influence of the religious ideas that emerged from the school of Saadiah Gaon.[41]

As evidence for this claim Baer cites a passage from a responsum of Saadiah to a certain heretic, apparently a Karaite, cited in Hebrew translation by Judah ben Barzillai in his commentary on *Sefer Yeṣirah.* In that context the "great light" is identified as the "light of the glory (*'or ha-kavod*), which is the created light (*'or ha-baruy*), the first of all things created and formed," the "resplendent light" (*'or ha-bahir*), also identified, as I mentioned above, as the "God of Israel" seen by Moses, Aaron, Nadab, Abihu, and the seventy elders, and as Akatriel, who was seen sitting on a throne in the Holy of Holies by R. Ishmael ben Elisha.[42] A comparison of the usage of the term "great light" in the three different sources leads to the following conclusions: (1) The specific usage found in *Sefer Josippon* is not present in this Saadianic text; (2) Donnolo employs the term in a theosophic and not an eschatological way, as is the case in *Sefer Josippon;* (3) Donnolo, in contrast to Saadiah, never explicitly—or implicitly, for that matter—describes the "great light" as being created. Hence we may conclude that the occurrence of the same expression in the different authors (even of the same time and the same geographical area, as in the case of Donnolo and *Sefer Jossipon*) does not necessarily mean that they are employing that given expression in the same way.

Donnolo's characterization of the "great light" as the instrument through which God creates the world suggests that this upper form of God, the splendor and fire, is identical with the *logos* or Torah in its pristine sense, which is, after all, the instrument of God's creativity, according to the standard rabbinic conception, reflected, for example, in the expression used in *Bereshit Rabbah* 1:1: "The Torah declared: I was the artisan's tool (*kele 'umanuto*) of the Holy One, blessed be He." Such an interpretation is supported by the fact that Donnolo mentions in this connection God's wisdom as well as evoking the image of God beginning to create the world by means of his great power two thousand years before the world was actually created.[43] One will immediately recognize the

[40] See the sources noted by Flusser in *Sefer Josippon* 1:301 n. 26. The term also occurs in some Hekhalot texts, but not in a technical theosophic sense. Cf. *Synopse,* §§ 105, 270; *Geniza-Fragmente,* p. 133.

[41] See Baer, "The Hebrew Book of Josippon," p. 192 n. 9; idem, "The Socioreligious Orientation of 'Sefer Ḥasidim,'" p. 60. See also Dan, *Esoteric Theology,* p. 32, who suggests an echo of the German Pietistic doctrine of the glory in the term "great light."

[42] *Perush Sefer Yeṣirah,* p. 20. The author employs the expression "great light" in the Saadianic sense, i.e., to refer to the created glory. See also, pp. 16–17, 35, and elsewhere.

[43] *Sefer Ḥakhmoni,* p. 34.

rabbinic allusions in this context: In the first instance, wisdom is interchangeable with Torah; therefore, if the *koaḥ ha-gadol* is identical with wisdom (and this, in fact, is suggested by another comment, that "God suspended the entire world by means of wisdom and His great power on emptiness"[44]), it is more than plausible to suggest that it is also to be identified as Torah. Moreover, the expression "two thousand years before the creation of the world" brings to mind the description in midrashic literature (e.g., *Bereshit Rabbah* 8:2) of the Torah as preceding the creation of the world by two thousand years. Indeed, in a previous part of this section of *Sefer Ḥakhmoni* Donnolo makes the point rather explicitly, recasting the midrashic image in light of the doctrine of letter-combination expounded in *Sefer Yeṣirah:*

> We have learned that two thousand years before the creation of the world the Holy One, blessed be He, played around with the twenty-two letters of the Torah[45] and He combined and rotated them and made from all of them one word. He rotated [the word] frontwards and backwards through all the twenty-two letters.[46] . . . All this the Holy One, blessed be He, undertook, for He wanted to create the world by means of His word and the epithet of the great name.[47]

In this passage Donnolo has informed us that in his mind the Torah, which is made up of the twenty-two letters, is identical with the word formed on the basis of those letters (*dibbur* or *ma'amar*) as well as with the epithet of the great name of God (*kinnuy shem ha-gadol*). The specific connection with the *logos* is also brought out in another passage that describes God as "containing and bearing everything, above and below, with His word and the power of His strength. . . . The Creator, blessed be He, contains and bears everything, and He is upon everything, in His word, as it says, 'He is the one who stretched out the heaven over chaos, who suspended earth over emptiness' (Job 26:7)."[48] The linguistic process (*ṣeruf ha-'otiyyot we-gilgul ha-dibburim*) is thus the first act of creation, followed by God's arranging in thought the celestial bodies (the dragon [*teli*], stars, constellations, zodiac signs, spheres, etc.) that would ultimately control events in the terrestrial realm. The central position accorded to the celestial bodies in the divine plan of creation is reflected in Donnolo's attributing to astrology the special distinction of being the science that provides the best intellectual means to gain knowledge of God's greatness.

Indeed, for Donnolo astrology becomes the secret wisdom by means of which God created the universe and through which human beings gain knowl-

[44] Ibid., p. 38.

[45] This image is based on the interpretation of Prov. 8:30 in *Bereshit Rabbah* 1:1; see also Ps. 119:77.

[46] There follows a detailed description of the process of combination and rotation, which involves both letters and their vowels. The presence of the technique of letter-combination in relation to combination of vowels in Donnolo has been noted by Idel in *Golem*, p. 75 n. 35.

[47] *Sefer Ḥakhmoni*, pp. 32–33; cf. Lipiner, *The Metaphysics of the Hebrew Alphabet*, pp. 130–131 n. 68.

[48] *Sefer Ḥakhmoni*, p. 83.

edge of this process.[49] While it is certainly the case that Donnolo thought of astrology as the highest science it is important to bear in mind that he does allow for a prior stage of divine creativity, which we have identified as the linguistic process by means of which the word of God, or the Torah, is formed. The word of God, generated on the basis of the twenty-two Hebrew letters, is identical with God's great power—also described in terms of various light metaphors—which comprises the ten ineffable *sefirot.* What is further implied in Donnolo's presentation, though not stated explicitly, is that the *sefirot* constitute a sphere beyond the celestial realms and that therefore gnosis connected with them, whatever form it takes, must be higher or more sublime than astrology. In the final analysis, for Donnolo, there is no positive gnosis of the *sefirot* in the sense of discursive knowledge; on the contrary, he insists on a number of occasions that human beings cannot really know the *sefirot* in any comprehensive or exhaustive way. The unknowability of the *sefirot* derives from the fact that they constitute God's "great power" (*koaḥ ha-gadol*) which is virtually identical with the image of God (*demut ha-'elohim*) as may be gathered from the similar terms used by Donnolo to describe the two, especially the characterization of each as an immeasurable and unfathomable light.

The theosophic interpretation of the *sefirot* is emphasized in Donnolo's interpretation of *Sefer Yeṣirah* 1:7, which I have cited above. For Donnolo the ten *sefirot* are said to be contained within the hypostatic glory called God's great power. Whereas the original text of *Sefer Yeṣirah* speaks of the *sefirot* forming a closed circle, with the first fixed in the last and the last in the first, Donnolo closes the circle with God: God is the beginning and end of the *sefirot,* which are set within his great power. To be sure, this is based in part on the continuation in *Sefer Yeṣirah,* "Know, think, and conceive that the Lord is one and the Creator is one, and there is no second to Him." That is, after the author of *Sefer Yeṣirah* describes the unity of the multiple *sefirot* in terms of the image of circularity, he must emphasize the oneness of God, inasmuch as the plurality of the *sefirot,* which may be construed as divine entities, or at least as having the status of such, might pose a challenge to the monotheistic idea of a singular God.

Yet what is lacking in *Sefer Yeṣirah* is the claim that the *sefirot* are indivisibly united or enclosed within God,[50] an interpretation later linked by theosophic kabbalists to the image "as a flame bound to the coal." It is precisely in this vein that Donnolo understands the passage: the *sefirot* are said to be fixed within God's great power like a flame bound to the coal. It is of interest to

[49] See Sharf, *Universe of Shabbetai Donnolo,* pp. 12–13; Kiener, "The Status of Astrology in the Early Kabbalah," p. 14.

[50] It is important to recall here the observation of Gruenwald in "Some Critical Notes," p. 492, that in some Neoplatonic texts, including Plotinus, there are to be found similar notions concerning the indivisibility of the emanations in their source. While Gruenwald does not rule out the possibility of some connection between *Sefer Yeṣirah* and the Neoplatonic writings, he does caution against such a position on the grounds that the terminology of *Sefer Yeṣirah* is "vague and slippery" and thus defies any scientific exactitude.

compare Donnolo's interpretation of this part of *Sefer Yeṣirah* with a passage from the Pseudo-Clementine *Homilies* 17: "He [God] is the Beginning and the End. For in Him the six infinite [ones, i.e., the Extensions] end, and from Him they take their extension toward the infinite."[51] Even if these Extensions are to be viewed numerically, as Pines suggests, it is evident from at least this statement that they constitute the pleroma or realm of fullness, for they are said to originate in and project from the divine.

A similar claim can be made with regard to Donnolo's conception of the *sefirot,* which are never identified by him as numbers or mathematical units, as they are by the other known tenth-century commentators on *Sefer Yeṣirah,* Saadiah Gaon and Dunash ibn Tamim (ca. 890–ca. 960),[52] and later by a variety of authors, including Solomon ibn Gabirol (ca. 1020–ca. 1057),[53] Abraham ibn Ezra, Judah Halevi,[54] and Judah ben Barzillai, whose commentary on *Sefer Yeṣirah* basically follows—indeed, to a great degree paraphrases—the commentary of Saadiah.

It must be noted, however, that in Dunash ibn Tamim's commentary there are a few hints that the *sefirot* are not ordinary numbers but rather signify powers or aspects in the divine world, understood in this context Neoplatonically, as the sphere of intelligible entities. For example, commenting on the image in *Sefer Yeṣirah* of the covenant of the one (*berit yaḥid*) set in the middle of the ten *sefirot,* he writes that the ten numbers are the "basis for all numbers" and "number one is in the middle, for from it all the numbers derive, but it is not a number." In the continuation of this passage Dunash states that the covenant of

[51] See Pines, "Points of Similarity," pp. 68, 85.

[52] Cf. Saadiah's commentary on *Sefer Yeṣirah,* ed. Kafiḥ, pp. 42, 51–52, 54, 67–68, 90–92, 105; *Sefer Yeṣirah with Commentary by Dunash,* p. 19; Vajda, "Commentaire kairouanais," pp. 126–127, 130–132. For the most recent discussion on Dunash's commentary, see Jospe, "Early Philosophical Commentaries," pp. 372–392. Most contemporary scholars have accepted, more or less, the mathematical approach as an accurate account of the original meaning of the text; see references in chapter 2, n. 65.

[53] Cf. Solomon ibn Gabirol, *Liqquṭim mi-Sefer Meqor Ḥayyim* II:27, ed. Munk, p. 9 (Hebrew text) (Zifroni ed., II:21, p. 46). For a discussion of this passage, see Liebes, "Rabbi Solomon Ibn Gabirol's Use of the *Sefer Yeṣira,*" pp. 78–79. See, however, Idel, "The Sefirot above the Sefirot," p. 278, where he notes that the term *sefirot* in the poem *Shokhen ʿad me-ʾaz* of Solomon ibn Gabirol functions in a specifically theological sense and does not connote mere numbers: by means of contemplating the ten *sefirot* one attains knowledge of the unity of God. As Idel also notes, this interpretation bears a strong similarity to the view of Eleazar of Worms, who in turn was undoubtedly influenced by Donnolo. For further discussion of these passages in ibn Gabirol, see Pines, "Points of Similarity," pp. 122–126; and Jospe, "Early Philosophical Commentaries," pp. 390–392. Finally, in this connection mention should be made of the usage of the term *sefirot* in a *piyyuṭ* on the Ten Commandments for Shavuʿot (falsely attributed to Saadiah Gaon; see I. Davidson, *Thesaurus of Mediaeval Hebrew Poetry,* 4 vols. [New York, 1924–38], 1:277, no. 6071); cf. *Maḥzor Romania* 129b. In this poem the Ten Commandments, referred to as the *maʾamarot,* "sayings of God," are said to parallel the ten *sefirot,* which are the principles of everything created: הלא הנם עשרת כעשרת בראשית כל ועשר הספירות וסודותיו ואדותיו יסודות. For a wide-ranging discussion of the correlation between the ten *maʾamarot,* the ten *dibberot,* and the ten *sefirot,* see Idel, "Sefirot above the Sefirot," pp. 268–277.

[54] See Jospe, "Philosophical Commentaries," pp. 394–402.

the one is an allusion to the Logos whence all speech derives.[55] It may be concluded, therefore, that Dunash has applied the Aristotelian notion (perhaps of Pythagorean origin) that one is not itself a number but is rather the measure of all numbers to the relationship of the Logos (which may be identified as well as the First Intellect) to the *sefirot*. In a manner similar to that of the Islamic Neoplatonist al-Kindi and that of his own teacher, Isaac Israeli (ca. 855–ca. 955), Dunash removes the True One (God) from the chain of emanation. The one that is the foundation of all numbers is not the Creator but the Logos or Intellect.[56] In light of this evidently Neoplatonic interpretation of the *sefirot* it makes perfect sense for Dunash to assert that included within the thirty-two paths of wisdom, which comprise the ten *sefirot* and the twenty-two letters, are "all the spiritual sciences (*ha-ḥokhmot ha-ruḥaniyyot*), for they are the beginning [or principle] of the [divine] unity (*hatḥalat ha-yiḥud*), [so that one may] contemplate things that are beyond nature."[57] In another place, commenting on the enigmatic statement in *Sefer Yeṣirah* (1:8) "Ten *sefirot belimah,* their vision is as swift as the flash of lightning, and there is no limit to their boundaries; one's discourse [about them] should be as swift as possible, and one's utterances should be as if driven by a storm; and before the throne they bow down," Dunash remarks that this section "elucidates more about the divine wisdom (*ḥokhmat ha-'elohut*) [i.e., metaphysics], which is appropriately [characterized] by the image (*dimyon*) of the ten *sefirot*."[58] Insofar as *ḥokhmat ha-'elohut* is specified as the science that deals with God's unity (*yiḥud*) and the spiritual entities (*ruḥaniyyim*), it follows that the *sefirot* must instruct one about some aspect of the divine and the angelic beings that make up the intelligible world. In a third passage the author states explicitly that the "ten ineffable *sefirot* are the power of [God] that spreads out in everything."[59] From these passages it may be concluded that for Dunash contemplation of the *sefirot* can teach one something about the unity of God as well as the spiritual realities. Dunash reflects here a Neoplatonic position that may have also been a central characteristic of the commentary on *Sefer Yeṣirah* by his teacher, Israeli.[60] Hence, even though the primary meaning assigned to the *sefirot* by Dunash is that of numbers, his position is fundamentally different from that of Saadiah.

The emphasis on the mathematical interpretation of the *sefirot* by Saadiah and Dunash, whatever differences there are between the two authors, can be easily explained in light of the resurgence of interest in Pythagoreanism in the

[55] Dunash's commentary, ed. Grossberg, p. 19; Vajda, "Commentaire kairouanais," p. 127.

[56] See Altmann and Stern, *Isaac Israeli*, pp. 151–164; Ivry, *Al-Kindi's Metaphysics*, pp. 19–21.

[57] Vajda, "Commentaire kairouanais," p. 127. For a slightly different reading, see p. 126, and the edition of Grossberg, pp. 19–20.

[58] Dunash's commentary, p. 34. For an entirely different reading of this passage, see the text established by Vajda, "Commentaire kairouanais," p. 148: הפרק הזה . . . ומורה על חכמת האומר אותו לפי שהוא דמיון יותר יפה לעשר ספירות, and translation on p. 147: "Ce chapitre . . . montre la sagesse de son auteur, car c'est une représentation encore plus belle des dix *sefirot*."

[59] Dunash's commentary, p. 46; cf. the reading in Vajda, "Commentaire kairouanais," p. 78.

[60] See Goldziher, "Fragment de l'original arabe du commentaire sur le Sefer Yeçirah par Isak Israéli"; Altmann and Stern, *Isaac Israeli*, pp. 108, 157–158, 170, 176 n. 1, 189–190, 209–215.

ninth and tenth centuries, as attested, for example, by Thābit ibn Qura's translation of the works of Nicomachus of Gerasa (ca. 100 C.E.) into Arabic[61] as well as by the elaborate mystical theory of numbers propounded by the Ikhwān as-Ṣafā'.[62] There is clear evidence that both Saadiah and Dunash were influenced by these trends, which no doubt had an impact on their reading of the ancient Jewish work *Sefer Yeṣirah*.[63] It is thus no mere coincidence that in Saadiah's list of nine cosmogonic theories in his commentary on *Sefer Yeṣirah*, the seventh view is the Pythagorean notion that the world was created from numbers, and the eighth view is that of *Sefer Yeṣirah* itself, that the world was formed out of the ten numbers and twenty-two letters. These two theories are listed next to each other, for in Saadiah's mind the latter represents the more perfect articulation of the former.[64] In the case of Donnolo, however, one finds no evidence of a Pythagorean interpretation of the *sefirot*. The commentary of Donnolo, in contrast to the mathematical approach of Saadiah and, to an extent, that of Dunash, reflects a theosophic understanding of the *sefirot* that anticipates the meaning of this term evident in later kabbalistic works.[65]

The fact that in southern Italy a theosophic interpretation emerged at roughly the same time the scientific or rational explanation was prevalent in the Muslim East is a significant fact that should be weighed carefully when one sets out to chart the history of Jewish esotericism. This point has been virtually ignored in the scholarly literature. One major exception is David Neumark, who noted that the commentaries on *Sefer Yeṣirah* composed in the tenth century reflected a struggle between those oriented toward philosophy, among whom he counts Saadiah and Dunash, and those oriented toward kabbalah, such as Shabbetai Donnolo. Neumark speaks of the relation of Donnolo to kabbalah in terms of the influence of *Sefer Ḥakhmoni* on later kabbalists, including the author/editor of *Sefer ha-Bahir*, specifically with respect to the

[61] Cf. W. Kutsch, ed., *Tabit b. Qurra's arabische Übersetzung der arithetike Eisagoge des Nikomachos von Gerasa* (Beirut, 1958). On the possibility of at least one Jewish disciple of Thābit ben Qura, see S. Pines, "A Tenth Century Philosophical Correspondence," p. 134 n. 106.

[62] See Brentjes, "Die erste Risala der Rasa'il Ihwan as-Ṣafa' über elementare Zahlentheorie." On Pythagoreanism in the Arabic milieu, see also Rosenthal, "Some Pythagorean Documents Transmitted in Arabic." For a discussion on Pythagoreanism in eleventh-century Byzantine thought, see P. Joannou, *Christliche Metaphysik, vol. 1, Die Illuminationslehre des Michael Psellos und Joannes Italos* (*Studia Patristica et Byzantina,* pt. 3), (Ettal, 1956), pp. 55–59.

[63] See M. Steinschneider, *Mathematik bei den Juden* (Berlin & Leipzig, 1893–99; repr. Hildesheim, 1964), pp. 62–63; S. Gandz, "The Origin of the Ghubar Numerals or the Arabian Abacus and the Articuli," *Isis* 16 (1931): 393–424; idem, "Saadia Gaon as a Mathematician," in *Saadia Anniversary Volume* (New York, 1943), pp. 141–195.

[64] See Jospe, "Early Philosophical Commentaries," p. 378. Vajda, in "Le commentaire de Saadia sur le Sefer Yecira," p. 75, has noted the closeness of the Pythagorean theory of numbers and the doctrine of *sefirot* in *Sefer Yeṣirah* according to Saadiah's explanation, despite his own effort to classify them as two distinct theories.

[65] Castelli, in *Commento,* pp. 21–27, esp. 24, concludes that according to Donnolo (and Eleazar of Worms) the *sefirot* are the "primary elements of the universe," which form an absolute unity. See Starr, *The Jews in the Byzantine Empire,* p. 55, where he translates the word *sefirot* as used by Donnolo as "spheres"—without, however, elaborating in any detail.

macrocosm-microcosm motif as well as the doctrine concerning the permutation of the Hebrew letters and names of God.[66] Neumark's view on this matter is well summarized in the following passage: "Shabbetai Donnolo expresses ideas that are not yet the distinctive teachings of the kabbalah, but that helped in the development of the latter. Yet at times he expresses ideas in a way that is very close to the formulation of the later kabbalah."[67] One may question Neumark's peculiar understanding of the evolution of philosophical and kabbalistic thought in medieval Judaism, but with respect to this issue he displays a remarkable sensitivity to Donnolo's text, although he does not fully articulate the implications of his own thinking. The importance of Donnolo's *Sefer Ḥakhmoni* to the development of "western kabbalah" has also been noted by Sharf, though his comments are in fact limited to the German Pietists, an influence that has been noted by other scholars as well. Indeed, what I am suggesting goes substantially further than the more limited claims of previous scholars, namely, that already operative in Donnolo is a theosophic notion of the *sefirot* that is the cornerstone for later kabbalistic thought.

That Donnolo operated with a theosophic conception of *sefirot* is evident from other texts in his *Sefer Ḥakhmoni* as well. For example, in his first extended comment on the term *sefirot* in *Sefer Yeṣirah* he writes:

> Ten ineffable *sefirot:* these are arranged in the image of the ten fingers on the hands and the ten toes on the feet, and the one God is set within the ten ineffable *sefirot.* Similarly, the covenant of unity is set within the ten fingers on the hands, which are five against five, in the tongue and mouth so that one may unify God (*leyaḥed ha-'el*). In the same way the covenant of unity is set within the ten toes of the feet, which are five against five, in the circumcision of the foreskin.[68]

Just as the one God is represented by the two covenants set within the fingers and toes of the human body, so the one God is set within the ten powers that Donnolo calls by the name *sefirot.* The point is repeated in another comment by Donnolo explaining the passage in *Sefer Yeṣirah* 1:5 (his reading is slightly different from the standard text, but I will cite it according to his reading), "Ten ineffable *sefirot.* Close your heart from meditating and your mouth from speaking. If your heart runs, return to God, for thus it says, '[the living creatures] were running to and fro' (Ezek. 1:14). Concerning this a covenant has been made": "[The covenant is made] by means of the tongue and mouth, that is, the holy language [through which one proclaims] the unity of God, and through the covenant of the foreskin so that one will remember God who has given him the covenant,[69] to strengthen his heart and to set in his mind that he cannot contemplate at all His divinity."[70] It follows that comprehension of the *sefirot* would amount to knowledge of God, and it is precisely for such a reason

[66] Neumark, *History of Jewish Philosophy* 1:121, 188, 190.
[67] Ibid., p. 258 n. 4.
[68] *Sefer Ḥakhmoni,* p. 35.
[69] Cf. Dunash's commentary, ed. Grossberg, p. 26; Vajda, "Commentaire kairouanais," p. 134.
[70] *Sefer Ḥakhmoni,* p. 38.

that this knowledge is not attainable by human beings. This step is taken explicitly by Donnolo when he comments on the language of *Sefer Yeṣirah,* "Ten ineffable *sefirot:* their measure is ten without end (*middatan ʿeser she-ʾein lahem sof*)":

> This is the import of what is written, "They have no end." This instructs us that there is no sage in the world who can know, comprehend, and delve into the knowledge of God, to discover the end and to reach the limit of these ten profound [impenetrable] *sefirot.* If a sage pursues them and seeks in his mind all the days of the world to comprehend them, it will not amount to anything. . . . For a person cannot delve with his mind to pursue in order to know these ten things, which are infinitely and endlessly deep.[71]

From this passage it is clear that for Donnolo knowledge of God involves knowledge of the ten *sefirot,* but that these are beyond the realm of human comprehension. To delve into the knowledge of God (*lehaʿamiq be-daʿat ha-ʾel*) would involve discovering and reaching the limit of the impenetrable *sefirot.* The contrast between Donnolo and Saadiah is brought out in clear terms when we compare their respective interpretations of this phrase in *Sefer Yeṣirah: middatan ʿeser she-ʾein lahem sof,* "their measure is ten without end." According to Saadiah, this characterization of the *sefirot* is meant to convey the notion that the ten primary numbers have no limit with respect to the combinations of them that human beings can produce, but they are limited in relation to God.[72] Hence, the claim that the *sefirot* have no limit does not at all, for Saadiah, imply that they are intrinsically related to God. For Donnolo this is precisely the force of the claim that the *sefirot* are ten without end, for they are indicative of—indeed, identical to—God's "great power" that cannot be fathomed by finite human minds.

The essential unknowability of the *sefirot* is reiterated several times by Donnolo, for example, his comment on the language of *Sefer Yeṣirah* 1:8, "Ten ineffable *sefirot,* their vision is as swift as the flash of lightning": "It is forbidden for a person to think about them even for a moment."[73] At one point Donnolo remarks that with the permission of God, the "one who grants knowledge and understanding," he has set out to explain "something of the solutions to the riddles of *Sefer Yeṣirah* that the Holy One, blessed be He, transmitted to Abraham, our patriarch, in His love for him, to teach him and his descendants after him about His divinity (*ʾelohuto*), unity (*yiḥudo*), greatness (*gedullato*), and power (*gevurato*), and His powerful works (*koaḥ maʿasav*), as it says, 'He revealed to His people His powerful works' (Ps. 111:6). For if it were not so, who would be permitted to consider and think in his heart in order to comprehend the simplest and smallest thing of all these matters?"[74] From this it can again be concluded that in Donnolo's mind *Sefer Yeṣirah* provides

[71] Ibid., pp. 35–36.
[72] Saadiah's commentary on *Sefer Yeṣirah,* ed. Kafiḥ, p. 54; cf. pp. 90, 105.
[73] Ibid., p. 37.
[74] *Sefer Ḥakhmoni,* pp. 36–37.

one with knowledge not only of the universe, referred to in the above citation as the force of God's actions (*koaḥ maʿasav*), but also of the divine nature itself, that is, God's unity, greatness, and power. Still, this knowledge is very limited, inasmuch as the finite human mind cannot grasp the ten powers, the *sefirot,* that ultimately comprise this unity, greatness, and power. What is visibly present within the phenomenological parameters of human experience is the anthropomorphic form that this *demut* assumes in the moment of prophetic disclosure.

Hai Gaon, Ḥananel ben Ḥushiel, and Nathan ben Yeḥiel

A very different approach to the problem of anthropomorphism and visionary experience can be discerned in other writings from the tenth and eleventh centuries that also had a significant impact on the development of medieval Jewish mysticism. Before proceeding to analyze the relevant ideas from this literature, a preliminary word is in order concerning the crucial talmudic text that informed the docetic orientation that I will describe in this section. In the previous chapter I noted that a decided turn toward a more rationalistic interpretation of mystical vision is evident in the Geonic material dating from the ninth, tenth, and eleventh centuries. While it cannot be proven conclusively that in Late Antiquity the Merkavah adepts understood their own experiences in a literal (i.e., corporeal) manner, it is evident that in this period a change in the understanding of the visionary experience occurred. It is entirely possible—indeed, very likely—that external influences such as the Neoplatonic doctrine of intellectual illumination influenced Jewish authors who sought to interpret prophetic and mystical visions attested in authoritative texts.[75] A similar process of interpreting divine epiphanies as inner, mental visions can be detected in contemporary Mu'tazilite theology and in Islamic mysticism. It must be noted, however, that a term central to subsequent discussions on the nature of visionary experience is found in a passage in the Babylonian Talmud, Megillah 24b, which does not seem to betray any significant external influence such as Neoplatonism. Given the central importance of this term, it would be beneficial to pause to consider the relevant text in some detail before proceeding with our analysis of the later sources.

At the end of the sixth mishnah in the fourth chapter of Megillah, one reads that R. Judah took issue with the view that a blind person can lead the congregation in the recitation of the blessings before the *Shema* (the liturgical proclamation of God's unity), including the blessing on the celestial luminaries, the sun, moon, and stars. R. Judah contends that one who is blind from birth cannot recite these blessings in order to fulfill someone else's obligation, for such a person has never seen the celestial lights. In the talmudic disputation on

[75] For a discussion of the Neoplatonic interpretation of prophecy in Jewish sources, see Altmann in *Isaac Israeli,* pp. 209–216; Sirat, *Théories,* pp. 61–88.

this mishnah an attempt is made to clarify the different positions. A baraita is cited in which the opponents of R. Judah's view pose the following argument: Many homiletically expound the details of the chariot even though they have never seen it, so analogously a blind man should be able to recite the blessings on the celestial lights even if he has never seen them in his life. The anonymous redactional voice of the talmud, the *setam*, here responds on behalf of R. Judah: In the case of the chariot "all depends on the discernment of the heart" (*'ovanta' de-libba'*), and thus the expounder can know the phenomenon by mental concentration without an actual seeing. The blind person, by contrast, can derive no benefit from the heavenly lights, and this is precisely the point of the blessing. The talmudic discussion continues with an effort to prove that R. Judah's view can be refuted. For our purposes, however, the conclusion is not relevant.

The key expression introduced by the *setam* is *'ovanta' de-libba'*, "discernment of the heart or mind,"[76] which implies that the vision of the chariot should not be construed as a physical seeing (an outer perception), but as a mental comprehension (an inner perception). This passing remark in the Talmud provided the terminology that colored much of the discussion in the Middle Ages on the nature of the chariot vision and thereby informed the intellectual development of mystical speculation within Judaism. It is especially in the thought of Hai ben Sherira Gaon that the contemplative interpretation of mystical and/or prophetic vision plays a central role. The views on this matter expressed by the leading Geonic figure developed in turn into a full-scale doceticism in the writings of the German Pietists, especially Eleazar of Worms, as will be explored in detail in the next chapter.

Our discussion of Hai's attitude toward visionary experience must begin with one of his responsa, which has been discussed previously by several scholars. In a response to a question concerning the talmudic legend of the four who entered Pardes, the mystical orchard, Hai describes certain techniques for one who desires "to contemplate the chariot and to gaze upon the palaces of the supernal angels." Such a person, prescribes Hai, "should sit and fast for several days, and place his head between his knees and whisper to the ground many songs and praises. . . . Then he will gaze inward and into the chambers [of his heart], like one who sees with his eyes the seven palaces. He contemplates as if he entered from palace to palace and sees what is in each one."[77] Two obvious conclusions can be drawn from this description: First, Hai did not question the validity of the claim that celestial palaces exist. Second, one who desires to gaze upon the celestial chariot should perform certain actions in order to conjure a mental image that is likened to an actual vision. The "as if" (*ke-'illu*) construction here is critical, for it suggests a transformative power

[76] See Halperin, *Merkabah in Rabbinic Literature,* p. 174; idem, *Faces of the Chariot,* pp. 318–319, 335. Cf. the Hebrew parallel to the Aramaic phrase *'ovanta' de-libba'* in the *Haggadat Shema' Yisra'el,* in Jellinek, ed., *Bet ha-Midrash,* 5:166, *binat levav,* already noted by Halperin.

[77] *Otzar ha-Geonim,* vol. 4, "Responsa to Tractate Hagigah," p. 14. See Idel, *Kabbalah: New Perspectives* p. 90.

under which one imagines that one is translated to the celestial realm even though no actual ascent occurs. The chariot vision is, therefore, contemplative or mental. It is clear from the relevant sources that Hai's conception of a mental vision is based on the talmudic expression "understanding of the heart," utilized by the anonymous redactional voice in B. Megillah 24b to explain R. Judah's view on the nature of the Merkavah vision. For Hai the ecstatic ascent described in the Hekhalot consisted of a mental vision—contemplation of the heart—rather than an actual journey whether in or out of body. Hai's view is brought into sharp relief when contrasted with the comment on the four rabbis who entered Pardes by the eleventh-century biblical and talmudic exegete Solomon ben Isaac of Troyes (Rashi), which was previously cited in the concluding paragraphs of the last chapter: "They mentioned a name and ascended." The ascent for Rashi is "actual" whereas for Hai it is contemplative or mental in nature. The latter orientation is clearly reflected in the comments on the same passage of the Tosafot, who contest the literal approach of Rashi: "'They entered Pardes': that is, by means of a name; they did not actually ascend, but rather it seemed to them that they had ascended."

Hai's view, adumbrated in the famous responsum mentioned above, is transmitted in his name by Nathan ben Yeḥiel of Rome in his talmudic lexicon, *Sefer he-ʿArukh,* where he comments on the expression "pure marble stones" used in the legend of the four rabbis who entered Pardes, according to the version in the Babylonian Talmud:

> This is explained in *Hekhalot Rabbati* and *Hekhalot Zuṭarti.* They [the mystics] would perform certain actions, pray certain prayers in purity, make [theurgic] use of the crown, gaze upon the palaces, see the divisions of angels according to their position, and [see] palace after palace. . . . They did not ascend on high but rather in the chamber of their heart they saw and contemplated (*roʾin we-ṣofin be-ḥadre libban*) like a person who sees and contemplates something clearly with his eyes, and they heard and spoke with a seeing eye (*ʿein ha-sokheh*) by means of the Holy Spirit. This is the explanation of R. Hai Gaon.[78]

It is noteworthy that in this passage the mystical vision of the chariot is interpreted with terms used in *Wayyikra Rabbah* 1:3 to describe the activity of the prophets (*she-sokhim be-ruaḥ ha-qodesh*): "They saw by means of the Holy Spirit." Indeed, the theory of mystical vision espoused by Hai is part of his larger view on the nature of prophecy as transmitted by Ḥananel ben Ḥushiel and Nathan of Rome. That Hai considered prophecy and mystical vision phenomenologically equivalent is evident from his responsum concerning the praxis to attain a vision of a chariot. In that context he argues against the view of his own father-in-law, Samuel ben Ḥofni (d. 1013), that visions and miracles were restricted to prophets. According to Hai, the miracles performed by the righteous and the visions perceived by them are identical to those of the prophets.[79] It follows, therefore, that just as mystical visions are to be consid-

[78] *Aruch Completum* 1:14.

[79] *Otzar ha-Geonim,* "Responsa to Tractate Ḥagigah," p. 15.

ered contemplative in nature, so too are the prophetic. It is possible that this effort to interpret both prophecy and the mystical vision of the glory as contemplative states indicates the influence of Neoplatonic thought.[80]

The same attempt to understand the mystical vision of the Hekhalot in light of prophetic vision is to be found in Ḥananel's commentary on the legend concerning the four who entered Pardes in B. Ḥagigah 14b: "They did not ascend to heaven but rather contemplated and saw by means of the understanding of the heart (*be-'ovanta' de-libba'*), like one who sees and looks through a speculum that does not shine."[81] In this case Ḥananel has combined two rabbinic idioms, "understanding of the heart" (*'ovanta' de-libba'*), which describes the chariot vision, and "speculum that does not shine" (*'ispaqlariyah she-'einah me'irah*), which is used to describe the experience of all prophets but Moses, who alone gazed through a speculum that shines.[82] The clearest application of this category to prophetic vision occurs in Ḥananel's commentary on passages in B. Berakhot 7a and Yevamot 49b. In the case of the former, commenting on the aggadic statement that God wears phylacteries, Ḥananel writes,

> The Holy One, blessed be He, makes His glory visible to those who fear Him and His pious ones through an understanding of the heart in the image of an anthropos sitting, as it is written, "I saw the Lord seated upon His throne, with all the host of heaven standing to His right and left" (1 Kings 22:19), and it is written, "I saw God sitting on the high and lofty throne and the skirts of His robe filled the Temple" (Isa. 6:1). [The glory appears] as one that has feet, as it is written, "[They saw the God of Israel] and under His feet there was the likeness of a pavement of sapphire" (Exod. 24:10). It is clear to us that the vision spoken of here is a vision of the heart (*re'iyat ha-lev*) and not a vision of the eye (*re'iyat ha-'ayin*). It is impossible to say that an image (*demut*) of God is seen through a vision of the eye. . . . It is possible to say that one sees through a vision of the heart the image of the glory (*demut kavod*) but not through an actual vision of the eye, for the verse states explicitly, "When I spoke to the prophets and through the prophets I was imaged" (*u-ve-yad ha-nevi'im 'adammeh*) (Hosea 12:11). This indicates that [God] showed to every prophet an image (*dimyon*) that he could see.[83]

Ḥananel thus equates R. Ishmael's vision of Akatriel in the Holy of Holies, according to the talmudic context, and the prophetic visions of Isaiah and Micaiah. In both cases an inner illumination of the heart is used to explain manifestations of the divine. What is seen of the divine is a purely mental image (*dimyon*). The term *demut kavod,* "image of the glory," no longer denotes a luminous substance existing autonomously outside the constitution of the human imagination. On the contrary, earlier aggadic traditions concerning this *demut* are semantically transformed, so that *demut* becomes *dimyon* in the sense of an image or phantasm within the mind. The midrashic usage of

80 Sirat, *Théories,* p. 92, makes this suggestion with respect to Ḥananel.
81 *Otzar ha-Geonim,* vol. 4, "Commentaries to Tractate Ḥagigah," p. 61.
82 B. Yevamot 49b.
83 *Otzar ha-Geonim,* vol. 1, Tractate Berakhot, appendix, p. 3.

dimmuyot to connote the external forms (*figurae*) in which God appears in this context become psychic phenomena, mental constructs by means of which the glory is imaged or visualized. The ontological significance of *demut* is radically altered by this psychologistic reading. The same point is reiterated in Ḥananel's commentary on the statement in B. Yevamot 49b that all the prophets gazed through the speculum that does not shine, while Moses alone gazed through a speculum that shines:

> All the prophets saw [the glory] within the speculum that does not shine, and it seemed to them that they had seen a visible object. This is like an elderly man whose vision is dim and he sees what is low as if it were high, one [thing] as if it were two, and the like, but it is not so. This is what is written, "and through the prophets I was imaged" (*u-ve-yad ha-nevi'im 'adammeh*) (Hosea 12:11), that is, the vision that they saw was an image (*dimyon*) and not an actual [entity] (*'iqqar*). Moses gazed upon the glory and the splendor of the *Shekhinah* through the speculum that shines from behind the *Shekhinah*. He requested [to see] more but it was not granted to him. . . . The view of all is that no creature has been granted permission to see the splendor and the glory that is greater than the glory of the *Shekhinah*.[84]

One can thus distinguish three levels, though only two are in any sense available in the prophetic visions. There is what is referred to scripturally as the face of God, the upper splendor or glory that no creature can see; the back of God, which is the aspect of the glory apprehended by Moses through a speculum that shines; and the vision of the glory apprehended by all other prophets through the speculum that does not shine. In the last instance the spiritual light of the glory is visualized as an anthropomorphic form through the intermediacy of the mental image (*dimyon*). The mystical vision described in the Hekhalot must be explained in the same way, according to Ḥananel: the body of the *Shekhinah* beheld by the *yorde merkavah,* with its refulgent splendor and incomprehensible proportions, is not a veridical reality but rather an image produced within the mind of the mystic.

Judah ben Barzillai al-Barceloni

The identification of prophecy and mystical vision implied in Hai Gaon and elaborated further by Ḥananel is challenged by Judah ben Barzillai al-Barceloni, whose own understanding of visionary experience represents an attempt to synthesize the Saadianic position with that of Hai, as transmitted especially by Ḥananel.[85] After citing Ḥananel's commentary on the passage in

[84] *Otzar ha-Geonim,* vol. 7, Tractate Yevamot, p. 314. For a slightly different version, see Judah ben Barzillai, *Perush Sefer Yeṣirah,* p. 12, quoted by Lewin, pp. 123–124.

[85] By contrast, Sirat, in *Théories,* p. 94, concludes with respect to Judah ben Barzillai's treatment of visionary experience, "Il a surtout utilisé Saadia, ne citant la vision intérieure et Rabbenu Hana-

Berakhot quoted above, according to which R. Ishmael's vision of Akatriel is equated with the prophetic visions of Isaiah and Micaiah, Judah ben Barzillai states categorically that one cannot compare the vision of the chariot mystics (*re'iyat ṣofe ha-merkavah*) with that of the prophets (*re'iyat ha-nevi'im*). "There is certainly a difference between them, for the Merkavah mystics were not prophets and we cannot say that the visions of the one were those of the other, for the visions of the prophets, in comparison to the visions of the Merkavah mystics, approximated an actual seeing" (*qerovim li-re'iyah mamash*).[86] Judah proceeds to establish this qualitative difference on semantic grounds: the verb used in connection with prophetic vision is *ra'ah,* whereas that of the chariot vision is *ṣafah.* The former denotes actual seeing, presumably with the physical eye, while the latter denotes mental vision or, in the language of the talmudic phrase, understanding of the heart. The content of vision in the case of prophecy is an external reality, in contrast to that of the mystical vision, which is a purely mental construction. Operating within his own epistemological values, Judah would affirm the primacy and veridicality of prophetic vision on the basis of this phenomenological distinction between outer and inner perception.

In his treatment of prophetic vision Judah seems to oscillate between the Saadianic position and that of Hai Gaon. That is, from one perspective he maintains, like Saadiah, that the object of the vision is external, whereas from another perspective it is a purely mental or contemplative construct. Judah begins with the theological presumption that God is incorporeal and therefore has no image (*demut*) or form (*ṣurah*). Whoever thinks that God has an image denies the essential principle of Jewish faith and is comparable to the Christians whom Judah in one place describes as "making images and bowing down to them."[87] On one occasion Judah does describe God as "being seen in the heart by all His creatures [i.e., humanity] but hidden from the eye . . . as it is written, 'No man shall see me and live' (Exod. 33:20)."[88] In this case, then, it would seem that God can be seen within the heart in a contemplative vision. Yet in most cases Judah emphasizes that what is seen cannot be God but must be an entity created by, and therefore ontologically distinct from, God. "Every vision that is mentioned with respect to an angel and/or prophet involves the created light that the Holy One, blessed be He, created . . . to show to the angels and prophets."[89]

This entity, the first light created by God, is also identified by several other

---

nel que pour mémoire." My analysis will show that this statement must be modified, inasmuch as Judah ben Barzillai does use Ḥananel's notion of internal or mental vision in a constructive way as part of his own theory of vision and does not simply mention it for the record. See also Scholem (*Origins,* p. 201), who treats the views of Judah ben Barzillai as following in an unbroken chain from Saadiah Gaon. See idem, *On the Kabbalah,* p. 93.

[86] *Perush Sefer Yeṣirah,* p. 22.

[87] Ibid., p. 14; see also pp. 79 and 82.

[88] Ibid., p. 84; cf. p. 177, where Judah uses similar language in the context of paraphrasing Saadiah.

[89] Ibid., p. 17; cf. pp. 31, 174–176, 185, 204.

names: glory (*kavod*), *Shekhinah*, Holy Spirit (*ruaḥ ha-qodesh*), and splendor (*hod*). Thus, commenting on the reference to the first of the *sefirot* enumerated in *Sefer Yeṣirah*, the "spirit of the living God," Judah writes, "[God] created the *Shekhinah*, which is the pure and holy spirit . . . this spirit, which is called the *Shekhinah* of His glory, is the Holy Spirit . . . from which the prophets heard the voice, and the spirit rested upon them, and the speech spoke with them, and it appeared to them as a form, as it is written by Moses, 'he beheld the likeness of God' (Num. 12:8)."[90] The Holy Spirit functions in the thought of Judah, as it does for Saadiah as well, as the source of both the auditory and the visual components of prophecy. Indeed, in some passages these two phenomena so converge that the auditory is itself visible and the visual audible: "The Creator shows some of the light of the glory He created to His angels or prophets, and similarly He shows them an image of the speech (*demut dibbur*) on the throne, and this is the *Shekhinah*."[91] It is plausible that reflected here is an echo of an ancient doctrine concerning the visible Logos that is identified as the divine Presence. The hypostasized word or speech is itself the enthroned glory that appears in an anthropomorphic form within the prophetic imagination. This epistemological convergence is particularly relevant in Judah's treatment of the Sinaitic revelation, as will be seen later on in this chapter.

It is of interest to note, moreover, that this characterization of the Holy Spirit as the anthropomorphic word has some kinship with cognate doctrines in Christianity. This remark is especially relevant in light of the fact that Judah specifies that one of the reasons he must expound in detail on matters pertaining to the Holy Spirit is the false interpretation of this notion found among the "wicked nations," by which he undoubtedly means Christians. In other words, the Christians interpret biblical references to the Holy Spirit (e.g., 2 Sam. 23:2) in a literal way, for they do not know how to interpret the figurative language of Scripture.[92] That the reference here is to Christians is evident from another passage, where in the same context Judah adds that the "heretics" of the nations interpret literally what should be taken figuratively, namely, anthropomorphic statements about the Deity or the Holy Spirit, and allegorize what should be taken literally, namely, the commandments.[93] It may be concluded, therefore, that a particular impetus for Judah's account of the Holy Spirit is the polemical stance that he adopts vis-à-vis Christianity. It is thus all the more striking that at some points in his discussion his conception of the anthropomorphic speech strikes the ear as close to descriptions of the hypostatic Logos according to Christian doctrine. Indeed, a stylized version of this may be found in a passage from the *ʿIshrūn Maqāla* ("Twenty Treatises") of David al-Muqammis (ca. 900) cited in Hebrew translation by Judah: "This is the mistake of the Christians who say that God lives according to [the attribute of] life, which is the Holy Spirit, and He lives according to wisdom, which is the Logos (*ma'amar*), which

[90] Ibid., p. 176; see also p. 119.
[91] Ibid., p. 205.
[92] Ibid., p. 75.
[93] Ibid., p. 77.

they call the Son."[94] This text is part of al-Muqammis's rejection of the Christian doctrine of the Trinity on the grounds that it is based on the notion of a multiplicity of attributes within God.[95] It is noteworthy that Judah would cite this text, which bears a similarity to his conception of the Holy Spirit, as being the enthroned image. Judah treated the topic of the Holy Spirit as a truly esoteric tradition that was transmitted only in an oral manner, and hence a *qabbalah* in the true sense of the term. Thus, in response to the question of why the rabbis never spoke of such a critical idea as the Holy Spirit, Judah writes, "The sages did not speak of this explicitly so that people would not come to contemplate what is above. . . . Therefore they would transmit this matter to their students and sages in a whisper and privately, through [oral] tradition (*qabbalah*)."[96]

Judah further distinguishes between the "beginning" of the luminous substance of the glory, referred to scripturally as the divine face, and the "end," identified as the back. No creature has seen the "beginning," but the "end" was seen directly by Moses through a speculum that shines and by all the other prophets indirectly through the speculum that does not shine. "The speech and the visions go forth to the angels and prophets from the end of the great light . . . from the end of the light the prophets see the divine visions and hear the voice go out from the spirit."[97] "Since all the prophets saw the created glory, which is called *Shekhinah*, on the throne of glory, they called it *Shekhinah*, for there the Creator caused His glory to dwell. The prophets saw the splendor of the *Shekhinah* to a degree from the end of the great light."[98] On occasion Judah also follows Saadiah in applying an allegorical approach to explain biblical theophanies, that is, the graphic descriptions of the glory's appearance are meant to be understood parabolically and figuratively. For example, in one instance he states that "most of what is said in the Torah concerning the glory of our God is certainly by means of parables and figurative language (*bi-meshalim we-dimyonot*)."[99] What is most intriguing, however, is Judah's

[94] Ibid., p. 79. Cf. *Dāwūd ibn Marwān Al-Muqammis's Twenty Chapters ('Ishrūn Maqāla)*, ed. and trans. S. Stroumsa (Leiden, 1989), pp. 192–193. The version is significantly different from that which one finds in the Hebrew text incorporated in Judah ben Barzillai: "This is the Christian doctrine of the Trinity, for they render God living with life, which is the Holy Spirit, and knowing with knowledge, which is the Logos, and which is what they call 'the Son'; this is sheer polytheism."

[95] See Vajda, "Le problème du l'unité de Dieu d'après Dawud ibn Marwan al-Muqammis," pp. 62–65.

[96] *Perush Sefer Yeṣirah*, p. 189, previously cited by Scholem, *Kabbalah*, p. 6.

[97] Ibid., p. 18; see also p. 234.

[98] Ibid., p. 204.

[99] Ibid., p. 27. It should be noted that in this passage the word *dimyon* is used synonymously with the word *mashal*, i.e., both connote "parable" or "figurative expression." Hence, in this context the word *dimyon* does not mean a mental image but rather denotes a metaphorical resemblance, i.e., *figura* or *similitudo*. See p. 41 where the term *dimyonot* clearly has the connotation of *typoi* or *figurae*. See references given in n. 102, below. On this usage in other medieval Jewish writers, both Sephardi and Ashkenazi, see A. Funkenstein, "Naḥmanides' Symbolical Reading of History," pp. 137–138, and revised version in idem, *Perceptions of Jewish History*, pp. 109–117;

appropriation of terminology used by those whose docetic orientation stood in marked contrast to Saadiah's realism. In effect, Judah attempts to combine the notion that the object of prophetic visions was a created light with the view that such forms inhere only within the mind. I will cite a key passage wherein the two intellectual currents converge:

> The Creator, blessed be He forever, created a light and a great fire for [His] glory, which is called the Holy Spirit as well as *Shekhinah* . . . no prophet can look at all upon the beginning of that great light. . . . From the end of the light the Creator shows lights and sparks according to His will to His angels, seraphs, and prophets. At times these sparks and lights emerge from the end of the light, whether for the angels or the prophets. There are occasions when they see the light in several images (*dimyonot*), visions, or dreams, or in a visible image (*demut re'iyah*) according to what God wills, as it is written, "and through the prophets I was imaged" (Hosea 12:11). . . . At times when God shows [the glory] He does so in the image of an anthropos [in the form] of fire or of the great light, and under his feet is a fiery and luminous throne. . . . All the prophets knew that all the forms they saw were created from light. . . . When God gives strength to the prophet in his eyes and his heart on account of his abundant sanctity, the Creator allows him to see something of the end of the light or the fire of the splendor of the *Shekhinah*, or some of the sparks that come out from the end of the light.[100]

To Saadiah's discussion Judah has added the key category of images, *dimyonot*. It can be shown that Judah utilizes two senses of the word *dimyon*. On occasion he uses the word *dimyon* as synonymous with *mashal* (allegory or figure of speech),[101] whereas in other contexts it is clear that he distinguishes between *mashal*, as a literary or rhetorical term, and *dimyon*, as an ontological category.[102] These represent, in accord with Saadiah's orientation, two distinct approaches to explaining anthropomorphic expressions used in specifically visionary contexts. Interestingly enough, a similar twofold approach can be found in Rashi's commentary to Hosea 12:11, "and through the prophets I was imaged": "I [God] appeared to them in several images. Another explanation: I will speak to them parabolically by means of allegories to make them comprehensible to those who hear them." By contrast, in several other commentaries on this verse, including those of Joseph Kara, Abraham ibn Ezra,[103] David Kimḥi, and the Karaite exegete Yefet ben Ali, the two terms *dimyonot*

S. Kamin, "'*Dugma*' in Rashi's Commentary," pp. 21–22. See Maimonides, *Introduction to Logic in the Hebrew Version of Moses ibn Tibbon*, p. 4 n. 7; Wolfson, *Crescas' Critique of Aristotle*, p. 400 n. 6. The philological connection between the roots *damah* and *mashal* is biblical in origin; see Isa. 46:5.

[100] *Perush Sefer Yeṣirah*, pp. 31–32.

[101] E.g., ibid., pp. 2, 3, 39, 43, 44, 57, 62, 63, 75, 76, 77, 83, 85, 88, 89, 99, 167, 168, 201, 203.

[102] E.g., ibid., pp. 41, 205.

[103] See U. Simon, ed., *Abraham ibn Ezra's Two Commentaries on the Minor Prophets* (in Hebrew), vol. 1, *Hosea, Joel, Amos* (Ramat-Gan, 1989), p. 119 n. 40. The editor fails to distinguish between ibn Ezra's use of *dimyonot* and the midrashic.

and *meshalim* are used interchangeably to denote figurative, parabolic, or allegorical expression. Judah, like Rashi, preserves something of the connotation of the term *dimyon* (or its equivalent *dimmuy*) in its original aggadic context, namely, a theophanic form in which God appears to the prophet. In Judah's case, however, there is a thread connecting the two usages of the word *dimyon,* for just as an allegory is a figurative expression of something in terms of some other idea or image, so the visual form of the glory is a depiction of this light in terms of something else that is not quite identical to it. In fact, the figure or shape the glory assumes appears exclusively in the mind of the prophet. That the latter usage of the term *dimyon* is based on the terminology of Ḥananel is confirmed by the fact that Judah explicitly cites Ḥananel's commentary on Berakhot.[104]

It is instructive, moreover, that Judah uses the expression "his eyes and his heart" to refer to the prophet's capacity for vision. Indeed, in this simple, passing, relatively insipid remark one can find evidence of Judah's distinctive attempt to combine the realist and docetic positions. The object visually apprehended by the prophet is the created light, the luminous splendor of the *Shekhinah.* Beams or rays of this light apparently hit the eye of the prophet (physically, not in a mental or spiritual sense), yielding the visual perception of the glory that encompasses the immediacy of sense perception. On the other hand, the light of the glory is visualized in terms of certain images that are produced within the heart or mind of the prophet and therefore constitute purely psychic phenomena. From that perspective the object of the visionary experience consists not of something as it is in actuality but only as it appears to be: "The angels and the prophets see in their visions as if they saw the image of the throne and as if an image of the glory were upon it, and as if the ophanim and beasts were carrying it."[105]

Judah thus compares the visualization of the glory to looking on one's image as reflected in a mirror made of iron or glass: just as no external object exists in the surface of a mirror, but merely an image reflected in rays of light, so, too, the forms in which the glory is seen are images within the mind. The analogy is not perfectly symmetrical, however, for in the case of the mirror reflecting an image of a man there is, within the limitations of medieval optics, a direct correspondence between external form and image, whereas in the case of the glory it would seem that there is no such correspondence. That is to say, the glory is an amorphous light that assumes shape only within the mind of the beholder. The experienced form of the glory is a mental construction for which there is no exact objective or spatially extended correlate. It is therefore assigned the status of illusory or faulty perception.

The last point is clarified further by Judah's own formulation of the distinction between Moses and all other prophets. The latter saw in terms of images because they did not have the perceptual or conceptual capabilities of Moses.

104 Cf. *Perush Sefer Yeṣirah,* p. 32.

105 Ibid., p. 189.

> Since they did not have the same capacity in their eyes and hearts as did Moses our master, [the glory] appeared to them from within these images (*mar'ot*), for they see their forms as the form of an anthropos. Sometimes they see them in the form of an elder and sometimes in the form of a youth. All these appearances are for them [mental] images (*dimyonot*) and not a [physical] vision (*re'iyah*). Just as there is no person in the mirror or glass [reflecting someone's image], so there is no form of a person within those lights [that come forth from the created glory]. By means of those great lights that they [the prophets] see there appears to them within these forms a form of an anthropos glorious in power, in the great light and in strength. This comes to them on account of the weakness and feebleness of their eyes and hearts, like a person whose vision is weak so that he sees that which is low as if it were high and that which is one as if it were two. Thus it is written, "and through the prophets I was imaged" (Hosea 12:11), for they are [mental] images and not a [physical] vision. But with respect to Moses, whose mind and heart were refined and whose eyes were brighter than all other people's, the Holy One, blessed be He, showed him His splendor and His glory, which He created for the honor of His name, for it is greater than all the other lights that the prophets saw. [Moses] looked at the end of the splendor of the *Shekhinah,* which is the great created light, and he had the visual capacity to see it with an actual vision (*re'iyah mamash*) and not [through] visions, dreams, or images. Therefore he saw, knew, and discerned that there is no form of an anthropos there, or any other [corporeal] form except the form of the splendor, the light, and the created great fire that is the form of the great light whose beginning no man can see.[106]

The appearance of the glory in the form of an anthropos is thus to be attributed to an inferior mode of prophetic experience. The prophets, whose eyes and hearts were weak, could not actually see the glory, that is, see it as it actually is, in its luminous essence. They could apprehend it only through mental images. Moses, by contrast, was capable of seeing the glory, or, to be more precise, the lower aspect of the glory referred to as the back or end, with an actual vision, that is, he saw the light as it is without its assuming the shape of anything corporeal within his consciousness. "Since the vision of Moses, our master, was refined he did not see images but looked and saw that there was no form there at all except for the forms of the created lights and fires. Therefore he did not speak through images, as it is written, 'With him I speak mouth to mouth, plainly and not in riddles, and he beholds the likeness of the Lord' (Num. 12:8)."[107] By a wonderful reversal of meaning, the "likeness of the Lord" (*temunat YHWH*) that Moses beheld, according to the scriptural record, is no image at all. Moses did not speak through figurative images because he had a direct perception of the created glory. The mark of his superior prophecy consists precisely in the fact that his immediate vision of the glory precluded his seeing any images or forms other than the light itself. Beholding no image is thus the true meaning of the claim that he beheld the "image of the Lord"![108]

[106] Ibid., pp. 34–35.
[107] Ibid., p. 35.
[108] See, however, ibid., p. 176, where the verse is interpreted in a somewhat different way.

All the other prophets saw the light as mediated through the images within their minds. These psychic images, however, are not completely arbitrary or subjectivistic. The images by means of which the glory is made visible are, in part, shaped by traditional assumptions regarding the nature of the glory. They are also conditioned by the particular historical moment in which the prophet has his experience. "In his mercy [God] appears in His glory to the prophets according to the matter and the time in which the prophets, the righteous, and Israel are living."[109] Judah expounds in greater detail upon this feature of the visionary experience:

> The prophets gaze upon the splendor of the *Shekhinah* and know that all the lights and images that appear to them are created. They see within these visions (*mar'ot*) as if they saw forms of a man made from fire and the great light. It appears to them in several images (*dimyonot*), according to the times and the situation in which Israel finds itself. It appeared to Moses from within a thorn bush, for Israel was among the thorns, in a time of great distress. It appeared to Moses and Israel upon the [Red] Sea as a youth engaged in warfare, and in the desert during the giving of the Torah it appeared "like the pavement of sapphire" (Exod. 24:10), that is, in the image of an elder sitting down. Thus it also appeared to Daniel regarding the future redemption in the form of an elder sitting down. . . . The prophets saw these images, for they saw the fires and lights created from the splendor of the *Shekhinah*. From these lights and flames they saw their image, which is the image of the anthropomorphic form of the splendor and the great fire . . . each and every prophet according to his capacity and the capacity of [the people of] Israel who were with him at the time, and in accordance with his period and that of Israel in which they were. All the images of the glory of our Creator [were not seen] with an actual vision (*re'iyah mamash*), as it is written, "and through the prophets I was imaged" (Hosea 12:11). But Moses our master . . . saw with an actual vision the great splendor that is the end of the created *Shekhinah*. He did not see any image (*demut*) of the glory of our Creator within the light, but rather the end of the form of the great light that our Creator created for His glory. Thus it says concerning him, "the glory of the Lord appeared" (Exod. 24:17).[110] [With (Moses) I speak mouth to mouth] "in a vision and not through riddles" (Num. 12:8). If you say that it is also written concerning all the other prophets, "I make Myself known to him in a vision" (ibid., 6), this vision (*mar'eh*) involved knowledge (*yedi'ah*) and not actual sight (*mar'eh mamash*). The Creator showed them created lights for their capacity for knowledge and their vision was not as refined as that of Moses. Images appeared to them from amidst the lights, but not in an actual vision. Moses our master saw the end of the great light, an actual vision of the light and not through images, riddles or [figurative] visions.[111]

It may be concluded, therefore, that Judah combined the view of Saadiah with that of Hai as articulated in the writings of Ḥananel. The glory is a created

[109] Ibid., p. 129; cf. pp. 134–135.

[110] In the biblical context the glory of God appeared as a consuming fire on the mountain before all of Israel and not exclusively to Moses. Judah's exegesis thus ignores the relevant context.

[111] *Perush Sefer Yeṣirah*, p. 39.

light, as Saadiah maintained, but the visible forms that it assumes—including, most importantly, the form of an anthropos—are psychic phenomena or mental constructions, as Ḥananel, following Hai, taught. The combination of these two currents, as I will set out to demonstrate in the succeeding chapters, had a decisive hand in shaping subsequent discussions on the nature of visionary experience in Jewish mystical sources.

Before leaving Judah ben Barzillai it is worthwhile mentioning one other area where he allows for the possibility of a vision of the *Shekhinah*, for this, too, presents important evidence for a mystical conception of vision that informed the later development of both Pietistic and kabbalistic conceptions.[112] I am referring to the vision that is connected specifically to the study of Torah. In earlier rabbinic sources a clear link was established between the study of Torah and the immanent dwelling of the *Shekhinah*. Moreover, several rabbinic passages stress that through study of Torah the supernatural phenomena of the Sinaitic revelation are recreated. By means of exegetical activity, therefore, a sage may receive divine illumination and in some cases may even be transformed into an angelic being.[113]

In these sources, however, there is no indication that Torah-study is a technique for inducing the appearance of the Presence, nor any suggestion that the text of the Torah is somehow viewed as a configuration of the divine light. The rabbinic notion, it seems, is simply that by studying God's word one fulfills the divine will and thus lives in the presence of God. In some midrashic texts, however, it is possible that in a more technical sense the Torah scroll represents the embodiment of the light of the *Shekhinah*, an idea that may have been informed in part by ancient practices that clearly indicate that the Torah shrine in the Synagogue (*'aron ha-qodesh* or *teivah*) parallels the Ark of the Covenant (*'aron ha-berit*): both are the locus of the Presence.[114] For example, in *Shir ha-Shirim Rabbah* 8:13, the point is made in a statement attributed to R. Joshua ben Levi cited by R. Simeon: "In every place that the Holy One, blessed be He, placed His Torah, He placed His *Shekhinah*." An interesting version of this motif is to be found in one of the recensions of the *Tanḥuma* in the statement attributed to R. Simeon bar Yoḥai, who compares the Torah to a king's daughter (one of several very common images used in rabbinic literature to describe the Torah in female terms[115]) set within seven palaces. The king reportedly says, "Whoever enters against my daughter, it is as if he entered against me."

112 See, by contrast, Scholem (*Origins*, p. 201), who concludes that Judah's commentary "does not betray the slightest hint of basic kabbalistic doctrines," or, put differently, his work "lacks all those gnostic symbols of the Shekhinah" characteristic of the *Bahir*.

113 Cf. the Genizah fragment in MS New York–JTSA Mic. 1370, fol. 3a, where it is reported that R. Mattiah ben Ḥeresh (second-century tanna) "was sitting and was occupied in [the study of] Torah, and the splendor of his countenance was [bright] like the sun and moon, and his visage was [radiant] like the ministering angels."

114 See Goodenough, *Jewish Symbols in Greco-Roman Times*, 4:115–116, 130–136; Prigent, *Judaïsme et l'image*, pp. 47–66, esp. 55–59.

115 I have studied the development of this motif in midrashic and kabbalistic sources in detail in "Female Imaging of the Torah."

The meaning of the parable is rendered immediately in the continuation of the text: "The Holy One, blessed be He, says: If a man desecrates My daughter, it is as if he desecrated Me. If a person enters the synagogue and desecrates My Torah, it is as if he rose and desecrated My glory."[116] The possible dependence of this statement on ancient Jewish mystical speculation is suggested by the fact that the Torah is compared parabolically to a princess hidden behind seven *hekhalot* (palaces). More important, a link is made between the Torah and the divine glory, in that the former, hidden within the ark in the Synagogue, is compared to the latter, which is said to be located in the Ark of the Covenant that was kept in the Holy of Holies of the Temple. The parallel between the throne of glory—the dwelling of the Presence, set between the cherubim on the Ark of the Covenant—and the scrolls kept in the Torah shrine is an ancient one in Jewish sources, expressing itself in a particular way in early Jewish mysticism.[117]

It is evident that such sources influenced the formulation of subsequent medieval authorities who explicitly identified Torah with the glory or Presence, a motif that was particularly important in both Pietistic and kabbalistic speculation. One interesting example, which may reflect an early attestation in medieval Jewish sources to the identification of the Presence and the Torah or Wisdom, is found in the following comment of Sherira ben Ḥanina Gaon (ca. 906–1006), elaborating on the statement attributed to R. Isaac in B. Soṭah 11a that applied Exod. 2:4, "And his sister stationed herself at a distance, to learn what would befall him," to the divine Presence:

> Know that the Presence (*shekhinah*) is [found] with the students [of Torah], and a light dwells among them; that light is called Presence (*shekhinah*) . . . and wisdom itself is one of the Presences (*shekhinot*), and thus it is written, "The Lord created me at the beginning of His course, etc." (Prov. 8:22), "I was with Him as a confidant" (ibid., 30). Regarding each verse it says the [name of the] Lord, which is one of the Presences (*shekhinot*), and she is called a sister to the sages, and consequently she is a sister of Moses standing at a distance.[118]

Wisdom is thus identified by Sherira as the Presence, or, to be more precise, one of the Presences (*shekhinot*), a usage that is found as well in one of the responsa of Sherira's son, Hai Gaon. The expression occurs in the context of Hai's discussion of various esoteric works of a magical or mystical nature: "We have heard strong rumors [to the effect] that some people who have been occupied with these [books] immediately perished, and all of this is on account of the holiness of the [divine] name, and the holiness of the Presences (*shekhinot*) and the angels that surround them, and the holiness of the chariot."[119] It follows from Hai's comment that the term *shekhinot* in these Geonic texts denotes a multiplicity of powers in the divine realm, the exact nature of which is not fully

[116] *Midrash Tanḥuma,* Pequde, 4.
[117] See Scholem, *Jewish Gnosticism,* pp. 20 n. 1, 24–25.
[118] *Otzar ha-Geonim,* vol. 11, Tractate Soṭah, p. 235.
[119] *Otzar ha-Geonim,* vol. 4, Tractate Ḥagigah, p. 21.

articulated. Although the further identification of the Presence and the Torah is not stated explicitly by Sherira, it is implied by the fact that wisdom in standard rabbinic thinking is identical with the Torah. The verses cited in the above passage are often applied by the sages to the primordial Torah. It is likely, therefore, that this is the underlying mystical intent of the opening statement, which clearly draws on older sources that state that the light, which is the *Shekhinah,* dwells with those who study the Torah, that is, the light itself is the divine wisdom, which is the Torah in some hypostatic sense.

A further step toward a mystical conception is discernible in Judah's commentary on *Sefer Yeṣirah*. This is particularly evident in Judah's exegesis of the talmudic passage interpreting the verse "In that day there shall be neither sunlight nor cold moonlight" (Zech. 14:6): "What is sunlight and cold moonlight (*'or yeqarot we-qipa'on*)? R. Eleazar said: The light that is heavy (*yaqar*) in this world shall be light (*qafuy*) in the world-to-come."[120] Judah cites two contemporary interpretations of R. Eleazar's explanation. The first, found in Ḥananel's commentary, identifies the light as a reference to the Torah; the second maintains that the light is the *Shekhinah* disclosed to the prophets. From his own vantage point Judah combines the two interpretations: "for the reward of the light of Torah is a vision of the splendor of *Shekhinah*. . . . [t]he one occupied with [the study of] Torah and who meditates upon it merits seeing the light of the *Shekhinah*."[121]

The light of Torah is thus the light of the *Shekhinah* that is manifest in prophetic visions; consequently, those who study Torah are accorded a vision of the splendor of the *Shekhinah*. Judah does not further qualify the nature of the vision accorded those who study Torah, but the expression that he uses, "a vision of the splendor of the Presence" (*re'iyat hod ha-shekhinah*), is the same one he employs to characterize prophetic vision. Interestingly, in another context one of the reasons Judah gives to explain the fact that God manifested his glory to Israel at the time of the Sinaitic revelation in the specific form of fire is that those who study the Torah merit the "light of *Shekhinah*" that is characterized as "fire consuming fire."[122] In another passage Judah equates the angels and the souls of the righteous who sit above and study Torah before the glory with different angelic beings who stand before the throne of glory. Although in that context Judah does emphasize the midrashic tradition regarding the inability of the angels to see the glory or even to know its place, it is significant that involvement with Torah is placed on the same level as standing before the glory—indeed, bearing the divine throne. From still other passages it would seem that for Judah the Torah is identical with the Holy Spirit. This is derived from the standard association of Torah with wisdom, on the one hand, and the further identification of wisdom with the Holy Spirit or the *Shekhinah,* on the other. It follows, moreover, that the vision of the splendor of the Presence is not

[120] B. Pesaḥim 50a.
[121] *Perush Sefer Yeṣirah,* p. 25.
[122] Ibid., p. 135.

simply the reward bestowed upon one who has fulfilled God's will, but flows from the text of the Torah, which is itself constituted by an emanation of this very light. Against this background we can better understand Judah's use of the rabbinic notion that the *Shekhinah* dwells among those who sit and study Torah together. Through study of Torah one merits the light of the *Shekhinah,* for Torah itself is composed of that very same luminous substance.

The most interesting evidence of a mystical conception of Torah is found in Judah's interpretation of the talmudic explanation (B. Giṭṭin 60a) of Zechariah's vision of the flying scroll (*megillah ʿafah*) as a vision of the folded Torah scroll:

> This vision that Zechariah saw was a visual image (*dimyon marʾeh*) and not an actual thing (*mamash*), but it was as if the Holy One, blessed be He, gave him power in his eyes and heart to see the measurement of wisdom, which is the Torah. . . . The Holy One, blessed be He, gave him power to see with his eyes as if he saw with a vision of his eyes and imagined in his heart a scroll 3,200 times greater than the whole world. Thus no human possesses knowledge to conjecture if the Holy One, blessed He, created the place of the Torah above the seven heavens in this measurement. [The Torah scroll] is an entity that is not [materially] real (*beriyyah she-ʾeino mamash*), as is the world, but is instead a form with measurements and dimensions, in the manner that [the glory] was shown to Isaiah. . . . The created world is an actually existing entity and thus [can be seen] with a vision of the eye (*reʾiyat ha-ʿayin*), whereas the vision of the Torah is not [attained] by means of a physical vision but through a vision of the heart (*reʾiyat ha-lev*).[123]

According to Judah's interpretation of the talmudic passage, Zechariah had a contemplative vision of the Torah scroll, which assumed enormous proportions. While no explicit mention is made of the *Shiʿur Qomah,* one is reminded here of precisely that tradition, though it is the Torah and not the Demiurge that is being measured.[124] Moreover, the identification of the Torah and the luminous glory is suggested by the fact that Judah compares Zechariah's vision of the Torah to Isaiah's vision of the glory. This comparison is not meant to suggest merely the fact that the means of vision in both cases are identical, but rather that the object of vision as well is similar in the visions of the two prophets.

123 *Perush Sefer Yeṣirah,* p. 67.

124 On the possible relation of the aggadic tradition concerning the flying scroll of Zechariah's vision to the anthropomorphic depiction of the Torah in ancient Jewish esotericism, see Idel, "Concept of the Torah," p. 43. Particularly relevant is the material of the German Pietists discussed at p. 42 n. 53. To the sources mentioned by Idel one could add *Sefer ha-Roqeaḥ,* p. 109, where Eleazar of Worms refers to the Torah under the throne of glory as the flying scroll. Several scholars have noted that in Qallir's *silluq* for *Sheqalim* the princess (*bat melekh*) is described in terms reminiscent of the *Shiʿur Qomah* measurements. It stands to reason that in this context the image *bat melekh* is employed to refer to the Torah; hence this is an early instance of the application of corporeal dimensions to the Torah. See Idel, p. 40 n. 49; Wolfson, "Female Imaging," p. 279. However, Cohen (*Shiʿur Qomah: Liturgy and Theurgy,* pp. 64–65) argues that the image of the *bat melekh* in Qallir's poem refers to the divine Presence and not the Torah.

The luminous nature of the Torah informs Judah's understanding of the Sinaitic theophany as well. For example, he emphasizes that the Israelites were illuminated by the divine light only after having heard the voice of revelation.[125] Indeed, as a result of this hearing and seeing they attained the status of angels[126] or prophets.[127] The critical point for Judah is that until they heard the voice they could not behold the light of the *Shekhinah:* "When the voice emerged [at Sinai] they were able to look and gaze upon the light that was in the end [of the glory] and the voice went forth. This matter is [alluded to] in the hearing of the voice or in its being seen."[128] There is thus a convergence of the two epistemic modes, the auditory and the visual. Because the populace was not accustomed to seeing the light of the Presence it was necessary for them to attain this vision through hearing the voice. Yet, the voice itself was constituted by this very light. This convergence is brought out most strikingly in the verse "And the people saw the voices" (Exod. 20:15), a *locus classicus* in Jewish sources to affirm the phenomenon of synesthesia as a supreme religious experience.

Mental Vision in Twelfth-Century Jewish Neoplatonism

It is necessary at this juncture to pause and consider the notion of prophecy as intellectual vision developed in mainstream medieval Jewish philosophical texts, for this, too, provides an important element in the reconstruction of the conceptual edifice within which medieval Jewish mysticism evolved. It is particularly in the Neoplatonic tradition that emphasis is placed on an intellectual vision of spiritual or incorporeal forms. For example, in the Pseudo-Empedoclean *Book of Five Substances,* an important medieval forgery that informed subsequent Jewish Neoplatonism, one reads about an "intellectual vision" (*ha-re'ut ha-sikhli*) through which one can know the "spiritual, intelligible forms" (*ṣurot sikhliyyot ruḥaniyyot*) that are the "impressions [or traces] of God" (*rishme ha-shem yitbarakh*) within the "world of the intellect" (*ʿolam ha-sekhel*).[129] These forms are akin to the Plotinian conception of intelligibles within the second hypostasis, Nous, which make up the intelligible world (*kosmos noetos*).

This Neoplatonic conception of a direct intellectual vision of incorporeal forms is utilized by various Jewish authors to explain biblical prophecy. For example, in his commentary on the verse "Then I, justified, will behold Your face; awake, I am filled with [the vision of] Your image" (Ps. 17:15), Abraham ibn Ezra characterizes the prophetic vision as "the knowledge of the work of God, for they are all universals (*kelalim*) made in wisdom and enduring eter-

[125] *Perush Sefer Yeṣirah,* p. 125.
[126] See ibid., p. 48.
[127] See ibid., p. 53.
[128] Ibid., p. 49.
[129] Kaufmann, *Studien über Salomon ibn Gabirol,* pp. 18–19.

nally. I am filled with the pleasure of Your image . . . and this does not occur in a dream but when one is awake. This vision is not a corporeal seeing (*mar'eh ha-ʿayin*) but a contemplative seeing (*mar'eh shiqqul ha-daʿat*), which truly constitutes the visions of God (*mar'ot 'elohim*)."[130] According to this passage, prophecy entails the contemplative vision of God's image, here equated with the divine face mentioned in the verse from Psalms, that amounts to a knowledge of the universals as they are contained within the Intellect, identified elsewhere by ibn Ezra as God's image.[131] This was, in ibn Ezra's view, the content of Mosaic prophecy as well. Thus in his commentary on Exod. 33:21 he states, "This is the sense of 'And you will see My back' (Exod. 33:2), from the perspective that He is the All. His glory fills all and from Him all derives, and all their images are [in the] All. This is the meaning of 'the image of God he has seen' (Num. 12:8)."[132] What Moses beheld was a contemplative vision of the Intellect, the All that derives from God that comprises within itself the universal forms of all things. This Intellect is further characterized in Scripture as the divine back or the divine image. In his commentary to Ps. 139:18, ibn Ezra interprets the process of prophetic illumination, called scripturally the "vision of God" (*mar'eh 'elohim*), in terms of the conjunction of the human soul to the Universal Soul (*be-hidabbeq nishmat ha-'adam ba-neshamah ha-ʿelyonah*) resulting in the vision of "wonderful images" (*temunot nifla'ot*). It is further specified in that context that this vision is contemplative or mental in nature. Similarly, in the Short Commentary on Exod. 23:20, ibn Ezra writes, "When the soul is directed toward the glory, the image of the forms and visions is renewed for it by the word of God."[133] Finally, in many places in his philosophical and poetical writings ibn Ezra—following the standard Hebrew usage of the Andalusian poets, which reflects in turn a technical Arabic idiom that goes back to Greek philosophical sources—speaks of a vision of God or the angels or intelligible forms through the rational faculty called by several names, to wit, the inner eye, the eye of the heart, and the eye of the intellect.[134]

Another important element in the explanation of prophetic vision in medieval Jewish Neoplatonists, including, for example, Isaac Israeli and Solomon ibn Gabirol, somewhat reminiscent of the notion espoused by Ḥananel, involves the claim that the visionary component of prophecy is explained in

[130] Cf. the interpretation of Ps. 17:15 given by the Karaite Aaron ben Elijah, in *ʿEṣ Ḥayyim*, ed. F. Delitzsch, p. 51. In this case beholding the divine image is also explained as an intellectual vision, but one that occurs after the death of the body. Only Moses was capable of attaining this level while his soul was still united with his body, as is attested by the verse "and he beheld the image of God" (Num. 12:8).

[131] See Wolfson, "God, the Demiurge, and the Intellect," pp. 95–101.

[132] *Perush ha-Torah le-Rabbenu 'Avaham 'ibn ʿEzra,* 2:219.

[133] Ibid., p. 306. For a fuller discussion of this text, see Wolfson, "God, the Demiurge, and the Intellect," pp. 107–109. Cf. Tanenbaum, "Beholding the Splendor of the Creator," pp. 335–344.

[134] *Iggeret Ḥay ben Mekitz,* pp. 82–83. See also, e.g., *The Religious Poems of Abraham ibn Ezra,* 1:26 (poem no. 2), 67 (no. 38), 69 (no. 39), 93 (no. 52), 97 (no. 54), 112 (no. 62), 120 (no. 66), 126 (no. 69), 304 (poem no. 163), 480 (no. 243), 515 (no. 258); 2:449 (no. 404); Abraham ibn Ezra, "Ten Poems," p. 84, poem no. 4, n. 4.

terms of the imaginative forms that play an intermediate role between corporeality and spirituality. This notion can be traced to the intermediate role accorded to the imagination between sense perception and reason in classical Neoplatonic sources such as Plotinus and Proclus, ultimately going back to Plato and Aristotle.[135] That is, the forms produced by the imagination impart knowledge of the spiritual entities to the soul in corporeal terms, but the images are not quite corporeal. In Israeli's view, as expressed in the *Kitāb al-Ustuqussāt* ("Book on the Elements"), the mechanics of prophetic vision are as follows: during sleep the spiritual forms (*ṣurot ha-ruḥaniyyot*), which are intermediate between corporeality and spirituality, are impressed upon the *sensus communis,* which is itself intermediate between the corporeal sense of sight and the imagination proper (*fantāsiya*), which is said to reside in the anterior ventricle of the brain. The *sensus communis* then transmits these forms, clarified by the intellect, to the imaginative faculty, which receives them in a more subtle way. "We mentioned that the forms with which intellect clarifies the spiritual forms are intermediate between corporeality and spirituality because they result from the imaginative representations of the corporeal forms, and are more subtle, spiritual, and luminous than the latter, which are found in our waking state and are full of darkness and shells.[136] The imaginative faculty transfers the images to the memory, where they are stored. In a state of wakefulness the person seeks to comprehend the spiritual meaning of these imaginative forms (*dimyonot*) through the cogitative faculty and will thus completely purify the forms of all vestiges of corporeality.[137] From Israeli's description it is evident that the intellect plays a critical role in the production of these imaginative forms; indeed, it seems that the imagination itself serves the rational soul.

A parallel to this notion of "imaginative revelation" may be found in the theory of prophecy advanced by the Muslim philosophers Alfarabi (ca. 873–950) and Avicenna (980–1037), although in their case it is clear that the spiritual forms apprehended by means of the imagination are understood in a more strictly Aristotelian sense as the universal forms that inhere in the Active Intellect. According to Alfarabi, the imaginative faculty has, in addition to the standard functions of retaining impressions of things apprehended by the physical senses and constructing new images on the basis of the sensory impressions, a third function: the figuration of the intelligible forms received from the Active Intellect in terms of perceptual symbols. The symbolic images produced in the imagination in turn impress themselves upon the perceptual faculty and the images are apprehended as sensible realities.[138] Avicenna similarly distin-

[135] See Bundy, "Theory of Imagination," pp. 19–82; Schofield, "Aristotle on the Imagination"; Warren, "Imagination in Plotinus"; Moutsopoulos, *Le problème de l'imaginaire chez Plotin;* idem, *Les structures de l'imaginaire dans la philosophie de Proclus;* Camassa, "Phantasia de Platone ai Neoplatonici"; Évrard, "φαντασια chez Proclus"; Cocking, *Imagination,* pp. 49–68.

[136] *Book on the Elements,* translated in Altmann and Stern, *Isaac Israeli,* p. 136.

[137] Ibid., pp. 135–137.

[138] See Rahman, *Prophecy in Islam,* pp. 36–45; Ur-Rahman, "Al-Farabi and His Theory of Dreams," p. 149. See also Cocking, *Imagination,* pp. 101–140.

guishes between two types of prophecy, imaginative and intellectual. In the case of the latter the universal intelligibles are received directly from the Active Intellect, whereas in the case of the former the prophet receives images from the celestial souls by means of his imaginative faculty.[139] The necessity for prophets of an inferior type to apprehend intelligible forms in sensory images bears a striking resemblance to the interpretation of the lower level of prophecy in Hai and his followers, although, of course, the rabbinic authors avoid the philosophers' technical jargon. Furthermore, the role of imaginative forms according to this understanding of prophecy is similar to the use of the concept of *dimyon* in the Jewish writers, including Judah ben Barzillai, as delineated above.

As is well documented, this view of prophetic vision in terms of the imaginative faculty's capacity to transform intellectual concepts into sense data, especially as formulated by Alfarabi, had a decisive influence on the conception of prophecy articulated by Maimonides.[140] Although Maimonides' views on prophecy had an important impact on developments in the literature of Jewish mystics in the thirteenth century—especially Abraham Abulafia but some theosophic kabbalists as well—a far more important figure in terms of influence on the kabbalists was Judah Halevi who, like Hai Gaon, Nathan of Rome, and Ḥananel, treated not only biblical prophecy but also the mystical experience related in some of the Hekhalot texts in terms of this inner vision.

Imaginary Visualization of the Enthroned Glory

In the remainder of this chapter I will examine some of the main features of Judah Halevi's presentation of prophetic and mystical vision, which, as will be seen more clearly later in this analysis, shared some basic presumptions with the mystical literature of subsequent generations. I will focus on only one aspect of Halevi's treatment of visionary experience, whether prophetic or mystical, which may have its origin in Jewish speculation on the vision of the chariot.[141] This is Halevi's claim that the spiritual forms can assume diverse shapes within the prophetic imagination—also identified by Halevi as the "inner" or "spiritual" eye (to be discussed more fully below)—collectively expressing the tangible or visible manifestation of the divine reality.[142] The spiritual forms are

[139] See Marmura, "Avicenna's Psychological Proof of Prophecy," p. 51.

[140] See his *Guide of the Perplexed* II:38, 41, 46; and see S. Pines's introduction to his translation of *The Guide of the Perplexed* (Chicago, 1963), lxxxix–xc; Breslauer, "Philosophy and Imagination"; Sermoneta, "La fantasia e l'attività fantastica nei testi filosofici della Maimonide." It must be noted that sometimes Maimonides reflects the Saadianic view of the created light as the object of prophetic visions. See *Guide* I:11, 25, 46, 64. Concerning Maimonides' attempt to preserve the objectivity of prophecy even in light of the central role played by the imaginative faculty, see Leaman, "Maimonides, Imagination, and the Objectivity of Prophecy."

[141] On Halevi's indebtedness to ancient Jewish mystical doctrines related to Merkavah mysticism, see Idel, "The World of Angels in Human Form," pp. 15–19.

[142] Cf. *Kuzari* I:99, IV:3, V:14. I have utilized the following editions of Halevi's philosophical dialogue: *Kitāb al-Radd wa-'l-Dalīl fī 'l-Dīn al-Dhalīl,* ed. D. H. Baneth and H. Ben-Shammai (Jerusalem, 1977); *Sefer ha-Kuzari,* trans. Yehuda ibn Tibbon (Warsaw, 1880); *Sefer ha-Kuzari,* trans. Y. Even-Shmu'el (Tel-Aviv, 1972).

thus configured symbolically within the prophet's imagination. Halevi informs us, moreover, that the most perfect of forms apprehended by the prophetic vision is that of the king or judge sitting on the throne of judgment. In his lengthy discourse on *Sefer Yeṣirah* in *Kuzari* IV:25 Halevi comments that the statement "the heart in the soul is like a king at war, the [constellation] Draco in the universe is like a king upon his throne, and the wheel in time is like a king in the country"[143] refers to three symbolic depictions of the *amr ilāhi* (*ha-ʿinyan ha-ʾelohi*), the divine matter, Draco symbolizing the intelligible world, the wheel the extended sphere of the sun, and the heart the realm of animate beings. The figurative expressions thus represent the providential role of the *amr ilāhi* in each of the three realms of being: the intelligible, the celestial, and the terrestrial. What is most important to this discussion is the fact that for Halevi the cosmological role of the *amr ilāhi* in the highest realm, that of the Intellects, is symbolized by the image of the king on the throne—the same image that serves as the highest form within the prophetic imagination. This point is reiterated in slightly different terms in one of Halevi's poems:

In His tent He set His Presence,
and placed visions for the prophets to look upon His image;
there is no form[144] and no plan, no limit to His understanding,
but only His visions in the eyes of the prophets, like an exalted and elevated king.[145]

The divine inherently has no form or image; within the eye of the prophet, which, as will be seen momentarily, should be identified as the imaginative faculty, the Presence can be envisioned in the form of an exalted king.

Here we would do well to consider more carefully Halevi's notion of prophetic vision and the specific role of imagination, for through such a consideration we can better appreciate Halevi's indebtedness to the Merkavah traditions, especially as they were interpreted in Geonic literature. Halevi rejects the standard medieval philosophic interpretation of prophecy as a state produced by the Active Intellect operating on the human intellect and imagination.[146] Thus in *Kuzari* I:87 Halevi writes that according to Jewish belief, "prophecy did not (as philosophers assume) burst forth in a pure soul, become united with the Active Intellect (also termed Holy Spirit or Gabriel), and be then in-

[143] *Sefer Yeṣirah* 6:2. See M. Schlüter, "Deraqôn und Götzendienst," *Judentum und Umwelt* 4 (Frankfurt am Main, 1982), pp. 130–142.

[144] Cf. *Dīwān des Abu-l-Hasān Jehuda ha-Levi* 3:5.

[145] Ibid., 231:

באהלו שת שכינתו
ושם מראות לנבואות להביט אל תמונתו
ואין תבנית ואין תכנית ואין קץ לתבונתו
רק מראיו בעין נביאיו כמלך רם מתנשא

[146] See Davidson, "Active Intellect in the Cuzari," pp. 366–367. For the intellectual background to this view of prophecy, see also Rahman, *Prophecy in Islam*, pp. 30–91.

spired."[147] Moreover, continues Halevi, Jews do not believe that "Moses had seen a vision in sleep, or that someone had spoken with him between sleeping and waking , so that he heard the words only in fancy [i.e., the imagination], but not with his ears, that he saw a phantom, and afterwards pretended that God had spoken with him." The implication of Halevi's rejection of the standard philosophic view is that from the Jewish perspective, as he presents it, the object of prophecy is a real objective entity, albeit spiritual in nature, that is apprehended by the individual.[148] The content of prophecy does not result from the prophet's intellectual conjunction with the Active Intellect as mediated through his imaginative faculty; it is, rather, an objectively verifiable datum,[149] although the means of verification may exceed the bounds of the normal processes of sense or intellection. For Halevi, that is, prophecy is more than a mere psychological state; it entails the same presumption of veridicality as normal sense experience, but in the case of prophecy the objective correlate of the vision is a spiritual form that, in the prophetic state, becomes tangible. Indeed, for Halevi, the fundamental paradox of prophetic revelation, that which the believing Jew cannot explain but must accept, is predicated on the fact that in the moment of prophecy the spiritual, incorporeal intention of God becomes tangible in both a visible and audible form known scripturally as the God of Israel.[150] Thus, in an elaborate discourse on the various divine names and the nature of prophetic revelation, Halevi notes, inter alia, that the verse "And under His feet there was the likeness of a pavement of sapphire" (Exod. 24:10) alludes to the fact that the nobles of Israel "perceived a spiritual form" (*al-ṣūrah al-rūḥāniyyah*) that is called "the God of Israel."[151] In the continuation of the same passage we are told that this "divine form" appears to human imagination in the most noble image, namely, that of a human being.

The means of ascertaining this form are decidedly mental or spiritual, that is, the prophet hears and sees in a way quite distinct from the physical senses. Halevi also contrasts prophetic vision with the process of rational insight or discursive reasoning. Thus in *Kuzari* V:14 Halevi states that the comprehension of matters pertaining to prophecy eludes the philosophers, for their faculty of reasoning is too limited. Only select individuals under the proper conditions possess the soul capable of "forming an image for themselves from the world in its totality, and they know God and His angels." The emphasis for Halevi is on the formation of an image by means of which one can attain knowledge of the divine realm. In IV:3 Halevi asserts that the prophets have an "inner eye"

[147] See, by contrast, *Kuzari* V:12, where Halevi presents a more straightforward philosophic account of prophetic illumination arising from the conjunction of the human intellect with the Universal Intellect. In that passage the philosopher of Halevi's exposition represents the opinion of Avicenna; see Pines, "Shiʿite Terms and Conceptions in Judah Halevi's *Kuzari*," p. 211.

[148] See Davidson, "Active Intellect in the Cuzari," pp. 389–390; Sirat, *Théories*, pp. 86–87.

[149] Rahman, in *Prophecy in Islam*, p. 38, draws a distinction between the views on prophecy of al-Farabi and Avicenna on the basis that the former, unlike the latter, tried to maintain the objective correlate for the psychological state of prophecy.

[150] See *Kuzari* I:89.

[151] *Kuzari* IV:3.

(*al-ʿayn al-bāṭinah*) or "spiritual eye" (*al-ʿayn al-rūḥāniyyah*) through which they see the spiritual forms. He goes on to identify this "inner eye" as the "internal sense" (*al-ḥus al-bāṭin*), which in turn may be identified with the imaginative faculty (*al-mutakhāyyilāh*)[152] through which the prophet apprehends the spiritual or incorporeal form. With respect to the relationship of this imagination to reason, Halevi appears to equivocate somewhat. On the one hand, he seems to allot a secondary role to reason, for he states that reason brings proofs for that which the spiritual eye has already seen, presumably in a direct, intuitive way, a view found elsewhere in Halevi.[153] On the other hand, he follows philosophic convention when he states explicitly in this very passage that the inner eye, the imaginative faculty, sees the spiritual forms only when "it is subject to the rational faculty," thereby implying that the imagination is secondary.

It is likely, as scholars have pointed out, that Halevi's conception of the inner eye is based on precedents in Islamic philosophy.[154] Moreover, his identification of the faculty that apprehends incorporeal spiritual forms as the imagination is reminiscent of Alfarabi's doctrine of prophecy taken over with some modification by Avicenna, as discussed above. The key difference between the views of Alfarabi and Avicenna, on one hand, and that of Halevi, on the other, is that the latter eliminates the role of the Active Intellect in bestowing these intelligibles on the imagination. For Halevi the prophet looks directly into the spiritual forms that are experienced in corporeal terms within the imagination. When a particular individual has met all the necessary religious and moralistic requirements for prophecy and is situated in the proper geographical place—the land of Israel—then "these [spiritual] forms are revealed to him, and they appear to him eye to eye, 'plainly and not in riddles' (Num. 12:8)."[155] In the context of IV:3, and in marked contrast to some other sections of the *Kuzari*,[156] the function that Halevi attributes to the imaginative faculty is apprehension of that which is incorporeal. A similar function is given in III:5, where Halevi describes one of the stages of the pietistic life as the exercise of the imaginative faculty to conjure images of certain major events and/or items

[152] For a historical survey of the relevant terminology, see Wolfson, *Studies*, 1:250–314.

[153] Cf. *Kuzari* I:15, II:48; Silman, *Thinker and Seer*, pp. 161–163.

[154] See Ivry, "The Philosophical and Religious Arguments in Rabbi Yehuda Halevy's Thought," p. 28. On possible Sufi connections, see Davidson, "Active Intellect in the Cuzari," p. 367 n. 4. See also Kaufmann, *Geschichte der Attributenlehre in der jüdischen Religionsphilosophie von Saadia bis Maimuni*, p. 166.

[155] *Kuzari* IV:3.

[156] In *Kuzari* V:12 Halevi, consciously portraying the philosophical view, depicts the "common sense" as the faculty that stores images of sensible objects after they have disappeared, whereas the "imaginative faculty" is described as "the faculty that combines all the images united in the common sense, and that separates them and adds changes to them without removing at all the images of the common sense." Farther on in the same section of the *Kuzari* Halevi notes that the highest function of the rational soul is such that the spiritual forms or intelligibles replace the images the vital soul had formed by means of the imaginative faculty. For the philosophical background of this passage, see Wolfson, *Studies* 1:286.

stored in the memory, such as the attempted sacrifice of Isaac, the Sinaitic theophany, the Tabernacle of Moses, the sacrificial cult, and the indwelling of the Presence in the Temple, in order to represent figuratively the divine matter. According to this passage, the symbolization of the divine matter in concrete images occurs within the imagination, but those images are supplied to the imaginative faculty by the memory, which retains select received traditions. In IV:3 Halevi expresses the matter in somewhat different terms, asserting that the relation of the inner sense to the incorporeal entity is parallel to the relationship between the outer sense and the sensible (physical) object. To be sure, Halevi emphasizes that in gazing on these spiritual forms with the inner eye the prophet sees forms appropriate to his nature and in accord with what he is accustomed to. Consequently, when the prophet describes the visionary experience he uses corporeal attributes, such as the image of God as the king or judge sitting on the throne. The image is appropriate from the perspective of the seer but inappropriate from the perspective of that which is seen: the spiritual form is not in its essence an enthroned king, but only appears as such in the mind of the prophet. Nevertheless, the experience is not purely subjective, for there is a correlation between the spiritual form and the mental image as constituted within the imaginative consciousness of the prophet. To take another example from a different domain, which sheds light on Halevi's conception of prophetic vision, in I:99 Halevi employs the midrashic motif that God showed Moses on Mount Sinai the prototype of the Tabernacle and all its parts. According to Halevi this means that God showed the forms to Moses "in a spiritual manner and he made them physically." Similarly, continues Halevi, David had a spiritual vision of the First Temple and Ezekiel of the last. This spiritual vision is contrasted sharply with the natural capacities of estimation, syllogism, and ratiocination. The critical point is that spiritual vision—the act of imagination—has an object that is outside the mind, an object that is incorporeal. Halevi clearly rejects as philosophically untenable the notion that God is a body; however, he puts forth a sophisticated phenomenology of religious experience predicated on the appropriation of anthropomorphic images (I:89, II:6). Halevi recognizes that religious ritual, especially sacrifices and prayer, demand some iconic representation of God located in sacred space (I:97, II:26). It is the imaginative faculty that fulfills this critical role of allowing that which is spiritual to be materialized in space. The Temple and Synagogue assume a talismanic function for Halevi in providing receptacles to draw down the divine matter, but in the absence of human imagination that spiritual force would not be visibly apprehended.

While the Islamic influence on Halevi's notion of prophetic imagination is clear enough, I would like to suggest another possible source that has been less readily acknowledged, namely, the theory of prophecy and mystical vision of Hai Gaon as transmitted by Ḥananel ben Ḥushiel and Nathan ben Yeḥiel of Rome.[157] In this context it is important to note that David Kaufmann has

[157] The possibility that Halevi's notion of prophecy as mental vision was influenced by Ḥananel's commentary on Berakhot 7a was noted by Even-Shmu'el in his translation of the *Kuzari*, p. 364.

suggested that Halevi's views regarding the distinctiveness of the Jewish people vis-à-vis the other nations, in terms of their immediate knowledge of God based on revelatory experience and the historical truth of prophecy, should be compared to similar ideas expressed by Nissim ben Jacob of Kairouan (ca. 960–1062).[158] Nissim singles out the prophets of Israel and the Jewish people collectively (specifically at the Sinaitic theophany) as possessing certain knowledge of God through direct experience, whereas the other nations acquire this knowledge only indirectly, through rational proofs and syllogistic reasoning.[159] The knowledge of God, which is unique to the Jews, is referred to periodically in the extant Hebrew translation of *Megillat Setarim* ("Book of Secrets") as *yediʿat ha-harggashot,* "sentient knowledge."[160] For Nissim, prophecy entails the immediacy of sense experience and this alone constitutes necessary knowledge that is absolute and irrefutable. To be sure, R. Nissim certainly denies that God possesses a body. What, then, is the object of the prophetic experience that is described as knowledge through the senses? In line with his Geonic predecessors, R. Nissim offers two possible explanations for passages that relate a visionary experience of the divine: either they are to be taken metaphorically or the object of the prophetic experience is in fact an angel, which is a form created by God.[161]

It is evident that Halevi has much in common with the views espoused by Nissim. Yet in at least one fundamental respect Halevi's description of the prophetic-mystical vision is closer to the position adopted by Hai, Ḥananel, and Nathan. That is, for Halevi, as for these writers, the locus of the vision is the imagination, a point not developed by Nissim. It thus seems to me that Halevi's position represents a kind of synthesis, or merging, of the respective views of Hai (and those who elaborated on his doctrine, especially Ḥananel) and Nissim: in the former, emphasis is placed on the heart as the spiritual organ of vision, while in the latter, the sensuous character of prophecy is underscored as the distinctive feature of the Jewish people. Inasmuch as Kaufmann has already duly noted the importance of Nissim for understanding Halevi's

[158] See Kaufmann, *Attributenlehre,* pp. 167–168 n. 121; S. Abramson, "Sefer Megillat Setarim," in *R. Nissim Gaon Libelli Quinque* (Jerusalem, 1965), p. 334.

[159] S. Poznanski, "Extracts from the Book Megillat Setarim of Rabbi Nissim ben Jacob of Kairouan," *Ha-Ṣofeh le-Ḥokhmat Yisraʾel* 5 (1921): 177–180 (in Hebrew). See also the fragment published by Abramson in "Sefer Megillat Setarim," pp. 344–345.

[160] Abramson, in "Sefer Megillat Setarim," p. 344, renders *yediʿat ha-harggashot* as a priori knowledge. This rendering is totally unsatisfactory, as it misses the very point of R. Nissim's claim, i.e., that a priori knowledge is prior to or independent of experience, and for R. Nissim the superiority of prophecy consists precisely in the fact that it is firsthand knowledge of an empirical, indeed sensuous, nature. See Kaufmann, *Attributenlehre,* p. 167 n. 121, where he accurately refers to R. Nissim's notion as "sinnlichen Wahrnehmung." It is noteworthy that in a German Pietistic text, perhaps composed by Eleazar of Worms, a very similar expression is employed. Cf. MS Oxford-Bodleian 2575, fol. 1b: "Even the glory they did not see with a vision of the eye but through comprehension of the heart. Although He showed them the glory in a vision of their hearts, He informed them with a sentient knowledge (*yediʿat hergesh*) of the potency of knowledge (*koaḥ ha-daʿat*) that is in every place." See above, n. 30.

[161] Poznanski, "Extracts," pp. 184–187.

doctrine of prophecy, I will concentrate on the impact Hai's interpretation of the chariot vision may have had on Halevi.

As I have shown, according to Hai's viewpoint prophetic and mystical vision alike are mental, a "seeing of the heart" (*re'iyat ha-lev*). While there is no definitive proof that these sources influenced Halevi directly, the common elements at least make the suggestion plausible. In suggesting that the Geonic interpretation of the Merkavah texts is a possible source for Halevi's notion of internal vision or the imaginative seeing of the heart (the crucial term employed by Halevi in his poems, as will be seen in detail below), I do not want to overlook the likelihood that he may also have been influenced directly by Islamic, especially Sufi, sources.[162] Similar theories explaining manifestations of the divine as inner illuminations of the heart can be found in both Muʿtazilite literature and Islamic mysticism.[163] Moreover, one should not ignore the possibility that figures such as Hai and Ḥananel were themselves influenced by Islamic thought in their interpretations of the Merkavah tracts.[164] Indeed, the role accorded the heart in the passages from Hai and Hananel is similar to the function of the heart (*qalb*) in Sufism as the seat of spiritual gnosis (*maʿrifa*) and internal vision (*baṣīra*). The Hebrew idiom Ḥananel (following a biblical precedent) uses in explicating the view of Hai Gaon, *re'iyat ha-lev,* which renders in turn the talmudic *'ovanta' de-libba'*, exactly parallels the commonplace Sufi term *ru'yat al-qalb,* which likewise connotes understanding of the heart. There is evidence as well that the motif of the heavenly journey (*miʿrāj*), attributed in the first instance to Muhammad (perhaps stemming from the influence of Jewish apocalyptic or mystical sources)[165] and secondarily to other adepts, was interpreted

162 See references to Kaufmann and Davidson given above, n. 154, and see below, nn. 168 and 177. The possible influence on Halevi of Islamic mysticism, especially Ismaʿīlīsm, has been suggested by several authors. See Kaufmann, *Attributenlehre,* pp. 166, 177 n. 135, 202 n. 180, 220–221 n. 205, 232 n. 221; I. Goldziher, "Le *Amr ilahi* (*ha-ʿinyan ha-'elohi*) chez Juda Halévi"; Pines, "La longue recension de la Théologie d'Aristotle dans ses rapports avec la doctrine ismaélienne"; idem, "Shiʿite Terms"; Efros, *Studies in Medieval Jewish Philosophy,* pp. 141–154. It would be of particular interest to compare Halevi's notion of the heart, or inner eye, as the locus of the imaginative form of the divine glory—the most perfect shape being that of an anthropos—with the role of theophanic imagination and the creativity of the heart in the thought of Muḥyī d-Dīn ibn al-ʿArabī. For a detailed analysis of this thinker, see Corbin, *Creative Imagination in the Sūfism of Ibn ʿArabī,* pp. 216–245.

163 See Altmann, *Studies,* p. 145, and references given to other scholarly literature in nn. 26–27.

164 The possibility that Hai's spiritualistic understanding of the vision of the chariot was influenced by Sufi mysticism (and particularly related to the function of the heart as the seat of mystical gnosis) was suggested by Jellinek in *Beitrage zur Geschichte der Kabbala,* pt. 2, pp. 15–16 n. 22. See also Bloch, "Die *Yorde Merkavah,*" pp. 69–72. And see Fenton's more recent "La 'Tête Entre Les Genoux.'" For the more general view that Hekhalot mysticism, dated to the latter part of the Geonic period, was derived from Islamic sources, see Graetz, "Die mystische Literatur in der gaonischen Epoche." On the relationship between members of the Geonic academy in Iraq and Muslim Pietists, see also the evidence adduced by Ariel, "'The Eastern Dawn of Wisdom,'" pp. 155–156.

165 Attributed on the basis of the traditional account of the nocturnal journey (*isrā'*) in Qur'ān 17:1; see also 53:4–18. See Horovitz, "Muhammeds Himmelfahrt." See also Newby, *A History of*

by Sufis not simply as a physical ascent from the sublunar world to the celestial throne but as a spiritual descent into the recesses of the inner self, the seven heavens corresponding to the *maqāmāt,* the stages of the Sufi path.[166] Thus, on a deeper level the vision of the throne is an internal image, which parallels the psychologistic or spiritualistic interpretation of Hai, who spoke of the mystic gazing into the chambers of his heart.

Even if we bracket for a moment the possible influence of Sufism on the Geonic interpretation of the Hekhalot praxis, the likelihood that Sufism had an impact on Halevi's notion of the heart as the organ of spiritual vision—the term used on occasion in the *Kuzari* (cf. II:24, 54)[167] and frequently in his poetry which parallels the inner or spiritual eye mentioned in the former[168]—should not be underestimated. It is important here to recall as well that the expression "eye of the heart" (*ʿein ha-lev*) is a commonplace in Andalusian Hebrew poetry of the Golden Period (tenth to twelfth centuries).[169] It is necessary to view Halevi, like any thinker or writer, in his proper historical, cultural, and literary context. Accordingly, we may say with confidence that Halevi adopted this terminology from his predecessors and peers. Yet I would argue that Halevi's particular use of these expressions is to be distinguished from what is found in the other sources.[170]

---

the Jews of Arabia from Ancient Times to Their Eclipse under Islam, pp. 62–63. For possible later reflections of Merkavah traditions in Islamic sources, see Halperin, *Faces of the Chariot,* pp. 467–490.

[166] See El-Azma, "Some Notes on the Impact of the Story of the Miʿirāj on Sufi Literature"; Sells, "Bewildered Tongue." For other sources see Altmann, *Studies,* pp. 42–44, and references to scholarly literature in nn. 11–18.

[167] It may be suggested that this understanding of the heart underlies Halevi's famous analogy comparing Israel to the heart of the nations; cf. *Kuzari* II:36. As Halevi repeats over and over again, only Israel have the divine matter that allows them to transcend the human species and become angelic or spiritual. This is significant, for it would indicate that Halevi placed the visionary capacity at the center of Judaism, perhaps echoing the older etymological connection between Israel and "the one who sees God."

[168] See Kaufmann, *Attributenlehre,* p. 202 n. 180; idem, "Jehuda Halewi," in *Gesammelte Schriften* 2:114–117 (Hebrew translation in idem, *Studies in Hebrew Literature of the Middle Ages,* pp. 177–179); Schirmann, *Hebrew Poetry in Spain and Provence,* 1:516–517, poem no. 222, n. 3; Ḥazan, *The Poetics of the Sephardi Piyyuṭ According to the Liturgical Poetry of Yehuda Halevi,* pp. 210–211. On the possible Sufi influence on Halevi's poetry, see Kaufmann, "Jehuda Halewi," p. 114 n. 4 (Hebrew translation, p. 177 n. 52).

[169] See Saadiah's poem in *Siddur R. Saadja Gaon,* p. 48, discussed by Mirsky, *From Duties of the Heart to Songs of the Heart,* p. 62; Eleazar ha-Bavli, *Dīwān,* p. 86; Samuel ha-Nagid, in Schirmann, *Hebrew Poetry* 1:113 (poem no. 32); *Liturgical Poetry of Solomon ibn Gabirol* 2:333 (poem no. 102), 462 (no. 135), 465 (no. 140), 516 (no. 176), 593 (no. 230); Isaac ibn Ghayyat, in Schirmann, 1:304 (poem no. 114); Moses ibn Ezra, *Shire ha-Ḥol,* 1:23 (poem no. 17), 59 (no. 60), 66 (no. 74), 86 (no. 85), 207 (no. 207), 134 (no. 131). See also the poems of Moses ibn Ezra in Schirmann, 1:412 (no. 169), 414 (no. 170); Zerachiah ha-Levi, *Shirat ha-Ma'or,* ed. I. Meisels (Jerusalem, 1984), p. 15.

[170] See, by contrast, Razhabi, in "Borrowed Elements in the Poems of Yehudah Halevi from Arabic Poetry and Philosophy," p. 173, who treats Halevi's notion of internal vision performed by the heart's eye in terms of Arabic philosophical precedents (and Sufi texts influenced thereby) without noting what I consider to be the key difference.

For the poets who embraced the general philosophical orientation of the Hispano-Arabic culture of their time the heart's eye is the means to attain an intellectual seeing of God or other immaterial entities (such as the angels and the rational soul). That is to say, in the Islamic-Jewish Neoplatonic tradition the vision of the heart is an intellectual intuition of that which is incorporeal and thus invisible in a physical sense. The eye of the heart (*'ein ha-lev*) is synonymous with the eye of the intellect (*'ein ha-sekhel*). A classic example of this is to be found in a passage from the *Rasā'il* of the Ikhwān as-Ṣafā', a tenth-century Neoplatonic text (possibly deriving from Ismā'īlī circles[171]) that had a wide influence on Muslim and Jewish writers in Arabic-speaking lands. According to one relevant passage, the believers, the sages, and the prophets are said to separate from the physical word and contemplate the spiritual world with the "eye of their hearts and the light of their intellects."[172] In a similar vein, the eleventh-century Jewish pietist Baḥya ben Joseph ibn Paquda speaks of the possibility of seeing God with the eye of the intellect. He thus implores the reader to strive to be illuminated by the "light of wisdom" so that he may see the truth of matters by a vision of the heart.[173] The standard viewpoint is also reflected by Maimonides in the *Mishneh Torah:* "The forms that are incorporeal are not seen by the eye, rather they are known through the eye of the heart, just as we know the Lord of everything without vision of the eye."[174] The "eye of the heart" is thus a figurative expression for the intellect, by means of which one acquires knowledge (either discursively or intuitively) of that which is without body.[175]

It is precisely such a conception that underlies the usage of this term in Andalusian Hebrew poetry. This does not, however, accurately reflect Halevi's usage, for the vision of the heart of which he speaks is not intellectual but imaginative, and the object that is seen is not the Neoplatonic form (or Aristotelian universal) but rather a spiritual entity that is constituted within the imagination (i.e., seen by the inner eye) as a tangible, almost sensuous, shape. Halevi, in contrast even to his Muslim predecessor Abū Ḥāmid al-Ghazzālī (1058–1111), to whom his thought has often been compared,[176] sharply con-

[171] For a review of the scholarly discussion, see Nasr, *An Introduction to Islamic Cosmological Doctrines*, pp. 25–40.

[172] *Rasā'il* (Cairo, 1928), 4:141 (cited by Razhabi, "Borrowed Elements," p. 173).

[173] *Sefer Torat Ḥovot ha-Levavot*, ed. J. Kafiḥ, pp. 347–348, 354.

[174] *Yesode ha-Torah* 4:7 (also mentioned by Razhabi).

[175] See Maimonides, *Guide of the Perplexed* I:4. From still other medieval sources it is evident that "heart" refers to the rational soul or the intellect, a usage related to, but divergent from, both biblical and rabbinic sources that treat the heart as the seat of thought and emotions. (The same connotations are implied in the Arabic *lubb*.) Of the many examples that could be cited I will mention one of the more striking ones, viz., Baḥya ibn Paquda's *Kitāb al-Hidāya ilā Farā'id al-Qulūb*, ed. J. Kafiḥ. The identification of the heart and the intellect is evident from the introduction (p. 14), where Bahya describes knowledge (*'ilm*) as the "life of their hearts and light of their intellects." Concerning this statement and parallels in other Arabic texts, see Rosenthal, *Knowledge Triumphant*, p. 321. See also the poem written by Baḥya in Schirmann, *Hebrew Poetry* 1:348, 351 (poem no. 139).

[176] See Kaufmann, *Attributenlehre*, pp. 119–140; idem, "Jehuda Halewi," pp. 123–124

trasts the function of the heart with that of the intellect.[177] The former, and not the latter, is the faculty that allows one to have direct gnosis of God and the world of spiritual realities. It seems likely to me that Halevi's identification of the heart or the inner eye as the imagination may indeed reflect the Geonic tradition recorded in the rabbinic materials discussed above. Specifically, the interpretation of prophetic experience and its application to Merkavah mysticism that is found in Halevi has its precedent in the view espoused by Hai and those who elaborated his doctrine. These sources, therefore, must be seen as an important channel for Halevi, perhaps supplying him with the basis to appropriate and transpose the Sufi notions that parallel the ideas found in the Jewish texts. Scholars have tended to focus on the external influence without giving sufficient attention to the internal sources that may have allowed for the assimilation, appropriation, and transposition of foreign materials or concepts.[178]

For Halevi, as well for his Geonic predecessors, the mystical vision of the chariot approximates the prophetic experience and both involve mental vision through images, which is depicted further as a seeing by means of the light of the glory of the Holy Spirit. For example, in *Kuzari* III:65 Halevi identifies the tanna R. Ishmael ben Elisha the High Priest as the one who is mentioned in the *Hekhalot, Hakkarat Panim,* and *Maʿaseh Merkavah*. "He knew all these secrets to the point that he merited a grade proximate to prophecy." That Halevi interpreted the visionary experience of the throne-world of ancient Jewish mysticism as phenomenologically equivalent to prophetic vision is evident as well from his description of R. Aqiva as one "who approached the level of prophecy until he had contact with [literally, made use of] the world of the spiritual entities, as it says, 'Four entered Pardes . . . one entered in peace and exited in peace.' Who was it? R. Aqiva."[179] Pines suggests that this passage must be understood against the background of the term *pneumata,* derived from Greek magical-

(Hebrew translation, pp. 184–185); Baneth, "Rabbi Judah Halevi and al-Ghazzālī"; Guttmann, "Religion and Knowledge in Medieval Thought and the Modern Period," pp. 21–23.

[177] See Baneth, "Rabbi Judah Halevi and al-Ghazzālī," p. 316 n. 4, where he points out that for al-Ghazzālī the heart is identified as the intellect or a power within the intellect; see also pp. 323–324 (English trans., pp. 193–195). Indeed, according to al-Ghazzālī, soul (*nafs*), spirit (*rūḥ*), intellect (*ʿaql*), and heart (*qalb*) denote different states (*aḥwāl*) of one spiritual entity (*al-laṭifāh al-rūḥāniyyah*); see Sherif, *Ghazali's Theory of Virtue,* p. 25. By contrast, Guttmann, in "Religion and Knowledge," p. 21, asserts that Halevi, like al-Ghazzālī, distinguishes between the heart, as the seat of religious knowledge, and the intellect. Cf. *Kuzari* II:26, where Halevi speaks of the heart as the locus of the external and internal senses. In IV:3 Halevi speaks of the intellect as being in the heart or the brain, but only in a metaphorical sense, inasmuch as the intellect cannot be found in physical place.

[178] The question of the transposition or transmutation of one cultural-literary form into another is especially acute with respect to Halevi's poetic composition, as it is for the Andalusian Hebrew poets in general. A typical account of this process is found in Razhabi, "Borrowed Elements," p. 165, with this description of the Jewish poet in Spain during the Golden Age: "In his soul there was no barrier between the Jewish culture and the secular culture, and at times there escaped from his pen, whether intentionally or not, foreign ideas and words." However, many of the examples Razhabi gives, especially in the case of Halevi, show that the ideas borrowed from Arabic texts resonated with ideas found in the traditional Jewish literature.

[179] *Kuzari* III:65.

theurgical texts of Late Antiquity, which was rendered in Arabic philosophic sources as *al-rūḥāniyyat.*[180] While this etymology may be correct, in this specific context it is important to emphasize what Pines fails to note, that here the world of spiritual entities, *ʿolam ha-ruḥaniyyim,* is identified with the aggadic Pardes, which is understood by Halevi as the celestial throne-world. That is to say, therefore, that in this case, at least, the spiritual entities comprise the objects known from this throne-world: the glory, the attendant angels, the chariot, and the throne. To be sure, the philosophical interpretation of this older motif is evident in the continuation of this very passage, where Halevi describes the fate of another rabbi who entered Pardes, Elisha ben Abuyah, as degrading the commandments "after contemplating the [separate] intellects."

In yet another passage in the *Kuzari* (II:4), where the merging of ancient Jewish theosophy and contemporary philosophic terminology is evident as well, Halevi notes that the "spiritual forms" (*al-ṣur al-rūḥāniyyah*) are called the "glory of the Lord" (*kevod YHWH*) and, metaphorically, simply the Lord (*YHWH*).[181] In that same context we are told that the glory (*kavod*) refers to "spiritual forms" that "are formed from the subtle spiritual substance (*al-jism al-laṭīf al-ruḥāni*) called the Holy Spirit (*ruaḥ ha-qodesh*)." The spiritual forms thus constitute the divine glory that derives from the Holy Spirit in a way reminiscent of Saadiah's notion of the theophanic forms deriving from the "second air," which he identifies as the Holy Spirit.[182] Finally, in another passage (IV:3), Halevi notes that biblical anthropomorphisms and theophanies, such as Exod. 24:10 and Num. 12:8, as well as *Maʿaseh Merkavah* and even *Shiʿur Qomah,* must be understood in light of the doctrine of *kavod* or *Shekhinah.*[183] That is, that which Scripture refers to as the God of Israel or the "image of God" is identical with the visible glory described in the Hekhalot text as well as the measurable Demiurge of the *Shiʿur Qomah* tradition. It may be concluded, therefore, that Halevi considered the mystical vision as belonging to the same phenomenological field as prophecy, even though the two are distinguishable in terms of degree.

"My Heart Has Seen": Poetic Dwelling and Prophecy

Support for the claim that the Geonic interpretation of prophetic and mystical vision had a decisive influence on Halevi may be gathered especially from his

[180] Pines, "On the Term *Ruḥaniyyot* and Its Origin and on Judah Halevi's Doctrine," p. 525.

[181] This is also reflected in the view of Abraham ibn Ezra that the upper world is "entirely the glory." See his Standard Commentary on Exod. 3:15, in *Perushe ha-Torah;* cf. Halevi's formulation in *Dīwān* 3:69 (poem no. 36): "the exalted ones are filled with the *kavod.*" The use of the term "glory" as a generic name for this immaterial angelic realm also underlies ibn Ezra's statement that "every glory is conjoined to God," i.e., every incorporeal angel, by virtue of its incorporeality, cleaves to the divine essence. Cf. ibn Ezra's Short Commentary on Exod. 33:32.

[182] Wolfson, *Studies* 2:93.

[183] In this regard, too, Halevi's view contrasts with that of Saadiah, who, according to one text that has been preserved in Judah ben Barzillai's *Perush Sefer Yeṣirah,* pp. 20–21, maintained that the object of the *Shiʿur Qomah* text was an aspect of the glory higher than the *Shekhinah* or the created glory that was apprehensible to human beings. Concerning this critical distinction in Saadiah, see Dan, *Esoteric Theology,* pp. 109–111; idem, "Kavod Nistar," pp. 73–76.

religious poetry, in which he often states that the seeing of the glory is performed by the heart or the heart's eye, which I take to be another way of describing the imagination. The first example is drawn from his poem *Yeʿiruni be-shimkha raʿayonai.* In Halevi's poetry the word *raʿayon* is often used synonymously with *dimyon* and therefore should be translated in such instances as "mental image" or "vision" rather than "rational thought" or "concept."[184] Moreover, the use of the metaphor of the heart's awakening to depict the prophetic vision is attested in the *Kuzari* as well. For example, in II:24 Halevi offers the following interpretation of the verse "I was asleep, but my heart was wakeful" (Cant. 5:2): "He [Solomon] designates the exile by the term 'sleep'[185] and the continuance of prophecy among them by the wakefulness of the heart."[186] Halevi's exegesis of the expression "my heart was wakeful" turns on the identification of the heart as the locus of prophetic vision. In the aforementioned poem, then, the images of the divine name that Halevi has in mind arouse him to further visions attained in a dream state:

My heart has seen You[187]
and believes in You
as if I had stood at Sinai;
I have sought You in my visions,[188]
Your glory passed over me,[189]
descending upon the clouds.[190]

[184] See Ḥazan, *Poetics of the Sephardi Piyyuṭ,* p. 210. Scheindlin, in *The Gazelle,* p. 165, renders *raʿayonai* in this poem as "meditations," by which he means intellectual meditations (see p. 168). Halevi may have been influenced by the conjunction of the words *raʿayon* and *lev* in Eccles. 2:22 and Dan. 2:30. Cf. *Dīwān* 4:235 (poem no. 124): את נתיבי רעיון אכונן. See also 3:164 (no. 89): בלבי ורעיוני; 182 (no. 99): יעירוני רעיוני וסוד לבי ומשאלו. Similar forms of expressions are used by other Andalusian Hebrew poets; see, e.g., Isaac ibn Ghayyat, in Schirmann, *Hebrew Poetry* 1:320 (poem no. 124), where רעיוני לבבה parallels חזיוני כתבה; 324 (no. 127): חדלו רעיוני parallels נסתמו חזיוני. See also Moses ibn Ezra, in Schirmann, 1:412 (no. 169): יעירוני שעפי לחזותך / ויראוני בעין לב נוראותיך. It is important to note in this context that in medieval Hebrew philosophical terminology the word *raʿayon* is generally used to translate the Arabic *khatir,* which can denote either the compositive animal imagination (sometimes rendered as *takhayyul*) or the faculty of estimation or cogitation (*wahm*). See Wolfson, *Studies* 1:286–287. See, however, Samuel ibn Tibbon's translation of Maimonides' *Guide* I:46, where *raʿayon* is identified as *dimyon,* i.e., imagination. See Wolfson, p. 255 n. 27; idem, *Philo,* 2:289 n. 39. See also the usage of the word *raʿayon* in Eleazar of Worms, *Ḥokhmat ha-Nefesh,* chap. 3, p. 15.

[185] This part of Halevi's interpretation reflects standard rabbinic exegesis on the verse. Cf. Targum on Cant. 5:2; *Shir ha-Shirim Rabbah* 5:2.

[186] Cf. *Dīwān,* 3:67 (poem no. 34):

ישן ולבו ער / בוער ומשתער /
צא נא והנער / ולכה באור פני

[187] Cf. Eccles. 1:16.

[188] Cf. Ps. 119:10.

[189] Cf. Exod. 34:5–6.

[190] *Dīwān* 3:65 (poem no. 32):

It is significant that here the poet's spiritual vision of God, attained in a dream, is likened to the prophetic theophany of the glory at Sinai; indeed, the poem is technically a *reshut* for the prayer of *barekhu* on the holiday of Pentecost, which celebrates, according to rabbinic interpretation, the Sinaitic revelation. The ultimate purpose of the visionary arousal—that is, the stirring of the heart to conjure an image of the divine—is to enable one to bless the name of the glory.[191] As the poem itself ends,

> My thoughts have awakened me from my bed,
> to bless Your glorious name, O Lord.[192]

Similarly, in another *reshut* written for *barekhu,* the poet boldly declares of God,

> He has an image that the eye does not see,[193]
> yet the soul in the heart discerns Him and gazes upon Him.[194]

In this case, too, the seeing of God is placed in a liturgical context: one visualizes the divine image so that one may bless it, and thus the poem concludes "Come and praise the Lord, and bless Him."[195] Other examples could be adduced to show that for Halevi the poetic experience—much like his remark concerning R. Ishmael's knowledge of Merkavah secrets and R. Aqiva's contemplation of Pardes—approximates the prophetic state.[196] This accords well

---

ולבי ראך ויאמן בך
כאלו מעמד היה בסיני
דרשתיך בחזיוני ועבר
כבודך בי וירד בענני

[191] The intrinsic connection between the inner vision and the act of praising God can be found in other Hispano-Jewish poets of the Golden Age. See, e.g., *Liturgical Poetry of Solomon ibn Gabirol* 2:464 (poem no. 138):

הגיג לבי בהביטי בקרבי
בכל עת ברכי נפשי אדוני

[192]

הקימוני שעפי מיצועי / לברך שם כבודך אדני

[193] Cf. Isa. 64:3.

[194] *Dīwān* 4:194 (poem no. 91):

כן לו דמות עין לא ראתה בלתי
נפש בלב תכיר אתו ותצפהו

It should be noted that in other poems Halevi states flatly that God has no image or form. In this regard Halevi followed conventional medieval philosophy, especially the views of Baḥya ibn Paquda. See Mirsky, *From Duties of the Heart,* pp. 50–51.

[195] בואי והודי את אדני וברכהו.

[196] See Komem's comprehensive study "Between Poetry and Prophecy." While the author documents fully the mystical tendencies of Halevi's poetry, specifically in terms of visionary experience, he does not mention early Merkavah sources. It should be noted that for Halevi the fulfillment of the traditional commandments is also a means—indeed, the only legitimate means—for the people of Israel to attain an angelic state, which is likened to prophecy. The key difference is that in the

with the testimony of other Spanish poets that their poetic inspiration was akin to prophecy.[197] Thus, for instance, Solomon ibn Gabirol records in several poems dreams he had that he considered a form of prophetic revelation, for through them he heard the divine voice and received a particular mission or disclosure of secrets.[198] And Abraham ibn Ezra, in one of his poems, boldly states,

> Hither and thither my eyes have seen wonders,
> and my ears have also heard prophetic visions.[199]

Perhaps even more telling is the statement in a poem of Judah ben Solomon al-Ḥarizi (1170–1235) describing the "generation of splendid poets who were called the band of prophets, / and among them was R. Judah Halevi."[200] This appears to be sound evidence that the poets (including Halevi) identified themselves as a distinct group within the larger society and defined their cultural vocation precisely in terms of the prophetic heritage. Thus, in the continuation of this text al-Ḥarizi writes that the poems seemed

> as if they were taken from the cherubim,
> or stolen from the language of the prophets:
> "and the spirit rested upon them—they were among those recorded,"[201]
> they prophesied and did not increase. . . .
> Mouth to mouth the prophecy spoke in them,

---

discussion of normative practice the visionary element is not central. Cf. *Kuzari* I:79, 98; II:34, 48; V:20; Silman, *Thinker and Seer,* p. 182. Other forms of pietistic behavior, especially song and dance, are likewise upheld by Halevi as means for cleaving to the divine matter; see *Kuzari* II:50. With respect to these forms Halevi may have been influenced by Sufi sources, which likewise emphasized dance as a means to induce mystical ecstasy. See Meier, "Der Derwischtanz"; Molé, "La dance exstatique en Islam"; Schimmel, *Mystical Dimensions of Islam,* pp. 179–186. On the other hand, Halevi could have drawn from earlier Jewish sources, as the use of dance in religious worship is attested in pre-Islamic Jewish texts, including the Bible. For discussion of the relevant sources, see Caquot, "Les danses sacrées en Israel et a l'entour."

[197] See Pagis, "The Poet as Prophet in Medieval Hebrew Literature," esp. p. 142.

[198] See Katz, *Openwork, Intaglios, and Filigrees,* pp. 38–41, 248–252.

[199] *Religious Poems of Abraham ibn Ezra* 1:139 (poem no. 75):

כי כה וכה פלאים ראו עיני
גם מחזות נביאים שמעו אזני

[200] Schirmann, *Hebrew Poetry* 2:137 (poem no. 312): דור המשוררים הנפלאים הקרואים חבל נביאים / אשר היה מהם הלוי רבי יהודה. I thank Prof. Menahem Schmelzer, who first pointed out this passage to me. In other passages al-Ḥarizi describes the poets in language appropriate to the prophets. See, e.g., 2:111 (poem no. 309), describing Isaac ibn Ghayyat: כי שירו צלחה עליו רוח נבואות; 114 (no. 309), describing the compositions of Halevi: כאלו היא מכוכבי רום גזולה / או מרוח הקדש אצולה; 136 (no. 312), describing the effects of the poems of Isaac ben Ḥisdai ibn Shaprut: ואז נפקחו במלאכת השיר העינים / ונפתחו השמים / ונראו מראות אלהים; 138 (no. 312), describing the situation after the death of the Spanish poets of the Golden Age, Solomon ibn Gabirol, Abraham ibn Ezra, Judah Halevi, and Moses ibn Ezra: נסתם חזון השיר ומוצאו / ונסתלק הכבוד ההוא ומוראו ולא יסף עוד מלאך יי להראה.

[201] Num. 11:26.

through poetic vision,
"plainly[202] and not in riddles."[203]

In the particular case of Halevi, a common denominator of the prophetic, mystical, and poetic consciousness is the notion of the glory as a spiritual form that assumes tangible shape within the imagination, the *visio spiritualis,* the seeing of the heart (*re'iyat ha-lev*), as these passages from his poems indicate:

The Creator, who brought forth everything
  from nothing,
is revealed to the heart but not to the eye.[204]

Unable to see His light with their eyes, their hearts
searched[205] and they saw the light of His glory.
  They were frightened.[206]

Man has no superiority over the beast,[207]
but that he may see their glorious Rock,
a vision of the heart and not of the eye.[208]

Even more poignantly, in another poem Halevi comments,

[202] Ibid., 12:8.

[203] Schirmann, *Hebrew Poetry* 2:137–138 (poem no. 312):

כאילו הם לקוחים מפי כרובים
או מלשון חוזים גנובים
ותנח עליהם הרוח והמה בכתובים
ויתנבאו ולא יספו
ופה אל פה נבואה דברה בם
בחזיון שיר במראה לא בחידות

[204] Ibid., 189 (poem no. 87):

יוצר המציא כל מאין
נגלה ללבב לא לעין

Mirsky, in *From Duties of the Heart,* asserts that this poem of Halevi reflects a passage in Baḥya ibn Paquda. Mirsky does not, however, take into account that for Halevi the word "heart" carries a different connotation than it does for Baḥya, i.e., for Halevi the term "heart" designates the imaginative faculty and not the intellect. See p. 57, where Mirsky interprets the use of the word "heart" (*lev*) in another one of Halevi's poems in the same way, as referring to the intellect (*sekhel*). In that context as well, however, the seeing of the heart of which Halevi speaks is an imaginative rather than an intellectual vision.

[205] Cf. Ps. 77:7.

[206] *Dīwān* 3:4 (poem no. 2):

ונלאו ראות אורו בעינם וחפשו
לבבם וראו אור כבודו ונבהלו

[207] Eccles. 3:19.

[208] *Dīwān* 3:204 (poem no. 113):

ומותר האדם   מן   בהמה אין
רק לראות צור כבודם   ראות לב לא ראות עין

To behold Him the eye fails,
but from my flesh[209] He is revealed to my heart.[210]

From these examples and others,[211] it may be concluded that in Halevi's poems the "eye of the heart" assumes the role of the "inner eye" described in the *Kuzari;* the vision of God located in the heart amounts to that which is conjured in the poet's imagination. Indeed, in the poem that begins *'Ahavim heʿelu be-lev lehavim,* Halevi mentions the "tablets of my heart" (*luḥot levavi*),[212] which are compared to the "tablets [of the Pact] inscribed on the one side and on the other" (cf. Exod. 32:15).[213] The point of the poem, alluded to in the biblical phrase that serves as its prelude, *mi-besari 'eḥezeh 'eloha* (Job 19:26), is to emphasize the extent to which the locus of one's knowledge and vision of God is centered in one's own physical and spiritual being. Thus Halevi maintains that one can "see" God from one's spirit, which is created from the spirit of God's mouth; from one's limbs, which are formed by God's hands; and from the tablets of the heart, which are likened to the tablets of the Pact, *luḥot ha-ʿedut,* inscribed on both sides. In still another poem, *Ya'atu lekha tushbaḥot,*[214] Halevi compares the hearts of those who worship God (*levav ʿovdekha*) to the tablets (*luḥot*) on which are carved the inerasable divine laws. In that context the heart that bears the imprint of the divine below is also

[209] A play on Job 19:26.

[210] *Dīwān* 3:6 (poem no. 5):

לחזותו עין כלה
ומבשרי ללבי נגלה

[211] Cf. ibid., 3:159 (poem no. 86): ובעין לב שרתיך; 3:272 (no. 144): מי כמוך יחיד הנסתר מאישון / הנגלה בלב; 288 (no. 145), reproduced in Wolfson, "Merkavah Traditions in Philosophical Garb," pp. 202–203; 4:201 (no. 97) cited in Wolfson, p. 229; 4:209 (no. 101): מה נפלא והוא נגלה / בעין הלב ומחשבותיו.

[212] This expression is based on a biblical idiom; see Jer. 17:1; Prov. 3:3, 7:3.

[213] *Dīwān* 2:272 (poem no. 51). On the symbolic correspondence of the Ark and the heart, see *Kuzari* II:28. On the comparison of the heart to the Ark, in which are hidden the tablets of the Pact, see *De Beatitudine capita duo R. Mosi ben Maimon Adscripta,* p. 2. It is possible that with respect to the image of the "tablets of the heart" Halevi was also influenced by a Sufi conception, as found, for example, in the *Iḥyā' ʿulūm ad-dīn* of al-Ghazzālī, wherein the heart is said to reflect the truths contained in the Well-Guarded Tablet (*al-lawḥ al-maḥfūz*), mentioned in the Qu'rān (75:22) and identified in the mystical literature with the Active Intellect or the Universal Soul. See Baneth, "Rabbi Judah Halevi and al-Ghazzālī," p. 325 n. 2.

[214] *Dīwān* 3:67–68 (poem no. 35):

ועלי לבב עובדיך
לוחות ושם עדיך
כי באצבעות ידיך
חקות אשר לא נמחות   חקקות על הלוחות

דרך נפשות קרבה
לדרך בכס מרכבה
כי ברוחך הטובה
על מי מנחות מונחות   וסביביו מנחות

compared to the throne that bears the glory above:[215] just as God dwells in the heart of the faithful, the faithful dwell alongside the throne of glory.[216]

One may assume that for Halevi the heart, equated with the tablets, is the divine essence, the *ʿinyan ha-ʾelohi,* that is embedded in the Jewish soul. This heart, moreover, is the inner eye or the imagination, on which are written the images—as the commandments are inscribed on the tablets—through which one sees God or the divine form in a concrete, tangible shape. This imaging of the formless God is the ultimate goal—and challenge—of the poetic dwelling.[217] To express the matter differently, for Halevi the imaginative visualization of God is a manner of expressing the sense of being filled with the immediacy of the divine Presence, the *ʿinyan ha-ʾelohi,* in one's heart. Thus in one of his poems, the *baqashah* (supplication) that begins with the words *ʾAvarekh ʾet YHWH ʾasher yeʿasani,* Halevi compares the "fear and trembling" of the process of poetic composition to various biblical accounts of visionary encounters with God, the glory, or an angel. Indeed, in the same poem Halevi implores the divine,

> Place my portion with Your unblemished saints. . . .
> Let me delight in the splendor of Your Presence,
> "Awake, I am filled with [the vision] of Your image" (Ps. 17:15).[218]

In this context we see a clear connection between the pious individual (*ḥasid*) and visionary experience of the image (*temunah*) of God, also referred to as the splendor of the Presence. This resonates well with the view expressed by Halevi in *Kuzari* V:12 to the effect that the pious is one level below the prophet.[219]

[215] On the correlation of the heart and the throne, and the possible Sufi influence, see discussion below. The association of the tablets and the throne in Halevi may also be derived from the aggadic tradition that the tablets were hewn from the sapphire stone of the throne or from a quarry beneath the throne. For references see Ginzberg, *Legends* 6:49–50 n. 258, 59 nn. 305–306. On the throne as the ontic source of the soul, and the heart as a sign of testimony of the divine, see *Religious Poems of Abraham ibn Ezra* 1:114 (poem no. 63): לכן יקר לבי לך אות מכסאך שרשי. One finds the correlation of the throne and the heart in Abraham Abulafia as well; see, e.g., the text quoted by Idel in *Language, Torah, and Hermeneutics in Abraham Abulafia,* p. 169 n. 80.

[216] See Fleischer, "Reflections on the Religious Poetry of Rabbi Yehudah Halevi," pp. 179–180.

[217] Cf. *Dīwān* 4:258 (poem no. 134): בלב רגז לראותך ונפשי לראותך חרדה; 263 (no. 135): עיני הדרך נכספה לראות / אך זאת כמוני בלי יאות. Cf. 2:306 (no. 89). See also the poem attributed to Halevi, though with a measure of reservation, in Schirmann, *New Hebrew Poems from the Genizah,* p. 251: יקר עצמך נעלה מראות . . . ואם על מרומים שכינתך—בחדרי לבבות תמונתך. Here, too, the divine image is said to be lodged in the chambers of the heart, i.e., the imagination. Compare this formulation to the language of Hai from Nathan of Rome's talmudic lexicon, cited above at n. 78.

[218] *Dīwān* 4:155 (poem no. 62):

ותן חלקי עם חסידיך התמימים . . . ותעדנני
בזיו שכינתך—ואשבעה בהקיץ תמונתך

[219] Cf. *Kuzari* III:103, where one is said to come close to the degree of prophecy through the doing of good deeds, sanctification, purification, and being close to the prophets. Halevi's association of pious behavior and the attainment of a degree that approximates prophecy had an impact

One of the essential images that informs this mental vision, as I have already indicated several times, is that of the enthroned glory. The point is evident from the poem *Mi-yadekha hayeta le-libbi:*

> One day I sought if the Lord was present,[220]
> for He transcends my physical sight;
> returning to my heart and my thoughts[221]
> I found Your throne as a witness, hidden within my recesses.[222]

In the above stanza God's throne, which ultimately is the locus of the numinous presence of the deity, is interiorized as an image within the poet's heart or imagination. It is possible that in this case Halevi may have been influenced by the correlation or identification of the heart (*qalb*) and throne (*ʿarsh*) common in Sufi literature.[223] From the continuation of the poem, however, it is evident that Halevi draws on another motif, found as well in other medieval Jewish poets who were also influenced by Islamic Neoplatonism,[224] concerning the identification of the throne as the ontic source of all souls.[225] Thus Halevi writes, "This is Your throne, the quarry of the soul" (*hu' kis'akha maḥaṣav neshamah*). Insofar as the throne is the "quarry of the soul," in Halevi's language, it follows that the soul is the locus for the imaging of that throne. The form of the throne is the objectivized self-image of the heart projected outward.[226]

In one of his most elaborate and personal accounts of the poetic experience, Halevi describes the state of ecstatic rapture in terms that deliberately echo the experience of the Merkavah mystic:

---

on the Jewish Sufism of Abraham Maimonides and his circle. See Fenton, *The Treatise of the Pool Al-Maqāla al-Ḥawḍiyya by ʿObadyāh Maimonides,* pp. 8–9, 58 n. 42; idem, *Deux traités de mystique juive,* pp. 75 n. 158, 77 n. 163.

220 Cf. Exod. 17:7.

221 Cf. Eccles. 2:22.

222 *Dīwān* 4:186 (poem no. 84):

יום בו אחפש היש אדני
כי נעלה מראות בעיני
שבתי ללבי ורעיוני
ואמצאה כסאך לעד בי טמון בחובי

223 See, e.g., Böwering, *The Mystical Vision of Existence in Classical Islam,* pp. 163–164, 191–193, 239, 253; Ibn ʿAṭāʾ Allāh, *Traité sur le nom Allāh,* ed., trans. Maurice Gloton (Paris, 1981), pp. 196–197; Nicholson, *Studies in Islamic Mysticism,* p. 114, citing a passage from Al-Jili (1365–1406).

224 See, e.g., *Liturgical Poetry of Solomon ibn Gabirol* 1:52; *Religious Poems of Abraham ibn Ezra* 1:114 (poem no. 63). See also the poem of Isaac ibn Ghayyat in Schirmann, *Hebrew Poetry* 1:304 (poem no. 114): חקרתיך—והנה בון זממי / בעין לב אמצאה אותך ואראה! קשורת כסאך נפש נפחתה.

225 Cf. *Dīwān* 3:257 (poem no. 138): ברכי [נפשי] אצולה מרוח הקדש; 4:188 (no. 86): דרשה נשמה דבק בכסאך / כי דמתה אל כרוב ומלאך. (On the association of the intellect and the cherub, on one hand, and the imagination and an angel, on the other, see Maimonides, *Guide of the Perplexed* II:6, interpreting *Qohelet Rabbah* 10:20.)

226 My formulation here is based on Corbin, *Creative Imagination,* p. 224.

> Bless the Lord, O my soul,[227] and join with the angels. . . . Give her passage[228] among the angels— in the dwelling of His servants and in the station of His angels, the servants of His kingdom, the messengers of His angelhood, and those who do His work. . . . Gaze upon the Rock from which you have been hewn.[229] . . . Lift your eyes and turn your face to the pure candelabrum[230] that is before the Lord, by whose light you will be illuminated. . . . And the Lord will shine His countenance upon you[231] and spread His wings over you.[232] . . . Then you will behold the resplendent light[233] that darkness cannot dim.[234]

In this passage the basic themes of the mystical experience described in the Hekhalot are all appropriated by Halevi (sometimes expressed through biblical idioms) in order to describe his own experience in the moment of ecstasy induced by poetic composition. He joins—indeed, becomes one with—the angels, utters hymns before God, and ultimately has a vision of the divine form, characterized as the resplendent light of the divine countenance. While much of the language here paraphrases scriptural texts, the frame that holds together the discrete parts seems to me to be the mystical experience known from the extant Merkavah compositions. From all the textual evidence that I have adduced, therefore, it may be concluded that the language and motifs of ancient Jewish mysticism were utilized by Halevi and set in his own Andalusian cultural milieu. Most important, the description of the visionary experience of the mystic is considered, phenomenologically speaking, on a par with prophecy and poetic inspiration. In all three cases the inner vision consists of an imaging of an incorporeal light in corporeal forms within the imagination. In great measure this provides the necessary phenonemological framework by which to understand visionary experience in medieval Jewish mysticism.

Prophetic Vision and the Apprehension of the Name

Let me conclude this chapter with a discussion of another motif in Halevi that has great affinity with an idea expressed in Jewish esoteric sources, namely, the conception of prophecy as the apprehension of the divine name. As I discussed in the previous chapter, the names of God occupy a central place in the world of

227 Ps. 103:1, and elsewhere.
228 Cf. Zech. 3:7.
229 Cf. Isa. 51:1. Cf. *Dīwān* 4:263 (poem no. 138): את צור לבבי את מקור חיי.
230 Cf. Exod. 31:8, 39:37; Lev. 24:4.
231 Cf. Num. 6:25.
232 Cf. Ezek. 16:8.
233 Cf. Job 37:21.
234 *Dīwān* 4:145 (poem no. 62):

ברכי נפשי את אדני והתחברי עם מלאכיו . . . ותני לך מהלכים—בין המלאכים—
במושב עבדיו ובמעמד משרתיו משרתי מלכותו—ושלוחי מלאכותו
ועושי מלאכתו . . . הביטי אל צור אשר ממנו חצבת . . . שאי עיניך—והסבי פניך—
אל המנרה הטהרה אשר לפני אדני אשר ממאורה תאירי . . . ויאר אדני פניו אליך—
ויפרש כנפיו עליך . . . אז תראי האור הבהיר אשר חשך לא ישופהו

ancient Jewish speculation on the chariot. Indeed, in some of the Hekhalot macroforms the *nomina barbara* assume both theosophical and magical-theurgical significance; that is to say, on the one hand, the names are said to reveal the nature of the divine essence, but, on the other, they serve as the principal means for the heavenly ascent to the throne as well as being an essential part of the hymns uttered by the angels and the mystic before the glory. These two functions cannot be separated, for the effectiveness of the names as magical-theurgical means is linked to the operative belief that the names indicate something of the divine (or angelic) essence. Insofar as the name of God reflects the essence of God—epitomized, for example, in the famous statement "He is His name and His name is He"[235]—it follows that the knowledge of God granted to the mystic in his ascent to the throne and vision of the glory will consist of knowledge of the names. The "seeing of the King in his beauty" is, in effect, a mystical vision of the letters that make up the divine names. Although Halevi does not discuss the actual Merkavah texts that espouse such a conception of the glory, it seems to me that his understanding of prophecy as the comprehension of the divine name is connected to this Jewish mystical tradition. Indeed, as will be seen farther on, Halevi on occasion employs precise terminology from the Hekhalot texts to characterize his conception of the name as a luminous substance. For Halevi the name is identical with the divine glory, which is characterized as light. These associations are standard themes in Jewish mystical literature that were expressed in both kabbalistic and Pietistic literature of the High Middle Ages. In the different currents of medieval Jewish mysticism the identification of the name and the glory served as the fundamental epistemic basis for the visionary experience of the divine.

Before proceeding to a discussion of the mystical conception of the name in Halevi, it must be noted that evidence for the cultivation of such an idea is found in the writings of other medieval Jewish Neoplatonists. In this context I will briefly mention four examples. In the poetry of Solomon ibn Gabirol the name is identified as the power of the Creator manifest in being through the divine will.[236] In Pseudo-Baḥya's *Kitāb Maʿānī al-Nafs* it is stated that the first of the entities that emanates from the One is called by the Greeks Active Intellect and by the Torah "glory," *Shekhinah*, and "the name."[237] According to Abraham bar Ḥiyya, the highest grade of prophecy, transcending the hearing of a voice and the vision of a form, is the explication of the divine name (*perush ha-shem*). Thus, reflecting on the verses "God spoke to Moses and said to him: I am the Lord. I appeared to Abraham, Isaac, and Jacob as El Shaddai, but I did not make myself known to them by the name YHWH" (Exod. 6:2–3), bar Ḥiyya writes, "This attests that the Holy One, blessed be He, informed Moses,

[235] *Synopse*, §§ 588. See Scholem, *On the Kabbalah*, p. 44.

[236] See Parnes, "The Mentioning of the Name in the Poetry of Solomon ibn Gabirol"; Levin, *Mystical Trends in the Poetry of Solomon ibn Gabirol*, pp. 80–91. On the influence of Merkavah mysticism on ibn Gabirol, see also Bargebuhr, *Salomo Ibn Gabirol*, pp. 74–76, 523–524, 565–567, 614; Liebes, "Rabbi Solomon Ibn Gabirol's Use of the *Sefer Yeṣirah*."

[237] Sirat, *A History of Jewish Philosophy in the Middle Ages*, p. 84.

our master, about the secret of the explicit name (*sod ha-shem ha-meforash*), which He did not disclose to the Patriarchs."[238] Even closer to Halevi's formulation is Abraham ibn Ezra, who speaks of the souls being conjoined to the angelic realm, that is, the separate Intellects, where they cleave to the glorious name, *shem ha-nikhbad* (the Tetragrammaton).[239] From these examples, and others that could have been cited, it is evident that Halevi's utilization of the ancient speculation concerning the name within a Neoplatonic context is not an isolated phenomenon but rather represents a discernible pattern in medieval Jewish Neoplatonism.

In *Kuzari* IV:15 Halevi writes that in the moment of prophecy, when the prophet achieves a state of being separated from his bodily existence by "cleaving to the angelic species," he is cloaked in the Holy Spirit (*ruaḥ ha-qodesh,* elsewhere described as *al-jism al-laṭīf al-ruḥāni,* the subtle spiritual substance) and by means of a prophetic vision apprehends the Tetragrammaton. The latter, Halevi notes, "is the specific and definite name, which instructs about the relation between God and His most perfect creatures on the face of the earth, namely, the prophets, whose souls are pure, and they receive the light that penetrates them like the light of sun in a crystal. . . . The explicit name instructs about the light that penetrates, and [it] attests that the light of God cleaves to men and penetrates them. . . . The matter of the Tetragrammaton cannot be comprehended by logic, and of it there is no proof except through prophetic vision." The prophet, cloaked in the light of the *ruaḥ ha-qodesh,* apprehends the divine name, which is a light that cleaves to the soul. This gnosis of the name, Halevi tells the reader in *Kuzari* IV:3, can be attained only through "the evidence of prophecy and internal vision."[240] Underlying Halevi's remarks is a decidedly mystical notion of the divine name that has its roots in the Merkavah texts, even though he has clearly borrowed technical Arabic terms from Islamic philosophy and mysticism to express these ideas. Accordingly, one can find in Halevi a correlation between the Tetragrammaton, on the one hand, and the luminous substance of the *kavod,* on the other.

This correlation is especially apparent in several of Halevi's poems. For example, in the poem *'Ish 'elohim gever,* a retelling of the Sinaitic revelation in alphabetic acrostic, Halevi discusses the second commandment, "You shall not take the name in vain," as follows: "Do not take in vain that which is hidden from His holy ones [i.e., the angels]. . . . [t]he splendor of the glory of His name called upon the multitude . . . kindling flames of fire."[241] Halevi has characterized the name as a luminous substance by substituting the name for the voice of God that is described as kindling flames of fire in Ps. 29:7. Specifically, there is a connection made between *hod* and *yaqar,* terms designating the luminosity of the glory, and the name. In another poem, *Barekhi nafshi 'et*

[238] *Megillat ha-Megalleh,* p. 43.

[239] See Wolfson, "God, the Demiurge, and the Intellect," pp. 101–106.

[240] Cf. *Kuzari* II:54.

[241] *Dīwān* 3:100 (poem no. 49): לא תשא לשוא גנוז לקדשיו . . . הוד יקר השם הנקרא על המוני . . . חצב להבות אש.

'adonai, the mystical conception of the name as a luminous Presence is evident as well:[242]

Bless the name—everlasting splendor,[243]
awesome and terrible.[244]

At the conclusion of that poem Halevi equates the divine name (*shem*), kingship (*malkhut*), and glory (*kavod*), all of which are identified as the light of God's countenance:[245] "Your name, Your kingship, and Your glory, O Lord, Lift up the light of Your countenance upon us."[246] In the *Kuzari* as well, the terms *kavod* and *malkhut* (or *mal'akhut*) both designate the visible form seen by prophets, the divine Presence (*Shekhinah*).[247] On occasion Halevi describes his own state of ecstatic inspiration in terms appropriate to the state of prophecy, as for example in the poem *Yodeʿe yegoni:*

His name is in me
like fire in my kidneys,[248]
bound to my heart,[249]
shut up in my bones.[250]

In this poem Halevi obviously draws on the prophet's description of God's word, "like a raging fire in my heart, shut up in my bones" (Jer. 20:9). For Halevi, however, the subject is not the prophetic word of God, the divine speech, but rather the very name of God, presumably the Tetragrammaton. The first words, "His name is in me" (*u-shemo ve-qirbi*), echo the biblical passage

242 Ibid., 258 (poem no. 138): ברכי את שם זהר העולם איום ונורא.

243 Cf. Isa. 60:19.

244 Cf. Hab. 1:7.

245 *Dīwān* 3:262 (poem no. 138): שמך מלכותך וכבודך אל נסה עלינו אור פניך יי.

246 Ps. 4:7.

247 Cf. *Kuzari* II:7, IV:3; *Dīwān* 3:23 (poem no. 64), 292 (no. 145), 4:145 (no. 62); Wolfson, *Studies* 2:89 n. 89; Efros, *Studies,* pp. 151–153. As Scholem noted in *Origins,* p. 223, there is an obvious similarity between Halevi's terminology and subsequent kabbalistic doctrine concerning the last of the ten emanations (*sefirot*), which is called by various names, including *kavod, Shekhinah,* and *malkhut.* Interestingly enough, Judah Halevi's name is mentioned in an anonymous document of Provençal origin extant in MS Vatican 236, fols. 82a–b, in conjunction with the kabbalistic idea that the tenth emanation, the divine glory, is identified as an angel—more specifically, the angel of the countenance (*sar ha-panim*) and the prince of the world (*sar ha-ʿolam*), i.e., Meṭaṭron. Concerning this text, see Scholem, *Origins,* pp. 224–226; the relevant comment is translated on p. 225. See chapter 5, n. 91 of the present book. Cf. Joseph Albo, *Sefer ha-ʿIqqarim* II:11. For a different explanation of the origins of the term *malkhut* as a designation for the glory in kabbalistic literature, see Dan, "Pesaq ha-Yirah veha-Emunah and the Intention of Prayer in Ashkenazi Hasidic Esotericism," p. 196.

248 On the conjunction of kidney and heart, used to designate one's inwardness, cf. Ps. 26:2, 73:21.

249 Cf. Ps. 73:21.

250 *Dīwān,* 3:89 (poem no. 47):

ושמו בקרבי   כאש בכליותי
קשור בלבי   עצור בעצמותי

describing the angel of the Lord, "for My name is in him" (*ki shemi be-qirbo*) (Exod. 23:21). This very verse played a crucial role in ancient Jewish esotericism, where it was read exegetically as a reference to Meṭaṭron, also designated as *Yah ha-Qaṭan,* for he was thought to have borne the Tetragrammaton within himself.[251] Halevi combines this image from Exod. 23 with that in Jer. 20 to create the notion of the name being inscribed on his heart[252] and inner parts like flames of fire. The name of God is itself the luminous substance that is within the poet. Thus, in another poem Halevi writes,

> Your name is before me—how can I walk alone?
> It is my beloved—how can I sit lonely?
> It is my lamp—how can my light go dim?
> How can I wander with it as a staff in my hand?[253]

Here the name of God is characterized in several ways, all of which tend to underscore the fact that it is a personalized dynamic entity—a point Halevi also makes in the *Kuzari* (IV:1, 3) when he states that the Tetragrammaton is the *nomen proprium* that designates the divine reality in its particularity and specificity, as is the function of proper names. The first verse brings to mind the passage in Ps. 16:8, "I have set the Lord before me always." For Halevi, however, it is specifically the name of God that is set before him in what is presumably a visual experience of a mystical nature. This name is the constant companion of the poet; indeed, it is his beloved (based on the imagery of Canticles), as well as his lamp—the ontic source of the poet's soul, characterized as a light—and, finally, the staff that supports the poet in his earthly peregrinations. In a recent discussion of this poem Raymond Scheindlin astutely observed, "This 'name of God' represents not merely the thought of God, but rather something divine that the poet feels to be an integral part of himself."[254] Indeed, the name of God for Halevi is a hypostatic entity, identical with the glory that is the ontological source of the soul of every Jew. The name is inscribed within the soul, for the soul is of the same substance as the name. Because of this consubstantiality the poet can be unified with the name. Thus in the poem *Yarshu le-miṣʿar ʾahuvekha* Halevi boldly commands, "Cleave to the name of God, / your strength, and hold fast to it."[255] In the moment of poetic composi-

[251] Cf. B. Sanhedrin 38b; *Reʾuyot Yeḥezqel,* ed. Gruenwald, p. 130, (and see editor's n. 119); *Synopse,* § 387.

[252] A similar notion is expressed, for instance, by the kabbalist Isaac of Acre, *ʾOṣar Ḥayyim,* MS Moscow-Guenzberg 775, fol. 54b: "The name of the King of kings, the Holy One, blessed be He, is inscribed on the heart of the enlightened ones from Israel, the pure souls upon whom He dwells."

[253] *Dīwān* 2:221 (poem no. 10):

שמך נגדי ואיך אלך לבדי
והוא דודי ואיך אשב יחידי
והוא נרי ואיך ידעך מאורי
ואיך אצען והוא משען בידי

[254] Scheindlin, "Redemption of the Soul in Golden Age Religious Poetry," p. 64.

[255] *Dīwān* 3:88 (poem no. 46): דבקי בשם אל אילותך ובו אחזי.

tion the poet, like the prophet, is cloaked in the Holy Spirit and apprehends the Tetragrammaton.[256] The object of the vision described in some contexts as the anthropomorphic configuration of the spiritual form within the imagination is here characterized as the mystical apprehension of the name. In the final analysis, for Halevi the visible glory, the aspect of the *Shekhinah* "revealed to the eye," is identical with the divine name, which is the light that emanates from the Holy Spirit, the "spiritual, hidden *Shekhinah*,"[257] and which comprises the totality of spiritual forms known from chariot speculation.[258]

Reflected in Halevi's writings is an older doctrine concerning the *kavod* that has its roots in the Jewish mystical tradition. To be sure, Halevi's philosophical formulation advances considerably beyond the more mythical presentation in the Merkavah texts, but there can be no doubt regarding the direct influence of the latter on the former. The "God of Israel," as the term is used in the Merkavah literature, refers to the manifest forms in the world of the throne that constitute the revealed aspects of the divine in the mystical vision. Halevi similarly maintains that the "God of Israel" is a spiritual form, expressed in the shape of the various inhabitants of the throne-world that are apprehended in a prophetic vision. In one place, as I have indicated, Halevi even describes this prophetic vision in terms of a person's cleaving to the angelic species (i.e., one strips away one's body and becomes a purely spiritual entity), being cloaked in the Holy Spirit, and comprehending the most sacred of divine names, the Tetragrammaton. While there is no exact parallel to Halevi's formulation in the Merkavah texts, it can easily be shown that each of the critical elements has a basis in the early forms of Jewish mysticism. Central to the latter is a visionary ascent that leads to a temporary transformation of the human being into an angel; this transformation, moreover, is often described in terms of the mystic surrounded by or cloaked in the light of the *kavod*. The culminating stage in the ecstatic vision, according to some textual units, is a mystical apprehension of the divine names—many of which are various permutations of the Tetragrammaton—as they are correlated with limbs of the divine body. In the case of Halevi, therefore, we have a striking example of a medieval Jewish intel-

[256] Cf. ibid., 261 (poem no. 138): ברכי . . . את שם קדוש ומקדש בפי כל חזה.

[257] See *Kuzari* V:23, and discussion in Davidson, "Active Intellect," p. 388.

[258] It is of interest to note that an older Jewish mystical tradition, reported by the Castilian kabbalist Jacob ben Jacob ha-Kohen of Soria in his commentary on Ezekiel's chariot vision, has great affinity with the views of Halevi: Jacob makes a distinction between an upper and lower glory, the former corresponding to the sefirotic gradations and the latter to the throne of glory, the encompassing electrum, seven seraphim, the cloud of glory, and eight cherubim. See "The Commentary on Ezekiel's Chariot," p. 8; see also p. 96 n. 11, where Farber notes the resemblance of this passage to Halevi's view. See also Idel, "World of Angels." The view of Halevi also resembles the position of the Pietist author Elḥanan ben Yaqar; see his *Sod ha-Sodot,* in *Texts in the Theology of German Pietism,* p. 3. This author interprets the biblical reference to God's back as the "last things" that God "emanated or created," which include the "glory, the chariot, and the celestial host."

lectual who sought to incorporate early forms of Jewish mysticism in the texture of a more sophisticated philosophical approach largely indebted to Islamic influences, especially Sufi and Ismaʿīlī thought. The complicated interweaving of the threads of philosophy and mysticism provides a literary profile of the medieval Jewish mysticism that took shape in Provence and northern Spain.

• CHAPTER FIVE •

Ḥaside Ashkenaz: Veridical and Docetic Interpretations of the Chariot Vision

THE THEORETICAL INTEREST in problems of divine revelation and prophetology by the Ḥaside Ashkenaz, a Pietistic movement that flourished in the twelfth and thirteenth centuries in the Rhineland, has been duly noted in the scholarly literature, yet the experiential component underlying these theosophical systems has been less appreciated. To state at the outset the thesis that I will set out to prove in this chapter: the theosophic understanding of the divine in the German Pietists (as in the case of the Provençal-Spanish kabbalists, to be discussed in the succeeding chapter) involves an ecstatic visionary component. Indeed, the theosophical systems elaborated by the Pietists and kabbalists indicate a fundamental convergence of ontology and epistemology, in that the knowing of the divine powers entails some vision of them. The ontological assumption equally shared by the Pietists and kabbalists regarding the luminous nature of the powers that fill the divine pleroma is inseparably linked to an epistemological assumption about the process of knowing these powers as one of illumination. I cannot enter here into a lengthy discussion on the sources for this ontology or metaphysics of light. Suffice it to say that these sources are indeed multiple. The image of God as light is a cross-cultural—if not a universal—phenomenon that has found expression in many different traditions. With respect to Judaism itself it can be said that the conception of God as a luminous being is found in the Bible, apocalyptic texts, and rabbinic aggadah, as well as the Merkavah literature and the whole range of liturgical poetry influenced by it. This conception is also instrumental in medieval Jewish philosophy, especially through the influence of Neoplatonism, according to which form is identified with light. For the Jewish mystics of the twelfth and thirteenth centuries, therefore, many different sources converged to form their ontology of light. It must be noted, finally, that in this medieval environment the Jewish mystics were not alone. On the contrary, in both Islamic and Christian cultures one can discern a widespread "aesthetics of light."[1] What is unique to the Jewish mystics, however, is the configuration of that light in terms of their respective theosophical structures, informed by specific religious and cultural patterns of thought and models of action.

I will principally discuss the problem of vision from the vantage point of the texts that were composed by members of the main circle of Judah ben Samuel he-Ḥasid of Regensburg (ca. 1150–1217) and Eleazar ben Judah of Worms (ca. 1165–ca. 1230). Mention of writings deriving from the independent group

[1] The term is borrowed from Eco, *Art and Beauty in the Middle Ages,* pp. 43–51.

identified by Joseph Dan as the "Circle of the Special Cherub" (*Ḥug ha-Keruv ha-Meyuḥad*)[2] will be made only for the sake of clarifying a position adopted by the main circle. My discussion of the latter will itself be divided into two parts, the first dealing with the more exoteric presentation of this problem and the second with what may be termed the esoteric presentation. As will be seen in more detail below, what I have called the exoteric presentation consists of the Pietists' own conscious effort to formulate ideas about the divine glory in philosophical terminology current in their day and in their environs. Although they did not have access to the entire range of Jewish, Islamic, or Christian philosophic texts, which were composed principally in Judeo-Arabic, Arabic and Latin, they did utilize a small number of primary sources (to be discussed more fully below). They thus attempted to conceptualize their ideas in these technical terms. On the other hand, it is clear that the Pietists received many older mystical-magical traditions, presumably both oral and written, that likewise informed their conception of the glory. I will consider these more mythical ideas in order to provide the ideational matrix for what I call the esoteric traditions promulgated by the German Pietists. I use the term "esoteric" to denote that which cannot be communicated fully in writing and which should be only alluded to partially in written form and transmitted orally.

When examining the religious worldview of the Pietists one cannot impose a measure of coherence or consistency that does violence to their own compositions. To an extent, the Pietists reflected ancient mystical traditions through the prism of contemporary philosophical discourse, but to the rational-minded their approach seems rather unsystematic. What is striking about the Pietists is their failure, or perhaps unwillingness, to recast the older mystical notions within a framework of a coherent metaphysics or ontology, despite their adaptation of a semi-philosophical theology.[3] In the writings of the Pietists we find a set of conflicting tendencies expressed through a web of linguistic and numerical associations rather than abstract philosophical concepts. The use of numerology and wordplay was a means by which Pietistic authors, especially Eleazar, contextualized older esoteric traditions within authoritative texts, most significantly Scripture and the normative liturgy. These devices, I assume, did not generate the ideas, but rather anchored preexisting notions in an accepted canon. The Pietists did attempt to provide some conceptual apparatus to explicate theosophical issues, but no schema so dominated their discussions as to

[2] See Dan, *Esoteric Theology*, pp. 156–164, 255–258; idem, *Studies in Ashkenazi Ḥasidic Literature*, pp. 89–111.

[3] See Scholem, *Major Trends*, pp. 86–87, 111–115; idem, *Kabbalah*, p. 42; Dan, *Studies*, p. 135; Sirat, *Théories*, p. 100. The claim of Ivan Marcus in *Piety and Society*, p. 10, that Joseph Dan's research has challenged Scholem's characterization of the Pietists' theological writings as eclectic and inconsistent is unacceptable on two counts: first, on occasion Dan himself has characterized the Pietists in terms similar to those of Scholem, and second, the majority of the texts that Dan used in his systematic presentation of the esoteric theology of the Pietists (which served as the basis for Marcus's observation) are the more philosophically oriented compositions known as *sifrut ha-yiḥud*. The truly esoteric writings of the Pietists indicate that Scholem's characterization is right on the mark.

force an eisegetical posture on their appropriation of multiple esoteric traditions. It is with respect to these traditions that the experiential aspect of the Pietists' concern with mystical visions surfaces most vividly.

While the theoretical aspects of Pietistic theology have been well analyzed in the scholarly literature, the mystical dimension—by which I mean the cultivation of visionary and ascent experiences—has been somewhat downplayed. The position adopted by Dan in his monographic study of what he calls the esoteric theology (*torat ha-sod*), published in 1968, epitomizes the point I am making. In a text that Dan attributes to Judah the Pious it is stated that the glory appears to prophets and those who enter the mystical orchard (*pardes*). Dan interprets the latter expression as a reference to the Pietists, leading him to observe, "This is the only example that I have found in the German Pietistic literature of the revelation of the glory to those occupied with the esoteric theology. Yet one should not conclude from this with certainty that the German Pietists involved with these matters merited to have a revelation of the glory."[4] Even in his discussion of the ceremony of the transmission of the divine name that is found at the beginning of the most esoteric of Eleazar's compositions, *Sefer ha-Shem* (the "Book of the Name"), Dan minimizes the "magical" elements implied, emphasizing instead that the principal concern is "theological" and "speculative"[5]—a view that has been challenged by Moshe Idel, who argues that the knowledge gained by transmission of the name has far greater "experiential implications."[6] It is noteworthy that in the context of discussing the relationship of the Pietists to the Hekhalot literature Dan himself expresses some uncertainty about this issue, pondering if the Pietists saw in these texts a truth that served merely as a "matter for speculation and study" or stood as "instruction and advice for the acquisition of a similar religious-spiritual path, i.e., ascent of the soul to the upper worlds for the sake of visionary experiences like those of the *yorde merkavah*." Although Dan admits that there are hints scattered in the Pietists' writings indicating that perhaps they may have encountered the texts of ancient Jewish mysticism in a more experiential fashion, finding that the very study of these texts facilitated the spiritual or mystical experience of an ascent, he still concludes that the general picture one receives from the writings of the Pietists is that the ancient Jewish mystical literature influenced the theological speculation of the Pietists but not their religious experiences.[7]

There is no conclusive textual evidence that the Pietists cultivated the practice of ascent to the chariot known from Hekhalot literature. Yet, it can be

[4] Dan, *Studies*, p. 170 n. 76.

[5] *Esoteric Theology*, p. 75.

[6] Idel, *Kabbalah: New Perspectives*, p. 323 n. 171.

[7] *Esoteric Theology*, pp. 26–27. The more modified view is reiterated by Dan in his *Jewish Mysticism and Jewish Ethics*, p. 55. In that context Dan specifies as examples of mystical phenomena in the writings of the Pietists the purification ceremony required before a master transmitted the secret of the divine name to a disciple and the creation of the homunculus (*golem*) through techniques elaborated in *Sefer Yeṣirah*.

shown that their interest in throne-mysticism was not merely speculative but was experiential in its orientation, a point made also by Idel.[8] Scholem himself had already cited manuscript evidence that reports that R. Samuel of Speyer, the father of R. Judah the Pious, ascended to heaven by means of the name of God, in the manner of the old Merkavah mystics.[9] If such a report is to be accepted as genuine, then we have clear evidence that in at least the case of Samuel, designated in the old sources as Samuel the prophet,[10] the interest in Merkavah had a definite experiential component. According to another tradition, R. Samuel made use of the divine names and once mentioned a name that caused the schoolhouse to be completely filled with light.[11] Underlying this legend is a specific technique of visualization, as will be seen further in this analysis.

In another place Scholem remarks that many of the Ḥaside Ashkenaz "attained the highest spiritual levels, and were considered to be masters of the holy spirit, or even prophets, a term applied to several men who are known for their activity in tosafist circles, e.g., R. Ezra ha-Navi ('the prophet') of Montcontour, and also to others who are otherwise completely unknown, e.g., R. Neḥemiah ha-Navi[12] and R. Troestlin ha-Navi from Erfurt.[13] These men's attainment of such spiritual heights was connected not only with their behavior on the ethical plane but also with the distinction they achieved in the realm of esoteric theosophy."[14] As I will attempt to show in the following discussion, occupation with

[8] *Kabbalah: New Perspectives,* pp. 27, 91–92. See also Marcus, *Piety and Society,* pp. 16, 109, 118, where he stresses the spiritual orientation of Eleazar of Worms's pietism as a guide to individual mystical experience. See also pp. 65–66, where Marcus notes that the Pietist authors invoked two different modes of religious authority: a received tradition from Sinai of esoteric lore about how to interpret the liturgy and Scripture, and an "intuitive, quasi-prophetic ability to perceive the will of the Creator which God has encoded in Scripture at Sinai." See also van Uchelen, in "Ma'aseh Merkabah in Sefer Ḥasidim," who contrasts the use of the term *ma'aseh merkavah* in *Sefer Ḥasidim* with the writings of Eleazar of Worms on the grounds that in the former the meaning is textual and exegetical, whereas in the latter it is esoteric and frequently connected to visionary experiences of the glory. See the fascinating statement of Eleazar (*Sode Razayya,* ed. Weiss, p. 135) that if an individual transmits the esoteric lore of the *Shi'ur Qomah* (involving the anthropomorphic measurements of God) in a whisper (the traditional way of transmitting secrets), then "he is placed on the throne of glory like Adam." From the context it is not clear if a mystical or an eschatological enthronement is implied, although it seems to me that the former makes better sense in context.

[9] See Scholem, *Major Trends,* p. 374 n. 77; idem, *Origins,* p. 248 n. 98.

[10] See, e.g., MS New York–JTSA Mic. 8122, fol. 95a. See also evidence adduced by Heschel in "On the Holy Spirit in the Middle Ages," p. 181 nn. 26, 31. In addition to the designation of Samuel the Pious as prophet, there are other legends regarding his magical powers to perform miracles or create a golem. See Dan, *The Hebrew Story in the Middle Ages,* pp. 162–186, 276–277; idem, "The Beginnings of Hebrew Hagiographic Literature"; Alexander-Frizer, *The Pious Sinner,* pp. 8–9.

[11] See Heschel, "On the Holy Spirit," p. 181.

[12] R. Neḥemiah ha-Navi is mentioned at the end of an Ashkenazi commentary on the forty-two-letter name of God in S. Mussayef, *Merkavah Shelemah* (Jerusalem, 1921), 31b.

[13] See Scholem, *Major Trends,* pp. 88, 370 n. 21; Heschel, "On the Holy Spirit," pp. 184–185.

[14] *Kabbalah,* pp. 37–38. On the other hand, on pp. 32–33 Scholem remarks that the attempt to discover numerological links through *gemaṭriah* between divine names and scriptural verses or

matters pertaining to the chariot by those who followed Samuel of Speyer constituted a decidedly mystical experience connected with visualizing the light of the glory both as an anthropomorphic shape and as the letters of the divine name. It is clearly the case, therefore, that the speculations on the nature of revelation expounded by the Pietists had an experiential underpinning, a point made by Colette Sirat as well: "Un second élément important de la théorie des révélations chez les hassidim est leur expérience personnelle des perceptions surnaturelles. En effet, les hassidim ont expérimenté la Présence divine, ils ont ressenti ce sentiment du 'numineux' que décrit R. Otto et nous voyons, pour la première fois dans la pensée juive du Moyen Age, un essai d'explication des visions surnaturelles qui soit en même temps une réflexion seconde sur le phénomène."[15] A fresh review of the relevant material, in both its exoteric and esoteric presentation, will help to sharpen our understanding of the ecstatic and mystical dimension of the theosophy espoused by the German Pietists—a critical link in the chain of transmission of Jewish esotericism from Late Antiquity to the Middle Ages. It will also provide a good window through which to examine the complexity of the problem of visionary experience in the literary remains of medieval Jewish mysticism.

Theological Reappropriation of Ancient Jewish Myth

Medieval Jewish mystics, both Pietists and kabbalists, were working with well-defined, textually rich theosophic traditions that stretched back hundreds of years. Awareness of these earlier theosophic traditions was available to the twelfth- and thirteenth-century mystics through various channels: fragments of ancient Jewish apocalyptic texts; rabbinic midrashim of an aggadic nature, concerned with the historical accounts of prophecy and revelation; the corpus of early Jewish mysticism, focused on the visionary ascent to the throne; liturgical poetry drawing extensively on the angelology and theology of the mystical sources; and medieval Jewish philosophical texts dealing with the theoretical problems of prophetic visions. It is ironic that the medieval philosophers—and here I include such thinkers as Saadiah ben Joseph, Solomon ibn Gabirol, Abraham ibn Ezra, Abraham bar Ḥiyya, Judah Halevi, and, to a much lesser extent, Maimonides—were deeply influenced by the earlier theosophy. I say

prayers, a process that began sometime in the Geonic period but reached a climax in the writings of Ḥaside Ashkenaz, represents "a decline in the practical use of this material during preparation for the soul's ecstatic ascent to heaven." Inasmuch as the Pietistic literature is saturated with this kind of material, the implication of Scholem's remark must be that the ecstatic ascent to the chariot by means of the names became less significant in this corpus. For an alternative approach, see Heschel, "On the Holy Spirit," pp. 182–186. See also text published by Kaufmann in "Notes et mélanges," in which reference is made to the "true prophet" who attempts to adjure Meṭaṭron to descend from above in order to answer a halakhic question regarding the knot of the phylacteries.

[15] *Théories,* pp. 97–98.

ironic because, as is well known, one of the main preoccupations of medieval Jewish philosophy, beginning in the ninth and tenth centuries, was to provide an ideological portrait of Judaism that sought to remove all anthropomorphisms from God. At the same time, these philosophers, beginning with Saadiah, had at their disposal earlier Jewish mystical texts that proferred a theosophical conception of God predicated on the visible form of divinity. As discussed in the preceding chapters, some of the technical terms that referred to that form are: *kavod, gevurah, demut, dimmuyot,* and *ṣurah*. To be sure, a radical semantic transformation occurred in the philosophical tradition: whereas the classical rabbinic authors, liturgical poets, and anonymous Jewish mystics employed these terms to refer to the apparently visible form or forms of divinity, Saadiah altered the meaning of the earlier Jewish esotericism by speaking of this glory or form as created and thus ontologically distinct from God. And that is precisely the point: biblical theophanies that mention the visible form of God need not be allegorically reinterpreted, for they are not really speaking about God, the uncreated and simple one, but rather a created light that is the first form brought into being by God. This conceptual reshaping was extremely important in safeguarding the continued existence of early Jewish mysticism through medieval times. The philosophical appropriation of esoteric motifs provided an intellectual out, as it were, that allowed one to continue to revere the mystical and mythical traditions without compromising the more rationalist understanding of God.

In the various stages in the development of German Pietism the Saadianic influence is evident, but combined with the influence of ancient Merkavah speculation, the interpretation of prophetical and mystical visions according to Hai Gaon and his followers—especially Nathan ben Yeḥiel and Ḥananel ben Ḥushiel—and other philosophical currents, such as the thought of Shabbetai Donnolo and the Neoplatonism of Abraham ibn Ezra.[16] (The influence of Abraham bar Ḥiyya is recognizable in certain Pietist cases, especially the *Ḥug ha-Keruv ha-Meyuḥad,* but not pronounced in Judah he-Ḥasid or Eleazar.[17]) The influence of these sources accounts for the Pietists' explicit and repeated rejection of anthropomorphism and their insistence that the Creator has no

[16] See Scholem, *Major Trends,* pp. 86–87, 107–118; Dan, *Esoteric Theology,* pp. 20–24, 39–40, 99–100, 104–116, 227–228. See the work of Farber cited below, n. 19. On the specific influence of Eriugena, see sources cited in n. 57. Scholem, in *Reshit ha-Qabbalah,* p. 118, suggests that the presence of the term *hawwayot* in the writings of Eleazar of Worms reflects a Neoplatonic influence, as we find in the contemporary occurrence of this term in the kabbalah of Isaac the Blind. See, however, Scholem, *Origins,* p. 281. See also Dan (*Esoteric Theology,* p. 94), who emphasizes the difference between the Pietistic and kabbalistic usage. For a different view, suggesting a common source, see Idel, "Sefirot above the Sefirot," p. 243 n. 21; and on the possibility of other common Neoplatonic sources that influenced the German Pietists and Provençal-Spanish kabbalists, see pp. 278–280, and idem, "Jewish Kabbalah and Platonism," p. 321.

[17] See G. Scholem, "Reste neuplatonischer Spekulation in der Mystik der deutschen Chassidim und ihre Vermittlung durch Abraham bar Chija"; Vajda, "De quelques vestiges du néoplatonisme dans la kabbale archaïque et mystique juive franco-germanique"; Dan, *Esoteric Theology,* pp. 157, 204–205; idem, "Pesaq ha-Yirah veha-Emunah," pp. 202–205.

material or representable form. As Scholem astutely observes, characteristic of the German Pietists was a "desire to synthesize the early material, including the anthropomorphic elements, with the spiritual interpretation that denies these elements."[18] Indeed, the older esoteric traditions, with a heavy emphasis on anthropomorphism, had a decisive impact on the spirituality and religious sensibility of the Pietists. This should not be underestimated.[19] Ephraim E. Urbach contrasted the approach of Eleazar with the blatant anthropomorphism found in a Pietistic commentary on the forty-two-letter name of God,[20] going so far as to say that the Qalonymide Pietists, especially Eleazar, fought against the anthropomorphic tendencies of the other Pietistic circles—a point corroborated from the evidence of Moses Taku as well as extant manuscript material, including a statement cited by Urbach concerning the burning of books that attributed anthropomorphic characteristics to God.[21] This is no doubt true, but the anthropomorphic speculations of the earlier texts surface time and again in the Pietistic writings, including those of Eleazar himself.[22] Indeed, given Eleazar's untiring effort to rid the divine of anthropomorphism, it is all the more striking that some of these traditions find their way into his work.

The assumption that one must make is that the Pietists experienced some tension between the anthropomorphic descriptions related in material they considered the sacred legacy of the Jewish past and a more contemporary rationalist theology. Shunning any systematic synthesis, they preserved the older esoteric traditions alongside the more or less contemporary philosophical concepts, often in "abstruse metamorphoses," as Scholem put it, so that one indeed finds in their theological and cosmological speculations a "reversion to

[18] *Kabbalah,* p. 42. See also *Major Trends,* pp. 86–87, 111–115; Idel, "Concept of Torah," pp. 47–48.

[19] See Dan, *Esoteric Theology,* pp. 25, 27–28; idem, "A Re-evaluation of the 'Ashkenazi Kabbalah,'" pp. 133–134, where he singles out the "myth of *Shi'ur Qomah*" as a point of similarity between theosophic kabbalah and German Pietism. On the other hand, see pp. 137–138, where Dan notes that one of the two key differences between the kabbalistic and Pietistic worldviews is the mythological nature of the divine, especially connected to the male-female polarity, the other difference being the theurgical element in the kabbalah. Farber, in "Concept of the Merkabah," pp. 296–302, suggests that the *Shi'ur Qomah* traditions in the circle of Judah he-Ḥasid are not to be taken as literally attributing corporeal dimensions to the glory, but rather are an expression of a "principle of ontological limitation and determination" expressed figuratively in mathematical terms. Farber compares this to the principle of *participatio* in Neoplatonism, which functions as a point of mediation between the infinite and finite. She concludes as well that there is a basic "phenomenological similarity" between the German Pietistic doctrine of *Shi'ur Qomah* and the kabbalistic approach; see pp. 401–432, 481. For a different attitude toward the role of anthropomorphism in the theology of the German Pietists, see Alexander-Frizer, *Pious Sinner,* pp. 77–78.

[20] Concerning this text, see Liebes, "The Angels of the Shofar and Yeshua Sar ha-Panim," pp. 186–187 n. 20.

[21] *'Arugat ha-Bosem,* ed. Urbach, 4:74. See Sirat, *Théories,* p. 97.

[22] In this regard it is of interest to mention the *Sefer ha-Qomah* recension of the *Shi'ur Qomah,* extant in MS Oxford-Bodleian 2257, fols. 16a–20a, which attributes the entire text to Eleazar of Worms. See Cohen, *Shi'ur Qomah: Texts and Recensions,* p. 7. See also the version of this text in MS Oxford-Bodleian 1791, fols. 58a–93b, which, according to the scribe's own testimony, is a copy made from the handwritten copy of Eleazar. See Cohen, *Shi'ur Qomah,* pp. 9–10.

mythology."[23] Scholem also correctly noted that in some cases Neoplatonic ideas incorporated by the German Pietists "underwent a process of retrogression from the metaphysical to the theological or Gnostical sphere, if not to pure mythology."[24] This is an important observation that must be borne in mind in any sustained examination of this complex body of literature. Despite the obvious acceptance of theological postulates informed by philosophical thought (e.g., the incorporeality of God), the German Pietists often appropriated mythical symbolism and imagery (typically anthropomorphic in nature) derived from midrashic and esoteric sources. In my view, the truly esoteric doctrine (*torat ha-sod*) cultivated by the German Pietists cannot be constructed solely on the basis of the *sifrut ha-yiḥud,* the genre of literature shaped by the explicit aim of expressing theological and anthropological views in terms of philosophical concepts.[25] This is not to say that this literature is completely devoid of esoteric material, but only that the secrets are encoded in these sources in philosophical terminology intended to conceal the esoteric matter from the purview of the learned who were not part of the inner circle of Pietists privy to the direct transmission of the mysteries and hidden lore.[26] Hence, to extract esoteric doctrines from these texts one must read them in light of, and in conjunction with, the other Pietistic sources (commentaries on the liturgy and the chariot vision of Ezekiel, treatises on the divine names, the glory, and the angels, and so on) that have an altogether different style and format. To assess properly the Pietistic thinking on matters such as the nature of the glory one must proceed from philosophical formulations toward the mythical.[27] In my presentation I will follow precisely this trajectory as I attempt to distinguish the exoteric pronouncements from the esoteric teachings.

The Exoteric Doctrine of Glory

Iconic Visualization of God as Image

The merging of early Jewish esotericism, Saadiah's philosophy, Donnolo's *Sefer Ḥakhmoni,* the Geonic material, and Neoplatonic writings is the distinguishing

[23] *Major Trends,* p. 87. See also reference to Dan's comment above, n. 19. The mythological aspects of the theological speculation of the German Pietists has also been recently emphasized by Liebes, "Die Natura Dei: On the Development of the Jewish Myth," in *Studies in Jewish Myth and Jewish Messianism,* pp. 50–51.

[24] *Major Trends,* p. 117. See *Kabbalah,* pp. 38–39.

[25] Concerning this genre of literature, see Dan, *Studies,* pp. 72–88.

[26] This point has already been emphasized by Dan in *Studies,* pp. 73–74; idem, "Pesaq ha-Yirah veha-Emunah," pp. 187–188.

[27] See, by contrast, the suggestion of Sirat in *Théories,* p. 97: "It est donc plausible que ce fut là une des raisons de la publicité que Juda le Pieux et Eleazar de Worms donnérent à la doctrine esotérique et qu'ils ont voulu ainsi extirper de la Communauté des croyances eronées." Sirat, basing herself on the view of Urbach (see n. 21), refers specifically to the anthropomorphic conception of God espoused by Moses Taku. In my opinion, the situation is precisely the reverse of what Sirat argues, i.e., the esoteric doctrine is informed by anthropomorphic conceptions that stand in marked tension with the philosophical formulations expressed in some of the Pietistic texts. The disclosure of the esoteric doctrine could not possibly combat anthropomorphic conceptions of God, but quite the contrary renders the positing of a nonanthropomorphic theology problematic.

feature of the theosophy of the German Pietists.[28] Thus, following in the philosophical tradition articulated by Saadiah, the Pietists state categorically that God—to whom they refer most frequently as the Creator (*ha-bore'*) or the One (*ha-yiḥud*)—has no image, body, or form. God's incorporeality is a corollary to divine unity, that is, given the fact that God is a simple unity—a unity without parts—God cannot be a body, which is by definition composite.[29] Moreover, since God is not a body, God cannot be said to occupy any place. God is therefore outside of all things. On the other hand, since God does not occupy any given place, God may be said to occupy all places. To put the matter in slightly different terms: God is nowhere, therefore God is everywhere. The concomitant affirmation of divine transcendence and immanence is expressed in one of the earliest documents that informed the Pietistic theology (attributed to various authors, including Samuel ben Qalonymous he-Ḥasid of Speyer and his son, Judah the Pious[30]), the *Shir ha-Yiḥud we-ha-Kavod* ("Hymn of the One and of the Glory"): "He surrounds everything and fills everything."[31] In the speculative thought of the Pietists, curiously enough, divine immanence is a product of God's transcendent unity and is not attributable to the visible aspect of God, the glory. This signifies an important shift from the biblical-rabbinic conception of the glory or *Shekhinah,* terms used to denote the divine immanence in the world. This is not to say that the Pietists did not entertain the possibility of the immanent indwelling of the glory; on the contrary, they not only entertained such a possibility, they considered the vision of the luminous form of the Presence to be the peak religious experience. What is noteworthy, however, is that from a technical theological standpoint divine immanence in the world—the sense of God's filling all things—is a characteristic attributed to the Creator and not the glory. The point is underscored in an interesting way in a passage from one of the manuscript versions of Eleazar's *Sefer ha-Shem:*

> The Creator has no boundary, circumference, or appearance, for if He appeared in a [certain] aspect (*gawwen*) He would have a boundary. Every created thing has a proximate boundary but the Creator is in the middle of everything and nothing is contiguous with Him as the spirit of life. . . . [The spirit] is not visible because it is too subtle to be seen, and how much more so its Creator. The created entities do not divide His unity, for just as the bread that is soaked in wine absorbs the wine and there is no place devoid [of the wine], so there is no place that is devoid of Him.

[28] See Scholem, *Major Trends,* p. 86; Dan, *Esoteric Theology,* pp. 20–24; Sirat, *Théories,* pp. 97–101.

[29] See, e.g., *Sha'are ha-Sod ha-Yiḥud we-ha-'Emunah,* pp. 146–147.

[30] On the attribution of this text to Judah the Pious, see A. Berliner, *Der Einheitsgesang* (Berlin, 1910), p. 13; I. Elbogen, *Der jüdische Gottesdienst in seiner geschichtlichen Entwicklung* (Leipzig, 1913), pp. 81, 383; and other sources quoted by Baer in *Seder 'Avodat Yisra'el,* p. 250. According to others, the poem was authored by Judah's father, Samuel ben Qalonymous he-Ḥasid of Speyer, or, as reported by Moses Taku in his polemical treatise *Ketav Tamim,* by Samuel together with a certain Bezalel; see Habermann in *Shire ha-Yiḥud we-ha-Kavod,* p. 11. For a review of this question, see Dan's introduction to the facsimile of the Thiengen 1560 edition of *Shir ha-Yiḥud,* pp. 7–15.

[31] *Shire ha-Yiḥud we-ha-Kavod,* ed. Habermann, p. 26.

> Just as the wine imparts an odor to the piece [of bread], so He reveals His actions.[32]

In this fascinating depiction of divine immanence Eleazar combines several modes of representation. Utilizing the geometrical imagery of the circumference and midpoint of a circle Eleazar expresses the paradox that God's transcendence is a factor of his omnipresence and his omnipresence a factor of his transcendence. God is visible in all things only because he is formless and therefore invisible. Interestingly, Eleazar also conveys this notion by comparing olfactory and ocular images: God's presence can be seen in his actions, just as the scent of the wine permeates the piece of bread soaked in it.

To explain the object of prophetic theophany and/or mystical vision the Pietists utilized the language of Saadiah, although they radically altered the original intent of his philosophical approach. A classic presentation of the different views is given in an anonymous text that Dan has attributed to Judah the Pious.[33] In this text three different views on the nature of prophetic revelation are offered: According to the first opinion, God is invisible and therefore what the prophet sees are images (*dimyonot*) in his mind, a process compared to a state of delusion or illusion (*'aḥizat 'einayim*) that may be conjured by magical means. The second opinion likewise maintains that God is invisible, but what the prophet beholds is the glory that emanates from God. Insofar as the glory has a fixed dimension it is visible; however, the place of the attachment or cleaving of the glory to God—that which is referred to scripturally as God's face (Exod. 33:20)—is not visible. The third opinion agrees with the second but maintains that the glory is a created light outside of God.[34]

Hence, the third view corresponds to that of Saadiah, the second to the Pietistic view based on Abraham ibn Ezra, and the first to a radical psychologistic understanding of prophecy that is informed in good measure by the thought of Hai Gaon as transmitted especially by Ḥananel.[35] As I will argue momentarily, in the Pietistic literature this psychologistic understanding develops into a pronounced doceticism. In another text attributed to Judah the Pious, a commentary on the prayer *'Aleynu*, there is again a discussion on the relation of the glory to the Creator, primarily from a liturgical perspective. In that context the Pietist author mentions two views. According to the first, the Creator

> shows to the [prophets] the glory so that they will know that the decree is from God.[36] Regarding the glory that the prophet sees it may be said that [God] creates

[32] MS Oxford-Bodleian 1638, fol. 52b. This passage is immediately succeeded by the discussion concerning the ritualistic requirements for the transmission of the divine name. See below, n. 226. The placing of these passages together suggests that the redactor of this manuscript version of *Sefer ha-Shem,* or the scribe who copied it, understood that according to Eleazar the transmission of the name occasions a visionary experience of the divine.

[33] Dan, *Studies,* pp. 134–147.

[34] Ibid., pp. 165, 169–171.

[35] See Dan, *Esoteric Theology,* pp. 130–143. Eleazar's ambivalence toward Saadiah's theory of the created glory has been noted by Verman in *Books of Contemplation,* p. 138 n. 98.

[36] Cf. MS Oxford-Bodleian 1566, fol. 136a: "He revealed His secret to His servants, the prophets, so that they would occupy their minds with the decrees of the Holy One, blessed be He."

> the glory and leads it according to His will to make known to the prophets the will of the Creator, and the prophet bows down to it.[37]

This view clearly employs Saadiah's understanding of prophetic vision. Immediately after this view is proposed, another possible position is stated, according to which

> the Creator places in the heart of the prophet a vision (*ḥezyon*), and the Creator governs that image (*dimyon*). . . . Within the image the Creator directs the image according to what He wills, so that the prophet will know the supernal Mind (*daʿat ʿelyon*) and bow down to Him and believe in Him. Thus he is bowing down to the Creator. It is written, "And they saw the God of Israel and under His feet, etc." (Exod. 24:10). The Creator is in that very image, and governs the image in accordance with what He wills . . . and that image is not separate from the Creator, blessed be He.[38]

This second explanation is meant to solve the theoretical problem stated toward the beginning of the text. If the visible form of the glory is characterized either as created, according to Saadiah, or as an image placed within the heart, according to an anonymous sage, then how can we address the prayer *ʿAleynu* (or prayer in general) to the glory, since that prayer contains the words "He is our God"? It is obvious that the reference here is to the dialogue between sages mentioned above. Prima facie, it would appear that the second view is comparable to the first view articulated in the former text, in that it posits that God is invisible and what the prophet beholds is a phantasm or image in his mind. In this case, however, there is an important new shift in the meaning of the term *dimyon*, "image," for the latter corresponds to the divine glory iconically apprehended in the moment of revelation. The Creator, therefore, is said to be present within the image.[39]

The initial theoretical problem of addressing prayer to an entity that is distinct from God is solved by the blurring of the ontological difference between the Creator and the image. One can worship the visible glory, an image within the mind, for the Creator is present in that very image; hence worshiping the image is akin to worshiping the Creator: "[The] glory corresponds to His will, to inform the prophet of the will of the Creator, and the prophet bows down to Him."[40] A similar view is espoused in a text extant in several manuscripts and attributed to R. Eleazar ha-Darshan,[41] although in this case the psychological nature of the imagined form is not emphasized: "The Creator produced a form (*yeṣirah*) called *Shekhinah* . . . and where He placed that form they bow down to the Creator, the Holy One, blessed be He, and they know that His desire and

[37] Dan, *Studies*, p. 83. I have translated according to the preferred reading in MS Oxford-Bodleian 1960, cited by Dan in n. 22.

[38] Ibid.

[39] Ibid., p. 83 n. 27.

[40] Ibid., p. 83.

[41] Concerning this thirteenth-century Ashkenazi figure, in some sources referred to as R. Eliezer, see Scholem, *Reshit ha-Qabbalah*, p. 204; idem, *Origins*, p. 109.

will is for them to worship Him in that place as if He himself were there."[42] In effect, the mental image functions iconically, that is, one worships the image as if it were an iconic representation of the deity.[43] To put the matter in somewhat different terms, the sacred presence of the divine, essentially formless and im-

[42] MSS Paris–BN 843, fol. 72a, New York–JTSA Mic. 1885, fol. 74a. See below, n. 180. Cf. MS New York–JTSA Mic. 1690, fol. 22b: "Our rabbis, blessed be their memory, said: When you pray, 'know before whom you pray,' and you are not permitted to imagine any form before Him, as it is written, 'to whom may you liken Me, to whom may I be compared' (Isa. 40:25). Therefore in the time of prayer a person should concentrate in his heart upon the glorious and awesome name which is YHWH, as I have explained above [regarding] 'I have placed the Lord before me always' (Ps. 16:8)." And cf. the similar formulation in MS Oxford-Bodleian 1938, fol. 69a: "A person is not permitted to imagine any form before Him. Therefore in time of prayer he should intend in his heart the glorious and awesome name of the four letters. . . . It appears that a person does worship with a perfect worship if he does not imagine his Creator, as it says, 'Know the God of your father and serve Him' (1 Chron. 28:9)." The iconic representation of God, necessary for proper worship, is thus achieved through forming an image of the Tetragrammaton. Cf. Isaac of Acre, *Sefer Me'irat ʿEinayim,* p. 217; *'Oṣar Ḥayyim,* MS Moscow-Guenzberg 775, fols. 100a, 129a; Gottlieb, *Studies in the Kabbala Literature,* pp. 234–236. As will be seen below, in the Pietistic literature the Tetragrammaton can assume the role and function of the visible form of the glory. On the meditative technique in thirteenth-century kabbalistic sources based on the imaginative visualization of the letters of the divine name, including the writings of Isaac ibn Laṭif and Isaac of Acre, see Idel, *Mystical Experience,* pp. 30–34.

[43] For the explicit prohibition on placing icons in the Synagogue, especially near the Ark, see Judah he-Ḥasid, *Sefer Ḥasidim,* § 1625, p. 396. Interestingly enough, in that context the word used to refer to the Christian belief in icons is *demuyot,* the very word employed by the Pietist authors to refer to mental images that the invisible spiritual realities assume within the imagination. The motif of worshiping mental icons expressed in the Pietistic writings bears a striking similarity to a strategy adopted by Eastern Christian theologians in the Iconoclastic debates that raged in the eighth and ninth centuries on the problem of God's incorporeality and the legitimacy of using icons in worship. The solution offered by the Pietists resembles the approach of John of Damascus, according to whom the physical icon was replaced by a mental image so that the worshiper would pray to that image as if he were bowing down to the iconic manifestation of God. Like the Pietists, John relates the mental image to the biblical idea of Adam having been created in the image of God. Moreover, the icon is treated as a mental image in the mind of God, i.e., the thoughts of God assume the character of pictorial figurations. The further step of locating the iconic representation in the mind of the worshiper is taken by Theodore of Studion. One final interesting similarity between the Pietistic view and John's treatment is his claim that the image in some sense is identical with the prototype of which it is an image. See Barasch, *Icon,* pp. 223–226, 273–274. Future research will have to determine if these phenomenological similarities can be linked to any specific historical causes. The channels of influence are very difficult to ascertain, but one must bear in mind that essential elements of the Pietistic worldview were shaped in geographical regions other than the Rhineland and in periods of time before the twelfth and thirteenth centuries. When assessing the Pietistic worldview one must recall that southern Italy, especially in the eighth and ninth centuries, assumes a central role as the context wherein some of the ideas, texts, and practices may have taken shape in an embryonic form. According to literary accounts by the Pietists themselves, the traditions and doctrines of an esoteric nature reached the Qalonymide family in southern Italy from both Palestine and Babylonia. (See Wolfson, "Theosophy of Shabbetai Donnolo," pp. 282–286.) Presumably, the esoteric doctrines were cultivated in those regions during the sixth, seventh, and eighth centuries, and perhaps even at an earlier time. The possibility of an adaptation of a Christian view at this nascent stage cannot be discarded. Alternatively, it may be the case that the parallel motifs expressed in the Jewish and Christian authors can be explained by similar historical conditions that produced similar results without causal connection.

ageless, is "localized" visibly and spatially in the mental image that functions as a symbol mediating between the transcendent and the immanent, the other and the given.[44] Yet the reader is warned that one must not extend this logic to the point of arguing that since God is omnipresent every place is appropriate for worship. "If you say that the Creator is outside the image and within it, for no prophet can differentiate between it and the Creator, and inasmuch as the Creator is in everything, let him bow down [in prayer] in any place that he wants, the matter is not so; for He desires the place where His glory is found and there He will fulfill the will of the one who prays."[45] The important point for this analysis is the first part of this statement: "the Creator is outside the image and within it, for no prophet can differentiate between it and the Creator."

A similar approach is taken by Eleazar of Worms. For example, in *Sefer ha-Shem* he writes that "He is within the image (*mar'eh*) and it appears to the mind of the prophet as the will of the Creator. The Creator and the images are not angels that are independent (*she-yiheyu be-khoaḥ ʿeṣem*), but rather [they represent] the will of the Creator as it appears according to the decree. . . . The Creator is outside the images and within them (*ha-bore' huṣ la-mar'ot u-ve-tokham*)."[46] In another text the language is even closer to that used in the commentary on *ʿAleynu* attributed to Judah:

> In the place that He makes His glory appear, there He desires the intention of the one who prays; thus one must set a fixed place for one's prayers. When a person worships in the place where His glory is, and the Creator is in His glory and governs it according to His will to inform the prophet of the will of the Creator, and he worships it, he believes in the Creator. . . . Within the image (*dimyon*) is the Creator who governs it. "They saw the God of Israel" (Exod. 24:10) and worshiped Him, the Creator within the image, "and through the prophets I was imaged" (Hosea 12:11).[47]

[44] My discussion here has been influenced by van der Leeuw (*Religion in Essence and Manifestation,* pp. 447–448), who has perceptively entitled his chapter "Endowment with Form in Worship." It seems to me that this formulation is entirely appropriate to characterize the Pietistic liturgical orientation. See the Ashkenazi tradition preserved in a commentary on Psalms in MS Oxford-Bodleian 1551, fol. 207b: "'I am ever mindful of the Lord's presence' (Ps. 16:8), when a person prays it should seem to him that the Holy One, blessed be He, is opposite him. This is the secret of 'He is at my right hand; I shall never be shaken' (ibid.), for [David] had a small Torah scroll and when he went out to war it was bound on his right arm and through its merit he was victorious."

[45] Text quoted in Dan, *Studies,* p. 83.

[46] MS British Museum 737, fol. 320b. On the imaginative visualization of the glory during prayer, see ibid., fols. 280a and 288b. Cf. Eleazar of Worms, *Ḥokhmat ha-Nefesh,* chap. 52, pp. 89–90: "What the supernal Mind decrees is within the images (*mar'ot*), and that Mind is in accord with what [God] decrees, and the images are in accord with the decrees. The Creator is outside the images and within them (*ha-bore' huṣ min ha-mar'ot u-ve-tokham*). The prophet can know the will of the Creator only through the images."

[47] *Shaʿare ha-Sod,* p. 155. Cf. the version of Eleazar's *Hilkhot ha-Kavod* extant in MS Oxford-Bodleian 2575, fol. 3a (the text is lacking in the printed version in *Sode Razayya,* ed. Kamelhar,

From the statements of Eleazar it is clear that the image plays a critical function: prayers must be directed to the formless Creator, but one can pray to a fixed form, for God is present in the image. Indeed, on a number of occasions Eleazar insists that intention in prayer should be directed to the Creator and not to the enthroned glory seen by the prophets. "When a person prays he should direct his heart [with proper intention], as it says, 'I have placed the Lord before me always' (Ps. 16:8). Therefore they established [in the formulation of blessings] 'Blessed are You, Lord,' like a person speaking to his friend."[48] Similarly, "A person should not think only about the glory that ap-

---

pp. 30–42): "Since it is written 'For I fill both heaven and earth' (Jer. 23:24), why does one need to pray in a Synagogue or in the Temple? Yet there is a place in which the Holy One, blessed be He, shows the created glory to the prophet according to the need of the hour. One might ask: How can one bow down to something created? And consider these verses: It is written, 'For I granted many visions, and through the prophets I was imaged' (Hosea 12:11). How could it be said, 'Yet my own eyes have beheld the King Lord of Hosts' (Isa. 6:5) when it is written 'no man shall see Me and live' (Exod. 33:20)? Rather the [vision] is nothing but a wonderful image (*dimyon*) and it appears as if he actually saw but it is nothing but a strong image. It is written, 'upon this semblance of a throne there was the semblance of a human form' (Ezek. 1:26); so, too, here [in the case of Isaiah] it is only an image." See fol. 3b, which more or less corresponds to the printed text in *Sode Razayya,* p. 32.

[48] *Sefer Razi'el,* 8d (cf. *Sode Razayya,* ed. Weiss, p. 7); see Scholem, *Major Trends,* p. 107. See also text cited below at n. 54. The point emphasized by Eleazar regarding the need to direct intention in prayer to the invisible Godhead rather than a lower visible divine power has a parallel in the writings of the circle of the Special Cherub, as is attested especially in the short treatise *Pesaq ha-Yir'ah we-ha-'Emunah* ("A Decision Concerning the Fear and Faith [of God]"). In that text, however, the term *kavod,* "glory," applies to the invisible entity (also referred to as the Holiness [*qedushah*] of God, or the *Shekhinah,* the divine Presence) and the visible form is called by the technical expression *keruv ha-meyuḥad,* the Special Cherub (or the Greatness [*gedullah*] and Kingship [*malkhut*]). More specifically, the worshiper is instructed to direct his prayer toward the enthroned and anthropomorphic Cherub in the east, the iconic and visible pole of the divine, but the intention ultimately must be directed from there to the invisible and imageless Presence of God in the west. The Cherub thus serves as a vehicle by means of which one gains contact with the Godhead. See Dan, "The Emergence of Mystical Prayer," pp. 93–102; idem, "Pesaq ha-Yirah veha-Emunah," pp. 200–201; idem, "Prayer as Text and Prayer as Mystical Experience." See also the statement of Shem Ṭov bar Simḥah cited by Scholem in *Reshit ha-Qabbalah,* p. 78 n. 1 (based on MS New York–JTSA Mic. 2430, fol. 65b; concerning this collection of German Pietistic secretes and its editor, see Scholem, *Major Trends,* p. 376 n. 122; Dan, *Esoteric Theology,* pp. 48, 255; idem, "The Vicissitudes of the Esoterism of the German Ḥasidim," p. 91; idem, "The Intention of Prayer from the Tradition of R. Judah the Pious"): "Therefore, a person should consider in his heart to pray so that his prayer will be received before the Creator, blessed be He, from the power of the Special Cherub who is emanated and created from His Great Fire. . . . No one should wonder how it can be said that the intention of a person should be [directed] to the Cherub so that through there his prayer will be accepted before the Cause of Causes, blessed be He, and that he should not direct his intention to the Cause of Causes. Did not the Holy One, blessed be He, make Moses our master, peace be upon him, hear His voice, saying, 'Pay heed to him and obey him, do not defy him, for he will not pardon your offenses, since My name is in him' (Exod. 23:21), in other words, do not exchange your intention but rather set your heart upon him in the time of your worship. Even though this is the case, they warned that one should not err and think that he has strength and power from himself. Rather, everything comes from His power. . . . Consider him in your worship, 'for My name is in him,' for his name is the great Meṭaṭron and he is called the lesser YHWH." Regarding the directing of prayers in the Ashkenazi liturgy to angelic beings ontically lower than the supreme Godhead, see also Liebes, "Angels of the Shofar."

pears opposite the exalted throne but rather about the Creator of all, who manifests His glory to those who are righteous in their hearts, for He is one and nothing resembles Him, blessed be He, and thus He 'is near to all who call Him' (Ps. 145:18). Therefore they established [in the formulation of blessings] 'Blessed are You, Lord,' like he who speaks mouth to mouth to one standing opposite him, as it says, 'I have placed the Lord before me always' (Ps. 16:8)."[49] And again, "In the blessing of his Master and his praise he should intend with all his heart, and when he says, 'Blessed are You, Lord,' he should think not about the glory seen in the heart of the prophets as it appears on the throne, but about the Lord who is God in the heavens, earth, air, sea, and the whole world."[50] An important parallel to this statement is found in an anonymous Pietistic text extant in manuscript:

> The essence of intention is in the first three blessings [of the eighteen benedictions], for they are the praise of the Creator, blessed be He. When a person says, "Blessed are You, Lord," he should think not about the glory seen by the prophets as it appears on the throne, but about the Lord who is God in the heavens above, without limit, whose place is hidden and concealed. For with respect to the visible glory (*ha-kavod ha-nir'eh*) the throne of glory is created to indicate to the prophets that there is a God. But with respect to Him there is no sitting and no image at all. It seems to me that one should also pray not to the hiding place of His glory (*ḥevyon ʿoz*) but to the great light (*ha-'or ha-gadol*), concerning which it is written, "for no man shall see Me and live" (Exod. 33:20), and within it are comprised the glory and strength, "God is the Lord," blessed be the name of the glory of His kingdom forever.[51]

The intention of prayer, at least in certain key parts of the liturgy, should be directed to the great light, which represents either God or the hidden glory, contrasted with the visible glory. In the continuation of the above text a distinction is made between those prayers that are directed to the great light and other prayers directed to the visible glory. The last point accords with the view affirmed by Eleazar in several other contexts wherein he insists that intention in prayer is directed toward the glory that is visible.[52] In particular, Eleazar connects this view with the statement attributed to Yose, that one who prays must cast his eyes downward and his heart upward.[53] For example, in one place he

[49] MS Paris–BN 772, fol. 90a.

[50] *Sefer ha-Roqeaḥ*, p. 9; and parallel in *Sha'are ha-Sod*, p. 153. See Dan, *Esoteric Theology*, p. 167.

[51] MS New York–JTSA Mic. 1878, fol. 108b, quoted in Idel, "Intention in Prayer in the Beginning of Kabbalah," p. 7. My thanks to Ephraim Kanarfogel for drawing my attention to this article. The reference there to MS JTSA Mic. 1873 should be changed to 1878; the correct number is given on p. 9.

[52] See Dan, *Esoteric Theology*, pp. 182–183.

[53] B. Yevamot 105b. See Zimmer, "Poses and Postures during Prayer," pp. 89–92. The Pietistic interpretation of this rabbinic dictum is discussed by I. Marcus in "Prayer Gestures in German Ḥasidism," to be published in the proceedings of the conference "Mystik, Magie und Kabbala im Aschkenasischen Judentum" (9–11 Dec. 1991, Frankfurt am Main, Germany). Cf. the passage

writes, "The Creator is actually close to you, that is, He fills everything and nothing is hidden from Him. It is written, 'for God is in heaven' (Eccles. 5:1), for the essence of His glory is seen above. . . . Thus the sages said in Yevamot, 'The one who prays should cast his eyes downward and his heart upward.' The Creator is next to him, but His glory is above, alongside the high and exalted throne."[54] Although the Creator is immanent in all things, intention in prayer should be directed upward to the glory. Yet in other texts, as I have indicated above, Eleazar, following his predecessors, insists that prayer be directed to the Creator. From a philosophical point of view, however, it is impossible to so direct one's intention, for the Creator is formless. Therefore, the role of the mental image is vital, for it facilitates the imaging of that which is without image. By means of the image one cay pray to the imageless Creator who, paradoxically, is both absent from and present in the image. This basic paradox of the religious phenomenology of prayer is alluded to by Eleazar in a comment on the passage in the morning liturgy, "David blessed the Lord in front of all the assemblage; David said: Blessed are You, Lord, God of Israel our father, from eternity to eternity" (1 Chron. 29:10):

> In a similar vein [to the opening of David's blessing], in all generations people say each and every day "Blessed are You, Lord," for it is written, "I have blessed the Lord before me always" (Ps. 16:8). The Lord is the all in all things. Therefore it says, "Blessed are You, Lord," like one who speaks [to another] mouth to mouth. "God of Israel," this refers to the glory that Israel the elder [i.e., Jacob] and all the prophets saw. This is a glorious form, a resplendent light without image except as it appears in the human imagination (*be-mar'eh 'adam ha-dimyon*). Lest one be startled if one sees [the glory] in another matter, the glory surrounds the prophet in a cloud all the time it is speaking with him. This should not be transmitted in writing but rather mouth to mouth, as the pious one did. The glory of God is not to investigate, lest one's heart be led astray to falsehood. It is written, "The glory of God is to conceal the matter" (Prov. 25:2).[55]

---

from *Sefer Ḥasidim* cited below at n. 243. See also the Ashkenazi text extant in MS New York–JTSA Mic. 1878, fol. 44a, partially cited below at n. 326.

[54] *Sode Razayya,* p. 37; also p. 31 (unless otherwise noted, all citations are from the Kamelhar edition). See also *Sha'are ha-Sod,* p. 154. Cf. the "secret of prayer" described in *Ḥokhmat ha-Nefesh,* chap. 53, p. 92: "The soul must think about the Creator who is standing opposite it and pray with intention, and it must bow down facing Jerusalem, for the essence of the glory is in the place of Jerusalem and in the land of Judah."

[55] MS Paris–BN 772, fol. 49a. See Urbach (*'Arugat ha-Bosem* 4:81–82), who cites this text from MS Vienna 108, fol. 31c. Urbach maintains (pp. 82–83) that the end of the passage that emphasizes the need to transmit this secret orally is an addition by one of Eleazar's disciples who reiterated the need for oral transmission after copying the master's explicit written explication of the secret. In my opinion this inference is unnecessary, for it can be shown that in a number of places in his compositions Eleazar alludes to an esoteric matter in writing but withholds the fuller explanation, maintaining that the appropriate means for transmitting such matters is through oral teaching. Typically, the need for secrecy is related to some erotic element in the divine realm. See below, n. 202.

Imagination and the Corporeal Symbolization of the Spiritual

Here we must pause and consider more carefully the role of imagination and the status accorded the imaginary in the Pietistic writings. It must be emphasized that the *dimyon,* the faculty by which one imagines, is not characterized by either of the two main functions attributed to the imagination in medieval Aristotelianism. That is, the *dimyon* is not construed by the Pietists as either representation through an image of an absent sensible object or as the presentation of that which is unreal (the imaginary) based on the sensory impressions retained in the imagination. To be sure, as we have seen, the Pietists use the expression *'aḥizat ʿeinayim,* optical delusion, to refer to the image of the glory visualized by the prophet. From one perspective, then, the images (*demuyot*) that are imagined are imaginary in the sense of being illusory or purely subjective. Yet from another perspective these images are the visible forms of that which is invisible but nonetheless ontically real—indeed, the ultimate reality, namely, the divine glory whose luminosity is intrinsically without shape. In that sense the images produced by the *dimyon* function as the symbolic depiction of the spiritual reality in concrete, tangible form. In the preceding chapter I discussed a similar notion in the thought of Judah Halevi and mentioned some of his sources in Jewish and Islamic Neoplatonism going back in some respects to classical Neoplatonic thinkers such as Plotinus and Proclus. Analogous theories of the role of imagination in medieval Christian literature can possibly be explained in terms of the influence of the same (or parallel) Neoplatonic sources transmitted to the Latin West, especially through John Scotus Eriugena.[56]

It cannot be proven with any degree of certainty—in fact, it is highly unlikely—that the Ḥaside Ashkenaz had direct access to or had the facility to utilize the aforementioned philosophical texts, although it has been suggested by several scholars that they may have known something of Eriugena's ideas.[57]

[56] On the centrality of imagination in the twelfth-century Platonic tradition, see Dronke, *Fabula Explorations into the Uses of Myth in Medieval Platonism.* My thanks to Bernard McGinn for calling my attention to this work. See also Bautier, "Phantasia-imaginatio"; Hamesse, "Imaginatio et phantasia chez les auteurs philosophiques du 12e et du 13e siècle." See also discussion of the symbolist mentality of the Victorines in Chenu, *Nature, Man, and Society in the Twelfth Century,* pp. 99–145.

[57] Scholem (*Major Trends,* pp. 108–109) raises the possibility that the German Pietists may have been influenced by an idea of Eriugena transmitted through the anonymous Hebrew paraphrase of Saadiah's *Book of Beliefs and Opinions.* See also Vajda, "De quelques vestiges du néoplatonisme," p. 166, and Scholem's comment published at the end of that article, p. 170; Idel, "Sefirot above the Sefirot," pp. 246 n. 41, 261 n. 110, 268. On the influence of Christian thought on Elḥanan ben Yaqar, see Vajda, "De quelques infiltrations chrétiennes dans l'oeuvre d'un auteur Anglo-Juif du XIIIe siècle," and the remarks of Dan in *Esoteric Theology,* pp. 38–39. I will not here enter into a lengthy discussion of the larger question concerning the influence of Christian monasticism on the Rhineland Jewish Pietists, but I will simply note that modern scholars have wavered between the assumption of parallel but independent developments (M. Güdemann, *Geschichte des Erziehungswesen und der Kultur der Juden in Frankreich und Deutschland* [Vienna, 1880]) and that of direct influence (Baer, "Socioreligious Orientation of 'Sefer Ḥasidim'"). Some recent scholars (Marcus,

On the other hand, it is plausible to suggest that common intellectual currents influenced their thinking along with that of thinkers in other religions, particularly Christianity, living in their time. The possible Neoplatonic understanding of the imagination in the thought of the German Pietists has been noted by Asi Farber, who, reflecting on the use of the term *dimyon* in the Pietistic literature, remarked that the Pietists accepted a Neoplatonized version of the images (*dimyonot* or *demuyot*) through which the glory is revealed. That is, the images are not merely epistemological constructs but ontological entities, which are, in fact, the paradigms of earthly realities that are experienced concretely within the imagination. The Pietistic conception thus reinterprets the images of Saadiah's philosophy by making them independent hypostases.[58]

In support of this interpretation let me mention here three examples from the many that could be cited; each of these illustrates another aspect of the Pietistic conception of the archetypal image. The first is a passage from Eleazar's commentary on *Sefer Yeṣirah* in which he characterizes the first of the ten *sefirot,* called *ruaḥ 'elohim ḥayyim,* "the spirit of the living God" (also identified as *ruaḥ ha-qodesh,* "the holy spirit") as the ether "in which were seen all the images (*dimyonot*) seen by every prophet and seer, and within it were heard the seven voices."[59] In this context, then, the *dimyonot* are more than just mental constructs; they are hypostatic entities that are said to be visible within the ether, the first of all created things. The images are the visual elements that parallel the seven audible voices of revelation. The second example is a teaching of Eleazar reported by his student Abraham bar Azriel: " 'And you shall see My back' (Exod. 33:20), the angels that are behind Me . . . that is, the images (*demuyot*) that are behind Me, 'but My face shall not be seen' . . . [that is,] the images that are before Me."[60] In this context the back of the glory is identified not with a single angel[61] but with a plurality of angels that are further characterized as the images through which the divine is manifest. These are to be

---

Piety and Society, pp. 150 n. 54, 151 n. 57; Schäfer, "Ideal of Piety of the Ashkenazi Ḥasidim") have challenged the assumption of Christian influence, stressing instead the internal Jewish trajectory. See n. 43, above.

[58] See Farber, "Concept of the Merkabah," pp. 271, 401–407, 410–414. Cf. the usage of the word *dimyonot* (images) as a parallel to *ṣurot* (forms) in Azriel of Gerona, *Perush ha-'Aggadot,* ed. Tishby, p. 105.

[59] *Perush Sefer Yeṣirah le-Rabbi 'Ele'azar mi-Worms* 3c.

[60] *'Arugat ha-Bosem,* 1:198. Cf. MS New York–JTSA Mic. 2430, fol. 74a; and see Farber, "Concept of the Merkabah" p. 407.

[61] See, by contrast, the tradition reported in *Sefer Mal'akhim,* attributed by Dan to Judah the Pious, to the effect that the angel behind God referred to in Exod. 33:20 is Raphael. See Judah he-Ḥasid, "The Book of Angels," ed. Dan, p. 115. According to another Ashkenazi tradition, reported in the commentary on the names of Meṭaṭron, the back of God mentioned in Exod. 33:20 refers to Meṭaṭron. Cf. MSS Cambridge Heb. Add. 405, fol. 306b; Oxford-Bodleian 2286, fol. 159b; Moscow-Guenzberg 90, fol. 128b; *Sefer ha-Ḥesheq* 6a. Concerning this text, see Dan, *Esoteric Theology,* pp. 219–224; idem, "The Seventy Names of Meṭaṭron"; Farber, "Concept of the Merkabah," pp. 237, 300, 423. A reflex of this tradition is found in the collection of Jacob ben Jacob ha-Kohen's teachings, *Sefer ha-'Orah,* MSS Milan-Ambrosiana 62, fol. 84a; Jerusalem-Schocken 14, fol. 67a.

contrasted with the higher angels, which are the images before the divine that cannot be seen, an idea that is reflected in older sources.[62] Finally, in a third text Eleazar writes that God "created glorious images (*demuyot nikhbadot*) and placed the thoughts (*daʿatanot*) of His decrees in the images, and among them is an image more splendid than the rest, and sometimes [it appears] in human form."[63] It is obvious from this passage as well that the *demuyot* are not purely mental constructs, but are ontic entities—angels—that manifest the divine will to the human imagination. In contrast to the second passage, this one states unequivocally that the angels are the theophanic forms that take shape within the mind. Such an identification is implied as well in a passage from *Sefer ha-Shem* of Eleazar: "It is customary for God to clothe the thoughts of His decrees, to show [them] to the prophets so that they will know that God has set His decrees. The prophet knows His thoughts according to the vision that he sees. At times this vision is called an angel."[64]

As Farber has also noted, one may connect the notion of images in Eleazar's writings with another conception he frequently mentions, namely, that the glory is manifest through nine forms of appearance or vision, usually identified as *maḥazot* or *mar'ot*.[65] The midrashic source for this notion is the statement attributed to R. Judah bar Ilai in *Wayyikra Rabbah* 1:14, that the prophets saw the divine through nine specula, whereas Moses saw through one speculum. In German Pietistic theosophy these nine mirrors are hypostasized and thus refer to ontic or archetypal images through which the glory is manifest.[66] An allu-

[62] See Targum Pseudo-Jonathan on Exod. 33:23, which renders the biblical statement "Then I will take My hand away and you will see My back" as "I will cause the groups of angels who serve before Me to pass and you will see the knot of the phylacteries of the arm." See also *Pirqe R. 'Eliʿezer* 46, 111b: "[God said to Moses,] Stand by the opening of the cave and I will cause the angels who serve Me to pass before you, as it says, 'And He answered, I will make all My goodness pass before you' (Exod. 33:19)." The influence of the latter text is clearly apparent in Eleazar's *Sode Razayya*, p. 6, where Exod. 33:19 is interpreted in terms of the "good attributes" (*middot ha-ṭovot*), which refer in this context to a class of angelic beings. On the association of God's face/presence with angels, see Olyan, *A Thousand Thousands Served Him*, pp. 108–109.

[63] *Sode Razayya*, p. 34.

[64] MS British Museum 737, fol. 223a. Cf. *Sode Razayya*, p. 6, where the angels are referred to as "images (*mar'ot*) whose thought is His decree." See Dan, *Studies*, pp. 31–32. Cf. *Ḥokhmat ha-Nefesh*, chap. 52, pp. 89–90. In that context Eleazar contrasts the images placed by the divine will in the minds of the prophets and the angels that act on their own power.

[65] See the extensive discussion in Farber, "Concept of the Merkabah," pp. 402–414. For a different interpretation of the terms "images" (*demuyot*) and "forms" (*mar'ot*) in the writings of Eleazar of Worms, see the brief comments of Funkenstein, "Naḥmanides' Symbolical Reading of History," p. 138. On the possibility that the word *dimyon* in medieval Jewish biblical exegesis is an equivalent for the Latin terms *imago, figura,* or *exemplar,* see Kamin, "'*Dugma*' in Rashi's Commentary on Song of Songs," pp. 21–22. See, however, the critique of Ta-Shema in "On the Commentary on the Aramaic Piyyuṭim in the Maḥzor Vitry," where he traces the use of the word *dimyon* to earlier sources.

[66] In this connection it is of interest to note the following comment in a poem of the eleventh-century poet Isaac ibn Ghayyat: "The splendor of the seven hidden palaces that are arranged / and the nine pure inner mirrors / that You have set between me and You" / (הוד שבעה היכלות צפונות סדורות / ותשע אספקלריאות פנימיות טהורות / ירית ביני וביניך). Cf. *The Poems of Rabbi Isaac Ibn Ghayyat,*

sion to such a construct is found in one of the recensions of *Sod ha-'Egoz* (the "Secret of the Nut"), a text that represents an early stage of Pietistic speculation on the nature of the chariot, which is compared structurally to the nut (perhaps based on Cant. 6:11):[67] "Nine visions of the glory [correspond to] nine leaves to every branch of the nut."[68] Eleazar refers to this notion as well on several occasions. To cite but two of the many relevant examples: "On the throne is the image of Jacob; thus in Scripture [the expression] 'my servant, Jacob' appears nine times, corresponding to nine types of splendor. . . . There are nine visions (*maḥazot*)[69] of the glory and it appears upon the image of Jacob."[70] In his commentary on the liturgy he remarks, "[The expressions] to place His name there, to cause His name to dwell there, appear nine times in the Torah, corresponding to the nine visions (*mar'ot*)."[71] From these and other passages it may be concluded that the Pietists affirmed the existence of nine theophanic forms through which the glory is manifest.

Inasmuch as the images seen by the visionary are the visible representation of the invisible realities, it may be said that for the German Pietists as well, the *dimyon* is the faculty that mediates between the corporeal and spiritual, and the images it produces are the visible representation of the invisible. Clearly, these images do not "objectively" represent truth, but neither are they entirely false or subjective. The imaginary is both real and illusory. This duality is highlighted by the Pietists' claim, discussed above, that God is both outside and within the image. The glory can be imagined in concrete forms, including most importantly that of an anthropos, for God, the transcendent One, is not the image; yet one can worship that very image, because God is present therein. The positive value accorded to the imagination is also underscored by the theological claim that it is the will of God itself that is responsible for placing these images within the prophet's mind. The point is well made in another passage in Eleazar's commentary on *Sefer Yeṣirah*. After stating unequivocally that God has no bodily image and therefore cannot be seen, Eleazar notes that God

---

p. 67. The reference here to the pure inner mirrors seems to signify something hypostatic and not merely a figure of speech. The parallel to the Pietistic interpretation of the aggadic motif is striking and demands further research.

[67] See Altmann, *Studies*, pp. 161–171; Dan, "*Ḥokhmath ha-Egoz:* Its Origin and Development"; idem, *Esoteric Theology*, pp. 207–210, 257–258; idem, "On the History of the Text of *Ḥokhmat ha-Egoz*," and the wide-ranging discussions in Farber, "Concept of the Merkabah."

[68] Altmann, *Studies*, p. 171.

[69] Cf. Eleazar's *'ofan le-shabbat teshuvah*, which begins with the words *'Or yisra'el u-qedosho*, in *Shirat ha-Roke'aḥ*, ed. Meiseles, p. 33: *'esh be-tesha' maḥazot lifne qadosh*, "the fire is in nine appearances before the Holy One."

[70] *Sode Razayya*, p. 29, and parallel in *Perush Sodot ha-Tefillah*, MS Paris–BN 772, fols. 76a, 134a; see Farber, "Concept of the Merkabah," p. 412, and my study "The Image of Jacob Engraved upon the Throne."

[71] MS Paris–BN 772, fol. 48b. Cf. MS Oxford-Bodleian 1566, fols. 37b, 41b. See also *Zohar Ḥadash* 94c (*Tiqqunim*): "Corresponding to the nine *sefirot* Ezekiel saw nine visions (*mar'ot*), concerning which it is said, 'The heavens opened and I saw visions of God' (Ezek. 1:1)."

"appears to the prophets by means of the presence of His glory through many images (*nir'eh la-nevi'im ʿal yede shekhinat kevodo be-dimyonot harbeh*), according to His desire and will, the one who creates images."[72] Hence, one of the technical names of God is "Creator of the images" (*bore' dimyonot*), for through these very images the invisible is made visible, thus rendering prophetic and mystical visions possible as well as providing a mechanism for liturgical worship. The images are more than allegorical or figurative tropes; they are signs of the spiritual reality experienced (and this is a critical term that needs to be emphasized) by the individual, and these signs possess a diaphanous quality that allows the nonrepresentable reality to be represented, that is, to be present as form in the imagination. The image is the symbolic figuration of the transcendent, and in the representation precisely that which is absent is made present.

Despite the correctness of the claim that, for the Pietists, the images must be viewed ontologically or hypostatically, in their writings they simultaneously developed the docetic posture alluded to in the aggadic texts and expanded in the Geonic material interpreting mystical and prophetic visions. That is to say, the images, which are of a spiritual, immaterial nature, assume concrete shape or form only within the mind of the one seeing the vision. A careful study of the relevant materials, both in manuscript and in print, indicates that the second posture is the one adopted in almost every instance by Eleazar of Worms, although in his case, too, one finds a modified notion of *dimyon*. Indeed, in one passage in his *Ḥokhmat ha-Nefesh* (the "Wisdom of the Soul"), Eleazar mentions explicitly the interpretation of the "first philosopher," a clear indication that he is referring to the dialogue discussed above. He writes,

> The first philosopher said that the images (*demuyot*) that are seen in [the magical technique of conjuring angelic visions called] the archons of the cup (*sare kos*) and the archons of the thumbnails (*sare bohen*)[73] and by means of delusions (*'aḥizat ʿeinayim*) are reflections and not [actual] bodies. . . . The image is a reflection corresponding to the person himself. Thus one says that these images are only in the mind . . . the idea changes and appears as images that have no substance . . . and this spirit appears as a delusion, in an image, [as it is written,] "in the image of God He created him" (Gen. 1:27).[74]

In another passage in the same composition Eleazar differentiates on legal grounds between the technique of conjuring images referred to as "the archons of the cup" (*sare kos*) and "the archons of the thumbnails" (*sare bohen*) and creating delusions (*'aḥizat ʿeinayim*) that have no external reality. The former is forbidden only by rabbinic ordinance,[75] whereas the latter is a scriptural prohi-

[72] *Perush Sefer Yeṣirah le-R. 'Eleʿazar mi-Worms* 3a.

[73] Concerning these techniques, see Dan, *Studies*, pp. 34–43; idem, *Esoteric Theology*, pp. 190–192.

[74] *Ḥokhmat ha-Nefesh*, chap. 48, p. 80; see also chap. 52, p. 91.

[75] In fact, the only reference to this magical practice in talmudic literature of which I am aware does not necessarily forbid it, but merely downplays its efficacy. Cf. B. Sanhedrin 101a. See the

bition.[76] In either case, however, one is dealing with mental images for which there are no objective correlates in the spatio-temporal realm. "It says, '[God ceased] from all the work of creation that He had done' (Gen. 2:3). What is the meaning of 'that He had done'? God gave permission for images of creatures to be seen in the human heart as, for example, the archons of the cup and the archons of the thumbnails that they see and the delusion (*'aḥizat ʿeinayim*) through which is seen the form of [one's] desire."[77]

It will be noted that at the end of the passage from *Ḥokhmat ha-Nefesh* in which Eleazar mentions the first philosopher he utilizes this very notion of a mental image to explain the biblical idea that man is created in the divine image, which is connected in other texts with the Pietistic conception of the celestial image (*ṣelem*)[78] that corresponds, as Scholem has written, to a kind of astral "archetype" that occupies a "sphere of noncorporeal, semi-divine existence."[79] In the most detailed formulation of the latter idea in Judah he-Ḥasid's *Sefer Ḥasidim* (the "Book of the Pious") there is already an implicit connection between the *ṣelem* and prophetic vision, as the relevant context has to do with the revelation of the divine glory to Moses, though there is no indication that the celestial *ṣelem* is treated as a mental image:

> It is written, "I will make all My goodness pass before you" (Exod. 33:19). The word "all" (*kol*) [in the expression "all My goodness," *kol ṭuvi*] numerically equals fifty [which corresponds to the fifty] gates of understanding.[80] Upon each and every gate there is appointed an angel. The expression "all My goodness" (*kol ṭuvi*) numerically equals [the word] *mazzal,*[81] [zodiacal sign], for [God] showed Moses the sign of their souls. . . . This is the meaning of "all My goodness before you." It should have been written "all My goodness before your eyes." Rather [the use of the expression "before you," *ʿal panekha*] alludes to the fact that the face of Moses is above when He passes above, over that very form, the angel comes down upon him and informs him. . . . Thus it says, "And God created man in His image,

commentary of Rashi, ad. loc., who renders the expression "archons of oil" (*sare shemen*) as "archons of the thumbnails" (*sare bohen*). (For the general influence of magical traditions on Rashi, see M. Catane, "Le monde intellectuel de Rashi," in *Les Juifs au regard de l'histoire,* ed. G. Dahan [Paris, 1985], pp. 83–84.) For further evidence of this practice from a Genizah fragment, see Schäfer, "Jewish Magic Literature in Late Antiquity and Early Middle Ages," p. 89. See also the fragment dealing with angelic adjuration in MS Oxford-Bodleian 1626, fols. 14a–b. See Daiches, *Babylonian Oil Magic in the Talmud and in Later Jewish Literature;* Trachtenberg, *Jewish Magic and Superstition,* pp. 219–222; Y. Bilo, "Pondering the 'Princes of the Oil': New Light on an Old Phenomenon," *Journal of Anthropological Research* 37 (1981): 269–278.

[76] *Ḥokhmat ha-Nefesh,* chap. 74, p. 127.

[77] Ibid., chap. 46, p. 73.

[78] See Dan, *Esoteric Theology,* pp. 218, 224–229.

[79] Scholem, *Major Trends,* pp. 117–118; idem, *Origins,* p. 112 n. 114; see also Mopsik, *Le livre hébreu d'hénoch,* p. 53.

[80] Cf. B. Rosh ha-Shanah 21b.

[81] Cf. B. Megillah 3b and the commentary of Rashi, s.v. *mazzalayyhu.* According to Rashi, the word *mazzal* in this context denotes the "archon of each person above." See also B. Sanhedrin 94a.

715-549-5671

> in the image of God He created him" (Gen. 1:27): one [image] above and one [image] below.[82]

Reiterating the same notion, Eleazar writes,

> Every angel who is an archon of the zodiacal sign (*sar mazzal*) of a person when it is sent below has the image of the person who is under it.[83] . . . And this is the meaning of "And God created man in His image, in the image of God He created him" (Gen. 1:27). Why is [it written] twice, "in His image" and "in the image"? One image refers to the image of man and the other to the image of the angel of the zodiacal sign that is in the image of the man.[84]

In an earlier Pietistic text that undoubtedly was one of Eleazar's sources, the prophetic vision is likewise described in terms of the intermediary of the celestial image: "Then the prophet sees the image above, and the sign (*mazzal*) that is the archon of that image in the image of [that] man. . . . Thus he sees the image and the speech of that image . . . he sees the image of the archon that is his sign."[85] What is apparently distinctive about Eleazar's interpretation is the claim that this celestial image takes shape only within the mind of one who perceives it. Similarly, in another work, *Shaʿare ha-Sod ha-Yiḥud we-ha-ʾEmunah* (the "Gates of the Secret of Unity and Faith"), Eleazar comments on the verse "God said, Let us make man in our image and in our form" (Gen. 1:26), but in this case extends his remarks to angelic beings in general and does not limit himself to the celestial image: "This [verse] does not imply that the Creator, blessed be He, has the form or image of His creatures, but rather the meaning of 'in our image' is that we [i.e., the angels implied in the plural form of the verse[86]] wish to be revealed to the prophets in the most desirable counte-

[82] *Sefer Ḥasidim*, § 1514, pp. 369–370. Cf. the Pietistic commentary on the Pentateuch printed as *Perush ha-Roqeaḥ ʿal ha-Torah*, 1:67–68. Concerning the attribution of this text, see J. Dan, "The Ashkenazi Ḥasidic 'Gates of Wisdom' "; idem, "The Commentary on the Torah of R. Eleazar of Worms." The influence of the Pietistic idea is discernible in *Zohar* 1:115b (Midrash ha-Neʿelam—hereafter abbreviated MhN), although in that case the operative term is *diyoqon* and not *dimyon* or *demut*, the terms generally employed in the Pietistic sources.

[83] In this context as well, it is evident that the angel spoken of is the celestial sign. It is significant that the Pietistic notion is not fatalistic or deterministic in its orientation, i.e., one's fate is not completely determined by the celestial form in whose image one is created. On the contrary, the morphological resemblance between earthly man and the celestial form endows the former with theurgical significance over the latter. See, e.g., the marginal commentary (derived from Eleazar of Worms) to Psalm 100 extant in MS Oxford-Bodleian 1097, fol. 8a: "Just as a person acts below, so his sign acts above, that is, the angel [which corresponds to the sign] before the supernal retinue. On account of a person being joyous in his heart, for he was worthy of being a servant of God, his joy is increased, as it is written, 'In the light of the king's countenance is life' (Prov. 16:15), that is, his sign, the angel, is happy and illuminates the king's countenance with life as well as the whole retinue above." The enduring influence of Ḥaside Ashkenaz is apparent in later literature; see, e.g., Pineḥas Eliyahu Horowitz, *Sefer ha-Berit ha-Shalem*, p. 466.

[84] *Ḥokhmat ha-Nefesh*, chap. 48, p. 80; cf. chap. 59, pp. 103–104; see Dan, *Esoteric Theology*, p. 226.

[85] MS Oxford-Bodleian 1567, fols. 60a–b, quoted by Dan in *Esoteric Theology*, p. 225 n. 8.

[86] See Targum Pseudo-Jonathan on Gen. 1:26; *Bereshit Rabbah* 8:4, pp. 59–60.

nance, which is the face of an anthropos, the image that is unique for us, the form of the glorious and honorable image that is seen by us."[87] In slightly different words, Eleazar reiterates this view in another work: "'Let us make man in our image and in our form' (Gen. 1:26). The meaning of [the word] image (*demut*) is like the honorable and important image (*dimyon*) that appears to us [i.e., the angels], and this is the image that is revealed to the prophets."[88] Hence, the meaning of the biblical claim that Adam was created in the divine image is that he was created in the theophanic image of the angels.[89] The conception espoused by Eleazar served as the basis for the following comment found in *Paʿaneaḥ Raza'*, compiled in the second half of the thirteenth century by the French exegete and tosafist Isaac ben Judah ha-Levi, whose first-hand knowledge of Pietistic doctrine is attested by the fact that he occasionally cites Judah the Pious and Eleazar of Worms: "'Let us make man in our image,' in the image of angels, that is, let us make man in that very image that the Holy One, blessed be He, showed to the prophets in the form of an anthropos."[90] It is important to note that the Pietistic conception of an angelic being contrasts sharply with the medieval Aristotelian conception that had gained currency amongst Jewish philosophers through the influence of Islam. To the Pietists the angel is not merely a disembodied intellect—in philosophical terminology, "separate intellect" (*sekhel nifrad*)—but rather an ethereal luminous body.[91]

[87] *Shaʿare ha-Sod*, p. 146. Cf. *Sefer Tagi*, MS Oxford-Bodleian 1566, fol. 242b, and the words of Eleazar cited in *ʿArugat ha-Bosem* 1:137. Cf. *Perush Sodot ha-Tefillah*, MS Paris–BN 772, fol. 177a, where Eleazar comments on the liturgical formulation for a wedding ceremony, "He who has created Adam in His image": "This refers to the countenance of the human face that is upon the throne." Eleazar interprets the continuation of the blessing, "in the image of the likeness of His form," as a reference to the erect posture of the human gait. Cf. *Ḥokhmat ha-Nefesh*, chap. 51, p. 88.

[88] Dan, *Studies*, p. 85. On the role of the image (*demut*) in the Pietistic writings, see also Sirat, (*Théories*, p. 104), who mentions specifically Shabbetai Donnolo and Abraham bar Ḥiyya as possible influences.

[89] The Pietists' reading of Gen. 1:26 is informed in part by Abraham ibn Ezra's exegesis of the verse, "the [expression] 'in God's image' [refers to] an angel" (*Perushe ha-Torah le-Rabbenu 'Avraham 'ibn ʿEzra*, ed. Weiser, 1:9). The intent of ibn Ezra's identification of the divine image with an angel is that one is created in the image of the Intellect or supernal anthropos, also identified as Meṭaṭron. See Wolfson, "God, the Demiurge, and the Intellect," pp. 98–99. See also *The Religious Poems of Abraham ibn Ezra*, ed. Levin, 1:62 (poem no. 35): לזאת בדמות מלאך בראתנו.

[90] Quoted in *Tosafot ha-Shalem: Commentary on the Bible*, ed. Gellis, 1:61.

[91] See *Sode Razayya*, pp. 3, 8. For a rejection of the medieval philosophical understanding of angels as separate intellects on the basis that the view of the rabbis is that angels possess bodies, albeit everlasting and therefore not subject to decay, see the text extant in MS New York–JTSA Mic. 1892, fol. 57a, quoted as well in Isaac of Acre, *Sefer Me'irat ʿEinayim*, p. 105. See also the anonymous letter in MS Vatican 236, fols. 82b–83a (concerning this text see chapter 4, n. 247). After presenting the philosophical view, as expressed especially by Maimonides, regarding the tenth separate intellect, i.e., the *agens intellectus*, identified with the rabbinic "Prince of the World," as the locus of prophetic visions, the author mentions that various sages, including R. Abraham the Head of the Court (i.e., Abraham ben Isaac of Narbonne), the *ḥakham* R. Abraham, R. Judah the Pious, and R. Eleazar (referred to here as Eliezer) of Worms, received the tradition "without demonstration or proof, in the way a person transmits a secret to his friend," that the angels are composed of both form and matter. This is presented, moreover, as the meaning of the

The angels are further described by the Pietists as clothing God's decrees or thoughts,[92] but the form the angel takes depends in each case on the particular person to whom the angel appears.[93] In one place Eleazar puts the matter thus:

> The angel [appears] in many images (*demuyot*), and this is [the import of the verse] "The one who looked like a man touched my lips, and I opened my mouth and spoke, saying to him who stood before me, My lord, because of the vision I have been seized with pangs and cannot summon strength" (Dan. 10:16). It does not say in the image of a man (*ki-demut 'adam*) [i.e., in the singular], but rather in the image of men (*ki-demut bene 'adam*) [i.e., in the plural], for the angel [can appear in] many images. The angel appointed over a man looks like that very man.[94]

The Pietistic conception is based on earlier views, as is attested, for instance, in various talmudic passages that report that angels descend to the world in the likeness (*demut*) of particular human beings. One especially noteworthy legend, which apparently belongs to the Hekhalot literature, reports that Gabriel was commanded by God to appear to the wife of the tanna Elisha in the image of her husband as she emerged from ritual immersion.[95] The couple were eventually blessed with a child, R. Ishmael the High Priest, whose countenance was said to be like that of Gabriel, the angel who transmitted to R. Ishmael the supernal secrets when he ascended to heaven.[96] What is especially important

---

biblical claim that Adam was created in the divine image, i.e., in the image of the angels, who possess body and soul. These sages "maintained that a reality is greater if the forms also have a body. Therefore there are some among them who think that the matter of the *Shi'ur Qomah* should be taken literally." In this connection it is also worthwhile to recall the interpretation of Gen. 1:26 in Ṭobiah bar Eliezer, *Midrash Leqaḥ Ṭov,* p. 15: the word *ṣelem* denotes the upright posture (*qomah zequfah*) characteristic of angels, and *demut* the face of the celestial beast underneath the throne.

92 See *Sode Razayya,* p. 7; *Sefer ha-Shem,* MS British Museum 737, fol. 223a.

93 The notion that an angel can change the appearance of his face is expressed in rabbinic literature; see, e.g., *'Avot de-Rabbi Natan,* version A, chap. 37, p. 109. In that case, however, the change in form is not dependent on the imagination of the one who sees the angel. On the other hand, the identification of angels as visions or phantoms occurs already in Josephus, where it is clearly part of his programmatic avoidance of anthropomorphic expressions in the Bible. See L. Feldman, "Josephus' Portrait of Jacob," *Jewish Quarterly Review* 79 (1988–89): 140 n. 87.

94 *Sode Razayya,* p. 11.

95 Cf. the talmudic legend in B. Berakhot 20a concerning R. Yoḥanan, of whom it is said that he used to sit at the entrance to the bathhouses so that when the women came out they would look at him and would have children with his beauty.

96 See *Liqquṭe Pardes,* attributed to R. Solomon ben Isaac (Amsterdam, 1715), 4a: *Shivḥe R. Yishma'el Kohen Gadol,* in *Ḥadashim Gam Yeshanim,* ed. Habermann, p. 86. See also *Midrash 'Eleh 'Ezkerah,* in Jellinek, ed., *Bet ha-Midrash* 2:65. In that context R. Ishmael's father is named R. Yose. For discussion of various medieval sources that cite or refer to this text, see Ch. M. Horowitz, *Uralte Tosefta's* (Frankfurt am Main, 1889), pt. 4, pp. 7–15. I have located another version of this legend in a Genizah fragment in MS New York–JTSA ENA 3021, 1, with the title *Zehirut ha-Ṭevillah,* followed by several sections from *Hekhalot Rabbati* (corresponding to *Synopse,* §§ 122–126, 130–138). The legend also appears in a collection of Ashkenazi material extant in MS Paris–BN 1408, fol. 67a. For a detailed description of this codex, see Sirat, "Le manuscrit hébreu n° 1408 de la bibliothèque nationale de Paris," esp. p. 346, where the specific text under discussion is mentioned. According to this version, the angel commanded by God to appear to

for our purposes is the claim that the angelic figure can assume the form of a particular human being and not merely a generic human shape. Such a notion is implied, in my view, in a statement found in the Pietistic writings to the effect that God sends an angel to each person in accordance with their thought or mental capacity.[97] The most elaborate account is given by Eleazar:

> The angels who are sent below [appear] according to the need of the hour and according to the will [of God]. Elijah made himself appear as a bear in order to bother R. Ḥiyya and his son [as is related in the Babylonian talmud, tractate] Bava Meṣiʿa [85b]. . . . At that moment Elijah was not a bear, but he appeared to them as such. Similarly, an angel came to Jacob in the image of Esau.[98] . . . The angels are very subtle bodies, like the spirit, which is subtle and not visible, for the body [of the angel] is from spirit and from fire. If He desires to reveal them He makes their bodies [literally, their burden] heavier, [as it says,] "Then one of the seraphs flew over to me" (Isa. 6:6), and in Daniel, "[I looked and saw] a man dressed in linen" (Dan. 10:5). For the Holy One, blessed be He, strengthened the light of the eye, as it says, "And the Lord opened the servant's eyes" (2 Kings 6:17). The Holy One, blessed be He, allows the angel to be seen distinctly and his body will be coarse and not subtle, and there is a conflict between him and those people who stand there and do not see him. . . . The angel is replete with images (*daʿatanot*) and the [particular] perspective of a person is according to the decree [that has been established].[99]

The angel is thus the subtle substance that assumes various forms in accordance with the individual's capacity as well as the divine decree at the given moment.

> On occasion the angels change into the form of an anthropos, as it says, "The one who looked like a man touched [my lips]" (Dan. 10:16), and sometimes into winds and into fire when they serve, as it says, "He makes the winds His messengers, fiery flames His servants" (Ps. 104:4). This is the [meaning of] "all the work of creation that God had done" (Gen. 2:3), that is, they made themselves in accord with the will of the Holy One, blessed be He.[100]

The same process explains prophetic visions: what the prophet sees—including and especially the divine glory—is a luminous form constituted

---

Elisha's wife is Meṭaṭron and not Gabriel. Moreover, in this case the legend purports to explain the unique role of R. Ishmael as recipient of the secret knowledge about the chariot, disclosed by Meṭaṭron. Thus God proclaims to Meṭaṭron, "I have a servant below who is just like you, and this is the one to whom you will transmit the secrets, as is [recorded] in the Book of Palaces." A similar version of this legend is found in Isaiah ben Joseph, *Ḥayye Nefesh,* MS New York–JTSA Mic. 1842, fols. 192a–b.

[97] See Judah he-Ḥasid, "Book of Angels," pp. 106–109; *Sode Razayya,* p. 4. On the relationship between angelic revelations and an individual's thoughts, see *Sefer Ḥasidim,* § 382, p. 117.

[98] Cf. *Bereshit Rabbah* 78:3, p. 921.

[99] *Sode Razayya,* p. 8. Cf. *Ḥokhmat ha-Nefesh,* chap. 52, n. 91.

[100] *Sefer Tagi,* MS Oxford-Bodleian 1566, fol. 245a.

within the imaginative consciousness of the prophet. "Thus he should do naught but the will of the Creator who created him, and he should not reflect on Him lest he go mad . . . yet he should acknowledge that He is one and He is imagined by the prophets [Hosea 12:11] according to the need of the hour."[101] In the Pietistic writings one can thus discern a thematic link connecting the nature of visions apprehended by prophetic comprehension, the magical techniques such as the archons of the cup and the archons of the thumbnails, and the astrological-anthropological doctrine of the celestial image.

Shi'ur Qomah and the Vision of the Glory: Veridical and Docetic Approaches in Eleazar of Worms

It will be worthwhile at this juncture to pursue in greater detail the exoteric Pietistic notion of the glory as it emerges especially from Eleazar's writings. Let me cite a typical passage, from *Sha'are ha-Sod ha-Yiḥud we-ha-'Emunah,* which has parallels in other texts of Eleazar:

> The Creator has no body, physical stature, image, or form at all. . . . The glory is an appearance of the resplendent light, which is called *Shekhinah,* and the will of the Creator shows and images that very light to the prophets according to the hour, to this one as that [form] and to the other as that. . . . From the resplendent light He created His glory . . . the appearance of the vision is in the heart of the one who sees. . . . The Creator is one and makes the glory appear according to His will. . . . The appearance of His splendor, which is His glory, is like a consuming fire, and they called it *Shekhinah*. . . . According to the will of the Creator is the appearance of His glory. Moses saw the splendor of the glory, the great resplendence, more than all the prophets. Within the vision are images (*dimyonot*), [as it is written,] "and through the prophets I was imaged" (Hosea 12:11). . . . The appearance of the images is according to the desire of His decrees, sometimes in the image of an anthropos and sometimes in another image, in accordance with His will He shows [the prophet] His glory in the place that He wills.[102]

In the continuation of this text Eleazar cites a passage from Ḥananel (as transmitted in the talmudic lexicon of Nathan of Rome) that distinguishes between two glories: the upper glory, called *Shekhinah* or the great splendor (*hod ha-gadol*), is an invisible, formless light, whereas the lower glory is that which is seen by the various prophets. With respect to the latter, one needs to make a further distinction: Moses had a clear vision of that lower glory through the speculum that shines and all other prophets beheld the glory through a speculum that does not shine, that is, through images that distort reality.[103] Eleazar

[101] *Perush Sodot ha-Tefillah,* MS Paris–BN 772, fol. 172a.

[102] *Sha'are ha-Sod,* pp. 147–148. Cf. the parallel to this passage in the text published by Dan in *Studies,* p. 86. See also Eleazar's *Hilkhot Ḥasidut* in *Sefer ha-Roqeaḥ,* pp. 21–22; *'Arugat ha-Bosem* 1:200–201.

[103] See *Sha'are ha-Sod,* pp. 148–149.

also follows Ḥananel's lead in characterizing prophetic vision as mental seeing (*re'iyat ha-lev*) rather than physical perception. Indeed, in his commentary on Ezekiel's chariot vision, Eleazar goes so far as to say that "Ezekiel saw in his heart the entire structure of the chariot from below to above."[104] It is of interest to note in this connection that in one Ashkenazi manuscript the views of Ḥananel and Nathan ben Yeḥiel are mentioned after a citation from Saadiah's *Book of Beliefs and Opinions* (according to the Hebrew paraphrase that circulated among the Pietists and greatly influenced their terminology[105]). After the views of the former are mentioned, the text reads, "And so R. Eleazar of Worms received from his teacher, R. Judah the Pious, who received from his father, R. Samuel the Pious."[106] Similarly, in one passage in *ʿArugat ha-Bosem* the author notes, after presenting R. Ḥananel's explanation of the nature of prophetic visions, which is said to likewise be the view of R. Nissim Gaon and Shabbetai Donnolo, "And this is our tradition (*qabbalatenu*) from the mouth of my teacher [i.e., Eleazar] and R. Judah [who received] from our rabbi Samuel the Pious."[107] The textual evidence does indicate that the Geonic interpretation of prophetic and mystical visions did indeed inform Eleazar's own approach, yielding a decidedly docetic orientation.

There is equally valid evidence, however, that the Pietists did not adhere rigidly to the notions of Hai Gaon and R. Ḥananel. That is, they also affirmed a more veridical approach, assuming, therefore, the existence of the luminous glory outside the mind. It is evident that in some passages Eleazar follows the orientation of Saadiah and asserts that the glory or Presence is a light created by God that is superior to the angels and assumes the measurements of the *Shiʿur Qomah*. Yet, in other passages, in contrast to the Saadianic view, the main circle of Pietists maintain that this glory, or "first light," is not created by but emanates from God (it seems that the major sources of influence were Donnolo and ibn Ezra); in that respect there is no ontological distinction between the Creator and the glory. The lower, visible glory likewise is not a created light outside of God but rather emanates from the invisible glory that emanates from the Creator. God, the hidden glory, and the revealed glory are thus three links in a continuous chain of being.

The theory of *kavod* put forth by the main circle of the German Pietists, especially as it is developed in the writings of Eleazar, is thus an attempt to combine the realist and docetic positions. On the one hand, the glory is an independently existing hypostasis, a luminous being that emanates from the One. On the other hand, this resplendent light is amorphous. The lower glory, a light that emanates from the first light, assumes various shapes in accordance with the divine will but only within the mind of the one who sees. There is

104 MS Paris–BN 850, fol. 48a.

105 See Dan, *Esoteric Theology*, pp. 22–23; Kiener, "The Hebrew Paraphrase of Saadiah Gaon's *Kitāb al-Amānāt wa'l-I'tiqādāt*," pp. 16–20.

106 MS Paris–BN 1408, fol. 40a. See Sirat, "Le manuscrit hébreu nº 1408," pp. 341–342.

107 *ʿArugat ha-Bosem* 1:200. For a slightly different formulation, cf. MSS New York–JTSA Mic. 2411, fol. 12b; Parma-Palatina 2784 (DeRossi 1390), fol. 78b.

therefore no presumption of veridicality with respect to these particular forms allegedly enjoyed by ordinary sense experience. That is, the phenomenological content of the experience does not correspond to something existing outside the mind, for the forms assumed by the glory are not independently existing realities but rather images lodged in the mind of the visionary with no ontic status as such. In Eleazar's own language, "The glory appears to the prophet, not [as it is] in actuality but [according to] the image of the appearance."[108] The visible glory thus has no definite form per se, but is revealed through the intermediary of images or forms that exist only in the mind of the one who is having the vision.[109]

The key concept in the Pietistic treatment of prophetic and mystical visions is *dimyon*, "image"—a term rooted, as we have seen, in the ancient midrashic tradition. I noted above that the Haside Ashkenaz employed this term in an innovative way to refer to the human faculty of imagining spiritual realities in concrete terms. It is necessary to reiterate, moreover, that the *dimyonot* themselves are treated ontologically by the Pietists, that is, these images are themselves the spiritual paradigms or archetypes of mundane realities that are apprehended by the imagination. What is true of these forms is equally applicable to the glory itself, which likewise is apprehended through imaginative forms constituted in the imagination as it interacts with the ontically independent entity. "The great Splendor," writes Eleazar, "is the *Shekhinah*, no one has permission to gaze upon it. . . . The [lower] glory alludes to the angel that changes to many forms. . . . At times it appears in the image of a human sitting on a throne, and he [the prophet] sees an awesome form. All is in the will of the Creator who makes His will visible according to the understanding of the heart."[110] Eleazar's words are very carefully chosen. The final expression, "understanding of the heart," had previously appeared, as we have seen in a previous chapter, in one talmudic context with reference to the chariot vision. As I have also noted, this locution was employed as well by several important rabbinic figures, including Hai Gaon and Ḥananel ben Ḥushiel, to explain either mystical or prophetic experience as contemplative in contrast to physical vision.[111] The usage of the term *dimyon* is also found in the writings of Ḥananel allegedly transmitting the thought of Hai Gaon. Thus, it may be said that the

108 *Perush Sodot ha-Tefillah,* MS Paris–BN 772, fol. 103a.

109 Cf. *Sode Razayya,* p. 47; *Perush ha-Merkavah,* MS Paris–BN 850, fol. 48a. The view of Eleazar is summarized well in a passage in a collection of Ashkenazi traditions extant in MS Paris–BN 843, fols. 72b–73a. The influence of Eleazar is also evident in the kabbalistic commentary on the *sefirot,* which in many manuscripts is attributed to his disciple R. Menaḥem (see Scholem, "Index to the Commentaries on the Ten *Sefirot,*" p. 505 n. 63). See, e.g., MS Munich 56, fol. 140b: "In truth the Creator has no image or form, except for His glory, which He shows to the prophets, and His will is within it, for He fills all worlds." Cf. MS Oxford-Bodleian 1938, fol. 64b.

110 Quoted in Dan, *Studies,* p. 87. See parallel in *Shaʿare ha-Sod,* pp. 151–152; and cf. *Perush ha-Merkavah,* MS Paris–BN 850, fol. 47a–b.

111 See the citation of Judah he-Ḥasid's *Sefer ha-Kavod* in *ʿArugat ha-Bosem* 3:78, where the expression is used to explain the vision of the thrones mentioned in Dan. 7:9. See also Eleazar's comment in his *Perush ha-Merkavah,* MS Paris–BN 850, fol. 48a.

docetic posture of Eleazar—that the form the inherently amorphous glory assumes depends on the images that do not exist outside the mind—is an elaboration of a tendency that has an earlier expression in Jewish sources. At times Eleazar's docetism is indeed quite pronounced. For example, in *Ḥokhmat ha-Nefesh* he states,

> All that was shown to the prophets, the mind saw, as is the case of the "archons of the cup" and the "archons of the thumbnails." All depends on [one's] thought. . . . the Creator places thoughts within the visual imagination (*maḥshevet ha-re'iyah*) and shows them to the prophet. Thus it is with respect to everything the prophets saw. . . . the vision that appears to the person is not due to a physical vision (*re'iyat ha-ʿeinayim*), for even a blind man can see the angel of death.[112]

Eleazar writes in slightly different terms in *Sefer ha-Shem,* commenting on the talmudic statement "The face of man is like a monkey in relation to the face of the *Shekhinah*" (B. Bava Batra 58a):

> "What form [can you] compare to him?" (Isa. 40:18). Rather [it is written] "and through the prophets I was imaged" (Hosea 12:11). One sees with one's heart. "Yet my own eyes have beheld the King, Lord of Hosts" (Isa. 6:5). According to the image (*dimyon*) that the prophet saw he knew the end of the decree. Concerning that which is said, "the face of the *Shekhinah,*" that is, according to the way it was seen in the mind of the prophets, for the Creator of all has no face. He appears instead in the image (*demut*) of an elder or in the image of a youth.[113]

Eleazar's statement reflects the ancient Jewish aggadic tradition according to which God appears primarily in two forms, either that of a young warrior (at the Red Sea) or an old man (at Sinai). As we have seen, in the midrashic sources the forms attributed to God are not to be understood as mental constructs solely dependent on the imaginative constitution of human consciousness. The forms—and here I again emphasize that the words used most frequently in the relevant texts are *dimmuyot, demuyot,* and, in later sources, *dimyonot*—assumed by God are not apparitional realities but are indicative of the divine nature. In other words, we have here a version in rabbinic literature of incarnation, by which term I mean the notion that God assumes the form of a human being.

In the Pietistic literature, by contrast, already evident in *Shir ha-Kavod* (the "Hymn of Glory"), the forms are not veridical, for they are only in the mind of the prophet. The position of Eleazar has an exact parallel in Elḥanan ben Yaqar's *Sod ha-Sodot* (the "Secret of Secrets"): "All these visions of God [through which He] appears by way of parables and allegories to speak to the prophets, as it says, 'I have multiplied visions and through the prophets I was imaged' (Hosea 12:11). . . . His appearances change into many things according to His will, as we have received from our rabbis, peace be upon them, that He was

112 *Ḥokhmat ha-Nefesh,* chap. 46, p. 75.
113 MS British Museum 737, fol. 378a.

revealed on the [Red] Sea as a youth and in Sinai as an elder full of mercy . . . all of these are visions of God, and in these visions there is nothing but a vision according to the will of God without any reality."[114] In one context Eleazar applies these theophanic images specifically to the angel's own capacity for vision: "The inner angels know the future through seeing the splendor of the glory, at times like an elder and at times like a youth."[115] In still other texts it is clear that the glory assumed these forms for the Israelites at the two key moments of their *Heilsgeshichte.*

To appreciate fully the approach developed by Eleazar it would be beneficial to consider, first, the reference to this midrashic notion in the Pseudo-Hai commentary on the forty-two-letter name of God included in *Sefer ha-Ḥokhmah,* a text that preserves older Ashkenazi traditions: "The Holy One, blessed be He, does not change His form . . . even though He appeared at the Sea as a youth, making war with a two-edged sword in His hand [Ps. 149:6], by means of the seventy-two-letter name in the secret of 216 letters, and at Sinai [He appeared] as an elder full of mercy, it is all one, for He reveals the *Shekhinah* in accordance with the needs of the hour."[116] In another passage in *Sefer ha-Ḥokhmah,* in a commentary on the seventy-two-letter name of God, one reads, "For the honorable Holy One, blessed be He, was revealed on the Sea as a warrior and on Mount Sinai He began [the Decalogue] with [the word] I, and was revealed as an elder sitting upon His throne of glory."[117] Similarly, in a Pietistic commentary on the various names of Meṭaṭron, we read in conjunction with one of these names, "*Gur 'aryeh* [a lion's whelp[118]] is numerically equivalent to *bore' baḥur* [i.e., the Creator is a youth], for when the Holy One, blessed be He fought upon the [Red] Sea He was revealed to Israel as a youth going to war, as it says, 'the Lord is a warrior' (Exod. 15:3), and when He was revealed to them on Mount Sinai He appeared as an elder expounding [Torah] in an acad-

[114] *Theological Texts of German Pietism,* p. 11, quoted and discussed in Farber, "Concept of the Merkabah," pp. 426–427. The docetic approach to prophetic vision is particularly strong in the case of the anonymous Pietistic work *Sefer ha-Ḥayyim* (regarding this text see Dan, *Esoteric Theology,* pp. 148–149). See, e.g., *Theological Texts of German Pietism,* pp. 4–5, where it is stated that prophetic vision in general is a dream state and the prophecy of Moses in particular is a vision of the heart.

[115] *Sode Razayya,* ed. Weiss, p. 119.

[116] MS Oxford-Bodleian 1568, fol. 6b. According to one tradition, the seventy-two-letter name of God is derived from Exod. 14:19–21, each verse consisting of seventy-two letters, making a total of 216, which are then divided into seventy-two triplets. The name is thus referred to by the word *'aryeh,* "lion," for the numerical value of this word is 216. On the word *'aryeh* functioning as a name of God, see Eleazar ben Moses ha-Darshan, *Sefer ha-Gimaṭri'ot,* MS Munich 221, fol. 109b.

[117] MS Oxford-Bodleian 1568, fol. 15a. Cf. the following statement in a commentary on the seventy-two-letter name, apparently written by Pietists of the circle that produced *Sefer ha-Ḥesheq,* extant in MS Munich 92, fol. 28b: "[The word] 'I' (*'anokhi*) [refers to] the glory, for the Holy One, blessed be He, showed the throne of glory upon the [Red] Sea . . . as it says in the *Book of Palaces,* the length of the Holy One, blessed be He, is 180 myriad parasangs and the length is 236 myriad parasangs as [is implied in] the number of *we-rav koaḥ,* as it says, 'Great is our Lord and full of power' (Ps. 147:5). He showed His length upon the Sea."

[118] Cf. Gen. 49:9.

emy."[119] In a second text, apparently from the same circle of Pietists,[120] we find the application of the other major aggadic image to God: "The forehead [of God] is called ASTGYHW . . . which is numerically equal to the father of the *demut yehudi* [i.e., Jewish image or image of a Jew,][121] for the Holy One, blessed be He, can be likened to a beautiful Jewish elder who is a scholar."[122]

In these four examples, especially the latter three, there is no indication that the forms through which God is manifest are considered purely mental. Even in the first case, which is closer in style and terminology to Eleazar, we are not told that the appearances of the Presence are imaginary forms.[123] In other writings of Eleazar, however, it is precisely this standpoint that dominates the discussion. Indeed, in one text of Eleazar, copied by Abraham bar Azriel in his *'Arugat ha-Bosem,* the docetic interpretation is presented in terms reminiscent of the first passage from *Sefer ha-Ḥokhmah* cited above:

> The Creator has no form or physical limbs, for He has no need of them. Proof of this is [the verse] "For you have seen no image" (Deut. 4:15), for if He had an image they would have known how He is, but it is written, "what form can you compare to Him?" (Isa. 40:18). . . . It is written with respect to the image in Ezekiel (1:26), "the semblance of a human form" (*demut ke-mar'eh 'adam*), but not "the form of a human" (*mar'eh 'adam*), for from the great, bright, lucid, and pure light [emanates a form] seated upon the high and lofty throne, and in the hands of the prophets it appears to them [Hosea 12:11] according to the need of the hour, sometimes as a youth and sometimes as an elder, as a judge or as one riding, standing, or sitting.[124]

The form in which the glory appears is determined in accordance with the needs of the hour, but is apprehended as such only within the prophetic imagination. These multiple forms, therefore, imply no ontic change in the status of the emanated light. As Eleazar puts it, "With regard to what we have found concerning changes in the *Shekhinah,* sometimes as a youth and sometimes as an elder, know that the reason [for this change] is that the glory appears to the prophets in accordance with the need of the hour."[125] The glory assumes multiple forms in accordance with the recipient, but in and of itself it remains immutable: "The *Shekhinah* sometimes appears to a prophet as another matter, yet the glory of the *Shekhinah* does not change but rather appears to him to do so."[126]

119 MS Cambridge Heb. Add., 405, fol. 314b.

120 See Liebes, "Angels of the Shofar," p. 186 n. 20.

121 That is, the name ASTGYHW = 485, which is also the numerical value of the expression *demut yehudi.*

122 Quoted in *'Arugat ha-Bosem* 4:76–77. Cf. the language of a text by R. Troestlin the Prophet, cited by Heschel in "On the Holy Spirit," p. 185 n. 54: "For the Holy One, blessed be He, says: I sit upon the beasts, and the numerical value is *demut yehudi,* for the Holy One, blessed be He, appears as a beautiful Jewish elder and sage."

123 Cf. *'Arugat ha-Bosem* 1:180.

124 Ibid., 1:137.

125 *Sode Razayya,* p. 41.

126 MS Oxford-Bodleian 1791, fol. 76b.

On other occasions Eleazar combines the midrashic tradition regarding the theophanous forms of God as elder and youth with the mystical notion of the measurement of the divine body as transmitted in the *Shiʿur Qomah*. The point is made in his *Sefer ha-Shem:*

> He manifested the form of a human face to the mind of the prophet, who saw according to the number (or measure) [implied in] "[Great is our Lord] and full of power" (*we-rav koaḥ*). . . . According to the vision [that one beholds] one knows His will and one knows the supernal Mind. . . . What image can you apply to him? Rather [it is written,] "and through the prophets I was imaged" (Hosea 12:11). He sees in his mind . . . according to the image (*dimyon*) that appears to the prophet he knows the [divine] decree. . . . But there are no faces above . . . when it says the "face of the *Shekhinah*" [it means] as it appears to the mind of the prophets, for the Creator of all has no face. He appears instead in the image of an elder or in the image of a youth.[127]

Eleazar has thus reinterpreted the earlier mystical tradition transmitted in the cluster of texts known as *Shiʿur Qomah* that ascribed corporeal dimensions to the enthroned divine form. From the point of view of the Pietistic theology, at least in its exoteric formulation, there is no divine form—God is not a body that possesses form—except what is apprehended in the mind of the visionary. Consequently, the measurements specified in the ancient esoteric work (the measurement most frequently cited by Eleazar is 236,000 myriad parasangs) are not attributable to the Creator or even to the glory in any objective way; they represent the proportions of the imagination, indeed, they are constituted within the imagination.

> The Creator is one and He manifests the glory[128] according to His will and desire, a wonderful, sublime, and radiant form . . . which He called the *Shekhinah,* sometimes it is seen without any form, a light that is not visible to any creature. . . . It says, "I have seen the Lord" (1 Kings 22:19), the particle (*ʾet*) comes to include His glory, and as it is seen by the eye His glory is great [in size], "Great is our Lord and full of power" (Ps. 147:5), [the expression "and full of power" (*we-rav koaḥ*)] numerically equals 236, for [the glory] is 236,000 myriad parasangs.[129]

Similarly, in his commentary on the prayers Eleazar writes, "He shows His glory in the hearts of human beings, 236,000 myriad parasangs."[130] "And concerning that which is written in the secret[131] of the Merkavah [regarding]

[127] MS British Museum 737, fol. 378a.

[128] The first letters of these four words in Hebrew, *yahid ha-boreʾ u-marʾeh ha-kavod,* spell out the Tetragrammaton, YHWH. This is an important point, inasmuch as comprised within the four-letter name are both the divine unity and the ability of God to manifest himself in the glory. I will return below to the theosophic implications of the relationship between the visible glory and the divine name.

[129] *Sefer ha-Roqeaḥ,* p. 21.

[130] MS Paris–BN 772, fol. 97b.

[131] The manuscript reads *be-sof,* "in the end," which I have corrected to *be-sod,* "in the secret." See, however, MS Oxford-Bodleian 1204, fol. 29d, where the reading is *be-sefer ha-merkavah,* "in

the measurement of the body (*shiʿur qomah*), this is according to the dimension that is seen by the eyes, but the greatness of the Creator cannot be fathomed."[132] "Above without measure the glory appears to the prophet, not in actuality but in the image of the appearance, for the inner beings and the electrum do not see it."[133] In his *Perush ha-Merkavah* Eleazar comments thus on the verse "Upon this semblance of a throne, there was the semblance of a human form" (Ezek. 1:26):

> The glory appeared to the prophets as a king sitting upon a throne. This is not to say that there is sitting [above] or any boundary to His unity. Rather, [the glory appears in this form] so that the prophet may know who is speaking to him. Concerning this it says in the *Sefer ha-Merkavah* [i.e., *Shiʿur Qomah*] the measurement of the creator, etc.[134]

For Eleazar, then, there is no distinction between prophetic and mystical visions, for in both cases the unique feature is the imaging of the luminous glory within the imagination, particularly as an anthropos.

> The Holy One, blessed be He, is very great and the essence of His abundant greatness cannot be seen by the eye nor spoken of by the mouth. That which was written in *Sefer ha-Merkavah* concerning the measure of the [divine] stature is in accord with prophetic vision. . . . Thus does the glory appear to those who fear the Lord who have seen in the intellect of the heart.[135]

> He showed the form of a human countenance (*parṣuf ʾadam*) to the heart of the prophet who saw [it] according to the number of [the words] "and full of power" [*we-rav koaḥ,* which equals 236 and corresponds to the standard measure of the divine stature, 236,000 myriad parasangs]. "Ascribe might to God" (Ps. 68:35). The image (*temunah*) applies only to the human countenance (*parṣuf ʾadam*), for he imagines (*yeṣayyer*) His appearance. "Know the God of your father and serve Him" (1 Chron. 28:9), for according to the vision one knows His will and knows the supernal Mind. . . . "They saw the God of Israel. They beheld God" (Exod. 24:10–11).[136]

In the above texts Eleazar repeats his basic notion that the anthropomorphic form described in the *Shiʿur Qomah* is the object of prophetic or mystical vision. The concluding remark of the first citation, "Thus does the glory appear to those who fear the Lord who have seen in the intellect of the heart," proves

---

the Book of the Chariot." That the latter reading is preferrable can be supported by the fact that in other contexts Eleazar cites the text of *Shiʿur Qomah* as *sefer ha-merkavah*. See, e.g., *Perush ha-Merkavah,* MS Paris–BN 850, fol. 67a.

132 MS Paris–BN 772, fol. 38b.

133 Ibid., fol. 103a.

134 MS Paris–BN 850, fol. 67a.

135 *Passover Haggadah with Commentary of R. Eleazar of Worms,* ed. M. Hershler (Jerusalem, 1984), pp. 175–176 (in Hebrew).

136 *Sefer ha-Shem,* MS British Museum 737, fol. 373a.

beyond any shadow of doubt that Eleazar considered it possible for the pious individual to have a mental vision of the glory on a par with prophetic experiences. In the second passage he adds that the image of God apprehended by the visionary is first and foremost a human face, a point supported by the numerological equivalence of the word *temunah* (image) and the expression *parṣuf 'adam* (human countenance), both equaling 501. This numerology is repeated on a number of occasions by Eleazar, of which I will mention just one example: "Concerning that which is said, 'the image of the glory of the Lord' (Ezek. 1:28), it is not [to suggest] that He has a countenance, but rather [the glory appears as an anthropos] so as not to frighten the prophet. 'You saw no image' (Deut. 4:15)—the [word] image (*temunah*) is numerically equivalent to human countenance (*parṣuf 'adam*). They saw several images (*dimyonot*) at Sinai face to face."[137]

So far, we have seen, the doctrine of revelation as it appears in some of the key passages in the Pietistic writings is decidedly docetic: the visible glory is a form that exists in the imagination. But one can also find evidence in the literature of the Pietists for the view that the glory is an emanated light that has objective existence outside the mind of the visionary. This light in one of its aspects has the capacity of appearing to the prophets in human form or as the measurable being related in the ancient Jewish mystical texts. Thus in one text, attributed by Dan to Judah the Pious, we find the following interpretation, based in part on ibn Ezra's commentary on Exod. 33:20, of the well-known passage transmitted in the name of R. Ishmael in the *Shiʿur Qomah,* "Whoever knows the measurement of the Demiurge is certain to be in the world-to-come, I and R. Aqiva guarantee this":

> The Creator has no limit. Concerning those verses that attribute dimensions to the Creator, "Great is our Lord and full of power" (Ps. 147:5), [the expression "and full of power," *we-rav koaḥ*] numerologically equals 236 [i.e., an allusion to the standard measure of the Demiurge in the *Shiʿur Qomah*], "who gauged the skies with a span" (Isa. 40:12), the measure is necessitated because of the created entities, for the Creator, blessed be He, has no limit. It was necessary for the glory to be greater than the created entities taken all together. From this viewpoint the enlightened one can know the One from the perspective of all things cleaving to it. Thus, it says "measure of the Demiurge," but He has no limit! What is intended is that

[137] *Sefer ha-Roqeaḥ,* p. 22. Cf. *Perush Sodot ha-Tefillah,* MS Paris–BN 772, fol. 40a; MS Oxford-Bodleian 352, fol. 197a; *Shaʿare ha-Sod,* p. 146; Eleazar ben Moses ha-Darshan, *Sefer ha-Gimaṭri'ot,* MS Munich 221, fol. 151b. See also *Maʿarekhet ha-'Elohut,* chap. 10, fol. 144a, where Eleazar of Worms is mentioned in conjunction with this numerology, although it is attributed as well to R. Isaac, i.e., Isaac ben Ṭodros. This numerology is utilized in the early kabbalistic tradition (perhaps of Geronese provenance) extant in MS New York–JTSA Mic. 2194, fol. 64a, as well as by Isaac of Acre in *Sefer Me'irat ʿEinayim,* p. 105, citing an anonymous text from "one of the great kabbalists." The numerology, perhaps under the direct influence of the Ḥaside Ashkenaz, is also evident in the long recension of *Sefer ha-ʿIyyun;* cf. Verman, *Books of Contemplation,* p. 67. See Scholem, *Origins,* p. 345. On the use of this numerology in Abraham Abulafia and Joseph Gikatilla, probably under the influence of German Pietistic sources, see Idel, "Maimonides and the Kabbalah," pp. 62–63.

the measure [applies to] that which cleaves (*davuq*) [i.e., the glory that emanates from and thus is attached to the One] and not as Saadiah explained [concerning a created glory].[138]

In the above text the measures of the *Shiʿur Qomah* tradition are removed from the Creator (the explicit reference in the sources to the *yoṣer bereshit*, the Demiurge, notwithstanding) and applied to the glory, characterized as emanating from and being united to the One. No qualification is found in this text to the effect that these dimensions are only images within the mind.

In the case of Eleazar of Worms various texts can be cited to prove that he, too, cultivated an ancient tradition that ascribed the corporeal measurements to the emanated glory without further specifying that the physical form is a mere image in the mind. On occasion Eleazar seems to reflect another ancient tradition, that the measurements of the *Shiʿur Qomah* apply to the angelic Meṭaṭron. Such a tradition, also attested in kabbalistic sources,[139] appears to be implied as well in the Ashkenazi commentary on the names of Meṭaṭron:

> *Ruaḥ pisqonit* [= 930] is the numerical equivalent of [the expression] *yah yah demut demut* [= 930], for he [Meṭaṭron] had two images (*demuyot*), at first the image of a man and in the end the image of an angel. *Ruaḥ pisqonit* is equal numerically to [the expression] *ke-rl"w 'elef ribbo parsah* [= 930], for this is the measure of the stature (*shiʿur ha-qomah*). This is to inform you that the Holy One, blessed be He, has no measurement, and He has no boundary or limit . . . and no eye has ever seen Him. Thus, when He selects a prophet to worship Him, he sees the splendor of His glory (*zohar kevodo*) on the throne in this measure.[140]

The first thing to note is that the statement that Meṭaṭron has two images, initially that of a man and latterly that of an angel, is obviously based on the earlier legend, expressed fully in the Hebrew Book of Enoch (*3 Enoch*), of the human Enoch being transformed into the angelic Meṭaṭron, an idea that is repeated on other occasions in this text, including most significantly this comment on one of the names of Meṭaṭron: "*We-ruaḥ* [the spirit] is numerically equivalent to *gever yah* [man-God], for at first he was a man and then he became through his righteousness an angel, for the Holy Spirit rested upon him and he became an angel."[141] Yet, according to the first text cited above, the

138 MS Oxford-Bodleian 1567, fol. 3b, quoted in Dan, *Studies*, p. 154.

139 See the statement of R. Abraham ben David of Posquiéres reported by his grandson, R. Asher ben David, in *'Oṣar Neḥmad* 4 (1863): 37, discussed by Scholem, *Reshit ha-Qabbalah*, pp. 75–76; idem, *Origins*, pp. 212–225; see also Isaac of Acre, *Sefer Me'irat ʿEinayim*, p. 40, and Idel, "Enoch is Meṭaṭron," pp. 156–157 (French trans., pp. 396–397). I have treated this topic at greater length in my study "Shiʿur Qomah and Meṭaṭron in the Writings of the German Pietists," to be published in the proceedings of the conference "Mystik, Magie und Kabbala im Aschkenasischen Judentum" (9–11 Dec. 1991, Frankfurt am Main, Germany). Some of the material in that article is repeated here.

140 MSS Cambridge Heb. Add. 405, fol. 302b; Oxford-Bodleian 2286, fol. 156a; Moscow-Guenzberg 90, fol. 127a; New York–JTSA Mic. 2206, fol. 11a.

141 MSS Cambridge Heb. Add. 405, fol. 305b. See also fol. 299b.

transformed Enoch still retains human characteristics insofar as the measurements of *Shiʿur Qomah* are applied to Meṭaṭron. The last point is especially highlighted in the printed version of the above passage, which concludes, "The Prince of the Countenance who serves Him is as big as this measurement."[142] Commenting on this text, Dan noted that "the author does not actually establish that the glory that is revealed to the prophets in the image of the *Shiʿur Qomah* is Meṭaṭron himself; rather he emphasizes that the image of Meṭaṭron, its measure and character, is like the image of the *Shekhinah* that is revealed to the prophets in the measure of 236,000 myriad parasangs."[143] There are statements in the Pietistic writings to support this interpretation, as will be seen in more detail below.

It seems to me, however, that the text is ambiguous enough to maintain an alternative view. In fact, it is entirely possible that underlying this text is an identification of Meṭaṭron with the *Shekhinah,* referred to at the end of the passage as the splendor of God's glory that appears on the throne in corporeal measurements. This identification, as Scholem noted, is found in other Ḥasidic writings as well as in early kabbalistic documents from Catalonia.[144] Scholem goes on to say that this identification "is clearly a promotion of Meṭaṭron, who in the Merkabah gnosis also bears the name Yahoel. The angel himself becomes a figure of the *kabhod.*"[145] Meṭaṭron, then, is the aspect of the glory that is depicted as the measurable anthropos who sits upon the throne and appears in prophetic visions. It must be noted that Dan, too, accepts the possibility of such an understanding of Meṭaṭron in the theology of the German Pietists, although he does not mention in this context the parallels in kabbalistic literature: "For the German Pietists Meṭaṭron was already a nearly-divine image, and sometimes actually divine; like his identification with the *Shekhinah* the German Pietists were inclined to draw him close to, and perhaps even identify him with, the divine glory itself."[146] A similar conclusion has been more recently affirmed by Farber, who comments on the passage quoted above, "It is reasonable to assume that before the author of this commentary was a tradition that maintained an identification between Meṭaṭron and the *Shiʿur Qomah*. . . . [P]erhaps this tradition already assumed the twofold nature of Meṭaṭron,"[147] that is, as an angel, on the one hand, and as the glory, on the other.

Indeed, it is evident from other passages in this Pietistic commentary that Meṭaṭron fulfills just this function. For example, the following meaning is attributed to one of Meṭaṭron's names: "*Zeraḥyah* is numerically equivalent to *ʾayeh ruaḥ* [where is the spirit?], for the Holy Spirit did not dwell on any other

[142] *Sefer ha-Ḥesheq,* § 25. On the attribution of the corporeal measurements of the *Shiʿur Qomah* tradition to Meṭaṭron, see the text published by Dan in *Studies,* pp. 153–154, and the parallel in Eleazar of Worms, *Ḥokhmat ha-Nefesh,* chap. 84, p. 144.

[143] *Esoteric Theology,* p. 223.

[144] See Scholem, *Origins,* pp. 187 n. 214, 214–215, 299 n. 198.

[145] Ibid., p. 187.

[146] *Esoteric Theology,* p. 219.

[147] "Concept of the Merkabah," p. 559.

person as on this one [Enoch], for he [Meṭaṭron] is revealed to the prophets and he is the angel of God."[148] In a second passage the link to *Shiʿur Qomah* is drawn as well: "*Zeraḥyahu* is numerically equivalent to *we-rav koaḥ* [great in power] for he [Meṭaṭron] is 236,000 myriad parasangs, and according to this measurement the Holy One, blessed be He, shines in His glory upon the throne, and He shows His glory to the one to whom He wills."[149]

Support for my interpretation may also be found in the following statement of Eleazar in his extensive commentary on the prayers: "'Unless You go in the lead' (*'ein panekha holkhim*) (Exod. 33:15) numerically equals [the expression] 'That is Meṭaṭron' (*zehu miṭaṭron*],[150] 'for My name is in Him' (Exod. 23:21), Shaddai is numerically equal to Meṭaṭron.[151] The *Shiʿur Qomah* is 236,000 myriad parasangs. 'It is the glory of God to conceal a matter' (Prov. 25:2)."[152] Eleazar thus considers the attribution of the *Shiʿur Qomah* measurements to Meṭaṭron to be a matter worth concealing. It is plausible that implied here is the identification of Meṭaṭron with the *Shekhinah*, of which I spoke above. It should be borne in mind, moreover, that the prooftext with which the passage begins, Exod. 33:15, explicitly mentions the divine countenance; hence the request of Moses that God accompany the people in their journey. Yet, according to Eleazar's interpretation, the reference to God's countenance is applied to Meṭaṭron. Presumably underlying this exegetical turn is the identification of the angel and the divine Presence.[153] Elsewhere in his writings Eleazar explicitly attributes these very characteristics to the glory. For example, in *Shaʿare ha-Sod ha-Yiḥud we-ha-'Emunah* he states that the resplendent light, which is the

148 MSS Cambridge Heb. Add. 405, fol. 306b; Oxford-Bodleian 2286, fol. 159b; Moscow-Guenzberg 90, fol. 128b.

149 MSS Cambridge Heb. Add. 405, fol. 309a; Oxford-Bodleian 2286, fol. 161a; Moscow-Guenzberg 90, fol. 130a.

150 That is, both expressions = 332, if the name Meṭaṭron is written without the *yod* (which equals 10), even though in this manuscript it is written with a *yod*. This expression occurs in B. Sanhedrin 38b and in a fragment on Meṭaṭron of Ashkenazi provenance in *Synopse*, § 389 (according to MS New York–JTSA Mic. 8128). In another passage from the same unit, § 396 (cf. § 733), Exod. 33:15 and 23:21 are applied to Meṭaṭron. On the other hand, the interpretation of Exod. 33:15 as referring to Meṭaṭron stands in open contrast to the reading of this verse in B. Sanhedrin 38b. See, however, Naḥmanides' commentary to the verse discussed in Wolfson, "By Way of Truth," pp. 139–140, 171–172.

151 Both = 314. Again, the numerology works only when the name Meṭaṭron is written without the *yod*, even though in the manuscripts it appears with it. For the usage of this numerical equivalence, see Rashi's commentary to Exod. 23:21; and cf. the Pietistic commentary on the names of Meṭaṭron, MSS Cambridge Heb. Add. 405, fol. 302b; Oxford-Bodleian 2286, fol. 156b; Moscow-Guenzberg 90, fol. 127b. See also Eleazar's comment in his *Perush ha-Merkavah*, MS Paris–BN 850, fol. 83a, cited below.

152 MS Paris–BN 772, fol. 110b. In this context it is of interest to note the identification of the divine name, the glory, and the angel of the countenance in a fragment on Meṭaṭron preserved in various manuscript codices; see *Synopse*, § 397. The manuscript witnesses indicate that this tradition is of Ashkenazi provenance.

153 My remarks here reflect an observation by Yehuda Liebes in a discussion we had regarding this text immediately before the lecture I delivered in Frankfurt (see n. 139). For a kabbalistic parallel, cf. MS Munich 357, fol. 3b.

glory, appears in various ways, "sometimes without a form, sometimes in human form, and sometimes as the *Shiʿur Qomah,* which comprises 236,000 myriad parasangs."[154] In a second passage near the end of this text Eleazar remarks that "what is said in *Sefer ha-Qomah*" is said with respect to the "measure of the visible glory" (*shiʿur ha-kavod ha-nirʾeh*).[155] It does not seem either coincidental or inconsequential that the measurements applied to Meṭaṭron in one place are ascribed to the glory in another. On the contrary, this may be related to a tacit identification of Meṭaṭron as an aspect of the glory. Whatever the intent of the secrecy that surrounds this notion, it is evident that Eleazar preserved a tradition that ascribed these corporeal dimensions to Meṭaṭron. No psychologistic reading is offered here to explain the seemingly gross anthropomorphism of the ancient Jewish mystical speculation.

Further evidence for what I have called the veridical approach is found, for example, in texts included in Eleazar's *Sefer ha-Ḥokhmah.* While one may question the veracity of the claim that Eleazar himself authored these texts, I do not think that one can seriously challenge the view that reflected here are Ashkenazi traditions, in some cases with much older roots, that had a great impact on the development of the Pietistic theosophy, especially in the case of Eleazar.[156] Thus, in one of the more celebrated passages of the commentary on the forty-two-letter name of God, attributed to Hai Gaon and included in the introduction to *Sefer ha-Ḥokhmah,* it is said of the divine Presence, *Shekhinah*—also identified as the crown (*ʿaṭarah* that is called Akatriel when the crown is on the head of the Creator), prayer[157] (*tefillah* or *ṣelotaʾ*), bride (*kalah*), daughter of the king (*bat melekh*), voice (*bat qol*), tenth kingship (*malkhut ʿasirit*), secret of all secrets (*sod kol ha-sodot*), and angel of the Lord (*malʾakh ha-shem*)—that "she herself is the size of 236,000 myriad parasangs, concerning which David said, 'Great is our Lord and full of strength' (Ps. 147:5), the numerical value [of the expression 'and full of strength' (*we-rav koaḥ*)] equals 236." The text goes on to specify that "the prophets saw the *Shekhinah,* for she is emanated," but not the Creator, who "is hidden from all, and has no measure or image."[158] The *Shekhinah,* then, is treated here as the manifestation of God on the throne as it is described in the *Shiʿur Qomah.* In a second passage from the same work the application of the ancient Jewish mystical speculation to the visual form of *Shekhinah* is given even more emphatically:

[154] *Shaʿare ha-Sod,* p. 152.

[155] Ibid., p. 155.

[156] See Scholem's observations in *Origins,* p. 184 n. 206; and the comments of Farber in "Concept of the Merkabah," pp. 142–143, 236–237, 254; Idel, *Kabbalah: New Perspectives,* pp. 193–196. See, however, Dan, *Esoteric Theology,* pp. 122–129.

[157] Cf. the Ashkenazi tradition preserved in MS Oxford-Bodleian 352, fol. 188a, which decodes the word *tefillah* in the liturgical expression *tefillah le-moshe,* "a prayer for Moses," as *tifʾeret paz yihyeh le-roʾsh ha-shekhinah,* "a splendor of fine gold shall it be for the head of the Presence." See also the Ashkenazi text extant in MS New York–JTSA Mic. 1786, fols. 43a–b, discussed by Idel in *Kabbalah: New Perspectives,* pp. 193–194, 372–373 n. 158.

[158] MS Oxford-Bodleian 1568, fols. 5a–b. See Scholem, *Origins,* p. 185.

> *SHQWSẒYT* [= 906] is numerically equal to [the expression] *demut u-demut* [= 906], for "on the semblance of the throne was a semblance of the appearance of a man" (Ezek. 1:26). Why is the word "semblance" (*demut*) repeated twice? For [the expression] *demut u-demut* numerically equals *we-rl"w 'elef we-ribbo' parsah* [236,000 myriad parasangs]. This is the measure of the appearance of the *Shekhinah* to the prophets, its length and width is such, and its measure is such, as it says, "Great is our Lord and full of power" (Ps. 147:5). *We-rav koaḥ* ("full of power") equals 236, which is the number of the measure of the *Shekhinah*.[159]

The representation of the enthroned figure of Ezekiel's vision as the object of the *Shi'ur Qomah* calculations is here supported by the supposed numerical equivalence of the expression *demut u-demut* and the measure of 236,000 myriad parasangs, which in Hebrew is *we-rl"w 'elef we-ribbo' parsah* (in fact, the two are not equivalent; the former equals 906 and the latter equals 913). This measure is applied specifically to the *Shekhinah,* which is visualized by the prophets, but not to the Creator, who is beyond any such dimensions or measurements. The point is reiterated in another Ashkenazi text that purports to be a tradition received from Judah the Pious, Joel the Pious, and Qalonymous the Pious: "The *Shekhinah* seen on the throne appears as very subtle, and whatever they saw was not a vision of the Creator, blessed be He, but rather He created something in the likeness of a human that sits on the throne of the Holy One, blessed be He. He showed them an image, numerically equal to 236,000 myriad parasangs; this is the stature of the one who sits on the throne."[160]

In a similar vein, in a commentary on the chariot known as *Perush Hafṭarah,* composed by one of the Pietists, it is said, "The vision of the stature of His great glory (*mar'eh qomat kevodo ha-gadol*), 'Great is our Lord, etc.' 'And full of power' (*we-rav koaḥ*) is numerically equal to 236, that is, the stature of the Holy One, blessed be He, is 236,000 myriad parasangs. . . . *rl"w* [i.e., the Hebrew consonants that equal 236] is the name of the visible Presence (*ha-kavod ha-nir'eh*)."[161] The last part of this citation is found as well in another passage incorporated in *Sefer ha-Ḥokhmah,* wherein the veridical orientation is also quite evident:

> The name of the visible Presence is *rl"w* and thus it is called *ANDPNSREL* [= 716], which numerically equals [the expression] He is 236,000 myriad parasangs

159 MS Oxford-Bodleian 1568, fol. 6b. See Idel, "Additional Fragments," p. 51. See also MS Moscow-Guenzberg 366, fol. 41a.

160 *Merkavah Shelemah* 30a. Cf. Simeon bar Samuel, *'Adam Sikhli,* 3b (pagination lacking in the original): "That which is said in the *Shi'ur Qomah* . . . is said with respect to the created glory that shows images (*dimyonot*) to the prophet. An example may be provided from the sun that shines upon the water and it shines correspondingly above, upon the wall, but the flashing does not touch the water, according to the opinion of R. Judah the Pious, may his memory be for a blessing."

161 MS Berlin Or. 942, fol. 151a. See, however, fol. 150b, whence it would appear that the anthropomorphic measurements of the *Shi'ur Qomah,* applied to the visible glory, are related to the immanence of the divine in all things (see Scholem, *Major Trends,* pp. 108–110) rather than to the manifest form of the glory that appears on the throne of the chariot (cf. *Major Trends,* p. 113).

(*we-hu' rl''w we-'elef parsah*) [= 716]. There are some who call [the *Shekhinah*] *ANRPNSREL*[162] [= 912] and it numerically equals *we-SHQWṢYT* [= 912], which is also the numerology of *we-rl''w 'elef ribbo' parsah* [i.e., the dimensions of the *Shiʿur Qomah,* 236,000 myriad parasangs], for of the Holy One, blessed be He, [it is said] "Great is our Lord and full of power" (Ps. 147:5), but "His wisdom is beyond reckoning" (ibid.). This [measurable being] is the *Shekhinah* that appears to the prophets, and the Creator created this form with several colors, as it says, "There was a radiance all about him" (Ezek. 1:27). The word radiance (*we-nogah*) has the same letters as the [word] color (*ha-gawwen*) . . . and this is the numerical equivalent of [the word] secret (*sod*) . . . and the numerical equivalent of [the expression] "God, the Lord who is one" (*'el YHWH 'eḥad*). For the *Shekhinah* has several colors and several appearances, to this prophet [it appears] in one way and to the other in another way. It is seen in seventy aspects according to the numerical value of [the word] radiance (*we-nogah*), for it has seventy names. But the secret (*sod*) [which also equals seventy] is that the Creator is "God, the Lord who is one" (*'el YHWH 'eḥad*) [which likewise equals seventy]. Even though He has seventy names . . . He is nevertheless "God, the Lord who is one."[163]

The name here given to the *Shekhinah* in its manifest form, especially in the first formulation, Andepanasarel, may be a compound of the Greek *anthropos* (or more precisely, according to one of its declensions, *anthropon*) and the Hebrew *sar-el,* the archon of God. The meaning implied in this name, therefore, would be that the anthropomorphic manifestation of the Presence is the angelic form. This notion is also implied in yet another passage from the Pseudo-Hai commentary on the forty-two-letter name (to be discussed more fully below) wherein the Presence is described, inter alia, as the angel of the Lord (*mal'akh ha-shem*), which is the size of 236,000 myriad parasangs.[164] The *Shekhinah,* then, is the angelic manifestation of God that assumes the corporeal dimensions specified in the esoteric tradition of the *Shiʿur Qomah.*[165]

Moreover, the *Shekhinah,* the measurable aspect of the divine, is described as a multicolored form created by God. The multifaceted nature of *Shekhinah,* expressed in its ability to appear in different forms to the prophets, is derived from the description in Ezekiel of the radiance that surrounded the semblance of the human form upon the throne, for the word for radiance, *we-nogah,* has the same consonants as the word for color or aspect, *ha-gawwen,* both equaling seventy.[166] This is further connected by numerology to the rabbinic notion

[162] This alternative reading is recorded as well in *Perush Hafṭarah,* MS Berlin Or. 942, fol. 151a. And cf. the text in *Merkavah Shelemah* 30b, where the name is given as ABRPNSREL.

[163] MS Oxford-Bodleian 1568, fol. 23a; see also MS New York–JTSA Mic. 1786, fol. 43b. See Farber, "Concept of the Merkabah," p. 410; Idel, "Additional Fragments," p. 52.

[164] MS Oxford-Bodleian 1568, fol. 5a.

[165] Scholem, *Origins,* p. 185.

[166] The description of the *Shekhinah* as that which comprises a multiplicity of colors is applied elsewhere in Eleazar's writings to the *ḥashmal,* the neologism used by Ezekiel to describe the luminous nature of the anthropomorphic form of the enthroned glory. This motif is expressed in a

of seventy aspects of Scripture[167] or, alternatively, the mystical notion of seventy names attributed to either God or Meṭaṭron.

Finally, this quality of *Shekhinah* is also connected to the word mystery (*sod*)[168] as well as to the phrase "God, the Lord who is one" (*'el YHWH 'eḥad*), for they too both equal seventy. The seventy names of God are the seventy aspects through which the glory appears, and these multiple forms together constitute a single unity, as is attested in the expression "God, the Lord who is one." It is instructive that in another context Eleazar interprets the word *sod*, which equals seventy, as a reference to the Torah, inasmuch as the latter comprises seventy facets of interpretation: "'The secret (*sod*) of the Lord is with those who fear Him' (Ps. 25:14). The Holy One, blessed be He, reveals His secret to those who fear Him. . . . [The word] *sod,* which is numerically equivalent to seventy, refers to the Torah that is explicated in accordance with seventy aspects."[169] It would not be incorrect, in my view, to combine the two

---

variety of ways, including the fact that 378 is the numerology of the word *ḥashmal* and the phrase *kol mine zohar,* i.e., "every kind of splendor." Cf. *Sode Razayya,* p. 13. A particularly illuminating formulation of this idea is found in *Perush ha-Merkavah,* MS Paris–BN 850, fol. 68a: "*Ḥashmal* is numerically equal to *kol mine zohar.* This is [the meaning of] through a splendor 'in the likeness of a *ḥashmal*' (Ezek. 1:4, 27). [The expression] 'in the likeness of a *ḥashmal*' instructs about the glory. Therefore Ezekiel saw by means of *ḥashmal* so that he could discern the glory." See also fol. 68b and the parallel in *Sode Razayya,* ed. Weiss, p. 169, where this idea is expressed in terms of another numerical equivalence: *ḥashmal* = *dimyon ṣiv'onim.* The latter term, literally the "image of colors," signifies that the *ḥashmal* comprises the multiple theophanic forms that appear in the imagination. Compare Judah the Pious, "Book of Angels," p. 113, where this idea is expressed in terms of the numerical equivalence of the expressions *ke-'en ḥashmal* ("in the likeness of an electrum") and *ke-zohar 'esh* ("like a fiery splendor"), i.e., both equal 533. Also relevant in this context is another passage in *Perush ha-Merkavah,* MS Paris–BN 850, fol. 69a (cf. 74a) and the parallel in *Sode Razayya,* ed. Weiss, p. 151, where Eleazar connects the word *sod,* "mystery," with *'ayin,* the Hebrew letter whose numerical value is seventy, the same as *sod.* The word *'ayin,* however, also refers to the eye. More specifically, Eleazar notes that "in the pupil of the eye is the countenance of the cherub." The two eyes, therefore, symbolically correspond to the two cherubim. On this identification see Wolfson, "The Image of Jacob Engraved upon the Throne," p. 167. It is likely that underlying this nexus of symbols is a contemplative praxis by means of which one can visualize the divine glory, which purportedly speaks through the cherubim (cf. Exod. 25:22, Num. 7:89). Ritualistically, the glory that appears between the cherubim is symbolized by the head phylacteries, which are, according to the locution of Scripture, "a reminder between your eyes" (Exod. 13:9) or "a frontlet between your eyes" (Exod. 13:16, Deut. 6:8). Underlying this symbolism is the further identification of the head phylacteries as the crown, which is the hypostatization of the Tetragrammaton. See "Image of Jacob," pp. 165–166.

[167] See *Bemidbar Rabbah* 13:15. For the earlier tradition regarding the multiplication of each divine word into seventy languages, see B. Shabbat 88b.

[168] On the connection between the word *sod* and the seventy names of God, see the passage from a kabbalistic commentary on the Tetragrammaton from the Iyyun circle, extant in MSS New York–JTSA Mic. 1805, fol. 51a; 1731, fol. 90b; 2194, fol. 33a.

[169] *Perush Sodot ha-Tefillah,* MS Paris–BN 772, fol. 89b. On the connection of seventy and esoteric knowledge, based on the numerical value of *sod,* see *Perush ha-Merkavah,* MS Paris–BN 850, fols. 68b–69a (quoted in n. 189, below) and parallel in *Sode Razayya,* ed. Weiss, p. 151. Cf. the Ashkenazi commentary on Psalms, MS Oxford-Bodleian 1551, fol. 206b.

traditions so that the *Shekhinah* in its multifaceted nature is identical with the Torah—a view that is found, for example, in the part of *Sefer ha-Ḥokhmah* that Eleazar himself composed.[170] What is critical from my perspective is the fact that the ability of *Shekhinah* to appear in these different forms, connected here with the *Shi*ʿ*ur Qomah* tradition, is not interpreted in purely mental or psychologistic terms.[171] Indeed, in one passage in his commentary on the liturgy Eleazar, reflecting on Ezekiel's throne-vision (especially Ezek. 1:26), remarks that the greatness (*godel*) of God is seen by the prophets with their physical eyes (*re*ʾ*ut* ʿ*einayim*):

> Upon that image of the throne that I see is the image of the appearance of a man, for the glory is not on the throne . . . the glory is above, very exalted, great and awesome. . . . [The words] great and awesome are juxtaposed, for [with respect to] the greatness that He shows to the prophets, according to the vision of the eyes, a limit is given to the greatness of His glory; praiseworthy is the one who knows and discerns it. "[Great is our Lord] and full of power." But His greatness has no limit as it is in itself.[172]

Vestiges of this approach can be detected in Eleazar's other compositions, as may be seen, for example, in the following passage from *Sod ha-Merkavah*, which combines the midrashic tradition concerning God's theophanous forms and the anthropomorphic measurements of ancient Jewish mystical speculation:

> The essence of the glory is seen above and the unfathomable fire of radiance is above, opposite the throne of glory, and within it the glory is seen in accordance with the will of the Creator, sometimes as an elder and sometimes as a youth, and the measure of the [bodily] stature is 236,000 myriad parasangs, as it is written, "Great is our Lord and full of power" (Ps. 147:5), [the expression] "and full of power" (*we-rav koaḥ*) numerically equals 236. . . . The stature of the visible glory is 236,000 myriad parasangs.[173]

In this context, then, the *Shi*ʿ*ur Qomah* measurements are applied to the visible glory (*ha-kavod ha-nir*ʾ*eh*) without any specification that the latter is merely a phantasm that inheres within the imagination of the prophet or mystic. On the contrary, it is specified that the glory is seen above, in the chariot realm, within the unfathomable fire that is opposite the throne of glory. In this case, then, it will not do to render the expression *ha-kavod ha-nir*ʾ*eh* as "the glory that is seen mentally by the prophet."

The "literal" attribution of the corporeal measurements of *Shi*ʿ*ur Qomah*

[170] Cf. MS Oxford-Bodleian 1568, fol. 25a, printed with slight textual variants in *Perush ha-Roqeaḥ* ʿ*al ha-Torah* 1:15. See Farber, "Concept of the Merkabah," pp. 236, 242, 609. I have elaborated on this theme in "The Mystical Significance of Torah-Study in German Pietism."

[171] Consider the interesting comment in Eleazar's *Perush Sodot ha-Tefillah*, MS Paris–BN 772, fol. 30b: "'With an outstretched arm,' this is the arm of Moses. It is also the arm of the Holy One, blessed be He, that He showed to His prophets."

[172] MS Paris–BN 772, fol. 71a; cf. fol. 97b.

[173] *Sode Razayya*, p. 31; cf. p. 41.

speculation to the *Shekhinah* is also evident in the following citation from Eleazar's *Commentary on Sefer Yeṣirah,* although in this text something of the docetic approach is preserved, as the appearance of God through the Presence is linked particularly to the phenomenon of images (*dimyonot*) that God creates in accord with his will:

> [The Creator] cannot be compared to a body or anything corporeal, nor can you mention any limb, not the mouth or the eye, as it is with the soul. He appears to the prophets by means of the Presence of His glory in many images (*dimyonot*) according to His will and desire, the one who creates images. With respect to the Presence of His glory it is said, "I beheld the Lord" (Isa. 6:1), "upon this semblance of a throne, there was the semblance of a human form" (Ezek. 1:26), "in our image, after our likeness" (Gen. 1:26), "and the Ancient of Days took his seat" (Dan. 7:9), "the heaven is My throne and the earth is My footstool" (Isa. 66:1). . . . And that which is said in the *Maʿaseh Merkavah* [regarding] the measurement of the stature of the Presence as 236,000 myriad parasangs . . . applies especially to the Presence of His glory, but the Creator of the world has no limit or boundary.[174]

The tension between the docetic and veridical orientation is particularly evident in a passage of Eleazar (which resembles in part the view of the second sage in the dialogue on the nature of the glory attributed by Dan to Judah he-Ḥasid[175]) cited by Abraham bar Azriel in his *ʿArugat ha-Bosem,* for, on the one hand, the measurements of *Shiʿur Qomah* are said to result from the vision of the glory within the heart of the visionary and yet, on the other hand, it is stated that these dimensions are attributed to the Creator (*yoṣer bereshit*) in order to make the point that the measurable glory indeed cleaves to—that is, is not ontologically distinct from—the transcendent One:

> Concerning that which is written in the *Shiʿur Qomah,* "I [i.e., R. Ishmael] and R. Aqiva guarantee that the one who knows the measure of the Creator is certain to be in the world-to-come." The Creator has no limit. And that which was said in the *Midrash Mah Rabu*[176] on the verse regarding the measure of the Creator, "Great is our Lord and full of power" (Ps. 147:5), this [expression "and full of power," *werav koaḥ*] numerically equals 236,000 myriad [parasangs], "[Who measured the waters with the hollow of His hand] and gauged the skies with a span" (Isa. 40:12). For the sake of prophetic vision this measure had to be shown to the prophet. . . . Those who fear God see the appearance of the glory in the intellect of their hearts. But the Creator has no limit. [The subject of the *Shiʿur Qomah*] should have been the vision of the glory, for the Creator has no limit. But [the measure is explicitly attributed to the Creator] in order to make the point that the measure [of the glory] cleaves [to the Creator].[177]

174 *Perush Sefer Yeṣirah le-R. ʾEleʿazar mi-Worms* 3a–b.

175 The relevant text is printed in Dan, *Esoteric Theology,* p. 138.

176 This relatively late midrash (see Jellinek, ed., *Bet ha-Midrash* 1:137–141, 6:36–70) is cited elsewhere by Eleazar or in his name. Cf. *Sode Razayya,* p. 54; *ʿArugat ha-Bosem* 1:187, 193.

177 *ʿArugat ha-Bosem* 1:202. Important evidence for the application of the *Shiʿur Qomah* to the *Shekhinah* may be found in other passages in Pietistic works. See, e.g., the text published by Dan in

Important evidence among Pietist authors for the application of the *Shi'ur Qomah* to the *Shekhinah* may be found in the following tradition (already mentioned above) preserved in an Ashkenazi commentary on the forty-two-letter name, reported in the name of three figures, Judah he-Ḥasid, Joel he-Ḥasid, and Qalonymous he-Ḥasid:

> "Upon this semblance of a throne, there was the semblance [of a human form]" (Ezek. 1:26). Why are there two images (*dimyonot*)? This is what is said in the *Book of Beliefs*[178] regarding the two glories (*kevodot*) above in heaven, one upon the throne and the other above. This is the explanation of the two images. The visible *Shekhinah* on the throne is seen in a most subtle way, and everything that they [the prophets] saw was not the appearance of the Creator, blessed be He, but rather He created [a form] in the likeness of a human and it sat upon the throne of the Holy One, blessed be He. He showed them an image (*demut*) according to the numerical equivalent of 236,000 myriad parasangs, and this is the stature of the one who sits on the throne. This was received from R. Judah Ḥasid and from R. Joel Ḥasid and from his brother R. Qalonymous Ḥasid.[179]

The veridical approach is likewise maintained in a tradition reported in the name of R. Eleazar ha-Darshan, an Ashkenazic authority who lived in the second half of the thirteenth century. R. Eleazar describes the *Shekhinah* as an entity that "changes according to the will of the Creator, as it says, 'For I granted many visions, and through the prophets I was imaged' (Hosea 12:11). At times the prophets and angels see it, and the limbs they measured in *Sefer ha-Qomah* refer to the limbs of the *Shekhinah*."[180] The force of this comment attributed to R. Eleazar is brought into sharp relief if one considers the position of his son, R. Moses ha-Darshan, in his *Shi'ur Qomah* commentary. Having denied categorically that God in any sense possesses physical limbs,[181] R. Moses ascribes the measurements of the *Shi'ur Qomah* tradition in one context to the throne itself[182] and in another to the Cherub that sits upon that throne.

Studies, p. 85, and another reference in n. 8; *'Arugat ha-Bosem* 1:33; the tradition reported in the name of R. Neḥemiah ben Zusman in *'Arugat ha-Bosem* 1:127–128, and the one in the name of R. Neḥemiah ben Solomon in 1:198. (Concerning this author, see Dan, *Esoteric Theology,* pp. 40, 66; *'Arugat ha-Bosem* 1:128 n. 2, where Urbach describes R. Neḥemiah as one of the editors or redactors of the main mystical corpus of Eleazar.)

178 This attribution is problematic inasmuch as the idea of two glories is not found in this work of Saadiah, although it is expressed in another work of his, the responsum to a heretic published in a Hebrew form in Judah ben Barzillai's *Perush Sefer Yeṣirah*.

179 *Merkavah Shelemah* 30a; cf. *'Arugat ha-Bosem* 4:78 n. 41.

180 MSS Paris–BN 843, fol. 72a, New York–JTSA Mic. 1885, fol. 74a. Cf. MS Munich 92, fol. 25a, where this text is cited as a tradition of Eleazar of Worms. On the image of the "limbs of the *Shekhinah*," see Scholem, *On the Mystical Shape*, p 297 n. 63. According to Scholem, the term originates with the German Pietists and from them exercises a major influence on the kabbalists.

181 Cf. MSS Rome-Angelica 46, fol. 3b; Milan-Ambrosiana 70, fols. 207b–208a (cf. Scholem, *Reshit ha-Qabbalah,* p. 228).

182 See MSS Rome-Angelica 46, fol. 2a; Milan-Ambrosiana 70, fol. 206a. Commenting on the adjective in the expression "the great God" (*ha-'el ha-gadol*), the author explains that "since

The Cherub is the one that sits upon the throne. And it is the image of the Holy One, blessed be He, when His shadow is still upon it.[183] This is the import of what is said, "and through the prophets I was imaged" (Hosea 12:11), for the appearance of the Cherub is like that of the shade, and the shade is [related to] the matter of prophecy. Occasionally it is seen like an angel, at other times as a human, a lion, a horse, a ram, in accordance with what He wills. It cannot be said that this [refers to] the Holy One, blessed be He, for it is said, "I am the Lord, I have not changed" (Mal. 3:6). It is instead the Cherub that changes and that appears in all these forms. . . . Concerning the Cherub it is said, "Your stately form is like the palm" (Cant. 7:8). . . . And this is what is said, "Great is our Lord and full of power" (Ps. 147:5). The numerical value [of the expression "and full of power," *we-rav koaḥ*] is 236. This is the Cherub. [The expression] "and full of power" (*we-rav koaḥ*) contains the letters [of the word] Cherub (*keruv*). This Cherub is referred to in the Torah [by the phrase] "the Lord and the one" (*YHWH we-'eḥad*). Thus you must say that it is this Cherub that appears to the prophets. After we have proven that the Cherub appears to the prophets, it must be said that the glory of the Lord is the Cherub, as it says, "And there appeared the glory of the Lord [in a cloud]" (Exod. 16:10). [The word] "appeared" (*nir'eh*) is numerically equivalent to the expression "this is the Cherub" (*zeh ha-keruv*). It is said, "It is the glory of God to conceal the matter" (Prov. 25:2). One must hide this and reveal it only to the humble.[184]

There are several critical notions operative in the above citation that are worthy of the reader's notice. First, as other scholars have pointed out, R. Moses' tradition regarding the enthroned Cherub that assumes the corporeal dimensions of the *Shi'ur Qomah* is reminiscent of the doctrine espoused by the other main circle of Pietists, the "Circle of the Special Cherub." This name, coined by Dan, is derived from the fact that one of the main theological claims found in this literary corpus is that the visible and measurable being on the throne, the anthropomorphic representation of the invisible, incorporeal, divine glory, is the special Cherub (*ha-keruv ha-meyuḥad*). While R. Moses does not employ this precise terminology, it is nevertheless evident that his position is close to this school of speculation. It has been suggested by Scholem and, more recently, by Farber, that these Pietistic speculations on the enthroned, measurable

---

[God's] throne [has a measure] that equals 236 [i.e., 236,000 myriad parasangs], the one who sits upon [the throne] is called great. And this is [the import of the verse] 'Great is our Lord and full of power' (Ps. 147:5), since His throne [equals the measure implied in the phrase] 'and full of power' [i.e., 236] He is called great."

183 Cf. the Ashkenazi commentary on the forty-two-letter name of God in MS Moscow-Guenzberg 366, fols. 40b–41a, where the *Shekhinah* is described as the anthropomorphic form upon the throne, also referred to as God's image (*demut*) and the shadow of His stature (*ṣel qomato*) that He showed to the prophets.

184 *Reshit ha-Qabbalah*, pp. 213, 217–219. The passage is partially copied in Naftali Herz Treves, *Siddur Mal'ah ha-'Areṣ De'ah*, section on daily prayers, s.v. *barekhu* (no pagination in the original). On the identification of the Presence as the Cherub, particularly when the former interchanges with Meṭaṭron, see Isaac of Acre, *'Oṣar Hayyim*, MS Moscow-Guenzberg 775, fol. 137b; see, however, fol. 7a, where Meṭaṭron is explicitly identified as the Cherub.

Cherub are related to older Jewish esoteric notions that were part of the world of throne mysticism.[185] In a separate study[186] I have argued that the Cherub—identified by various key terms, including, the image of Jacob engraved on the throne, the back of God, the smaller countenance, the throne of glory, the Splendor of Israel—also assumes a central role in the esoteric doctrine of the Qalonymide circle. The Cherub is the lower glory that is identified as the visible pole of the revelatory experience for both prophet and mystic. Moreover, this lower glory, or Cherub, is a throne for the upper glory that rides or sits upon it. The moment of enthronement—also characterized, on the basis of the key passage in *Hekhalot Rabbati* (discussed in chapter 3) as the upper glory embracing and kissing the image of Jacob—is treated as one of the most esoteric traditions by Eleazar; he mentions it several times in his writings, occasionally emphasizing the secrecy that surrounds this notion. It is likely that the shared speculation on the enthroned Cherub, simultaneously the object of prophetic and mystical vision, points to an older tradition that influenced these two independent circles. It is, therefore, all the more instructive that R. Moses "contemporizes" this tradition by arguing, much like Eleazar of Worms in the texts examined above, that the Cherub is the image of God, that is, the form that inheres in the imagination of the seer. Thus the view espoused by R. Moses contrasts sharply with the more veridically oriented tradition reported in the name of his father, R. Eleazar.

The full impact of the veridical approach can be ascertained only by a closer examination of the more esoteric stratum of the theosophic writings of the German Pietists. Whatever the theoretical understanding of the possibility of seeing God that emerged among the Pietists, it is clear that they received much older traditions that assumed that the vision of God's glory as an anthropomorphic form was possible. Moreover, the esoteric understanding of this vision involved the further identification of this glory with the divine name. Hence, seeing the light of the glory meant contemplating the name. On the other hand, knowing the name entailed a vision of the glory. Indeed, in the mystical vision light and letter symbolism converge: the anthropomorphic shape is itself composed of the letters of God's name.

The Esoteric Doctrine of the Glory and the Name

Transmission of the Name and the Account of the Chariot

For the German Pietists, theosophic gnosis entailed mystical illumination of the sort I have just described. In the main circle of German Pietists, as may be detected principally from the writings of Eleazar of Worms, it is clear that the

[185] Scholem, *Major Trends*, pp. 113–114; idem, *Origins*, p. 211; Farber, "Concept of the Merkabah," p. 309. See also Altmann, *Studies*, p. 167 n. 28.

[186] Wolfson, "The Image of Jacob Engraved upon the Throne."

rabbinic esoteric tradition—*maʿaseh merkavah,* the "account of the chariot"—was understood as speculation on the divine names and especially the four-letter divine name, the Tetragrammaton. A telling proof of this can be found in this comment in Eleazar's *Sefer ha-Shem,* a treatise entirely dedicated to an exposition of the divine names: "The account of creation (*maʿaseh bereshit*) may not be expounded by three, nor laws pertaining to forbidden sexual relations (*ʿarayot*), and the secret of the name (*sod ha-shem*) is not revealed to three, but only to one or two."[187] It is evident that this statement is based on the mishnaic passage in Ḥagigah 2:1, "*ʿArayot* may not be expounded by three, nor *maʿaseh bereshit* by two, nor the *merkavah* by one." Eleazar has retained two of the three esoteric disciplines enumerated by the sages of the Mishnah and replaced the third, study of the chariot (*merkavah*), with the secret of the name (*sod ha-shem*). This is not a mere coincidence but rather reflects the Pietistic view, itself based on earlier sources,[188] that speculation on the chariot is connected with the mystical knowledge of the divine name.[189] Further evidence for this identification may be gathered from a statement in Eleazar's commentary on the liturgy concerning the seventy-two-letter name derived from Exod. 14:19–21: "In these three verses . . . you will find all the letters of the [Hebrew] alphabet except for *gimmel.* This is to declare that one needs to join three letters together [to form a name]. In addition, it is to instruct one that the account of the chariot is not expounded to three, as it is stated in the tractate Ḥagigah."[190] In this case we see a specific connection made between the seventy-two-letter name of God and the account of the chariot, a view that is

[187] MS British Museum 737, fol. 201a.

[188] See Idel, *Mystical Experience,* pp. 14–16; idem, "Defining Kabbalah." Especially significant is the comment of the northern French exegete Samuel ben Meir (ca. 1080–ca. 1174) that the "secrets of the Torah" mentioned in B. Pesaḥim 119a include the account of the chariot (*maʿaseh ha-merkavah*), the account of creation (*maʿaseh bereshit*), and the explication of the (divine) name (*perusho shel shem*).

[189] On the secrecy pertaining to the divine name in the Pietistic literature, see Dan, *Esoteric Theology,* pp. 74–76. See, in particular, *ʿArugat ha-Bosem,* 2:154, for a discussion of the esoteric character of the name as the locus of great secrets. See also *Perush Sodot ha-Tefillah,* MS Paris–BN 772, fol. 126a, where Eleazar comments on the verse "Bless the Lord, O my Soul, all my being, His holy name" (Ps. 103:1): "The name (*'et shem*) includes the chariot and the upper and lower secrets." And see *Perush ha-Merkavah,* MS Paris–BN 850, fols. 68b–69a: "[The letter] *ʿayin* numerically equals *sod.* This is [the meaning of the verse] 'The secret of the Lord is for those who fear Him; to them He makes known His covenant' (Ps. 25:14). That is to say, the great secret of the name (*sod ha-gadol shel ha-shem*) is not transmitted except to those who fear [God]. But 'to them He makes known His covenant,' to those who fear [God] so that they can teach it to the children of Israel. . . . 'The secret of the Lord is for those who fear Him,' this refers to those who are pure of heart, faithful to their Creator. For them God 'draws out mysteries' (Job 12:22) and He brings to light His secret."

[190] MS Paris–BN 772, fol. 36a. For the continuation of the passage, see below, n. 192. Cf. the parallel in *Sefer ha-Shem,* MS British Museum 737, fol. 192a, and *Perush ha-Roqeaḥ ʿal ha-Torah,* 2:73; and see Abraham Abulafia, *Sitre Torah,* MS Paris–BN 774, fol. 139a. On the connection of the letter *gimmel* and esoterica, see the comment by R. Benjamin ben Abraham in a commentary on *'Otiyyot de-R. ʿAqiva',* MS Vatican 291, fol. 17b: "*gimmel* is crowned with three crownlets according to the mysteries of Torah."

known from other Jewish sources as well.[191] This interpretation is a specific application of the more general identification of *ma'aseh merkavah* with mystical knowledge of the divine name.

It is clear that for the Pietists this speculation was not merely theoretical but represented the occasion for a contemplative vision of the name. Indeed, knowledge of the chariot entails meditative ascent by means of the divine name. Thus in his *Perush ha-Merkavah,* after specifying some of the requirements necessary for the transmission of the glorious name (*shem ha-nikhbad*),[192] Eleazar comments that the one who "knows it [the name] and walks with a straight heart is like one of the ministering angels, and he is received from camp to camp, for he is like an angel and his soul is bound to the high and exalted throne."[193] Although the technical language of *yeridah la-merkavah,* "entry to the chariot," is not used here, it is obvious that Eleazar's description of the adept who knows the name is drawn from the Hekhalot mystical praxis. That is, the one who possesses knowledge of the name is transformed into an angelic being and thus receives passage through the heavenly realms until his soul is bound to the throne.[194] In another passage from the same treatise Eleazar notes that just as the prophet "saw the chariot" by the River Chebar, so too

[191] See the tradition cited in Abraham ibn Ezra's Standard Commentary on Exod. 14:19 (ed. Weiser, 2:93) from a *Sefer Razi'el:* "The one who wants to inquire of [the meaning of] a dream should recite at the beginning of the night the verse 'In the thirtieth year' (Ezek. 1:1), for it comprises seventy-two letters." Cf. ibn Ezra's Short Commentary on Exod. 3:13 (2:245), where the same tradition is reported in the name of *Sefer ha-Razim;* see also *Sefer ha-Shem,* ed. Lippmann, 10a; *The Religious Poems of Abraham ibn Ezra* 1:136 (poem no. 74). On the tradition connecting the seventy-two-letter name and the first verse of Ezekiel, cf. Farber, ed., "Commentary on Ezekiel's Chariot," p. 1: "The one who mentions this verse [Ezek. 1:1] should have the proper intention concerning the vision of the dream. And if you ask why this verse alludes to seventy-two letters which [correspond to] the seventy-two names, you should know that the seventy-two holy names of the Holy One, blessed be He, are rooted and unified in the essence of the chariot, and they are like pillars of shining lights. . . . Ezekiel the prophet saw visions of God which are called the chariot, and since the seventy-two names are unified in the chariot this verse is based on seventy-two letters which correspond to the number of seventy-two names." See also p. 198 n. 12, where Farber mentions the ibn Ezra source. On the connection of the seventy-two-letter name and prophecy, see also the comment of Isaac of Acre in *'Oṣar Ḥayyim,* MS Moscow-Guenzberg 775, fol. 16b: "The secret [of the seventy-two-letter name] is *'aryeh* [which numerically equals 216, the number of letters in the three verses, Exod. 14:19–21, whence the seventy-two-letter name is derived], and through its power the prophets prophesied, 'A lion (*'aryeh*) has roared, who can but fear? [My Lord has spoken, who can but prophesy?]' (Amos 3:8)."

[192] For an alternative specification of the moral attributes required for transmission of the name, see *Perush ha-Tefillah,* MS Paris–BN 772, fol. 36a: "In the thirteen verses in the Pentateuch, where there occurs [the formulation] 'to love the Lord' or 'you shall love the Lord,' all the letters appear except for the *gimmel.* This indicates that the name is not taught to one who is haughty or who moves hurriedly [to sin; cf. Prov. 19:2] or one who is angry." On the particular connection between transmission of the name and subjugation of sexual desire, see n. 202, below.

[193] MS Paris–BN 850, fol. 49b. On the necessity of mentioning the name on an empty stomach, thereby enabling one to attain a spiritual state akin to that of the angelic beings, see the fragment of *Sefer ha-Shem* in MS New York–JTSA Mic. 1885, fol. 2a.

[194] From other Pietistic texts it is clear that prayer was viewed in a mystical vein as an occasion for ascent to the chariot. See Farber, "Concept of the Merkabah," p. 237.

> whoever is occupied [with the study of] the chariot (*ha-ʿoseq ba-merkavah*) or the glorious name (*shem ha-nikhbad*) [i.e., the Tetragrammaton], he and his students, to whom he wants to transmit this, should go and bathe in water, and cover their whole bodies in water, and their clothes should be soaked in water. . . . they should immerse themselves and get dressed in white clothes[195] and stand in water up to their thighs. And the rabbi should begin [to cite the blessing], with fear and trembling, with [proper] intention in mind, looking at the water. . . . Blessed are You, O Lord, our God, king of the universe, God of Israel, You are one and Your name is one, and You have commanded us to conceal Your great name, for Your name is awesome. Blessed are You, Lord, and blessed is the name of Your glory forever, the glorious and awesome name, Lord, our God. "The voice of the Lord is over the waters" (Ps. 29:3). Blessed are You, Lord, the one who reveals His secret to those who fear Him, the one who knows all secrets.[196]

A careful scrutiny of this passage indicates that Eleazar's conception of the divine name is based largely on some of the Hekhalot compositions, specifically *Hekhalot Zuṭarti* and *Maʿaseh Merkavah*. An outstanding feature of both these macroforms is the emphasis placed on the divine name as the concentration of power as well as the focus of mystical vision. The liturgical formula proposed by Eleazar concerning the different aspects of the name is reminiscent of passages found in the aforementioned Hekhalot texts. Indeed, one of the expressions used by Eleazar, "You are one and Your name is one" (*'atah 'eḥad we-shimkha 'eḥad*) is found verbatim in *Maʿaseh Merkavah*.[197] Moreover, it is evident from other passages in his own writings that Eleazar assigns a theurgical significance to the knowledge of the name, a motif that is prevalent in *Hekhalot Zuṭarti* and, to an extent, in *Maʿaseh Merkavah*. It follows that, inasmuch as the name represents the power of God—indeed, in a sense is interchangeable with God—the one who acquires knowledge of the name is imbued with the power to perform magical acts and adjurations. The emphasis in the blessing on the need to conceal the name resonates with a distinctive element of *Hekhalot Zuṭarti*, as I have previously mentioned, namely, knowledge of the name is treated as esoteric lore that cannot be readily disseminated. Finally, in Eleazar's writings it is evident that the name is depicted as a fiery or luminous

[195] For similar requirements as preparation for the ecstatic praxis of letter-combination in Abulafia's kabbalah, see Scholem, *Major Trends*, p. 136; Idel, *Mystical Experience,* p. 39. The notion that white clothing symbolizes purity is an ancient motif. See, e.g., P. Rosh ha-Shanah 1:3, 57b. On the symbolic import of white clothes as a sign of purity in medieval Christian mysticism, see Cleve, "Semantic Dimensions in Margery Kempe's Whyght Clothys."

[196] MS Paris–BN 850 fols. 58a–b. Cf. the *Sefer ha-Qomah* of Moses ha-Darshan (MSS Rome-Angelica 46, fol. 6a; Milan-Ambrosiana 70, fol. 211b), where it is reported that before one utters a certain praise of God one must ritually immerse oneself or pour nine measures of hot water over oneself.

[197] See *Synopse,* § 589. The formulation is obviously based on Zech. 14:9. See also the formulation in the magical text extant in MS New York–JTSA Mic. 8128, fol. 15a, printed in Herrmann and Rohrbacher-Sticker, "Magische Traditionen der New Yorker Hekhalot-Handschrift," p. 124: "He is one and His name is one (*hu' 'eḥad u-shemo 'eḥad*)."

substance, a conception that is particularly striking in *Maʿaseh Merkavah,* where the name assumes hypostatic dimensions.[198] Indeed, in at least one passage from that macroform the divine name is characterized as being "etched in burning fire" (*ḥaṣuv be-ʾesh lehavah*),[199] words that echo the verse "the voice of the Lord kindles flames of fire" (*qol YHWH ḥosev lahavot ʾesh*) (Ps. 29:7). One may detect from the end of Eleazar's passage (as well as from the parallel text in *Sefer ha-Shem* to be cited below) that he, too, identified the voice of God described in Psalm 29 as the name of God, an identification that allowed for the liturgical use of that very psalm in the techniques required for transmission of the name or the secret of the chariot.[200]

Study of the chariot and of the divine name—which are, from Eleazar's perspective, identical pursuits—must be transmitted orally from master to disciple. This theme is repeated by Eleazar on several occasions, of which I will here cite two important illustrations: "Whoever thinks about these matters will be perturbed if he does not receive that this wisdom [of the chariot] is a sublime wisdom that should not be written but only transmitted from mouth to mouth."[201] "The whole explanation [of the chariot] should not be explained except mouth to mouth, the master to the disciple, with the proper clothing and ritual immersion, and in a place of purity, for Ezekiel saw the chariot upon the river Chebar."[202] The transmission of the name likewise requires a ceremony of

[198] See *Synopse,* §§ 548, 551, 552.

[199] Ibid., § 549 (according to MS Oxford-Bodleian 1531).

[200] The recitation of Psalm 29 is imbued with magical powers, specifically over water, in a baraita in B. Pesaḥim 112a, but there the issue does not seem to have to do with the identification of the voice as the name. See, by contrast, the blessing on the Tetragrammaton extant in MS Florence Medicea-Laurenziana, Plut. 44.13, fol. 84a.

[201] MS Paris–BN 850, fol. 49a.

[202] Ibid., fol. 58a. See also fol. 71a, where in the context of discussing the cherubim Eleazar again notes that "everything should not be revealed in writing but only from mouth to mouth." See also the language in *Sefer ha-Shem,* MS British Museum 737, fol. 181b: "The glorious name (*shem ha-nikhbad,* i.e., the Tetragrammaton) as well as the forty-two-letter name should not be disclosed [orally] except to the humble." And cf. the comment of Eleazar recorded in *ʿArugat ha-Bosem* 1:204, regarding a passage in *Hekhalot Rabbati,* cited as *Sefer ha-Merkavah,* which describes the eating and drinking of the angels who guard the seventh palace (cf. *Synopse,* § 214): "it is known that above there is no eating or drinking, but if I were to write the explanation one who was not worthy would see it and err to the point of the matter being perverted. A person should consider in his heart that he should not heed the matter with his heart except by means of a tradition (*qabbalah*)." Despite the fact that Eleazar did commit a large percentage of the Ashkenazi secrets to writing, and thereby broke the link of esotericism and orality (see Dan, *Esoteric Theology,* pp. 15–18; idem, "Re-evaluation of the 'Ashkenazi Kabbalah'," pp. 127–128), the fact is that there are still a number of places in his writings wherein he briefly alludes to a secret and explicitly informs the reader that the matter cannot be fully revealed except through oral transmission. In some passages Eleazar appropriates the rabbinic notion that esoteric matters must be transmitted "in a whisper." See, e.g., *Sode Razayya,* ed. Weiss, pp. 135 (see n. 8, above), 151. In that respect I am in agreement with the view of Farber concerning the existence of superesoteric traditions among the German Pietists that were transmitted orally from teacher to disciple and not committed to writing. Typically, these superesoteric traditions involved bisexual symbolism in the divine realm reminiscent of kabbalistic theosophy. See Farber, "Concept of the Merkabah," pp. 117, 126, 237, 254, 621, 628–630. See also my study "Image of Jacob"; Idel, "Sexual Metaphors and Praxis," p. 221 n. 79

purification involving immersion in a ritual bath of purification, the donning of white clothes, and the utterance of specific blessings. Eleazar begins *Sefer ha-Shem* with a description of the method required for the transmission of the name very similar to, albeit more elaborate than, the ceremony he described in his *Perush ha-Merkavah,* cited above:

> YHWH–His unique, glorious, and awesome name. We will explain its meaning according to the capacity to speak and to know about the glory of the supernal name of the Lord and His fear. . . . The [name] is transmitted only to the meek, who do not get angry, and to the God-fearing,[203] who perform the commandments of their Creator. It is transmitted only over water, as it is written, "The voice of the Lord is over the waters" (Ps. 29:3). Before the master teaches his disciples they should bathe in water and immerse themselves in [the ritual bath that measures] forty *se'ah.*[204] They should don white clothes and fast on the day he will teach them [the name], and they should stand in the water up to their ankles. Then the master opens his mouth in fear and says: Blessed are You, O Lord, our God, king of the universe, Lord, God of Israel, You are one and Your name is one, and You have commanded us to conceal Your great name, for Your name is awesome. Blessed are You, Lord, who reveals His secret to those who fear Him, the One who knows all secrets. The master and his disciples should look at the water and say, "The ocean sounds, O Lord, the ocean sounds its thunder, the ocean sounds its pounding, more majestic than the breakers of the sea is the Lord, majestic on high" (Ps. 93:3–4). "The voice of the Lord is over the waters, the God of glory thunders, the Lord, over the mighty waters" (Ps. 29:3). "The waters saw You, O God, the waters saw You and were convulsed; the very deep quaked as well" (Ps. 77:17). "Your way was through the sea, Your path, through the mighty waters; Your tracks could not be seen" (ibid., 20). Afterwards they should go near the water or to a synagogue or study-house where there is water in a pure vessel, and the master should say: Blessed are You, Lord, our God, king of the universe, who has sancti-

---

(French trans., p. 352 n. 78); Ginsburg, *The Sabbath in the Classical Kabbalah,* p. 176 n. 231. There is a clear link in the Pietistic sources between transmission of the name and subjugation of sexual desire. Cf. the following remark in the Pietistic work in MS Oxford-Bodleian 1566, fol. 38a: "This is [the meaning of the verse] 'This shall be My name forever' [*shemi le-ʿolam*] (Exod. 3:15), [the word *shemi* signifies that] *shem yod* [i.e., the name that begins with *yod,* the Tetragrammaton] is written *le-ʿolam,* [the name is transmitted] to the one who in the world (*ʿolam*) is pure of all transgression. . . . *Shemi le-ʿolam,* the unique name (*shem ha-meyuḥad*) is revealed only to one who has abrogated the desire for women from his heart." The second interpretation is based on the fact that the word *le-ʿolam,* written in the defective, can be read as *leʿalem,* to conceal. Cf. B. Pesaḥim 50a; Qiddushin 71a. In the Pietistic source, transmission of the Tetragrammaton is linked to nullification of sexual desire. Cf. *Sefer ha-Shem,* MS British Museum 737, fol. 213a: "The unique name is not revealed except to one who has nullified the lust for women." For a convenient review of the German Pietists' attitude toward sexuality, see Biale, *Eros and the Jews,* pp. 72–82.

203 *Baʿale yir'ah*—literally, "masters of fear"— one of the code names for the Pietists. See the quotation from *Sefer ha-Shem* below, n. 275.

204 The traditional ritual bath of purification (*miqveh*) had to hold a required measurement of forty *se'ah.* Cf. M. Menaḥot 12:4; B. Yoma 31a. The purificatory nature of water is an ancient motif in Jewish folklore and ritual. See Patai, *Water,* pp. 12–45.

fied us with His commandments and commanded us and separated us from the nations[205] and revealed to us His secrets and instructed us in the knowledge of His great and awesome name.[206]

The connection of transmission of the name over a body of water to the appearance of the luminous glory is brought out as well in the Pietistic work *Sefer Tagi,* without, however, a detailed account of the actual mystical practice: "Three [things] require water: the explicit name, that is, the Tetragrammaton, is not transmitted except over water.[207] A king is not anointed except over water. One studies Torah over water. Therefore [the glory] is made visible to the prophets over water."[208] The textual bases for this comment are a passage in *Qohelet Rabbah* 3:15 that explicitly states that the divine name is transmitted only in a pure place and over water[209] and a passage in B. Horayot 12a that mentions the law concerning the anointing of a king by water,[210] as well as a tradition relating that R. Mesharsheya would advise his sons to recite their learning by a stream so that their studies would be as prolonged as the continual flow of running water.[211] The Ḥaside Ashkenaz extended this legend to a precept about Torah-study in general, that one should study Torah over water. Implicit here is the mystical identification of the Torah and the name, on one hand, and the name and the glory, on the other: Torah should be studied by water, for the esoteric dimension of Torah is the divine name, which is, at the same time, the luminous glory that appeared in a prophetic vision by a body of water. It is thus no mere coincidence that in the text from *Sefer Tagi* mention is made of both the transmission of the name and the vision of the glory. It should be noted as well that the idea that the glory appears on or near a body of water

205 Cf. Lev. 20:24, 26.

206 MS British Museum 737, fols. 165b–166a. Cf. MSS Paris–BN 825, fol. 193a; Munich 92, fol. 1a.

207 This formulation is reported in the name of the mystics (literally, "sages of the truth," *ḥakhme ha-'emet*) by Baḥya ben Asher in his commentary to Lev. 16:30 (ed. Chavel, 2:505): "It is a tradition of the mystics that the name is not transmitted except over water, as it says, 'The voice of the Lord over the water' (Ps. 29:3)." As we have seen, this verse is also interpreted by Eleazar of Worms as a reference to the divine name. Cf. Scholem (*On the Kabbalah,* p. 136 n. 1) who already suggested that Eleazar was the probable source for Baḥya. The text I have cited contains the exact phrase used by Baḥya.

208 MS Oxford-Bodleian 1566, fol. 233a.

209 This midrashic passage as a possible source for the German Pietistic practice of transmitting the name was previously noted by Dan, *Esoteric Theology,* p. 75 n. 10.

210 The biblical precedent for this law is 1 Kings 1:32ff. Cf. T. Sanhedrin 4:10; Maimonides, *Mishneh Torah,* Kele ha-Miqdash 1:11, Melakhim 1:11. See Patai, *Water,* p. 11.

211 In light of this source, Scholem's remarks in *On the Kabbalah,* p. 137, that the magical significance of water as an appropriate medium for initiation (as described in *Sefer ha-Malbush* and *Sefer ha-Shem*) does not occur in talmudic literature or any other Jewish traditions should be slightly modified. On the *topos* of the Torah as a body of water and the transformative power of Torah-study to turn the sage into a fountain or spring, see Fishbane, "The Well of Living Water," esp. pp. 14ff. See also the passage from *Sefer ha-Melammed* on the comparison of Torah to water extant in MS Vatican 300, fols. 23a–23b. It is recommended that the text should be studied on the seventh day of Passover, which commemorates the splitting of the Red Sea.

is based on much older sources, including apocalyptic, midrashic, and mystical texts.[212] The Pietists combined the various traditions, for in their view the name, the glory, and the Torah are identical.

That transmission of the name, construed as the esoteric discipline of the chariot, entails a vision of the Presence is implied in a second passage from *Sefer Tagi:* "The ones below are not worthy of making [theurgic] use of (*lehistammesh*) this light[213] so that the chariot (*maʿaseh ha-merkavah*) and the light of the *Shekhinah* would be below."[214] In a third passage from this text, commenting on the expression *we-ruaḥ ʾelohim meraḥefet ʿal pene ha-mayim*, "the spirit of God was sweeping over the waters" (Gen. 1:2), a clear connection is made between water and the prophetic spirit:

> [The word] *meraḥefet* has six crownlets[215] [corresponding to] the six voices written in the chariot,[216] excluding [the verse] "And I heard the voice of someone speaking" (Ezek. 1:28). . . . Thus it is written, "like the sound of mighty waters" (ibid., 24). When were the waters mighty? I would say at the time of creation. Then the Holy One, blessed be He, decreed to unite His spirit over the prophets. "A spirit passed by me" (Job. 4:15). "And the spirit of God was sweeping over the waters" (Gen. 1:2). The one who makes his heart like water will contemplate the faces of the two cherubim.[217]

It should be noted that the techniques adduced by Eleazar were not entirely his innovation, but were based on long standing traditions in Jewish esoteric literature regarding the necessary praxis for uttering the divine name:[218] one must fast, ritually immerse oneself in water, and put on clean clothing, usually specified as white. Similar techniques for the recitation of the divine name are known from other Jewish esoteric works, including the ecstatic kabbalah of Abraham Abulafia, which influenced Isaac of Acre and later sixteenth-century kabbalists, such as Ḥayyim Vital.[219] One also finds that medieval authors specify similar techniques as a preparation for the making of an homunculus (*golem*).[220] For example, Eleazar himself in one context notes that one who

[212] See *Reʾuyot Yeḥezqel*, ed. Gruenwald, pp. 112–113; Idel, "On the Metamorphosis of an Ancient Technique of Prophetic Vision in the Middle Ages." On the nexus between water and the indwelling of the Holy Spirit, see the comment of R. Jonah ben Amittai in P. Sukkah 5:1, 55a. On the connection of water and the appearance of the divine Presence, see also the following tradition in MS New York–JTSA Mic. 2194, fol. 48d: "Thus the throne is established upon seven rivers corresponding to the seven clouds of glory. . . . In every place where the *Shekhinah* is there is water."

[213] The idiom "to make use of the light" is used in classical aggadic midrashim. Cf. *Bereshit Rabbah* 41:3, p. 405, and other references cited there in n. 4.

[214] MS Oxford-Bodleian 1566, fol. 244a.

[215] That is, the ornamental crownlets placed over the letters in the Torah scroll.

[216] Cf. Ezek. 1:24–25, where the word *qol*, "voice," is repeated six times.

[217] MS Oxford-Bodleian 1566, fol. 225a.

[218] See, e.g., *Synopse*, §§ 670, 966.

[219] See Scholem, *Major Trends*, p. 136; Idel, *Mystical Experience*, p. 39, and other examples adduced on p. 50 n. 114. For the influence of Abulafian techniques on Vital, see also Meroz, "Aspects of the Lurianic Teaching on Prophecy," pp. 71–72.

[220] See texts quoted by Idel in *Golem*, pp. 60, 63.

studies *Sefer Yeṣirah* should purify himself—undergo purification through ritual immersion—and don white clothes. It is likely that this is connected with the practical creation of a *golem* by means of pronouncing the different letter-combinations outlined in the ancient Jewish text.[221] Given the employment of these techniques in texts concerning recitation of the name or golem-making, it seems reasonable to conclude that for Eleazar study of the chariot, which was equivalent to contemplating (and perhaps also reciting) the name, involved a mystical praxis. He therefore went to great lengths to provide the necessary steps that one had to take before one orally received the name from the master. Finally, it is evident that, reflecting a much older technique in Jewish esotericism, water was treated by the Pietists as one of the appropriate mediums for visualization of the divine glory. The significance of the water is thus twofold: it provides the means for ritual purification and the medium through which the glory can be seen.

It is likely that the Pietists were especially indebted to the Babylonian, Geonic magical text *Sefer ha-Malbush* (the "Book of the Garment"), which was preserved and copied by the German Pietists as part of the ancient Jewish esoteric lore. According to this text the utterance of divine or angelic names on a body of water resulted in the appearance of various images. Thus in one passage the following technique is recommended: "On the night of the eighth [day] he should go out to the water and call out the name upon the water. At that moment he will see in the air by the water the image of a form. If it is green, he knows that he is still impure. . . . If he sees the image as red, he knows that he has been purified from underneath."[222] The visualization of the external image is a projection of the psychological state of the visionary; what appears outside the mind is, to borrow the locution of the Jungian analyst Erich Neumann, a "psychic image-symbol" that derives from the interior state of the individual and is projected on the external world.[223] The visual image is, in effect, a symbolic depiction of an internal psychic condition.[224] While there are significant differences between this text and the Pietists' own understanding of visionary experience, the issue of water as the proper medium for recitation of the name, eventuating in a vision of an image, cannot go by unremarked. It is evident with respect to this matter, among others, that the Pietists were not simply passive recipients of older texts but were active participants in these magical-mystical techniques and creative innovators of ideas and practices based on older texts.

[221] See Dan, *Esoteric Theology*, pp. 63–64; Scholem, *On the Kabbalah*, p. 185 (full Hebrew text reproduced in Scholem, *Elements of the Kabbalah and Its Symbolism*, p. 406); Idel, *Golem*, pp. 56–57.

[222] MS Oxford-Bodleian 1960, fol. 110b.

[223] Neumann, *The Origins and History of Consciousness*, p. 294.

[224] Cf. MS Oxford-Bodleian 1960, fol. 111a: "You see nothing but smoke passing before you. . . . Conjure these angels by means of the names written on the supernal garment (*malbush shel ma'alah*), and you shall call it [the name] and in whatever form (*ṣurah*) or image (*dimyon*) that you desire the matter [i.e., the angelic form] will be seen when the name is mentioned (*bi-she'at zekhirat ha-shem*)."

In a second passage from *Sefer ha-Shem* Eleazar relates the reception of the divine name to the visionary experience connected with chariot imagery:

> YHWH is called the glorious name (*shem ha-nikhbad*), as it is written, "to revere this glorious Name" (*leyir'ah 'et ha-shem ha-nikhbad*) [= 1078] (Deut. 28:58). [This expression] equals numerically "to revere the four letters" (*leyir'ah dalet 'otiyyot*) [= 1078], for it is glorious and it is not uttered as it is written on account of its great holiness. Other glorious names are above in the light surrounded by a cloud. Therefore the [expression] "They have placed My name there" (*samu shemi sham*) appears fifty-two times in the Pentateuch, and fifty-two times [the word] cloud, to indicate that a cloud surrounds the glorious name above. Therefore the one who studies the name should wear beautiful clothes. The name is not mentioned unless beautiful clothes are worn, the garments of honor. . . . Each of the names has a resplendent light and an enveloping cloud.[225] The names of God are written about the throne of glory, on the pillars of glory.[226]

Implicit in the above description is the view that knowledge of the divine name, which involves the practical or even theurgical mentioning of the name (referred to by the technical term *hazkarat ha-shem*),[227] entails some vision of the light that is contained in the name. The Pietist must wear the proper clothes, which correspond to the clouds that surround the names, for by wearing the proper clothes one is capable of apprehending the light hidden within the clouds. The proper attire functions, like the body of water and the cloud, as a medium that reflects and thus makes visible the luminous glory.[228] Interestingly enough, one does not find prominent in the writings of the Ḥaside Ashkenaz the notion of the investiture of the divine name by the mystic initiate, an idea that is found in much older sources. In his discussion of the rite of initiation for transmission of the name in Eleazar of Worms, Scholem mentions a related tradition preserved in *Sefer ha-Malbush*, which, as we noted above, did in fact influence the Pietists. This text depicts in graphic terms the ritual of

[225] Cf. the text in MSS Oxford-Bodleian 1566, fol. 42a; 1567, fol. 54a.

[226] MS British Museum 737, fol. 172a; for a slightly different version of this passage, see MS Oxford-Bodleian 1638, fol. 52b.

[227] In some of the Hekhalot compositions the terms *lehazkir* and *hazkarah* denote the technical uttering of the name of God, the Tetragrammaton. Similar usage is detected in rabbinic sources; see, e.g., *Sifra on Leviticus*, Nedavah, 2:4, 4a; *Sifre on Numbers* 39, p. 43; *Sifre on Deuteronomy* 306, pp. 341–342. The term *hazkarot* (or, alternatively, *'azkarot*) is used in rabbinic literature to refer to the occurrence of the divine name, especially the Tetragrammaton. Cf. P. Berakhot 4:3, 8a; Ta'anit 2:2, 65c; B. Berakhot 28b; *Midrash Tehillim* 29:2, 116b.

[228] The intermediary role accorded the garment is known from one of the texts attributed by Dan (*Studies*, p. 172) to Judah he-Ḥasid: the sun is said to shine on a colored garment, red or green, and a reflection of that garment is said to be seen on the wall. In that context, however, the garment is used parabolically to refer to the chariot, and the wall is the river in which the chariot is reflected. See Idel, "On the Metamorphosis," pp. 1–2. On the cloud as a medium for visualization, see the description of the *ḥashmal* in *Perush ha-Merkavah*, MS Paris–BN 850, fol. 77a: "A cloud is between it and the glory, and through the cloud it sees the supernal Mind, 'beholding visions of the Almighty' (Num. 24:16), as a person who sees through a speculum." Cf. MS Oxford-Bodleian 1638, fol. 58a. For a slightly different version of this text, see *Sode Razayya*, ed. Weiss, p. 170.

putting on the divine name, which is here understood concretely as a garment of deerskin parchment inscribed with the magical names of God. The critical passage reads as follows: "Then go into the water up to your loins and put on the venerable and terrible Name in the water."[229] Despite the obvious similarity to the ritual described by Eleazar, it is noteworthy that in the Pietistic text one finds no mention of putting on the name. It seems, rather, that in the Pietistic context the correlation is made between the clouds surrounding the name and the garment worn by the mystic. Yet, as will be seen below, something of this older idea is reflected in Eleazar's writings when he describes the creation of a garment for the glory by means of mentioning the divine name.

The image of the cloud covering the name is reminiscent of a similar image used by Eleazar to describe the appearance of the divine word at Sinai. Commenting on the words in the Rosh ha-Shanah liturgy, "You were revealed in the cloud of Your glory upon Your holy nation to speak with them," Eleazar writes,

> The word of God is like white fire clothed in a black and dark cloud.[230] . . . Thus it was revealed in a cloud that surrounds the glory. . . . "Upon Your holy nation"—at that time [at Sinai] Israel were holy, as it is written, "a holy nation" (Exod. 19:6), for they separated from their wives for three days[231] and were like the ministering angels. Therefore His glory was revealed in order to speak to them. The word that goes out from the mouth of God is a fire brighter in its whiteness than any other fire in the world, and the brightness blinds the eyes like one who looks at the sun when it is in its strength. Therefore the glory, the will of His word, is fire; the form of a cloud and darkness surround it. According to the needs of the hour the word goes out, for the Holy One, blessed be He, places the Presence of His throne of glory between the dark waters, and the Presence is in the clouds.[232]

According to this passage, the fiery word of God, enveloped by the cloud and darkness, was apprehended by the (male) Israelites who at that time were in a state of holiness characteristic of angelic beings. The ritualistic necessity of wearing appropriate clothes when one mentions the name reflects the ontic reality that the word or glory appears within the envelopment of the cloud or darkness. The donning of white clothes by humans who mention the name is paralleled by a description of the four camps of angels who surround the throne of glory and who sanctify the name of God: "They immersed themselves three times in pure fire and dressed themselves in pure white fire in order to mention the unique and glorious name."[233] It is of interest to bear in mind a tradition reported by Eleazar: "When the priests mentioned the name in the Temple,

[229] Quoted in Scholem, *On the Kabbalah,* p. 137.

[230] Cf. Deut 4:11–12. This image is also reminiscent of the aggadic motif concerning the primordial Torah being written in white fire upon black fire. See Scholem, *On the Kabbalah,* p. 38 n. 2.

[231] Cf. Exod. 19:15.

[232] MS Paris–BN 772, fols. 157b–158a.

[233] Ibid., fol. 133a.

518,400 angels descended, filling the entire world."[234] In this case the mentioning of the name does not draw down the glory itself but summons a host of angels, which are, much as the glory itself, luminous bodies. Hence, one sees again the connection that is made in the Pietistic view between the act of uttering the divine name and causing the light to descend from above. In a fundamental sense, for Eleazar the angels are identical with the letters of the names.[235] By uttering the name, then, one not only causes the light of the glory to be illuminated but is in the process mimetically transformed into an angelic being. The magical and mystical aspects of the praxis of mentioning the name are inseparable.

In his expansive commentary on the liturgy Eleazar points out, in language almost identical to the passage from *Sefer ha-Shem* cited above, that the mentioning of the name has the theurgical impact of creating a luminous garment for the glory, which is itself nothing but the letters of the divine name:

> When Israel bless the name of His glory, the glory is increased, as it is written, "Your faithful ones shall bless you, they shall talk of the majesty of Your kingship, and speak of Your might" (Ps. 145:10–11). "The glorious majesty [of Your splendor]" (ibid., 5). And this is [the meaning of] "Blessed is His glorious name" (Ps. 72:19), for the name is glorified in a bright cloud. Know that [the expression] "to place His name there" is written in the Torah fifty-two times and there are fifty-two times in the Torah that the [word] cloud is mentioned. That is to say, there is a cloud for each name.[236] . . . It is written, "Your glorious name" (1 Chron. 29:13), for [the name] is clothed and glorified in splendor. [The expression] "Your glorious name" [*le-shem tif'artekha*] is numerically equivalent to "the four letters" [*'arba'ah 'otiyyot*][237] which is the Tetragrammaton [YHWH]. When Israel mentioned the name in the Temple, then "His glory filled the whole world, amen and amen" (Ps. 72:19).[238]

[234] *Sode Razayya,* p. 8. On the theurgical power of the priestly blessing, see Targum to Cant. 3:7.

[235] On the connection between angels and letters, see the tradition of Eleazar of Worms in *'Arugat ha-Bosem* 1:131: "All the angels were created in the image of the letters and they stand before the throne of glory." Cf. Abulafia, *Ḥayye ha-'Olam ha-Ba'*, MS Oxford-Bodleian 1582, fols. 45a, 52a (translated in Idel, *Mystical Experience,* p. 31); and the passage published by A. Jellinek in "*Sefer ha-Ôt,* Apokalypse des Pseudo-Propheten und Pseudo-Messias Abraham Abulafia," in *Jubelschrift zum siebzigsten Geburtstage des Prof. Dr. H. Graetz* (Breslau, 1887), p. 86 (translated into English in L. Jacobs, *The Jewish Mystics* [London, 1990], p. 60). See also the Ashkenazi tradition reflected in *Synopse,* § 393, which is a prayer to the effect that when one mentions the name one should not be destroyed by fire. The implication here seems to be that mentioning the name results in some sort of conflagration, a point underscored in the continuation of the passage, which emphasizes that the angels are made of fire.

[236] On the correlation of the seventy-two names of God and the word "cloud" (*'av,* whose consonants *'ayin* and *bet* equal 72), see MS New York–JTSA Mic. 1878, fol. 87a.

[237] The numerology here is perplexing, as the first expression, *le-shem tif'artekha,* equals 1471 and the second, *'arba'ah 'otiyyot,* equals 1101. See, however, *'Arugat ha-Bosem* 2:154, where it is stated that the word *tif'artekha* is numerically equal to the expression *'arba'ah 'otiyyot,* i.e., both equal 1101. It may be assumed that Eleazar had such a numerical equivalence in mind in this context as well.

[238] MS Paris–BN 772, fol. 110a.

In a second passage from *Sefer ha-Shem* Eleazar elaborates on this theme, adding several images, including, most significantly, the motif of the completion of the throne:

> When Israel mentioned the name as it is written [i.e., the Tetragrammaton] in the Temple, then glory and majesty were before Him, and this is [the meaning of the verse] "Glory and majesty are before Him; strength and splendor are in His temple" (Ps. 96:6). This is "the glory of His name" (ibid., 8), and this is "a glorious name" (Isa. 63:14). Then the glory is clothed in beauty, splendor, and majesty, and the throne is complete, and "joy is in His place" (1 Chron. 16:27). This is "for Your name is called upon Your city" (Dan. 9:19), "they rejoice in Your name all day long" (Ps. 89:17). The numerical value of "Your name is like finest oil" (*shemen turaq shemekha*) [= 1456] (Cant. 1:3) equals that of [the expression] "the four letters of Your name" (*'arba'ah 'otiyyot shemekha*) [= 1456].[239]

The proper utterance of the divine name results in the investiture of the divine glory in a garment of splendor and majesty. The girding of the glory is connected more specifically with the completion of the throne. I surmise that in the Pietistic setting the latter expression signifies the enthronement of the glory. For the Pietists, following the relevant Hekhalot passages, the moment of enthronement is a *hieros gamos* in which both the (male) glory and the (female) throne are aggrandized. Significantly, the glory can occupy the throne only after it has been attired by means of the mentioning of the name. Indeed, the purpose of the garment is to prepare the glory for its sitting upon the throne,[240] a moment whose erotic element is alluded to in the above text in the citations of 1 Chron. 16:27 and Dan. 9:19. Moreover, the linkage of the image of the fine oil to the divine name in Cant. 1:3 in this context suggests that the utterance of the name results in the overflow of the divine efflux from the glory to the throne, an alternative way of signifying the sacred union.

From still other texts it is certain that the main circle of Pietists, influenced in part by Abraham ibn Ezra, identified the Tetragrammaton in one of its aspects with the glory: knowledge of the name amounts to some vision of the light of the glory. Thus, in one of the texts attributed by Dan to Judah the Pious, we read:

> Moses alone saw the great glory. Thus [it says in Scripture] "And the Lord [YHWH] spoke to Moses," "And the Lord [YHWH] said," using this name [YHWH]. Therefore Jethro said: "Now I know that the Lord [YHWH] is greater than all gods" (Exod. 18:11). The Lord is unique, He is God of gods, He and not an angel. At times [YHWH] is used as the name of His essence (*shem 'aṣmo*), referring to the Creator, and at times it refers to the form (*ha-to'ar*) that appears to

[239] MS British Museum 737, fol. 169a. Cf. MSS Oxford-Bodleian 1638, fol. 51b; Oxford-Bodleian 1953, fol. 43a; and New York–JTSA Mic. 2430, fol. 67a, where the enclothing of the glory by means of the utterance of the name is linked specifically to Yom Kippur.

[240] This symbolic use of the image of the garment in Pietistic sources is an elaboration of earlier literature; see chapter 3, n. 84.

> the prophet. It has already been written in *Sefer ha-Kavod* [the "Book of the Glory"] that the form is according to the decrees [of God's will]. It says [in Scripture], "I am the Lord." Does He appear to the prophet in such a way? The testimony and proof is in the expression "the Lord of hosts," that is, He appears as a form within the [celestial] hosts, as in the case of Micaiah, Isaiah, and Daniel.[241]

In this passage there is an innovative use of Abraham ibn Ezra's notion, expressed on several occasions in his writings, that the Tetragrammaton can function either as a proper noun (*shem ha-ʿeṣem*) or as an adjective (*shem ha-toʾar*). In the former instance the name appears by itself, whereas in the latter it is joined to another term such as the expression "Lord of Hosts" (*YHWH Ṣevaʾot*). The Pietistic author has utilized ibn Ezra but radically altered his intent especially with respect to the second usage. In the first instance the Pietist has preserved ibn Ezra's meaning intact, though he has slightly altered the technical language, for he refers to the Tetragrammaton as *shem ʿaṣmo,* "the name of His essence," rather than *shem ha-ʿeṣem,* "the essential name." This is a very slight deviation that does not affect the meaning. By contrast, with respect to the second usage there is a major shift. The Pietistic author employs ibn Ezra's locution *shem ha-toʾar,* but for him it is no longer an adjective in a strict grammatical sense. That is, he employs the term *toʾar* to denote the form that the Tetragrammaton assumes as it appears to the prophets. Moses alone saw the great glory that is depicted in Scripture in terms of knowing the Tetragrammaton in its essential aspect. Other prophets had a knowledge of that name, but only as it assumed a particular form (*toʾar*) within the angelic hosts. In both cases, however, there is a correlation between the name and the revealed glory. This tradition seems to have influenced the anonymous *Shir ha-Yiḥud* that Habermann attributed to a French *payyeṭan* living in the thirteenth or fourteenth century: "Blessed be the name of His glory from His place, and exalted in the majesty of His throne of glory; how pleasant it is when His glory is revealed in the name *Yod-He* [i.e., the Tetragrammaton] that is the seal of His splendor."[242]

Ontic Identification of Torah, Name, and Glory

In addition to the identification of the name and the glory, in Pietistic literature one finds the further identification of the name and the glory with the Torah. This identification is predicated on the fact that the Torah is equated with the name of God, which in turn is equated with the glory. The correlation of the divine name and the glory or Presence, on the one hand, and the Torah, on the other, is implicit in the following passage in *Sefer Ḥasidim:*

> When a person prays the *Shekhinah* is facing him, as it says, "I constantly place the Lord before me" (Ps. 16:8). Even though it says "the Lord before me," he should

[241] Quoted in Dan, *Studies,* p. 153; see also *Esoteric Theology,* p. 135.
[242] *Shire ha-Yiḥud we-ha-Kavod,* p. 64.

only cast his intention above to the heavens. Since he does not know where the Temple is he should think in his heart during his prayer as if the glory were facing him within four cubits, and its height is above heavenward. . . . Similarly, the one who reads the Torah on the seventh, second, or fifth day, when he reaches a name [of God], if he can have the intention he should [cast his] intention toward Him. The one who sits in the east should consider in his heart as if the *Shekhinah* were facing west and his face is opposite him. . . . The one who passes before the Ark (*ha-ʿover lifne ha-teivah,* i.e., the one who leads the public prayers) . . . should intend in his heart as if the *Shekhinah* in heaven corresponds to the Ark. . . . When [the cantor] says [the *qaddish*] *yitgaddal* [*we-yitqaddash shemeih rabba*', "magnified and sanctified be His great name"], they should turn toward the Torah scroll, and if he is worthy, he should take hold of the Torah, and the people should intend their heart toward the Torah. Therefore, [the congregation should] say, "Exalt [the Lord our God] and bow down to His footstool" (Ps. 99:5), for the Torah is His footstool. [The expression] *hadom raglav* [His footstool] is written five times in Scripture, corresponding to the Torah scroll, which comprises the Pentateuch, and the two staves in the Torah scroll correspond to "His legs are like marble pillars" (Cant. 5:15).[243]

For the Pietist, the divine Presence is thought to be present in the place of worship, especially in the holy Ark that contains the Torah scroll. This is to be understood in a rather technical sense, for the Torah represents the embodiment of the divine glory. For example, in an anonymous commentary on the seventy names of God, deriving from the Pietists, the identification of Torah and the glory is made explicitly: *ha-torah—kevodo shel ha-qadosh barukh hu*', "the Torah [is] the glory of the Holy One, blessed be He."[244] This identification underlies the remark cited above from *Sefer Ḥasidim* that when the cantor says the *qaddish,* in which the name of God is sanctified, the congregation should turn to the Torah scroll.[245] Moreover, the Torah is identified as the footstool of God, which provides the ideational basis for the ritual of bowing down to the Torah. One can find further evidence for these ideas in Eleazar's commentary on the liturgy. Thus, in the context of discussing the prayer uttered when the Torah is taken from the Ark, which includes the recitation of Ps. 99:5, he notes,

"His footstool" (*hadom raglav*) refers to the Torah, and this is [the import] of what R. Simeon [bar Isaac] wrote in the *yoṣer* for *Shavuʿot* [describing the primordial Torah]: "I approached His feet, I dwelt in His shadow." Thus [the expression]

[243] *Sefer Ḥasidim,* § 1585, p. 387.

[244] MS Jerusalem-Sassoon 290, p. 585, cited by Idel in "Concept of Torah," p. 42 n. 53.

[245] In a passage from *ʿArugat ha-Bosem* 3:204, it is made clear that the sentence in the *qaddish,* "may His name be blessed, etc.," corresponds to the Torah, inasmuch as the name is equated with the Torah: "In the verse 'in the beginning' (Gen. 1:1) there are seven words and twenty-eight letters, and similarly in the verse 'And God spoke' (Exod. 20:1). This indicates that for the sake of the Torah He created the world, the seven words corresponding to the seven days of the week. . . . Thus they instituted [the saying of *qaddish,* which includes the passage] 'may His great name [be blessed]' seven times a day, and it has seven words and twenty-eight letters."

hadom raglav occurs five times in Scripture,[246] corresponding to the five [occurrences of] *melekh ha-kavod*[247] [the glorious king].[248]

In a second passage from the same work Eleazar offers a similar mystical explanation for the *qaddish,* but in this case the principal focus is on the visualization of the *Shekhinah* in the Ark, the place in which the Torah scroll is enshrined: "*Yitgaddal,* the cantor who goes before the Ark (*ha-yored lifne ha-teivah*), should place his life in his hand, and pray with all the intention of his heart, and when he says *yitgaddal* he should cast his eyes to the holy Ark, for the *Shekhinah* rests in it, as it says, 'I constantly place the Lord before me' (Ps. 16:8)."[249]

In this connection it is of interest to consider the tradition reported by Eleazar in *Sefer ha-Roqeaḥ* in the name of Ḥizqiyyah, the brother of the RaBaN, R. Eliezer ben Nathan of Mainz (ca. 1090–ca. 1170):[250]

> When the Torah scroll is returned to its place [in the Ark], and when one bows down to it, the verse "Exalt the Lord our God [and bow down to His footstool]" (Ps. 99:5) is said. In the blessings of the Torah, too, we bow down to the glory of the Torah. When we return [the Torah], "Let them praise [the name of the Lord, for His name alone is sublime; His splendor covers heaven and earth]" (Ps. 148:13) is said, to indicate that one does not bow down because of the divinity that is in the Torah (*'elohut she-ba-torah*), but rather he bows down to the Holy One, blessed be He, for His Presence rests upon it [the Torah], and not because it, too, is a god, for "His name alone is sublime" (ibid.).[251]

This tradition rejects the explanation that one bows down to the Torah because it is divine in the normative sense of comprising the words of God or in the mystical sense of being identical with the glory. Rather, the reason for bowing down is that the *Shekhinah* itself dwells upon the Torah and is thus located in the Ark that contains the scrolls. We may detect in this explanation a polemical statement against the full identification of Torah and the divine glory, a position articulated on occasion in Pietistic sources, including Eleazar himself. Indeed, the Torah shrine in the thought of the Ḥaside Ashkenaz is comparable to either

[246] Isa. 66:1; Ps. 99:5, 132:7; Lam. 2:1; 1 Chron. 28:2. In a sixth occurrence, Ps. 110:1, the reference is not to the Temple or the earth as the locus of the divine presence.

[247] Ps. 24:7, 8, 9, 10 (twice).

[248] MS Paris–BN 772, fol. 135a; see also *Siddur Mal'ah ha-'Areṣ De'ah* of R. Naftali Herz Treves, section on the *yoṣer* of Sabbath, s.v. *gaddelu la-YHWH 'itti u-neromemah shemo yaḥddav* (Ps. 34:4).

[249] MS Paris–BN 772, fol. 62a; cf. MS Oxford-Bodleian 1097, fol. 17a. Cf. also MS Oxford-Bodleian 1102, fol. 14b; *Siddur of R. Solomon ben Samson of Garmaise,* p. 76.

[250] See *Sefer ha-RaBaN,* § 73, cited by Urbach in *'Arugat ha-Bosem* 4:52 n. 76.

[251] *Sefer ha-Roqeaḥ,* p. 208; cf. the formulation on p. 109, where Eleazar notes that on Rosh ha-Shanah and Yom Kippur an infant is circumcised after the reading of the Torah "because the Presence is near the Torah." This passage also seems to reflect the idea that the ritual of circumcision is connected with the visible manifestation of the divine Presence. For a discussion of this motif in midrashic and kabbalistic sources (principally the *Zohar*), see Wolfson, "Circumcision, Vision of God, and Textual Interpretation."

the Ark in the Temple or the throne of glory.[252] This nexus of symbols is evident in one passage in *Sefer Ḥasidim,* wherein we find the following sequence of ideas: The Sabbath corresponds to the seven heavens or, alternatively, the seven thrones.[253] Thus, the throne is mentioned seven times in the Sabbath liturgy, "for in each of the heavens there is a throne, one corresponding to the other." By tallying the numerological equivalence of the seven references to the throne (*kisse'* = 81, *kiss'o* = 87, *kisse'* = 81, *kiss'akha* = 101, *we-khiss'o* = 93, *kiss'o* = 87, *kisse'* = 81) one comes up with the sum of 611, which is the numerical value of the word Torah. Having established these correspondences, Judah concludes, "There is no throne without the Torah, and this is [the import of the poem] 'At the time before creation He established the Torah and the throne.'[254] Therefore the Torah is read on the Sabbath. And there occurs seven times in Scripture [the expression] 'enthroned on the cherubim' (*yoshev ha-keruvim*).[255] Therefore, [on the Sabbath] seven [sections in the Torah] are read, and it is as if the *Shekhinah* were placed on the throne of the cherubim."[256]

The correlation of the Torah and the throne is not to be taken in a merely figurative or rhetorical way. On the contrary, the force of these images is that they function as religious symbols, activating specific modes of pietistic behavior: just as the Presence dwells (ontically and not metaphorically) upon the throne, so it rests upon the Torah scroll encased in the holy Ark. The full significance of the symbolic understanding of Torah, and its implicit function as a talisman, is made evident in the concluding statement that reading the seven sections of Torah on the Sabbath is equivalent to placing the *Shekhinah* upon the throne of cherubim: the reading of Torah has the (theurgical) effect of enthroning the *Shekhinah*. That this is so is based on the fact that the ontic status of the Torah is that of the throne. I noted above that in both *Sefer Ḥasidim* and Eleazar's commentary on the liturgy one finds the explicit identification of the Torah as the divine footstool.

The more specific correlation of the Torah and the throne appears in *Sefer Tagi:* "The Torah and the throne of glory are one pair (*zug 'eḥad*), for the

[252] The correlation of the two is biblical in origin; see Jer. 17:12.

[253] The correlation of heaven and throne is linked exegetically to Isa. 66:1. On the tradition of the seven thrones corresponding to the seven heavens, see *Sode Razayya,* p. 16; *Perush ha-Tefillot,* MS Paris–BN 772, fol. 123a, where this tradition is cited in the name of a midrash. See text cited below, n. 259. See also Meir ibn Gabbai, *'Avodat ha-Qodesh,* pt. 3, chap. 41, p. 359, where the seven thrones in the seven heavens are referred to as seven images (*dimyonot*), which in turn correspond to the divine emanations. The idea of a throne located in each of the seven heavens is already found in the apocalyptic text *Ascension of Isaiah* and has a reflex in the Jewish mystical tract *Re'uyot Yeḥezqel;* see Gruenwald, *Apocalyptic,* pp. 59, 137. See also Jacob ben Jacob ha-Kohen, "Commentary on Ezekiel's Chariot," ed. Farber, pp. 92–93 n. 25, 156–157 n. 19.

[254] See Goldschmidt, *Maḥzor la-Yamim ha-Nora'im,* vol. 2, *Yom Kippur,* p. 408. As Goldschmidt notes, this poetic image is based on earlier aggadic sources wherein the Torah and throne are listed among the various things created before the world.

[255] 1 Sam. 4:4; 2 Sam. 6:2; 2 Kings 19:15; Isa. 37:16; Ps. 80:2, 99:1; 1 Chron. 13:6.

[256] *Sefer Ḥasidim,* § 637.

tablets were taken from the throne of glory.[257] . . . Just as the *Shekhinah* is upon the throne, so it is upon the Torah and upon the Ark in which there is the Torah and the tablets. Thus the Torah is His throne."[258] Eleazar likewise alludes to such a notion when he writes that "the Torah is in His throne as it is in the Ark."[259] The consubstantiality of the Torah and the throne also assumes eschatological significance:

> The fire of the throne serves the supernal ones and the fire before the throne of glory serves the lower ones, for just as the Torah was given in fire, so the sacrifice is burnt in fire, and before the soul that ascends enters beneath the throne the angel purifies it by the fire that is before the throne . . . and they place it under the throne and there one sees the secrets and mysteries of Torah. . . . The tablets are from the throne; [the word] *luḥot* [tablets, written in a defective form without a *waw*] through *a''t ba''sh* is *kisse'* [throne], for the tablets and the Torah were in the throne.[260]

The point is reiterated in another passage: "The word *luḥot* is written without a *waw*, for through *a''t ba''sh* this numerically equals the word *kisse'*, to indicate that they were given from underneath the throne, and the one who fulfills the Torah is placed under the throne, as it says, 'The teaching of the Lord (*torat YHWH*) is perfect, restoring life' (Ps. 19:8) [of the soul] to under the throne of glory, and this is [the meaning of] 'the life of my lord will be bound up in the bundle of life' (1 Sam. 25:29)."[261]

From these texts we may postulate that the mystical import of the verses from Psalms uttered by the congregants when the Torah is removed from and returned to the Ark is that the Torah is identical with the name or the glory that is upon the throne. The issue is far from being merely theoretical or theological in some abstract sense. On the contrary, the theosophic ideas occasion a mystical experience for the pious individual realized within the framework of the traditional synagogue practice, and that experience is of a decidedly visual character. An allusion to this is found in the following exegetical comment of Isaac ben Judah ha-Levi: "'He put a veil over his face' (Exod. 34:33): from here [it is

257 For other references to the aggadic motif of the tablets being hewn from the sapphire stone of the throne of glory, see Ginzberg, *Legends* 6:49–50 n. 258, 59 nn. 305–306.

258 MS Oxford-Bodleian 1566, fol. 224b. Cf. Eleazar's *Perush ha-Tefillot,* MS Paris–BN 772, fol. 90b; *'Arugat ha-Bosem* 1:161. Eleazar's influence may be detected in Baḥya ben Asher's commentary on Exod. 31:8 (ed. Chavel, p. 327). See Idel, *Language, Torah, and Hermeneutics,* pp. 168–169 n. 77.

259 *Sode Razayya,* p. 38. See also the passing reference to this motif in Eleazar's *Sod Ma'aseh Bereshit,* printed in *Sefer Razi'el,* 17b (cf. *Sode Razayya,* ed. Weiss, p. 51): "Therefore one bows down to the Torah, which is His footstool in the Ark. Similarly, He made seven thrones in the heavens."

260 *Sode Razayya,* p. 19. And cf. the text from *Sefer ha-Kavod* cited in Abraham bar Azriel, *'Arugat ha-Bosem* 1:161.

261 MS Vatican 460, fol. 18a. The correlation of the soul and the throne is drawn explicitly in *Ḥokhmat ha-Nefesh,* chap. 54. One of the points Eleazar makes is that, inasmuch as the Torah and the soul share one ontic source in the throne, the soul can be compared to the Torah.

derived] that when [worshipers] come from the Ark and the reading of the Torah they cover their faces."[262] That is, just as Moses had to cover his face because it was illuminated with the radiance of the divine Splendor, so one who returns from the Ark and the reading of the Torah has to cover his face because it is illuminated with the radiance of the Presence that dwells upon the Torah scroll.

The tradition referred to above concerning the identification of the Torah and the name is found in other texts in the Pietistic corpus. In *Sefer ha-Shem* Eleazar affirms the identification of the name and the Torah: "YWHW is numerically equal to twenty-six, and since the Torah was given after twenty-six generations [from Adam] it is dependent on His great name."[263] The point is made elsewhere in the same work, but in that context the theosophical notion serves as the basis for a mystical understanding of the religious obligation to study Torah: "The four letters YHWA:[264] [the letters YHW] numerically equal twenty-one, and when one considers the pronunciation with an A the sum is twenty-two, corresponding to the twenty-two letters of Torah. This indicates that [with respect to] the one who studies Torah it is as if he mentioned the name (*ha-lomed torah ke-ʾillu mazkir ha-shem*)."[265] To study Torah has the effect of mentioning the name, which, as we have seen from other passages in the Pietistic corpus, involves the vision of the luminous form of the glory. The point is also made in another passage in *Sefer ha-Shem:* "The glorious name (*ha-shem ha-nikhbad*) is with those occupied in Torah, and it illuminates their eyes."[266] In this case as well, the text is rendered comprehensible only in light of the tacit identification of the Torah, the name, and the luminous glory.

The identification of these three things is implicit in a tradition recorded on a number of occasions by Eleazar, commenting on the scribal practice of marking the Tetragrammaton by writing three *yods,* with a line extending from the last *yod* over all three, thus forming the letter *bet,* which is characterized as a

[262] *Paʿaneaḥ Razaʾ,* 63b.

[263] MS British Museum 737, fol. 173a.

[264] This form may have been suggested by Eccles. 11:3; see Reisel, *The Mysterious Name of Y.H.W.H.,* pp. 39–41, 60–61, and other references given on p. 104 n. 206. It should be noted that these four letters were considered by various medieval writers to constitute one of the forms of the Tetragrammaton, indeed the hidden name of God. In thirteenth-century mystical literature this tradition was prominent, especially in the writings of the Iyyun circle and Abraham Abulafia. See Scholem, "Seridim ḥadashim mi-kitve R. ʿAzriʾel mi-Gerona," p. 219 n. 2; idem, *Origins,* p. 315 nn. 238–239, p. 337; Idel, *Mystical Experience,* pp. 18, 22, 31 (see esp. Abulafia's *Ḥayye ha-ʿOlam ha-Baʾ*, MS Oxford-Bodleian 1582, fol. 47a). Cf. MS Oxford-Bodleian 1610, fol. 72b. A possible polemic against this view in the writings of the Provençal kabbalist Isaac the Blind has been noted by Pedaya in "'Flaw' and 'Correction' in the Concept of the Godhead in the Teachings of Rabbi Isaac the Blind," p. 182. On the tradition regarding the four vowel letters AHWY, functioning as a divine name, cf. Abraham ibn Ezra, *Sefer Ṣaḥot,* 4b, 47b; *Sefer ha-Shem,* 6b–7a; *Perushe ha-Torah,* ad Exod. 3:15, ed. A. Weiser, 2:27; Judah Halevi, *Sefer ha-Kuzari* IV: 3. For a mystical treatment of this tradition, which may reflect some Ashkenazi influence as well, see Asher ben David, *Perush Shem ha-Meforash,* p. 3.

[265] MS British Museum 737, fol. 190b.

[266] Ibid., fol. 178a.

crown.[267] In his explanation of the prayer uttered on Rosh ha-Shanah after each blowing of the shofar, *Ha-yom harat ʿolam ha-yom yaʿamid mishpaṭ,* Eleazar refers to this iconic tradition:

> [This prayer] has thirty-two words, corresponding to the thirty-two paths [of wisdom] by means of which the world was created. . . . Therefore the name [YHWH] is written with three *yods,* which equal thirty, and the crown is like a *bet* [which equals two]; thus there are thirty-two, corresponding to the numerical value of *kavod.* . . . May God have mercy on us through the merit of Torah, which begins with the *bet* of *bereshit* (Gen. 1:1) and ends with the *lamed* of *le-ʿeine kol yisraʾel* (Deut. 34:12).[268]

The chain of images is reiterated by Eleazar in a second passage, related to the opening words of the three verses of the Priestly blessing in Num. 6:24–26:[269]

> *Yevarekhekha, yaʾer, yissaʾ* [comprise] three *yods* that correspond to the ten *sefirot,* the ten *maʾamarot,*[270] and the ten *dibberot* [commandments]. Therefore there are three *yods* in the name YYY and the *bet* surrounding [them]. Thus there is [a sum of] thirty-two [*lamed-bet*], which corresponds to the thirty-two paths by which the world was created.[271] Thus [the Torah] begins with the bet of *bereshit* (Gen. 1:1) and ends with the *lamed* of *le-ʿeine kol yisraʾel* (Deut. 34:12).[272]

[267] Concerning this scribal tradition and discussion of some of the sources that may have influenced Eleazar's formulation, see the note of M. Steinschneider, *Monatsschrift für Geschichte und Wissenschaft des Judentums* 40 (1896): 130–132; Lauterbach, "Substitutes for the Tetragrammaton," pp. 46 n. 22, 54 no. 50, 59–61. For additional sources, see B. Lewin's introduction to his edition of the *'Iggeret R. Sherira Ga'on* (Haifa, 1929), pp. xxxi–xxxii. See also M. Beit-Arié, "Stéréotypies et individualités dan les écritures des copistes hébraïques du moyen âge," in *L'écriture: Le cerveau, l'œil et la main,* ed. C. Sirat, J. Irigoin, E. Poulle (Brepols, Turnhout, 1990), p. 213. The scribal tradition of writing the Tetragrammaton with three *yods* was appropriated and reinterpreted by Provençal and Spanish kabbalists as well. See, e.g., Isaac ben Jacob ha-Kohen, *Perush Mirkevet Yeḥezqel,* published by G. Scholem in *Tarbiz* 2 (1931), p. 194, and further references provided on p. 204 n. 8. See also evidence adduced by Idel in "Sefirot above the Sefirot," pp. 245–246, and idem, "Kabbalistic Material from the School of R. David ben Judah he-Ḥasid," p. 176.

[268] MS Paris–BN 772, fol. 163b. See the Ashkenazi commentary on Psalms in MS Oxford-Bodleian 1551, fols. 215a, 222a.

[269] Cf. Ṭobiah bar Eliezer, *Midrash Leqaḥ Ṭov,* p. 185. See the tradition of Eleazar in the name of Judah the Pious in MS New York–JTSA Mic. 8122, fol. 89a. A similar linkage of the three *yods* of the name and Num. 6:24–26 is found in a passage of Menaḥem ben Solomon's *Midrash Sekhel Ṭov* found in *Sefer Assufot* of R. Eliezer ben Joel Halevi (the Rabiah); see *Midrash Sekhel Ṭov,* ed. Buber, introduction, p. xxxix; Lauterbach, "Substitutes for the Tetragrammaton," pp. 60–61. See also Ephraim ben Shimson, *Perush Rabbenu 'Efrayim ʿal ha-Torah,* 2:66, ad Num. 4:26.

[270] That is, the ten sayings through which the world was created; cf. M. Avot 5:1.

[271] Eleazar briefly alludes to this tradition in *Sefer ha-Roqeaḥ,* p. 207. Cf. the passage in *Sefer Assufot* of the Rabiah, published by M. Gaster in the *Report of the Judith Montefiore College* (London, 1893), pp. 61–62, cited by Steinschneider, *Monatsschrift für Geschichte und Wissenschaft des Judentums* 40 (1896): 131, and Lauterbach, "Substitutes for the Tetragrammaton," p. 60.

[272] MS Paris–BN 772, fol. 84b. Cf. *Sefer ha-Shem,* MS British Museum 737, fol. 203b. Cf. Simeon bar Samuel, *'Adam Sikhli,* 1b: "The Holy One, blessed be He, transmitted this name of the

Eleazar thus draws on the correspondence between the thirty-two paths of wisdom through which the world was created—an idea first articulated in *Sefer Yeṣirah*—the glory (*kavod,* whose numerical value is thirty-two), and the Torah (which begins with the letter *bet* and ends with *lamed,* whose sum is thirty-two).[273] This is represented orthographically as well, through the scribal tradition of marking the Tetragrammaton by three *yods,* which equal thirty, and a half-circle extending from the last *yod* over all three, which is designated as the crown and is compared to a *bet,* whose numerical value is two.[274]

In a parallel to this text in *Sefer ha-Shem,* the ontic identification of the Torah and the glory is rendered even more explicitly:

> In [the first words of the verses Exod. 14:19–21] *wa-yissa'*, *wa-yavo'*, and *wa-yeṭ,* there are three *yods* in one name [i.e., the seventy-two-letter name]. Therefore the name [YHWH] must be written with three *yods,* YYY, and the crown is like a *bet.* Thus there are thirty-two [three *yods* = 30 + *bet* = 2] to inform us that [God] created the world by means of thirty-two paths. Thus the Torah begins with the *bet* of *bereshit* and ends with [the *lamed* of] *yisra'el.* Thus there is thirty-two (*lamed-bet*), which is the numerical value of [the word] *kavod* (glory). There is no glory but the Torah (*'ein kavod 'ela' torah*).[275]

The final statement is derived from earlier sources, such as, the comment in Avot 6:3, where it signifies that honor must be paid to the scholar. It is evident that Eleazar has theosophically recast the rabbinic saying to identify the Torah itself as the glory of God. The homology of the Torah, the glory, and the name is symbolized by the fact that the first and last letters of the Pentateuch are *bet* and *lamed,* which equal thirty-two, the numerical value of the word *kavod,* "glory," and the orthographic representation of the name as three *yods* plus a *bet.*

---

three *yods* to Moses our master, peace be upon him, in Egypt when He told him to place a drop of blood on the two doorposts and the lintel [cf. Exod. 12:7; see following note]. The pious one, may the memory of the righteous be for a blessing, said that the three *yods* should be written one next to the other [in a straight line]. There are those who say that the three *yods* allude to the ten emanations (*sefirot*), the ten utterances (*ma'amarot*), and the Ten Commandments (*dibberot*). Perhaps they also allude to the three *yods* of [the words of the priestly blessing] *yevarekhekha, ya'er, yissa'*."

[273] Cf. the commentary on Psalms influenced by Ashkenazi traditions extant in MS Oxford-Bodleian 1551, fol. 215a: "'Glorious king' (*melekh ha-kavod*) (Ps. 24:10)—[the word *kavod,* "glory"] has the numerical value of thirty-two [*lamed-bet*]. The Torah begins with a *bet* and ends with a *lamed.* The name of redemption is that of thirty-two, the three *yods,* [corresponding to three drops of] blood on the two doorposts and the lintel (cf. Exod. 12:7) [together with a *bet*]. Five times [in Psalm 24] the word *kavod* is written, corresponding to the five books of the Pentateuch."

[274] Concerning the tradition of writing the divine name with three *yods* together with a *bet,* thereby attaining the sum of thirty-two, see the commentary on *qaddish* extant in MS Paris–BN 850, fols. 14b–15a.

[275] MS British Museum 737, fol. 203a. Cf. fols. 205b–206a: "YYY, three *yods* and a *bet* on their back, that is its crown. Thus there are thirty-two. Therefore *Sefer Yeṣirah* begins [by referring to] thirty-two paths [of wisdom]. . . . Why thirty-two? For the Torah begins with *bet* and ends with *lamed.* To teach you that everything is alluded to in the Torah, but it is hidden from people, and the secrets of Torah were not transmitted except to those who fear him [see above, n. 203]." See also Isaac ha-Levi, *Pa'aneaḥ Raza'*, 4b; and cf. Abulafia, *Ḥayye ha-'Olam ha-Ba'*, MS Oxford-Bodleian 1582, fol. 50b.

The Glorious Angel and the Vision of the Name as Anthropos

In the final analysis, the ontic identification of the Torah, the name, and the glory is predicated on the phenomenological convergence of light and name symbolism experienced in the mystical vision. This convergence is also expressed in another way in the Pietistic writings, when it is posited that the letters of the divine name may assume tangible or concrete shape as an anthropomorphic form. This possibility is explicitly affirmed in the anonymous text *Sefer ha-Navon,* written by someone who apparently had knowledge of the main circle of the German Pietists:[276]

> The name [YHWH] appears in its letters to the angels and prophets in several forms and radiance and it appears in the image of the appearance of an anthropos, as it says, "Above the expanse over their heads was the semblance of a throne, in appearance like sapphire, and on top, upon this semblance of a throne, there was the semblance of a human form" (Ezek. 1:26) . . . it appears in "the semblance of a human form," this refers to the *Shekhinah* and the angel of the glory (*mal'akh ha-kavod*) which is the Tetragrammaton.[277]

According to this text, then, the four-letter name of God assumes the anthropomorphic form of the *Shekhinah,* which is the angel of the glory (*mal'akh ha-kavod*) that appears in the prophetic vision. Here we have come upon one of the key elements in the esoteric doctrine of the German Pietists, one that reflects a much older idea in Jewish esotericism and that finds expression in the kabbalistic literature as well. Indeed, it may be said that the medieval Jewish mystics recovered the mythic dimension of a biblical motif regarding the appearance of God in the guise of the highest of angels, called "angel of the Lord" (*mal'akh YHWH*), "angel of God" (*mal'akh ha-'elohim*), or "angel of the Presence" (*mal'akh ha-panim*), which sometimes appears in the form of a man.[278] Evidence for the continuity of the exegetical tradition of an exalted angel that is in effect the manifestation of God is to be found in a wide variety of later sources, including Jewish apocalyptic,[279] Samaritan,[280] Jewish-Christian,[281]

[276] See Dan, *Esoteric Theology,* pp. 60–61.

[277] Quoted in Dan, *Studies,* pp. 119–120. On the parallels to this motif in the writings of Abulafia, see Idel, *Mystical Experience,* pp. 100–105.

[278] See Gen. 16:9–13, 18:2, 21:7, 22:11, 31:11, 33:11–13; Exod. 3:2ff., 14:19, 23:21, 32:34; Josh. 5:13–15; Judg. 2:1, 4, 5:23, 6:11ff., 13:3ff.; Isa. 63:9; Ps. 34:8. Cf. Eichrodt, *Theology of the Old Testament,* 2:24; Stier, *Gott und sein Engel im Alten Testament;* Hirth, *Gottes Boten im Alten Testament;* H. Röttger, *Mal'ak Jahwe—Bote von Gott* (Frankfurt, 1978).

[279] See Rowland, *Open Heaven,* pp. 94–113. It is also of interest to note that in the Qumran literature one finds the notion that the divine Presence is represented by the angels that dwell among the sect. See Bokser, "Approaching Sacred Space," p. 283; Schiffman, *The Eschatological Community of the Dead Sea Scrolls,* p. 50.

[280] See Fossum, *Name of God,* pp. 177ff., 319ff.

[281] See J. Daniélou, "Trinité et angélologie dans la théologue judéo-chrétienne"; idem, *The Origins of Latin Christianity* (London, 1977), pp. 149–152; Rowland, "The Vision of the Risen Christ in Rev. 1:13ff."; Carr, *Angels and Principalities,* pp. 143–147; Fossum, "Jewish Christian Christology and Jewish Mysticism."

Patristic (polemical writings presumably reflecting the belief of certain Jewish thinkers),[282] Gnostic,[283] early Jewish mystical,[284] and sectarian.[285] This tradition of angelophany figured prominently as well in the literature of both the German Pietists and the Provençal-Spanish kabbalists. In both cases we find evidence for the identification of, or the blurring of the distinction between, the glory and an angelic being, the anthropomorphic manifestation of the divine revealed to prophets and mystics.[286] More specifically, in some of the earliest kabbalistic sources the *Shekhinah* is identified in one of her aspects with Meṭaṭron.[287]

The blurring of the distinction between the divine and an angel is evident, for instance, in the following Ashkenazi tradition: "Know that [the word] *'elohim* is numerically equal to eighty-six; if you add the [five] letters [of the word itself] the sum is ninety-one, which is the numerical value of [the word] *mal'akh* [i.e., angel]. And this [is the import of the verse] 'An angel of the Lord appeared[288] to him in a blazing fire out of a bush' (Exod. 3:2), [the angel] refers to God Himself."[289] An interesting presentation of this Ashkenazi tradition is to be found in the following comment of Ephraim ben Shimshon, interpreting the reference to the angel who redeems (*ha-mal'akh ha-go'el*), mentioned in Gen.

282 See Pines, "God, the Divine Glory, and the Angels according to a Second-Century Theology."

283 See Quispel, "Gnosticism and the New Testament"; idem, "The Origins of the Gnostic Demiurge"; idem, "The Demiurge in the Apocryphon of John."

284 In some literary units of the Hekhalot literature it is very difficult, if not impossible, to differentiate between God and his angel. See Scholem, *Jewish Gnosticism,* pp. 43–55; idem, *Kabbalah,* p. 19; Farber, "Concept of the Merkabah," pp. 246, 258, 261, 559. The attribution of divine characteristics to the highest angel also underlies traditions about Meṭaṭron, the demiurgical angel in ancient Jewish esotericism. See Fauth, "Tatrosjah-Totrosjah und Meṭaṭron in der judischen Merkabah-Mystik." The confusion is especially evident with respect to the names of God and Meṭaṭron. See Rohrbacher-Sticker, "Die Namen Gottes und die Namen Meṭaṭrons."

285 See Wolfson, "The Preexistent Angel of the Magharians and al-Naḥawandi."

286 Cf. the identification of the tenth *sefirah* as the Prince of the Divine Countenance or Prince of the World, according to the tradition reported in the epistle of Samuel ben Mordecai to Yequtiel ha-Kohen against the opponents of Maimonides, cited by Scholem, *Origins,* p. 225; see Septimus, *Hispano-Jewish Culture in Transition,* p. 167 n. 14. Cf. also the following tradition, reported in the name of R. Ezra, in MS Vatican 283, fol. 70a (and MS Munich 56, fol. 209b): "We have received that this angel is the glory, and he is called the angel of the covenant (*mal'akh ha-berit*)." Cf. Ezra's comment included in Azriel of Gerona, *Perush ha-'Aggadot,* pp. 10–11. See also my study "The Secret of the Garment in Naḥmanides"; the secret of the garment involves basically the same motif of the glory taking on the form of an angel.

287 See Scholem, *Origins,* pp. 187 n. 214, 214–215, 299; see also above, n. 165; Benamozegh, *Israël et l'humanité;* pp. 251–252.

288 The manuscript reads ויבא, but I have corrected it in accordance with the masoretic text, וירא.

289 MS New York–JTSA Mic. 1822, fol. 36a; cf. MS Moscow-Guenzberg 366, fol. 23b; and the following passage from a commentary on *Sefer Yeṣirah* in MS Paris–BN 680, fols. 204b–205a: "Contemplate it [the name Shaddai] and you will know that this is the name of the angel of God (*mal'akh ha-'elohim*). . . . This is [the import of the verse] 'I am sending an angel' (Exod. 23:20), [the word *mal'akh*] has the numerical value of 91, and it is the concealment of the name. Thus it is said, 'Pay heed to him and obey him, do not defy him, for he will not pardon your offenses, since My Name is in him' (ibid., 21), for his name is that of his Master." The pronounced influence of Ashkenazi traditions on this commentary is evident.

48:16, which seems to substitute for the word *'elohim* in the preceding verse:

> Thus it is [established] in the secret of the chariot (*sod ha-merkavah*) that the Holy One, blessed be He, is mentioned as an angel in the secret of the angels, [a sphere] in the secret of the spheres, and that is the throne. All of these are emanations that emanate from the splendor of His great infathomable and limitless light. Thus it is written in Exodus (3:2), "An angel of the Lord appeared to him in a blazing fire out of a bush," and immediately after it is written, "God called to him out of the bush" (ibid., 4), and it is written, "for he was afraid to look at God" (ibid., 6). Therefore the word *mal'akh* [angel] numerically equals *ha-'elohim* [the divine].[290]

The identification of the *Shekhinah* with the angel of God is evident as well in a passage from the Pseudo-Hai commentary on the forty-two-letter name contained in Eleazar's *Sefer ha-Ḥokhmah:*

> On every side of the *Shekhinah* are crowns of royalty, and this one itself is of the size of 236,000 myriad parasangs. Concerning this, David said, "Great is our Lord and full of power" (Ps. 147:5), [the expression "full of power," *we-rav koaḥ*] numerically equals 236. "His wisdom is beyond reckoning" (ibid.). Jeremiah said concerning it, "But the Lord is truly God: He is a living God, the everlasting King" (Jer. 10:10), this [i.e., the expression "everlasting King," *melekh 'olam*] numerically equals 236. She governs the world according to her, and she is called the angel of the Lord (*mal'akh ha-shem*) on account of [her] mission,[291] but in her there is no separation. Thus the verse said, "I am sending an angel before you" (Exod. 23:20). This refers to the *Shekhinah*, for the word *mal'akhi* ["My angel"] is [spelled out as] *m''m lm''d k''f yw''d,* which has the numerical value of *Shekhinah* [= 385].[292]

290 *Perush Rabbenu 'Efrayim 'al ha-Torah,* 1:154. See also the identification of the face of God (*pene'elohim*) as angels (*mal'akhim*) in Eleazar ben Moses ha-Darshan, *Sefer ha-Gimaṭri'ot,* MS Munich 221, fol. 120b.

291 As Idel remarks in *Golem,* p. 311 n. 5, this is based on a midrashic principle to the effect that angels are named in accordance with their mission.

292 MS Oxford-Bodleian 1568, fols. 5a–b. The Hebrew text is printed in Dan, *Esoteric Theology,* p. 121. The expression *mal'akhi* in Exod. 23:23 is applied to Meṭaṭron in the anonymous Pietistic commentary on the names of Meṭaṭron; cf. MSS Camb. Heb. Add. 405, fol. 313a; Moscow-Guenzberg 90, fol. 132a; Oxford-Bodleian 2256, fol. 163b. Cf. *Perush ha-Roqeaḥ 'al ha-Torah* 2:129, where, according to one interpretation, the angel mentioned in Exod. 23:23 (*mal'akhi*) is identified as Meṭaṭron. However, according to an alternative interpretation mentioned there (the text is also cited from MS Oxford-Bodleian 268 in *Tosafot ha-Shalem,* ed. Gellis, 2:348), the word *mal'akhi* ("my angel") is transposed into the name *mikha'el* (Michael). Cf. *Sode Razayya,* ed. Weiss, p. 98; *Zohar Ḥadash,* 13a–b (MhN); David ben Aaron Ḥazzan, *'Iggeret 'Aseret Monim,* MS Oxford-Bodleian 1637, fol. 35b (regarding this author see B. Richler, "Hebrew Manuscripts That Have Been Split Up," in *Assufot,* ed. M. Benayahu [Jerusalem, 1987], 1:121, no. 39 [Hebrew]); see also the magical treatise extant in MS Florence Medicea-Laurenziana 44.13, fol. 92a. The angel mentioned in Exod. 23:20 is identified as Michael in several midrashic sources as well; see *Midrash Leqaḥ Ṭov,* p. 170; *Midrash 'Aggadah,* p. 162; see Baḥya ben Asher's commentary to Exod. 23:20, ed. Chavel, 2:244, in which he cites this explanation in the name of R. Ḥananel; and cf. Benamozegh, *Israël et l'humanité,* p. 250.

The author of the text utilizes numerology (specified at the end of the translated passage) in order to support the identification of the *Shekhinah* with the *mal'akh ha-shem,* the highest of the angels. In fact, however, in this passage the *Shekhinah* is characterized in a twofold way: on the one hand, the corporeal dimensions of the *Shiʿur Qomah,* which characterize the theophany of the glory on the throne, are assigned to the *Shekhinah;* on the other hand, the *Shekhinah* exercises providential care over the world, and in this capacity assumes the form of an angel. It is this twofold nature that underlies the statement that "she governs the world according to her," with both aspects curiously being referred to in the feminine.[293]

Even though the *Shekhinah* has two dimensions, ultimately she is one ontic entity, as the author emphasizes with his claim that "she is called the angel of the Lord on account of [her] mission, but in her there is no separation." Given the fact that Exod. 23:20 is cited as a prooftext, it is likely, as Scholem has observed, that the angel spoken of here is none other than Meṭaṭron (linked exegetically to this verse, e.g., in B. Sanhedrin 38b), who is further identified with the *Shekhinah* herself in her capacity as ruler of the world.[294] I have noted above that within the Pietistic literature a related notion is found, according to which the corporeal measurements of *Shiʿur Qomah* are applied to both the *Shekhinah* and Meṭaṭron.

It is relevant to note here as well that the blurring of the distinction between the glory and the highest angel, Meṭaṭron, may also be implied in the etymology of the name Meṭaṭron given by Eleazar as derived from the Latin *metator* (messenger, leader, guide, or one who shows the way)[295] and the suffix *ron* meaning song or praise:[296]

> He is called Meṭaṭron, which is [derived from] *metator* in a foreign language, which means one who leads (*manhig*), as [it says] in *Bereshit Rabbah,* "the Holy One became a *meṭaṭron* for them"[297] and a leader. Therefore [the angel] is called Meṭaṭron because he governs the world. And it says *ron* [i.e., to utter praise] each day. Concerning him it is said "do not defy him . . . for My name is in him"

[293] See Idel, *Golem,* p. 311 n. 4. I think my reading provides a partial answer to Idel's query. It should also be borne in mind, as Idel himself has shown, that Meṭaṭron is sometimes depicted in feminine images; see Idel, "Additional Fragments," pp. 51–52, where Ashkenazi material is discussed.

[294] Scholem, *Origins,* p. 187.

[295] This etymology was made popular by Nathan ben Yeḥiel of Rome's *Sefer he-ʿArukh,* s.v. *metator.* It is employed as well by the Geronese kabbalists. Cf. Scholem, *Origins,* pp. 298–299; Wolfson, "By Way of Truth," pp. 171–172 n. 218. See also Moore, "Intermediaries in Jewish Theology," pp. 62–68.

[296] Cf. the poem *Le-'el naʿaraṣ be-sod qedoshim maʿriṣim u-maqdishim* in *Maḥzor Romania,* 1:33 (the page is incorrectly marked as 29) where there is play on the name Meṭaṭron and the word *ron,* i.e., song or praise: *u-meṭaṭron yeranen ron.* Cf. the kabbalistic anthology, *Migdal David,* by David ben Isaac, MS Jerusalem-JNUL Heb. 8° 397, fol. 161a.

[297] Cf. *Bereshit Rabbah* 5:4, p. 34. There the reading is, "The voice of the Holy One, blessed be He, became a *meṭaṭron* [or, according to some texts, *meṭaṭor*] upon the water." See also *Sifre on Deuteronomy* 338, p. 388.

(Exod. 23:21). Shaddai is numerically equal to Meṭaṭron. . . . Why is his name numerically equal to Shaddai? For he gives testimony concerning the Holy One, blessed be He, that it is worthwhile to worship and praise Him.[298] . . . The great name is inscribed on his heart, "for My name is in him."[299]

In the continuation of this text Eleazar emphasizes in a number of ways that Meṭaṭron should not be confused with the divine, refuting the earlier tradition that emphatically states that Meṭaṭron sits upon a throne: "He stands . . . and he has no throne upon which to sit, but when he writes[300] there is something like sitting, but not in actuality. It merely seems that he is sitting, for he is judge over them all."[301] Despite the fact that Eleazar attempts to avoid treating Meṭaṭron as a full-fledged divine being, it is evident that he reflects, like other Pietistic authors, older traditions wherein the line is somewhat obscured. This no doubt underlies Eleazar's own statement that Meṭaṭron governs the world, a task that one would expect to be attributed to the Creator. In one of the passages in the older *Shiʿur Qomah* fragments there is an intimation of the demiurgical characterization of Meṭaṭron in the description of him as being written "with the letter by which heaven and earth were created."[302] Such a tradition survived and continued to be influential in medieval authors, as I have argued specifically in the case of ibn Ezra, who identified Meṭaṭron as the *yoṣer bereshit* in whose image the human is created.[303]

The providential role accorded Meṭaṭron by Eleazar is affirmed in a passage included in *Sefer ha-Ḥokhmah* that may very well have been an important source for his own formulation: "The Prince of the Countenance is called Meṭaṭron, he is all-powerful (*ha-kol yakhol*). Thus, the numerical value of Meṭaṭron [= 314] is [equal to the expression] 'he who governs the whole world' (*ha-manhig kol ha-ʿolam* = 314). This is the numerical value of Shaddai [= 314], for he said 'enough' to everything and he is omnipotent."[304] It is

[298] There follows a passage from a *Shiʿur Qomah* fragment (cf. *Synopse*, §§ 485–487) cited as *Maʿaseh Merkavah*.

[299] MS Paris–BN 850, fols. 83a–b. For a partial translation of this text from a different manuscript, cf. *3 Enoch*, ed. Odeberg, p. 127.

[300] This reflects one of the older traditions regarding Meṭaṭron as the heavenly scribe who writes down the merits of Israel. See *3 Enoch*, ed. Odeberg, p. 95.

[301] MS Paris–BN 850, fol. 83b. On the emphasis of Meṭaṭron as standing opposite the divine glory and bowing down to it, see the text extant in MS Oxford-Bodleian 1925, fol. 149a. It must be noted that in other Pietistic sources the earlier mythic tradition that Meṭaṭron is the scribe who sits in heaven is transmitted without qualification. See, e.g., *ʿArugat ha-Bosem* 2:195, 3:78.

[302] Cf. *Synopse*, §§ 389, 396, 733. On the demiurgical character of the angel Meṭaṭron as the hypostatic form of God, see Stroumsa's wide-ranging study "Forms of God." See also Dan, "Anafiel, Meṭaṭron, and the Creator."

[303] See Wolfson, "God, the Demiurge, and the Intellect."

[304] MS Oxford-Bodleian 1568, fol. 21a. Cf. *Perush Hafṭarah*, MS Berlin Or. 942, fol. 154a. It would appear from this text that Meṭaṭron is identified as the *ṣaddiq*, the righteous one that sustains the world, the *axis mundi*. See ibid., fol. 155b. It is possible, therefore, that implicit here is a phallic understanding of Meṭaṭron, a motif further developed in kabbalistic sources. See chapter 7, n. 40.

evident from this passage that Meṭaṭron is the demiurgical angel in whose power is invested providential care of the cosmos. The force of this characterization is underscored by the fact that the author of the above text applies the talmudic etymology of the divine name, Shaddai, "I am the one who said to the world 'enough,'"[305] to Meṭaṭron. The same tradition is expressed in the anonymous Pietistic commentary on the names of Meṭaṭron referred to above, but in this case there is an effort to qualify the boldness of the claim by making the demiurgical angel subservient to God: "Meṭaṭron numerically equals Shaddai, for he said to his world 'enough' and it was decreed, and Meṭaṭron bears the entire world by his great power, and he hangs onto the finger of the Holy One, blessed be He."[306]

Perhaps one of the strongest proofs that the identification of Meṭaṭron and the Presence was posited by certain Pietistic authors is found in the critique of this view included in *Sefer ha-Qomah* of Moses ben Eleazar ha-Darshan. The relevant comment occurs in the context of explicating some of the names of Meṭaṭron in the spirit and language of the Pietistic commentary on these names[307] already mentioned several times in this chapter:

> *Ruaḥ Pisqonit* is numerically equal to *ke-rl"w 'elef ribbo parsah* [i.e., both expressions = 930] and this is the measure of the Prince of the Countenance. If someone were to ask: Is it not written, "Great is our Lord and full of power" (Ps. 147:5)?—the response is that the glory reveals himself to the prophet in that measure, but the Cause of Causes has no measure . . . he cannot do anything if the Holy One, blessed be He, does not assist him. This is to exclude those who say that the Prince of the Countenance is the *Shekhinah* and the *Shekhinah* is called the Prince of the Countenance. It is not so, but rather the Prince of the Countenance is from the power of the *Shekhinah*. He is appointed as ruler and judge over the whole world, but Heaven forbid one should say concerning the Prince of the Countenance that he is the *Shekhinah* or that the *Shekhinah* is the Prince of the Countenance. If, however, you find that someone calls the *Shekhinah* by [the name] Meṭaṭron, this is not a mistake. This is another secret that is explained in the name of R. Tam . . . which he found in this book. Thus all of them [i.e., the names of Meṭaṭron] are explained in the book of Neḥemiah the son of R. [Solomon],[308] may the memory of the righteous be for a blessing.[309]

[305] Cf. B. Ḥagigah 12a.

[306] MSS Cambridge Heb. Add. 405, fol. 302b; Moscow-Guenzberg 90, fol. 127b; Oxford-Bodleian 2286, fol. 156b. In a second passage from this work the role of world-sustainer is applied to Meṭaṭron as well. See MSS Cambridge Heb. Add. 405, fol. 301a; Moscow-Guenzberg 90, fol. 126a; Oxford-Bodleian 2286, fol. 155a.

[307] See Liebes, "Angels of the Shofar," p. 185 n. 10.

[308] Here I have followed Scholem's suggested emendation in *Reshit ha-Qabbalah*, p. 201 n. 2.

[309] MSS Rome-Angelica 46, fol. 8a; MS Milan-Ambrosiana 70, fol. 215a; partially transcribed in Scholem, *Reshit ha-Qabbalah*, p. 201.

On the one hand, R. Moses categorically rejects the identification of the angelic Meṭaṭron and the divine Presence;[310] on the other hand, he does allow for the attribution of the name Meṭaṭron to the *Shekhinah,* an aspect of the tradition that he considers to be esoteric (*sod*). The precise nature of that secret is not revealed, but it seems to me plausible to suggest that it involved some tradition, as one finds in kabbalistic sources, that distinguished an upper and lower Meṭaṭron, one angelic and the other divine, and thus allowed the name to be ascribed to the *Shekhinah.* In one context R. Moses utilizes the orthographic distinction, already attested in the *Shiʿur Qomah* fragments,[311] between writing Meṭaṭron with seven letters (MYṬṬRWN) or six (MṬṬRWN) to make this very point, a strategy also used by various Spanish kabbalists for this purpose.[312] It may be concluded, therefore, that attested in the Pietistic writings is the tradition that the glory is identified with an angelic being that is also described as the anthropomorphic figuration of the deity—even though, as is surely the case, the Pietists themselves tried to distinguish the glory and the angel and some of them even openly criticized those who failed to uphold such a distinction.

Perhaps the most significant affirmation of the glorious angel in the Pietistic sources is a formulation found in several writings of Eleazar already noted above: "the glory alludes to the angel that changes to many forms." The import of this statement is not simply that the angel changes according to the command of the glory, but that the glory itself is the angel that has the capacity to assume multiple theophanic forms.[313] Another text that affirms in a striking

[310] Cf. MSS Rome-Angelica 46, fols. 2a, 11b; Milan-Ambrosiana 70, fols. 206a, 220b–221a (transcribed by Scholem in *Reshit ha-Qabbalah,* p. 202). See *Sefer ha-ʾOrah,* MS Jerusalem-Schocken 14, fol. 63a, where the sin of Nadab and Abihu is specified as thinking that Meṭaṭron was God. The traditional rejection of the identification of Meṭaṭron and the divine Presence (cf. the reading of Exod. 23:21 in B. Sanhedrin 38b, and the famous story concerning Elisha ben Abuyah and Meṭaṭron in B. Ḥagigah 15a) is reiterated in various medieval commentaries, e.g., R. Solomon ben Isaac of Troyes and R. Meir ha-Levi Abulafia. See Septimus, *Hispano-Jewish Culture in Transition,* p. 167 n. 18.

[311] See *Synopse,* § 389; Cohen, *Shiʿur Qomah: Texts and Recensions,* pp. 105, 159, 208. See Scholem, *Major Trends,* p. 70; Cohen, *Shiʿur Qomah: Liturgy and Theurgy,* p. 128.

[312] Cf. MSS Rome-Angelica 46, fol. 11b, Milan-Ambrosiana 70, fol. 221a. Cf. Scholem, *Le-Ḥeqer Qabbalat R. Yiṣḥaq ben Yaʿaqov ha-Kohen,* pp. 15, 28–29 nn. 97–98 (= *Tarbiz* 2 [1931]: 202, 214–215 nn. 97–98), 182–183 n. 3 (= *Tarbiz* 5 [1934]: 186–187 n. 3). See also Jacob ben Jacob ha-Kohen, "Commentary on Ezekiel's Chariot," pp. 27, 124–125 n. 16; Idel, *Mystical Experience,* p. 165 n. 209. Other relevant kabbalistic sources are cited by R. Margaliot in *Malʾakhe ʿElyon* (Jerusalem, 1988), pp. 88–89.

[313] It is of interest to compare the Pietistic idea of the glory that symbolizes the angel that changes to many forms to the description of the Presence, the last of the ten emanations in *Zohar* 1:232a, as the "angel that is sometimes male and sometimes female. . . . There are angels sent into the world that change to many aspects, sometimes female and sometimes male, sometimes judgmental and sometimes merciful. . . . In this manner that angel [i.e., the Presence] has many aspects, and all the aspects of the world are present in that place. This secret [is alluded to in the verse] 'Like the appearance of the bow which shines in the clouds on a day of rain, such was the appearance of the surrounding radiance. That was the appearance of the semblance of the Presence of the Lord' (Ezek. 1:28). Just as all the aspects are within her, so she governs the whole world." See Scholem, *On the Mystical Shape,* p. 186; Tishby, *Wisdom of the Zohar,* p. 379.

way the ontic identification of the glory and an angel is found in the *Sod ha-Yiḥud,* attributed to Judah the Pious but in all probability written by someone else: "This is the image of the honorable glory, Akatriel Yah, the Lord of Hosts. There is a midrash that attests that Akatriel is an angel, and those enlightened in the secret of the unity will comprehend."[314] The secret alluded to here, designated as the secret of unity (*sod ha-yiḥud*), seems to me to hinge on the blurring of the ontological distinction between the glory, named Akatriel, and the angelic hypostasis. This tendency may be traced to certain Geonic figures, including Saadiah, who in some places distinguished between the upper, transcendent glory and the lower, visible glory that is to be identified further as Akatriel, the highest angel.[315] It is noteworthy that a parallel phenomenon is found in kabbalistic texts, for example, in the identification of the last of the ten emanations, *Shekhinah,* and the first of the angels, Meṭaṭron, that is found in some of the earliest kabbalistic documents. In some of these sources one even finds that the precise term used by the author of *Sefer ha-Navon,* "angel of the glory" (*mal'akh ha-kavod*), is applied to the *Shekhinah.*[316] The

[314] Quoted in Dan, *Studies,* p. 81. Cf. the Ashkenazi text extant in MS Oxford-Bodleian 1791, fol. 80a, where Akatriel, mentioned in the talmudic legend (B. Berakhot 7a), is interpreted as an angel. See also the fragment of a text preserved in MS Oxford-Bodleian 2575, fol. 1a.

[315] See Judah ben Barzillai, *Perush Sefer Yeṣirah,* p. 22, who cites two opinions with respect to the nature of Akatriel: according to one view (attributed to Saadiah), this name refers to an angel (this is also the view of R. Nissim of Kairouwan as well as an eighth-century apocalypse; see Scholem, *Jewish Gnosticism,* p. 53 n. 32), and according to another view (attributed to other Geonim) it refers to a being that derives from the light of the glory itself. For a possible polemic against Saadiah, see the commentary of Ḥananel ben Ḥushiel to B. Berakhot 7a, in *Otzar ha-Geonim,* ed. B. Lewin, vol. 1, Tractate Berakhot, appendix, p. 5: "There are those who say that Akatriel is an angel, but we have received that he is the glory." This text is copied in Judah ben Barzillai, *Perush Sefer Yeṣirah.* See Farber, "Concept of the Merkabah," p. 558. In a fragment comprising Hekhalot material extant in some manuscripts (cf. *Synopse,* § 597) it is evident that Akatriel is the name applied to the enthroned glory surrounded by angels, which is to be distinguished from the transcendent God, designated by the traditional appellation "the Holy One, blessed be He." See also the tradition preserved in the Ashkenazi text included in *Merkavah Shelemah* 23b (Farber, in "Concept of the Merkabah," p. 237, suggests that the author of this composition is Eleazar of Worms): "[The word] *ba-seter* has the numerical value of Akatriel [i.e., both = 662], and this name the Holy One, blessed be He, teaches when He is sitting in secrecy above, and no creature can see Him." The numerical equivalence of the name Akatriel and the expression *ba-seter* (cf. Isa. 48:16; for a different vocalization, *be-seter,* cf. Ps. 91:1) is found as well in Eleazar's commentary on the liturgical poem *Ha-'oḥez be-yad middat mishpaṭ* (see Scholem, *Origins,* p. 125 n. 129), extant in several manuscripts, e.g., MS Munich 92, fol. 26b. See also the Ashkenazi text included in *Sefer ha-Ḥokhmah,* MS Oxford-Bodleian 1568, fol. 5a, where this numerology is employed, and in another Ashkenazi text extant in MS New York–JTSA Mic. 1786, fol. 43b. The last source is cited and discussed by Idel, *Kabbalah: New Perspectives,* pp. 195–196, 374 n. 196.

[316] See, e.g., MS Oxford-Bodleian 2456 (Christ Church 198), fol. 12a; see also the formulation of Ezra of Gerona in *Perush ha-'Aggadot,* p. 11. Cf. the formulation in the thirteenth-century moralistic treatise *Sefer ha-Yashar* (Jerusalem, 1978), chap. 5, p. 58: "The angels are forces that have neither body nor form, but they are capable of clothing themselves in form. . . . Some of them [appear] in the shape of an anthropos, and that is the most precious in their eyes, for that is the form in which the angel of the glory (*mal'akh ha-kavod*) appeared, as it says, 'upon this semblance of a throne, there was the semblance of a human form' (Ezek. 1:26)." Concerning this work, see Shokek, "The Affinity of Sefer ha-Yashar to the Circle of Geronese Kabbalists."

appearance of *Shekhinah* in an angelic form that is visualized as an anthropos, according to Naḥmanides, is also implied in the secret of the garment (*sod ha-malbush*), to which he refers in his commentary to Gen. 18:1. It is also evident that kabbalists shared with the Pietists the identification of the name and glory, in that utterance of the former eventuates in a vision of the latter. To cite one example from what appears to be an early Geronese text:

> As a consequence of our mentioning the glorious name (*shem ha-kavod*), He is unified with us, and is blessed in His blessing. The meaning of the name is known to the enlightened, according to the matter, "Behold the name of the Lord comes from afar" (Isa. 30:27). And the meaning of the glory of the Lord is, as it is written, "the appearance of the glory of the Lord" (Exod. 24:17), and it is written, "you shall behold the glory of the Lord" (ibid., 16:7), and it is written "The Lord our God has shown us His glory" (Deut. 5:21), and many more such as these.[317]

From the textual examples adduced, it is obvious that the name is here treated hypostatically as the luminous and visible Presence of God.

In the Pietistic conception as well, the glory is further identified as the name that is visualized as an anthropos. One is here reminded of the mystical vision in Abulafia's ecstatic kabbalah. In that case, too, the letters of the Tetragrammaton (and other divine names) have the capacity to appear within the imagination of the mystic as an anthropomorphic form (which, in the thought of Abulafia, is an allegorical depiction of the Agent Intellect).[318] It stands to reason that in this matter, as in several others, Abulafia was influenced by the literature of the German Pietists.[319] What is essential to note is the correlation between mystery (*sod*) and the name, on one hand, and the name and the glory (*kavod*), on the other. This suggests that for the Pietists visualization of the glory (in one of its most sublime forms, as the measurable anthropos who sits upon the throne) is concomitantly a mystical apprehension of the name. This tradition is confirmed in a teaching of Eleazar reported by his disciple Abraham bar Azriel, that the number 236—that is, the measurement of the *Shiʿur Qomah*—derives from the four letters of the name by means of a complex numerology.[320] Significantly, the teaching of Eleazar is cited in the context of an explication of a passage from a late midrashic work, the *Alphabet of R. Aqiva,* which attributes the measurements of *Shiʿur Qomah* to the body of the Presence (*guf ha-shekhinah*).[321] The juxtaposition underscores the fact that the name is identical with the glory, and both may assume in the mystical vision the shape of an anthropos.

In one of the theosophic texts attributed by Dan to Judah the Pious the

[317] MS Oxford-Bodleian 2456 (Christ Church 198), fol. 15b.

[318] See Idel, *Mystical Experience,* pp. 100–105.

[319] Ibid., pp. 9, 22–24, 100; idem, *Language, Torah, Hermeneutics,* pp. 50–51; see above, nn. 219 and 235.

[320] *ʿArugat ha-Bosem* 1:128. For a later attestation of a similar tradition, see Menaḥem Azariah of Fano, *Kanfe Yonah,* pt. 2, § 53, 47b.

[321] *Batte Midrashot* 2:370; see Scholem, *Major Trends,* p. 66.

symbolic nexus of the name and the glory is expressed in terms of the image of the crown worn by the righteous.[322] The Pietists, like the kabbalists, removed this image from its eschatological context in both Jewish apocalypses and talmudic-midrashic literature and understood it as a symbolic depiction of a mystical state of communion with the glory or divine Presence. Moreover, the Pietists combined the image of the eschatological crown with that of the crown worn by the glory, an older motif rooted in ancient Merkavah mysticism. According to that tradition, the crown is made of the prayers of Israel and is placed on the head of the glory by one of the highest angels, either Sandalphon or Meṭaṭron. It is evident, moreover, that in the esoteric theosophy cultivated by the German Pietists the liturgical crown is treated hypostatically as a divine emanation, sometimes identified as the *kavod* or *Shekhinah* and others times as the image of Jacob engraved on the throne of glory.[323] To cite one of the relevant passages from this work:

> When Sandalphon mentions the name over the crown,[324] the name carries the crown like a magnet.[325] . . . When he adjures the name, the crown is cloaked in splendor before the glory,[326] and this is [the meaning of] "Blessed is the name of His glory forever" (Ps. 72:19). And similarly it is done with respect to the righteous who receive the face of the Presence. It is written, "we extol the name of Your splendor" (1 Chron. 29:13). "The name of Your splendor" (*le-shem tif'artekha*) is numerically equivalent to [the expression] "the four-letter name" (*le-shem ben*

[322] On the symbol of the crown in Ḥaside Ashkenaz, see Scholem, *Origins,* pp. 98, 104, 184–186; Farber, "Concept of the Merkabah," pp. 231–244; Idel, *Kabbalah: New Perspectives,* pp. 194–197; and my study "The Image of Jacob." It is worthwhile to consider the mystical, theosophic, and magical uses of the image of the crown in light of the social practice in Ashkenaz, renewed in the late Middle Ages, of brides, and perhaps also bridegrooms, donning crowns during the wedding ceremony, a practice attested as well in the iconic depictions of crowned brides in Ashkenazi manuscripts from the mid-thirteenth century onwards. See Feuchtwanger, "The Coronation of the Virgin and of the Bride."

[323] Cf. *Sode Razayya,* ed. Weiss, pp. 4–5 (*Sefer Razi'el,* 8a–b), pp. 147–148 (MS Oxford-Bodleian 1638, fol. 56a).

[324] Cf. B. Ḥagigah 13b.

[325] Cf. MSS Oxford-Bodleian 1567, fol. 73a; Paris–BN 850, fols. 119b–120a, 120a, 121b.

[326] In an Ashkenazi text, extant in MS New York–JTSA Mic. 1878, fol. 44a, there is a description of the ascent of the crown prepared by Sandalphon from the prayers of Israel to Meṭaṭron and from there to the image of Jacob engraved on the throne. At that juncture the crown is said to be "clothed in a glorious fire that no eye can gaze upon on account of its great splendor. Immediately all the beasts, ophanim, electrums, seraphim, and the throne of glory offer splendid praise to the glorious king. Then the crown expands infinitely, and it increases and is elevated, facing the consuming fire that shines without end, without image or form." The text parallels the description in *Pesiqta Rabbati* 20, 97a–b, but in the midrashic context no mention is made of the image of Jacob. Cf. the Ashkenazi commentary on the hymn *Ha-'Aderet we-ha-'Emunah* (MS Vatican 228, fol. 107b), which describes the ascent of the crown made from the prayers of Israel in similar terms: "when it reaches the image of Jacob our father that is engraved on the throne of glory, then it expands according to the glory and is completely glorified." Concerning this text, see Dan, "Ashkenazi Ḥasidic Commentaries on the Hymn *Ha-'Aderet we-ha-'Emunah.*" See also Eleazar's *Perush ha-Merkavah,* MS Paris–BN 850, fol. 71b.

> *ha-'arba' 'otiyyot*).[327] The nine times [in Scripture that the expression] "to place His name" (*lasum shemo*) [is employed] and [the nine times that the expression] "to cause His name to dwell" (*leshaken shemo*) [is employed] correspond to the nine visions that come over the righteous.[328] Corresponding to this are three times [that the splendor of the Presence is mentioned], "the glory of the Lord has shone upon you" (Isa. 60:1), "Upon you the Lord will shine, and His glory will be seen over you" (ibid., 2). These [three] correspond to "the name of splendor" (*shem tif'eret*) (ibid., 63:14), "the name of His holiness" (*shem qodsho*) (Ps. 145:21), "the name of His glory" (*shem kevodo*) (Ps. 72:19).[329]

In this passage, then, the name is equated with the divine splendor or holiness, which are synonymous with the radiant glory. The beatific vision of the righteous—depicted by the symbolic crown—is here understood as the contemplative vision of the name. The vision of the name, in turn, results in the crowning of the righteous in divine splendor. A structural similarity is thus established between the crowning of God by the prayers of the righteous and the crowning of the righteous by the vision of the Presence. Just as the angelic adjuration of the name lifts the crown to the head of the enthroned glory, so the utterance of the name causes the righteous to be crowned in glory. Again, we see that in the religious experience cultivated by the German Pietists the threads of magic and mysticism are not easily disentangled.

The connection between the different visualizations of the glory and various divine names is brought out in a passage in Eleazar's commentary on the liturgy:

> "The glorious majesty of Your splendor" (Ps. 145:5) . . . the splendor of His majesty has no limit but He reveals to the prophets . . . the glory, He shows them the great glory. . . . By means of the glory the will of the Creator is made visible. . . . "And Your wondrous acts" (ibid.), for the majesty of Your glory is called among the angels master (*'adon*), that is, Adonai; among the prophets it is called YHWH; and among the Patriarchs, El Shaddai. This is [the meaning of] "that which I have done in my heart." This is not transmitted except to one who understands of his own accord.[330]

In a more abbreviated fashion Eleazar expresses the same idea in a second passage from this work: "The One, blessed be He, has no body or form, and He cannot be compared to any creature. . . . His glory is seen by the prophets . . . sometimes in the name Elohim and sometimes in [the name] El

[327] The two phrases as they appear in the manuscripts are not equivalent, for *le-shem tif'artekha* equals 1471 and *le-shem ben ha-'arba' 'otiyyot* 1523. The obvious correction consists of erasing the word *ben* which equals 52, in the second phrase; if that sum is removed from 1523, one gets the desired 1471.

[328] Cf. MS Paris–BN 772, fol. 41b.

[329] MSS Oxford-Bodleian 1566, fol. 37b, 1567, fol. 49b. Cf. *Sode Razayya*, ed. Weiss, p. 90.

[330] MS Paris–BN 772, fol. 97b.

Shaddai."[331] In another text, a sustained reflection on Exod. 6:3, the correlation of the divine names and the varied forms of the manifestation of the glory is affirmed as well: "Just as we know with respect to the [divine] names that there is one level above another, so, too, with respect to the images of the glory (*demuyot shel kavod*) that there is amongst them a level higher than the rest."[332]

Evidence for the cultivation of techniques to induce a vision of the glory among the Pietists may be gathered from a passing remark in Eleazar's commentary on Ezekiel's chariot. While discussing the electrum (*ḥashmal*) mentioned by Ezekiel, which is one of the various ways to describe the appearance of the anthropomorphic glory, Eleazar reports the following story:

> My teacher [Judah the Pious] told me that once he and his father [Samuel] were in the synagogue, and there was a plate full of oil and water placed before them. The sun shone on that plate and a splendor, unlike any other, emerged from it. His father said to him: Son, consider that splendor, for such was the matter of the splendor of the electrum.[333]

Although it is not specified that Judah the Pious and his father, Samuel, employed meditative techniques that utilized a vessel of water placed in the sunlight as a medium to behold the glory,[334] it would not be incorrect, in my view, to understand this narrative in precisely such terms.[335] The plate of oil and water, with the rays of sunlight shining on it, conjures an image of the electrum, which is the appearance of the glory. Eleazar refrains from describing the elec-

[331] Ibid., fol. 171b. Cf. fol. 64a, where the angels called *qedoshim*, "the holy ones," are distinguished from other angels, inasmuch as they see the vision of Shaddai in the speculum that shines.

[332] MS Oxford-Bodleian 1791, fol. 80b.

[333] MS Paris–BN 850, fol. 47b. See Scholem, *Major Trends*, pp. 103, 374 n. 77.

[334] See Idel, "On the Metamorphosis." For similar techniques of visualization in zoharic literature, see chapter 7, n. 200. In this connection it is of interest to consider the comment of Rashi on the mishnaic prohibition of bringing out fire from water on festivals: "They would take a clear glass vessel (*zekhukhit levanah;* concerning this term, see chapter 6, n. 24) and place it in the sun when the sun is very hot. The glass emits a flame and they bring some flax and place it on the glass and it is ignited. I have thus understood from a *yoṣer* composed by one of the sages of Lombardy." In the standard editions of the Babylonian Talmud a note has been added here to the effect that the reference is to Shabbetai Donnolo's commentary on *Sefer Yeṣirah*. Indeed, there is a passage in that work that is quite similar to Rashi's description; see *Sefer Ḥakhmoni*, ed. Castelli, p. 28; [Similar language is found in a responsum of Sherira Gaon in *Teshuvot Ge'one Mizraḥ u-Ma'arav*, ed. J. Mueller (Berlin, 1888), no. 145, 36a; cf. Judah ben Barzillai, *Perush Sefer Yeṣirah*, p. 198.] Prof. Menahem Schmelzer informed me that Solomon Buber already corrected the reference in Rashi's comment in the way suggested above in his edition of Ṭobiah bar Eliezer's *Midrash Leqaḥ Ṭov* 4a, n. 71. It is likely that the German Pietists were also influenced by the passage of Donnolo. Cf. *Sode Razayya*, pp. 14–15; *'Arugat ha-Bosem* 1:154–155.

[335] It should be noted that in another Pietistic text the vision of the glory is described, inter alia, in terms of the shining of the sun in water, in milk, and on the wall. See Dan, *Studies*, p. 170. See also *Ḥokhmat ha-Nefesh*, chap. 53, p. 92, where the presence of the *Shekhinah* with the Jewish people in exile is described metaphorically in terms of the phenomenon of the sunlight shining upon water in a vessel; the splendor that the sunlight produces on the surface of the water represents the *Shekhinah*.

trum in any more detail, except to note that the splendor of the electrum is like that of the sun and moon shining together.[336] It is clear that Eleazar considered study of the chariot to be an experiential, and not merely an exegetical, undertaking. Thus he specifies that the wisdom connected to speculation on the chariot cannot be written but should be transmitted orally. Even this oral transmission is severely limited by a host of qualifications pertaining to the intellectual, religious, and moral character of the potential recipient. But the one who is worthy to receive these secrets is, to repeat a passage already cited above, "given the glorious name [YHWH], the secret, for whoever knows it and walks with a straight heart is like one of the ministering angels. He is received from camp to camp, for he is like an angel and his soul is bound to the high and exalted throne."[337] Knowledge of the chariot is thus equated with the meditative ascent by means of the divine name.

For the German Pietists knowledge of the name, a knowledge that involves the mentioning of the name, results in a visionary experience on a par with prophetic revelation. Thus, in a telling remark preserved in R. Moses ben Eleazar ha-Darshan's commentary on *Shiʿur Qomah,* we read that he "who knows [the name of God] and prays by means of it, the *Shekhinah* rests upon him and he prophesies like the ancient prophets."[338] An intrinsic connection is made between the divine name (the Tetragrammaton) and prophecy. Although the visual component of the prophetic experience is not elaborated on in this context, it seems to me a plausible inference to draw, given the frequent characterization of prophecy as the vision of the luminous glory.

That the Pietists considered themselves capable of attaining such ecstatic

336 It is likely that the secret here involves the unification of masculine and feminine potencies within the mysterious electrum, symbolized respectively by the images of the sun and moon. On the feminine character of the moon in the Pietistic writings, see Wolfson, "Image of Jacob," pp. 154–156 n. 116, 159–160 n. 129; Liebes "De Natura Dei," pp. 50–51. On the luminous quality of the electrum, see n. 166, above. The androgynous quality of the electrum is expressed in Eleazar's writings in terms of the distinction between the *ḥashmal* (Ezek. 1:4, 27) and *ḥashmalah* (ibid., 8:2), expressions that are identical in meaning in Scripture but that the Pietists interpret as a reference to two distinct entities. It is evident from a number of passages that the secret related to this distinction concerns the attribution of gender to the electrum, which is, after all, the manifestation of the glory (cf. Ezek. 1:27 and *Pirqe R. ʾEliʿezer* 4, 9b–10a). See Farber, "Concept of the Merkabah," pp. 112–115, 553–554, 623–624. On the virtual interchangeability of the *ḥashmal* and the glory that appears from between the cherubim, supported by the numerical equivalence of *ḥashmal* and the expression *ʿal keruvim* ("upon the cherubim"), see "Book of Angels," p. 116. In the final analysis, in Eleazar's writings the dual aspect of the *ḥashmal* is parallel to, and in some contexts virtually identical with, the bisexual nature of the cherubim. See, in particular, *Perush ha-Merkavah,* MS Paris–BN 850, fols. 76b–77a, and the material collected in *Sode Razayya,* ed. Weiss, pp. 167–173; Wolfson, "Image of Jacob," pp. 176–177. The esotericism surrounding the vision of the electrum is directly related to the erotic nature of the divine glory. See n. 202, above. The secrecy pertaining to oral discourse about the vision of the *ḥashmal* and *ḥashmalah* is emphasized in another passage in Eleazar's *Perush ha-Merkavah,* MS Paris–BN 850, fols. 77b–78a. See also fols. 68b–69a (quoted in n. 189, above) and *Sode Razayya,* ed. Weiss, p. 173.

337 MS Paris–BN 850, fol. 49b. Cf. *Sode Razayya,* ed. Weiss, p. 138.

338 MSS Rome-Angelica 46, fol. 2a; Milan-Ambrosiana 70, fol. 206a. Cf. Scholem, *Reshit ha-Qabbalah,* p. 222; and discussion in Idel, *Kabbalah: New Perspectives,* p. 169.

states is attested by a comment made by one of their fiercest opponents in the thirteenth century, Moses Taku.[339] In one place in his polemical work *Ketav Tamim* Moses refers to the Pietists as those "who make themselves prophets and habituate themselves in the [theurgical] mentioning of the holy names."[340] Moses goes on to compare the ecstatic techniques of the Pietists to those of the magicians.[341] The important point for our analysis is the connection made in his remarks between mentioning the name and prophetic illumination. I see no reason to doubt the veracity of this report: the Pietists did make use of the divine names for the purpose of attaining some sort of prophetic vision. Moreover, the techniques for attaining a vision of the glory are comparable to the magical techniques employed to conjure images of angels reported by the Pietists and mentioned previously in this chapter. Moreover, as Idel has shown, there is evidence from both the anonymous Pietistic work *Sefer ha-Ḥayyim* and Eleazar's *Sefer ha-Ḥokhmah* to confirm the veracity of Taku's claims that different Pietistic groups utilized the pronunciation of divine names in order to induce prophetic and visionary experiences.[342]

It can be safely concluded, therefore, that the experiential component is central and not tangential to the Pietistic theosophy. Their speculative treatises on the nature of the glory, angels, and prophecy, their exegetical commentaries on liturgical and biblical texts, their mystical works on esoteric subjects such as Ezekiel's chariot vision and the different names of God, as well as their more magical or folkloristic interests, all attest to the essential role ecstatic vision plays in the Pietistic worldview. With respect to the critical phenomenological question—what is the nature of that which is visualized?—there are basically two approaches evident in their thinking: the veridical and the docetic. These two approaches can be correlated with the two major intellectual influences on the German Pietistic worldview: the ancient theosophical tradition that assumed that the glory is the enthroned anthropos, also identified with the divine name, and the medieval philosophical conceptions of the glory as a created or

339 See Scholem, *Major Trends,* p. 109; Dan, *Esoteric Theology,* pp. 31, 34; idem, introduction to facsimile edition of Moses Taku's *Ketav Tamim,* pp. 7–27.

340 *'Oṣar Neḥmad* 3 (1860): 84. On Taku's critique of the two stages of linguistic creation to produce a calf (based on the legend in B. Sanhedrin 65b) by means of *Sefer Yeṣirah,* which parallel the technique disclosed by Eleazar of Worms, see Idel, *Golem,* p. 59. On the theurgical use of divine names by Ashkenazi authorities, see also the evidence reported by R. Solomon ben Abraham ibn Aderet in *She'elot u-Teshuvot ha-Rashba* (Vienna, 1812), no. 548, 72a. See following note.

341 Judah he-Ḥasid's involvement with magic by use of divine (as well as demonic) names is attested in a statement of Isaac of Acre (MS Oxford-Bodleian 1911, fol. 7b), cited by Goldreich in his edition of *Sefer Me'irat 'Einayim,* p. 409 n. 11; on Judah's clairvoyant powers, see also the statement of Isaac of Acre in the name of R. Oshaya, p. 58. Mystical and magical traditions about the Ḥaside Ashkenaz survived into a much later period. Thus, for example, in *Sefer Ma'ase Nissim* of Joseph the Sexton of Worms (1604–1678), there is a tale concerning Eleazar of Worms travelling to Spain to instruct Naḥmanides in the ways of kabbalah. In the context of that tale we learn that the soul of Eleazar ascended to heaven and that he used holy names to effect magical and supernatural occurrences. See S. Eidelberg, *R. Juspa, Shammash of Warmaisa (Worms): Jewish Life in 17th Century Worms* (Jerusalem, 1991), pp. 65–70.

342 *Kabbalah: New Perspectives,* pp. 98–99.

emanated light that takes shape within the human imagination. The difference in opinion between Judah and Eleazar—or even within one man—is an accurate gauge for ascertaining the difficulty the medieval Jewish mystic, operating within a more philosophically acute environment, had in appropriating the ancient theosophical traditions. The docetic tendency, as it appears in the Pietistic literature, is one way the medieval mystic dealt with the conflict between, on the one hand, assuming that God is essentially formless and invisible and, on the other, accepting the mystical tradition that posited as a peak experience the vision of God as an anthropomorphic form upon the throne, achieved by mentioning the divine name. With respect to this conflict of interests the Pietists are not unique. Indeed, medieval Jewish mystical literature abounds with affirmations of God's visible form, followed immediately by some manner of qualification. In sum, it may be said that in the classical period of medieval Jewish mysticism, the twelfth and thirteenth centuries, various traditions, some older and some more recent, converged to help give shape to the rich and diverse—but not always consistent—world of Jewish mystics. The seeing of the divine form loomed large in the center of this world.

• CHAPTER SIX •

Visionary Gnosis and the Role of the Imagination In Theosophic Kabbalah

Ontology of Light and Mystical Vision

Any discussion on the nature of mystical vision must begin with an analysis of the phenomenon of light and light symbolism as it is operative in the given religious tradition of the particular mystic. The frequency with which the religious experience is associated with the phenomenon of light is a well-attested fact in the history of religions. Moreover, the symbolism of light is repeatedly associated with mystical experience. Indeed, the ontology of light gives shape to and generates the mystic experience, which is essentially a state or process of illumination. In the varieties of medieval Jewish mysticism this is certainly the case.

One of the dominant and striking features of the various circles of kabbalistic speculation in the twelfth and thirteenth centuries is the use of light symbolism to depict the nature of the divine. It would seem that the light imagery is primarily a symbolic complex describing the theosophic structure and secondarily, that this complex is transferred to a level of experience. That is, for the kabbalist the primary function of the light symbolism is theosophic in nature, used to describe the divine reality; only in a secondary sense does this symbolism function to describe the phenomenological pole. In other terms, the light imagery depicts an exterior light in the divine realm that has an ontologically independent status, whereas the interior light of the mystical experience is a derivative phenomenon. Mystical illumination, therefore, would be a consequence of the luminous nature of the divine. Yet it is the case, as will be shown in more detail in this chapter and the next, that the ontological and phenomenological poles are inseparably interwoven. What is conceived of metaphysically as the ultimate nature of being, that is, light, coincides with what is experienced in the mystical experience of illumination.

While many relevant texts could be cited to support my contention that the convergence of the ontological and phenomenological poles characterizes the theosophy of the kabbalists, I would like in this context to cite two passages in particular, one that describes the potencies of the divine chariot as luminous names and another that deals more directly with the sefirotic hypostases. The first is taken from an extensive commentary on Ezekiel's chariot, composed in the second half of the thirteenth century by the Castilian kabbalist Jacob ben Jacob ha-Kohen:

> The names above are the true essence, and they are divine powers hewn from the quarry of the intelligible light and from the pure, holy wondrous light. They are appointed to do everything, and every action is realized through them. They are interpreted truthfully by the holy prophets, the great sages, and the select few who make use of them in all good things before the Holy One, blessed be He, and not for another matter that is not the will of God. . . . All this comes to teach you that the names above with the true essence are hewn from the quarry of the light of life, for the intelligible grades are called kings and their glorious names are called princes. He who knows and comprehends the essence of the names, and knows how to mention them properly and correctly, as they are mentioned by the angels, his prayer is immediately received and approved. The enlightened will comprehend this secret that I have revealed concerning the matter of the name.[1]

The mystical secret connected to the name that this kabbalist has revealed, as we learn from Jacob's exegesis of Exod. 3:13–15, involves both the visual manifestation of the letters of the name in fiery forms, related to the motif expressed in older Jewish esoteric literature concerning the ascension of the letters to the throne of glory, and the proper recitation of the names. In this case the mystical illumination that ensues from knowledge of the names, which constitute the divine essence above in the realm of the chariot, is virtually identical to the magical use of the names. Significantly, for this kabbalist there is no vocational difference between prophet, sage, and theurgical mystic.[2]

The second textual example is taken from the fourteenth-century kabbalist Joseph ben Shalom Ashkenazi, who commented thus on the words of *Sefer Yeṣirah* 1:8, "Ten ineffable *sefirot,* their appearance is like lightning": "There

[1] "Commentary on Ezekiel's Chariot," p. 3; see sources cited and discussed by Farber on pp. 78 n. 12, 80 n. 1.

[2] On the illuminative nature of mystical gnosis of the divine name, cf. the anonymous commentary from the *Ḥug Sefer ha-Temunah,* the circle of the "Book of the Image," on the seventy-two-letter name of God, extant in several manuscripts (a version of this text was printed as part of *Sefer Razi'el;* cf. Scholem, *Catalogus Codicum Cabbalisticorum Hebraicorum,* p. 7 n. 1). Cf. MS New York–JTSA Mic. 8115, fols. 66b–67a (MSS Cambridge Heb. Add. 671, fol. 84a; Oxford-Bodleian 1938, fols. 196a–197a): "Then you will know something of the ways of the Supernal who illuminates the eyes of His sages, as it is written, 'A light shines for the upright in the darkness' (Ps. 112:4). They vindicate [those of] a pure intellect and place them in the supernal light, as it says, 'For the commandment is a lamp, the teaching is a light' (Prov. 6:23). If he comprehends God, blessed be He, to place his intellect [in a] straight way, to comprehend the form, combination, holy number, and vocalization of the glorious, awesome, and explicit name in holiness and purity, fortunate is he and his offspring. If he constantly directs his attention to God, then he will comprehend His light, and his intellect will be filled with the light of the angels, 'for he is an angel of the Lord of Hosts' (Mal. 2:7). For this form engraved on the throne . . . [consists of] the twenty-two letters of the Torah, which are the mystery of the letters *AHYH* [i.e., the name *Ehyeh,* whose consonants equal twenty-one, together with the word itself, equals twenty-two, corresponding to the number of letters in the Hebrew alphabet], and they are the light of every creature, the angels above and Israel below. One letter is engraved in them and among them, as it says, 'For My name is in him' (Exod. 23:21), 'in the midst of this people' (Num. 14:14)." According to this text, as we saw in the last chapter in the case of the German Pietists, knowledge of the name has the power to transform a human into an angel.

are those who explain [the words] 'their appearance is like lightning' [in the following way]: when a prophet or a mystic[3] comes to gaze upon these holy lights [i.e., the *sefirot*] he knows that at times they shine in relation to him and they appear as if they were lightning, and then they immediately are hidden, and they shine again and are hidden."[4] The luminous nature of the divine emanations is experienced only in the context of the phenomenological relationship, yet the latter is made possible by the fact that the emanations are constituted by light. It will be seen in the course of our analysis that this circle is a central component of the kabbalistic worldview: one is illuminated by visually contemplating the illuminations above, but the illuminations above are available only to one who is so illuminated.

Before proceeding with a discussion of light and mystical vision, it would be in order to turn our attention briefly to the question of "origins" of kabbalistic speculation understood in a historical vein. The sudden outburst of the different mystical and pietistic trends in northern France, Germany, Provence, and northern Spain in the twelfth and thirteenth centuries is a phenomenon that has never been fully explained historically. It is doubtful that we will ever be able to account comprehensively for this phenomenon (which Scholem revealingly referred to as the "origins" of kabbalah[5]) in historical terms if we continue to view history in a naive empiricistic and sequential way. To borrow standard terms from structuralist theory, derived ultimately from the linguist Ferdinand de Saussure, a history of ideas must be charted diachronically and synchronically, and what is necessary to account for both axes is a methodology recently termed by Ioan Couliano "morphodynamics," that is, a description that considers both the morphology of ideal objects, or systems of ideas, and their complex patterns of interaction in time as they cross the surface of history in an apparently unpredictable way.[6]

One must at the outset recognize the fundamentally syncretistic character of kabbalistic writing and therefore set out to discern multiple tracks, at times intersecting and at other times running parallel. Reflecting on the issue of the ultimate origins of ancient Gnosticism, Robert McL. Wilson observed that it is necessary to recognize several spheres of influence without claiming that any one of them is dominant.[7] Is it not plausible to adopt just such an approach when discussing the problem of the origins of kabbalah? Indeed, the very articulation of the question in this fashion seems to me problematic. By setting the issue in this way one must assume that the particular phenomenon (or class of phenomena) whose origins one is seeking to describe can be defined and de-

[3] *Ha-meyaḥed,* literally, "one who unifies," which I take to mean the one who is united with God, i.e., the mystic.

[4] *Perush le-Sefer Yeṣirah,* attributed to the RABaD, in *Sefer Yeṣirah,* 27a. For further discussion of this text, see Idel, *Kabbalah: New Perspectives,* p. 106.

[5] On Scholem's passionate concern for origins, a concern he shared with Walter Benjamin, see the comments of Handelman, *Fragments of Redemption,* p. 8.

[6] Couliano, *Tree of Gnosis,* pp. 1–22.

[7] See Wilson, "Jewish Christianity and Gnosticism," p. 264.

marcated. But is such a monolithic orientation appropriate to a literature as complex and multifaceted as kabbalah? Would it not be more appropriate to view kabbalah as a religious orientation that expresses itself in various historical manifestations, rather than a historical phenomenon that embraces elements of a religious nature? In the effort to chart the development of kabbalah, we would do better to isolate currents or streams that run through the ever-changing landscape of the relevant texts.

One can distinguish at least four main streams that converged to give shape to medieval kabbalah with respect to the particular issue at hand: images and motifs culled from the aggadic-midrashic literature, Merkavah mysticism, theosophic-mythic speculation preserved in texts like *Sefer ha-Bahir,* and Neoplatonism. Each of these contributed significantly to the characterization of the divine in terms of light imagery. Indeed, the fusion of these different conceptual schemata in the complex symbolism of kabbalah was made possible by the shared acceptance of an ontology of light to characterize both the divine nature and the quintessential human experience of that nature. This is epitomized in one of the more popular etymologies of the key term used to name the divine emanations in kabbalistic texts, the word *sefirot,* said to derive from *sappir,* which means sapphire, conveying the notion of luminosity or "sapphirine reflections."[8] It is this onto-theological presumption that provides the phenomenological datum of the mystical experience: to know God as light is to be mystically illuminated. The point is well captured in this characterization of the divine emanations:

> "And there in a cloud appeared the Presence of the Lord" (Exod. 16:10), in order that the glory that is within it would not be seen, as it says, "He made darkness His screen" (Ps. 18:12), "a cloud and thick darkness are around Him" (Ps. 97:2), that is, surrounding the Holy One, blessed be He, there is a cloud and thick darkness. This is to say, the inner glory that is within it is not seen, even by His servants and messengers who are sent before Him, but the thick darkness itself is the transparent and translucent light, as the sages, blessed be their memory, said in the prayer, "[You appeared to them] in bright clouds,"[9] and these are the *sefirot.* Their light in relation to His light is like the light of the candle in relation to the sun, and they are like a clear glass that shines and illuminates, showing to the eye what is within it. The tenth *sefirah* is the speculum that does not shine, and it is like a glass mirror, and the one who looks at it sees His image within it, and that which is within it is not seen outside it. . . . Therefore this *sefirah* is called the cloud of glory, for the glory is concealed in it. The rabbis, blessed be their memory, called it the speculum that does not shine because of the glory that is hidden within it. When the Holy One, blessed be He, wills to talk to His prophets, this *sefirah* becomes filled from

[8] See Scholem, *Origins,* p. 81; idem, *Kabbalah,* pp. 99–100.

[9] This is taken from the beginning of the *shofarot* section recited in the *musaf* service on Rosh ha-Shanah. Cf. Goldschmidt, *Maḥzor la-Yamim Nora'im,* vol. 1, *Rosh ha-Shanah,* p. 271. The expression *ʿarfale ṭohar* is employed in one of the prayers included in the Hekhalot text *Maʿaseh Merkavah;* cf. Schäfer et al., *Synopse,* § 590.

the inner glory, according to their level, and they hear the word, but the one who speaks is not seen by them, for He is hidden within it.[10]

According to this text, the divine manifestations, referred to on the basis of a standard liturgical expression as "bright clouds" (*ʿarfale ṭohar*), are the covering that hides the inner glory, *kavod penimi.* The function of the clouds, however, is not only to obstruct vision but to allow that which they conceal to be revealed. This is alluded to in the claim that the "thick darkness itself is the transparent and translucent light." The specific locus of the vision is the tenth *sefirah,* the *Shekhinah,* the cloud of glory, for through it the lights above are seen. As is to be expected, the anonymous kabbalist has recast biblical prophecy in light of his own theosophic assumptions. The content of the prophetic vision is thus related to the sefirotic emanations. More specifically, the explanation of the prophetic epiphany offered here preserves the concomitant concealment and disclosure of God, a dialectic that is presented along gender lines. The last of the divine hypostases is feminine in relation to the upper potencies and is thus designated by the talmudic expression "speculum that does not shine."[11] That is, the *Shekhinah* vis-à-vis the rest of the *sefirot* is characterized as pure passivity and receptivity; like a mirror or prism, the *Shekhinah* reflects the luminous but invisible forms from above. The masculine potency is the inner glory that in and of itself is hidden but is revealed through the lower, feminine potency, the cloud of glory. The erotic nuance is underscored by the comment that when God wills to talk to the prophets this emanation becomes filled with that inner glory.[12] The concealed phallus, the ultimate and obsessional object of the mystic's gaze, is specularized through the speculum that resists representational form, as it has nothing of its own.[13] But lacking all form—indeed, constituting the very essence of lack and negativity—allows the feminine to disclose the form of the hidden glory. The divine woman is an "optical apparatus" that refracts the light and renders the veiled image visible, like the rainbow that is manifest in the covering of the cloud.[14] The eye can

[10] MS New York–JTSA Mic. 1727, fols. 18a–b.

[11] B. Yevamot 49b, where Moses is contrasted with all other prophets, inasmuch as he alone saw through a speculum that shines, whereas they perceived the divine through a speculum that does not shine. From the context it is clear that seeing God through the speculum that shines entails, paradoxically, a formless or imageless vision.

[12] See the similar formulation in *Sefer ha-Bahir,* § 130, where the land that is above—i.e., the feminine potency of the divine, corresponding to the land of Israel—is said to be filled from the glory of the name, i.e., the masculine potency.

[13] Here again my analysis has been influenced by the work of Irigaray. See especially *Speculum of the Other Woman,* pp. 144–151. On the concealed nature of the masculine *Yesod* contrasted with the revealed nature of the feminine *Shekhinah,* especially in zoharic literature, see Liebes, "Messiah," pp. 139–140 (English trans., pp. 26–28). See chapter 7, n. 41 of the present work.

[14] Cf. *Zohar* 1:18a–b, and the passage of Joseph of Hamadan cited in chapter 7 at n. 48. To avoid potential misunderstanding let me state emphatically that I do not deny the obvious fact that in kabbalistic sources the *Shekhinah* is represented in the typically feminine images of mother, daughter, and bride. It is necessary, however, to understand these images within the larger androcentric mentality of the medieval kabbalists. As I have argued in several studies and in the next

contemplate the interior image, the speculum that shines, only through the external sheath, the speculum that does not shine. Here we come again upon the fundamental and enduring paradox in the kabbalistic understanding of the mechanics of vision and the implied iconicity of the divine: what has form is invisible and what is visible has no form.

The reinterpretation of prophecy along these lines is, indeed, rather widespread in kabbalistic literature. The implication of such claims is not merely theoretical, but reflects the assumption that contemplation of the *sefirot* was considered a vehicle for prophetic experience.[15] It is appropriate to reiterate Abraham Abulafia's description, mentioned in the introduction to this book, of some of the early theosophic kabbalists as "prophets for themselves."[16] To be sure, Abulafia himself devised a mystical praxis that was primarily concerned with inducing a state of ecstasy defined as prophecy. The gist of his contention against the theosophic kabbalists concerns not the fact that they considered themselves worthy of prophecy but that the principal focus of their experience was visual—the main object of contemplation was the sefirotic lights—whereas for Abulafia and his followers priority was given to the auditory and verbal element of prophecy (even though visualization of the letters of the divine

---

chapter, according to kabbalistic phallocentrism, the feminine is ontologically localized in the male organ. Thus, the engendering mythic structure of kabbalistic symbolism may be referred to as the androgynous phallus. The unification of masculine and feminine symbolically signifies the ontological reintegration of the female to the male. Representations of the *Shekhinah* as an autonomous feminine persona are characteristic of the state of exile and fragmentation. Even the image of the *Shekhinah* as a bride adorned for her wedding is a transition between exile and redemption. The latter is fully represented when the bride enters the nuptial chamber and is transformed therein into the crown of the bridegroom. This transformation represents the final restoration of the female to the male, for the bride has become the corona of the penis. The point is succinctly expressed by Moses de León in *Sefer ha-Mishkal,* p. 115: "Therefore our rabbis, blessed be their memory, would say, 'Come forth, O Bride,' when the Sabbath began and the day was sanctified, like one who waits for the bride to enter the nuptial chamber. But during the day [of Sabbath] the [layer of] dew surrounded their heads and they were crowned by 'a crown of beauty and a diadem of glory' (Isa. 28:5)." Moses de León contrasts the ontic status of the *Shekhinah* on Friday night, the eve of Sabbath, and the day of Sabbath: in the former she is like a bride waiting to enter the nuptial chamber, but in the latter she has been transformed into the crown on the heads of the male rabbis. The quotation from Isaiah suggests an eschatological understanding of this process. In my opinion, as I will argue at length in the next chapter, it is the latter aspect of the feminine that is the ultimate object of visualization in the kabbalistic tradition.

[15] It is clear from the relevant literature that the designation of *Shekhinah* as the locus of vision was not merely a theoretical explanation of biblical prophecy but was considered the medium for mystical visions as well. In one striking example from an actual mystical diary from the period, the *'Oṣar Ḥayyim* of Isaac of Acre, the author reports that a spiritual and distinguished disciple who was also a colleague (*talmid ḥaver ruḥani watiq*) reported that he had a dream in which he saw Isaac writing the words "in the tenth year Elijah the prophet came to me." See MS Moscow-Guenzberg 775, fol. 10b; and Gottlieb, *Studies in the Kabbala Literature,* p. 234. Isaac interprets "the tenth year" as a reference to the *Shekhinah,* the tenth *sefirah,* also alluded to by the fact that there were seven words in the statement and *Shekhinah* is the seventh of the lower *sefirot* that correspond to the seven days of the week. Isaac's point, then, is that the *Shekhinah* is the locus of the *gilluy 'eliyahu,* the revelation of Elijah.

[16] Abulafia's letter *We-Zot li-Yehudah,* p. 16; also cited by Idel, *Mystical Experience,* p. 77.

names in luminous or anthropomorphic forms is not lacking in the ecstatic kabbalah). Abulafia's statement is significant, inasmuch as it accurately reflects the preoccupation of theosophic kabbalists with ocular imagery and the actual visualizing of these divine emanations, a process that they portrayed as a mode of prophecy.

In light of Abulafia's remarks one would do well to recall that the *Zohar* itself occasionally refers to the kabbalists, disciples of R. Simeon bar Yoḥai (sometimes designated as *maskilim,* as will be discussed more fully below), as "true prophets" (*nevi'e mehemne*) upon whom the Holy Spirit dwells.[17] In one context we read, "When the lower splendor, Adonai [i.e., the tenth gradation or *Shekhinah*] joins with the supernal splendor, YHWH [i.e., the sixth gradation or *Tif'eret*] the hidden name [YAHDWNHY, i.e., the combination of the two names[18]] is produced, which the true prophets know and [by means of which] they [visually] contemplate the supernal splendor."[19] In a second passage, which describes the visualization technique of placing a vessel of water in the sunlight, reference is made again to the "true prophets" who contemplate the upper emanations (the central three *sefirot* symbolized by the celestial beasts that bear the throne) through the colors that are reflected in the speculum that does not shine, that is, the *Shekhinah.*[20] I will discuss this passage at greater length in the following chapter; suffice it here to note that the term "true prophets" does not refer to ancient seers but rather to contemporary kabbalists who apprehend the sefirotic lights through specific means of visualization. That theosophic kabbalists assumed the posture of prophets and advocated the possibility of visionary experiences on a par with classical prophecy is evident in the "secret of prophecy" (*sod ha-nevu'ah*), one of a cluster of twenty-four kabbalistic secrets extant in manuscript, composed by Joseph Angeleṭ,[21] who was active in the fourteenth century:

> At the beginning he sees that which is visible, and his power expands to the mind of the One who produced them, and he binds his spirit above, and draws the spring

[17] See *Zohar* 2:154a; Heschel, "On the Holy Spirit," p. 180 n. 24. See also *Zohar* 2:190b, where the spirit of prophecy is said to have rested on Simeon bar Yoḥai, referred to as "the holy lamp." In that context it is evident that the prophetic spirit is connected more specifically with the disclosure of secrets. An actual practice to induce prophecy underlies the description of the garment (*malbush*) in Joseph Gikatilla's *Sod Yod-Gimmel Middot,* in Scholem, *Catalogus,* p. 224. Another attestation in late-thirteenth-century Castile of a technique being utilized to attain prophetic illumination is found in Moses of Burgos's introduction to the kabbalistic reworking of the commentary on the forty-two-letter name. See G. Scholem, "R. Moses of Burgos, the Disciple of R. Isaac," *Tarbiz* 5 (1934): 56–58 (in Hebrew). In this case the means of achieving such a state were related specifically to recitation of the divine names, reminiscent of the German Pietists and Abraham Abulafia, who may have been the teacher of Moses of Burgos. See Idel, *Mystical Experience,* p. 19.

[18] See Verman, "The Development of Yiḥudim in Spanish Kabbalah," pp. 32–33.

[19] *Zohar* 1:110b.

[20] *Zohar Ḥadash* 39d. See also *Zohar* 2:245a.

[21] On the attribution of these kabbalistic secrets to Joseph Angeleṭ, see Idel, "Types of Redemptive Activity in the Middle Ages," p. 264 n. 46. See also the comments of Liebes in "How the Zohar Was Written," pp. 64–65 n. 293 (English trans., p. 225 n. 298).

> downward. Initially he thinks about the reasons for that which is revealed, and afterwards, bit by bit, [he considers] that which is hidden. For this he needs [to be like] clear glass, so that foul material will not impede [his] comprehension. . . . And the enlightened one of a good intellect (*ha-maskil sekhel ṭov*)[22] should purify his body and sanctify it from impurity, and cleanse his palms, as it is written, "He who has clean hands" (Ps. 24:4), and he should purify his inside as his outside, as it is written, "and a pure heart" (ibid.). Then "he shall carry away (*yissa'*) a blessing" (ibid., 5), the secret of prophecy, as it says, "Portions were served (*wa-yissa' mas'ot*) from his table; but Benjamin's portion was several times that of anyone else" (Gen. 43:34).[23]

It is obvious that in the above passage Angeleṭ is not talking about a process limited to the classical prophets in the ancient past of Israelite history. Rather, he is addressing "contemporary" prophets who are the enlightened mystics (*maskilim*). Angeleṭ describes their prophetic experience as a contemplative ascent (reminiscent of the Geronese mystics, to be discussed in the following section) resulting in the binding of the human and divine minds, a process that is set into motion through visualization exercises, moving from what is revealed to what is hidden. Indeed, Angeleṭ alludes to the fact that the mystic himself becomes a medium for visualization with his reference to the clear glass (*zekhukhit levanah*),[24] a term he uses elsewhere in this text to convey the idea that a human being can become a physical vessel to receive the divine influx.[25] Finally, he specifies the need for purificatory rites that the mystic must undertake if he is to receive the prophetic inspiration. There is no distinction here between prophet and mystic, at least not in terms of the possibility of visually comprehending and being in communion with the divine. Although Scholem tries, from the vantage point of his own systematic categorization of the three stages in the historical development of religion, to distinguish between prophetic revelation and mystical experience, he admits that in the case of some sources it is often difficult to maintain such a distinction, for the prophet is often portrayed as the perfect mystic of any given ideological system. Yet, as will be seen momentarily, Scholem is not always consistent on this matter and often takes what seems to me to be a rather rationalistic approach in his treatment of the visionary aspect of the kabbalistic tradition.

[22] The expression is based on 2 Chron. 30:22.

[23] MSS Oxford-Bodleian 1630, fols. 57a–b; New York–JTSA Mic. 1915, fols. 26a–b.

[24] This term had already been used in one talmudic passage in the sense of a medium for visualization; cf. B. Megillah 6a, reiterated in *Bemidbar Rabbah* 13:16. See also the intriguing comment in P. Sukkah 4:7, 54d, to the effect that since the destruction of the Temple, coagulated wine (*yayin qarush;* cf. B. Sukkah 12a) and clear glass (*zekhukhit levanah*) have ceased to exist. In the continuation of the passage it is further explained that the reference is specifically to clear glass that is layered or coiled up (*she-hayetah mitqappelet*). Cf. *Midrash 'Eikhah Rabbah* 4:2, ed. Buber, p. 144; B. Soṭah 48b. See also comment of Rashi cited in chapter 5, n. 334.

[25] Cf. MS Oxford-Bodleian 1610. fol. 55a, where Aaron, Moses, and Miriam are said to have been "like clear glass, prepared to receive the divine overflow that illuminated them." See also fol. 55b, where the talmudic statement regarding the disappearance of clear glass with the destruction of the Temple (see previous note) is reinterpreted along this line.

While the kabbalists were clearly interested in speculating on and developing the metaphysical intricacies of their theosophic doctrines, underlying these speculations was a deeply experiential (and predominantly visual) component, a point often overlooked in scholarly accounts of kabbalistic literature. For his part, Scholem fluctuates between a genuine appreciation of the mystical underpinning of theosophical gnosis and a more restrained attitude toward kabbalistic texts. For example, he describes the *Zohar* in the following way: "If I were asked to characterize in one word the essential traits of the world of Kabbalistic thought, those which set it apart from other forms of Jewish mysticism, I would say that the Zohar represents Jewish theosophy, i.e., a Jewish form of theosophy." Scholem clarifies his terminology by noting that "theosophy signifies a mystical doctrine, or school of thought, which purports to perceive and to describe the mysterious workings of the Divinity, perhaps also believing it possible to become absorbed in its contemplation. Theosophy postulates a kind of divine emanation whereby God, abandoning his self-contained repose, awakens to mysterious life; further, it maintains that the mysteries of creation reflect the pulsation of this divine life."[26] It is evident that in this context Scholem places great emphasis on the experiential dimension of theosophy: the theosophist does not merely describe the workings of the divine; he perceives them and may even be absorbed in contemplation. While it may be the true that in the history of kabbalah an original perception of God was externalized and transformed into mere book learning, in the case of the *Zohar* the object of gnosis, the *sefirot,* "still had the unbroken reality of mystical experience."[27] It may not be inappropriate here to recall Scholem's characterization of ancient "gnosis" as a "mystical esotericism for the elect based on illumination and the acquisition of a higher knowledge of things heavenly and divine."[28] In a fundamental sense, this seems to be an accurate reflection of Scholem's own view regarding kabbalistic gnosis. Elsewhere Scholem similarly acknowledges that ecstatic mystical experiences may lie at the bottom of many kabbalistic writings, for the visionary element breaks through time and again, even though most kabbalists were reticent to discuss such experiences at length. Notwithstanding this recognition of the visual underpinning of theosophic gnosis, Scholem concludes that kabbalistic meditation and contemplation assumed a "more spiritualized aspect." Scholem singles out the *Zohar* by noting that mystical ecstasy plays an insignificant role in this work. He even goes on to suggest that part of the success of the *Zohar* can be traced to this attitude of restraint, which presumably struck a familiar chord in the Jewish heart.[29]

It is possible that one could remove the contradiction here by stating that Scholem distinguishes between ecstasy proper, involving an ascent or translation to otherworldly realms, and mystical experience of the *sefirot,* although I am not inclined to resolve the tension in this way. It seems, rather, that Scholem

[26] *Major Trends,* pp. 205–206.
[27] Ibid., p. 207.
[28] *Jewish Gnosticism,* p. 1.
[29] *Major Trends,* pp. 121–123.

affirms contradictory positions, on the one hand asserting that mystical experience underlies the zoharic theosophy, and on the other denying that ecstasy figures prominently in this book. The force of his denial of the mystical or ecstatic component is captured in his claim that kabbalistic contemplation takes on a more spiritualized aspect. What Scholem intends by this expression is made clear in another passage, where he is even more emphatic in his denial of the visionary element in theosophic kabbalah. In that context Scholem asserts that the contemplation of the *sefirot* has nothing to do with visions but is solely a matter of intellectual ascent. Meditation in the kabbalistic tradition is an activation of the intellect rather than the imagination.[30]

From these remarks it would appear that in Scholem's assessment, kabbalah is first and foremost an intellectual discipline that provides one with knowledge of the divine and its relationship to humanity—particularly the Jewish people—and the world. Kabbalistic texts, according to this reading, place primary emphasis not on experience and praxis but on theory, a body of esoteric lore, a specific program of study characterized by a system of symbolism, and a derivative method of exegesis. Most striking is Scholem's claim that concentration on theosophic matters is solely a matter of intellect. This flies in the face of the explicit claim of many kabbalists that the esoteric lore is not attained through the exercise of reason but rather as a received tradition—hence the force of the very term "kabbalah."

While the critical scholar may raise doubts regarding the historical legitimacy of these claims, it is nevertheless the case that most kabbalists accorded, at best, a secondary role to intellect. From their viewpoint it is simply incorrect to locate the locus of contemplation of the *sefirot* in the intellect. Indeed, Scholem's statement that meditation initially activates the imagination and subsequently the intellect reflects his own rational bias, which cannot be upheld in the face of the overwhelming textual evidence. As I will argue below, in a considerable number of kabbalistic texts priority is given to imagination as the primary means for attaining visionary gnosis of the divine pleroma, which cannot be perceived by the senses or conceived by the intellect. The imagination is elevated to a position of utmost supremacy; it is, in effect, the divine element of the soul, which enables one to gain access to the realm of incorporeality.

Indeed, sufficient textual evidence exists to demonstrate that from the early stages of the development of kabbalistic thought and practice in the formative period (twelfth to fourteenth centuries) a central role was accorded the imagination as the means by which one visualized (the operative term is *leṣayyer*) the sefirotic lights or letters of the divine names and thereby attained a state of prophecy or ecstatic ascent to the higher realms of being.[31] Any experience of

[30] *Kabbalah,* p. 370.

[31] Some of these techniques have been discussed by Idel in *Kabbalah: New Perspectives,* pp. 104–106; see idem "Kabbalistic Prayer and Colors"; idem, *Mystical Experience,* pp. 30–37. And see the text published by Idel, "Intention and Colors," pp. 1–14. According to this text, the visualization of the sefirotic lights is achieved by means of imagining the letters of the Tetragammaton in terms of various permutations, which in turn are correlated with different colors.

the *sefirot* that is referred to as mystical must involve some sort of imaginative translation into the divine pleroma, which is, properly speaking, an ecstatic state. Through the activation of the imagination an intermediate position between the spiritual and physical worlds is attained, inasmuch as the former is visualized in terms of the latter. It would not be inappropriate, in my opinion, to designate the sefirotic pleroma by the technical Sufi term *ʿālam al-mithāl* (*mundus imaginalis*), translated in some kabbalistic sources as *ʿolam ha-demut,* "the world of the imagination." While this technical terminology was indeed employed by ecstatic kabbalists under the direct influence of Sufism,[32] I would extend its application to the theosophic kabbalists as well, for from a phenomenological perspective the sefirotic pleroma comprises the imaginal archetypes of the spiritual forms of divinity.

A particularly poignant expression of the central role accorded the imagination in kabbalistic epistemology is found in the following commentary in the *Zohar* on Prov. 31:23, "her husband is known in the gates" (*nodaʿ ba-sheʿarim baʿlah*): "This refers to the Holy One, blessed be He, who is known and comprehended according to what one imagines in one's heart (*lefum mah dimeshaʿer be-libbeih*), each one according to what one can comprehend through the spirit of wisdom, and according to what one imagines in one's heart, so [God] is known in one's heart. Therefore, [He] is known in the gates, in these imaginings, but no one can comprehend and know Him as He is."[33] The word *shaʿar,* "gate," is here associated with the word *shaʿer,* "to imagine," a wordplay that enables the zoharic authorship to affirm a view clearly docetic in its orientation. That is, one knows the divine in accordance with what one imagines in one's heart (and, as will be seen in detail in the next chapter, mystical gnosis in the *Zohar* is almost always visionary in nature), but God as he is in his true essence is unknowable. Thus, the intent of the biblical idiom "God is known in the gates," is that the divine *sefirot* are depicted in the gates of the imagination. Simply put, imagination provides the vehicle through which one can have access to God. In the absence of imagination there is no form, and without form there is no vision and hence no knowledge. Indeed, the *Zohar* abounds with detailed, graphic descriptions of the sefirotic realm, at times articulating an intensely anthropomorphic theosophy. Knowledge of the divine realm is mediated through the visionary imagination. It is thus difficult to verify Scholem's view from the sources themselves.

I would like to emphasize here that there is sufficient textual evidence to suggest that the study of the *sefirot* itself, as viewed from within the tradition, was considered an exercise in imaginary visualization. Speculation on the *sefirot* was intended to provide a vehicle for experience as the assumption of the

[32] See Idel, "Mundus Imaginalis and Likkute HaRan," pp. 73–89.

[33] *Zohar* 1:103b. See Matt, *Zohar: The Book of the Enlightenment,* p. 66, and relevant notes on p. 221. The author of the *Zohar* employs a similar locution to explain the phenomenology of dreams; see *Zohar* 1:149a, 194a. See also the description of the second emanation, *Ḥokhmah,* in an anonymous kabbalistic text, MS Oxford-Bodleian 1938, fols. 64b–65a: "We have permission to meditate upon it in the heart, for thought can imagine it and give it a measure in the heart."

kabbalists was that these emanations constitute the *deus revelatus*. Lest I risk being labelled a reductionist on this point, let me emphasize that I am not suggesting that every kabbalist assumed the same thing with respect to the nature of the divine pleroma and its visibility. There are, to be sure, important differences in details from one kabbalist to another. And if, as the old saying goes, God lives in the details, then it is certainly the case that the portrait of God in kabbalistic documents depends very much on the rich details that vary from source to source. Yet it seems to me that there is a shared presumption in the theosophical kabbalah regarding the *sefirot* as the visible aspect of the hidden God—bracketing for a moment the philosophical consideration of whether one adopts an essentialist or instrumentalist view of the divine emanations.[34] To put the matter somewhat differently, the *sefirot* constitute the theophanic image that represents the visible shape assumed by the hidden Godhead. The emanative process, therefore, should be viewed as the projection of the imageless divine into an image.

A striking metaphor conveying the mythical notion of the unfolding of the imageless One is employed in a kabbalistic text, *Midrash R. Shimʿon ha-Ṣaddiq* (the "Midrash of R. Simeon the Just"), part of the literary corpus known as *sifre ha-ʿiyyun,* the "Books of Contemplation."[35] According to this composition, the Primordial Ether, also identified as the Holy Spirit, is described as a "mirror through which everything[36] is manifest to all creatures. . . . Thus they said that before the creation of the world . . . the Primordial Ether (*ha-ʾawir ha-qadmon*) was alone . . . and the power of the Holy One, blessed be He, was hidden within it. His glory was not recognized at all until this Ether split and His splendor was seen and His glory revealed. At that moment He brought forth one potency and He called it Primordial Wisdom (*ḥokhmah qedumah*)."[37]

In a separate study I have focused on the specifically feminine nature of the Primordial Ether in the Iyyun material.[38] The gender issue is especially relevant

[34] For a review of the different theoretical conceptions of the *sefirot,* see Scholem, *Kabbalah,* pp. 96–116; Idel, *Kabbalah: New Perspectives,* pp. 136–153.

[35] The two most comprehensive studies of these mystical compostions are Scholem, *Origins,* pp. 309–362, and Verman, *Books of Contemplation.* On the particular source, the "Midrash of R. Simeon the Righteous," and its place in the Iyyun corpus, see Scholem, *Reshit ha-Qabbalah,* p. 256 n. 3.

[36] Following the reading in the two manuscripts that I consulted: *she-ha-kol,* i.e., everything. See, however, the reading in the printed version found in Moses Boṭarel's commentary on *Sefer Yeṣirah* 39c: *she-ha-ʾel,* i.e., God. According to this reading the Primordial Ether is the mirror through which the divine reality itself is manifest.

[37] MSS Munich 215, fols. 292b–293a; Oxford-Bodleian 1960, fol. 152a. The text has been cited and analyzed by Scholem; see references in n. 39. On the role of the Primordial Ether in the Iyyun material, see Scholem, *Origins,* pp. 331–347; Verman, *Books of Contemplation,* pp. 153–156.

[38] See Wolfson, "Erasing the Erasure / Gender and the Writing of God's Body in Kabbalistic Symbolism." See especially the text transcribed and translated in Verman, *Books of Contemplation,* pp. 202–203, wherein the Primordial Ether is described as a female androgyne: "sometimes she is emanated and sometimes she emanated; sometimes she is influenced and sometimes she influences. She is two-faced: the tree of life and the tree of knowledge."

in the above passage, inasmuch as the Primordial Ether is described as the mirror through which everything is seen. Again, it can be seen that the role of iconic representation—the objective pole of the ocularcentric gaze—is attributed to the feminine. What is perhaps even more intriguing is the fact that here this function is expressed through the image of the splitting open of the Ether to reveal the glory hidden within it. Both Scholem and Pines have suggested that the image of the split Ether is derived from the poetry of Solomon ibn Gabirol, whereas Liebes has argued that this image (in ibn Gabirol and the Iyyun texts) reflects the myth of the cosmic egg in ancient Orphic cosmogony.[39] Leaving aside the question of the historical feasibility of Liebes's argument, there can be little doubt regarding the validity of the comparison from an ideational perspective. That is, in the Iyyun sources, as well as in the zoharic material based thereon, the image of the splitting of the Primordial Ether conveys the notion of the division of the primordial androgyne into a masculine and feminine polarity. For our purposes it is significant that in the kabbalistic material the cosmogonic myth is understood in essentially visual terms: the breaking of the etḥeral covering (symbolic of the vagina) accounts first and foremost for the disclosure of the glory (the male organ) that was concealed within the hidden depths of the Godhead. The initial act of creation is a self-impregnation that results in the extension of the Infinite into the finite, the splintering of the imageless One into a multiplicity of forms. Through the feminine speculum the masculine form is revealed.

It is evident from other texts belonging to the Iyyun corpus that the myth of the primary fissure is employed to explain the visual projection of the divine. For example, in an Iyyun work that reflects a more standard sefirotic terminology, *Sefer ha-Yiḥud* (the "Book of Unity"),[40] the first of the emanations, *Keter* (Crown), is described as the "encompassing resplendent light in which there is made a kind of cleavage[41] that changes from one matter to another until it splits. Through this splitting the ten emanations (*sefirot*) come to be from the flux (*meshekh*) that issues from it."[42] In the commentary on the ten *sefirot* from the same literary corpus we read, "This Ether is the name of the Holy One, blessed be He . . . and when it arose in His thought to bring forth His actions the Ether split, then His splendor was perceptible and the glory of the Holy One, blessed be He, was seen, and He brought forth these matters and

[39] Scholem, "Traces of Gabirol in the Kabbalah," p. 168; idem, *Origins*, pp. 341–343; Pines, "He Called Forth to the Nothing and It Split"; Liebes, "Kabbalistic Myth of Orpheus," pp. 445–446 (English trans., pp. 82–83). See idem, "Tsaddiq Yesod Olam," p. 102 n. 160, where Liebes remarks on the "mythical catastrophe" that is expressed by the use of the image of the breaking forth (*beqiʿah*), found in kabbalistic sources from the Iyyun circle and zoharic texts of the thirteenth century as well as Sabbatian authors of the seventeenth century.

[40] See Scholem, *Reshit ha-Qabbalah*, p. 258 n. 13.

[41] The word I have rendered as "cleavage" is *ṣedeq*. It is possible that in this context the term is meant to convey the image of a sieve, usually called in the Hebrew source *kevarah*. On the symbol of the sieve for the vagina, see Halperin, "A Sexual Image."

[42] MSS Paris–BN 825, fol. 202b; Vatican 211, fol. 4a. The text is quoted by Pines in "He Called Forth to the Nothing," p. 339 n. 2.

they are the ten *sefirot belimah.*"[43] The splitting of the Ether signifies the opening of the feminine that allows the masculine splendor to be seen in the image of the ten luminous emanations.

Similar imagery is employed in other theosophic kabbalistic texts as well, for the sefirotic edifice is the self-configuration of the divine. From a philosophical standpoint, the revelatory experience of the kabbalists is a mirror image of the myth of origins that is projected onto the divine. That is, just as the concealedness of the male is disclosed through the opening of the feminine when the Infinite breaks through its own aura, so, too, the mystic below visually apprehends the hidden male through the prism of the feminine. In light of this fundamental aspect of the life-world of the kabbalists, the characterization of kabbalistic literature as merely theoretical simply misses the mark. In a text that appears to be quite early, the centrality of vision within a theosophic context is unambiguously affirmed: "These are the ten *sefirot* in which God, blessed be He, is seen, and by means of them He governs the worlds."[44] The mystical underpinning of theosophic gnosis is illustrated in a striking way as well in the following passage, attributed to the kabbalist Joseph ben Ḥayyim: "Therefore I will explain the ten *sefirot,* the divine principles, according to the kabbalah, so that one may cleave to them, as it is written, 'This is my God and I will glorify Him' (Exod. 15:2), [the word *we-'anvehu,* 'I will glorify Him,' can be read as] I and He (*'ani we-hu'*).[45] When one cleaves to them [the *sefirot*], the divine Holy Spirit enters into him, in all his sensations and all his movements."[46] This kabbalist explicitly announces his intention in explaining the ten *sefirot,* namely, to enable the reader of his text to cleave to these paradigms that correspond to various human activities.[47] The illuminative nature of kabbalistic wisdom is also apparent in an anonymous commentary on the *sefirot,* written in all probability in Castile in the latter part of the thirteenth century:[48]

> I will enlighten you and lead you in this way, to inform you of the mystery of unity (*sod ha-yiḥud*) through which the King is unified and the knowledge of His truth through which He is elevated, to show you the force of His comprehension, the wealth of the glory of His splendor and His kingdom, and the majesty of the splendor of His greatness in all the places of His dominion. I will show you the splendor to secure you in the Supernal Crown [first *sefirah*], to cover you in the splendor of the faithful Wisdom [second *sefirah*], to open for you the gates of

[43] *Catalogus Codium Cabbalisticorum Hebraicorum,* p. 204; also quoted by Scholem in "Traces of Gabirol," p. 168 n. 31.

[44] MS New York–JTSA Mic. 1805, fol. 14b.

[45] Cf. M. Sukkah 4:5.

[46] MS Paris–BN 843, fol. 37a. See also MS New York–JTSA Mic. 1885, fols. 74b–75a (previously cited by Idel; see following note).

[47] See Idel, *Kabbalah: New Perspectives* p. 350 n. 333, where he cites the relevant passage from the JTSA manuscript (see previous note) and remarks on the similarity between the approaches of Joseph ben Ḥayyim and Abulafia, related especially to the discussion of the ten *sefirot* as human activities and the emphasis placed on cleaving to them.

[48] See Scholem, "Index to the Commentaries on the Ten *Sefirot,*" p. 18.

> Understanding [third *sefirah*], to allow you to cleave to the attributes of Mercy, Strength, and Beauty [fourth to sixth *sefirot*], to make you take delight in Eternity, Majesty, the Foundation, and the Crown [seventh to tenth *sefirot*]. Then your soul will don the garment of splendor and beauty, grace and love, and you will be crowned with the resplendent light that surrounds the Presence, and this is the secret in which is contained the mystery of the upper and lower knowledge.[49]

The goal of gnosis of the sefirotic pleroma is the unitive experience with the Presence, the last of the ten emanations, which is here characterized as the donning of the garment and the wearing of the crown of resplendent light. Time and again in kabbalistic texts, union with the *Shekhinah* is depicted in terms of this imagery, especially the crown.[50]

What is essential to emphasize in this context is that the unitive or illuminative experience results from a visual knowledge of the *sefirot*, a knowledge that scholars all too often consider merely theoretical or discursive in nature. Thus R. J. Zwi Werblowsky, utilizing Rudolf Otto's distinction between mysticism and theosophy, concludes that the ecstatic experiences cultivated by sixteenth-century kabbalists served only as a means for gnosis or esoteric knowledge. Generalizing from this observation Werblowsky contests the view expressed by Scholem that "under the cover of the bewildering and often bizarre theosophical speculations of the kabbalists there hides a genuinely mystical life." Werblowsky offers the following critique, focusing primarily on Lurianic kabbalah: "The fact remains, nevertheless, that the discursive and even dialectical elements are so prominent in kabbalistic literature that we may almost speak of an intellectualistic hypertrophy. . . . More often than not kabbalistic literature is less the record of the *cognitio experimentalis dei* than the substitution of a theosophical *pilpul* for the halakhic one of the rabbinic lawyers."[51] Scholem's formulation is closer to the mark, though he is not always consistent on this point, as I noted above. Indeed, in a later characterization of the theosophic element in kabbalah Scholem seems to embrace the very formulation of Werblowsky: "Speculations of this type occupy a large and conspicuous area in kabbalistic teaching. Sometimes their connection with the mystical plane be-

[49] MS Milan-Ambrosiana 62, fol. 118a.

[50] See, e.g., the interpretation of the passage in the Sabbath liturgy describing Moses, "a crown of splendor (*kelil tif'eret*) You placed on his head," extant in MS Vatican 231, fol. 109a: "For he was united with *Malkhut,* and the crown of splendor is *Yesod,* placed on top of *Malkhut,* which was on his head." The feminine Presence sits atop the head of Moses (or the mystic), and the crown on the head of the Presence is the masculine gradation, *Yesod,* that corresponds to the phallus. Cf. the interpretation of this liturgical passage in Judah ben Yaqar, *Perush ha-Tefillot we-ha-Berakhot,* pt. 1, p. 104, discussed in Wolfson, "Female Imaging of the Torah," pp. 292–293. See also the secret related to the crown of Moses (*kelil moshe*) in MS Oxford-Bodleian 2396, fols. 4b–5a, where the image of the crown is explicitly connected to the motif of communion (*devequt*) with the divine.

[51] Werblowsky, *Joseph Karo,* p. 40; see, however, p. 50, where Werblowsky describes the process of "automatic thinking" operative in the kabbalists in sixteenth-century Safed, i.e., a method of producing discursive, intellectual doctrines in a spontaneous manner without any conscious effort or intention. In such a case, it would appear, the primary issue is the mystical experience of receiving a supernatural revelation, not the discursive knowledge that results therefrom.

comes rather tenuous and is superseded by an interpretative and homiletical vein which occasionally even results in a kind of kabbalistic *pilpul* (casuitry)."[52]

It is, however, misconceived to isolate—in the kabbalistic tradition in general and in Lurianic kabbalah in particular—theosophic gnosis from mystical ecstasy. Indeed, the literature of the kabbalists, especially the disciples of Luria, is precisely what Werblowsky says it is not, namely, the record of their experiential knowledge of God. To the outsider it may appear that kabbalistic texts are an exercise in dialectics, a thicket of theosophical ruminations that conceal the living face of divine reality. But to the initiate these texts are a mapping of the divine, an iconic representation by means of which one is afforded an opportunity to behold the luminous presence of God. Theosophic kabbalah is, as Scholem correctly observed with respect to Luria, a kind of "visionary thinking" that evolves from "mystical inspiration."[53] Scholem's own characterization of ancient Gnosticism, to which I have already referred, as a mystical esotericism based on illumination that results in a higher form of knowledge, is a perfectly apt description of theosophic kabbalah in its classical manifestations. This body of lore, too, is predicated on a mystical esotericism that is based not on reason or logical discourse but rather on illumination from above that leads the adept to the acquisition of a higher knowledge of things heavenly and divine. Possession of secret gnosis is what distinguishes the kabbalist from other members of the religious community, and this gnosis is decidedly experiential, involving a visionary quality that in some cases is described in unitive terms.

The visual dimension of kabbalistic gnosis is captured by kabbalists' technical designation *maskilim*, the "enlightened ones," based on Dan. 12:3, "and the enlightened will shine like the splendor of the firmament." The term *maskil*, the active participle of the verb *lehaskil*, is applied to the kabbalists in a technical sense, for they have a vision of the divine realities. In that regard the term *histakkelut* has the connotation of contemplative vision in a way that parallels *contemplatio* in the Latin Neoplatonic tradition, translating the Greek *theoria*.[54] At the heart of the kabbalist's *Weltanschauung* lies ecstatic vision; indeed, the phenomenological boundaries of his world, axiologically and ontically, are determined precisely by this visual relationship. Moreover, the ocularcentric orientation of theosophic kabbalists is related to a phallocentrism that informs every aspect of their religious thinking and practice. Not limited, like the rest of the Jewish males, by temporal or spatial constraints, the kabbalist places the vision of God at the center of his worship; indeed, his worship is

[52] *Kabbalah*, p. 4; see also Idel, "Defining Kabbalah," p. 98.

[53] *Major Trends*, pp. 255, 258.

[54] See Sed-Rajna, "L'influence de Jean Scot sur la doctrine du kabbaliste Azriel de Gérone," p. 455 nn. 5–6. See also Scholem, *Origins*, p. 224; Pedaya, " 'Flaw' and 'Correction'," p. 211 n. 96. Particularly relevant is the description of the masters of esoteric lore given by Shem Ṭov ibn Gaon in *Badde ha-'Aron u-Migdal Ḥananel*, p. 47: "the enlightened kabbalists upon whom the pure spirit appeared" (*ha-maskilim ha-mequbbalim 'asher hofi'a 'aleihem ruaḥ ṭahorah*). Compare the passage from Moses of Burgos cited in chapter 7, n. 149.

determined by the very vision that involves the dialectic of the male seeing and being seen. The point is dramatically underscored in a passage from an anonymous Castilian kabbalistic text, *Sefer ha-Yiḥud* (the "Book of Unity"), in which the author struggles with the obvious clash between traditional aniconism and the visionary demands of mystical gnosis: "How can faint and weary eyes see the faces that see but are not seen? . . . But permission to see and to contemplate is attained by those worthy 'to behold the king in his beauty' (Isa. 33:17). They enter the chamber of the king and 'eat of its luscious fruit' (Cant. 4:16), and they delight in the entertainment of the bridegroom and bride."[55] The kabbalists are designated as those worthy of beholding the king in his beauty, for the visionary element is an essential feature of their spiritual being. The mystics experience what is withheld from others: they see the faces that see but are not seen, that is, the sefirotic emanations, which collectively constitute the countenance of God. Significantly, the visual encounter is described, partially on the basis of the verse from Canticles, as a partaking of the fruit inside the king's chamber. It is obvious that this image metaphorically represents the erotic union of the mystic with the divine Presence. The visionary consumption that the mystic enjoys is linked, moreover, to the sacred union of the masculine and feminine aspects of the Godhead. In the final analysis, the object of the mystic's gaze is the divine phallus, cryptically alluded to in the biblical idiom of seeing the king in his beauty. That is, the beauty of the king is the aspect of God that corresponds to the male organ exposed when there is union above. This is the implication of the mystic's taking delight in the joyful play of the bridegroom and bride. The intensely erotic element of the mystical vision is connected to the phallus in a twofold way: it is by virtue of the phallus that the mystic is granted permission to see what is obscured in the ordinary field of human experience and that which is seen is the divine phallus disclosed in the moment of coitus. The erotic and basically phallic nature of vision that informs the phenomenological foundation of the kabbalistic understanding of mystical vision is epitomized in a comment of Elijah ben Solomon Zalman, the Gaon of Vilna (1720–1797): "It is known that all union is dependent on sight, as it is written, '[When the bow is in the cloud] I will see it and remember the everlasting covenant . . . [the sign of the] covenant that I have established' (Gen. 9:16–17). It is known that the establishment of the covenant (*haqamat berit*) is in [sexual] copulation."[56] The biblical idiom, *haqamat ha-berit,* is here understood as signifying the erection of the penis that is necessary for sexual intercourse, and that is dependent on the vision of the bow in the cloud: the union

[55] MS Vatican 236, fol. 164a. It is relevant to note that the expression "entertainment of the bridegroom and bride" (*mazmuṭe ḥatan we-khallah*) appears in B. Ḥagigah 14b in conjunction with the description of the gathering of the ministering angels to hear the exegetical discourse on the chariot by R. Joshua in the presence of R. Joseph ha-Kohen. The author of *Sefer ha-Yiḥud* has appropriated this expression and applied it specifically to the sexual union of the divine bridegroom and bride. The role of the mystic as the intermediary that facilitates the *hieros gamos,* a fairly common idea in kabbalistic literature, is expressed in another passage in *Sefer-ha-Yiḥud;* cf. MS Vatican 236, fols. 171a–b. On eating as a metaphor for sexual union and mystical communion, see n. 90, below.

[56] *Be'ur ha-Gera le-Sifra di-Ṣeni*ʿuta, 2b.

of the masculine in the feminine. In the phenomenal plane of kabbalistic ritual and myth, eros and vision are harnessed in an inseparable bond.

Although theosophic kabbalists in general placed the vision of God at the center of their religious existence, it should be noted that some kabbalists emphasized the supremacy of the auditory over the visual as the primary epistemological mode.[57] Indeed, as Scholem notes, the two main competing images characterizing the *sefirot* in the early kabbalistic sources were visual (light) and auditory (letters and sounds). Although the two systems were often meshed together, one can still discern a pattern in some kabbalists that indicates a priority given to the faculty of hearing over seeing.[58] Other kabbalists, by contrast, affirmed the superiority of the eye over the ear.[59] (In this respect the kabbalistic literature reflects a contemporary debate in medieval Jewish philosophy, with some philosophers privileging the sense of hearing as the primary epistemological mode and others the sense of sight.[60]) In still other kabbalistic sources the sefirotic emanations are said to be experienced concomitantly as audible voices and visible lights. Mystical knowledge, in contrast to normal modes of perception, entails synesthesia, wherein the two epistemic modes converge and interpenetrate.[61] It seems to me, therefore, that even in those contexts that indicate the supremacy of hearing over seeing, the two systems,

[57] The privileging of the auditory over the visual is evident in several passages in *Sefer ha-Bahir* (§§ 69–70, 79, 88) that reflect a later Provençal redaction. See Scholem, *Reshit ha-Qabbalah,* pp. 62–63; Pedaya, "Provençal Stratum in the Redaction of *Sefer ha-Bahir,*" pp. 154–155. According to a tradition expressed in a variety of bahiric passages, gnosis of God is attained through the ear, which structurally corresponds to the letter *'alef,* which symbolically depicts the first of the emanations, divine Thought. Cf. the text of Azriel of Gerona in Scholem, "Traditions of R. Jacob and R. Isaac ben Jacob ha-Kohen," pp. 233–234. On the privileging of hearing, consider also this statement in MS Oxford-Bodleian 1938, fol. 6a: "The reason why Israel placed 'we will do' before 'we will hear' is that hearing is closer to the level of the soul, for hearing is spiritual and the soul is spiritual." Finally, we find the view expressed by certain kabbalists that the primacy accorded to the auditory over the visual is related to the presumed oral nature of kabbalah. That is, the reception of esoteric knowledge through oral transmission is placed on a higher cognitive level than mystical vision. Gnosis is attained not as a consequence of one's own personal visions, but only through direct contact with an authoritative master. See, e.g., the text of R. Jonathan, *'Or ha-Sekhel,* MS New York–JTSA Mic. 1831, fol. 3b; Isaac of Acre, *Me'irat 'Einayim,* p. 11.

[58] In a number of early Geronese texts the faculty of sight is associated with the feminine potency and the faculty of hearing with the masculine. See, e.g., MS Oxford-Bodleian 1945, fols. 58b, 59b–60a, 61a; Jacob ben Sheshet, *Sefer ha-'Emunah we-ha-Biṭṭaḥon* 12, ed. Chavel, p. 288; idem, *Meshiv Devarim Nekhoḥim,* ed. Vajda, p. 189. See also Baḥya ben Asher's commentaries to Gen. 29:32 (ed. Chavel, 1:259), Exod. 4:11 (2:37), Num. 27:13 (3:197), and his statement in *Kad ha-Qemaḥ* cited by Kaufmann, *Die Sinne,* pp. 142–143 n. 8. See Recanaṭi, *Perush 'al ha-Torah* 29d–30a, 90c.

[59] See, e.g., "Commentary of R. Isaac of Acre to the First Chapter of *Sefer Yeṣirah,*" pp. 389–390; *'Oṣar Ḥayyim.* MS Moscow-Guenzberg 775, fol. 47a. It is noteworthy that in this mystical diary R. Isaac records both visual and auditory revelations. See Gottlieb, *Studies in the Kabbala Literature,* pp. 231–234.

[60] See Kaufmann, *Sinne,* pp. 140–143.

[61] Cf. *Sefer ha-'Orah* of Jacob ben Jacob ha-Kohen, MS Milan-Ambrosiana 62, fol. 88b: "The voices were changing of themselves in black and white fire like the letters of the tablets [were written] black fire upon white fire, inclining towards the redness."

light and sound, are so conflated that it is impossible to speak of hearing the divine voices without seeing them. The question that remains to be asked concerns the exact nature of that visual experience. In truth, no one approach was adopted universally and categorically by the kabbalists. On the contrary, we find a range of opinions involving, most typically, contemplative vision, imaginative vision, and, in some rare cases, physical vision.[62] In the remainder of this chapter I will explore in detail the mode of imaginary visualization of the sefirotic potencies in selected kabbalistic texts, for I consider that epistemic mode to be the most important form of visual representation of God in the relevant literature.

Prophecy, Mystical Vision, and Contemplation: Imagination and the Visio Spiritualis in Thirteenth-Century Kabbalah

It is evident from some of the earliest sources, as I have already noted, that the kabbalists considered visionary gnosis of the *sefirot* phenomenologically on a par with prophetic experience, which was understood to be a contemplative or mental vision. For example, Isaac the Blind of Provence comments that the vision (*ṣefiyyah*) of the *sefirot* is the "contemplation of one thing from another" (*hitbonenut davar mitokh davar*), for the vision consists of the fact that "each cause [i.e., *sefirah*] receives from the cause above it, for the attribute [or measure, *middah*] draws from the attribute that is hewn, and that which is hewn from the engraved, and that which is engraved from the inscribed, and that which is inscribed from that which is hidden."[63] In an evidently Neoplatonic fashion, Isaac characterizes the vision of the sefirotic lights as consisting of contemplating the different links in the ontological chain. The force of Isaac's claim is rendered more explicit in an alternative reading of the above passage: "The vision consists of each and every cause drawing close and ascending, and contemplating the cause above it" (*we-ha-ṣefiyyah hi' she-kol sibbah we-sibbah mitqarevet u-mitʿalah we-ṣofah mi-sibbah ha-ʿeloyonah mimenah*).[64] The idea expressed here is based on the Neoplatonic notion that intelligible forms gazing upon or contemplating their source create an overflow of light from above that has the effect of unifying the links in the chain of being. To cite one representative example from the Pseudo-Empedoclean *Book of Five Substances,* a Neoplatonic text that was known in the Middle Ages in both philosophical and kabbalistic circles: "When the forms that are caused look upon their cause,

[62] See, e.g., Judah Ḥayyat's commentary on the anonymous kabbalistic work *Maʿarekhet ha-'Elohut,* 114b, where he distinguishes two kinds of vision of the Presence: sensory vision (*re'iyah be-ḥush ha-ʿayin*) and an inner vision (*re'iyah penimit*), the latter being the higher mode of visual experience.

[63] Isaac the Blind, *Perush Sefer Yeṣirah,* appendix to Scholem, *Kabbalah in Provence,* p. 6. See paraphrase of Isaac's view in *Be'ur le-Ferush ha-Ramban,* attributed to Meir ibn Sahula, 2a.

[64] MS Berlin Or. 942, fol. 54b. For a slightly different version, see MS New York–JTSA Mic. 2325, p. 104.

they are united with it until the effect and the cause become one thing. And their unity results from their looking with one glance at the Foundation of the Foundations, blessed be He, and when they look with one glance He causes in one moment an efflux of His light."[65]

Isaac the Blind applies the imagery of vision as a metaphor for the emanative process to describe the sefirotic potencies. The point is made as well in Azriel of Gerona's commentary on the same text in *Sefer Yeṣirah:* "Another explanation of 'their appearance [was like that of lightning]': The vision (*ṣefiyyah*) is the power drawn from above to below, and that power is called vision, for the one gazes upon the other to receive its word."[66] It is likely that such a notion is implied in the terse remark in an anonymous text on the *sefirot* that I consider to be quite early, extant in manuscript. Utilizing the description in Esther 1:14 of the seven ministers of Persia and Media who "had access to the royal presence," this text describes the upper seven emanations as "beholding the face of the King" (the Cause of Causes).[67] In another anonymous fragment, perhaps composed in the Geronese circle of Ezra and Azriel, we likewise come upon the image of the sefirotic emanations having the capacity to see the divine essence, designated as the Cause of Causes:

> Neither something nor nothing is said about Him. Not something because He certainly is! And not nothing because the prophets saw Him as an elder and sometimes as a youth. At other times they saw only the glory. . . . This is a wondrous form that no eye has seen.[68] Even though the angels are created without matter and are emanated, He is hidden from them. . . . But the *sefirot* that are proximate [to the divine] see Him. . . . We know that everything is contained in Him: the *sefirot* are emanated and no separation is appropriate.[69]

Two points about this text are noteworthy: first, the prophets were able to see the Cause of Causes directly, as either an elder or youth (reflecting the aggadic tradition discussed at length in the previous chapter); second, the emanations, which are not ontically distinct from the Cause of Causes, are described as having a vision of God, in contrast to the angels, who cannot see Him.[70] What is crucial to emphasize is that Isaac the Blind appropriates this ontological conception, Neoplatonic in origin, and formulates it within a psychological framework in order to edify the nature of religious—or, more specifically, mystical—experience: the locus of the vision is the heart of the individ-

[65] See Kaufmann, *Studien über Salomon ibn Gabirol,* pp. 20–21; see also p. 28.

[66] In *Kitve Ramban,* ed. Chavel, 2:455.

[67] MS New York–JTSA Mic. 1777, fol. 17b.

[68] Based on Isa. 64:3.

[69] MS New York–JTSA Mic. 8558, fol. 8b.

[70] The idea of sefirotic vision figures in the writings of other kabbalists as well. Consider, e.g., Joseph ben Shalom Ashkenazi's *Perush le-Sefer Yeṣirah* 1:6 (attributed to RABaD): "There are those who explain [the expression] 'their vision' [as follows]: The vision (*ṣefiyyah*) refers to the fact that *sefirot* look and contemplate one another. . . . Similarly, the creatures look upon the paths of the creatures above them . . . and through their contemplation sparks of light are cast upon the *ḥashmal* [made up of] various colors."

ual, that is, the imaginative faculty.[71] In another passage, Isaac interprets the word *ke-mar'eh,* which is to be rendered here "as a vision," as "contemplation that has no substance" (*hitbonenut she-'ein bo mamash*).[72] The import of this statement is that what is seen by one who contemplates the *sefirot* are mental images of the spiritual entities rather than sensible data corresponding to something existing outside the mind. The text continues:

> The vision is the subtle and pure splendor [seen in accordance with] the comprehension of the one who receives. . . . "Their appearance is like lightning"—this refers to the subtlety and purity of the comprehension of the one who receives . . . the attribute [or measure] is that which is received by the separate realities [*nifradim,* i.e., the ontic realm beneath the *sefirot*], for the prophets saw the attributes in accordance with their comprehension and by means of their ability to receive they expanded their thought . . . for from that which he comprehends he can recognize that which he cannot comprehend. Therefore the potencies (*middot*) arose, for language can comprehend only that which comes out from Him,[73] since a man cannot comprehend the potency of the [divine] speech and the letters (*middat ha-dibbur we-ha-'otiyyot*), but only the potency [of language] itself (*middatah be-ʿaṣmah*). There is no potency outside the letters. All the sublime potencies are given to be meditated upon (*lehitbonen*), for each potency receives from the potency above it, and they are given to Israel, to contemplate from the attribute seen in the heart, to contemplate to the Infinite.[74]

It is significant that Isaac thematically links together the visionary experience of prophecy and the contemplative ideal of mystical intention in prayer: just as the prophets visualized the separate entities of the sefirotic realm, so, too, the mystic can contemplate and meditate on the divine potencies as they take shape in the heart, that is, the imagination. It seems to me, moreover, that it is precisely this process of imaginative visualization of the *sefirot* that underlies the teaching of Isaac concerning the mystical significance of prayer recorded by his disciple Ezra ben Solomon of Gerona:

> The pious one, our teacher, blessed be his memory, said: The essence of the worship of the enlightened (*maskilim*) and those who meditate on His name (*ḥoshve shemo*)[75] is "and cleave to Him" (Deut. 13:5). This is a cardinal principle in the

[71] See Jacob ben Sheshet, *Sefer ha-'Emunah we-ha-Biṭṭaḥon* 19, ed. Chavel, p. 413.

[72] Appendix to Scholem, *Kabbalah in Provence,* p. 5.

[73] On this difficult phrase, see the extensive discussion in Scholem, "The Concept of Kavvanah in the Early Kabbalah," pp. 175–176 n. 13.

[74] Appendix to Scholem, *Kabbalah in Provence,* pp. 5–6. Cf. idem, "Concept of Kavvanah," pp. 165–166; idem, *Origins,* pp. 300–301.

[75] The expression is taken from Mal. 3:16. I have rendered it in accordance with its distinctive usage in this context. See also Scholem, *Origins,* p. 302. On the association of the designation *maskilim* and knowledge of the "secret of the glorious name" (*sod ha-shem ha-nikhbad*), see *Sefer ha-Bahir,* § 139, which clearly reflects the redactional setting of the Provençal kabbalists. See Pedaya, "Provençal Stratum," pp. 150–155, where she discusses several passages in the *Bahir* in light of the mysticism of the divine names in the kabbalah of Isaac the Blind and his disciples. Although

> Torah with respect to prayer and blessings, that one must harmonize one's thought and one's faith as if it cleaved above, to unify the name in its letters and to comprise within it the ten emanations (*sefirot*) like a flame bound to the coal.[76] With his mouth he mentions it according to its appellation [Adonai], but in his heart he unites it in accordance with its structure and how it is written [YHWH].[77]

It is especially noteworthy that the heart is specified as the locus of the unification of the letters of the Tetragrammaton that comprise the ten divine emanations, an idea obviously based on the fact that prayer is designated in traditional rabbinic sources as *ʿavodah she-ba-lev,* "worship in the heart." Although the matter is not specified in detail, I think it is fair to assume that the unification of the letters of the name is predicated on and facilitated by some form of visualization of these letters within the imagination. Hence, Isaac the Blind taught that as the enlightened mystic pronounces with his mouth the name Adonai he imagines the letters YHWH in his heart, which, as I have suggested, is the seat of the imaginative faculty. The mystical significance of the heart as the center for the unification of the *sefirot* comprised in the letters of the Tetragrammaton is reiterated in an anonymous text that also reflects the Provençal-Geronese tradition: "The righteous, pious, and men of action [mentally] concentrate (*mitboded*)[78] and unify the great name, blessed be He [YHWH], and stir the fire on the pyre of the heart chamber[79] in their hearts. Then from the pure thought all the *sefirot* are unified and bound one to the other, until they are drawn up to the fount of the flame whose sublimity has no end."[80]

Through the proper mental concentration the name is unified within the imagination, a process that is compared to the kindling of a fire on the pyre in the hearth chamber in the Temple, where the priests used to warm themselves. From the context, moreover, it is evident that this imagery is meant to underscore that the unification of the name in the heart of the mystic substitutes for the offering of sacrifices on the fires of the altar whose mystical purpose it was

---

Pedaya does not mention the passage to which I have referred, her discussion is important to provide a fuller background.

[76] The image is taken from *Sefer Yeṣirah* 1:8.

[77] Quoted by Ezra in his *Perush le-Shir ha-shirim,* ed. Chavel, p. 522; see also Azriel of Gerona, *Perush ha-ʾAggadot,* p. 16; MS New York–JTSA Mic. 1915, fol. 20b. See Idel, *Kabbalah: New Perspectives,* pp. 54, 298 n. 128.

[78] Scholem, in "Concept of Kavvanah," p. 168, translated the term *mitboded* as "withdraw to live in solitude," but it seems to me that Idel is correct in his suggestion that here the term connotes mental concentration rather than physical seclusion. See *Kabbalah: New Perspectives,* pp. 53–54, where the relevant text is translated and explicated. For the background of this usage in medieval philosophical texts, see Idel, "*Hitbodedut* as Concentration in Jewish Philosophy." On the further development of this term in later mystical literature, especially the Abulafian tradition and its influence on sixteenth-century kabbalists, see idem, "*Hitbodedut* as Concentration in Ecstatic Kabbalah."

[79] This whole expression, *u-maʾaḥizin ʾet ha-ʾesh bi-medurat bet ha-moqed,* is derived from M. Shabbat 1:11.

[80] MS Berlin Or. Quat. 833, fol. 98a, quoted in Scholem, "Concept of Kavvanah," p. 178, n. 38; for an alternative English rendering, see p. 168.

to unify the divine forces. In that sense the mystic takes the place of the priest, a motif stressed in other Geronese material.[81] For example, commenting on the verse "My beloved has gone down to his garden to the bed of spices, to browse in the gardens and to pick lilies" (Cant. 6:2), Ezra notes that the expression *yeridah,* "descent," as opposed to *ʿaliyyah,* "ascent," is used to characterize the divine process in a time of exile. He notes further that the expression "to pick lilies" refers to "the time of exile, when there are no sacrifices, thanks-offerings or meal-offerings, and the spiritual things [*ha-devarim ha-ruḥaniyyim,* i.e., the *sefirot*] ascend and are drawn to the place of their origin. . . . Therefore, one must try to draw down the blessing to the patriarchs [i.e., the fourth, fifth, and sixth *sefirot*] so that the children will have some emanation. Hence the emanation and the drawing-forth are called gathering."[82]

In the time of exile, when there is no Temple and consequently there are no sacrifices, the emanations ascend and gather into their place of origin; the activity that draws down the flow of divine energy is the liturgical worship of Israel, and especially the prayers of the kabbalists, who know the proper theurgical intentions and the pronunciation of the divine name. That the theurgical act of prayer is endowed with redemptive qualities is highlighted in a second passage from this work that links the twin injunction to know God and worship him to the first of the Ten Commandments, "I the Lord am your God who brought you out of the land of Egypt, the house of bondage" (Exod. 20:2):

> "I the Lord am your God," for knowledge is the foundation and root of everything. Concerning this the rabbis, blessed be their memory, said, "Whoever has knowledge it is as if the Temple were built in his life."[83] The meaning of this is that such a person knows how to unify the unique name [*shem ha-meyuḥad,* the Tetragrammaton] and it is as if he built the palace above and below. . . . If there is no knowledge no worship is possible, neither the worship of sacrifices or that of prayer. . . . The pious one [i.e., R. Isaac the Blind] said to his disciples: When you pray, know before whom you stand, thus it says, "Know the God of your father, and serve Him" (1 Chron. 28:9), after the knowledge the labor of service should be in his bosom. "Who brought you out of the land of Egypt"—there is an allusion here to the fact that every person is obligated to unify His name, for that redemption was not by means of an intermediary, an angel, or a seraph, but rather the Holy One, blessed be He, in His essence and glory went forth. Therefore a person must know how to unify the name, He is one and not two . . . and he must unify Him in the ten *sefirot* in the Infinite.[84]

It is very significant that Ezra connects the religious obligation to unify the divine, understood kabbalistically as uniting the ten emanations in their Infi-

[81] See Pedaya, "The Spiritual vs. the Concrete Land of Israel in the Geronese School of Kabbalah," pp. 255–264. See also Brody, "Human Hands Dwell in Heavenly Heights."

[82] *Perush le-Shir ha-Shirim,* ed. Chavel, p. 504.

[83] B. Berakhot 33a.

[84] *Perush le-Shir ha-Shirim,* ed. Chavel, p. 521. See Idel, *Kabbalah: New Perspectives,* p. 298 n. 124, where he adduces the relevant texts of Ezra and Azriel in a similar context.

nite source, to the part of the verse that describes the redemption from Egypt. The essential kabbalistic praxis, as taught by Isaac the Blind, is thus given overt, messianic implications.[85] In the absence of a Temple the kabbalist functions as a priest, for he can draw down the divine energies to sustain the different realms of existence. The point is affirmed unequivocally by Azriel of Gerona: "The name and throne are not complete until [the time that] Amalek is avenged. Therefore they had to offer sacrifices and pronounce the unique name from the threshold of the Temple Court and inward. In the time of the exile [there are] enlightened ones (*maskilim*) of Israel and individuals in whom is the knowledge to bless and sanctify the name in secrecy and openly; it is as if the Temple were built in their days."[86] For my purposes it is necessary to reiterate that the theurgical and soteriological obligation of the kabbalist is accomplished through the faculty of the imagination, symbolically depicted as the heart, for that is marked as the locus of mystical intention that involves as an essential component the visualization of the sefirotic lights encased in the letters of the divine name.[87]

The docetic dimension of Isaac's theosophic conception of prophecy is underscored by his insistence that these *middot* are visualized only in accordance with the visionary's power of receiving them; indeed, this constitutes a distinctive quality of the prophet. The docetism is, as I have already remarked, contextualized within a Neoplatonic framework: the prophetic contemplation of the *sefirot* represents the last link in a chain of emanation through which the spiritual light is progressively condensed until it assumes some tangible shape. This shape, however, is seen only within the heart of the visionary in accord with his capacity to receive the influx from above. Thus there is a configuration of the spiritual forms within the imagination of the mystic.[88]

[85] On the implicit messianic element of the kabbalistic ideology and praxis of Isaac and his students, see Pedaya, "'Flaw' and 'Correction.'"

[86] Scholem, "Seridim ḥadashim," pp. 218–219.

[87] For another example (also of likely Geronese provenance) of the heart depicted as the locus for the unification of the sefirotic powers, especially the masculine and feminine potencies, consider MS New York–JTSA Mic. 1915, fol. 22a, a kabbalistic explication of the structural parallelism between the Tabernacle and the human body: "The Tabernacle, its utensils, the Ark, and the cherubim all are symbolized in the form of man, and just as the Tabernacle and its utensils are a throne to the Presence, so the body of the holy man is a throne for the Presence. The great secret is [alluded to in the verse] 'in every place where I cause My name to be mentioned I will come to you and bless you' (Exod. 20:21), that is, if I find a chariot upon which I can mount in the limbs of a person, in the likeness of the throne that receives the one who rides upon it, then I will rest upon one. . . . Know that by the fulfillment of the commandments one sanctifies his body. . . . The one who reads the Torah and studies Mishnah and Talmud, the tablets in his body are like the pattern of the tablets in the ark. [The masculine] *Tif'eret* and [the feminine] *Malkhut* are united within his heart, since he unifies *Tif'eret* and *Malkhut* by means of the Written Torah and the Oral Torah. Hence, the body of man is verily called a temple, and in him are tablets wherein all the *sefirot* are united through the secret of *Tif'eret* and *Malkhut*."

[88] It is worth noting that a similar conception is found in the *Periphyseon*, bk. 2, 576D–577A, of John Scotus Eriugena, a text whose possible influence on the Provençal and Geronese kabbalists, especially Azriel, has been noted in the scholarly literature. See Scholem, *Origins*, pp. 314, 422–

The docetic orientation of Isaac was adopted by Ezra of Gerona, as is attested, for example, in his comment on R. Yoḥanan's statement that the eating mentioned in Exod. 24:11, "They beheld God, and they ate and drank," is an "actual eating" (*'akhilah vada'it*) and not, as other rabbinic sages maintained, a figurative expression for being nourished by the Presence.[89] Elaborating on this text, Ezra employs an analogy quite common in the literature of medieval mystics who characterize the direct experience of God as "tasting"[90] or "eating": "See how wonderfully this sage spoke, for the base food, that derives from one cause after another, the one receiving from the other, nourishes the person and sustains him; how much more so the one who is conjoined [to the divine] and sees with the eye of the heart (*'ein ha-lev*) the Cause of Causes, he is nourished and derives pleasure, and this is the essential and definitive eating."[91] For Ezra the "eye of the heart" is the imaginative faculty, a usage that may be traced back to Judah Halevi. In chapter 4 I suggested that this medieval commonplace in Islamic and Jewish sources assumed a new meaning for Halevi. Whereas other authors designated the intellect or rational faculty as the "eye of the heart," in his poetry Halevi employed this terminology to refer to the imagination. Similarly, in *Kuzari* IV:3, Halevi calls the imagination (*al-mutakhāyyilāh*), also identified as the internal sense (*al-ḥus al-bāṭin*), the inner eye (*al-ayn al-bāṭinnah*) or spiritual eye (*al-ayn al-rūḥānniyah*). Halevi's pronounced influ-

---

423, 440; Sed-Rajna, "L'influence de Jean Scot," pp. 453–463; Idel, "Sefirot above the Sefirot," pp. 242 n. 17, 243 n. 20, 267–268, and nn. 145–153. According to Eriugena, two kinds of images are impressed upon the memory: sensible images and images of the intelligible realities or primordial causes. Just as the sensible images are impressed upon the external sense, the latter are impressed upon the internal sense, associated in the medieval Neoplatonic and Aristotelian traditions with imagination, on the one hand, and memory, on the other. Hence, one of the central functions of the imagination is to store images of the primordial causes. This is remarkably close to the view expressed by Isaac and developed by his disciples, concerning the capacity of the imagination to visualize the sefirotic entities. Although it is plausible that the Provençal and Catalan kabbalists drew on other Neoplatonic texts that resonate with the views of Eriugena, the fact that in other respects his ideas have parallels in the kabbalistic writings strengthens the conjecture that he may have been a source for this notion of imaginative seeing.

[89] See *Wayyikra Rabbah* 20:10; *Bemidbar Rabbah* 2:25. Cf. *Zohar* 1:104a, where the two rabbinic interpretations are conflated. See also *Zohar* 2:126a.

[90] This metaphor was, of course, suggested by Ps. 34:9. Another possible source for the metaphor of eating to connote intense and direct experience of God may have been Canticles (see, e.g., 2:3, and Caroline Walker Bynum's discussion in *Holy Feast and Holy Fast*, pp. 150–186), for the erotic connotation of eating would have been naturally transferred to religious experience, given the allegorical reading of the text, which is not supplanted by the mystical-symbolic interpretations offered by the kabbalists. On the use of eating as a metaphor for sexual union in classical rabbinic sources, see chapter 1, n. 131. On eating as a metaphor for *devequt*, or mystical union, see the brief discussion in Gottlieb, *Studies in the Kabbala Literature*, p. 237, and Idel, *Kabbalah: New Perspectives*, pp. 70–73 where he discusses the particular image of swallowing as a metaphor for mystical union.

[91] *Liqquṭe Shikheḥah u-Fe'ah*, 4a–b; also cited in Azriel of Gerona, *Perush ha-'Aggadoṭ*, p. 15; Recanaṭi, *Perush 'al ha-Torah* 48d. The teaching of Ezra is alluded to as well in Jacob ben Sheshet, *Sefer ha-'Emunah we-ha-Biṭṭaḥon* 8, ed. Chavel, p. 377. For a parallel, see Ezra's *Perush le-Shir ha-Shirim*, ed. Chavel, p. 486.

ence on the Geronese kabbalists is a well-attested fact in scholarly literature;[92] I suggest that the expression "eye of the heart," or simply "the heart," to designate the imaginative faculty is one more illustration of this influence.

Returning to Ezra's text: As a consequence of cleaving to the Godhead, the Cause of Causes, one sees the divine by means of the eye of the heart, that is, one forms a visual image within the imagination, a process that is compared to an act of consumption. Just as the food one eats can sustain one, for it is part of a continuous chain of being, so in the spiritual plane all things are connected, and contemplative seeing can sustain one, for by visualizing the divine potencies one draws down the flow of energy from the higher ontological plane. Also implied in the notion that one contemplates the *sefirot* by means of the imagination is the assumption that each individual contains or is constituted by this very ontic structure. As Ezra himself puts it in several places in his writings, "A person is composed of all the spiritual entities" (*ha-'adam kalul mi-kol ha-devarim ha-ruḥaniyyim*).[93] Insofar as man does contain the divine emanations within himself, it must follow that these spiritual realities are rendered accessible through a process of looking at one's inner self through an imaginary visualization. Essentially, this is a version of a motif widely attested in Islamic and Jewish philosophy, as well as in mystical literature influenced by the latter: self-knowledge is consummated in the knowledge of God. According to a saying found in tenth-century Islamic and Jewish sources and cited frequently in later medieval Jewish literature: "He who knows himself knows his Lord."[94] Ezra's statement is no doubt related to the theme of man as a microcosm. What is particularly interesting in his case is the designation of the imagination as the faculty by which knowledge of the divine through self-contemplation is achieved.

It may be shown elsewhere in Ezra's writings that he considered prophecy as contemplative illumination ensuing from a state of union or conjunction of man and God, a description that is indebted largely to the writings of Abraham ibn Ezra.[95] He writes in his commentary on the talmudic aggadot, "For [the prophet] would sit and study, and he would cleave with his thought above . . . for every light needs the light above it, to draw it down to it, for each and every light is according to the subtlety of its inwardness."[96] In a fuller version of this text preserved in the commentary on the aggadot by Ezra's younger contemporary Azriel of Gerona, we read,

[92] See Kaufmann, *Attributenlehre*, pp. 166–167 n. 120; Tishby's remark in Azriel of Gerona, *Perush ha-'Aggadot*, p. 34 n. 15; Scholem, *Origins*, pp. 222–224, 410–411 n. 107; Idel, "World of Angels in Human Form," pp. 15–19. See also the source cited in chapter 4, n. 247. The influence of Halevi on the Geronese kabbalists has also been noted by Pedaya in her studies cited above, nn. 81 and 85.

[93] See *Perush ha-'Aggadot le-Rabbi 'Azri'el*, p. 5; *Perush le-Shir ha-Shirim*, ed. Chavel, p. 528; MS Oxford-Bodleian 1947, fol. 26b; and *Sod 'Eṣ ha-Da'at*, by Ezra, cited in Scholem, *On the Mystical Shape*, p. 66. See Idel, *Kabbalah: New Perspectives*, pp. 43, 290–291 nn. 29–30.

[94] See Altmann and Stern, *Isaac Israeli*, pp. 203–208; and Altmann, "The Delphic Maxim in Medieval Islam and Judaism," in *Studies in Religious Philosophy and Mysticism*, pp. 1–40.

[95] See Idel, *Kabbalah: New Perspectives*, p. 45; "Types of Redemptive Activity," p. 274.

[96] MS Vatican 295, fol. 107a.

> As [the prophet] was sitting and studying, and would cleave his thought above, the wondrous entities [i.e., the *sefirot*] were engraved upon his heart, and by means of this emanation and this cleaving of thought the entities were increased and expanded, and from the joy they were revealed to him. In this manner was the drawing down of prophecy (*hamshakhat ha-nevu'ah*), for the prophet would concentrate [his mind] (*mitboded*) and intend his heart and cleave his thought above. And in accordance with the cleaving of prophecy (*devequt ha-nevu'ah*) the prophet would see and know what would occur in the future.[97]

The prophetic vision, induced by study of a text, results in the contemplative communion (*devequt*) of the prophet's thought with the divine thought. In this state of *devequt* the prophet engraves or inscribes the sefirotic powers upon his heart, and this in turn causes an overflow of the *sefirot,* which are then disclosed to him.

In my view, the heart must again be understood as the imagination within which the spiritual realities, the *sefirot,* are visualized. The main philosophical sources for this notion of imaginative revelation were Jewish Neoplatonists such as Isaac Israeli and Judah Halevi, authors who were certainly studied by this circle of kabbalists in Gerona.[98] Ezra used the Neoplatonic conception of the imagination as the faculty that apprehends incorporeal spiritual forms to explain the visualization of the *sefirot* that results from the contemplative ascent to and communion with the highest recesses of the divine realm.[99] In this connection it might be well to recall a description of the process of visual ascent by means of the imagination found in the *Fons Vitae* of Solomon ibn Gabirol. While the influence of ibn Gabirol on other aspects of Geronese (and Provençal) kabbalah has been duly noted in the scholarly literature,[100] to the best of my knowledge this element has escaped the attention of scholars. Yet the similarities in approach to the understanding of prophecy as a visual ascent facilitated by the imagination are striking. Ibn Gabirol speaks about the possibility of "imagining the intelligible realities in one's imagination" and the means to accomplish this consist of visualizing the intelligible realities in terms of the sensible, inasmuch as the latter are patterned after the former. Hence, from the lower one can proceed to the upper, from what is revealed to what is hidden, from the compound to the simple, from the effect to the cause. Ibn Gabirol

[97] *Perush ha-'Aggadot le-Rabbi 'Azri'el,* p. 40. On the tradition of the righteous cleaving above to the Presence as a result of their desire to be in the celestial academy, see the Geronese text in MS New York–JTSA Mic. 2194, fols. 58c–d, 59a.

[98] On the influence of Israeli, see Scholem. "Traces of Gabirol in the Kabbalah," pp. 171–173; Altmann, "Isaac Israeli's 'Chapter on the Elements,'" p. 32; Altmann and Stern, *Isaac Israeli,* pp. 130–132, 164. On the influence of Halevi, see sources cited above, n. 92.

[99] See discussion of Ezra's view of prophecy as a contemplative act in Idel, *Kabbalah: New Perspectives,* pp. 42–44. Idel has noted the Neoplatonic background of Ezra's thinking and has also emphasized the critical role of the imagination. See further *Mystical Experience,* p. 147 n. 29, where Idel employs the expression "visual imagination" to characterize the meditative technique of visualization implied in the Geronese material reworked by Recanaṭi.

[100] See Scholem, "Traces of Gabirol"; idem, *Origins,* pp. 341–343.

describes this process of imaginary visualization as a mental ascent that resembles the Geronese kabbalists' description of the ascent of the soul to the sefirotic pleroma:

> If you want to imagine these substances and the way in which your essence extends to them and surrounds them, you must ascend in your intellect to the last of the intelligibles, to cleanse and purify your intellect from all the impurity of the sensibles, to redeem it from the captivity of nature, to reach through the faculty of your intellect the ultimate boundary of what you can apprehend regarding the truth of the intelligible substance, until in the final analysis you are almost stripped from the corporeal substance as if you did not recognize it at all. Then, in effect, you comprise the entire physical world in your essence, and you place it entirely in a corner of your soul, and when you do this you understand the smallness of the sensible in relation to the greatness of the intelligible. Then the spiritual essences will be as if they were resting in your hands, and you will contemplate them as if they were before your eyes as they are, surrounding you and hidden from you, and you will see your essence as if you yourself were of these very essences. At times you will think that you are only a part of them because of the bond between you and the physical essence, and at times it will seem to you that you are the sum of all these substances and there is no difference between you and them, on account of the unity between your essence and their essence, and the conjunction of your form and their form.[101]

The imagination, therefore, is the vehicle for the contemplative ascent to the spiritual realm and the ultimate conjunction of the individual and the intelligible forms, the reunion or reunification of the soul and its spiritual root. For the Geronese kabbalists as well, seen clearly in the case of Ezra, the imagination is the faculty by means of which one can produce the form of the spiritual entities, the *sefirot,* and through which one ascends to be reunited with these entities. The references to ascent of the soul found in the writings of the Geronese kabbalists are due primarily to the influence of Neoplatonism, and the resemblance to ibn Gabirol's description should be considered one more example of this influence.

That this is the intent of Ezra's conception of prophetic illumination is supported by the interpretation of Ezra found in the works of Menaḥem Recanaṭi. In his commentary on the Torah, Recanaṭi describes the prophetic process in terms reminiscent of Ezra:[102] "When the pious and men of action were [engaged in a state of mental] concentration (*mitbodedim*) and were involved in the supernal secrets, they would imagine through their imaginative faculty (*hayyu medamim be-khoaḥ ṣiyyur maḥshevotam*) as if these entities [the *sefirot*] were engraved in front of them, and when they bound their souls to the supernal soul these entities were increased and blessed, and revealed themselves

[101] *Meqor Ḥayyim* III:56. Cf. Judah ben Samuel Campanton, *'Arba'ah Qinyanim,* MS New York–JTSA Mic. 2532, fols. 45a–b.

[102] As noted already by Idel in *Kabbalah: New Perspectives,* p. 43.

from the Nothingness of Thought (*'afisat ha-mahshavah*) [the highest *sefirah*], like a person who opens a fountain of water and it spreads continuously."[103] In his kabbalistic exposition of the commandments Recanaṭi employs similar language: "Now understand this great secret, which all of Israel do not comprehend but the enlightened ones do comprehend: when the pious ones would concentrate their thoughts (*mitbodedim*) and reveal the hidden mysteries, they would imagine through their imaginative faculty (*medammim be-khoaḥ ṣiyyur maḥshevotam*) as if the entities [i.e., *sefirot*] with which they were occupied were engraved before them."[104] Again it is emphasized that the prophets visualized the sefirotic hypostases through the imagination.

That Ezra served as the basis for Recanaṭi can be shown from several of Ezra's texts. For example, in *Sod ha-ʿEṣ ha-Daʿat* (the "Secret of the Tree of Knowledge"), which almost certainly derives from Ezra, as Scholem already surmised,[105] it is stated explicitly that the soul of the prophet, like that of the righteous one, ascends until it reaches the supernal soul, with which it is united in complete union (*nefesh ha-navi' mityaḥedet ʿim ha-neshamah ha-ʿelyonah yiḥud gamur*).[106] Another passage of Ezra that influenced Recanaṭi's formulation is a description of the contemplative ascent through prayer found in Ezra's commentary on the aggadot: "The ancient pious ones would elevate their thought to the place of its source, and they would recite the *miṣwot* and the words, and through this recitation and the conjunction of thought (*ha-maḥshavah ha-deveqah*) the entities were blessed and increased, and they received the influx from the Nothingness of Thought, like a person who opens a fountain of water and it spreads here and there."[107] In this account—unlike the others, which deal with the prophetic process—no mention is made of the heart or the imaginative faculty. What Ezra implies, however, Recanaṭi makes explicit: as a result of the union of the soul with the Universal Soul—alternatively expressed as the cleaving of thought to divine Thought or Wisdom[108]—images of the *sefirot* are etched on the prophet's imagination; hence, it is through the imagination that one has a revelatory experience of the divine powers.

[103] *Perush ʿal ha-Torah* 37d; cf. 90b–c, where the same principle is applied to intention in sexual relations, i.e., through proper mental activity one has the capacity to form the shape of the fetus contained in the semen.

[104] MS Vatican 209, fol. 28a. This text is noted as well by Idel in *Mystical Experience,* p. 147 n. 29.

[105] *On the Mystical Shape,* p. 65.

[106] Hebrew text published by Scholem in *Elements of the Kabbalah,* p. 195. For a different English rendering, see Scholem, *On the Mystical Shape,* p. 67; see also Idel, *Kabbalah: New Perspectives,* p. 42.

[107] *Liqquṭe Shikheḥah u-Fe'ah* 8a (cf. *Perush ha-'Aggadot le-Rabbi ʿAzri'el,* p. 40). See also *'Iggeret ha-Qodesh,* ed. Chavel, p. 333; Mopsik, *Lettre sur la sainteté,* pp. 248–249, 305–306 n. 149.

[108] See, e.g., Ezra's comment in *Liqquṭe Shikheḥah u-Fe'ah* 5b (cf. *Perush ha-'Aggadot le-Rabbi ʿAzri'el,* p. 20): " 'Say to Wisdom, You are my sister' (Prov. 7:4), that is, to conjoin [human] thought to [divine] Wisdom as if they were one thing."

A similar idea is implied in a passage of Azriel wherein he explains the mechanics of vision in relation to dreams. He remarks that the ability to clarify and discern the images of thought (*dimyone maḥshavah*) is dependent on the degree of purity of the individual soul. The one whose soul is not pure cannot distinguish between true and false imaginings. By contrast, the "visionary who has a pure soul sees everything without confusion, interruption, or doubt, and the vision is fixed in his mind and inscribed in his intellect and burns in him like fire. . . . The vision that the soul sees occurs at the time that a person sleeps, and his soul ascends and draws down from above the life force; in drawing down the life of the spirit it draws down the paths of the light of the intellect and knowledge to warn the soul about the future so that it will rest in the repose of the eternal life."[109] Admittedly, in this text no mention is made of the imagination; on the contrary, the emphasis is on the intellective powers of the soul. However, I do not think it would be misleading to conclude that it is the faculty of imagination that facilitates the mental ascent of the soul to the divine realm, whence it draws down the emanative flux that eventually translates into concrete images. To appreciate Azriel's remarks one must bear in mind the Neoplatonic conception of imaginative revelation that has been discussed above.

The role of the imagination in the visualization process is underscored by another comment of Azriel in his catechetical commentary on the theosophic doctrine of the *sefirot*, known as *Shaʿar ha-Shoʾel* (the "Gate of the Inquirer"). Responding to the supposed question concerning the nature (*mahut*) of the divine emanations, Azriel asserts,

> When the [divine] essence is clothed in the imagination (*be-hitlabesh ha-ʿeṣem ba-dimyon*) we should liken the first power to a hidden light, the second power to the light that comprises every color—and this light is in the likeness of blue (*tekhelet*), which is the completion (*takhlit*) of all colors, but there is in it no known color—the third power to a green light, the fourth power to a white light, the fifth power to a red light. The sixth power is composed of the white and red. The seventh power is a red power inclined toward the white. The eighth power is a white power inclined toward the red. The ninth power is composed of the white and red, and from the red inclined toward the white and the white inclined toward the red. The tenth power is composed of every color.[110]

What is instructive about this passage is Azriel's explicit claim that the divine essence assumes specific forms—according to the language of the text, "is clothed"—through the imagination (*dimyon*).[111] By means of the imaginative

[109] *Perush ha-ʾAggadot le-Rabbi ʿAzriʾel*, p. 76.

[110] *Perush ʿEser Sefirot ʿal Derekh Sheʾelah u-Teshuvah*, printed with Meir ibn Gabbai, *Derekh ʾEmunah*, p. 5.

[111] See discussion in the *Perush ha-ʾAggadot le-Rabbi ʿAzriʾel*, pp. 104–105, regarding the *dimyonot* (images) that parallel the *yeṣirot* or *ṣurot* (forms). See below, n. 130. For later use of this text see Moses of Kiev, *Shoshan Sodot*, 51a, who glosses Azriel's comment *be-hitlabesh ha-ʿeṣem ba-dimyon* with the statement, "It is imaged by many different colors, as it says, 'and the light dwells with Him' (Dan. 2:22)."

faculty one can visualize the emanations in terms of different lights and colors. It is likely, moreover, that such a process of imaginative representation is alluded to in another comment in the same text:

> [E]ven though there is no boundary above . . . there is a boundary for everything that is grasped through the meditation of the heart (*hirhur ha-lev*) and the allusion of thought (*remez ha-maḥshavah*)[112] which emanates below to be found in speech and seen in action. Everything that is bounded has a measurement and corporeality, for everything that is grasped in the meditation of the heart is called a body (*guf*), even the spirit. Therefore, the *sefirot,* the principle for everything that is bounded (*kelal le-khol mugbal*), are the root (*shoresh*). This boundary that is without boundary (*ha-gevul ha-hu' mibeli gevul*) emanated; thus it says[113] [of the *sefirot*], "their measure is ten which have no end."[114]

The corporeal form assumed by the divine emanations, referred to paradoxically as the "boundary that is without boundary," takes shape within the imagination, here alluded to by the term heart (*lev*), as I have argued above with respect to both Isaac the Blind and Ezra of Gerona. It is the imagination, therefore, that is the locus of the anthropomorphic configuration of the divine pleroma, a point that Azriel states explicitly in yet a third passage from this work:

> Concerning that which you asked, if they [the *sefirot*] have a measure, boundary, and corporeality. This is mentioned explicitly in the Torah, the Prophets, and the Writings. In the Torah, as it is written, "in our image, after our likeness" (Gen. 1:26); in the Prophets, "and upon the likeness of a throne, etc." (Ezek. 1:26); and [in the Writings] it is written, "my beloved is white and ruddy" (Cant. 5:10). In the words of the sages,[115] "the one who knows the measure of the Creator is sure to be in the world-to-come, I and Aqiva guarantee this matter," as it says in Midrash Mishle.[116] We have found in the midrash,[117] "R. Ḥanina said: At first, whoever pointed out the icon of the king was killed; now the children enter the schoolhouse and point out the divine name with a finger."[118]

The anthropomorphic characterization of God implied in the three biblical texts, the passage from *Shi'ur Qomah* (assumed to be a rabbinic source), and

[112] This is a technical term in Isaac the Blind's kabbalah; see his *Perush Sefer Yeṣirah* in appendix to Scholem, *Kabbalah in Provence,* p. 3.

[113] Cf. *Sefer Yeṣirah* 1:7.

[114] *Perush 'Eser Sefirot 'al Derekh She'elah u-Teshuvah,* p. 5.

[115] That is, the statement found in various textual recensions of *Shi'ur Qomah;* cf. *Synopse,* §§ 711, 953.

[116] Referring to the oft-cited text of this midrashic compilation, which is clearly related to the esoteric tradition. Cf. *Midrash Mishle,* pp. 84–86. Part of the passage has been translated by Scholem in *Major Trends,* p. 71, where he duly notes the connection of this text to Jewish esoteric speculation.

[117] *Midrash Tanḥuma,* Bemidbar, 10; see also *Bemidbar Rabbah* 2:3; *Shir ha-Shirim Rabbah* 2:13.

[118] *Perush 'Eser Sefirot 'al Derekh She'elah u-Teshuvah,* p. 7.

the midrashic text is applied by Azriel to the sefirotic pleroma. Perhaps most intriquing of all is the final midrashic citation, wherein a parallel is drawn between an iconic representation of a king and the letters of the Tetragrammaton. Indeed, from the kabbalistic perspective the Tetragrammaton comprises the ten *sefirot,* which together constitute the iconic form of *deus revelatus* in the image of a heavenly anthropos.

The full implications of the themes discussed above are drawn in a brief text on the mystical significance of prayer, *Shaʿar ha-Kawwanah la-Mequbbalim ha-Rishonim,* attributed by Scholem to Azriel of Gerona[119]—an attribution challenged by Idel, who suggests that the text was composed in the late thirteenth or early fourteenth century.[120] As a background to this text, it must be noted that the use of the imagination for meditative techniques involving visualization of divine names is well documented in thirteenth-century mystical sources, both in the circle of the German Pietists and among the theosophic and ecstatic kabbalists. According to one passage extant in manuscript (which opens with the statement "the tradition regarding prayer, and this is a tradition that R. Azriel received from the great rabbi, R. Isaac, blessed be his memory), "The first name refers to the Supernal Crown (*Keter ʿElyon*), the first gradation, and the second name is the tenth gradation, which is the Diadem (*ʿAṭarah*), and afterwards it will ascend a bit, that is, the tenth gradation [will ascend] to the Supernal Crown, which is the first gradation, and he should imagine in his mind the [letters of the] Tetragrammaton, which is the Supernal Crown."[121] The theosophic process connected here with mystical intent in prayer involves the ascent of the tenth emanation to the first, thereby unifying the sefirotic pleroma, represented by the unification of the divine name. In conjunction with this process it is necessary for the initiate to imagine in his mind the very letters of the name; indeed, it seems that it is the imaging of the letters that fosters the uniting of the sefirotic grades above. A slightly different, but not altogether unrelated, notion occurs in the *Shaʿar ha-Kawwanah la-Mequbbalim ha-Rishonim,* mentioned above, ascribed to Azriel but more likely composed in a later generation. Essentially, this text presents evidence for a visual meditation on light symbols that clearly reflect the gradations of the pleroma. That the locus of these visionary symbols is the imagination is stated at the outset:

> Whoever fixes a thing in his mind with complete firmness, that thing becomes for him the principal thing. Thus, when you pray and recite benedictions, or [otherwise] wish to direct the intention to something in a true manner, then imagine (*dimmah*) that you are light and all about you is light, from every direction and every side, and in midst of the light a stream of light, and upon it a brilliant light, and opposite it a throne and upon it a good light. . . . Turn to the right and you

[119] Scholem, "Concept of Kavvanah," pp. 171–174; idem, *Origins,* pp. 416–419. See also Idel, *Mystical Experience,* p. 78.

[120] Idel, *Studies in Ecstatic Kabbalah,* p. 144 n. 22.

[121] MS Cambridge Heb. Add. 505, fol. 7b, quoted by Idel in "Writings of R. Abraham Abulafia," p. 261.

> will find pure light, to the left and you will find an aura which is the radiant light, between them and above the light of glory, and around it the light of life. Above it is the crown of light that crowns the objects of thoughts, illumines the paths of ideas, and brightens the splendor of visions. This illumination is inexhaustible and unending, and out of its perfect glory come grace and blessing, peace and life for those who keep the path of its unity.[122]

The visual meditation outlined in this text culminates in a description of the union of the human and divine wills in which the divine will is clothed in the human will and draws it up into the realm of divine potencies. From the stage of imaging the different lights, which correspond to aspects of the divine, one reaches the source, "the perfect glory of the withdrawing light (*'or ha-mitʿalem*) that has neither form nor image, measure nor magnitude, extent nor bounds, neither limit nor ground nor number, and which is in no way finite."[123] There is thus a progression in the meditational practice, from conjuring images of the sefirotic lights to a state of imagelessness, an emptying of the mind of all images or forms when one attains the highest grade if not the Infinite (*Ein-Sof*) itself. At this point the individual's will and the will of God are completely unified: "And he who in this manner lifts himself by the strength of his intention from one thing to another until he reaches the Infinite must direct his intention in a way that corresponds to that which he wishes to accomplish, so that the upper will clothes itself in his will."[124] The ultimate goal of the proper intention in prayer is the mystical merging of the human and divine wills, but this process eventuates in the opening up of the upper channels and the consequent overflow of the divine effluence from grade to grade:

> When the upper will and the lower will in its identification, in its adherence to unity, become one, then the stream gushes forth with sufficient strength to accomplish its intention. . . . For to the extent to which his will adheres to an object that conforms to the upper will, the impulse (of the divine Will) clothes itself in it and draws itself up. . . . And he draws down the effluence that crowns the secret of things and essences . . . he draws along the effluence from stage to stage and from cause to cause until his actions are completed in conformity to his will.[125]

At the conclusion of the passage the author makes clear that he considers the visual technique of ascent and descent to be akin to prophecy: "And this is the highest path of prophecy along which he who makes himself familiar with it is able to ascend to the rank of prophecy."[126]

Commenting on this text Scholem perceptively notes: "The true *kavvanah* described in this text is therefore identical with the path of prophecy, which passes through the realization of the perfect *debhequth* with God, that is, the

[122] I have utilized the English rendering in Scholem, "Concept of Kavvanah," pp. 172–173, with some slight modifications.

[123] Ibid., p. 173.

[124] Ibid.

[125] Ibid., pp. 173–174.

[126] Ibid., p. 174.

cleaving of human thought and will to the thought and will of God. . . . The illumination, which is to be obtained through *debhequth,* can therefore be distinguished from prophecy only by its degree and not by its nature. The prophet is here, as so often in medieval thought, none other than the perfect mystic."[127] Mystical intention in prayer is thus equated with the path of prophecy, for both involve the ascent to the sefirotic pleroma, which is accomplished through the activity of the creative imagination.[128]

The Provençal and Geronese kabbalists thus identified the imagination as the locus of the visual presencing of the imageless Infinite. The docetic orientation is underscored in another text that reflects the particular idiom of Isaac the Blind's Geronese disciples, especially Azriel. It is also of interest to note that in this text Judah Halevi's technical philosophical term *ʿinyan ʾelohi,* "the divine matter," is utilized to refer to the influx that proceeds from the Godhead: "All the images (*ha-dimyonot*) are comprised within the Root of Roots, and it is possible for Him to appear in any one of them He wills, for all is inscribed in Him, and He is revealed in the attribute that is appropriate for the need of the hour; thus the divine matter (*ha-ʿinyan ha-ʾelohi*) changes in the imagination of the thought of the one who sees (*be-dimyon maḥshevet ha-roʾeh*) according to the change of his intention from attribute to attribute, but there is no change from the perspective of [the divine] essence."[129] Analogous to the concept of *dimyonot* in the theosophy of the German Pietists, the images in the kabbalistic literature are not purely subjective but are rather the ideal or archetypal forms contained in the Godhead or the aspect of it that corresponds to divine Thought;[130] they are, however, only imagined as specific forms with determi-

[127] *Origins,* p. 419.

[128] Mention should be made of the fact that the Geronese tradition concerning the role of imagination in the process of contemplative prayer, study, and prophecy is applied in the case of the anonymous *ʾIggeret ha-Qodesh* to sexual cohabitation. That is, according to this text, probably written in the last decade of the thirteenth century, during intercourse the man is required to cleave to the divine by ascending via his imagination to the sefirotic realm, whereas the woman is supposed to cleave to the man by having an image of him in mind. Cf. *Kitve Ramban* 2:331–334. See also above, n. 107.

[129] MS Vatican 283, fol. 71a. This text was previously quoted by Scholem, "Seridim ḥadashim," p. 216 n. 3.

[130] See *Perush ha-ʾAggadot,* p. 82, where Azriel speaks of the sefirotic entities being formed in the "images of Thought" (*dimyone ha-maḥshavah*). In this context it is evident that the word *dimyon* has the connotation of "form," akin to Platonic ideas that inhere within Thought. See also Jacob ben Sheshet, *Meshiv Devarim Nekhoḥim,* p. 78, where the term *dimyonot* connotes images or archetypal forms of spiritual realities. Idel, in "Jewish Kabbalah and Platonism," pp. 328–330, discusses these references as well as two critical passages from Naḥmanides wherein the terms *dimyon* and *ṣiyyur* appear in the sense of "prefiguration" but at the same time have the metaphysical connotation of the form that inheres in the divine Thought. See as well the text from Jacob ben Sheshet translated and discussed in Wolfson, "Beautiful Maiden without Eyes," pp. 163–164. Cf. the passage in MS New York–JTSA Mic. 1815, fol. 21a, where the word *ṣiyyurim* is used to connote these archetypal forms. See also the kabbalistic commentary on the *maḥzor* by Isaac ben Ṭodros, MS Paris–BN 839, fol. 192a, where the rabbinic statement that the soul is comparable to God in five ways (cf. B. Berakhot 10a) is linked to the notion that the soul is bound to the "bundle of life" (*ṣeror ha-ḥayyim*) in five images (*dimyonot*). It is evident that in that context as well, the

nate shape within the human imagination. By so locating the image of God within human imagination the theosophic kabbalists are able to preserve concomitantly both elements of the tradition—aniconism, on the one hand, and the corporeal and anthropomorphic representation of the deity, on the other.

Interestingly, this halfway position of the image between being and nothingness is affirmed explicitly in the following kabbalistic text: "The secret of 'it arose in [His] thought to create:' it is alluded to here in the beginning of the Torah and the outset of the order of letters that the word create (*bara'*) connotes image (*ṣiyyur*). . . . This is not to say that it is in something real or in nothing, but rather it is something that comes forth from nothing but has not yet attained [a state of] being, like an image on the wall. Thus it is the way of people to say, 'I have formed an image of something in my thought.'"[131] What is significant for the purposes of my analysis is the characterization of the mental image as situated between being and nothing. By linking the corporeal representation of God to the realm of images the kabbalists are able to both affirm the corporeal figuration of God implicit in the esoteric texts and preserve the traditional account of God's essential incorporeality. The dialectical resolution of these clashing orientations within the imagination is brought out in the following commentary on the *sefirot, Sod we-Yesod ha-Qadmoni,* attributed to the Iyyun circle:

> What is the essence of the Creator? He is a living essence that is compared to the appearance of the image of the soul and its form, that is, the shape of the anthropos, but it is spiritual, like the brain or ether that is a form and not a body. The Holy One, blessed be He, is similar to this; He may be compared and yet He is incomparable. Heaven forfend, He has no image or form, but rather the image of His intellect is like a soul that is imagined (*meṣuyeret*) in the shape of a body (*binyan ha-guf*); thus He takes shape in the *sefirot*. The one who wishes to understand this should think about the subtlety and the essence (*ha-daqut we-ha-mahut*), but not [corporeal] substance (*ha-mamashut*). Further, the Holy One, blessed be He, overflows to all the *sefirot,* and all the *sefirot* draw from His power, and He is seen through the intermediaries, but He is elevated and exalted above them, for there is no limit to His exaltation. This is [the import of] "there was the semblance of a human form" (Ezek. 1:26), and not an actual human.[132]

It is significant that in this text the divine is characterized as an intellect that is compared to a soul that assumes corporeal form (*binyan ha-guf*), but that form takes shape only within the imagination. In other parts of this work, reflecting an approach typical of the material belonging to this circle, the au-

---

latter term designates archetypal forms or images of spiritual entities. The technical use of the term *dimyonot* is also discernible in the Iyyun text *Sod Yedi'at ha-Meṣi'ut,* MS Jerusalem-Schocken, 6, whose close relationship to the style and language of Azriel of Gerona was previously noted by Scholem, *Reshit ha-Qabbalah,* p. 256, n. 5.

131 MS New York–JTSA Mic. 2469, fol. 146a.

132 MS Munich 54, fol. 288a.

thor speaks at length about intellectual lights that comprise the pleroma, lights comprehended by means of an intellectual vision. These lights, moreover, are correlated with images culled from earlier forms of chariot speculation. It is also characteristic of this text and the related literature that the light metaphors converge with linguistic symbolism, the letters, especially of the divine names, being described as luminous forms. In this context I will cite one example, for it is particularly instructive of the centrality of the visionary component in the theosophical structure. Commenting on the two forms of the letter *pé,* the author writes, "They are called the form of the intellect (*ṣurat ha-sekhel*), and their path is called the great light (*'or ha-gedullah*), which is called *Ḥazḥazit,* that is, the place of the origin of the vision of the prophets (*ḥezyon ha-ḥozim*)."[133] In this passage prophetic vision is treated as a form of intellectual vision, whereas in the first passage cited above the locus of the visualization of the divine intellect is the imagination.

It should be noted that in other kabbalistic writings, including those of the Geronese kabbalists, one can find support for the view that mystical vision, reflecting the ontic status of the eschatological state, is an intellectual comprehension or contemplation.[134] For example, Naḥmanides comments on the talmudic teaching that Moses saw through a speculum that shines:[135] "The term seeing (*re'iyah*) is brought [in the sense of] contemplation of the intellect (*histakkelut ha-sekhel*) and elevation of understanding (*'illuy ha-havanah*)."[136] This intellectual vision represents the ultimate state of prophecy, which can be realized to an extent by the mystic. In the continuation of this text Naḥmanides describes the righteous in the Garden of Eden as reaching the very level of Moses:

> For the people of that world will attain the level of Moses, our rabbi, whose soul rose above his body until his physical faculties were annihilated, and he was clothed in the Holy Spirit every moment, as if his sight and hearing were only through the eye of the soul (*'ein ha-nefesh*). . . . The body is annihilated and the soul separates from its faculties when the Holy Spirit emanates upon a person and he sees by means of vision itself when he sees Michael and Gabriel, and this is true vision and the proper hearing. . . . Thus we have come to deal with the mysteries

[133] Ibid., fol. 291a. The term *ḥazḥazit* used to designate the locus of prophetic visions, and identified further as the "wheel of greatness" (*'ofan ha-gedullah*), is found in the base text of this circle of speculation, *Sefer ha-'Iyyun,* in its various recensions; see Verman, *Books of Contemplation,* pp. 46 n. 51, 70, 83, 103.

[134] Some kabbalists went even further and, following a stricter Maimonidean approach, spoke of a mystical vision freed from the corruptions of the imagination. See, e.g., Isaac of Acre, *'Oṣar Ḥayyim,* MS Moscow-Guenzberg 775, fol. 28b. In the case of this kabbalist one may surmise that the ecstatic kabbalah of Abulafia played a major role in informing his conception of purifying the rational faculty of all images. See below, n. 180. On the other hand, it must be recalled that Isaac of Acre himself assigned an important role to the imagination as the faculty that forms mental images of the letters of the divine names on which the adept meditates; see Idel, *Mystical Experience,* p. 33.

[135] B. Yevamot 49b.

[136] *Kitve Ramban* 2:297.

of prophecy (*sodot ha-nevu'ah*) and visions of the pious (*re'iyot ha-ḥasidim*) who see angels.[137]

It must be noted, however, that while Naḥmanides clearly delineates the prophetic experience as an intellectual vision wherein the bodily senses are completely obliterated, he also assigns an essential role to the process of visualizing sensible images as a means of attaining a state of union with the divine. Thus, in a passage that precedes the one just cited, he specifies that it is by virtue of contemplating the concrete forms of the spiritual entities that God placed in the terrestrial Garden of Eden (a physical locality) that one can gain visual knowledge of the divine realms and thereby be conjoined to the glory:

> [God] formed (*ṣiyyer*) in that glorious place all that occurs in the supernal world, that is, the world of souls, in a physical form (*ṣiyyur gashmi*), so that one may contemplate from there the roots of all that is created, corporeal, psychical, and angelic, and to comprehend the Creator, blessed be He, from the comprehension of all that is created. . . . Thus, those who dwell in the Garden of Eden, which is the most precious of places, learn from the forms of the [spiritual] entities all the supernal secrets, and their souls ascend by means of this study, and they see visions of God in the company of the glory of the supernal ones (*we-ro'eh mar'ot 'elohim be-ḥevrat kevod ha-ʿelyonim*) from that place. They comprehend all that a created being can know and contemplate like Moses our master, peace be upon him, at Sinai, in the matter as it is written, "[Note well, and follow the patterns for them] that are being shown you on the mountain" (Exod. 25:40).[138]

It may be concluded, therefore, that Naḥmanides remained within the general framework of the Neoplatonic tradition insofar as he posits the visualization of corporeal images as the means of reaching the higher spiritual forms. However, the precise function of the imaginative faculty in this process is not clarified in Naḥmanides' account.

Shekhinah as the Archetypal Image

A related motif developed in thirteenth-century kabbalistic material similarly underscores the critical role accorded the imagination in the spiritual practices and theosophical beliefs of Jewish mystics. This is the valorization of the *Shekhinah,* the feminine potency of the divine, as the archetypal image, in some cases also identified as the imaginative faculty within the human soul. According to the standard theosophic reinterpretation of prophecy in thirteenth-century materials (not to mention later sources based on the earlier texts), the locus of visualization is the Presence, designated by the rabbinic idiom "the speculum that does not shine." The feminine aspect of the Godhead is the optical apparatus through which the masculine aspect, and particularly the

[137] Ibid., p. 299.
[138] Ibid., p. 296.

membrum virile, is seen. In a typically medieval posture, image and imagination are linked to the feminine.[139]

To be sure, this identification draws on earlier rabbinic sources wherein the *Shekhinah* is designated as the locus of revelatory experience. This view, a commonplace in thirteenth-century kabbalistic texts, is expressed, for instance, by Ṭodros Abulafia in this comment on the verse "You shall see My back but My face you shall not see" (Exod. 33;23): "The explanation of all this is that he saw the image of the great name (*temunat ha-shem ha-gadol*) but not the upper faces. [The rabbis,] blessed be their memory, said in the *Sifre,* 'the image of God did he see' (Num. 12:8), this is the appearance of the back (*mar'eh 'aḥorim*), and this is sufficient for the enlightened."[140] The aspect of the divine that is visible is the hinder part, the Presence, the image of the great name—the Tetragrammaton that corresponds to the masculine potency. The frontal aspect of God remains hidden, revealed only through the back (*'aḥor*), the speculum that is the other (*'aḥer*). Thus, the author of a zoharic passage wherein several of Jacob's dream-visions are discussed remarks that the word *mar'eh* refers to the "mirror in which all the images (*diyoqnin*) are seen." The biblical locution, therefore, is *wa-'ere' ba-ḥalom,* "I saw in a dream" (Gen. 31:10), for Jacob saw the divine image through El-Shaddai, that is, the *Shekhinah,* "for it is a mirror in which another image is seen, and all the upper images are seen in it." Utilizing this symbolic explanation of the visual experience, the dream-vision of Jacob's ladder (Gen. 28:12) can be explained as well: "What is the ladder? The grade upon which all other grades are dependent, and that is the Foundation of the World."[141]

The object of the vision is the phallic *Yesod,* the cosmic pillar symbolized as the ladder, but only as it is seen through the prism of the feminine speculum in a nocturnal dream-vision. The characterization of mystical vision is in line with the kabbalists' account of biblical theophany: the masculine form projects through the aperture of the feminine. It is precisely this dynamic that constitutes the nature of the image in theosophic kabbalah: it is an opening, an optic hole, by means of which the concealed is disclosed. The image is at the same time a paradigm ontically related to the archetype of which it is an image. The faculty of the imagination facilitates the double reflection and thereby allows one to behold the image within the image.

A relatively early textual attestation of this idea is found in Ezra's commentary on Canticles. The relevant passage is based on a comment in an earlier midrashic source to which I referred in the opening chapter of this book. For the sake of comparison I will cite the passage again in this context: "'I have likened you, my darling' (Cant. 1:9). The expression 'I have likened you' (*dimitikha*) connotes images (*demuyot*). This teaches that through an image

139 See Culianu, *Eros and Magic in the Renaissance,* pp. 3–27, esp. 17–23. See also Raschke and Gregory, "Revelation, the Poetic Imagination, and the Archaeology of the Feminine"; Ross-Bryant, "Imagination and the Re-Valorization of the Feminine."

140 *'Oṣar ha-Kavod ha-Shalem* 4d.

141 *Zohar* 1:149b.

(*dimyon*) God was revealed to Israel; as a person who sees his friend and says, This is the one, so Israel looked upon the Holy One, blessed be He, and imagined (*medammim*) Him."[142] Utilizing the midrashic tradition explaining the theophany at the splitting of the Red Sea, Ezra writes in his own commentary to this verse, "Israel gazed (*mistakkelin*) upon the Presence like one who imagines (*medammeh*) his friend and says, This is the one. In that manner Israel gazed upon the Presence, and imaged (*mar'im*) her, saying, 'This is my God, and I will glorify Him' (Exod. 15:2)."[143] Ezra thus appropriated the midrashic tradition, but he applied it specifically to the vision of the Presence, the last of the ten hypostatic gradations, rather than to a vision of God in a generic sense. In contrast to the other texts of Ezra that I have examined above, according to this passage the focus of the imaginative vision is not divine Thought or Wisdom, one of the highest emanations, but the *Shekhinah,* the lowest of them. This notion reached its climax, as will be seen below, in the specific identification by some kabbalists, especially in the generation of the *Zohar,* of the *Shekhinah* as the archetypal image or even the imaginative faculty.

An interesting development of this motif is found in Jacob ben Sheshet, who describes the *Shekhinah* as that aspect of the divine that can be visually constituted within the prophetic imagination:

> At the Sinaitic theophany [God] granted power and permission to the prophets to ascend, each one according to his ability. There is support for my words from what is said, "I appeared to Abraham, Isaac, and Jacob as El Shaddai" (Exod. 6:3), that is, [God] appeared to them in the vision of the glory that is designated to speak to the prophets. But "I did not make Myself known to them [by the name YHWH]" (ibid.) through a comprehension of the essence of the throne (*be-hassagat ʿeṣem ha-kisse'*). . . . Know that the vision consists of [God] showing Himself in one of the appearances (*mar'ot*) that does not consist of comprehension of the essence, like the appearance of images formed in the heart (*mar'ot ha-dimyonot ha-misṭayyerot ba-lev*) on the basis of a thing that is known, together with comprehension of its essence and substance, not through something else.[144]

This passage underscores the point that no one can have direct knowledge of the divine hypostases; at best the vision of this realm is mediated through the images that are conjured by the imagination, again designated by the term "heart." The specific object of the imaginary consciousness is, moreover, the *Shekhinah,* referred to as *mar'eh ha-kavod,* the "vision of the glory," inasmuch as it is the visible aspect of the divine, comprising the various forms (*mar'ot*) through which the glory is seen.

Ezra's language seems also to have influenced the Castilian kabbalist Isaac ben Jacob ha-Kohen, who was active in the second half of the thirteenth century. Specifically, Isaac combines the notion of an angel, or separate intellect,

[142] *Midrash Zuṭa,* p. 13.

[143] *Perush le-Shir ha-Shirim,* ed. Chavel, p. 487. Cf. Baḥya ben Asher's commentary to Gen. 9:6, ed. Chavel, p. 120.

[144] *Sefer ha-'Emunah we-ha-Biṭṭahon* 6, ed. Chavel, p. 374.

being clothed in human form (understood in terms of Maimonides' conception of prophecy as mediated through the Active Intellect, the last of the ten grades of angels) and Ezra's view regarding the imaginative revelation of the spiritual forms. Describing the traditional notion of the "four camps of the Presence," Isaac writes,

> There is no corporeal image or physical form there at all, but only spiritual emanation. Not all the angels, but only the tenth grade, appeared to the prophets, each one according to his level. . . . [When he has a vision] the faculties of the prophet are weakened and change from form to form, until he is clothed in the power of the form that is revealed to him, then he is transformed into an angelic form. He is transformed into this form so that he can receive the prophetic power, and the engravings of the spiritual forms are engraved on his heart.[145]

Although the influence of Ezra is discernible here, an important difference between the two kabbalists must be noted. According to Ezra, the *sefirot* themselves assume visible shape within the imagination, whereas for Isaac it seems that the angelic forms are what is seen by the prophet. It is likely that Maimonides' conception of prophecy is evident here as well, for it is only the tenth grade of angels, corresponding to the *agens intellectus,* that appears in prophetic visions. Moreover, the final claim, that the prophet receives the spiritual forms in his heart, may reflect Maimonides' notion that all prophets with the exception of Moses received the intellectual overflow mediated through the imagination. On the other hand, it may be closer to the Neoplatonic tradition in which the imagination is the power that receives spiritual forms of an ontological (and not merely psychological) nature. There is, however, another important source for Isaac ha-Kohen's formulation: the German Pietists whose thought had an important impact on this kabbalistic circle. The influence of the Pietistic conception is even more pronounced in this comment of Isaac's older brother, Jacob ben Jacob ha-Kohen:

> What you see regarding all the forms of the letters formed within the *'alef* comes to teach you that the Holy One, blessed be He, appears to His prophets and servants in several appearances (*mar'ot*) and visions (*ḥezyonot*). This is what is written, "To whom, then, can you liken Me, to whom can I be compared? says the Holy One" (Isa. 40–25), that is, I can appear to My prophets and servants in several appearances for the power of all the forms (*ṣurot*), appearances (*mar'ot*), and images (*dimyonot*) is in My capacity, in My power and strength they are contained and formed. Even though Scripture says that the Holy One, blessed be He, is revealed in several different images, do not think that it is so. There are before Him powers that change in several different ways, and these are the powers of the angels.[146]

[145] Scholem, "Traditions of R. Jacob and R. Isaac," p. 92.

[146] Ibid., p. 202. See also the comment of another Castilian kabbalist writing in the latter part of the thirteenth century, Isaac ibn Sahula, in his commentary on Canticles, ed. Green, p. 417: "The explanation of 'I have likened you, my darling' (Cant. 1:9), that is to say, I have likened You to the ministering angels when You come close to me."

The various images by which God is manifest are angelic powers that can assume different forms in the prophetic imagination. By identifying the multiple theophanic figurations as angels Jacob ha-Kohen is able to maintain a common medieval philosophical attitude regarding the immutable nature of God. It should be obvious, however, that these changing angelic potencies are not really ontically distinct from the divine. This point is underscored by the initial analogy employed by Jacob ha-Kohen: just as the forms of all the letters are contained in the first letter, so, too, God appears in a multiplicity of images.[147] It is evident, moreover, that for Jacob, as well as for his brother Isaac and other kabbalists with similar views, the imaginary seeing of the theophanic forms had a transformative quality. Thus, in another work, a collection of Jacob ha-Kohen's teachings, *Sefer ha-'Orah* (the "Book of the Illumination"), the imagination is described as facilitating the transformation of the Israelites at Sinai from corporeal beings into angels: "Through the imagination (*ha-dimyon*) they imagined mental images (*dimyonot sikhliyyot*), and from the power of those very images they lost their senses and remained as ministering angels, deriving pleasure from the splendor of the Presence, and that entire event was as it is written concerning the revelation of the Torah at Mount Sinai."[148] Given the juxtaposition of this statement to a discussion of the vision of the voices at Sinai (according to the accepted reading of Exod. 20:15), it is reasonable to assume that the object of the imaginative visualization was indeed the voices of revelation. This reading is borne out by another version of the text in a second manuscript: "Thus the voices (*qolot*) appeared to them [as] mental images, and from the power of those images they lost their senses and remained as ministering angels, deriving pleasure from the splendor of the Presence herself."[149]

The portrayal of the *Shekhinah* as the archetypal image is most fully developed in the zoharic corpus. In one context in the main body of the *Zohar* the mater is put in the following way: the biblical term *maḥazeh* refers to the *Shekhinah,* for she is the prism (*ḥezu*) in which "all the supernal images

[147] This idea, as I stated above, is based on a conception expressed by Eleazar of Worms, discussed extensively in the previous chapter, viz., that the glory represents an angel that changes into multiple forms (*dimyonot*) that are seen within the prophetic or mystical imagination. The influence of the German Pietistic motif of the glory that interchanges with an angel is evident in a tradition reported by Moses of Burgos in the name of his teacher, Jacob ha-Kohen, extant in MS Cosantanse 181, fol. 106b, printed by Scholem in "R. Moses of Burgos, Disciple of R. Isaac," *Tarbiz* 5 (1934): 319–320 (in Hebrew). See also MSS Oxford-Bodleian 1945, fol. 18a; Moscow-Guenzberg 131, fol. 161a, quoted by Farber in Jacob ben Jacob ha-Kohen, "Commentary on Ezekiel's Chariot," p. 124 n. 16. According to this passage, Meṭaṭron is associated with the attribute of judgment and the divine Presence with the attribute of mercy. The rabbinic statement (B. Sanhedrin 38b) that the name of Meṭaṭron is like that of his Master, based on Exod. 23:21, is interpreted in terms of the dynamic of one attribute acting in light of the other. Moreover, the divine Presence, identified as an attribute of God, is called "angel" on account of the fact that the providence of the world occurs through that attribute.

[148] MS Milan-Ambrosiana 62, fol. 90b.

[149] MS Florence Medicea-Laurenziana 44.14, fol. 7b; See also fol. 6a, where Moses is described as being clothed in the "splendor of the perfection of the intellect, and he resembled the ministering angels, and he participated in the power of the Presence."

(*diyoqnin ʿilaʾin*) are seen,"[150] or, alternatively expressed, she is "the prism in which the upper forms are seen, like a mirror in which all the images are seen."[151] In another zoharic text we read,

> "The likeness of the four beasts" (Ezek. 1:5). The likeness of what? The likeness of the supernal beasts, for from those that are visible those that are hidden and invisible are seen. Thus it is called likeness (*demut*) and it is called image (*ṣelem*). . . . Here is a supernal secret: when the river comes forth from Eden all the souls that are the fruit of the Holy One, blessed be He, come out from it, and the one that takes them does so at the time they come out before the Holy One, blessed be He. Each one enters into an image, to assume form in that place that is called likeness (*demut*), and they are the four beasts. Each one is formed there in the image that is appropriate to it. From there all these images are formed according to their form, like one that enters a mold to be formed.[152]

A parallel formulation of this role of the *Shekhinah* as the image that imparts form is found in *Sefer ha-Yiḥud ha-ʾAmiti* (the "Book of True Unity"), another composition of the Iyyun circle that may in fact have been a source for the zoharic text cited above:

> This is the power of the Presence that receives all the entities [i.e., the *sefirot*]; they enter into it without an image and emerge from it with matter, form, and an image. [The Presence] is the form of an image (*toʾar demut*) like a coin, seal, or instrument that fixes a form. There would be no divine matter without the Presence.[153]

In both of these passages the Presence is portrayed as actively imparting form to that which emerges from her, like a stamp that imprints the material surface with a particular form. The feminine potency is therefore a matrix that gives shape to the other forms. Specifically, these forms consist of the four angelic beasts beheld by Ezekiel. At one point the *Zohar* comments that the description of the four beasts in the verse "Each of them had a human face" (Ezek. 1:10) implies that "all the images were comprised within them, for they are the great faces,[154] and the engraved faces are formed within them like the explicit name [YHWH] that is engraved on the four sides of the world, east, west, north, and south."[155]

In the continuation of this passage it becomes apparent that the idea being expressed is the structural parallel between four of the ten *sefirot*—the middle triad or three Patriarchs, plus the tenth, which corresponds to David—and the four angelic beasts that are contained within the *Shekhinah*. The engraving of these angelic forms upon the throne is described as an elaborate process that

[150] *Zohar* 1:91a.

[151] Ibid., 88b. For fuller discussion of this passage and the one cited in the previous note, see Wolfson, "Circumcision, Vision of God, and Textual Interpretation," pp. 199–201.

[152] *Zohar Ḥadash* 38b–c.

[153] MS New York–JTSA Mic. 1822, fol. 7a.

[154] In contrast to the "smaller faces," or cherubim; cf. B. Ḥagigah 13b.

[155] *Zohar* 1:18b.

involves each of the forms gazing upon the face of the divine anthropos. "The [face of the] anthropos gazed upon them all, and all of them rose and gazed upon him. Thus all of them were formed in their engravings, in this form by the mystery of the one name that is called Awesome, and then it is written concerning them, "Each of them had a human face."[156] The contemplative gazing (*histakkelut*) results in the production of each angelic form, specularized through the image of the *Shekhinah*.[157] In this case as well, the ocular gaze is fundamentally phallic in nature.

The motifs outlined above are especially developed in *Tiqqune Zohar* and *Ra*ʿ*aya Mehemna,* two works belonging in an extended sense to the zoharic corpus but composed by an anonymous Spanish kabbalist in the early fourteenth century. According to this kabbalist, the last of the *sefirot,* the *Shekhinah,* is identified as the locus of visionary experience, inasmuch as she is the "figure (*ṣiyura*ʾ) of the upper and lower realities, and all the images (*diyoqnin*) of the *sefirot* and their names are formed within her, and in her are inscribed the souls, angels, and holy beasts."[158] Older traditions about the visibility of the Presence are here recast in a purely docetic way: *Shekhinah* continues to be designated as the *dimyon,* the image, and hence is viewed as the source of visionary imaginings (*dimyonot*), but the images assumed by the *Shekhinah* exist solely within the imagination of the visionary.[159]

The *Shekhinah* is thus characterized as the symbolic image or likeness (*temunah*) seen in prophetic vision, as the verse itself relates concerning Moses, "he beholds the likeness of the Lord" (*u-temunat YHWH yabiṭ*) (Num. 12:8). The *Shekhinah,* however, is not visible in and of itself, but only in a secondary ontological state and only in accordance with the imagination of the recipient of the vision: "Even that image is [not seen] in her place, but only when she descends to rule over the creatures, and emanates upon them, she appears to them, each one in accordance with their sight, vision, and imagination (*yitḥaze lon le-khol ḥad ke-fum mar*ʾ*eh we-ḥezyon we-dimyon dilhon*), and this is the import of the verse 'and through the prophets I was imaged' (*u-ve-yad ha-nevi*ʾ*im* ʾ*adammeh*)."[160]

Although it is not stated explicitly in this context, it can be shown from other passages that in her descent to govern the world the *Shekhinah* assumes an angelic garment (what some kabbalists, following Naḥmanides, referred to as

[156] Ibid., 19a. Cf. *Zohar* 1:149b (*Sitre Torah*), 3:48a–b, 135a, 154a.

[157] Cf. *Zohar* 3:118b.

[158] *Tiqqune Zohar* 22, 65a.

[159] According to *Zohar* 2:116b (Raʿaya Mehemna—hereafter abbreviated RM), a distinction is made between a sage, who sees the masculine and feminine potencies of the divine with the "eye of the intellect," and the prophet, who sees them with his very eyes by means of *mar*ʾ*eh* and *ḥezyon,* i.e., diurnal and nocturnal visions. Cf. the characterization of the Presence or glory in R. Asher ben David's *Perush Shem ha-Meforash,* p. 2, as that which "appears to prophets according to their level and according to their mission. . . . According to the mission it changes from appearance to appearance." R. Asher emphasizes the visionary aspect of the *Shekhinah* throughout this work, relating it especially to biblical theophanies. See pp. 12–14.

[160] *Zohar* 2:42b.

sod ha-malbush, "the secret of the garment"). Thus on several occasions in these works we find the idea that the highest of angels, Meṭaṭron, is the body of the *Shekhinah*[161] or the chariot consisting of the images of the four beasts in which she is revealed.[162] Elsewhere the five archangels, Michael, Gabriel, Uriel, Nuriel, and Raphael, are described as the garment of the *Shekhinah*. These traditions are clearly elaborations of an earlier motif, as I have discussed in conjunction with the Ḥaside Ashkenaz, concerning the interchange of the glory (*Shekhinah*) and the exalted angel (in some cases identified as Meṭaṭron). Or, to put the matter in biblical terms, the angelic presence is the theophanic manifestation of the divine. The anonymous author of *Tiqqune Zohar* and *Raʿaya Mehemna* has added the idea that the specific form of the angelic appearance of the divine glory varies in accordance with the imagination of each one to whom the *Shekhinah* is manifest. The profoundly docetic orientation of this kabbalist is expressed in another passage from *Tiqqune Zohar:*

> The *Shekhinah* is the image (*dimyon*) and appearance (*mar'eh*) of everything. The image, as it is said, "and through the prophets I was imaged" (Hosea 12:11). Concerning her it is said, "he beheld the likeness of the Lord" (Num. 12:8). She is called image (*dimyon*), for all the aspects [seen by] by prophets (*parṣufin di-nevi'ei*) are inscribed within her.[163] And she is called vision (*mar'eh*), for all the lights that are above her are seen through her, as it is written, "I make Myself known to him in a vision" (Num. 12:6). . . . She rides upon the four beasts, which include the face of a man, the face of a lion, the face of an ox, and the face of an eagle. To the one who is a human she appears in human form, and to the one who is like the other beasts she appears in the form of the beasts of the throne, to each one in accordance with his capacity (*le-khol ḥad ke-fum ḥeileih*).[164]

In yet another passage the *Shekhinah* and *Binah* are together designated as "visions of God" (*mar'ot 'elohim*), linked exegetically to Ezek. 1:1, but a difference is maintained between the two: "The supernal Mother [*Binah*] is the concealed vision that has no image (*dimyon*); the lower Mother [*Shekhinah*] is the

[161] On possible sources for the identification of Meṭaṭron as the body of the Presence (*guf ha-shekhinah*), see Idel, "World of Angels in Human Form," p. 57; and Farber, "On the Sources of Rabbi Moses de Leon's Early Kabbalistic System," p. 83 n. 35.

[162] *Tiqqune Zohar,* introduction, 14b. Cf. *Zohar* 3:230b (RM): "The angel Meṭaṭron is the chariot of the *Shekhinah*." And cf. Joseph of Hamadan, *Sefer Tashak,* ed. Zwelling, p. 350: "Therefore it says, 'the heavens opened and I saw visions of God' (Ezek. 1:1), he saw the chariots of the Maṭrona that are called Meṭaṭron, but he did not see the chariots of the Holy One, blessed be He."

[163] Cf. Moses Cordovero, *Pardes Rimmonim* 23, s.v. *dimyon:* "The [word] *dimyon* refers to *Malkhut* and she is called in this way when she sits on the throne of glory. . . . When she comprises all the visions and aspects of the prophets she is called *dimyon*." See also the commentary of Judah Ḥayyat to *Maʿarekhet ha-'Elohut* 144a, and Joseph Albo, *Sefer ha-ʿIqqarim* III:17, where an association is made between the speculum that does not shine and the imaginative faculty. For a critique of this text, see Ḥayyim ben Benjamin of Genazzano, *'Iggeret Ḥamudot,* p. 12. On the nexus of the imagination (*dimyon*), prophecy (with the exception of Moses), and the *Shekhinah* described as the speculum that does not shine, see Joseph Gikatilla, *Shaʿare 'Orah,* ed. Ben-Shlomo, 1:248.

[164] *Tiqqune Zohar* 18, 31b.

revealed vision that has an image, and concerning her it is said, 'through the prophets I was imaged' (Hosea 12:11). 'Imaged' (*'adammeh*): she is the image for every prophet, to each one in accordance with his capacity."[165] The nature of that image and the means by which it is apprehended are purely mental:

> This vision [i.e., *Shekhinah*] is composed of the ten *sefirot*. . . . she has several visions (*ḥezyonot*), images (*dimyonot*), and forms (*mar'ot*), and everything is known by the intellectual eye of the heart (*'ein ha-sekhel de-libba'*), concerning which it is said, "The heart knows, the heart understands." Concerning that which is said, "and through the prophets I was imaged," the image (*dimyon*) is in the intellect of the heart (*sekhel de-libba'*) and not an image of the eye (*dimyon de-'eina'*).[166]

The *Shekhinah* is thus described as the locus of all the archetypal images that are visually apprehended in the prophetic experience. The feminine axis of the divine is, in effect, the *mundus imaginalis,* the realm of spiritual forms whose materiality (and hence phenomenality) is constituted in the human imagination.[167] It is highly significant that the first of the seventy interpretations of the first word of Scripture, *bereshit,* which make up the content of the *Tiqqunim,* begins precisely on this point:

> *Bereshit: bet reshit.* This is "the gate to the Lord through which the righteous enter" (Ps. 118:20). This is the gate for the righteous who have permission to enter there; others who are not righteous are driven out from there. In her are inscribed, depicted, and engraved the upper and lower images (*diyoqnin*). The form of a man is inscribed there, and this is the image of man. The form of a lion is there to the right, the form of an ox to the left, and the form of an eagle in the middle. . . . The four letters of the holy name, YHWH, shine upon them. The king of all the beasts is man (*'adam*), which is numerically equivalent to YHWH.[168] The image of man (*demut 'adam*) is the holy *Shekhinah,* for she is his image (*deyoqneih*); she is his seal (*ḥotam dileih*), concerning which it is written, "Let me be a seal upon your heart" (Cant. 8:6). Thus the *Shekhinah* says [to the Holy One]: Even though You ascend above, Your image is never removed from me, like the seal that is in the place to which cleaves the impression of the master of the seal. The image of the seal through which He is known is not removed from her. . . . The seal of the Holy One, blessed be He, is certainly the *Shekhinah.*[169]

165 Ibid., 30, 74b.

166 *Zohar* 3:280b (RM).

167 An interpretation of the prophetic experience as the revelation of one's own form is found as well in an anonymous kabbalistic text, where it is stated that one's form "is comprised in the *Shekhinah,* and when the *Shekhinah* is revealed to him he sees his form as if he looks in a mirror." See MS Oxford-Bodleian 1954, fol. 68a, quoted in translation by Idel in "Universalization and Integration," p. 36.

168 That is, the word *'adam* (anthropos) numerically equals forty-five, which is also the value of the word YHWH when it is written out in full. On the correlation of the four letters of the Tetragrammaton and the four creatures in Ezekiel's vision of the chariot, see Joseph of Hamadan, *Sefer Tashak,* ed. Zwelling, pp. 360, 370.

169 *Tiqqune Zohar* 1, 18a; cf. 21, 67b; 70, 121a; *Zohar Ḥadash* 33a–b.

The *Shekhinah* is the image (*dimyon*) manifest in prophetic visions, for she is the likeness of the anthropos (*demut ʾadam*), that is, the image of the masculine aspect of the divine.[170] More specifically, it is evident that in the above passage the *Shekhinah* is portrayed as the phallus of the divine anthropos. This is alluded to in the depiction of the *Shekhinah* as the seal (*ḥotam*) of the image of the man. In the next chapter I will elaborate on this aspect of the theosophic myth. Suffice it here to note that the visual image of the divine, the *Shekhinah*, is compared to a seal on which is imprinted the impression of the master of the seal. That seal is also represented as the Tetragrammaton, whose letters correspond to the four theophanic figures of Ezekiel's chariot.

It is of interest to compare the above texts with the view expressed in a passage from one of the Hebrew theosophic works written by the author of *Tiqqune Zohar,* where it is said that the *Shekhinah*

> is called *ṣelem* on account of the fact that she is like the likeness above (*ki-deyoqno shel maʿalah*), and she is called *demut* on account of the fact that she is comparable to the image above (*she-domah le-dimyon shel maʿalah*), and this is the secret of "and through the prophets I was imaged," that is, to the souls that resemble the likeness above (*deyoqno shel maʿalah*) the Holy One, blessed be He, is revealed in the image above (*dimyon shel maʿalah*). The image is the Spirit that is the median line in the image of *Tifʾeret.*[171]

In this context, then, the image is linked with the masculine potency, *Tifʾeret,* in whose image is the feminine *Shekhinah,* and hence the force of the verse from Hosea is that the prophets experienced the former through the latter. The imaginal forms that inhere within the feminine Presence actually derive from the masculine potency that is hierarchically above the feminine. Indeed, according to another text, the locus of the images or forms is in *Yesod* (Foundation) or *Ṣaddiq* (Righteous), symbolized by the letter *ṣaddi,* the grade that corresponds to the phallus of the divine anthropos:

> The *Ṣaddiq* is the pillar that supports everything, and through him that which is above everything is known, for the *Ṣaddiq* contains all the *sefirot,* and in him everything is united in one unit. It is [symbolized by] the palm branch (*lulav*), the bond of all the *sefirot.* In the letter *ṣaddi* are formed all the forms (*ṣiyyurin*) of the palaces that surround the supernal Garden of Eden, the various forms of the act of creation that the righteous inherit, and in it shine the points of Torah that are points in the palace that is the lower Presence. These [points] shine on the forms like pearls that shine on the head of a crown and like the stars that shine in the firmament. On account of all the points of the stars it is said, "And God placed

[170] Cf. *Tiqqune Zohar* 62, 94b. In this connection it should be noted that some kabbalists link the word *demut* specifically to the male potency; e.g., MS Oxford-Bodleian 1938, fol. 63a: "Concerning that which is said, 'Let us make man in our image, after our likeness' (Gen. 1:26), [this is] the image (*demut*) of the male . . . the image that is distinguished in the male is that which is distinguished in God. 'After our likeness,' refers to *Yesod,* which is the masculine and is distinguished in man."

[171] *Sefer ha-Malkhut* 23a.

them in the firmament of the sky to shine upon the earth" (Gen. 1:17), that is, the lower Presence.[172]

The forms become visible through the feminine, but their ontic source is actually in the masculine, the *Ṣaddiq*. There are kabbalistic sources that explicitly connect the phallic aspect of the divine and the production of images. I will cite two brief examples, both deriving from the Iyyun circle. The first is drawn from the treatise *Sod ʿEser Sefirot we-Sod ha-Gewanim* (the "Secret of the Ten Emanations and the Secret of the Colors"), which, as its name indicates, establishes a correlation between the divine attributes (also referred to as the *mar'ot 'elohim,* "visions of God"[173]) and colors.[174] In the delineation of the ten gradations, the ninth, which corresponds to *Yesod* or the divine phallus, is described as "the king in the power of the imagination" (*melekh be-khoaḥ dimyon*).[175] This image is repeated in a second passage from the same composition, where this gradation—called, among other things, the secret of Torah (*sod ha-Torah*) and the covenant of peace (*berit shalom*)—is again identified as the king, which is the power of the imagination (*koaḥ dimyon*).[176]

The second example that locates the power of imagination in this aspect of the divine is taken from a commentary on the thirty-two paths of wisdom, one of several such commentaries written at different times by members of this literary circle.[177] According to this text, the thirty-two paths divide into three groups. The first group corresponds to the ten *sefirot,* even though the names given to each power reflect the nonsefirotic stage of speculation. The ninth of those powers is identified as the light that bestows form (*'or ha-meṣuyyar*). The implication of this name is drawn explicitly in the description of Ṣiyoriel—the corresponding power in the second decade, which consists of angelic beings that parallel the sefirotic entities—who is said to "give shape to all the forms (*ṣurot*) hidden in the power that bestows form."[178] Although in this case the precise language of imagination is not used, it is evident that the bestowing of forms is related to this capacity of the mind. As will be seen in detail in the following chapter, the contextualizing of the imaginative faculty in the phallus is a central tenet of zoharic theosophy; indeed, one might very well speak of the phallic imagination as the critical element in the ecstatic-mystical experience underlying many of the homiletical and theoretical discussions in the *Zohar,*

[172] *Tiqqune Zohar* 70, 120b–121a. Cf. the *Sod ha-Ḥashmal* of Joseph Gikatilla, 41a, wherein both *Yesod* and *Shekhinah* are portrayed as a source of forms and images; the former is linked with the word *ṣelem* and the latter with *demut.*

[173] MS Vatican 171, fol. 133b.

[174] See Scholem, *Reshit ha-Qabbalah,* p. 260 n. 21; idem, "Index to the Commentaries on the Ten *Sefirot,*" p. 508 n. 93.

[175] MS Vatican 171, fol. 133a.

[176] Ibid., fol. 133b.

[177] See Scholem, *Reshit ha-Qabbalah,* pp. 257–258 n. 11.

[178] MS New York–JTSA Mic. 8558, fol. 6a. A version of this text is printed in the anthology of kabbalistic works compiled by Judah Koriat, *Ma'or wa-Shemesh* 24b; see Scholem, *Reshit ha-Qabbalah,* p. 258 n. 11.

for it is through the capacity of the creative imagination that the mystic imputes measure to the divine form. The author of *Tiqqune Zohar* likewise locates the forms or images in the divine phallus, but the manifestation of those forms in specifically visible images is effected through the medium of the feminine divine Presence, which is, in fact, an aspect of the phallus, the corona of the penis. Moreover, the tangible shapes that those forms assume are dependent on the mental capacity of the recipient, especially his imaginative faculty.

Reverberations of Imaginative Seeing in Later Kabbalistic Literature

The centrality of the role of the imagination as the vehicle for revelatory experience continued to have a decisive influence in subsequent kabbalistic literature. In the concluding section of this chapter I would like to round out my discussion of this motif by examining some of the relevant sources in which the imaginative visualization of the divine is further elaborated. For example, in his *Masoret ha-Ḥokhmah* (the "Tradition of Wisdom") the early sixteenth-century kabbalist Abraham ben Eliezer Halevi includes as the first in a list of eight advantages to the study of kabbalah the pleasure that the soul experiences when one contemplates "those forms engraved upon the heart, until it appears to him as if he were seeing them with his actual eye." It is significant that the first advantage noted in this context is the pleasure that results from one's imagining the forms of the emanations as they are inscribed within the heart. The veridicality of the experience is such that the individual considers that he is actually seeing these emanations with his own eyes. The implication here is that by contemplating the imaginative forms of the *sefirot* one attains a state proximate to prophecy. Hence, in the continuation of this text, when describing the eighth advantage the author makes it clear that in his opinion, through knowledge of kabbalah one receives the illumination of the Holy Spirit and may even "reach the boundary, so that if he were to gain more of this wisdom it is possible that he would ascend to the level of prophecy."[179] In still other passages Abraham ben Eliezer singles out the importance of the imagination as a faculty for visual meditation. Thus, drawing on sources from the thirteenth century—including, most importantly, Isaac of Acre, whose views were at least in part informed by Abraham Abulafia[180]—he writes,

[179] MS New York–JTSA Mic. 1737, fols. 30a, 31a, published (on the basis of MS Vatican 431, fols. 43a, 44a) in G. Scholem, "The Kabbalist R. Abraham ben Eliezer Halevi," *Qiryat Sefer* 2 (1924): 127 (in Hebrew).

[180] Some of the relevant passages are discussed in Idel, *Mystical Experience*, pp. 30–34. The texts of Abraham ben Eliezer Halevi were not discussed by Idel in that context, but see his "Writings of R. Abraham Abulafia," p. 263; see also p. 275 n. 68, where Idel remarks specifically on the affinity of Isaac of Acre and Abraham ben Eliezer. The influence of Abulafia on Isaac of Acre has been studied extensively by Idel; see *Mystical Experience*, pp. 80–82, 85, 115–118, 134, 141; *Studies in Ecstatic Kabbalah*, pp. 81–83, 92–95, 112–119, and relevant notes.

> And so there are angels when an individual mentions their names he must focus on them by means of the imaginative faculty, and imagine them in the form of human beings. Their faces are faces of flame, and their whole bodies a raging fire, some are white fire, some green fire, and some red fire, it is all according to the imagination from which they derive. Similarly, in mentioning some of the names [of God] one must intend certain known intentions. There is a name concerning which one must concentrate on whether its letters are written before him in red fire or green or white, or in the likeness of gold or silver, and there are some letters that are infinitely enlarged. Each one is in accordance with what is needed in that particular matter, and according to the attribute that is drawn from it. Permission has not been given to write all this explicitly, lest it come to someone who is not worthy, and he will destroy the world.[181]

The last comment echoes a remark of Halevi in another work, *Hora'ah 'al She'elat ha-Mal'akhim* ("A Directive Concerning the Question of Angels"), which, as Scholem noted,[182] also reflects the influence of Abraham Abulafia's *ḥokhmat ha-ṣeruf,* the wisdom of letter-combination: "The mentioning of the [divine] names (*hazkarat ha-shemot*) is necessary to form spiritual images (*ṣiyyurim ruḥaniyyim*) by the increase of the imagination (*be-tigboret ha-dimyon*)[183] in a variety of forms, each one in accordance with what it is and in accordance with the attribute that derives from it, and that very name draws from it; permission has not been given to write all this, lest it come into the hands of someone unworthy, who will destroy the world."[184] The recitation of divine names eventuates in the augmentation of the imagination, which produces spiritual images of different forms in accordance with the specific name and the divine attribute to which it is correlated.

Further evidence can be seen for the development in the sixteenth century of meditative techniques based on the role accorded the imagination in the visualization of the divine hypostases. For example, Eleazar ben Moses Azikri (1533–1600), in his mystical diary, *Milei di-Shemaya* ("Words of Heaven"), placed the visual encounter between man and God at the center of the mystic's worship:

> You should constantly see your Creator with the eye of your intellect, for "the Lord looks down from heaven on mankind to find a man of understanding (*maskil*), a man mindful of God" (Ps. 14:2). That is, with the eyes of his intellect he seeks Him, and when he sees Him it makes an impression, as in the case of the ostrich, for when she looks well at her egg the [baby] ostrich is formed and takes shape within it, and [the egg] breaks open and [the ostrich] comes out.[185] So, too, with respect

[181] MS New York–JTSA Mic. 1737, fol. 33b.

[182] Scholem, "The Kabbalist R. Abraham ben Eliezer Halevi," p. 110 n. 2.

[183] Curiously, these critical words are missing in the revised version of Scholem's study, printed in the introduction to the facsimile edition of *Abraham ben Eliezer Ha-Levi, Ma'amar Meshare Qiṭrin, Constantinople 1510* (Jerusalem, 1977), p. 18 (in Hebrew).

[184] *Kerem Ḥemed* 9 (1856): 146, quoted by Scholem (see references in the two previous notes).

[185] Cf. Ḥayyim Vital, *'Eṣ Ḥayyim* 8:1, 34b, where a similar analogy is employed to demonstrate the generative power of the looking of the eyes (*histakkelut 'einayim*) in the Adam Qadmon to

to God, when He looks at you He causes all kinds of bountifulness and blessings to flow upon you. Thus it says, "all your males shall appear" (Deut. 16:16). The [rabbis] interpreted [the word] *yera'eh* [appear] as *yir'eh* [will see], for just as a man comes to be seen (*lera'ot*), so he comes to see (*lir'ot*).[186] For the masses of people this occurs on the three festivals of the year in the time of the Temple, but for the enlightened ones (*maskilim*) [this occurs] on a regular basis, every day, at any time, in every place. When you look heavenward with the intention of the heart, the arousal of the will of every will will be stirred, blessed be He and blessed be His name forever and ever.[187]

In this passage the eye of the intellect is specified as the means by which one looks upon the divine. In still other passages in his diary Azikri upholds the intellect as the faculty of vision. In one context Azikri mystically interprets the verse "I have placed the Lord before me constantly" (Ps. 16:8) as the need to contemplate God without interruption through the eye of the intellect, for by so doing one draws down the efflux of light from above.[188] Indeed, following a much older motif, expressed in medieval Jewish sources, Azikri notes that the aspect of the human soul that derives from the throne of glory is the intellect; hence, the verse extols the wise man as one who has eyes in his head (cf. Eccles. 2:14).[189] The intellect, therefore, is the bond that connects man and God. Yet, it can be shown from another passage in this diary that parallels the text I cited above that it is the imagination that is assigned the role of facilitating the visual encounter:

The imagination is active [in the prophetic process], as R. Moses [ben Maimon] proved. Some of the philosophers say that the imagination through which a person imagines his friend acts in him like the egg of an ostrich, for when she gazes in a fixed way upon it the ostrich takes shape in it and comes out, like the egg of a chicken upon which the chicken sits. In this manner when a person, who is made in the image and likeness of the King of the world, concentrates his mind upon Him, he draws forth from Him the will and light. He is renewed and becomes a new creature, as it says, "to peoples yet to be born, for He has acted" (Ps. 22:32).[190]

While the vision of God is surely not a physical perception—Azikri stresses that the vehicle of vision is the eye of the intellect rather than a physical eye—it is nonetheless facilitated by the imagination, which translates the spiritual forms into concrete sensible images. Indeed, the seeing of the divine gradations

---

produce the vowel points (*nequddot*) that come streaming forth from the eyes. It stands to reason that there is an underlying sexual connotation to the process as well, the points corresponding to drops of semen.

186 Cf. *Mekhilta de-Rabbi Shim'on bar Yoḥai*, p. 159; *Sifre on Deuteronomy*, 143, pp. 195–196; B. Ḥagigah 2a.

187 *Milei di-Shemaya*, p. 103; cf. pp. 120, 174–175, 176.

188 Ibid., p. 120.

189 Ibid., pp. 174–175.

190 Ibid., p. 176. See, however, *Sefer Ḥaredim*, pt. 1, chap. 5, p. 37, where Azikri cautions one about the dangers of the imagination when thinking about the nature of God.

is not possible unless they assume tangible shape in the human imagination. Ḥayyim Vital affirmed this position as well in his description of the prophetic process in his *Shaʿare Qedushah* (the "Gates of Holiness"), which I cite in full:

> The Holy Spirit (*ruaḥ ha-qodesh*) rests on a person when he is awake, when the soul is in his body and does not leave it [as in sleep]. But [the prophetic state involves] the matter of separation [of the soul from the body], for he removes [from his mind] all [mundane] thoughts entirely. And the imaginative faculty in him, which is a faculty that derives from the elementary animal soul, prevents him from imagining or thinking about any matter pertaining to this world, as if his soul had left him. Then his imaginative faculty transforms his thoughts until he imagines that he ascends to the upper worlds to the roots of his soul . . . and the forms of all the lights will be inscribed in his thought as if he imagined and saw them, as is the way of the imaginative faculty to imagine in his mind things of this world even though he does not [actually] see them. . . . The [divine] light and influx reaches the rational soul that is in his body, and from there it reaches the vital soul and the imaginative faculty that is within it. And there these [spiritual] matters assume a corporeal form in the imaginative faculty so that [the prophet] can comprehend them as if he actually saw them with the [physical] eye (*we-sham yiṣṭayyeru ha-ʿinyanim ha-hem ṣiyyur gashmi be-khoḥo ha-medammeh we-ʾaz yevinem ke-ʾillu roʾeh ʾotan be-ʿayin mamash*).[191]

Vital goes on to say that at times the sefirotic light descends and takes the form within the imaginative faculty of an angel who is seen or heard. In a separate discussion on the wisdom of interpreting the chirping of birds (*ṣifṣufe ʿofot*) contained in *Shaʿar Ruaḥ ha-Qodesh* (the "Gate of the Holy Spirit"), Vital offers several explanations for the identity of the birds. One of those is relevant to our discussion, as it involves a process not unlike that of the prophetic imagination:

> Sometimes [the chirping of birds is to be explained] in another manner, for the soul of some righteous person comes from the upper world and is clothed in that form and image; it is not an actual creature or bird, but only appears and is seen in this way, and he reveals secrets of Torah. Indeed, according to the level and stature of the person who sees them, they appear before him, and on occasion they appear before two people at once, and before one person it appears in the form of a bird or another creature, and before the second person it appears in another manner; it all depends on the level of the person who sees them.[192]

It is apparent that Vital's description of the prophetic process is reminiscent of Maimonides' description of prophecy as the overflow of the Active Intellect to the rational faculty and then to the imagination.[193] There are, however,

[191] *Shaʿare Qedushah,* pt. 3, chap. 5, pp. 89–90.

[192] *Shaʿar Ruaḥ ha-Qodesh,* 5d.

[193] See Werblowsky, *Joseph Karo,* pp. 69–70. See also Vital's statement in the fourth part of *Shaʿare Qedushah,* printed in *Ketavim Ḥadashim le-Rabbenu Ḥayyim Vital,* p. 22. Let me note, parenthetically, that Vital's explanation may have been based more directly on a passage in Joseph

important differences between Maimonides' conception of prophecy and that of Vital. The most obvious one is that for Maimonides the intellectual overflow has its source in the Active Intellect, the last of the separate intellects, whereas for Vital the source of the overflow of the divine light is the *Ein-Sof* itself. The point was articulated in *Sefer ha-Berit* (the "Book of the Convenant") by R. Pineḥas Eliyahu Horowitz, whose ideas on prophecy were heavily influenced by Vital: "The prophetic overflow does not come from the Active Intellect, for it is a thing that does not exist except in their discourse; rather the prophetic overflow comes from the awesome and glorious Lord, for the Lord places the overflow of His holy spirit, the spirit from above, upon the prophet, as it says, 'Would that all the Lord's people were prophets, that the Lord put His spirit upon them' (Num. 11:29)."[194]

Secondly, according to Vital, the imagination has the additional, and in fact primary, function of serving as a vehicle for celestial ascent, in this case an ascent of the prophet to his soul-root in the sefirotic realm. The imagination, then, is the means by which the forms of the *sefirot,* referred to by Vital as *ṣiyyure kol ha-ʾorot,* are inscribed in the prophet's mind. The soul ascends via the imagination to the divine world, which is the ultimate object of vision; for Maimonides the prophet receives an overflow from the Active Intellect, but there is no direct contact with God. On precisely these grounds various kabbalists criticized the philosophical understanding of prophecy as mediated through the Active Intellect. For example, Moses of Kiev, in his kabbalistic anthology *Shoshan Sodot,* commented on the verse "I beheld my Lord seated on a high and lofty throne" (Isa. 6:1): "It is not as the opinion of the philosophers that the prophet sees the Active Intellect, for how could a prophet call that by the name Lord which designates the essence of [God's] lordship?"[195] The distinction I am drawing was noted as well in *Sefer ha-Berit,* though in that context the author was not focusing specifically on Vital: "According to the philosopher, the intellectual soul of the one who is righteous and pure of heart ascends to the Active Intellect, but according to the kabbalists, he is with holy souls more important than he, for he ascends to the countenance of the Lord in the mountain of God . . . and there he sees true things, and the soul shows all this to the body from a distance through the imaginative faculty, for the imagina-

---

ben Shalom Ashkenazi's kabbalistic commentary on *Bereshit Rabbah,* which utilizes the Maimonidean explanation of prophecy, albeit in a theosophical garb, i.e., the influx is said to overflow from the *Shekhinah,* identified as the imaginative faculty (*koaḥ ha-medammeh* or *koaḥ ha-dimyon*), to the Active Intellect (which must be here identified as Meṭaṭron), and from there to the rational faculty in man, and finally to the imagination. Cf. *A Kabbalistic Commentary of Rabbi Yoseph ben Shalom Ashkenazi on Genesis Rabbah,* pp. 221–222. The likelihood that this was a source for Vital is strengthened by the fact that a lengthy passage on the nature of prophecy, cited in the name of the philosophers in Joseph ben Shalom Ashkenazi's text, is also found in the fourth part of Vital's *Shaʿare Qedushah,* according to some manuscripts. Cf. also p. 223, and n. 38, where attention is drawn to the citation of this passage by Vital. See also Idel, *Kabbalah: New Perspectives,* p. 106.

[194] *Sefer ha-Berit ha-Shalem,* p. 478.

[195] *Shoshan Sodot,* 15b.

tion is a necessary thing, [as it says,] 'and through the prophets I was imaged.'"[196]

The critical role accorded to imagination in the prophetic experience—presented in language reminiscent of Vital—involves both an ascent to the divine realm and a drawing down of the efflux to the lower worlds. The vision of prophecy, in contrast to that of a dream, occurs when the soul is still connected to the body, although one should separate one's thought as if one's soul had departed from this world and the imagination had stopped thinking about corporeal matters: "Thus he should think and form in his imagination (*yeṣayyer be-dimyono*) the gradations of the roots of his soul in all the worlds, and he should imagine that he ascended to those worlds, one level after another, in those roots that he has there, from one to the other, and he should imagine in his imagination that he saw the lights that are there."[197] The text goes on to describe in elaborate detail the process of visual imagination that results in both the ascent to the divine pleroma and the drawing down of the light to the mundane realm; what is significant for our purposes is the fact that the faculty that facilitates and actualizes the *ascensio mentis* is the imagination. Despite the basic similarity between the role accorded the imagination in the kabbalistic perspective espoused by Horowitz and the treatment in classical medieval Jewish philosophical writings, such as Maimonides', a sharp distinction is drawn between the view of the kabbalist and that of the philosopher, on the grounds that, according to the former, the prophet draws down the flux of light and energy directly from the divine rather than through the intermediary of the Active Intellect.

There is yet a third difference that must be noted. It seems to me that the view espoused by Vital is closer in its orientation to the Neoplatonic approach of Ezra of Gerona than to the Aristotelian scheme, even though Vital clearly was influenced by Maimonides' formulation, perhaps through the medium of Joseph ben Shalom Ashkenazi. That is, for Vital the *sefirot* themselves, which are akin to spiritual forms (*ṣurot ruḥaniyyot*) in a Neoplatonic ontology, assume a physical form (*ṣiyyur gashmi*) within the imagination, and from the internal senses of the imagination this form is transferred to the external senses through which it is experienced as if it were corporeal. The major difference between the two approaches is captured in the description of prophetic imagination in Yoḥanan Alemanno's commentary on Canticles, *Shir ha-Maʿalot li-Shelomo* (the "Song of Solomon's Ascents"), in the context of delineating the seven guidances provided by the Active Intellect to the human soul; the sixth guidance is connected to the imagination. Using the example of the prophets as a model, Alemanno states that the imagination, guided by the Active Intellect, "forms veridical images taken from the subtle, spiritual forms (*ha-ṣurot ha-daqot ha-ruḥaniyyot*) and the separate substances (*ʿaṣamim nivdalim*)." These images are experienced in concrete form (*mugshamim*) "just as a person imagines a sen-

[196] *Sefer ha-Berit ha-Shalem,* p. 289.
[197] Ibid., p. 472.

tient living being and copies it upon the wall as if he were alive." Alemanno's view is thus consistent with the older Neoplatonic conception expressed in kabbalistic literature, for prophecy consists of the imaginative figuration of the spiritual forms. "It is not as most people think," continues Alemanno, "that the images of the prophets are like dream-images compounded from sensible impressions that remain in the realm of imagination. . . . On the contrary, these [images] are copies of the separate forms within the imagination."[198]

The difference between the Neoplatonic and Aristotelian approach is highlighted if we bear in mind that according to Vital even Mosaic prophecy required imagination. Indeed, the distinction between Moses and all other prophets is not, as Maimonides argued, that the latter required imagination and the former did not. Rather, the distinction consists of the fact that Moses alone was capable of receiving the imagined form through his physical senses and experiencing the concertized form with all five external senses. It follows that for Vital the imagination plays an essential role in the prophetic experience in a way that has no place in the Maimonidean scheme. Indeed, in the fourth part of *Shaʿare Qedushah,* long maintained by kabbalists themselves to be the most recondite part of the text and hence unfit for publication (it was finally published in 1988), the role of the imagination in the contemplative ascent is underscored as well. Vital reiterates the view that the one who wishes to attain the prophetic inspiration of *ruaḥ ha-qodesh* must separate the soul from the body "as if the soul went out from the body and ascended to the heavens."[199] The imaginative faculty is the means by which this separation from the body and the heavenly ascent are achieved. During the ascent the imagination plays a critical role as well. As Vital writes, "You should ascend in your thought from heaven to heaven, until the seventh heaven, called Aravot, and imagine (*we-yeṣayyer*) that there is a great, white curtain upon Aravot, and upon it are drawn (*meṣuyyar*) the letters of the Tetragrammaton, in square letters (*ketav ʾashurit*), in a color that is known, in very thick script, each letter like a mountain and white as snow."[200] Other visual meditative techniques, dependent on the imagination, are specified in this text, as they are in *Shaʿar Ruaḥ ha-Qodesh,* but what I have cited is sufficient to make the point: the imagination serves as a means for the ascent, which eventuates in the cleaving of the soul to its divine root. Through this cleaving there is an increase in the upper *sefirot,* which results in a downward influx of the divine light, resulting in the configuration of that light within the visionary's imagination. In another passage Vital

198 I have utilized the text published in A. M. Lesley, "*The Song of Solomon's Ascents* by Yoḥanan Alemanno: Love and Human Perfection According to a Jewish Colleague of Giovanni Pico della Mirandola" (Ph.D. diss., University of California, Berkeley, 1976), p. 578; for a different English rendering see p. 210. The Hebrew text was published under the title *Shaʿar ha-Ḥesheq* by R. Jacob Barukh in Livorno, 1790. I have consulted the reprint of this version (Halberstadt, 1862), 39a.

199 The text is printed in *Ketavim Ḥadashim le-Rabbenu Ḥayyim Vital,* p. 6.

200 Ibid. Cf. *Shaʿar Ruaḥ ha-Qodesh* 4c–d, where Vital discusses the practice of forming visual images of the letters of the Tetragrammaton.

depicts the very purpose of human existence in terms of the necessity to comprehend the secrets of Torah so that one can imagine in his soul the supernal matters. The effect of sin is that it pollutes the soul so that "it cannot see and comprehend the true perfection, which is the secrets of Torah; that the [divine] form may cleave to him (*lehidabbeq bo ṣurah*), for this reason he was created. Therefore, he is asked [upon death], 'Have you gazed upon the *Shiʿur Qomah,*' which are the secrets of Torah."[201] The sinful soul is like a copper mirror so full of stains and rust that no form can be seen in it. The pure soul, by contrast, is like a clear mirror in which the "supernal holy things take shape" (*mitṣayyarim bah ha-qedoshim ha-ʿelyonim*). The mandate, therefore, is for every soul to repent and purify itself in order "to enter the [mystical] orchard of wisdom (*pardes ha-ḥokhmah*) so that the holy, supernal things will take shape (*yiṣṭayyeru*) within his soul."[202] The process of configuration of the spiritual entities is one that is achieved through the agency of the imagination (*koaḥ ha-meṣayyer*). Hence the prophetic task of imagining the *sefirot* becomes the ultimate calling of *homo religiosus*.

By way of summary, let me again note that my discussion has been limited to a very small percentage of the material in medieval Jewish mystical sources that deals with spiritual visions and the role of imagination. From what I have discussed, however, it should be apparent that a proper appreciation of the imaginative faculty is crucial to understanding the nature of visionary experience in these sources. What the different mystics have in common is a belief that the imagination is the faculty that allows the formless essence of the hidden God to be manifest as a visible presence in the heart of the pious soul. As I have emphasized, in medieval Jewish mysticism this idea is expressed in terms borrowed from various philosophical systems. Yet the concern with the imaging of the imageless God is rooted in the biblical and rabbinic traditions, whose mythopoeic conception of a deity capable of assuming incarnational form greatly informed the kabbalistic mind.

Within the theosophic kabbalist tradition the imaginative faculty is singled out as the means of visualizing that which cannot be perceived by the senses or conceived by the intellect. Not only is the imagination not to be seen as subordinate to reason, as the medieval Aristotelians would have it, but it is elevated to a position of utmost supremacy; it is, in effect, the divine element of the soul that enables one to gain access to the realm of incorporeality. A full-scale phenomenological analysis of the imagination is critical in reevaluating one of the most significant, and yet problematic, aspects of the Jewish mystical tradition, namely, its acceptance of anthropomorphic and corporeal images as a legitimate mode of religious discourse. Although medieval Jewish mystics struggled with this part of the tradition, often qualifying their own use of such images, there can be no question that it is one of the key elements of kabbalistic theosophy and pietism. The central role accorded the imagination in theosophic kab-

[201] *ʿOlat Tamid* 46a–b.
[202] Ibid., 46b.

balah, as is the case of the German Pietists, allowed the mystics to appropriate traditions regarding God's manifest form without compromising the basic Jewish antinomy to idolatry based on the belief that God is formless and imageless. By locating the anthropomorphic shape of God within the imagination both extremes are avoided, for the image is a symbolic characterization and as such functions as an intermediary between corporeality and spirituality. This insight is essential if we wish to appreciate the anthropomorphic speculations and the visions of the medieval Jewish mystics. The corporeal figuration of the divine is not to be taken either literally or metaphorically; it is symbolic and as such allows the formless to be manifest in form, but only within the imagination.

The point is well captured in the following passage from the anonymous kabbalistic work, *Maʿarekhet ha-ʾElohut,* written in the early part of the fourteenth century:

> Know that a person's physical form is made in the [likeness of the] supernal image (*demut ʿelyon*), and the supernal image is the [sefirotic] edifice. . . . Now that you know the human form (*ṣurat ha-ʾadam*), if you have received through oral transmission, you can comprehend the truth of the prophetic vision seen by the prophets. The rabbis, blessed be their memory, called this vision the measure of the stature (*Shiʿur Qomah*). . . . Concerning this it is said in Scripture, "Let us make man in our image and in our likeness" (Gen. 1:26), and regarding the vision it is said, "and through the prophets I was imaged" (Hosea 12:11). R. Isaac [ben Ṭodros] said that [this is alluded to] by the sign that the [word] *temunah* [image] numerically equals [the expression] *parṣuf ʾadam* [human countenance]. I have also found this in the words of R. Eleazar of Worms.[203]

Within the Jewish mystical tradition the problem of anthropomorphism is inseparable from the question of visionary experience. Hence, the mystery of *Shiʿur Qomah* is correlated with prophetic vision. What the prophets saw is that which is described in the esoteric *Shiʿur Qomah,* which in turn is linked exegetically to the biblical claim that Adam was made in God's image. That the anthropos is made in God's image implies that God is in the image of the anthropos. In the mystical vision attested in the Jewish sources, anthropomorphism and theomorphism converge. The phenomenological basis for this convergence, the figural corporealization of God within the human imagination, is provided by Hosea 12:11, *u-ve-yad ha-neviʾim ʾadammeh,* "through the prophets I was imaged."

[203] *Maʿarekhet ha-ʾElohut,* chap. 10, 144a. See also chapter 5, n. 137 of the present work.

• CHAPTER SEVEN •

The Hermeneutics of Visionary Experience: Revelation and Interpretation in the Zohar

Interpretative vs. Revelatory Modes

Mystical experience, like experience in general, is contextual. If that is the case, it follows that mystical visions will always be shaped, informed, and determined by one's institutional affiliation. The claim that the vision is conditioned by preexperiential criteria renders the very notion of an immediate visionary experience of God or things divine problematic, if not impossible. While the mystic may present his or her experience as a direct encounter with God or one of the angels—comprising, therefore, an immediacy unknown to normal everyday consciousness—the fact is that this experience is shaped by prior experiences that are, more often than not, recorded in texts that have been appropriated as part of the canon of a particular religious tradition. A certain "anxiety of influence," therefore, is clearly discernible in the visionary literature of the different mystical traditions: vision is always, to an extent, revision.

The weight of prior visionary experiences is particularly strong in mystical writings that evolve within religions that are principally exegetical in nature, of which Judaism is, of course, a prime example. For the Jewish mystic, commentary on previous visions will often provide the dominant forms of mystical expression. The midrashic recasting of visions recorded in literary documents into new visions is a predominant feature of the different stages of Jewish mysticism, as I argued in the concluding section of chapter 3 with respect to the particular vision of the chariot in postbiblical apocalyptic and mystical literature. This instance is representative of a larger phenomenon: textual study itself provides the occasion for visionary experience. Indeed, the notion of an "inspired" or "pneumatic" exegesis is a well-known feature in Jewish texts, especially pronounced in apocalyptic and mystical circles, as I also indicated at the conclusion of chapter 3. It is, however, conventionally assumed that such a modality should be contrasted with the more normative rabbinic scriptural interpretation (*midrash*), which flourished in a context wherein access to immediate divine revelation had ceased. Midrashic activity, it is assumed, presupposes a distance from God. In the absence of direct communication with God through prophetic revelation, one discerns the will of God from the study of sacred Scripture.[1]

[1] See, for instance, Halivni, *Midrash, Mishnah, and Gemara*, p. 16.

More recent discussions, however, suggest that midrashic activity itself should be viewed as a revelatory mode. Exegesis of Scripture is a means of reexperiencing the seeing of God, particularly at the historical moment of Sinai.[2] Needless to say, contemporary scholars of such an orientation have taken their cue from traditional sources, such as the following midrashic comment on the verse "Your neck with strings of jewels (*ba-ḥaruzim*)" (Cant. 1:10):

> [A] When they string together (*ḥorzim*) words of Torah, and the words of Torah to the Prophets, and the Prophets to the Writings, the fire burns around them, and the words are as joyous as when they were given from Sinai. Were they not originally given in fire, as it says, "The mountain was ablaze with flames to the very skies" (Deut. 4:11)?

> [B] Ben Azzai was sitting and interpreting, and the fire surrounded him. They went and told R. Aqiva: Rabbi, Ben Azzai is sitting and interpreting, and the fire is burning around him. He went to him and said to him: I have heard that you were interpreting, and the fire was burning around you. He said to him: Indeed. He said to him: Perhaps you were occupied in [the study of] the chambers of the chariot (*ḥadre merkavah*)? He said to him: No, but I was sitting and stringing together words of Torah, and words of Torah to the Prophets, and the Prophets to the Writings, and the words were as joyous as when they were given from Sinai, and they were as sweet as at their original giving. Were they not originally given in fire, as it is written, "The mountain was ablaze with flames to the very skies"?[3]

The intent of the first part of this pericope, [A], is to establish, by an artful play on the word *ḥaruzim*, that the necklace worn by the female beloved described in Canticles 1:10 is prepared by students of Scripture who string together (*ḥorzim*) biblical verses by some associative method.[4] Underlying this activity is the hermeneutical assumption of the basic unity of Scripture in its diverse parts; hence, a verse from one section can illuminate that of another if the exegetical prowess of the interpreter is equal to the task. As a result of this activity the fires of Sinai are rekindled, for through the interpretative process the moment of revelation is reexperienced.

The second part, [B], is a specific narrative that illustrates the point. In the initial comment of R. Aqiva to Ben Azzai we encounter an additional element. That is, R. Aqiva assumes that the supernatural occurrence of the fire surround-

[2] See Boyarin, *Intertextuality and the Reading of Midrash*, pp. 110, 118–122; idem, "The Eye in the Torah"; Fraade, *From Tradition to Commentary*, pp. 25–68.

[3] *Shir ha-Shirim Rabbah* 1:10; for a slightly different version of this narrative, set in another midrashic context, see *Wayyikra Rabbah* 16:4, pp. 354–355. For discussion of this and other related texts, see Urbach, "Traditions about Merkabah Mysticism," pp. 7–9; Boyarin, *Intertextuality*, pp. 109–110.

[4] For discussion of midrashic hermeneutics as linking up words of Scripture, see Bruns, *Hermeneutics Ancient and Modern*, pp. 109–110. On the image of textual units constituting the jewelry and ornamentations by which the Torah (as bride) is adorned, see reference below at n. 133.

ing Ben Azzai must be linked especially to theosophic speculation, in the idiom of the text, being occupied with the study of the chambers of the chariot.[5] Ben Azzai's response indicates that it is not esoteric study that eventuates in this revelatory experience but rather the basic scriptural study involving the linking of texts to texts like the stringing of beads to make a necklace. On the one hand, this comment may be an implicit polemic against esotericists who concentrated on theosophic speculation in their exegetical studies, specifically the esoteric study of Ezekiel's chariot. On the other hand, a positive and decidedly mystical valence is applied to scriptural hermeneutics in general. Through the process of interpretation, the Sinaitic epiphany is relived. The presumption of this anonymous midrashist is well captured by Gerald Bruns: "Revelation is never something over and done with or gone for good or in danger of slipping away into the past; it is ongoing, and its medium is midrash, which makes the words of Torah rejoice 'as when they were delivered from Sinai' and 'as sweet as at their original utterance.'"[6]

Indeed, within the midrashic imagination, broadly defined, there is no hard-and-fast line in the traditional vernacular of the rabbis separating text from exegesis, written from oral Torah. The blurring of boundaries is evident at both ends: the base text of revelation is thought to comprise within itself layers of interpretation, and the works of interpretation on the biblical canon are considered revelatory in nature. To cite Bruns again, the rabbis "imagined themselves as *part* of the whole, participating in Torah rather than operating on it at an analytic distance. . . . [I]t follows that the words of interpretation cannot be isolated in any rigorously analytical way from the words of Torah itself."[7]

Interpretation, therefore, can be viewed as an effort to reconstitute the original experience of revelation. A bold formulation of this viewpoint is given by Daniel Boyarin: "The memory of having seen God in the Bible and the desire to have that experience again were a vital part of Rabbinic religion. They constituted, moreover, a key element in the study of Torah, the making of midrash."[8] This claim is critical in the evaluation of the relationship between the normative rabbinic hermeneutics and the revealed exegesis of apocalyptic and mystical sources. The revelatory status of scriptural interpretation is a central component in medieval Jewish mysticism as well. I will discuss in detail below the convergence of the modes of revelation and interpretation in the *Zohar,* arguably the main theosophic kabbalistic corpus of the thirteenth century.

At this juncture let me note two other examples from medieval literature that support the contention made above. The first is drawn from a Pietistic composition, *Perush Hafṭarah,* a commentary on Ezekiel's chariot vision. Commenting on the word *niftehu,* "opened," in the first verse of Ezekiel, "the heavens opened and I saw visions of God," the Pietist author notes that the numerical

[5] See Dan, "The Chambers of the Chariot."

[6] "Midrash and Allegory," p. 637.

[7] *Hermeneutics Ancient and Modern,* p. 115.

[8] "The Eye in the Torah," p. 534; also p. 541: "The hermeneutic practice of midrash was understood as a means to reachieve such moments of seeing God."

value of the word *niftehu* is the same as the word *midrash* (both equal 544), for "that is the name that opens the gates of heaven."[9] The full implication of this numerology is clear: it is the activity of midrash, scriptural interpretation, that provides the key to open the heavens so that one can have visions of the divine and thereby reexperience the revelation of the chariot granted to the prophet. The biblical text is a mirror in which the reader can see the reflection of the chariot.

The revelatory function of exegesis is further affirmed in a striking way in an anonymous kabbalistic work of the fourteenth century, *Sefer ha-Temunah* (the "Book of the Image"): "Thus everything is found in the tradition of the kabbalists who comprehend everything by means of the prophets from the verses that indicate the matter in verses that are known to those who comprehend. These [scriptural verses] are called 'chapter headings,' for they are the limbs of the body, and the *sefirot* are in a human image, for man is a microcosm, as it says, 'Let us make man in our image and in our likeness' (Gen. 1:26)."[10] According to this text, one gains knowledge of the anthropomorphic form of the divine structure by studying Scripture, for that, too, can assume the shape of an anthropos, the verses being likened to limbs of the body.[11] Reading Scripture is a form of iconic visualization. Gnosis of the divine is attained through study of the sacred text, which in the final analysis is a manner of self-knowledge, inasmuch as the human, too, is created in the shape of God, which is the Torah.

Before proceeding to the detailed analysis of the relationship between revelation and interpretation in the *Zohar,* it is necessary to underscore again that within the Jewish mystical tradition—with some very few exceptions—it is incorrect to distinguish sharply between exegesis and experience. A growing sentiment among scholars of Jewish mysticism, spurred especially by the work of Idel,[12] is that there has been for the most part in the academic treatment of medieval Jewish mysticism an overconcentration on the hermeneutics of mystical texts and a concomitant neglect of the ecstatic experiences that often underlie these literary compositions.[13]

What is necessary to redress this scholarly imbalance is not a focus on experience divorced from interpretation, for, heeding Bernard McGinn's words cited in the Introduction, we must recognize the interdependence of one on the other. It is evident from the kabbalistic sources themselves that one cannot separate

[9] MS Berlin Or. Quat. 942, fol. 149b.

[10] *Sefer ha-Temunah,* 25a.

[11] See Scholem, *On the Kabbalah,* pp. 44–50; Idel, "Concept of Torah," pp. 49ff., esp. 72–73.

[12] See *Kabbalah: New Perspectives,* pp. 27–29. In an effort to counter the description of kabbalah as predominantly theoretical rather than practical, Idel has in his own research paid far greater attention to the experiential side of kabbalistic thought, including the motifs of *devequt* (pp. 35–58) and *unio mystica* (pp. 59–73), as well as a variety of other meditative or contemplative techniques intended to induce religious ecstasy (pp. 74–111). Even in his discussion of kabbalistic hermeneutics, Idel includes a section on pneumatic interpretation and union with the Torah, thereby focusing on a relatively neglected aspect of the Jewish mystical tradition concerning the experiential dimension of study (pp. 234–249).

[13] See Gruenwald, "The Midrashic Condition."

the interpretative and revelatory modes: the nature of mystical experience is such that it is conditioned and shaped by the concepts and symbols that inform the particular kabbalist's worldview as it is applied hermeneutically to the canonical texts of the tradition. On the other hand, the experience itself transforms the kabbalist as reader of the text. Kabbalistic hermeneutics is, as Idel puts it, "an experiential study of Torah,"[14] or as Bruns, building on the work of Idel, expresses it, a "hermeneutics of experience rather than of exegesis."[15] Indeed, Bruns's description of the "mystical hermeneutics" of al-Ghazzālī as an appropriation of an "archive of interpretation" that surrounds a text seems to me to be perfectly apt for describing the hermeneutical principle that underlies much of the kabbalistic literature. The understanding of a text is not mediated by one's tradition; rather, one's understanding of tradition is mediated by one's experience of the text.[16] Mystical hermeneutics as a "hermeneutics of experience" is equally applicable to both theosophical and ecstatic kabbalah, but my immediate focus in this chapter is one specific instance of the theosophical trend, namely, the *Zohar.*

Any attempt to understand the religious texture of the *Zohar* must take into account the fact that the theosophical ruminations contained in this anthology are not merely speculative devices for expressing the knowable aspect of God, but are practical means for achieving a state of ecstasy, that is, an experience of immediacy with God that may eventuate in union or communion. The texts themselves, at the compositional level, reflect the mystic's experience of the divine pleroma and the reintegration of his soul with its ontic source. Behind the multifaceted symbols and interpretations of biblical verses found in the *Zohar* is a fraternity of mystics[17] ecstatically transformed by contemplation of the divine light refracted in nature, the soul, and the Torah. There is indeed genuine ecstatic experience underlying the hermeneutical posture of the *Zohar.* The revelatory character of exegesis is perhaps best seen in the zoharic correlation of the rite of circumcision and visionary experience of the *Shekhinah,* on the one hand, and the dynamic of textual study as an opening of the biblical text, on the other. There is a basic phenomenological structure common to both, namely, the disclosure of that which is concealed. It can be assumed that the writing of the zoharic text proceeded from some such experience of divine immediacy wherein the veiled aspect of divinity is exposed. Students of Jewish mysticism are apt to lose sight of the deeply experiential character of this work, which is nominally and structurally a midrash. Both visualization of God and the hermeneutical task are predicated on a physiological opening (the protrusion of the circumcised penis), corresponding to an ontological opening within the divine (the unveiling of the phallus from within the covering of the vulva).[18]

[14] *Kabbalah: New Perspectives,* p. 229.

[15] *Hermeneutics Ancient and Modern,* p. 135.

[16] Ibid., p. 134.

[17] The notion of a circle of kabbalists responsible for the production of the *Zohar* has been advanced by Liebes in "How the Zohar Was Written."

[18] See my study "Circumcision, Vision of God, and Textual Interpretation."

For the zoharic authorship, therefore, there is a basic convergence of the interpretative and revelatory modes; the act of scriptural interpretation is itself an occasion for contemplative study and mystical meditation. There is no question of the kabbalist needing to pass from a state of theoretical description to actual realization of his mystical wishes. One cannot, especially from the standpoint of the *Zohar,* separate theory and praxis, gnosis and ecstasy, contemplation and imaginative representation.

The typological patterns of mystical experience are aspects of the hermeneutical relationship. Here one encounters the fundamental circle that marks the way before the scholar: the conditions of mystical experience are informed by the very structures of thought that the kabbalist assumes to be operative in the biblical text that he is interpreting. The midrashic condition[19] of the *Zohar* is thus inscribed within the circle of experience and interpretation: the vision that generated the text may be reenvisioned through interpretive study. This has important ramifications for understanding the textual and phenomenological parameters of visionary experience in Jewish mystical sources. Study itself was viewed as a mode of "visual meditation"—a technique known in medieval Christian mysticism as well[20]—in which there is an imaginative recreation of the prophetic vision within the mystic's own consciousness.

The currents of medieval Jewish mysticism in the formative period of its literary genesis, the twelfth and thirteenth centuries, are to be sharply contrasted with their Christian and Islamic counterparts. Whereas this period saw an impressive proliferation of (autobiographical) visionary tracts composed by Christian and Islamic mystics, in the case of Jewish mystics the evidence is quite scanty. In fact, with the exception of the prophetic treatises written by the ecstatic kabbalist Abraham Abulafia and his disciples (e.g., the anonymous author of *Sha'are Ṣedeq*), the record of angelic visions of Jacob ben Jacob ha-Kohen collected in the work *Sefer ha-'Orah,* and a mystical diary written by Isaac ben Samuel of Acre (one of the first mystics to combine theosophical and ecstatic trends of Kabbalah) that records that kabbalist's visual and auditory revelations of Meṭaṭron, there are no other textual attestations of first-person accounts of mystical visions in the formative period of European kabbalah. Even in the subsequent history of Jewish mysticism the examples of actual accounts of personal visual or auditory revelations are extremely limited.[21] But

[19] This expression is appropriated from the work of Gruenwald. See "Midrashic Condition" and "Midrash and the 'Midrashic Condition.'" As Gruenwald notes, the "midrashic condition" is a mental attitude that entails creation of meaning rather than concern for the lexical or philological understanding of a text.

[20] See, e.g., the discussion of visual meditation in the case of Bernard Clairvaux in Jantzen, "Mysticism and Experience." As Jantzen shows, according to Bernard the content of mystical vision (which is contemplative in nature and not physical sense perception) is supplied by meditation on Scripture. God—or, more precisely, the Word—appears in sundry ways, constituted by images drawn from representations of Jesus in the Gospels. Cf. Gregory Palamas, *Triade* II.3.18, in Meyendorff, *Grégoire Palamas: Défense des saints hésychastes,* p. 427.

[21] As noted by Scholem in *Major Trends,* pp. 15–16, 37–38, 121–122. Here I mention some of the better known examples in the history of Jewish mysticism of visionary diaries: the anonymous

one should not be misled by appearances. The fact that the genre of visionary literature is limited in Jewish mysticism does not diminish the status of visions and visionary experience for Jewish mystics. It is simply a matter of knowing where to look. That is, many of the exegetical treatises, especially commentaries on Ezekiel's chariot, as well as the more speculative works on theosophy, are implicitly visionary. Typically, concern with laying out the structure of Ezekiel's vision or that of the theophany at Sinai is a veil covering descriptions of the particular mystic's own visions. As with other medieval biblical commentaries, one has to know how to read the mystical commentaries in order to discern the underlying experiential component, often hidden, perhaps for political or social reasons, in the cloak of the ancient character whose authoritative stature is beyond the reach of criticism or censure. The Moses portrayed in the *Zohar,* for instance, is less a depiction of the biblical Moses than it is a product of the kabbalist's religious imagination—indeed, it is a self-portrait. This point is obvious enough, but it is nevertheless often missed when scholars evaluate the visionary component of medieval kabbalah.

Revelation

Gershom Scholem has argued that historical documents attest to the fact that in the twelfth century two distinct modes of legitimization of mystical doctrine were operating in kabbalistic circles. One consisted of the mystical revelations of Elijah, the other of mystical midrash, particularly as evidenced by *Sefer ha-Bahir.*[22] Elsewhere Scholem has written that innovations were made during the history of kabbalah, either on the basis of new interpretations of older traditions or as a result of novel inspiration or revelation.[23] Kabbalistic literature, in

Sefer ha-Meshiv (see Idel, "Inquiries"); *Maggid Mesharim* of Joseph Karo (see Werblowsky, *Joseph Karo*); *Sefer Gerushin* of Moses Cordovero; *Sefer Milei di-Shemaya* of Eleazar Azikri (see Pachter's edition, cited in chapter 6, n. 187); *Sefer ha-Ḥezyonot* of Ḥayyim Vital (see Tamar, "Messianic Dreams and Visions of R. Ḥayyim Vital"; Oron, "Dream, Vision, and Reality in Ḥaim Vital's *Sefer ha-Ḥezyonot*"); *Gei Ḥizzayon* of Abraham Yagel (see Ruderman, *A Valley of Vision*); the recorded dreams of the Sabbatian Mordecai Ashkenazi (see Scholem, *The Dreams of R. Mordecai Ashkenazi*); the experiential and visionary notations to the scriptural commentaries of Moses David Valle, the designated messiah in the circle of Moses Ḥayyim Luzzatto (see Tishby, "The Experiential and Visionary Notations of Rabbi Moses David Valle"); and the *Megillat Setarim* of the nineteenth-century Ḥasidic master Isaac Judah Jeḥiel Safrin, which is based in great measure on the aforementioned work of Vital. Visions were a large part of Ḥasidic spirituality, though only some were committed to writing. See, e.g., the dream visions of the Baʿal Shem Ṭov's grandson, Moshe Ḥayyim Ephraim of Sudlikov, described at the end of his *Degel Maḥaneh 'Efrayim* (Brooklyn, 1984), p. 177.

[22] *Origins,* pp. 39–44, 49–53. Concerning the midrashic character of *Sefer ha-Bahir,* see Dan, "Midrash and the Dawn of Kabalah"; Stern, *Parables in Midrash,* pp. 216–224. In this connection it is of interest to note that Abraham Abulafia enumerated three sources for his mystical knowledge: oral reception from teachers, written works of a kabbalistic nature, and auditory revelations from heaven (*bat qol*). Cf. *Sefer ha-Hesheq,* MS New York–JTSA Mic. 1801, fol. 5b; *Ḥayye ha-ʿOlam ha-Ba',* MS Oxford-Bodleian 1582, fol. 44b.

Scholem's view, is thus colored by a duality between supernatural illumination and traditional exegesis.

I shall argue, by contrast, that in the zoharic corpus the two modes, revelation and interpretation, are identified and blended together. This convergence is due to the fact that the underlying theosophic structure provides a shared phenomenological basis. In the mystic's hermeneutic relation to the text he once again sees God as God was seen in the historic event of revelation. In short, from the point of view of the *Zohar,* visionary experience is a vehicle for hermeneutics as hermeneutics is a vehicle for visionary experience. The combining of these modalities was a potent force that had a profound influence on subsequent generations of Jewish exegetes.

The nexus between textual study and visionary experience having been established, interpretation of Scripture was no longer viewed as simply fulfilling God's ultimate command, to study Torah, but was rather understood as an act of participating in the very drama of divine life. *Interpretatio* itself became a moment of *revelatio,* which, in the language of the *Zohar,* further involves the process of *devequt,* "cleaving to God."[24] For example: "Praiseworthy is the portion of one who enters and departs,[25] who knows how to contemplate the secrets of his Master and to comprehend (*le'itdabbeqa'*) them. Through these mysteries one can cleave (*le'itdabbeqa'*) to his Master."[26] And, "'Those who consider His name' (Mal. 3:16) [refers to] all those who contemplate words of Torah to cleave (*le'itdabbeqa'*) to their Master, to know the secret of the holy name and to establish the wisdom of His name in their hearts."[27] And, "All those engaged in Torah cleave (*mitdabbeqin*) to the Holy One, blessed be He, and are crowned in the crowns of the Torah."[28]

Ecstatic Death and the Vision of the Presence

To grasp the correlation of interpretative and revelatory modes in the *Zohar,* it is necessary to analyze each component of the equation separately. The first question, then, concerns the zoharic understanding of revelation. Scattered

23 *Major Trends,* p. 120.

24 The zoharic usage of *dvq* in the double sense of "comprehension" and "cleaving" reflects the medieval philosophical usage of the word *devequt* to describe the state of conjunction between human and divine (or Active) intellects; see J. Klatzkin, *Thesaurus Philosophicus: Linguae Hebraicae et Veteris et Recentioris* (Berlin, 1928), 1:128–129.

25 An oft-repeated technical expression in *Zohar* for mystical hermeneutics, based on the legend of the four rabbis who entered Pardes. According to one version, R. Aqiva alone entered and exited in peace; see T. Ḥagigah 2:4; B. Ḥagigah 14b; *Shir ha-Shirim Rabbah* 1:28. On the use of the expression "to enter and to exit" in zoharic literature, see Liebes, "Messiah," pp. 154–155 nn. 240–241 (English trans., pp. 35, 178 n. 110); Matt, *Zohar,* p. 279, s.v. "entered . . . emerged;" Wolfson, "Forms of Visionary Ascent as Ecstatic Experience in Zoharic Literature," pp. 211–212.

26 *Zohar* 2:213b; cf. 1:130b.

27 *Zohar* 2:217a.

28 *Zohar* 3:36a; cf. 19a; *Zohar Ḥadash,* 27d. Underlying these and some other passages—and the examples could be greatly multiplied—is the assumed identification of the Torah and God; see below, n. 175. On the image of the crown as a symbol for mystical union, see discussion below.

throughout the voluminous corpus of the *Zohar* are many valuable, at times contradictory, insights concerning the nature of revelation. Let me note at the outset that the zoharic authorship occasionally rejects out of hand the very possibility of a visionary experience of the divine. Thus, we read, "R. Jose said: What is the meaning of the verse 'And they saw the God of Israel' (Exod. 24:10)? Can one look upon the Holy One, blessed be He? Is it not written, 'For no man shall see Me and live' (ibid., 33:20)? But here it says, 'And they saw!' "[29] To deal with the apparent textual discrepancy between Exod. 24:10 and 33:20, two possible interpretations of the former are presented: the object of the vision described therein was either the rainbow, symbolic of the divine Presence,[30] or Meṭaṭron, the angel referred to both as *na'ar* (youth) and as the brightness of the light of the Presence. The *Zohar,* in this context, thus begins from the premise that God is not visible; the bold assertion of Exod. 24:10 must be interpreted in such a way as to remove the anthropomorphic and iconic implications of a literal reading.

There are, however, two ways to understand the reluctance of the *Zohar* to read Exod. 24:10 as an explicit affirmation of a vision of God. On the one hand, it may be argued that in the mind of the *Zohar* such a possibility is theoretically impossible: God is a transcendent being who has no visible (either mentally or sensibly) image or form. Such a posture is unequivocally adopted, for instance, by Moses de León in one of his Hebrew theosophic works, *Sheqel ha-Qodesh.* After discussing the various grades of prophetic experience he cautions the reader, "In any event, God, may He be blessed, is removed from every idea and thought, for no one can comprehend [Him] and He, may He be blessed, has no image or form. Thus the Torah speaks in human language in order to settle their minds."[31]

De León goes on to say that at times even in the sensible world people see images that have no basis in reality, as, for example, one who sees mirages while wandering through the desert. The images seen by prophets likewise have no reality-base but are merely the means by which the prophet visualizes and

[29] *Zohar* 2:66b.

[30] The use of the rainbow as a symbol for the feminine Presence in kabbalistic literature is based on biblical and rabbinic precedents wherein the divine glory is compared to the rainbow; cf. Ezek. 1:28; B. Ḥagigah 16a; *Bereshit Rabbah* 35:3, p. 330. This usage in widespread in kabbalistic texts that influenced the zoharic formulation. See, e.g., Naḥmanides' commentary on Gen. 9:12, ed. Chavel, 1:64–65; Ṭodros Abulafia, *Sha'ar ha-Razim,* pp. 127–128; idem, *'Oṣar ha-Kavod ha-Shalem,* 24c; and the anonymous *sod ha-qeshet* ("Secret of the Rainbow") in MS New York–JTSA Mic. 1887, fols. 15a–b. On the nexus between the rainbow (*qeshet*) and the divine glory (*kavod*) in ancient Jewish esotericism and subsequent mystical literature, see Farber, "Concept of the Merkabah," pp. 269–270. In the symbolic universe of the kabbalists the rainbow may also be utilized as a symbol for the masculine potency *Yesod;* see below, n. 40. On the dual signification of this symbol, cf. the anonymous text in MS New York–JTSA Mic. 1878, fol. 48b. On the connection of the prohibitions on looking at the rainbow and gazing at the moon, both symbols for the divine Presence, see the tradition of Meir Abulafia reported by his nephew, Ṭodros Abulafia, in *'Oṣar ha-Kavod,* 16d; and *Sha'ar ha-Razim,* p. 49 n. 19. And cf. the formulation in Moses of Kiev, *Shoshan Sodot,* 58a, discussed in H. Lieberman, *'Ohel Raḥel* (Brooklyn, 1980), 1:94–95.

[31] *Sheqel ha-Qodesh,* p. 19.

comprehends that which lies beyond visualization and comprehension, just as the anthropomorphic expressions in Scripture are only the means by which finite minds comprehend the truth. It may be suggested, however, that this formulation does not genuinely express de León's kabbalistic orientation but should be seen instead as an apologetic presentation of kabbalistic theosophy, perhaps in response to an actual or imagined critic who would have challenged the doctrine of *sefirot* on the grounds that it introduces multiplicity into the Godhead. Indeed, on other occasions in his writings de León espouses a view that is far more compatible with the mythic portrayal of the divine in zoharic kabbalah, which also accepts the possibility of a visual experience of the sefirotic emanations.

The overwhelming evidence from the *Zohar* and related literature points us in another direction: the problem for the zoharic authorship is not the theoretical possibility of seeing God, but only the possibility of having such a vision during one's corporeal lifetime. Indeed, on several occasions the *Zohar* notes that at the moment of death the individual soul, freed from its physical encasement, sees the *Shekhinah*. Echoing the view attributed to R. Dosa in earlier midrashic compilations, the *Zohar* not only affirms the possibility of a postmortem visual experience of God, but contends that one may not leave this world until one has seen the *Shekhinah*.[32] The verse that serves as the scriptural prooftext to substantiate this claim is Exod. 33:20, "You may not see Me and live." Following the precedent of the midrashic reading of this verse, the *Zohar* asserts that in one's lifetime one cannot see the divine Presence, but upon one's death one can—indeed, must—have such an experience.

The denial of the vision of God applies only to the existential situation of embodiment. At death the soul is ecstatically released from its imprisonment in the physical body and the liminal moment is marked by a visual encounter with the divine. In zoharic literature, moreover, death is represented as the erotic union of the soul with the feminine *Shekhinah*.[33] Just as the unitive experience of the mystic is a kind of ecstatic death, so in turn is death a kind of mystical union. Ironically enough, the ejaculation of semen into the female—an act that may result in the generation of new life within the womb—is a spiritual dying for the male. The correlation of Eros and Thanatos is most powerfully represented in the dramatic portrayal of Simeon bar Yoḥai's death near the conclusion of the zoharic text. In the process of explicating Ps. 133:4, "There the Lord ordained blessing, everlasting life," R. Simeon is said to have perished when he reached the word "life," which in this context denotes the *semen virile* that flows from *Yesod*, the divine phallus, to the female genitals, symbolized by the scriptural expression in the preceding verse, "mountains of

[32] See *Zohar* 1:79a, 98a (MhN), 218b, 226a; 245a; 3:88a, 147a. Cf. *Pirqe Rabbi 'Eli'ezer* 34, 80a. See also Maimonides, *Guide of the Perplexed* III:51; Moses de León, *Mishkan ha-'Edut*, MS Berlin Or. Quat. 833, fol. 45a; idem, *Book of the Pomegranate*, pp. 250, 393 (Hebrew section).

[33] See *Zohar* 2:48b; 3:120b. On the thematic connection of death and sexuality in Western culture, see Bataille's provocative study *Death and Sensuality*.

Zion." The death of the master occurs precisely at the moment when he exegetically reaches the point of describing the orgasmic climax of the *hieros gamos* in the divine realm.[34] What is essential for the purposes of this study is that the ejaculatory death is depicted in visual terms as a seeing of the Presence.

The Phallus Unveiled: Eros and Vision

That the limitation of seeing God is connected in zoharic literature to the shackles of the body, on the one hand, and the erotic nature of the vision, on the other, rather than to the theoretical rejection of visionary experience as such, is substantiated by the following passage:

> It has been taught: R. Jose said: When the priest spreads out his hands it is forbidden for the people to look upon him, for the *Shekhinah* rests upon his hands.[35] R. Isaac said: If it is the case that the [people] do not see [the *Shekhinah*], what does it matter to them [if they look upon the priest's hands]? For thus it is written, "For no man shall see Me and live," that is, in their lifetime they do not see [God] but in their death they do. He said to him: Inasmuch as the Holy Name is alluded to by the fingers of the hands,[36] and one must fear [God], it follows that even though [the people] do not see the *Shekhinah* they should not look upon the hands of the priests so that they will not be impertinent with respect to the *Shekhinah*.[37]

The problematic issue is not seeing God as such, but rather the attainment of such an experience in this life. The body is the barrier preventing one from seeing the *Shekhinah,* and once this barrier is removed then the vision is possible—indeed, necessary—as a precondition for the ontic translation to the divine pleroma. Notwithstanding the inherent obstacle to the vision of the divine, it is still improper for one to gaze at the hands of the priests wherein the Presence dwells, for the ten fingers correspond to the ten *sefirot* contained within the Tetragrammaton; this is the import of the statement that the "Holy Name is alluded to by the fingers of the hands."[38] This theme is repeated in

[34] *Zohar* 3:296b (*Idra Zuṭa*). See Liebes, "Messiah," p. 192 (English trans., p. 63).

[35] The zoharic view is based on the opinion attributed to Judah bar Naḥmani in B. Ḥagigah 16a that one's eyes are dimmed by looking at one of three things: the rainbow, a prince, and the priests. As is made clear in the talmudic explication of this teaching, the common denominator of all three items is the indwelling of the divine Presence. In the case of the priestly blessing in the time of the Temple, this indwelling was further connected to the explicit utterance of the Tetragrammaton.

[36] Cf. *Zohar* 3:146b: "It has been taught: When the priest spreads out his hands he must not join the fingers together, so that each of the holy crowns will be blessed separately, as is appropriate, for the Holy Name must be articulated in its inscribed letters without mixing one with the other." See the interpretation of this text reflected in later practices in Ḥayyim ha-Kohen of Nikolsburg, *ʿAvodat Kehunah,* 6b. See also *Zohar* 2:208a, where it says that in all blessings (with the exception of Havdalah, said at the end of the Sabbath) the fingers of the hands are raised so that "the Holy Name will be crowned by them." Cf. *Zohar* 2:67a; MS Oxford-Bodleian 1610, fol. 74a; Ginsburg, "The *Havdalah* Ceremony in Zoharic Kabbalah," pp. 210–211.

[37] *Zohar* 3:147a.

[38] The correspondence of the ten fingers to the ten divine emanations, at times connected more specifically with the hands of the priests spread out during the priestly blessing, is a motif expressed

another zoharic context that combines the restriction on looking at the rainbow and the injunction against looking at the priest's hands mentioned separately in the Babylonian Talmud (Ḥagigah 16a): "It is forbidden for a person to look at the rainbow, for it is the appearance of the supernal image; it is forbidden for a person to look at the sign of his covenant [i.e., the *membrum virile*], for it symbolizes the Righteous of the world [*ṣaddiq yesod ʿolam*]; it is forbidden for a person to look at the fingers of the priests when they spread out their hands, for the glory of the supernal King rests there."[39] The juxtaposition of these two rabbinic teachings, the prohibitions on gazing upon the rainbow and looking at the hands of the priests, brings to light a fundamental element in the zoharic understanding of visionary experience. Implicit here is the application of the word "bow" (*qeshet*) to *Yesod,* the aspect of the divine that corresponds to the phallus.[40] It is the latter, the ultimate object of mystic visualization, that

---

in earlier sources as well; see, e.g., *Sefer ha-Bahir,* § 124, reflecting in turn *Sefer Yeṣirah* 1:3, wherein the ten *sefirot* are compared to the ten fingers; see also discussion in the concluding part of chapter 2. The zoharic authorship may also have been drawing on other traditions regarding the divine name and the hands of the priests. See, e.g., the Ashkenazi tradition recorded in Pseudo-Eleazar, *Perush ha-Roqeaḥ ʿal ha-Torah,* 3:24–25, according to which the three *yods* of the three words that begin each verse of the priestly blessing in Num. 6:24–26 constitute the Tetragrammaton, which, according to a scribal tradition, was written with three *yods.* The first part of this text has parallels in the writings of Eleazar of Worms (see chapter 5, n. 272) and is based on earlier sources (see chapter 5, n. 267). Cf. *Zohar* 3:147b. On the marking of the Tetragrammaton by the priests' hands, see also Baḥya ben Asher's commentary on Exod. 17:12, ed. Chavel, 2:156; Isaac of Acre, *ʾOṣar Ḥayyim,* MS Moscow-Guenzberg 775, fol. 46b; Judah ben Solomon Campanton, *ʾArbaʿah Qinyanim,* MS New York–JTSA Mic. 2532, fol. 19b. In his commentary to Num. 6:27 (ed. Chavel, 3:34) Baḥya notes an alternative tradition that the priest's hands mark the letters of the name Shaddai rather than YHWH. This tradition is also alluded to by Abraham Abulafia in *ʾOṣar ʿEden Ganuz,* MS Oxford-Bodleian 1580, fol. 64a, where he also mentions the tradition that the one who performs the circumcision should form the letters of the name Shaddai with his fingers.

[39] *Zohar* 3:84a.

[40] This symbolism is based on the fact that in rabbinic literature the word *qeshet* euphemistically signifies the phallus; see, e.g., B. Soṭah 36b; Sanhedrin 92a. See Scholem, "Colours and Their Symbolism in Jewish Tradition and Mysticism," *Diogenes* 108 (1979): 89–90; 109 (1980) 69–71. This usage is rather widespread in kabbalistic literature. See, e.g., MS Oxford-Bodleian 1598, fol. 112a (concerning this text see Scholem, "Index to the Commentaries on the *Sefirot,*" p. 508 n. 93); MS Oxford-Bodleian 1628, fol. 72a (see Scholem, "Index," p. 509 n. 102); *Tiqqune Zohar* 18, 32b; Cordovero, *Pardes Rimmonim,* 23:19, s.v. *qeshet;* Isaiah Horowitz, *Shene Luḥot ha-Berit* 274b (Horowitz explicitly connects the prohibition of looking at the rainbow with the taboo of looking at the sexual organ, inasmuch as the secret of the rainbow is the gradation that corresponds to the phallus). Needless to say, numerous other examples could have been cited. See the text of Moses of Burgos cited below, n. 149. See also Jacob ben Jacob ha-Kohen, *Sefer ha-ʾOrah,* MS Milan-Ambrosiana 62, fol. 105b (cf. MS New York–JTSA Mic. 1869, fols. 24b–25a), where the rainbow is identified as the "great light" that is "derived from the intelligible light that is the level of Meṭaṭron." The mystical significance of the claim that the rainbow is the image of the appearance of the glory is that the rainbow corresponds to Meṭaṭron (on the relationship between Meṭaṭron and the divine Presence in Jacob's writings, see chapter 5, n. 61). In the same context Jacob ha-Kohen informs the reader that this aspect of the angelic realm corresponds to both the place of the intellect and the phallus. Moreover, Jacob reports having a vision of the rainbow with his eyes and his heart. In my opinion the phallic character associated with Meṭaṭron (for the possible Ashkenazi source for this motif, see chapter 5, n. 304) also underlies Jacob ha-Kohen's identification of Meṭa-

must be concealed from the ordinary gaze of human beings,[41] a point underscored as well by the explicit statement that it is prohibited to look at the sign of the covenant. Unlike the former passage, wherein it is stated that one should not look at the hands of the priests out of respect for the *Shekhinah* even though the latter cannot be seen by mortal human beings, in the second redac-

---

ṭron as the *sar shalom,* the archon of peace, inasmuch as the word *shalom* can be used euphemistically to designate the male organ. Cf. Jacob ha-Kohen, *Perush ha-'Otiyyot,* p. 206, where the letter *gimmel* is identified as peace (*shalom*) and associated further with the covenant (*berit*), i.e., the penis. See also Moses of Burgos's commentary on the forty-two-letter name in MS Oxford-Bodleian 1565, fol. 99b, where the first three letters of the name ABG"Y are said "to instruct about Absalom, for the father (*'av,* composed of the letters *'alef* and *bet*) is the third (*gimmel*) that is peace (*shalom*)." For a slightly different reading see the printed version in *Liqquṭim me-Rav Hai Gaon,* 5a. On the phallic connotation of the word *shalom* in earlier rabbinic sources, see Wolfson, "The Tree That Is All," pp. 49–50 n. 68. In my opinion the phallic status of Meṭaṭron also underlies Jacob ha-Kohen's identification of Meṭaṭron with the divine goodness, linked exegetically to Ps. 31:20 and Exod. 33:19. Cf. MSS Bar-Ilan 47, fols. 14a, 15b; Jerusalem-Schocken 14, fols. 53a. 54b. See also the exegesis of Exod. 2:2 in MSS Milan-Ambrosiana 62, fol. 79b, and Vatican 428, fol. 28b. Finally, the association of Meṭaṭron with the phallus may underlie the identification of this angelic being with the letter *yod,* the letter that traditionally signifies the sign of the covenant of circumcision incised upon the penis. On the relation of the *yod* and Meṭaṭron in Jacob ha-Kohen's *Sefer ha-'Orah,* see MSS Milan-Ambrosiana 62, fols. 100a, 105b–106a, 110b; Vatican 428, fol. 24a. On the identification of Meṭaṭron and the letter *yod,* signifying the tenth separate intellect, in other thirteenth-century Castilian texts, see Farber, "On the Sources of Rabbi Moses de Leon's Early Kabbalistic System," pp. 79–80 n. 28; Wolfson, "Letter Symbolism and Merkavah Imagery in the Zohar," pp. 203–205; idem, "God, the Demiurge, and the Intellect," pp. 83–84 n. 28. The phallic position of Meṭaṭron also seems to be underscored in a kabbalistic interpretation on Ezekiel's chariot extant in MS Oxford-Bodleian 1938, fol. 16b, where the image of the *ḥashmal* is associated with Meṭaṭron. See also *Tiqqune Zohar* 70, 119b, and the parallel in *Zohar Ḥadash* 116b. And compare *Tiqqune Zohar,* Introduction, 7a: "The rainbow is the Righteous, Foundation of the world, and Meṭaṭron is his appearance below. This is what Ezekiel saw, for it contained all images." Finally, mention should be made of the fact that the phallic nature of Meṭaṭron is also suggested in the writings of Abraham Abulafia. See, e.g., *Mafteaḥ ha-Shemot,* MS New York-JTSA Mic. 1897, fol. 61a, where Meṭaṭron is identified explicitly as the potency that has dominion over procreation. This power is linked more specifically to the name Shaddai, which has the same numerical value as the name Meṭaṭron. The appearance of this view in all of these sources strongly indicates that the phallic role accorded Meṭaṭron reflects a much older doctrine of Jewish esotericism.

[41] See *Zohar* 3:73b–74a (*Matnitin*), where the secret of illicit sexual relations (*sod 'arayot*) is couched in visual terms. On the essential concealment of *Yesod,* the grade that corresponds to the male organ, from the purview of human vision, see Liebes, "Messiah," pp. 140–141 (English trans., pp. 27–28). On the central role of the divine gradations that correspond in the visual experience to the testicles, see *Zohar* 3:133b (*Idra Rabba*); see also formulation in *Sod 'Ilan ha-'Aṣilut le-R. Yiṣḥaq,* p. 84. Finally, it is worth mentioning that the male organ is described as the locus of divine concealment and disclosure in a commentary on *Sefer Yeṣirah,* MS Paris–BN 680, fol. 203a: "When the corona is revealed it resembles a *yod* . . . and this is a great holiness, for when she is small she has the numerical value of a *yod,* but when the *yod* is in the plēnē form [i.e., *yod-waw-dalet,* 10 + 6 + 4] it has the numerical value of *kaf* [i.e., 20], and the *kaf* in plēnē form [*kaf-pe,* 20 + 80] is *qof* [i.e., 100], which is the holiness (*qedushah*) and the concealment of the Creator, blessed be He." In a state of elongation the male organ signifies the holiness of God that is his concealment, whereas the diminished state is the disclosure of the corona that corresponds to the feminine potency.

tional setting it is clear that the possibility of seeing the *Shekhinah* is assumed, for the very looking at the priests' hands is akin to gazing at the glory of the supernal King, which is symbolically equivalent to looking at the rainbow or the phallus. Even in those passages, where the *Shekhinah*, the feminine potency of the divine, is designated as the locus of vision, it can be shown that in the kabbalistic literature in general, and the *Zohar* in particular, the *Shekhinah* is visualized as only part of the male organ; indeed, in the visual encounter the *Shekhinah* is the protruding aspect of the divine phallus, the corona of the penis, and not a distinct feminine entity. This is not to deny that the *Zohar* on occasion describes in graphic detail the female genitals of the divine persona over and against the male organ; indeed, in one striking passage the vagina (which corresponds to the *Shekhinah*) is described as the "place to conceal that penis that is called Mercy."[42] Sexual intercourse is a reverse counterpart to circumcision: in the latter the element of the penis that is revealed is the female corona, whereas in the former the penis is concealed by the female genitals. The visible aspect of the *Shekhinah* is linked to the sign of the covenant. Thus, from the standpoint of mystical vision, the feminine is localized as part of the masculine.

From still other zoharic passages it can be shown that the restriction on seeing the divine was predicated precisely on the fact that such a vision is not only theoretically possible but involves the mythic dynamic of copulation in the Godhead. Thus, in the context of specifying certain gestures required when one prays, the *Zohar* states that a person "must close his eyes in order not to see the *Shekhinah*. In the book of R. Hamnuna the Elder it says that the angel of death is summoned to the one who opens his eyes during prayer or does not cast his eyes to the ground, and when his soul leaves [this world] he does not see the light of the *Shekhinah* and does not die by a kiss."[43] It is evident from this text that the divine Presence is inherently visible, for it is precisely on account of the visibility of the Presence that one must close one's eyes. The one who keeps his eyes opened is denied a vision of the Presence at the appropriate time, namely, the moment of death, when the soul is separated from the body.

A similar rationale is connected with the ritual of falling on one's face during the supplication prayer: "It is necessary to fall on one's face. What is the reason? For at that moment it is the time of sexual union, and every person must be ashamed before his Master and cover his face with great shame, and contain

42 *Zohar* 3:142a (*Idra Rabba*); cf. 3:29a (*Idra Zuṭa*).

43 *Zohar* 3:260b; see also text from *Zohar* 3:187b cited below at n. 196 (the two sources are conflated by Azikri in *Milei di-Shemaya*, ed. Pachter, p. 117). For discussion of the zoharic text and its influence on subsequent authors, see Zimmer, "Poses and Postures during Prayer," pp. 92–94. See also Gries, *Conduct Literature*, pp. 220–222. On the closing of the eye as part of a meditation technique in ecstatic kabbalah, see Idel, *Studies in Ecstatic Kabbalah*, pp. 134–136. The notion of departing from this world by a kiss is found in rabbinic texts to contrast the death of select righteous persons with the death of ordinary folk who die through the agency of the Angel of Death. The *Zohar* appropriates this term and applies it to the death of the comrades. See Matt, *Zohar*, p. 284. On the use of death by a kiss in other kabbalistic texts to designate the state of the soul's cleaving to the Presence, see Idel, *Kabbalah: New Perspectives*, pp. 44–45, And see now extended discussion of this motif in Fishbane, *The Kiss of God*.

his soul in that union of souls."[44] The prohibition on looking at the divine, enacted in this particular prayer gesture, is based not on the inherent invisibility of God, but rather on the fact that one must not gaze at the divine partners at the moment of sexual union. The shame that one must have at that moment is related to the primordial taboo on gazing at the divine phallus that is disclosed during the act of coitus. It is the nature of the phallus to be veiled, and in the event of its unveiling the appropriate emotion is shame.[45] This theme is widely repeated in kabbalistic literature. For example, in one anonymous text it is stated that "in the time of union and cleaving it is inappropriate to look; therefore it says, 'And Moses hid his face, for he was afraid to look at God' (Exod. 3:6)."[46] According to another text the talmudic dictum (B. Ḥagigah 16a) that looking at the rainbow amounts to exhibiting a lack of respect for the honor of the Creator is explained in terms of the one who "contemplates with the eye of his heart the matter of the perfect union."[47] Within the symbolic universe of the theosophic kabbalist the recommendation not to look at the rainbow, the word *qeshet* serving as a symbol for the penis, is to avoid visually contemplating the moment of sacred union above, between the masculine and feminine potencies of the divine, when the male organ is exposed. As Joseph of Hamadan expressed the matter,

> The covenant (*berit*) that is seen in the cloud on a rainy day signifies the colors of the attribute of the *Ṣaddiq*. . . . Ezekiel the prophet, may peace be upon him, alluded to this when he said, "Like the appearance of the bow which shines in the clouds on a day of rain, such was the appearance of the surrounding radiance. That was the appearance of the semblance of the Presence of the Lord. When I beheld it, I flung myself down on my face" (Ezek. 1:28). From here [it is deduced that] it is forbidden to look at the phallus (*berit*) and the one who sees the phallus should fall on his face.[48]

[44] *Zohar* 2:129a. See Liebes, "Messiah," p. 179 n. 313 (English trans., p. 185 n. 156).

[45] See J. Lacan, *Ecrits: A Selection,* trans. A. Sheridan (New York and London, 1977), p. 288.

[46] MS Paris–BN 843, fol. 75b. Cf. MS New York–JTSA Mic. 1878, fol. 5a: "It is the honor of royalty (*kevod malkhut*) not to look at the King except by way of concealment (*derekh hastarah*), as it is written, 'And Moses hid his face, for he was afraid to look at God' (Exod. 3:6)."

[47] MS Berlin Or. Quat. 942, fol. 60a. Cf. MS New York-Columbia x893 Ab92, fols. 18a–b.

[48] Joseph of Hamadan, *Sefer Tashak,* ed. Zwelling, pp. 52–53. See also pp. 67–68, where Hamadan interprets the aggadic statement that in the days of R. Joshua ben Levi the rainbow was not seen (cf. *Bereshit Rabbah* 35:2, pp. 328–329) as containing an allusion to one of the mysteries of Torah. According to his explanation, the secret involved the unity of the masculine and feminine attributes. That the rainbow is not seen indicates symbolically that the *Shekhinah* is contained in the other attributes. In the continuation of this passage Hamadan asserts that the phallus (*berit*) and the rainbow (*qeshet*) are one reality that manifests itself either as the attribute of mercy (the masculine phallus) or as the attribute of judgment (the feminine rainbow). It is of interest to compare and contrast Joseph of Hamadan's passage with the description of the appearance of the rainbow in Moses de León's *Shushan ʿEdut,* pp. 363–364: "The rainbow (*qeshet*) is a great mystery (*sod gadol*) and it is seen in a cloud, for its nature is such that it exists in a cloud. Thus you should know that the rainbow [appears] on a rainy day and it is called the sign of the covenant (*'ot berit*). However, the [word] *qeshet* is in a feminine form, as it says, 'and it shall serve as a sign of the

In another kabbalistic text, apparently written within the circle of Naḥmanides, the prohibition of looking at the aspect of God that corresponds to the phallus is emphasized in similar terms. After delineating the respective correspondence of the last two emanations, *Yesod* and *Shekhinah,* to the penis and the corona, the anonymous author states, "On account of the holiness one should not look upon it, and with respect to this they said 'whoever looks at the rainbow, etc.' If this is the attribute corresponding to one's prayers one should not look."[49] Implied in the last remark is an obvious visual technique applied during prayer: one visualizes the divine attribute that corresponds to the particular prayer one is reciting. However, in the case of the attribute that corresponds to the phallus, one is obligated not to conjure a visible image for fear of uncovering that which must be veiled. In still other kabbalistic texts, as we have seen in the case of the *Zohar,* the issue is related especially to the prayer of supplication.

> A person closes his eyes and places his hands over them, and appears as someone who has died, that is, he is like someone without hands, eyes, or feet, and all of his actions are abandoned for the Lord. . . . There is another hidden secret: at the moment one prays [the prayer of the eighteen benedictions] in his worship he intends the true unity, and the action that a person does below causes an act above, resulting in the copulation and union above. A person must hide out of shame for his Master and close his eyes in order not to look at the moment of copulation. Even though it is impossible to see above, "for no man shall see Me and live" (Exod. 33:20), nevertheless the knowledge of the sages constitutes their vision. On account of this they said that it is forbidden to look at the fingers of the priests when they spread out their hands, for the Presence rests on their hands at that moment, and it is forbidden to look at the Presence. Even though it is impossible to see, as we said, he must hide his eyes.[50]

---

covenant' (*we-hayetah le-'ot berit*) (Gen. 9:13). . . . Yet when the rainbow is seen, then the sign of the covenant is within it and judgment vanishes from the world. Therefore, when the rainbow is not seen, then the forces of strength [increase]. . . . Whenever the rainbow is seen in the cloud, then the sign of the covenant is within it. This is the secret of 'I will remember My covenant' (ibid., 15), for there is no memory without the sign of the covenant. Therefore they instituted the blessing [on seeing the rainbow], 'Blessed be You who remember the covenant' (*barukh zokher ha-berit*), for then she is composed of the colors that are seen within her from the All. . . . Know that the secret of the matter of the rainbow and the covenant are joined together (*sod 'inyan ha-qeshet we-ha-berit be-yaḥad neḥbarim*). Therefore [the rabbis] ordained that a person is forbidden to look at the rainbow so that he would not humiliate the *Shekhinah,* and he should not look within it." The passage has several conceptual and philological parallels in *Zohar* 1:7b. Clearly, the rainbow functions as an androgynous symbol, but it is the masculine aspect, the *'ot berit,* that endows the feminine, the *qeshet,* with visible form. It is obvious, moreover, that the rationale offered here for the rabbinic teaching that one should not look at the rainbow involves the exposure of the phallus in the unification of male and female. Cf. *Tiqqune Zohar* 18, 36a; 58, 92b.

49 MS New York–JTSA Mic. 1878, fol. 9a.

50 MS Florence Medicea-Laurenziana 44.13, fol. 23a; see also MS New York–JTSA Mic. 1822, fol. 47a.

The motif is elaborated as well by Isaac of Acre, but in contrast to the anonymous text just cited he assumes that the Presence can actually be seen by the mystic visionary:

> The Diadem is the revealed world and she is greatly seen by the humble enlightened ones, until in the chamber of chambers they are embarrassed by her more than other people, and rightfully this is the way it is. Therefore the rabbis, blessed be their memory, instituted the recitation of the supplication prayer, related specifically to her, with closed eyes so that they would not contemplate her. Observe that the rabbis, in every matter of modesty of which they speak, mention the Presence, because she is revealed greatly and is seen by the one who has received and God, blessed be He, has given him eyes to see. Notice that the rabbis, blessed be their memory, forbade the wearing of the fringe garment, which symbolizes the Diadem, at night.[51]

The position of the zoharic authorship accords with the view expressed by Isaac of Acre: the necessity of covering one's eyes is to prevent one from beholding the sacred union when the male potency enters the female. The full mythos underlying this ritual is predicated on the possibility of seeing God—indeed, precisely that aspect of God that corresponds to the phallus, a view exegetically linked in the *Zohar* to the verse "From my flesh [i.e., the circumcised flesh] I will see God" (Job 19:26).[52] While the vision is not of a corporeal nature, it is evident that it is not simply a metaphor for gnosis; there is actual vision grounded in the modality of sensory experience and the placing of the hands over the eyes purposefully obstructs that vision. For the most part people in the material plane are not capable of seeing the divine Presence, but this has little to do with the medieval rationalist's insistence that God is intrinsically invisible because He possesses no visible form. On the contrary, the embodied perception of the glory, especially in terms of the structure of the union of male and female localized in the androgynous phallus, is the basic phenomenological presupposition of theosophic kabbalah in general and zoharic kabbalah in particular. The vision of the Presence is ultimately a seeing of the corona of the divine phallus, the *'aṭeret berit*. That is the implication of the verse from Job, from the flesh—that is, the penis—God is seen. This complex gender transformation provides the conceptual underpinning for the connection of the rite of circumcision to visualization of the divine.[53]

[51] *Me'irat 'Einayim,* p. 85.

[52] See Wolfson, "Circumcision, Visionary Experience, and Textual Interpretation," p. 206. The valorization of the phallus at the locus of seeing God privileges the masculine and relegates the feminine to a secondary status. On the other hand, it should be noted that to some extent the kabbalistic treatment of the rite of circumcision involves a feminization of the masculine, inasmuch as the incision of the penis results in an opening of the body that corresponds to the feminine aspect of the divine; see "Circumcision," pp. 204–205. On the possibility that this is already adumbrated in midrashic texts, see Boyarin, "'This We Know to Be the Carnal Israel'," pp. 493–497.

[53] An important text that may have served as a source for the *Zohar* is Jacob ben Jacob ha-Kohen, *Sefer ha-'Orah,* MS Florence Medicea-Laurenziana 44.14, fol. 6b: "God, blessed be He, sealed His name on His creatures who emanate from the mystery of His unity at the beginning of

The *Zohar* thus embraces the paradox that the divine phallus is both concealed and revealed.[54] The essential feature of the mystic vision as a seeing of the veiled phallus is set out in the following description of prophecy, for it is the assumption of the kabbalists who participated in the circle of the *Zohar,* as I stated explicitly in the previous chapter, that they were the "true prophets"; they perceived no historical gap between themselves and the classical prophets of ancient Israelite history.

> This is the one [splendor] that is seen and all the colors are hidden in it, and it is called Adonai. Three colors appear below this [i.e., three colors are seen within the *Shekhinah*], and three colors above [corresponding to the three central emanations, *Ḥesed, Din,* and *Raḥamim*]. . . . When the lower splendor, Adonai, unites with the upper splendor, YHWH, the hidden name is produced through which the true prophets knew and contemplated the upper splendor. This is YAHDWNHY, the appearance of those that are hidden, as it is written, "like a *ḥashmal* in the flame" (Ezek. 1:4).[55]

The vision of the prophet is conditioned by the union of the male and female potencies, represented as the upper and lower splendors, the former corresponding to YHWH and the latter to Adonai.[56] The union of these produces

---

the [creation] process and they are Israel. . . . He commanded them regarding circumcision, which is a precept that has the sealing of the name, as it says, 'Who among us can go up to the heavens' (*mi yaʿaleh lanu ha-shamaymah*) (Deut. 30:12), the first letters spell *milah* [circumcision] and the last YHWH. Thus they merited [the theophanous experience of] Mount Sinai, to see the splendor of the voices, the lightnings, and the clouds." R. Jacob thus develops the exegesis of Deut. 30:12 found in the German Pietistic literature, which underscores the correlation of the divine name and circumcision (see Wolfson, "Circumcision and the Divine Name," pp. 87–96; on the influence of the Pietistic exegesis on Castilian kabbalists, see pp. 96–112). It is on account of the seal of circumcision that the Israelite males were worthy to see supernatural phenomena at Sinai, including most significantly the visible voices. Consider also the mystical exposition of the rite of circumcision in *Sefer ha-'Orah,* MS Milan-Ambrosiana 62, fol. 99b: "The corona resembles a *yod,* for it is the first letter of the explicit name [YHWH]. In this form it is engraved on the flesh of the holy nation, for the world was created for the sake of Israel so that in the future they would receive this commandment and the Torah." On the nexus between circumcision and the indwelling of the Presence, see also the comment in the anonymous kabbalistic commentary on prayers extant in MSS Berlin Or. Quat. 942, fol. 8a; Oxford-Bodleian 1925, fol. 10a; and Paris–BN 188, fol. 177b. Regarding the provenance of this text, see Idel, "Writings of R. Abraham Abulafia," pp. 77–78, 84. The correlation of a vision of the Presence and the rite of circumcision, rooted in the midrashic traditions, is also found in German Pietistic sources. The point is epitomized in the Ashkenazi commentary on Psalms extant in MS Oxford-Bodleian 1551, fol. 208b: "[The expression] *be-ṣedeq 'eḥezeh fanekha,* 'Then I, justified, will behold Your face' (Ps. 17:15), is numerically equal to *Shekhinah* with a surplus of eight [i.e., the former expression has a sum of 377 and the latter 385], for the one who is circumcised is worthy [to see] the *Shekhinah,* as it says, *ki 'im galah sodo 'el* [*ʿavadav ha-nevi'im*]. 'Without having revealed his secret to [His servants the prophets]' (Amos 3:7), the final letters [of *'im galah sodo 'el*] spell *mahul* [circumcised], for [such a person] merits the *Shekhinah.*"

[54] See *Zohar* 2:186b. Cf. the description of *Yesod* by Isaac ha-Kohen, in *Perush Ṭaʿame ha-Nequddot we-Ṣurotan,* as a door that is "sometimes open and sometimes closed" ("Traditions of R. Jacob and R. Isaac ben Jacob ha-Kohen," p. 268).

[55] *Zohar* 1:100a–b (*Sitre Torah*).

[56] The union of masculine and feminine as the essential phenomenological datum of prophecy is

the name YAHDWNHY that is visually contemplated by the prophets and mystics. Through the vision of the Presence in a state of union with the upper masculine potency one comprehends the unity of the pleroma represented by this name, which is constituted by a combination of the masculine YHWH and the feminine Adonai. The prophetic vision accorded the kabbalist is essentially a vision of the phallic *Yesod* through the covering of the *Shekhinah*. This is alluded to at the end of the above passage in the reference to the *ḥashmal* that is seen from within the fire: the *ḥashmal*—the term used in the vision of Ezekiel to describe the form of the anthropomorphic glory or, more specifically, the part of that form from the loins upward—corresponds to the male potency, specifically the penis, and the fire to the feminine aspect that envelops the masculine. Symbolically, the fiery covering parallels the corona of the penis. The object of the mystical vision is the union of male and female localized in the aspect of God that is the phallus. The phallic character of the *ḥashmal*—and by extension the erotic aspect of the prophetic-mystical vision—underlies the following zoharic commentary on the verse "In the center of the fire the likeness of the *ḥashmal*" (Ezek. 1:4):

> It has been established that [the word "*ḥashmal*" refers to] the fiery beasts that speak, and they are the splendor that shines, it goes up and down, the fire that is burning. It exists and does not exist, for there is no one who can understand it in one place. No eyes or vision can master it. It is and it is not, in one place and then in another place. It goes up and down. In this appearance is hidden that which is hidden and concealed that which is concealed. This is the mystery called *ḥashmal*. Prophets must see, know, and contemplate within this with the vision of the heart and eye more than anything else. . . . All that they contemplate to see and to know is the speculum that does not shine. No prophet was worthy of contemplating the speculum that shines but Moses, the faithful prophet, for all the keys of the house were placed in his hand. When all the other prophets reached this *ḥashmal* to contemplate with their eyes, their thoughts were confused and the heart was not settled, and because of it they abandoned all corporeal images. Consequently, they saw within what they saw in silence.[57]

---

emphasized by earlier kabbalists as well, e.g., Naḥmanides; see Wolfson, "Secret of the Garment," p. xl; and cf. the kabbalistic explanation on prophecy, apparently from the school of Naḥmanides, extant in MS New York–JTSA Mic. 1878, fols. 13a–b: "The prophecy of Moses our master, peace be upon him, was above that of the other prophets. This is [the intent of] the statement of [the rabbis], blessed be their memory, that his prophecy was through a speculum that shines and the other prophets through a speculum that does not shine, for his prophecy was through the great name [YHWH]—face, that is, [the male] *Tif'eret*, to face, that is, [the female] *'Aṭarah*. Thus it is written, 'Face to face the Lord spoke to you' (Deut. 5:4), 'with him I speak mouth to mouth' (Num. 12:8). Concerning that which the Torah says, 'he is trusted throughout my household' (Num. 12:7) . . . his comprehension was in [relation to] the house [i.e., the female Presence] and his contemplation was in the great name [the male potency]. The prophecy of the patriarchs also involved the great name [masculine] and the glorious name [feminine]. However, they experienced and contemplated only through the glorious name."

[57] *Zohar Ḥadash*, 38b.

The implication of the zoharic text can be ascertained from the following passage of Moses de León in his *Shaʿar Yesod ha-Merkavah,* a commentary on Ezekiel's chariot vision: "*Ḥashmal*—the beasts of fire that are joined as one in the mystery of proper unity and oneness when everything is bound together in one knot."[58] The vision of the *ḥashmal* is, in effect, a vision of the three upper beasts, that is, the central *sefirot,* as they are united in one bond in *Yesod,* the divine phallus. Even closer to the language of the *Zohar* is the continuation of de León's text: "This is the mystery of the *ḥashmal* that we mentioned above, the mystery of the beasts united as one, and they are called *ḥashmal* . . . and the mystery of these beasts [is that they] are called in their unity *ḥashmal.* This is a known mystery in the depths of wisdom, and [the *ḥashmal*] is called YAHDWNHY, the mystery of the supernal beasts united in one name."[59] From the zoharic texts and their parallels in de León's writings it may be concluded that the mysterious *ḥashmal* of Ezekiel's vision is interpreted theosophically as a reference to the divine phallus that comprehends within itself the upper three gradations, which are the fiery beasts. Most significant, the incandescent phallus is concealed from the vision of the prophet and/or mystic. Thus, commenting on the biblical text "I saw the likeness of the *ḥashmal*" (Ezek. 1:4), the zoharic authorship reflects, "'In the likeness' (*ke-ʿein*), that is, like the eye (*ke-ʿeinaʾ*) that cannot contemplate in contemplation, but it is closed and opened, opened and closed. Thus is the *ḥashmal* concealed and not seen at all except through the hidden vision that no one can understand or comprehend at all."[60]

Seeing the Voices

The visual experience of the divine normally denied to mortal human beings was attained by the Israelites at Sinai and by mystic visionaries in the time of the composition of the *Zohar,* although it is cloaked in the narrative wrapping of second-century Palestine. Indeed, the capacity of the kabbalist to see the *Shekhinah* places him squarely on the level of the one who visually experienced the Sinaitic epiphany and who thereby attained the status of an angelic or spiritual being. There are various treatments of the nature of the visionary experience of the Sinaitic theophany in the *Zohar.* One of the key texts,[61] an interpretation of Exod. 20:15, "And all the people saw the voices" (*we-khol ha-ʿam roʾim ʾet ha-qolot*), raises the obvious problem that troubled classical and medieval exegetes alike: why does Scripture employ the predicate "saw" in conjunction with the object "voices," thereby mixing an optical and an auditory meta-

[58] MS New York–JTSA Mic. 1805, fol. 18b. Cf. Joseph of Hamadan, *Sefer Tashak,* ed. Zwelling, p. 356: "What is the *ḥashmal*? When he joins Meṭaṭron with Yahoel. Thus it says, 'Like a *ḥashmal* in the flame' (Ezek. 1:4), this alludes to the unity of the Holy One, blessed be He."

[59] MS New York–JTSA Mic. 1805, fols. 20b–21a. The text is printed in Meir ibn Gabbai, *ʿAvodat ha-Qodesh,* pt. 4, chap. 19, p. 467.

[60] *Zohar Ḥadash,* 41a.

[61] *Zohar* 2:81a–b.

phor? In response to this query, the *Zohar* offers three possible interpretations. The first, attributed to R. Abba, is based on a close, more or less literal, reading of Scripture, attested especially in several Geonic authors,[62] and suggests that the incorporeal voices of divine speech were embodied in the physical media of darkness, cloud, and thick fog,[63] which allowed them to be seen by the human eye. From such a vision the Israelites were illuminated by the supernal light of God. The second view, attributed to R. Jose, maintains that these voices, the content of the vision, were nothing other than the *sefirot* themselves, the potencies of God, which shone forth. It thus makes perfect sense to speak of an "actual seeing" of these voices, for the latter are in essence of a luminous nature.[64] A third view, attributed to R. Eleazar, offers yet another, though not unrelated, interpretation. According to him, the voices likewise refer to the *sefirot,* but the vision of these voices was mediated through the last of them, the *Shekhinah.*[65] This is alluded to in the verse by the accusative particle *'et,* which functions in the *Zohar* as a mystical symbol for the last gradation, the completion of divine speech, inasmuch as this word comprises the first and last consonants of the Hebrew alphabet.[66] A reference to this zoharic view is to be found in Moses de León's *Mishkan ha-ʿEdut:*

> I have seen in the secrets of Torah a deep matter concerning the verse "And all the people saw the voices," the secret of the speculum that does not shine [i.e.,

[62] Cf. the explanation of revelatory experience in Saadiah's commentary on *Sefer Yeṣirah,* ed. Kafiḥ, p. 31; Judah ben Barzillai, *Perush Sefer Yeṣirah,* p. 273. Saadiah's explanation is also cited by pseudo-Baḥya in *Sefer Torot ha-Nefesh,* p. 18; see also Jacob ben Sheshet, *Meshiv Devarim Nekhoḥim,* p. 191; Recanaṭi, *Perush ʿal ha-Torah,* 26a. See Sirat, *Théories,* p. 23; idem, *La lettre hébraïque et sa signification,* pp. 24, 35 n. 31.

[63] Cf. Deut. 4:11, 5:19–20. Cf. *Zohar* 1:11b: "Darkness is fire, as it is written, 'When you heard the voice out of the darkness' and 'The mountain was ablaze with flames to the very skies, darkness, etc.'" A likely source for the equation of darkness and elemental fire may have been Maimonides, *Guide of the Perplexed* II:30.

[64] Cf. *Zohar* 2:194a: "All [of Israel] saw the upper lights illuminated in the speculum that shines [i.e., *Tif'eret*], as it is written, 'And all the people saw the voices' (Exod. 20:15)." An alternative interpretation of this verse that likewise emphasizes the visionary characteristic of the Sinai event is to be found in *Zohar* 2:146a: "When the Holy One, blessed be He, was revealed on Mount Sinai, He gave the Torah in ten words (or commandments). Each and every word produced a voice and that voice divided into seventy voices [cf. B. Shabbat 88b: *Midrash Tanḥuma,* Shemot, 25; *Shemot Rabbah* 28:4]. All of [the voices] shone and sparkled before the eyes of Israel, and with their very eyes they saw the splendor of His glory, as it is written, 'And all the people saw the voices.'" See also the graphic description in *Zohar Ḥadash* 41b–c of Israel's seeing the engraving of the letters of the first word of the Decalogue, *'anokhi,* on the tablets of stone, which resonates with the description of revelation in the targumic fragment cited in n. 73, below.

[65] Cf. *Zohar* 2:83b. Cf. Naḥmanides' commentary to Gen. 15:1 (1:89), and Deut. 5:19 (2:369); MS Oxford-Bodleian 1645, fol. 88a: "'They saw the God of Israel,' the prophecy of the [Israelite] people was by means of the glorious name (*shem ha-nikhbad,* i.e., the Presence) through the medium of a cloud and thick darkness. The elders prophesied through it without any intermediary, and Moses actually saw Him, as it says, 'and you shall see My back.'"

[66] See *Zohar* 1:15b, 30b, 53b, 60a, 208a, 247a; 2:90b, 126a, 147b; *Tiqqune Zohar,* 30, 74b; MS New York–JTSA Mic. 1805, fol. 21b. In interpreting this seemingly insignificant word, the kabbalists follow an ancient midrashic practice attributed particularly to the school of Aqiva; see B. Pesaḥim 22b.

> *Shekhinah*]. They said that this speculum is hidden and takes form. She stands and is momentarily seen, then returns and is hidden as at first; she takes form and afterwards is hidden and removed. This is the hidden secret of the verse "all the people are seeing" (*we-khol ha-ʿam ro'im*). It is written *ro'im* [in the present tense] and not *ra'u* [in the past tense].[67]

The use of the present tense implies that the activity of seeing described here is not completed, for indeed, the object of vision, the *Shekhinah,* is characterized by a ceaseless dialectic of appearing and hiding. De León affirms the ongoing possibility of reliving the theophanic moment of Sinai that was marked by the manifestation of this particular grade. As will be seen in more detail below, it is precisely through the activity of Torah-study that the enlightened kabbalists are afforded the opportunity to see the *Shekhinah* as she was seen at the historical event of revelation.

R. Eleazar's interpretation that at Sinai Israel had a vision of the *Shekhinah* has its antecedents in a host of midrashic and aggadic statements that emphasize the unique theophanous quality of the Sinaitic revelation. In terms of kabbalistic precedents, the notion that *Shekhinah* is the locus of the revelatory experience at Sinai is first expressed in *Sefer ha-Bahir.* The relevant section begins with an exegetical reflection on Exod. 20:15: "'All the people saw the voices' [refers to] those voices of which David spoke."[68] This statement is followed by a detailed enumeration of the seven occurrences of the expression "voice of the Lord" (*qol YHWH*) in Ps. 29:3–9, which had already been applied exegetically to the Sinaitic revelation in classical rabbinic sources.[69] Moreover, the *Bahir* appropriates the view attributed to R. Yoḥanan that the Torah was given in seven voices[70] and gives it a theosophic interpretation: "Thus you have learned that by means of seven voices the Torah was given, and the Lord of the world was revealed through all of them to [Israel], and they saw Him, as it is written, 'All the people saw the voices.'"[71] The voices mentioned in Exod. 20:15 are those enumerated in Ps. 29:3–9, that is, the seven voices through which the Torah was given, which, according to the kabbalistic symbolism in the *Bahir,* represent the divine potencies. Inasmuch as these potencies are essentially light it follows that one can speak of the seeing of the voices in a literal sense, and the initial exegetical problem of using a visual predicate with an auditory object is solved. The seeing of the voices recorded in Scripture therefore signifies that the people of Israel had a vision of God who was re-

[67] MS Berlin Or. Quat. 833, fol. 35a.

[68] *Sefer ha-Bahir,* § 45. On a similar hypostatization of the seven voices in Ashkenazi tradition, see MS Oxford-Bodleian 1208, fol. 6b, where Psalm 29 is interpreted in terms of the "seven voices that go out before the Presence."

[69] Cf. *Mekhilta de-Rabbi Ishmael,* ʿAmaleq, 1, p. 188, and Baḥodesh, 1, p. 205; *Mekhilta de-Rabbi Shimʿon bar Yoḥai,* p. 142; *Sifre on Deuteronomy,* 343, p. 397; *Shir ha-Shirim Rabbah* 1:13; B. Zevaḥim 116a. And see esp. the formulation in *Midrash Yelammedenu* cited in *Yalqut Shimʿoni* ad Psalm 29, 2:709. See also the *piyyuṭ* of Eleazar Qallir, in *Jubelschrift zum neunzigsten Geburtstag des Dr. L. Zunz* (Berlin, 1884), p. 204.

[70] B. Shabbat 88a; *Midrash Tanḥuma,* Shemot, 25; *Shemot Rabbah* 28:4.

[71] *Sefer ha-Bahir,* § 45.

vealed through the seven emanations. To an extent, the bahiric view is based on the exegetical posture of R. Aqiva, who reportedly interpreted Exod. 20:15 as follows: "They saw and heard that which was visible. They saw the fiery word coming out of the mouth of the Almighty as it was hewn upon the tablets."[72] According to Aqiva, then, seeing the voices involved a mystical perception of the fiery letters of God's speech as they were engraved on the stone tablets.[73] From another comment attributed to Aqiva, in which Exod. 20:15 figures as a key prooftext, it appears that the voices seen at Sinai amounted to a vision of the visage of God: "R. Aqiva interpreted the verse [Cant. 2:14] as referring to the time that Israel stood before Mount Sinai, 'O my dove, in the cranny of the rocks,' for they were hidden under the cover of [Mount] Sinai. 'Let me see Your face,' as it says, 'And all the people saw the voices' (Exod. 20:15)."[74] The kabbalistic explanation offered in the *Bahir* is an elaboration of this midrashic view, for the vision of the divine voices was, in effect, a mystical apprehension of God.

The position of the *Bahir* is modified somewhat in the continuation of the text, where it is emphasized that the seeing of the seven voices was mediated through the last of them, which corresponds to the *Shekhinah*. This notion is expressed in three consecutive passages, each one employing somewhat different terminology. In the first instance, responding to the textual discrepancies regarding God's addressing the people at Sinai from the heavens (Exod. 20:22) and His descending from the mountain (Exod. 19:20, 2 Sam. 22:10), the *Bahir* states that "His great fire, which is one voice, was on earth, while the other voices were in heaven, as it is written, 'From the heavens He let you hear His voice to discipline you; on earth He let you see His great fire; and from amidst that fire you heard His words' (Deut. 4:36)."[75] There is thus no contradiction between the different scriptural accounts, for God spoke from heaven but was heard primarily from the earth. More specifically, the locus of the divine

[72] *Mekhilta de-Rabbi Ishmael,* Baḥodesh, 9, p. 235 (cf. the view of Bar Qappara in *Midrash Samuel* 9:4, p. 74). In contrast to Aqiva, two other interpretations of Exod. 20:15 are given in the aforementioned midrashic source: R. Ishmael's view that "they saw what is visible and heard what is audible," and the opinion of Judah the Prince that the seeing of the voices is meant "to proclaim the excellence of the Israelites, for when they stood before Mount Sinai to receive the Torah they interpreted the divine word as soon as they heard it." For a parallel to Judah's explanation, see *Sifre on Deuteronomy* 313, p. 355; see Urbach, *The Sages,* pp. 266–267. Cf. *De Migratione Abrahami* 47–49, where Philo's view seems to approximate that of Judah. See Wolfson, *Philo,* 2:37–38. From other places in the Philonic corpus, however, it seems that he interpreted Exod. 20:15 in a way akin to Aqiva; see *De Decalogo* 32–33, 46–47; *De Vita Mosis* II.213; Chidester, *Word and Light,* pp. 30–43.

[73] It would be fruitful to compare the view attributed in rabbinic sources to Aqiva to the midrashic gloss to Exod. 20:2 found in M. Klein, *Genizah Manuscripts of Palestinian Targum to the Pentateuch* (Cincinnati, 1986), 1:264: "The first commandment as it emerged from the mouth of the Holy One . . . like meteors, like lightning, [and] like torches of fire; a torch of fire to His right, and a torch of fire to His left; it sprang forth and flew in the heavenly space. And all of Israel saw it, and feared it. And it would return and be engraved upon the two tablets of the covenant."

[74] *Shir ha-Shirim Rabbah* 2:31.

[75] *Sefer ha-Bahir,* § 46.

epiphany—both visually and aurally—is the "great fire" (*'esh ha-gedollah*), the *Shekhinah,* the only one of the seven voices that is immanent on earth, the other six being in heaven. The point is exegetically linked to "[The Lord spoke to you out of the fire;] you heard the sound of words but perceived no shape—nothing but a voice" (ibid., 12), which, according to the *Bahir,* implies that "they saw an image, but not every image, as it is written, 'you perceived no shape—nothing but a voice,' and it is written, 'you heard the sound of words.'"[76] The meaning of the seemingly cryptic remark, "they saw an image, but not every image," is that the Israelites saw the image (*temunah*) of God that is identical with the singular voice (*qol*), that is, the *Shekhinah,* which comprises all the other voices that were not seen directly. The expression *kol temunah* refers specifically to the attribute of God that corresponds to the phallus, designated as *kol,* inasmuch as it comprises within itself all the other potencies. The Israelites thus were vouchsafed a vision of the *Shekhinah,* which is the image of God, but not of *Yesod,* which is the image that is the All. In a third passage the issue is clarified even further: "One verse says, 'All the people saw the voices' (Exod. 20:15), and another verse says, 'The voice of the words that you heard' (Deut. 4:12). How is this possible? At first they saw the voices. And what did they see? The seven voices . . . and in the end they heard the speech that went out from them all. We have learned that there were ten [words] and the rabbis said that all of them were said in one word.[77] So all of these [seven voices] were said in one word."[78]

Just as the rabbis had claimed that the ten words of revelation were uttered in one, so, too, the seven voices, which correspond to the seven lower *sefirot,* are all contained in one voice (*qol*) or speech (*dibbur*), that is, the *Shekhinah.* That the one word that contains all the others refers to *Shekhinah* may be gathered from the continuation in the *Bahir:* "Ten utterances (*ma'amarot*)[79] [correspond] to the ten kings. Perhaps they could not be spoken by one? The word *'anokhi* ["I"] is written in [the beginning of the Decalogue] and it comprises all ten. And what are the ten kings? Seven voices and three words."[80] All ten utterances, composed of the seven voices and three words, are contained within

[76] Ibid., § 47.

[77] Cf. *Mekhilta de-Rabbi Ishmael,* Baḥodesh, 4, p. 218: "The Holy One, blessed be He, said all the ten commandments in one word, and afterwards specified each commandment by itself." And *Midrash Tanḥuma,* Yitro, 11: "the ten words [of revelation] all emerged from the mouth of God in one voice."

[78] *Sefer ha-Bahir,* § 48.

[79] In this context the word *ma'amarot* is used to refer to the ten words of revelation. Elsewhere in the *Bahir* (§ 138) the *ma'amarot* stand for the utterances by means of which the world was created, which correspond to the ten *sefirot,* which in turn correspond to the ten sayings (*dibberot*) of revelation (§ 124).

[80] Ibid., § 49. Cf. A. Hebbelynck, "Les mystères des lettres grecques," *Muséon* 1 (1900): 34–36, where the divine pleroma is represented by a decade broken up into the "three hypostases of the indivisible Trinity" and the seven days of the week (the six days plus the Sabbath). This work, a fourth-century text that comprises older traditions, including ideas of a Judeo-Christian provenance, is an important source for the study of early Jewish esotericism.

the Presence, which is designated by the first-person pronoun *'anokhi,* the subjective pole of the divine pleroma and the personal voice of revelation. Paradoxically, the first word of the Decalogue (*'anokhi*) symbolizes the last of the divine emanations, the audible and visible aspect of the pleroma that comprises within itself all ten powers. That the *Shekhinah* is the visible manifestation of the hidden God is stated in what appears to me to be one of the older tradition-complexes incorporated in the *Bahir.* The following parable is given to explain in what sense the pleroma of divine Wisdom is called "blessing" (*berakhah*), the place to which every knee bows down (cf. Isa. 45:23): "To what may this be compared? To those who seek to see the face of the king, but they do not know the whereabouts of his house. At first they asked: Where is the house of the king? and afterwards they asked: Where is the king?"[81] The way to find the king, therefore, is through his house, that is, the *Shekhinah,* which is the visible representation of the hidden God.

What is implied in the enigmatic passages from the *Bahir* is developed further by thirteenth-century Spanish kabbalists, of whom I will here mention two examples. The first is Ezra of Gerona, who comments that although there are two aspects of Torah, written and oral, which correspond respectively to the sixth (masculine) and tenth (feminine) divine emanations, the medium of revelation of the former is the latter. "The Oral Torah [*Shekhinah*] emanates from the Written Torah [*Tif'eret*], which maintains her. . . . The two *torot* were given by means of the *Shekhinah* . . . for the inner voice [of revelation] was not discernible or heard until the end, which is the tenth *sefirah.*"[82] My second example is Naḥmanides, who writes in his commentary to Exod. 19:20,

> [The Torah] was given to Moses in seven voices [i.e., the seven *sefirot*], which he heard and comprehended. But with respect to Israel, they heard it in one voice [i.e., the *Shekhinah*], as it says, "a loud voice and no more" (Deut. 5:19). And it says, "You heard the sound of words but perceived no shape—nothing but a [single] voice" (ibid., 4:12). And here, too, [Scripture] alludes [to this]: "And all the people saw the voices" (Exod. 20:15), the word *qolot* (voices) is [written] without a *waw* [signifying the plural form], for they [Israel] saw all the voices as one [i.e., the *Shekhinah*].[83]

[81] *Sefer ha-Bahir,* § 4.

[82] *Perush le-Shir ha-Shirim,* ed. Chavel, p. 487. Cf. the passage translated and discussed by Scholem in *On the Kabbalah,* pp. 49–50: "The form of the Written Torah is that of the colors of white fire, and the form of the Oral Torah has colored forms as of black fire. . . . And so the Written Torah can take on corporeal form only through the power of the Oral Torah." Scholem attributed the text to Isaac the Blind; see, however, Idel, in "Kabbalistic Material from the School of R. David ben Judah ḥe-Hasid," p. 170 n. 9, suggests that the text was authored by a certain kabbalist, R. Isaac, who wrote at the end of the thirteenth or the beginning of the fourteenth century. See idem, "Infinities of Torah in Kabbalah," p. 145. It is worthwhile to compare that text with another kabbalistic passage extant in MS Oxford-Bodleian 1945, fol. 38b; see also fol. 66b.

[83] Naḥmanides' commentary to Exod. 20:2, 1:388. See also his commentary to Gen. 15:1, p. 89; Exod. 3:13, p. 291; Deut. 5:19, 2:369; 34:10, p. 504. In contrast to the view expressed by Naḥmanides, other kabbalists, such as Ezra of Gerona, maintained that at Sinai Moses beheld but

The opinion attributed in the *Zohar* to R. Eleazar follows this line of interpretation by maintaining that the vision of the upper lights at Sinai was mediated through the *Shekhinah*. In another context the *Zohar* puts the matter as follows: "When the Torah was given to Israel they saw and gazed directly upon the other mirror [*Shekhinah*] and the upper gradations, and they desired to gaze upon and see the glory of their Master. Thus they saw the supernal glory of the Holy One, blessed be He."[84] In yet another zoharic passage we read, "It has been taught: when God revealed himself on Mount Sinai all of Israel saw as one who sees a light in a crystal. From that light each one saw that which Ezekiel the prophet did not see. Why? For those upper voices were revealed [or, according to a variant reading, inscribed] in one, as it is written, 'And all the people saw the voices.' By Ezekiel, however, the Presence was revealed in her chariot and no more. Ezekiel saw as one who sees from behind many walls."[85]

According to the *Zohar*, and other thirteenth-century kabbalistic works as well, the vision of God accorded to all prophets with the exception of Moses,[86]

---

five *sefirot* (based on the opinion of R. Ḥelbo, cited in B. Berakhot 6b, that the Torah was given in five voices). See *Perush le-Shir ha-Shirim*, ed. Chavel., p. 488; Azriel of Gerona, *Perush ha-'Aggadot*, p. 7. See, however, Ezra's commentary on the aggadot extant in MS Vatican 441, fol. 49a, where, after mentioning the passage from Berakhot, he summarizes the various positions as follows: "The ten [voices], and the seven, and the five, everything was one [or perhaps: all these views are identical]." Cf. Ṭodros Abulafia's interpretation of R. Ḥelbo's view in *'Oṣar ha-Kavod,* 4a, to the effect that the five voices, which correspond to the five *sefirot,* were contained in the *Shekhinah*, the locus of the theophanic vision. For an effort on the part of a kabbalist to harmonize the different aggadic views regarding the revelation of Torah in seven voices, five voices, or one voice, see MS Oxford-Bodleian 1945, fol. 38a.

84 *Zohar* 1:91a. Cf. 2:146a: "Whatever Israel saw at that time [i.e., at Sinai] they saw from one light [i.e., *Shekhinah*] that received all the other lights [i.e., the upper *sefirot*], and they desired to see it."

85 *Zohar* 2:82a. The expression "as if from behind a wall" is used on several occasions in zoharic literature to characterize an inferior mode of visualization. See, e.g., *Zohar* 2:69b, 130b, 213a; 3:174b; *Zohar Ḥadash* 38a, 39d. This expression is used as well by Moses de León in several of his Hebrew theosophic writings; see, e.g., *Sha'ar Yesod ha-Merkavah,* MS Vatican 283, fol. 169b: "concerning the upper [celestial creatures] there is no seeing except by a slight contemplation as if from behind a wall."

86 Employing the terminology of B. Yevamot 49b, many kabbalists maintained that all prophets with the exception of Moses beheld the *Shekhinah,* the "speculum that does not shine"; Moses, by contrast, beheld the divine through *Tif'eret,* i.e., the "speculum that shines." Cf. Azriel of Gerona, *Perush ha-'Aggadot,* pp. 33–34; *Zohar* 1:131a, 170b–171a; 2:23b, 82b, 245a; 3:174a, 198a, 268b; *Zohar Ḥadash* 38b, 42c, 77a; *Tiqqune Zohar* 18, 32a; Moses de León, *Sheqel ha-Qodesh,* p. 16; Gikatilla, *Sha'are 'Orah* 1:70, 149–150, 159, 248–249 (cf. Goetschel, "The Conception of Prophecy in the Works of R. Moses de León and R. Joseph Gikatilla," pp. 222–224); Isaac of Acre, *Me'irat 'Einayim,* pp. 41–43. Cf. *Zohar* 2:82b: "all prophets vis-à-vis Moses are like a female vis-à-vis a male." To be sure, not all kabbalists accepted this interpretation. See, e.g., Ṭodros Abulafia, *Sha'ar ha-Razim,* p. 79, where it is stated that even Moses comprehended the speculum that shines, i.e., *Tif'eret,* only indirectly, through the medium of the two cherubim, which, according to this kabbalist, symbolize the ninth and tenth gradations, *Yesod* and *Shekhinah*. Other kabbalists also attempted to lower the level of Mosaic prophecy, especially in terms of visualization, although a clear distinction between Moses and other prophets was always maintained. See, e.g., *Me'irat 'Einayim,* pp. 55, 134; MS Paris–BN 843, fol. 75a; MS Oxford-Bodleian 1945, fol. 67b.

was said to be mediated through the last of the divine grades, the feminine Presence.[87] The Presence is the archetypal image that contains all images, the prism or mirror that reflects all the supernal forms.[88] One might even go so far as to say that for the kabbalists the Presence is not only the locus of prophetic experience but also the "objective correlate" or "sensory pole" of prophetic vision. On several occasions Naḥmanides criticized Maimonides on precisely this score: the latter contrasted prophetic vision with actual seeing too sharply, implying that the contents of a prophetic vision have no basis in concrete external (or spatial) reality.[89] The position of the *Zohar,* in full concord with Naḥmanides, would be that the object of prophetic vision does not exist only in the mind of the prophet but is an objective reality. On the other hand, as I argued in the previous chapter, for the zoharic authorship, as for other kabbalists, the form or forms that the spiritual reality assumes are constructed within the imagination. This is not to say that the imagined object is purely subjective insofar as it is constituted by an intentional act of imaging. The point is rather that in the prophetic vision the spiritual forms of the divine pleroma are configured in the last of the gradations, and the latter corresponds to the imagination, for it is perceived in distinct forms only by the imagination. Indeed, human imagination is a mirror that reflects the divine mirror in such a way that by imaging the image of the divine anthropos the visionary, in effect, is seeing his own pneumatic being projected outward. This double reflection should not be construed, in contemporary terms, as a form of psychological reductionism, inasmuch as the ontological presupposition underlying the kabbalistic psychology is that the soul itself is of the same substance as God. The kabbalistic perspective, in contrast to the Maimonidean view, maintains that the images seen in the imagination correspond to an external or transcendent reality, the divine Presence. Thus, in a passage from *Midrash ha-Neʿelam* on the book of Ruth, it is stated that the prophets—with the exception of Moses—"saw the

[87] Cf. *Zohar* 1:85a, 88b, 91a–b, 183a, 203a, 240b; 2:245a, 247b, 257b; *Tiqqune Zohar* 18, 31b; 19, 39b; *Zohar Ḥadash,* 111b (*Tiqqunim*). See Scholem, *Origins,* p. 451. It should be noted, however, that on occasion the zoharic authorship, in line with accepted kabbalistic symbolism, refers to the two gradations above the Presence, *Neṣaḥ* and *Hod* as the source of prophetic inspiration. Cf. Azriel of Gerona, *Perush ha-'Aggadot,* p. 49; *Zohar* 1:1b, 183a; 2:104b, 171a, 251b, 257b, 276b; 3:35a, 68a (RM); 90b; *Tiqqune Zohar,* introduction, 2a–b, 11b, 13a; 21, 49a; 55, 88b; 70, 123b; *Zohar Ḥadash* 119c (*Tiqqunim*); Gikatilla, *Shaʿare 'Orah* 1:149–150; Moses de León, *Sheqel ha-Qodesh,* p. 58 (cf. Goetschel, "Conception of Prophecy," pp. 222, 232); Baḥya's commentary on Num. 12:6, ed. Chavel, 3:72–73. Yet, even in these contexts, it is abundantly clear that the medium of prophetic vision is the *Shekhinah.*

[88] Cf. *Zohar* 1:13a, 88b, 91a, 183a; 2:186b.

[89] See Naḥmanides' lengthy critique, in his commentary to Gen. 46:1 (ed. Chavel, 1:246–51), of Maimonides' discussion of prophecy in the *Guide of the Perplexed* I:27, and in his commentary to Gen. 18:1 (1:103–105) of Maimonides' interpretation of angelic revelations in the *Guide* II:4. See also my "Secret of the Garment in Naḥmanides." It should be noted that in some cases Maimonides does allow for an "objective" correlate to prophetic visionary experience, viz., the "created light" (the *Shekhinah*), which God has made especially for this purpose. Cf. *Guide* I:11, 25, 46, 64. This reflects the Saadianic conception of the "created glory"; see chapter 4, section on Saadiah Gaon.

images from above as a sort of body" (*she-ro'im dimyonot shel maʿalah kemin guf*).[90] To see the spiritual images in concrete, tangible form is precisely the distinctive quality of the prophetic vision. The point is elaborated on by Moses de León, who contrasts the prophecy of Moses with that of all other prophets:

> [In the case of] the prophecy [of Moses], his vision was devoid of all corporeal matters. He saw the matter clearly from within the speculum that shines, which does not take shape at all in a corporeal vision (*she-'einah nigshemet bi-re'iyat gufni kelal*). It is rather a true splendor, pure and clear. This is not so with respect to the rest of the prophets, who saw from within a speculum that does not shine, for it takes shape in accordance with their vision (*nigshemet kefi re'iyatam*), and they do not see it except as a corporeal image (*demut guf*).[91]

While de León, like the aforementioned zoharic text, contrasts the imaginary seeing of the divine in bodily forms with a purer seeing that is imageless, the significant point for my analysis is the characterization of the former. It is, after all, this latter kind of seeing that is achievable by the kabbalists and thus best informs us about their particular religious orientation.

To return to the zoharic interpretation of revelation: It follows that the interpretation of R. Eleazar places the Sinaitic theophany in the spectrum of normal—that is, other than Mosaic—prophetical experience wherein the locus of visionary experience is the last gradation. It is noteworthy, moreover, that the Sinaitic vision is contrasted with that of Ezekiel's vision of the chariot in Babylonia: whereas Israel saw all the upper gradations as reflected in the Presence as if in a crystal, Ezekiel merited seeing the Presence only as reflected in her chariots, that is, the angelic beings beneath the divine realm. It would appear from the view of R. Jose, however, that at Sinai Israel achieved a higher level of prophetic consciousness. Indeed, in another passage,[92] also attributed to R. Jose, the *Zohar* presents an alternative explanation, according to which those at Sinai were said to be on a par with Moses, thereby exceeding the experiential level of other prophets. In this case as well, the *Zohar* contrasts Israel's vision at Sinai with that of Ezekiel. In the scriptural account of the latter's vision words like "image," "likeness," and "appearance" are constantly employed, for Ezekiel saw what he saw "as if from behind a wall," whereas Israel saw God "face to face." "Ezekiel saw the image of the supernal chariots, for he saw from a place that was not so bright." Israel saw a vision of the five upper voices[93] through which the Torah, according to one rabbinic view, was given, whereas Ezekiel saw five corresponding gradations below the divine realm: the stormy

[90] *Zohar Ḥadash*, 77a. According to an alternative version the text reads, "they saw the images above as a sort of form (*gawwen*)." I would suggest that the reading "as a sort of body" at some point was changed by a copyist because of its radical implications.

[91] *Mishkan ha-ʿEdut*, MS Berlin Or. Quat. 833, fol. 3a.

[92] *Zohar* 2:82b. See also 194a; and Isaac of Acre, *Me'irat ʿEinayim*, p. 5.

[93] This accords with the view of Ezra of Gerona; see above, n. 83. Cf. *Zohar* 2:84b, 90a, 206a. De León affirms the same view in several of his Hebrew theosophic writings; see *Book of the Pomegranate*, p. 162 (Hebrew section); MS Munich 47, fol. 336a.

wind, a huge cloud, the flashing fire, a radiance, and the electrum (see Ezek. 1:4). At Sinai, then, Israel achieved something of the status of Moses. The *Zohar* notes, accordingly, that Scripture says with respect to Moses, "And the Lord descended on Mount Sinai and called to Moses" (Exod. 19:20), and analogously, with respect to the nation, "the Lord descended in front of all the people on Mount Sinai" (ibid., 19:11). Hence, at Sinai the king's "head" and "body" were revealed, whereas Ezekiel saw only the "lower hand" or "feet" of God. Ezekiel, like Isaiah, had a vision of the Presence, but even that was a lower level of visualization.[94]

As to the specific content of the visionary experience at Sinai, we learn, moreover, that the vision had a decidedly gnostic element, that is, through the vision the people were able to gain esoteric knowledge of the divine attributes. "It has been taught: R. Jose ben R. Judah said: Israel saw here [at Sinai] that which Ezekiel the son of Buzi did not see; and they all comprehended the supernal, glorious Wisdom."[95] A clear link between the visionary and epistemological is thus formed: through the vision, theosophical knowledge was gained. Knowledge, according to the *Zohar,* is essentially of a visionary nature; the word the *Zohar* employs for mystical contemplation, *histakkelut,* should be rendered "visualization," for the visual contemplation of the divine form lies at the heart of mystical knowledge. It is within this framework that one must understand the further connection made between the seeing of the voices and the process of interpretation. In earlier midrashic sources, as well as in Philo, the seeing of the voices described in Exod. 20:15 was already understood as a conceptual vision expressed through interpretation. When Israel saw—that is, comprehended—the words of the divine revelation, they immediately interpreted them. Drawing on this ancient motif in Jewish thought, the *Zohar* elaborates on the hermeneutical quality of the visionary experience at Sinai:

> The ten words of the Torah [i.e., the Decalogue] contain all the [613] commandments,[96] comprehending what is above and below, the principle of the ten words of

[94] The zoharic authorship, together with several other thirteenth-century kabbalists, relegated Ezekiel's chariot vision to a lower ontological realm below the divine pleroma. To be sure, as is evident from the various kabbalistic commentaries on Ezekiel 1, the particular details of the prophet's vision all have a symbolic correspondence to the upper realm, but in essence the throne-world of that vision was concerned with the "lower chariot," i.e., the realm of angels below the sphere of divine potencies. See Scholem, *Major Trends,* pp. 206–207; Tishby, *Wisdom of the Zohar,* pp. 587–595; Farber in Jacob ben Jacob ha-Kohen, "Commentary on Ezekiel's Chariot," pp. 94 n. 3, 170 n. 1.

[95] *Zohar* 2:82a.

[96] This notion can be traced to Geonic and late medieval midrashic sources. See Saadiah's commentary on *Sefer Yeṣirah,* ed. Kafiḥ, pp. 47–48; idem, *'Azaharot le-'Aseret ha-Dibberot,* in A. Jellinek, *Qunṭres Taryag* (Vienna, 1878), p. 5 n. 14; Judah ben Barzillai, *Perush Sefer Yeṣirah,* p. 278; *Bemidbar Rabbah* 13:16, 18:21; *Sefer ha-Bahir,* § 124; Ezra of Gerona, *Perush le-Shir ha-Shirim,* ed. Chavel, p. 521; *Zohar* 2:90a–b, 93b; Moses de León, *Book of the Pomegranate,* pp. 219, 340–341, 342 (Hebrew section). See Wolfson, "Mystical Rationalization of the Commandments in *Sefer ha-Rimmon,*" pp. 224–225.

creation. . . .[97] These [ten words] were carved on the tablets of stone, and all that was hidden in them was visible to their [the Israelites'] eyes, for they all knew and considered the secret of the 613 commandments of the Torah contained in them. All was visible to them, all was understood in the minds of Israel, and all was revealed to their eyes. In that time all the secrets of Torah, above and below, were not removed from them, for they saw with their eyes the splendor of the glory of their Master. Since the day God created the world there was nothing like His revealing His glory on Sinai.[98]

Through a vision of the divine glory, the last of the emanations in the sefirotic pleroma, the people of Israel were able to penetrate the depths of Torah, to gain the hidden (i.e., kabbalistic) secrets of the 613 commandments contained in the Decalogue. The ten words of revelation correspond to the ten words of creation, which in turn correspond to the ten divine gradations. According to the *Zohar,* then, at Sinai the people of Israel gained knowledge of the esoteric, as well as the exoteric dimension of Torah, through a vision of the glory. The esoteric dimension is fundamentally an understanding of the sefirotic pleroma expressed specifically as the comprehension of secrets contained in the Decalogue. Thus, by seeing the glory the Israelite people were capable of acquiring mystical knowledge embodied in the Torah.

Interpretation

The Enlightened Will Shine: Mystical Hermeneutics as Theophany

As we have seen, the *Zohar* upholds a special kind of visionary experience at Sinai: the Israelite people were said to have seen either the upper five gradations directly, thereby achieving the level of Moses, or the last gradation as reflecting the upper five. In the text cited at the close of the last section, the people likewise were said to have seen the divine glory, and at the same time all the secrets of the Torah. Indeed, according to that passage, these secrets were available to Israel precisely because they beheld the splendor of the glory. Visual experience, therefore, grounds theosophical comprehension; gnosis flows out of a mystical seeing. It can be further argued that in the mind of the zoharic authorship the process of kabbalistic hermeneutics is, in some sense, an imitation of the historical event of revelation. Consider, for example, the following passage: "Thus it was that on that day the colleagues (*ḥavrayya'*) saw the face of the *Shekhinah* and they were encompassed by fire. The face of R. Abba was burning like a flame from the joy of Torah. It has been taught: that whole day none of them

[97] That is, the ten words by which the world was created; cf. M. Avot 5:1. For references to the correspondence between the logoi and the commandments, see Ginzberg, *Legends* 3:104–106, 6:43 n. 237, 45 n. 243; M. Kasher, *Torah Shelemah* (New York, 1973), 9:43 n. 72; Moses de León, *Book of the Pomegranate,* p. 219 n. 20 (Hebrew section).

[98] *Zohar* 2:93b–94a; 2:82b, 156b.

left the house and the house was bounded by smoke. Among themselves they were innovating words of Torah as if on that very day they had received the Torah on Mount Sinai."[99] Here, too, the zoharic view is rooted in a long-standing rabbinic tradition according to which exegetical activity, or study of Torah, was linked to the Sinaitic theophany. Several rabbinic passages, as I have already indicated, even stress that through interpretation of the Torah the supernatural phenomena of the Sinaitic event are recreated. Moreover, in a host of rabbinic sources the illuminative nature of Torah-study is emphasized: the countenance of the sage is described as shining with the brightness of the celestial lights and illuminating others.[100] It is plausible that precisely such a characterization underlies the rabbinic idea, clearly evident in the zoharic passage cited above, that he who receives the face of the sage is as if he received the face of the *Shekhinah*. In the *Zohar* the correlation of hermeneutics and revelation is focused specifically on the fact that in both, comprehension of the text is related to a vision of the glory. Yet, whereas those present at Sinai comprehended esoteric truths of the Torah through a vision of the glory, the mystics gain a vision of the glory through intense study of the Torah.[101] It may be argued, moreover, that, according to the *Zohar,* the mystic must experience some prior spiritual illumination before he can contemplate the *Shekhinah* and see the light of Torah. This point, it seems to me, underlies the following interpretation of Dan. 12:3, the *locus classicus* in the *Zohar* to refer to the mystical-theurgical character of kabbalistic hermeneutics.[102]

> "And the enlightened will shine like the splendor of the sky" refers to the pillars and supports of that palanquin. "The enlightened" (*ha-maskilim*) are the upper pillars and supports [i.e., the kabbalists] who contemplate (*mistakkelei*) with their understanding the palanquin [*Shekhinah*] to the extent that it is necessary. . . . "They will shine," for if they did not shine and were not illuminated, they would not be able to gaze upon and contemplate that palanquin to the extent that is necessary. . . . "The splendor" (*zohar*): that which illuminates the Torah. "The splendor" that shines upon the heads of that beast [i.e., *Shekhinah*] and these heads are the enlightened who shine perpetually and who contemplate that firmament and the light that emerges from there, which is the light of Torah that shines constantly without pause.[103]

[99] *Zohar* 1:94b. On the relation between theosophic exegesis and the Sinatic revelation, consider *Zohar* 1:216b: "It has been taught: R. Jose said, From the day that R. Simeon left the cave, these words were not hidden from the fellows, and they would contemplate the supernal secrets, and they were revealed among them as if they were given at that moment on Mount Sinai." See also the telling remark in *Zohar Ḥadash* 93c (*Tiqqunim*): "The Holy One, blessed be He, inclines the heavens and the heavens of the heavens toward the [mystical] fellowship [of R. Simeon] in the manner of [the event at] Sinai."

[100] See sources discussed in Aalen, *Die Begriffe 'Licht' und 'Finsternis'*, pp. 272–283.

[101] On gaining a vision of the divine glory through study of a text, see the legend in *Zohar* 1:56b concerning Abraham and Enoch looking at the book of the generations of mankind given originally by God to Adam.

[102] See Giller, *The Enlightened Will Shine,* pp. 21–32.

[103] *Zohar* 1:15b–16a.

In this context the mystics not only contemplate (or visualize) the palanquin—a symbolic reference to *Shekhinah* based on Canticles 3:9[104]—they are the very pillars and supports on which it rests. However, in order for them to contemplate the splendor (*zohar*) of the *Shekhinah*—the masculine potency that corresponds to the phallic *Yesod*,[105] as reflected in Torah—they must be illuminated by it, a process that is here depicted as the light shining on their heads. Mystical enlightenment thus consists of the illumination of the divine phallus on the heads of the kabbalists, which results in their ability to comprehend mysteries of Torah that emerge from the feminine Presence.[106]

Crowning and Visionary Union with the Phallus

One should take note here of the subtle gender transformation that is implied in the depiction of mystical illumination: the kabbalists, whose heads are illumined, are feminized as they receive the efflux from the phallic splendor. That this illumination entails a crossing of gender boundaries is evident from the related image of the crown or diadem employed in the *Zohar*, following earlier kabbalistic sources, to convey the notion that the mystics are united with the divine in visual contemplation.[107] Alternatively, it may be said that the crowning of the kabbalists is a ritual reenactment of circumcision, whereby the corona of the penis is disclosed. As I intimated above, in the complex gender symbolism of theosophic kabbalah the corona of the penis corresponds to the feminine aspect of the Godhead, the *Shekhinah*, and hence the act of crowning must be viewed as a feminization.

The underlying theosophic assumption here is that the phallus is the ontic source of both masculinity and femininity. This idea is already expressed in a passage in *Sefer ha-Bahir*, where it is stated that the letter *ṣaddi* (i.e., the

104 See, e.g., *Zohar* 1:29a.

105 On the phallic connotation of the word *zohar*, see the interpretation of Dan. 12:3 in *Zohar* 1:100a–b, and the parallel in *Zohar Ḥadash* 104b–c (erroneously printed as part of the *Tiqqunim* section); *Zohar* 2:2a; *Zohar Ḥadash* 106b–c. These passages will be discussed in detail below.

106 The influence of the zoharic imagery is particularly evident in one of the hymns Isaac Luria composed for the Sabbath meals, in which he describes the overflowing of the divine grade that corresponds to the phallus on the heads of the kabbalists, resulting in their uttering mystical secrets to crown the table (symbolizing the Presence). See Liebes, "Hymns for the Sabbath Meals Composed by the Holy Ari," p. 551. Cf. *Zohar* 2:153b.

107 On the crown as a symbol for mystical union in the *Zohar* and Moses de León's Hebrew theosophic texts, see the preliminary remarks in Wolfson, "Mystical-Theurgical Dimensions of Prayer in *Sefer ha-Rimmon*," pp. 52–55. For the use in Geronese kabbalistic texts of the image of being crowned in light for the state of *devequt*, see the evidence adduced by Idel in "Universalization and Integration," pp. 35–36, and further references at p. 199 n. 27. For a variety of other references to the act of coronation as a symbol for *hieros gamos*, see Ginsburg, *Sabbath in the Classical Kabbalah*, s.v. "coronation or crowning of divinity on Shabbat." See also *Zohar* 2:127a–128a, 210b; and see references in chapter 6, n. 50. Another pertinent image is that of the coronation of the righteous in the Garden of Eden by the righteous on earth, i.e., the kabbalists, when they study Torah at midnight; see *Zohar* 2:209a; 3:144b–145a. To be sure, the use of the image of the crown in kabbalistic literature to refer to the state of mystical illumination and union draws on much older motifs connected with this symbol, but the matter cannot be pursued in this context.

Ṣaddiq, the Righteous, who is in the position of the phallus) orthographically can be broken into a *yod* on top of a *nun*, the former symbolizing the male potency (the sign of the covenant of circumcision) and the latter the female (perhaps related to the word *neqevah*).[108] Contained within the one letter is the duality of male and female. One should speak, therefore, of an androgynous phallus. To put the matter in slightly different terms, we have here another example of a one-sex theory: the feminine (specifically the clitoris) is but an extension of the masculine (the penis).[109] This commonplace biological conception allowed the medieval kabbalists to affirm the bisexuality of the Godhead without introducing any metaphysical duality. On the contrary, the contextualization of the female in the male organ allows the kabbalists to envision the penis as the locus of the union of both genders. To cite one of many relevant examples from zoharic literature, "'Blessings light upon the head of the righteous' (Prov. 10:6). The head of the righteous is the holy corona."[110] The feminine aspect is localized as part of the phallus, the head that is disclosed in the ritual of circumcision. The act of uncovering the corona is mystically transformed into an occasion for the revelation of the divine diadem; indeed, circumcision is understood in kabbalistic literature as a rite of symbolic androgynization[111] as a result of which the feminine attribute of God appears through the semiological opening that is inscribed upon the penis. This point is underscored in an anonymous thirteenth-century kabbalistic text, where it is noted that the rite of circumcision "alludes to the perfect unity, and the matter of the androgyne (*du-parṣufim*) is explained in it; examine and discover with respect to the exposure of the corona."[112]

The symbolic correlation of the corona of the penis and the feminine *Shekhinah* is facilitated by the philological coincidence that the word *'aṭarah*, "crown," is the technical name of that part of the male anatomy as well as one of the designations of the *Shekhinah*.[113] Insofar as the male organ is the ontic source of both male and female, the religious significance of circumcision lies in the

[108] *Sefer ha-Bahir*, § 61.

[109] See Laqueur, *Making Sex*.

[110] *Zohar* 1:162a.

[111] See Eliade, *The Two and the One*, pp. 111–114.

[112] MS Paris–BN 843, fol. 39b. Cf. Moses de León, *Sheqel ha-Qodesh*, p. 67; idem, *Sefer ha-Mishkal*, p. 133; idem, *Book of the Pomegranate*, pp. 227–229 (Hebrew section); Gikatilla, *Sha'are 'Orah*, 1:114; Isaac of Acre, *Me'irat 'Einayim*, p. 44.

[113] See, e.g., *Zohar* 1:29b, 74a, 162a; 2:22a, 58a, 100b. For other references to this motif, see Wolfson, "Circumcision, Vision of God, and Textual Interpretation," p. 205 n. 53, to which many more sources could be added. An important parallel is found in the protokabbalistic material in the German Pietistic literature that suggests links to much older sources. See references in chapter 5, nn. 322, 326. In my view, in the Pietistic sources, and in the older texts they utilized, the crown assumes a phallic signification, especially evident in the image of the extension of the crown in its ascent to sit upon the head of the glorious king. The feminine imagery is applied to the manifest image of the divine that corresponds to the corona of the penis. Paradoxically, the female potency is symbolized by the most concrete of male images. The corona of the penis underscores the androgynous nature of the *membrum virile*, a potent element in Jewish esotericism. See my study "The Image of Jacob," especially the revised English version.

fact that by means of this ritual the androgynous unity of God is established. The point is affirmed as well in the following remark by Isaac of Acre: "[The word] *qeshet* (bow) [refers to] *ʿAṭarah* according to the form, for if you contemplate the arc of the penis (*qeshet ha-gid*) you will see the form of the letter *waw,* and the corona is in the form of a *yod.* Thus she is composed from the All (*kelulah min ha-kol*) and everything is one."[114] Just as the *yod* is part of the *waw,* so too the *Shekhinah,* the corona of the penis, is part of *Yesod,* the arc of the male organ. Within the symbolic representation of theosophic kabbalah the feminine is located in the male's reproductive organ. The point is epitomized in the following statement: "The sword is the Foundation, and this is the saying of the rabbis, may their memory be for a blessing,[115] 'the fiery ever-turning sword' (Gen. 3:24), sometimes female and sometimes male."[116] The fiery sword placed at the east of Eden symbolizes the attribute of God that corresponds to the phallus, the Foundation, which comprises both male and female.

The notion of an androgynous phallus has important ramifications for understanding the phenomenological structure of the mystical vision in the kabbalistic sources. In light of the gender metamorphosis suggested above, the object of visualization, the *Shekhinah,* is identified as the corona of the penis. Seeing God amounts to seeing that aspect of the phallus that reveals what is veiled. The dialectic is poignantly captured by Moses de León: "This is called a secret since its matter is hidden, the concealed secret of the Creator, and understand. In its secret is the moon that stands and is hidden. . . . Thus, it is called a concealed secret and it is hidden with her, and in its secret she stands and is swept away. Indeed, the secret of this matter is so that it will bind within itself the secret of the crown (*ʿaṭeret*)."[117] The essential concealedness of the divine phallus is connected especially to the corona that extends and is revealed. But the corona corresponds to the feminine potency, the *Shekhinah,* that is together

[114] *Me'irat ʿEinayim,* p. 2.

[115] *Bereshit Rabbah* 21:9, p. 203.

[116] MS Paris–BN 680, fol. 164b. This passage appears in the concluding section of a commentary on the account of creation in the book of Genesis, attributed to the Catalonian kabbalist Joseph bar Samuel. This commentary is printed in Jacob ben Sheshet, *Sefer Meshiv Devarim Nekhoḥim,* pp. 193–196 (see p. 11 n. 3, where the Paris manuscript is mentioned) and in Isaac of Acre, *Me'irat ʿEinayim,* pp. 16–17. The passage I have translated, however, is not found in either of these versions.

[117] *Book of the Pomegranate,* pp. 227–228 (Hebrew section). Cf. the words of Moses of Burgos in his commentary on the forty-two-letter name of God, MS Oxford-Bodleian 1565, fol. 102a, quoted in Scholem, "Traditions of R. Jacob and R. Isaac ha-Kohen," p. 288: "In the section 'Consecrate to Me every first-born' (Exod. 13:2), which is written in the phylacteries, sublime mysteries are alluded to in the mind of the kabbalists; they instruct about the foundation of the grade that is the opening of the portal and entrance to the comprehension of the supernal mysteries, for the section 'Consecrate to Me every first-born' is contained (*kelulah*) in the Foundation (*yesod*) that is called All (*kol*). R. Jacob, my teacher, may his memory be for blessing, explained that the words *qaddesh li* ('consecrate to Me') have the same numerical value as the word *middat* (the word *middah,* 'attribute,' in a construct state) [i.e., both expressions equal 444] to illustrate that the very holy attribute (*middah ha-qedoshah*) is the one that is speaking and she too is called All (*kol*) for she is contained in the attribute of the Foundation (*kelulah be-middat ha-yesod*)."

with the male, *Yesod*. That the former is contextualized as part of the male organ summons us to the realization that the feminine is fully integrated as an aspect of the masculine. In the final analysis, the union of male and female so central to kabbalistic theosophy and theurgy—in fact, the cornerstone of its engendering myth and praxis—is in fact a reconstitution of the male androgyne.[118] Hence, the image of the crowning of the kabbalists should be considered a process of feminization, but the latter needs to be understood in light of the specific gender assumptions of the socio-cultural context that informed the mentality of medieval kabbalists. When so understood it is obvious that the feminization implies that the kabbalists are crowned in the light of the corona of the penis; in a fundamental sense, therefore, they are ontically identified with that aspect of the divine anthropos.

The conception of the crown as the locus of visualization is found, for example, in a tradition of Isaac the Blind reported by Jacob ben Sheshet:

> [The word] strength alludes to the Oral Torah, which is her strength and her crown. Permission has not been granted to write [the Oral Torah], and there is an illusion to this in the verse "all the glory of the king's daughter is inward" (Ps. 45:14). That is, she is hidden and concealed from the eye. It has already been said that it is forbidden to look at the rainbow, for it is "the appearance of the image of the glory of the Lord" (Ezek. 1:28), and this is the place of the diadem (*maqom ha-ṣiṣ*). Thus I received in the name of the pious one, R. Isaac, the son of the great R. Abraham [ben David], blessed be his memory.[119]

From one perspective the Presence, symbolized as the crown or the Oral Torah, must be concealed from human vision. This is the meaning of the verse from Psalm 45 concerning the inwardness of the glory of the princess as well as the rabbinic dictum that one should not gaze at the rainbow. However, from an-

[118] See Wolfson, "Woman—The Feminine as Other."

[119] *Sefer ha-'Emunah we-ha-Biṭṭaḥon* 16, ed. Chavel, p. 401. On the correlation of the diadem (*ṣiṣ*) and the faculty of vision (*haṣaṣah* or *histakkelut*), see MS Oxford-Bodleian 1945, fol. 57b; *Zohar* 2:217b, 218b; *Zohar Ḥadash* 67d. On the association of the traditional fringe garment (*ṣiṣit*), the priestly diadem (*ṣiṣ*), and visionary experience (*histakkelut*), see *Zohar* 3:174b–175a (*Piqqudin*). According to that passage the *ṣiṣ* corresponds to the masculine supernal world, i.e., *Binah*, and the *ṣiṣit* to the feminine lower world, i.e., *Malkhut*. Just as the former is an object of visual contemplation, so, too, the latter. Moreover, the gazing upon the *ṣiṣit*, following the explicit injunction of Num. 15:39, is to lead one to remember the *ṣiṣ*. We see once again the ontically subservient status accorded the feminine. The positive valorization of the fringe garment consists in the fact that it leads one to the priestly diadem, i.e., that the feminine is a means to attain the masculine. The theurgical goal of vision, therefore, is to contain the female in the male, to raise the *ṣiṣit* to the level of *ṣiṣ*. These three motifs are connected in the *sod ha-ṣiṣit*, the secret of the ritual of the fringe garment, included in Jacob ha-Kohen, *Sefer ha-'Orah*, MS Milan-Ambrosiana 62, fol. 96b: "Another reason: know that the matter of *ṣiṣit* is from the term 'gazing' (*habaṭah*), as it says, 'peering (*meṣiṣ*) through the lattice' (Cant. 2:9). The 613 commandments are dependent upon the matter of the fringe garment, and regarding he who looks upon that fringe garment it is as if he contemplated all the 613 commandments. . . . This commandment is a substitute for the crown (*keter*) that is the garment (*malbush*) of all the *sefirot*." Whatever the precise meaning of the last passage, it is likely that the association of the crown and the fringe garment is based on the wordplay of *ṣiṣit* and *ṣiṣ*, attested in the zoharic text as well.

other perspective it is precisely this attribute of God, the diadem (*ṣiṣ*), that is the locus of vision (*haṣaṣah*) for the contemplative mystic. The paradoxical nature of the diadem as that which is revealed and concealed in the visionary encounter is also underscored in the following comment: "The rainbow (*qeshet*) is the place of the diadem (*ṣiṣ*), that is, *ʿAṭarah* [the Presence] that corresponds to the diadem. I have seen regarding this [an explanation of the verse] 'the bow appears in the cloud' (Gen. 9:14), that is, the cloud of glory wherein there is the glory. That cloud and the glory are as though [they were] one thing."[120] The masculine glory (*kavod*) is enveloped by the feminine cloud (*ʿanan*), and the latter allows the former to be seen. This is the mystical secret of the verse "the bow appears in the cloud"—the masculine potency is seen from within the feminine.

One of the common motifs reinterpreted by thirteenth-century kabbalists in this mystical vein is the eschatological teaching of Rav (B. Berakhot 17a) to the effect that in the world-to-come the righteous sit with their diadems on their heads and derive pleasure from the splendor of the Presence. In the relevant kabbalistic literature this is associated with another eschatological teaching attributed to R. Eleazar in the name of R. Ḥanina (interpreting Isa. 28:5) that in the future God will become a diadem for the head of each and every righteous person (B. Megillah 15b). Commenting on these talmudic statements, Ezra of Gerona wrote, "You must know that the matter of the diadem is a symbol for the soul that enters and cleaves and is crowned by the resplendent light."[121] The eschatological crown thus functions as a symbol for the union of the soul and the divine Presence, for the former is encompassed by the light of the latter, which is also symbolized as the diadem (*ʿAṭarah*).[122] Ṭodros Abulafia commented on the same talmudic passages along similar lines: "The diadem is a world unto itself, and the Holy One, blessed be He, places a crown of kingship on the head of every righteous person, for 'the lifebreath returns to God who

[120] MS Paris–BN 680, fol. 141a.

[121] *Liqqute Shikheḥah u-Fe'ah*, 3b; Azriel of Gerona, *Perush ha-'Aggadot*, p. 12.

[122] Cf. Naḥmanides' commentary to Exod. 16:6 (ed. Chavel, 1:365): "Those of the world-to-come are sustained by virtue of their deriving pleasure from the splendor of the Presence, by cleaving to it through the diadem on their heads, and the Diadem is the attribute called in this way, as it says, 'the Lord of Hosts shall become a crown of beauty' (Isa. 28:5), and concerning her it says, '[And gaze upon King Solomon] wearing the crown that his mother gave him' (Cant. 3:11)." Cf. *Me'irat ʿEinayim*, p. 8. On cleaving to the Presence in Naḥmanides, see Wolfson, "By Way of Truth," p. 152 n. 141; to the sources mentioned there, one might add Naḥmanides' statement in *Kitve Ramban* 1:192. On the association of the letter *yod*, the eschatological crown, and the corona of the penis, consider Jacob ha-Kohen, *Perush ha-'Otiyyot*, p. 215: "Moreover, the form of the letter *nun* comes to teach us that he who subdues and weakens the power of the *membrum virile* so that he does not defile himself in impurity and adultery, and he subdues and weakens the evil inclination like the *nun* that is bent, the Holy One, blessed be He, binds His name to the crown that is on his head in the world-to-come, and this letter is the *yod*. Therefore, you should imagine the form of the letter *yod* in the head of the *nun* like a crown to indicate that he who separates himself from adultery the Holy One, blessed be He, crowns him with the letter of His holy name. . . . Know that the Holy One, blessed be He, metes out to man measure for measure, for the letter *yod* is inscribed and sealed through the covenant of circumcision."

bestowed it' (Eccles. 12:7), and the soul of the righteous person is crowned and adorned by the splendor of the Presence and they derive pleasure from her; therefore, one does not have a need for eating or drinking, for this is actual eating."[123] The eschatological vision is characterized as a state of being crowned by the Presence, also referred to as eating, which is obviously to be understood as a symbol for integrative union, an approach we have seen as well in Ezra of Gerona. What is even more significant is that the theosophic kabbalists applied this eschatological image to the mystical state of union attainable by select individuals in this world. Thus, for example, in an anonymous kabbalistic commentary on the rabbinic legend of the four sages who entered Pardes, the fate of Ben Azzai, who "looked and died," is described in the following terms:

> He gazed at the radiance of the Presence, like a person who looks with his weak eyes at the full light of the sun and his eyes are weakened, and sometimes he becomes blinded because of the strength of the light that overcomes him. Thus it happened to Ben Azzai: the light that he gazed upon overwhelmed him from his great desire to cleave to it and to derive pleasure from it without interruption, and after he cleaved to it he did not want to separate from that sweet radiance, and he remained immersed and hidden within it. His soul was crowned and adorned from that radiance and splendor to which no creature can cleave and afterwards live, as it says, "for no man shall see Me and live" (Exod. 33:20). But Ben Azzai only gazed at it with a slight vision, and his soul departed and remained hidden in the place of its cleaving, which is a most precious light. The death was the death of the pious whose souls are separated from all the affairs of the lowly world and whose souls cleave to the ways of the supernal world.[124]

In this characterization the rabbinic sage Ben Azzai represents a typology of mystical experience. Reflecting on this text, Idel noted that contained here is an image of integration or immersion in the divine light that follows a state of

[123] *'Oṣar ha-Kavod,* 6b. Similar mystical interpretations of the eschatological crown of the righteous are found in the writings of Moses de León. As representative examples, see *Shushan 'Edut,* pp. 343–344; *Sheqel ha-Qodesh,* pp. 97–98. In both sources de León identifies the eschatological crown with the *Shekhinah,* but in the latter source he more openly characterizes this crown as the corona of the penis. Accordingly, the eschatological image of the righteous sitting with their crowns on their heads signifies the ontic restoration of the feminine to the masculine, the reconstitution of the male androgyne. Precisely this image was utilized by subsequent kabbalists, including Isaac Luria and his disciples, to depict the ontic status of the feminine in the messianic era. On eating as a metaphor for sexual union, especially when it is applied to the righteous, see Moses de León, *Sod 'Eser Sefirot Belimah,* p. 381: "The matter is the secret of the ninth [emanation], which is the Righteous who constantly eats (*ṣaddiq ha-'okhel tamid*), and his eating is to satisfy his soul." Cf. *Zohar Ḥadash* 48d, where the midrashic notion of the righteous gazing on the radiance of the Presence being an "actual eating" is applied to angels, who are said to eat and drink from the light of the Presence. On the use of the crown as a symbol for communion with the Presence in an eschatological setting, see also *Zohar Ḥadash,* 26a (MhN); the commentary of Isaac ibn Sahula on Canticles, ed. Green, p. 444; Joseph of Hamadan, *Sefer Ṭa'amey ha-Mizwoth,* ed. Meier, p. 60.

[124] MS Vatican 283, fol. 71b.

devequt, the cleaving of the human soul to its divine origin. The image of being crowned or adorned by the divine radiance presupposes the entry of the soul of the mystic into the divine light. This entry signifies a type of apotheosis or transformation of the mystic visionary, but not total fusion or union.[125] Indeed, the images of crowning or adornment denote a form of unitive experience, but one that is akin to sexual union wherein self and other are not totally merged or absorbed into one entity. The language of entry or being immersed does seem to suggest such a notion, which is enhanced further by the image of deriving pleasure from the radiance of the Presence. Indeed, one finds in the case of other kabbalists, such as in the Hebrew theosophic writings of Moses de León, that the state of *devequt,* or union between mystic and the feminine Presence, is depicted in terms of the metaphor of wearing a crown.

Previously, I emphasized the gender metamorphosis implied by the act of coronation: the mystic is identified with the feminine aspect of the divine and therefore becomes female in relation to the male God. It must be pointed out, however, that in some contexts the very same process is symbolically reversed, that is, the crowning represents the unification of the male mystic with the feminine Presence by virtue of the effulgence that encircles and envelops the head of the mystic. In such cases the crown symbolizes the corona of the penis that unites with the *Shekhinah*. Again the phallic connotation of the crown is evident, and it is precisely that aspect of God that is the locus of visionary experience. Thus, in one passage the zoharic authorship reflects on the verse "O maidens of Zion, go forth and gaze upon King Solomon wearing the crown that his mother gave him on his wedding day, on his day of bliss" (Cant. 3:11): "Whoever sees that diadem sees the beauty of the King to whom peace belongs."[126] The *Shekhinah,* symbolized as the diadem worn by King Solomon, is the visible aspect of the divine, but it is itself only part of the male organ, the corona of the penis. The beauty of the king is represented by the circumcised penis, which corresponds to that gradation of the divine also designated as peace (*shalom*), that is, *Yesod*. The image of the masculine king wearing the crown connotes perfect unity of male and female, which, as I noted above, involves a reconstitution of the male androgyne. That the visualization of the divine crown by the mystic also connotes a form of sexual union can be shown from other texts in the *Zohar,* sometimes linked exegetically to the same verse in Canticles, wherein the image of the crown or the process of crowning is used

[125] See Idel, "Universalization and Integration," p. 36.

[126] *Zohar* 2:100b. The connection of beauty and the divine phallus, or the attribute of *Yesod,* is underscored in *Zohar* 3:65–66a: "'From Zion, perfect in beauty, God appeared' (Ps. 50:2), that is, from Zion, the beauty of the world, Elohim appeared." To appreciate what is implied here one must bear in mind that Elohim corresponds to the *Shekhinah* and Zion to *Yesod*. The point of the zoharic text, therefore, is that the Presence is manifest from the divine phallus. It is likely that the word *mikhlal,* "perfect," is connected to *kelil,* "crown." If that assumption is correct, then the biblical expression "perfect in beauty" (*mikhlal yofi*) probably refers to the corona of the male organ. Cf. *Zohar* 1:186a; 3:118a.

to denote the union of the masculine and feminine aspects of the pleroma.[127] To cite one representative example:

> When the Matrona [*Shekhinah*] departs from the King [*Tif'eret*] and they are not found in union, the Supernal Mother [*Binah*] departs from the King and she does not feed him, for the King without a Matrona is not crowned in the crowns of the Mother. . . . When he is joined to the Matrona she crowns him in several crowns, in several splendors of the supernal and holy crowns, as it is written, "O maidens of Zion, go forth and gaze upon King Solomon [wearing the crown that his mother gave him on his wedding day]" (Cant. 3:11). When he unites with the Matrona, then the Supernal Mother crowns him, as is fitting.[128]

In another passage the image of the crown is deployed to depict concomitantly the union of male and female elements within the divine realm and the union of the mystic with the Presence:

> Come and see: It is written, "A river issues from Eden to water the garden" (Gen. 2:10). That river [*Binah*] overflows its sides when [*Ḥokhmah*] unites with it in perfect union. Then that Eden [*Ḥokhmah*] is in that path which is not known above or below, as it says, "No bird of prey knows the path" (Job 28:7). They are found in [a state of] harmony, for the one never separates from the other. Then the springs and streams come forth and crown the Holy Son [*Tif'eret*] with all these crowns; then it is written "wearing the crown that his mother gave him" (Cant. 3:11). At that moment the Son inherits the portion of his Father and Mother, and he delights in that pleasure and comfort. It has been taught: When the Supernal King is in [a state of] royal comfort[129] and he sits with his crowns, then it is written, "When the king was on his couch, my nard gave forth its fragrance" (Cant. 1:12), that is, *Yesod,* which emits blessings to unite the Holy King and the Matrona. Consequently, blessings are bestowed upon all the worlds and the upper and lower beings are blessed. Now the holy spark is crowned by the crowns of that gradation, and he and the comrades send up the praises from below to above, and she is crowned in those praises. Now blessings must be drawn out from above to below for all the comrades by means of that holy gradation.[130]

The author of this passage craftily weaves together the theosophic exposition and narrative discourse that provides the literary framework for that exposition. As a result of the kabbalistic interpretations of the relevant verses that unfold within the text, the master of the mystical fellowship, R. Simeon, desig-

[127] See *Zohar* 1:168b–169a; 2:57b–58a, 84a, 205b–206a, 277b; 3:5a, 96b, 148b (in that context the diadem is also identified, on the basis of Ps. 19:6, with the bridegroom's nuptial chamber), 263a. Cf. *Zohar* 2:22a, where the image of crowning is used to denote the overflow of blessings from *Binah* to *Malkhut,* the upper and lower feminine gradations.

[128] *Zohar* 3:77b; cf. 102b.

[129] Literally, "comforts of the kings" (*tafnuqe malkhin*). This idiom occurs several times in zoharic literature; see *Zohar* 1:216b; 2:2b. In the present context it obviously has sexual connotations.

[130] *Zohar* 3:61b–62a.

nated here "the holy spark,"[131] is crowned by the divine splendor—a process that parallels the description of the worlds being blessed by the overflow of the divine pleroma as a result of the union between the Holy One and the Presence through the agency of *Yesod,* the conduit that corresponds to the phallus. R. Simeon is the earthly counterpart of this particular gradation and thus is crowned by the splendor of the Presence.[132] The Presence, in turn, is crowned by the praises that R. Simeon and other members of the mystical fraternity send up by means of further homiletical and exegetical insights. A similar circle is discernible in the passage that describes the practice of the comrades studying Torah on the night of Pentecost, which, according to the rabbinic understanding, celebrates the Sinaitic theophany. The different aspects of Torah-study are compared to jewelry and ornaments[133] with which the kabbalists, "children of the palace of the bride," adorn the Presence who stands on their heads like a crown. On the next day, when they enter the nuptial chamber, the Holy One "blesses them and crowns them with the crown of the bride."[134] A second passage describing the same practice says that on the night of Pentecost "the Community of Israel [i.e., the Presence] crowns them, and she comes to unite with the King, and the two of them crown the heads of those who are worthy."[135]

The state of wearing a crown thus symbolizes the union that allows for the study of Torah, which, in turn, results in adorning the bride with jewels and preparing her for union with the groom. Indeed, being crowned signifies a state of visionary communion with the Presence that is a prerequisite for the disclosure of mystical secrets. Thus, R. Simeon reportedly said to his comrades during the "Small Assembly" (*Idra Zuṭa,* the last gathering of the mystical fellowship wherein the master revealed his final teachings, culminating with his ecstatic death), "Now I want to reveal words before the Holy One, blessed be He, for you are all crowned upon your heads."[136] Only the mystics who participated in the esoteric fraternity merited unification with the Presence, symbolized by the image of wearing the crown. "All the hosts of heaven opened up at that time: 'Praiseworthy are you, righteous ones, those who preserve the Torah, those who are engaged in [the study of] Torah, for the joy of your Master is among you, and the crown of your Master is crowned upon you."[137] The point is also underscored in the following passage: "It is written, 'A capable wife is a crown for her husband' (Prov. 12:4):[138] it is the secret of faith for a person to

[131] See Liebes, *Sections of the Zohar Lexicon,* pp. 139–140.

[132] Cf. *Zohar* 3:145a (*Idra Rabba*) where R. Simeon is described as the Sabbath day—i.e., the seventh of the six days, which corresponds to *Yesod*—who is crowned and more holy than the other days, i.e., the other comrades in the fraternity. The phallic role of R. Simeon in zoharic literature has been studied in great detail by Liebes, "Messiah."

[133] Cf. *Midrash Tanḥuma,* Ki-Tissa, 18.

[134] *Zohar* 1:8a.

[135] *Zohar* 3:98a.

[136] *Zohar* 3:291b.

[137] *Zohar* 2:211a.

[138] The zoharic reading of this verse represents a theosophic recasting of the midrashic interpretation, which notes that a man is crowned by his wife. Cf. *Bereshit Rabbah* 47:1, p. 470.

cleave to his Master and to fear Him constantly, not to deviate to the right or left; thus it has been established that a person should not go after idolatry, which is called a 'wife of whoredom' (Hosea 1:2)."[139] From this context, then, it is obvious that cleaving to the divine is facilitated by means of union with the feminine Presence, which, in this passage, is described as wearing a crown on one's head. To turn from this secret of faith is to exchange the "capable wife"—that is, the feminine Presence[140]—for the "wife of whoredom," the demonic feminine aspect, or Lilith. It is the particular distinction of the kabbalists that they are crowned by the splendor of the light of the Presence. A clear indication that the motif of coronation in these passages (and in many others that could have been cited) refers to the ecstatic experience of an actual group of mystics is found in the zoharic interpretation of Jacob's reply to Esau, "The children with whom God has favored your servant" (Gen. 33:5). After a detailed discussion wherein these children are understood midrashically as the Jewish children who died an innocent death, the zoharic authorship casually remarks: "Now the children are the sages, for the Holy One, blessed be He, grants them secrets of Torah, to be crowned in them and to be perfected by them."[141] One learns further that the evil eye has no control over these sages, for the good eye of the Holy Spirit dwells upon them. It is obvious that this comment is a historical aside that casts light on the hermeneutical enterprise of the zoharic authorship. The kabbalists of the zoharic circle, referred to by the generic term "sages," experience what is attributed to R. Simeon and his colleagues.

It is through the mechanism of the circumcised phallus that Jewish males cleave to the feminine Presence[142] so that there will be unity above, between the masculine and feminine aspects of the Godhead.[143] The same structural dy-

[139] *Zohar* 1:38b.

[140] Cf. *Zohar* 2:83b; 3:42b, 96b, 178b (*Piqqudin*).

[141] *Zohar* 3:203a.

[142] See *Zohar* 1:93a; 3:166a. It should be noted that in some passages it is emphasized that as a result of circumcision the Jewish males are mystically bound to the *sefirah* of *Yesod,* which corresponds to the phallus in the divine anthropos. Cf. *Zohar* 1:216a; 2:61b; Matt, *Zohar,* p. 246. It is evident, however, from these passages that the cleaving of the male Jew to *Yesod* is to facilitate the union of that attribute with the feminine Presence. This dynamic is linked exegetically by the *Zohar* to the verse "And your people, all of them righteous, shall possess the land for all time" (Isa. 60:21). Cf. *Zohar* 1:59b, 216a, and elsewhere. This dynamic also underlies the ontic difference between Muslims and Jews, for the latter alone can be bound to the masculine potency, whereas the former achieve a partial communion with the feminine potency. Cf. *Zohar* 2:32a, 86a; Isaac of Acre, *Me'irat 'Einayim,* p. 113; Joseph Angeleṭ, *Livnat ha-Sappir,* MS British Museum 27,000, fol. 338a; Wolfson, "Circumcision and the Divine Name," pp. 98–99; Kiener, "The Image of Islam in the Zohar," pp. 58–59.

[143] Conversely, the one who is not careful with respect to the phallus, especially one who commits onanism, is prevented from seeing the Presence upon the death of the body. Cf. *Zohar* 1:57a, 69a, 219b; 2:103a, 214b, 263b; 3:90a; Moses de León, *Shushan 'Edut,* p. 353; idem, *Book of the Pomegranate,* p. 230 (Hebrew section); idem, *Sefer ha-Mishkal,* p. 75; Tishby, *Wisdom of the Zohar,* p. 1366. Underlying this idea is the further correlation of the phallus and the eye; hence, in sixteenth-century sources it is emphasized that the rectification for the sin of spilling semen in vain is the shedding of tears. I have discussed some of the relevant sources in my study "Weeping, Death, and Spiritual Ascent" (see chapter 3, n. 85). Cf. *Zohar* 2:60b, where seeing the face of the *Shekhinah* is linked to the sexual purity connected with laws of menstruation.

namic underlies various passages in the *Zohar* that address the relationship of the kabbalist to the text of Scripture, sometimes also depicted in feminine imagery, following earlier aggadic usage. That is, by studying Torah the mystic not only crowns God[144] but is himself crowned by the divine splendor, a technical term that is associated in the *Zohar* with mystical comprehension.[145] The enlightened kabbalists (*maskilim*) who are worthy of contemplating the divine secrets are said to be illuminated "with the crown of splendor that is supernal to all."[146] There is a fundamental convergence here of the ontological and phenomenological poles, for what is conceived of metaphysically as the ultimate nature of being—light—coincides with that which is experienced in the mystical experience of illumination. Thus the word *zohar* is interpreted in a twofold manner: on the one hand, it symbolically refers to one of the divine gradations and, on the other, it characterizes the state of the *maskilim* when they contemplate the former. Conversely, the union of human and divine can be depicted in terms of the masculine deity being crowned by the words of exegesis uttered by the mystic. It follows, therefore, that the sexual imagery connected with the motif of coronation is quite fluid, for the mystic is depicted as male when he is crowned with the splendor of the divine Presence, but he may also be portrayed as female when the male aspect of the Godhead is crowned by the mystic. Especially noteworthy in this regard is this zoharic passage:

> It has been taught: The images of all those who are occupied with [the study of Torah] during the night are engraved above before the Holy One, blessed be He, and the Holy One, blessed be He, takes delight in them all day and looks at them. That voice [of one engaged in Torah-study] rises and breaks through all the firmaments until it ascends before the Holy One, blessed be He. . . . Now the Holy One, blessed be He, engraves the image of R. Simeon above, and his voice ascends and is crowned by the holy crown until the Holy One, blessed be He, is crowned by it in all the worlds and is glorified by it.[147]

According to this text, God derives pleasure all day long from the iconic representations of the righteous who study Torah during the night, namely, the fraternity of kabbalists responsible for the composition of the *Zohar*. Interestingly enough, the delight that God derives from these images is associated particularly with his looking at them, another indication that the scopic gaze has phallic connotations. Moreover, the voice of R. Simeon is singled out as the one that presently ascends and becomes a crown upon God's head. Hence the masculine and feminine roles are inverted: the masculine element of God is

[144] In numerous contexts the zoharic authorship describes the activity of crowning God by the words of Torah studied in the mystical fellowship; see *Zohar* 2:128a, 129a, 143a, 201b, 214a, 217a; 3:61a (quoted below), 174a. To be sure, this motif is a variation of the older esoteric idea of God being crowned by the words of prayer of Israel, an idea that appears frequently in the *Zohar* as well; see 1:132a, 167b, 2:213b, 218a; 3:260b.

[145] See Gottlieb, *Studies in the Kabbala Literature,* pp. 210–211. See also the text of Meir ibn Gabbai cited and discussed by Ginsburg in *Sabbath in the Classical Kabbalah,* pp. 294–295.

[146] *Zohar Ḥadash* 105a.

[147] *Zohar* 3:61a.

crowned by the mystic. This motif complements the other, which is predicated on the mystic being crowned by the feminine aspect of God.

Mystical Fellowship as Constitution of the Divine Face

The close connection between those engaged in mystical hermeneutics and the *Shekhinah* is emphasized in any number of passages in the *Zohar*. For example, in one place we read that the righteous (the mystical fellowship of R. Simeon) are called the "face of the Presence" (*'anppe shekhinta'*) because the "Presence is hidden within them. She is concealed and they are revealed. Those who are close to the Presence are called her face. And who are they? Those whom she adorns together with her to be seen before the supernal King."[148] The hierarchical relationship imposes a reversal in the gender valence: the Presence, who is feminine vis-à-vis the supernal divine potency, is the revealed aspect of the concealed phallus. In relation to the Presence, however, the mystical righteous, who also stand in the position of the phallus, are revealed and she is hidden. The mystics, therefore, are accorded the role and status of the corona, the protruding and revealed element of the phallus. In that sense they are the "face" of the Presence.[149] In another place we read that R. Simeon specifically

[148] *Zohar* 2:163b; cf. Matt, *Zohar,* p. 250. In the continuation of this text mention is made of the principle that a person's face reflects the spiritual level to which he or she is attached. The latter idea is, no doubt, based on earlier physiognomic traditions that have found their way into this medieval text; see esp. *Zohar* 2:73a. Hence, the face of the righteous one is like the face of the Presence. Cf. Azikri, *Milei di-Shemaya,* ed. Pachter, p. 122. On the history of physiognomic texts in Jewish mysticism and their influence on the *Zohar,* see Scholem, "Cheiromancy in the Zohar"; idem, "Ein Fragment zur Physiognomik und Chiromantik aus der Tradition der spätantiken jüdischen Esoterik"; Gruenwald, "Further Jewish Physiognomic and Chiromantic Fragments"; idem, *Apocalyptic,* pp. 218–224. For a later kabbalistic development of this motif, see Fine, "The Art of Metoposcopy," pp. 85–86. Other tales that disseminated from sixteenth-century Safed describe individuals afraid to look at Luria or Vital for fear of gazing at the face of the Presence; see *Toledot ha-Ari,* pp. 174, 192; *Sefer ha-Ḥezyonot,* p. 36.

[149] See *Zohar* 3:6b, 25b, 148a, 265b. The zoharic view is well reflected in a text of Moses of Burgos (who may have served as a literary or oral source for ideas expressed in the zoharic literature), from his commentary on Zechariah's vision of the menorah, MS Mussayef 92, fol. 2b, quoted by Scholem in "Traditions of R. Jacob and R. Isaac," p. 288: "Setariron is the archon of the Foundation of the world (*sar yesod ʿolam*), and he is Sandalphon, and in him is the secret of the Foundation of the crown (*sod yesod ʿaṭeret*), and the Foundation is the face of the crown (*pene ha-ʿaṭarah*). . . . The Foundation is the face of the crown, that is, the light of her face." On the angel Setariron and his connection to the divine phallus, *Yesod,* see another fragment from the same text published by G. Scholem in "R. Moses of Burgos, the Disciple of R. Isaac," *Tarbiz* 5 (1934): 181 (in Hebrew): "The fourth [angel] is called Setariron and he is the archon of the Righteous, Foundation of the world (*ṣaddiq yesod ʿolam*), and he is called this on account of the foundation (*yesod*) that is hidden in the median line, and he is the covenant of peace and the supernal mystery (*seter ʿelyon*), and this is the secret of 'O you who dwell in the shelter of the Most High' (Ps. 91:1)." Implicit here is the identification of this divine gradation, *Yesod,* as the locus of esotericism, *sod.* See also the text of Moses of Burgos published by Scholem in "R. Moses of Burgos, the Disciple of R. Isaac," *Tarbiz* 4 (1933): 217 (in Hebrew): "It is known to the enlightened kabbalists (*maskilim ha-mequbbalim*) that the emanation (*sefirah*) that has been mentioned is set in the position of the concealed foundation (*ha-yesod ha-neʿelam*) that is the foundation of the world . . . and the bow

gave the name "Peniel" to two of his comrades, R. Eleazar and R. Abba, for "they saw the face of the *Shekhinah*."[150]

In light of the fact that in the *Zohar* the vision of the face of the *Shekhinah* is connected to seeing the unveiled phallus, it is possible that underlying the visionary experience is a latent homoeroticism, in terms of the relationship of the mystics to both God and one another. Support for my contention may be gathered from the following zoharic interpretation of the verse "Three times a year all your males shall appear before the Sovereign, the Lord" (Exod. 23:17):

> What is [the meaning of] "your males?" All those who guard the holy covenant [i.e., the phallus] and do not sin by means of it, these are the sons of the King, and every day He is glorified through them and He remembers them. Thus it is said "your males," the ones who possess a holy covenant, for the King remembers them every day. There is no glory before the supernal King as the one who guards the covenant. Therefore they must appear three times a year before Him.[151]

Following in the footsteps of other kabbalists, the author of this passage exploits the presumed philological connection of *zakhar* (masculine) and *zakhor*

(*qeshet*) that is compared (*muqash*) to the glory, the appearance of the glory of the Lord [cf. Ezek. 1:28], is alluded to in the final letters [of the expression] *berakhot le-ro'sh ṣaddiq*, 'blessings light upon the head of the righteous' (Prov. 10:6) [i.e., the last letters of these three words are *taw, shin,* and *qof,* which spell *qeshet*], which alludes to a hidden secret (*sod nistar*)." The discussion on the procreative quality of this gradation ends with the following code of esotericism: "This is a great secret about which no enlightened one is permitted to speak." On *Yesod* as the locus for the study of the secrets of Torah, see p. 225 of the same work. This correlation also underlies Moses' insistence, in his kabbalistic reworking of a commentary on the forty-two-letter name of God, that the name should not be transmitted to someone whose sexual desire has not abated. See G. Scholem, "R. Moses of Burgos, the Disciple of R. Isaac," *Tarbiz* 5 (1934): 54–55 (in Hebrew).

150 *Zohar* 1:9a. These three figures in the *Zohar,* R. Simeon, R. Eleazar, and R. Abba, represent the three pillars that sustain the mystical fellowship whose total number is ten. These ten symbolically correspond to the ten divine emanations, and the three rabbis correspond to the three central emanations, Lovingkindness (*Ḥesed*) on the right, Strength (*Gevurah*) or Judgment (*Din*) on the left, and Mercy (*Raḥamim*) or Beauty (*Tif'eret*) in the center. See Liebes, "Messiah," pp. 98–99, 130–132 (English trans., pp. 9–10, 20–21). Cf. *Zohar* 2:209a, where three of the colleagues are identified as lights that come from the *Shekhinah*.

151 *Zohar* 3:165b. See also 2:124a, 183a; 3:168a; and compare the discussion of *Zohar* 2:38a below in n. 155. An extraordinarily bold and graphic affirmation of the phallomorphic and homoerotic elements of the visionary experience is found in Joseph of Hamdan; see ed. Meier, *Sefer Ṭa'amey ha-Miẓwoth,*" pp. 232–233: "On the three festivals one must make a pilgrimage [to the Jerusalem Temple] as it says, 'Three times a year all your males shall appear before the Sovereign Lord, the God of Israel' (Exod. 34:23). . . . The males see His face on the appointed times of the festivals, for the bridegroom comes to unite with the bride, which corresponds to the Community of Israel, and the holy and pure pipe, which is the secret of the covenant, is disclosed. Therefore it says, 'all the males shall see the face of the Sovereign Lord, the God of Israel.'" According to Joseph of Hamadan's reading, the verse describes the seeing of God, and thus he changes the passive "will be seen" to the active "shall see." Moreover, this vision is tied exclusively to the males because in the Temple the masculine and feminine aspects of the Godhead are joined and in the process of this union the male organ, symbolically described as the "holy and pure pipe," is revealed. Only the males, therefore, can behold God's face, which is another symbolic reference to the phallus, the "secret of the covenant."

(remember). God's memory is linked especially to the males who are sexually pure. There is no greater glory before God than the circumcised Jewish males who are innocent of sexual transgression. The mandate to appear before God in the Temple, which is prescribed three times a year by Scripture, is here understood exclusively in terms of the phallus. The focal point of the visual encounter is the male organ. Whereas other zoharic texts emphasize that the divine phallus is the object of the mystic's vision, this text emphasizes that the mystic's phallus is the object of God's vision. The phallocentric orientation of this passage borders on homoeroticism, inasmuch as the singular bond that connects the male deity and male worshiper is the penis.

The homoerotic implications of the constitutive seeing of the face of the *Shekhinah* is suggested by one passage in particular: "R. Ḥiyya and R. Jose met one night in the Tower of Tyre. They stayed there as guests and took joy in one another. R. Jose said: How glad I am that I saw the face of the *Shekhinah*."[152] On one level, it is evident that this text simply implies, in line with a rabbinic orientation, that conversing in words of Torah with a colleague is equivalent to seeing the face of the *Shekhinah*. Going beneath the surface, however, it is obvious that the vision is here connected to the joyous bonding of the two male mystics in the Tower of Tyre. The setting of this narrative drama in that location is not inconsequential; the obvious phallic connotation of the tower sheds light on the meaning of the text as a whole. The mutual discourse of R. Ḥiyya and R. Jose constitutes the unveiling of the hidden phallus that is expressed as a seeing of the face of the *Shekhinah*. The joy that the mystics take in one another is a form of homoerotic pairing.

In other places in the *Zohar* the homoerotic signification of the mystical fraternity is applied to the comrades at large. In several critical contexts this motif is linked exegetically to the verse "How good and how pleasant it is that brothers dwell together" (Ps. 133:1). Significantly, the continuation of the biblical text describes the overflowing of fine oil from the head to the beard of Aaron (ibid., 2), an image that is interpreted on numerous occasions in the *Zohar* in overt sexual terms.[153] The homoeroticism of the mystical fraternity is underscored especially in this zoharic passage:

> It has been taught: R. Jose said: One time the world needed rain. R. Yeisa, R. Ḥizqiyah, and the rest of the comrades went before R. Simeon. They found that he and his son, R. Eleazar, were going to see R. Pineḥas ben Yair. When [R. Simeon] saw them, he opened up and said, "A song of ascents. Of David. How good and how pleasant it is that brothers dwell together." What is the meaning of "that brothers dwell together?" And it is said [of the cherubim], "they shall face each other" (Exod. 25:20, 37:9). When they are gazing at each other face-to-face, it is written, "how good and how pleasant," but when the male turns his face from the female, woe to the world. . . . Another interpretation: "How good and how pleas-

[152] *Zohar* 2:94b.

[153] See *Zohar* 1:88a, 258b; 2:87b; 3:7b, 34a, 39a, 88b, 132b (*Idra Rabba*), 209a, 295b (*Idra Zuṭa*).

> ant, etc." These are the comrades at the time that they sit as one and are not separated from one another. At first they appear as warriors engaged in battle who want to kill one another. Afterwards they are transformed by the love of comradeship. What does the Holy One, blessed be He, say? "How good and how pleasant it is that brothers dwell together." [The word] *gam* [in the expression *gam yaḥad*, "together"] signifies the inclusion of the *Shekhinah* with them. Furthermore, the Holy One, blessed be He, listens to their words and it is pleasing to Him, for He takes joy in them.[154]

Ostensibly this entire passage is about the union of masculine and feminine, symbolized most perfectly in the face-to-face gaze of the cherubim. The juxtaposition of Ps. 133:1 and Exod. 25:20 (37:9) indicates that the assemblage of the mystical brotherhood is a form of union akin to the unification of the male and female cherubim. When the comrades confront one another in textual study, they are united in a face-to-face encounter, being transformed thereby from warriors into lovers.[155] Although the union is posed as heterosexual, in

[154] *Zohar* 3:59b. Concerning this passage and its relationship to the *Idra Rabba,* see Liebes, "Messiah," p. 163 n. 273 (English trans., p. 180 n. 128). The homoerotic quality of God's relationship to the righteous, who constitute the face of the *Shekhinah* or the corona of the phallus, is emphasized in any number of places in zoharic literature that describe God's taking delight with the righteous. See *Zohar* 1:72a, 82b, 136b, 178b, 245b, 255a; 2:173b, 217b; 3:193a; and elsewhere.

[155] In my opinion, the claim of R. Simeon at the beginning of the *Idra Rabba* that "we are dependent on love" (*Zohar* 3:128a) likewise involves a homoerotic connotation. More specifically, it is clear from the context that the assembly of the mystics represents the collective constitution of the divine phallus. The issue, however, is not the preparation of R. Simeon, the earthly counterpart to *Yesod,* for his union with the *Shekhinah* (as suggested by Liebes in "Messiah," pp. 157–165 [English trans., pp. 37–43]), but rather the reconstitution of the androgynous phallus by restoring the female aspect of the phallus (the corona, represented by the fraternity who are the face of the *Shekhinah*) to the male aspect of the phallus (R. Simeon, who is the position of *Yesod*). The homoerotic implications of R. Simeon's role as the phallic center of the mystical fraternity are suggested by the following passage in *Zohar* 2:38a: "It is written, 'All your males shall appear before the Sovereign Lord' (*yera'eh kol zekhurkha 'et pene ha-'adon*) (Exod. 34:23). Who is the *pene ha-'adon?* This is Rashbi. Those who are male from the [divine aspect of] masculinity come to appear before him." It is significant that the visual encounter between God and the male Israelites is here applied more specifically to R. Simeon and the male mystics. Cf. *Zohar* 2:190b, where the love of the mystical brotherhood is likewise emphasized and where it is stated that the lack of love creates a blemish in the Torah that is effectively a rupture of the union of male and female. Significantly, the union is also represented in that context by the figures of Abraham, Isaac, and Jacob, who loved and embraced one another. Again, one sees from this context that the homoerotic bonding of males can theosophically symbolize and actualize the union of male and female in the Godhead. In that context as well, the bonding of the mystical fellowship is depicted as a face-to-face visual encounter. Thus, R. Simeon says to his colleagues, "The word is a secret, but I will tell it to you, my beloved children, the beloved children of my soul. What shall I do? They said it to me in a whisper, but I will say it openly. When we see face-to-face, all faces will agree to this" (*Zohar* 2:190b–191a). For a different explanation of the idiom "face-to-face" in this context, see Matt, "New-Ancient Words," p. 189. The sense of textual combat in the *Zohar* is captured beautifully by Matt on pp. 193–194. Finally, it should be noted that the homoerotic overtones of the relationship between the mundane *ṣaddiq* and his divine counterpart can be heard even where heterosexual imagery is employed to describe the male's relationship to God. Consider, e.g., *Zohar* 1:66b: "Come and see: When there is a *ṣaddiq* in the world the *Shekhinah* is not removed from him and

fact the bonding involves only male figures. The concluding statement, that the *Shekhinah* is joined with the mystics, signifies that the male fraternity constitutes the *Shekhinah*. That is, the comrades are the face of the *Shekhinah* that is rendered visible through their exegetical activity and hermeneutical engagement with Scripture. The vision of the *Shekhinah* is dependent on the union of masculine and feminine,[156] but in zoharic symbolism the feminine is ontically part of the masculine. Accordingly, homoerotic relations can be depicted theosophically in heterosexual terms.

On other occasions it is the master himself, R. Simeon, who is singled out on account of his symbolic correspondence to *Yesod* and his mantic power to cause the *Shekhinah* to shine in the place wherein he engaged in textual interpretation: "R. Isaac said: One day I went with [R. Simeon] on the road and he opened his mouth in [explication of the] Torah. I saw a pillar of cloud fixed from above to below and one splendor shone within that pillar."[157] Drawing, moreover, on earlier rabbinic sources wherein a nexus is established between study of Torah and the dwelling of the Presence, the *Zohar* emphasizes time and again that through study one cleaves to, or is united with, the *Shekhinah*.[158] To cite three salient examples:

> "The wise shall obtain honor" (Prov. 3:35): Whoever is engaged in the [study of] Torah merits inheriting the supernal portion in the glory of the holy, supernal

---

her desire is for him. As a result of this the desire from above is directed toward her in love as the desire of a male for a female. . . . Thus [it is written,] 'But I will establish My covenant with you' (Gen. 6:18). I aroused my desire on account of you." The erotic relationship of the earthly *ṣaddiq* (i.e., the male kabbalist) and the *Shekhinah* arouses the desire of the divine *ṣaddiq* (i.e., *Yesod*) for the *Shekhinah*. Hence, the meaning of God's statement to Noah, "But I will establish My covenant with you," is that the erection of the divine phallus (= the establishing of the covenant) is achieved through the efforts of the earthly *ṣaddiq*. The implicit meaning of the zoharic text is made explicit by Moses de León in *Sod 'Eser Sefirot Belimah*, pp. 381–382: "It is said that every sage is jealous of another sage and every warrior is jealous of another warrior, but the Holy One, blessed be He, is not like this. He is called *ṣaddiq* and when there is a *ṣaddiq* on earth He loves him. . . . This is a hidden mystery: a husband always hates his wife when she loves someone other than him. But [in the case of] this [divine] *ṣaddiq*, the eternally living one (*ḥei ha-'olamim*), His woman constantly loves the earthly *ṣaddiq*. The eternally living one knows this and He arouses His love for the world even more and with greater affection. . . . This is the secret of 'But I will establish My covenant with you,' for there is no erecting of this covenant (*qimah li-verit zo*) except by another *ṣaddiq*. Understand this, for everything is correct to 'those who have attained knowledge' (Prov. 8:9)." The sexual arousal of the divine *ṣaddiq* by means of the earthly *ṣaddiq* may have a homoerotic aspect, even though it must be readily admitted that it is expressed within the framework of heterosexual images.

156 Cf. *Zohar* 3:59a.

157 *Zohar* 2:149a. See also 3:79b: "When R. Abba and the colleagues saw R. Simeon they would run after him and say, 'The Lord will roar like a lion, and they shall march behind Him' (Hosea 11:10)." Cf. *Zohar Ḥadash* 60a, where R. Simeon is described in eschatological terms as the "crown of the righteous who will sit in the Garden of Eden to receive the face of the *Shekhinah*, and they will see the Holy One, blessed be He, who takes delight with the righteous."

158 *Zohar* 1:135b, 164a, 245a; 2:94b, 134b (RM), 149a, 155b, 188b; 3:22a, 35a, 36a, 60b, 61a, 213a, 268a–b, 298a; *Zohar Ḥadash* 28b (MhN), 95a (MhN). For other references, see Tishby, *Wisdom of the Zohar*, p. 770 n. 43.

King. . . . And who is that? That which is called the glory of the Lord who does not ever depart from them.[159]

Whoever is engaged in Torah, it is as if he is engaged in the palace of the Holy One, blessed be He, for the supernal palace of the Holy One, blessed be He, is the Torah.[160]

Come and see: When a person draws close to the Torah, which is called good, as it is written, "the teaching of your mouth (*torat pikha*) is good to me" (Ps. 119:72), he draws close to the Holy One, blessed be He, who is called good, as it is written, "The Lord is good to all" (Ps. 145:9), and he then comes close to being righteous, as it says, "Happy is the just man, for he is good" (Isa. 3:9). When he is righteous the *Shekhinah* rests upon him and teaches him the highest secrets of Torah, for the *Shekhinah* is joined only to one who is good, for the Righteous [masculine *Ṣaddiq*] and Righteousness [feminine *Ṣeddeq*] go together as one.[161]

Elsewhere, those who rise at midnight to be engaged in the study of Torah are called "comrades of the Holy One, blessed be He, and the Community of Israel," that is, the masculine *Tif'eret* and the feminine *Shekhinah,* for when they utter words of interpretation they "cleave to the wings" of *Shekhinah* and their words are "brought forth and dwell in the bosom of the King."[162] The study of Torah, especially of esoteric matters, serves as a means to unite *Tif'eret* and *Shekhinah,* which are symbolically correlated with the Written Torah and the Oral Torah, and thus the hermeneut stands in the position of *Yesod,* the conduit that connects the two. This function is realized only by the kabbalist who is mystically united with the *Shekhinah* through study. Thus, according to the *Zohar,* the Talmudic dictum that Sabbath eve is the most appropriate time for the scholar's marital duty (B. Ketuvot 62b; Bava Qama 82a) must be explained in light of the fact that during the week the scholar, that is, the mystic exegete, is united with the *Shekhinah* and therefore must be separated from his earthly consort.[163] Whereas all other people are mandated to have sexual intercourse during the week after midnight, the mystics at that time rise to study Torah, for in that activity they are united with the feminine Presence; only on Friday nights do they have intercourse with their earthly wives so that they may symbolically represent the hierogamy above.

The reference to the fellows who rise at midnight to study is, no doubt, to the mystical fellowship of R. Simeon bar Yoḥai, which, as Liebes has argued, is not

159 *Zohar* 3:268b. Cf. 3:35a.

160 *Zohar* 2:200a.

161 *Zohar Ḥadash* 29a.

162 *Zohar* 3:22a.

163 See *Zohar* 1:50a; 2:63b, 89a; 3:49b, 78a, 81a, 143a (*Idra Rabba*). Cf. Ginsburg, *Sabbath in Classical Kabbalah,* pp. 114, 292–293; idem, *Sod ha-Shabbat,* pp. 34–36, and relevant notes, pp. 119–121. The model here again is the aggadic view of Moses, who separated permanently from his wife after receiving the Torah on Mount Sinai. See Liebes, "Messiah," p. 122 (English trans., p. 15).

simply the imaginative construction of one idiosyncratic individual (Moses de León), but in all probability reflects an actual historical group of kabbalists. Most significant is Liebes's claim that the composition of the *Zohar* in its multiple redactional layers grew out of the study meetings of such a group; hence, incorporated in the *Zohar* are the attempts of the various members of the circle to explain shared doctrines, themes, and motifs, each from his own exegetical standpoint.[164] By positing a theory of multiple authorship, one need not forfeit the thematic and literary integrity of the whole. On the contrary, the circle theory enables us to begin to see the complicated relations that pertain between different strata of the *Zohar* and we can appreciate the sense of fellowship that actually bound together the kabbalists in late-thirteenth-century Castile, who were indeed "reapers of the field," continuously seeking to clarify the complicated theosophic doctrines they both inherited and innovated. One must, therefore, acknowledge authorial complexity without ignoring coherency and specificity. Liebes has noted, moreover, that there is evidence in the *Zohar* and the Hebrew theosophic writings of Moses de León for kabbalistic rituals that were enacted by members of this group.[165]

On such ritual—indeed, perhaps the central one, which informed the entire mystical community—involved the midnight study of Scripture in light of the emerging theosophy. This was the stage for the narrative drama that unfolds in the pages of the *Zohar.* The mythology of the *Zohar* is anchored in a historical reality. The study group produced the anthology of texts called *Sefer ha-Zohar* on the basis of the claim that the ones who were in the group were ecstatically illuminated by the divine splendor in the moment of interpreting scriptural verses. The common bond of this mystical fraternity was the inspired exegesis of Scripture. Furthermore, the study meetings were endowed with theurgical significance, inasmuch as the masculine and feminine aspects of the Godhead were unified by means of kabbalistic discourse. It is necessary to reintegrate the theurgical and mystical elements of the religious experience of the kabbalist, for it makes no sense to speak of effecting the nature of God if one is not experiencing God in some immediate and direct sense. The theurgical significance of the composition of the *Zohar,* rooted in the mystical experience of visual communion with the divine, has been well understood by kabbalists themselves through the generations. To cite here two examples from seventeenth-century sources: Abraham Azulai wrote, "Know that the essence of the intention of R. Simeon bar Yoḥai, peace be upon him, in the composition of the *Zohar* . . . was to provide a support for her [the *Shekhinah*], to unite her with her husband . . .

[164] See Liebes, "How the Zohar Was Written," p. 7 (English trans., p. 89).

[165] Ibid., p. 5 n. 16 (English trans., p. 196 n. 19). See *Book of the Pomegranate,* p. 70 n. 6 (Hebrew section), where I raised the possibility that de León's reference to the "masters of the covenant of faith" (*ba'ale berit ha-'emunah*) denoted his own circle, which I further identified as the "circle of the Zohar." While other scholars, including Jellinek and Scholem, had already employed this terminology to refer to a literary group, I had in mind a community of mystics who were functioning as an actual social unit, i.e., performing specific actions and holding common beliefs. Liebes's study has considerably advanced the conversation in this direction.

for he and his comrades were occupied in the [study of] secrets of Torah, and this causes the unification of the Holy One, blessed be He, and his *Shekhinah* by means of the secret, for the secret (*sod*) is [also called] *raz* and this numerically equals *'or* (light)."[166] In a similar vein, Naftali Bachrach wrote, "R. Simeon bar Yoḥai was the righteous one, foundation of the world, and by means of his studying this [esoteric] wisdom with which he was occupied . . . he united [the masculine] *Ze'eir 'Anpin* with his female [counterpart, i.e., *Shekhinah*]. . . . This is the secret of all those who write mystical books: they repair the world of action by the secret writing of these esoteric truths. The esoteric truth unites *Ze'eir 'Anpin* with his female counterpart in the most inward way."[167] Both kabbalists acknowledge that the literary composition of the *Zohar* served the theurgical task of uniting the feminine and masculine aspects of the divine. Bachrach goes beyond Azulai and claims that the composition of all written kabbalistic texts serves this purpose. Reversing the traditional code of esotericism, which did not encourage the writing down of secrets, Bachrach sees the activity of writing as the most sacred of religious duties. The kabbalist can achieve the unification of male and female in the Godhead through the writing of mystical texts, for he, like Simeon bar Yoḥai, stands in the position of *Yesod,* the phallus that both marks the difference between male and female and acts as a copula connecting them. From the kabbalistic vantage point, writing of secrets is a decidedly phallic activity[168] that ensues from an ecstatic state wherein the mystic is united with the divine Presence.

Going beyond all previous midrashic or aggadic sources, the zoharic authorship posits that hermeneutical activity is not merely a divinely inspired state, but the very means to behold the divine.[169] That is, through the mystical study of Scripture the kabbalist can see the divine light hidden in the text, for the letters themselves are nothing but the configurations of that light.[170] "There is no word in the Torah that does not have several lights shining to every side. . . . The supernal Wisdom shines in it for the one who needs it."[171] The words of

[166] *Ḥesed le-'Avraham* 6a.

[167] *'Emeq ha-Melekh* 144c.

[168] On the phallic character of writing in medieval Christian culture, see Leupin, *Barbarolexis*. For a discussion of this issue in classical Greek texts, see DuBois, *Sowing the Body,* pp. 130–166. For further discussion of this motif in kabbalistic sources, see Wolfson, "Erasing the Erasure."

[169] See *Zohar* 1:72a, 92b, 115b; 2:200a; *Zohar Ḥadash* 28a.

[170] This is substantiated in parts of the *Zohar* by means of the numerical equivalence (found already in German Pietistic sources and the works of Abraham Abulafia based thereon) between *raz* "mystery," and *'or,* "light." Inasmuch as both words equal 207, it may be said that one who knows the mystery of the text can see the light hidden therein. Cf. *Zohar* 1:140a (MhN); 3:28b (RM); *Zohar Ḥadash* 8d (MhN), 94b, 104a (*Tiqqunim*); *Tiqqune Zohar* 19, 39b. On the kabbalistic notion of the letters as configurations of divine light, see Scholem, "The Name of God and the Linguistic Theory of the Kabbalah"; idem, *On the Kabbalah,* p. 63. In the final analysis, the kabbalistic notion that words of Scripture are the concretization of divine light represents a version of the Neoplatonic conception of God's accommodating self-revelation, i.e., the divine light is concealed in a variety of veils so that human beings can perceive it.

[171] *Zohar* 3:202a. In that context the different lights that shine in each word of Torah correspond to the various types of meaning, to wit, the literal or contextual, the homiletical, the allegori-

Torah are likened to garments[172] that cover this divine light, and only the mystic, who contemplates the esoteric sense hidden in the words of the text, can again apprehend this light. As de León succinctly expressed it in his *Mishkan ha-ʿEdut,*

> Our holy Torah is a perfect Torah, "all the glory of the royal princess is inward" (Ps. 45:14). But because of our great and evil sins today "her dress is embroidered with golden mountings" (ibid.). . . . Thus God, blessed be He, laid a "covering of dolphin skin over it" (Num. 4:6) with the visible things [of this world]. Who can see and contemplate the great and awesome light hidden in the Torah except for the supernal and holy ancient ones? They entered her sanctuary and the great light was revealed to them. . . . They removed the mask from her.[173]

Of the various levels of interpretation of the Torah,[174] the deepest or most profound is that which envisions the text as a *corpus symbolicum* of the divine world. Each word of Scripture is potentially a symbol of the divine life, and as such participates in this life. Kabbalistic exegesis, therefore, is a form of revelatory experience, for the study of Torah not only generates a visionary experience but itself constitutes such a vision. To appreciate fully this last claim one must bear in mind several of the standard principles accepted by kabbalists of the late thirteenth century. The Torah in its mystical essence is nothing other than the divine Name, the Tetragrammaton, which itself comprises the theosophic structure of the ten gradations.[175] Hence the Torah (mystically conceived) is identical with God. Although this tacit assumption is clearly the foundational principle that lies behind almost every word of the *Zohar,* it is stated quite explicitly in one place that "the Holy One, blessed be He, is called the Torah."[176] A bit further on in the same context, one reads that the "Torah is nothing but the Holy One, blessed be He."[177] It follows, inasmuch as the Torah is nothing other than the divine edifice, the study of the Torah itself necessarily entails some sort of visionary experience of God. The zoharic viewpoint is well captured in this statement of Joseph of Hamadan:

---

cal, the mystical, and the legalistic. See n. 174. Cf. the description of the radiance of the letters of the opened Torah scroll in *Zohar* 3:164b. For a later reverberation of the zoharic motif, see Vital, *Shaʿar ha-Kawwanot* 48c, where Luria is described as gazing on the letters of the Torah scroll in order to draw forth the great light.

[172] See *Zohar* 1:103b; 3:152a, 164b; *Zohar Ḥadash* 96c (*Tiqqunim*). On the theme of the garments of Torah, see Tishby, *Wisdom of the Zohar,* p. 1083; Cohen-Alloro, *The Secret of the Garment in the Zohar,* pp. 45–49.

[173] MS Berlin Or. Quat. 833, fol. 1b. See Cohen-Alloro, *Secret of the Garment,* p. 47.

[174] By the latter part of the thirteenth century, kabbalists generally distinguished between four levels of interpretation: the literal, homiletical, allegorical, and mystical. See Scholem, *On the Kabbalah,* pp. 53–61; Tishby, *Wisdom of the Zohar,* pp. 1085, 1091–1092; van der Heide, "Pardes." See also below, n. 226.

[175] See Scholem, *On the Kabbalah,* p. 39; Tishby, *Wisdom of the Zohar,* pp. 1079–1082; Idel, "Concept of Torah," pp. 49–58.

[176] *Zohar* 2:60a; cf. 3:265b.

[177] *Zohar* 2:60b.

> Therefore the Torah is called by this name, for it instructs [us] about the pattern of the Holy One, blessed be He . . . the Torah, as it were, is the shadow of the Holy One, blessed be He . . . and inasmuch as the Torah is the form of God He commanded us to study it so that we may know the pattern of the upper form. As some kabbalists[178] said concerning the verse "Cursed be he who does not raise up the words of this Torah" (Deut. 27:26), is there a Torah that falls? This is rather a warning to the cantor to show the writing of the Torah scroll to the community so that they will see the pattern of the upper form. How much more so [is it incumbent] to study the Torah so that one may see the supernal mysteries and see the actual glory of the Holy One, blessed be He. All the time that one studies the Torah one is actually sitting in the shadow of the Holy One, blessed be He.[179]

By studying the letters of the Torah, or even by simply gazing on the open Torah scroll, one apprehends the form or image of the divine.[180] For the kabbalist, seeing the text is tantamount to seeing the shape of God. Isaac of Acre put the matter as follows: "The words and letters . . . are like the garment of a person, the literal sense and commentaries the body, and the true kabbalah and the great powers and secrets . . . are the soul, and this is [the meaning of] what is written, 'From my flesh I will see God' (Job 19:26)."[181]

Textual Study, Mystical Enlightenment, and Prophetic Revelation

It is through interpretation of the Torah, in accord with kabbalistic principles, that the mystic participates again in the act of revelation, now understood in a decidedly visual sense. This experience exceeds the normal range of prophetic visionary experience, however, for the kabbalist attains that which the Israelite attained at Sinai. Thus, in one passage the *Zohar* explains the talmudic dictum that "the sage is better than the prophet" (B. Baba Batra 12a) by noting that "those who are [mystically] engaged in Torah" stand on a higher level in the sefirotic world than the prophets; they "stand above, in the place that is called Torah, the pillar of all faith, and the prophets stand below, in a place that is called *Neṣaḥ* and *Hod.*"[182] Below the prophets are those who "utter words by the Holy Spirit," for they are linked particularly to the last *sefirah*. Those engaged in Torah are on the highest level, which corresponds symbolically to the

178 Cf. Naḥmanides' commentary to Deut. 27:26, ed. Chavel, 2:472.

179 *Sefer Ṭaʿamey ha-Miẓwoth*, ed. Meier, p. 58. See parallels in *Sefer Tashak*, ed. Zwelling, pp. 72, 88, and esp. 93. Hamadan's text has been discussed by Idel in "Concept of Torah," pp. 64–65. See also the passage from a late-thirteenth-century kabbalistic text, *Sefer ha-Yiḥud*, translated and discussed by Idel in "Infinities of Torah," p. 145. See also Fishbane, *Garments of Torah*, pp. 42–43.

180 Cf. the statement of Judah Ḥayyat in his commentary to *Maʿarekhet ha-ʾElohut*, 95a: "The Torah is the image (*demuto*) of the Holy One, blessed be He, and from its perspective one can compare the form, which is the soul, to its Creator."

181 *Meʾirat ʿEinayim*, p. 110.

182 *Zohar* 3:35a.

Written Torah in the divine realm, that is, *Tif'eret,* the sixth gradation, the *sefirah* of Moses, also called the pillar of all faith (*qiyyuma' de-khol meheimanuta'*).[183] It is clear that the expression "those engaged in Torah" (*de-mishtaddelei be-'oraita'*) refers specifically to the mystics who study and interpret Torah according to the symbolic universe of theosophic kabbalah.[184] The theosophic exegete, therefore, is the enlightened one, the *maskil,* who attains the level of Moses. It is thus no mere coincidence that the zoharic authorship places the following assertion in the mouth of R. Simeon: "'I have seen now what no man has seen since Moses ascended the second time to Mount Sinai, for I have seen the [sefirotic] faces illuminated like the light of the bright sun. . . . Moreover, I have known that my face is illuminated, but Moses did not know and did not consider."[185] Or, again, according to a second utterance of R. Simeon, commenting on the premature death of three of the comrades in the Great Assembly, "Perhaps, God forfend, a decree of punishment has been given to us, for by our hands that which was not revealed since Moses stood on Mount Sinai has been revealed."[186] According to yet another zoharic passage, the scriptural account of Mosaic prophecy is applied to R. Simeon:

> It has been taught: "Do not come near a woman during her period of uncleanness to uncover her nakedness" (Lev. 18:19). R. Judah taught: The generation in which R. Simeon bar Yoḥai dwells is all righteous, all pious, all fearers of sin. The Presence dwells among them unlike other generations. Therefore these [esoteric] matters are made explicit and not hidden. In other generations this was not the case and matters pertaining to the supernal secrets could not be revealed, and those who knew them were afraid [to disclose them]. When R. Simeon communicated the secret of that verse [Lev. 18:19] the eyes of the comrades shed tears, and all that he said was revealed in their eyes, as it is written, "With him I speak mouth to mouth, plainly and not in riddles" (Num. 12:8).[187]

It seems hardly insignificant that this verse is applied to R. Simeon. On the contrary, this application underscores the fact that the kabbalistic gnosis is rooted in a prophetic state; indeed, the prototype of kabbalistic masters reaches the very level of Moses, the ideal of all prophets. The interpretative prowess of the kabbalist stems from a direct communication of these matters through a supernatural process of a revelatory nature that is a reenactment of the Sinaitic

[183] Concerning this expression, see Liebes, *Sections of the Zohar Lexicon,* pp. 379–380.

[184] See, e.g., *Zohar* 1:189b–190a; 2:61b, 95a, 202a; 3:22a, 36a, 73a, 96a, 112a, 153a (*Piqqudin*); *Zohar Ḥadash* 70d. In *Zohar Ḥadash* 97c (*Tiqqunim*) to be "engaged in Torah study" is given the particular theurgic meaning of uniting the feminine and masculine potencies of God. The expression *le'ishtaddel be-'oraita'* can also have the less technical meaning of simply being occupied with Torah study. See, e.g., *Zohar Ḥadash* 80d–81a (MhN); *Zohar* 1:132b, 168a, 184b, 242b; 2:27a, 46a, 83b, 161a–b; 3:98b.

[185] *Zohar* 3:132b (*Idra Rabba*).

[186] Ibid., 144a (*Idra Rabba*). It is clear that the author of this unit conceived of the contents of the Great Assembly as another Sinaitic revelation. On the parallel theurgical powers of R. Simeon bar Yoḥai and Moses to perform miracles, see esp. *Zohar* 2:149a.

[187] *Zohar* 3:79a. See Liebes, "Messiah," p. 144 (English trans., p. 29).

epiphany. The special connection between mystical hermeneutics and the revelatory experience of Sinai is also implied in another passage in the *Zohar,* in which four levels of meaning in Scripture are distinguished: the narrative, depicted as the garment; the laws and rituals, which correspond to the body; the kabbalistic meaning, which is the soul; and the innermost meaning, which is the soul of souls. Regarding the third and fourth levels the *Zohar* reflects, "The sages, servants of the supernal King, who stood at Mount Sinai contemplate but the soul that is the essence of everything, the Torah itself, and in the future they will contemplate the soul of the soul of Torah."[188] It is evident that "the sages who stood at Sinai" refers to the kabbalists who in the present behold the real Torah, which corresponds to *Tif'eret,* the sixth emanation, and in the messianic future will comprehend an even deeper level of secrets in the Torah, which corresponds to *Keter,* the first of the emanations. Through exegesis, therefore, the kabbalists reexperience the Sinaitic revelation.

That the kabbalist, according to the *Zohar,* is on a par with Moses is stated openly in another passage (briefly discussed in the preceding chapter) wherein Mosaic prophecy is contrasted with that accorded to the Patriarchs, Abraham, Isaac, and Jacob. Whereas the Patriarchs had visions of the "lower colors" as reflected through the prism of the *Shekhinah,* Moses alone beheld the "upper colors" that are "concealed and invisible." After having established the different modes of prophetic vision, the *Zohar* interprets Dan. 12:3, "And the enlightened (*maskilim*) will shine like the splendor (*zohar*) of the sky" thus: "Who are the enlightened ones? This refers to the wise one who comprehends by himself those matters that no man can speak with his mouth. These are called enlightened. 'They will shine like the splendor of the sky.' Which sky? The sky of Moses, which stands in the middle [of the divine edifice]. The splendor of this [sky] is hidden, and its color is not revealed."[189] It is quite evident that the enlightened, the *maskilim,* are the mystics, or more accurately, the theosophic kabbalists.[190] Accordingly, the zoharic authorship attributes to the enlightened the quality of understanding on their own, a character trait already singled out in the Mishnah as appropriate for one desiring to engage in *ma'aseh merkavah,* speculation on the divine chariot (Ḥagigah 2:1). Moreover, we are told that the enlightened "shine like the splendor of the sky," which is identified further as the "sky of Moses."[191] The latter term refers symbolically to *Tif'eret,* the divine gradation, which, as was mentioned above, corresponds to Moses. That is to say, therefore, that the mystic is capable of reaching the level of Moses. Quite remarkably, the continuum of experience for prophet and mystic

[188] *Zohar* 3:152a. See Matt, *Zohar,* p. 205.

[189] *Zohar* 2:23a.

[190] See *Zohar* 2:2a, where the enlightened (*maskilim*) are identified specifically as "those who are occupied with the mystery of wisdom." See also *Zohar Ḥadash* 105a (*Matnitin*), 105c, 106b. And see *Tiqqune Zohar,* introduction, 17a (parallel in *Zohar Ḥadash* 93d [*Tiqqunim*]), where the *maskilim* of Dan. 12:3 are interpreted explicitly as a reference to R. Simeon and his circle. See Giller, *Enlightened Will Shine.* On the technical use of the term *maskilim,* see also chapter 6, n. 55.

[191] Cf. *Zohar Ḥadash* 94b (*Tiqqunim*).

appears to be one and the same. That implies two things: first, classical prophecy is reinterpreted as a mode of mystical experience involving visualization of the *sefirot,*[192] and second, revelatory experience of God is still a distinct possibility for the kabbalist. Hence, the *Zohar* in one place refers to the theosophic kabbalists as "those engaged in wisdom to visualize the glory of their Master."[193] The goal of theosophic gnosis—the wisdom with which the kabbalist is engaged—is visualization of the glory.

Vision of the Closed Eye

In the continuation of the zoharic passage cited above, wherein the visionary experience of the enlightened mystic is compared to that of Moses, a specific technique for achieving a vision of the sefirotic realm is set forth; although the experience is designated as knowledge (*yediʿah*), in contrast to seeing (*yirʾah*), it is evident that the knowledge intended is itself essentially of a visual nature and thus draws on sensory modes of perceptual experience. This technique, one of two such procedures mentioned in the *Zohar* to induce visionary experiences (the second one is noted below), involves the rotation of the closed eye, which creates an array of colors said to symbolize the upper hidden colors that shine but are not visible, that is, the three central gradations, Lovingkindness (*Ḥesed*), Judgment (*Din*), and Mercy (*Raḥamim*), which also correspond to the three Patriarchs and the three members of the mystical fellowship mentioned at the outset of this particular narrative unit.[194] "The secret is: the eye that is closed and opened, when it is closed it sees the speculum that shines, and when it is opened it sees the speculum that does not shine."[195] In a paradoxical turn, the possibility of a vision of the upper colors within the speculum that shines (*Tifʾeret*) is linked to the eye that is closed,[196] whereas the vision of the lower colors within the speculum that does not shine (*Shekhinah*) is linked to the eye that is opened. Similarly, in another context it is stated that the "splendor of the speculum is not seen at all except through the rotation of the eye when it is closed. They rotate it in circular motion and in that rotation the speculum that

[192] In this connection it is of interest to note the following comment in MS New York–JTSA Mic. 8558, fol. 9b, which accompanies a standard diagram of the ten *sefirot:* "The prophets knew only the colors and forms and in accordance with the color they comprehended the attribute." Underlying this passing remark is the assumption that the prophetic experience was determined by a vision of the sefirotic emanations that may have been induced by specific techniques.

[193] *Zohar* 2:247b.

[194] See Liebes, *Sections of the Zohar Lexicon,* pp. 291–292; and the reference to Idel below, n. 200.

[195] *Zohar* 2:23b; cf. 1:42a.

[196] Cf. the comment in *Zohar* 3:187b, which describes the following experience of the wonder-child (*yanuqa*ʾ): "When he made the blessing [over the cup of wine] he closed his eyes for a moment, and afterwards he began to speak: Comrades, greetings for you from the good Master to whom the whole world belongs." In this context, then, the closing of the eyes creates a trance state by which the wonder-child ascends to the divine pleroma. On closing the eyes during prayer, see also above, n. 43.

shines is seen; no one can bear that color except the one who sees the splendor shine in the closed eye."[197] In yet another context there is an allusion to the technique of rotating the closed eye to envision the three central *sefirot,* specifically in the context of mentioning the three divine names in Deut. 6:4, which allude to the threefold unity of the divine:[198] "Only in the vision of the Holy Spirit they are known, and by means of the closed eye it is known that the three are one."[199] The same praxis is elaborated on by de León, although in this case the technique of rotation of the closed eye is combined with another technique, known from the *Zohar* and de León's Hebrew writings, which consists of placing a dish of water in the sunlight to create shadows of light dancing about on a wall, creating, in effect, visual traces of the central three sefirotic lights, also identified as the upper celestial creatures (*ḥayyot*) characterized by ceaseless circular motion.[200] As I noted in the preceding chapter, in one passage in the *Zohar* this technique of the dish of water is associated with the "true prophets"—the kabbalists—who employ this medium to visualize the upper sefirotic colors as reflected in the *Shekhinah.*[201] De León describes the process as follows:

> "And the creatures ran to and fro, in the appearance of a flare" (Ezek. 1:14). From here is the mystery of the supernal chariot, the speculum that shines, the splendor devoid [of form], which is not comprehended by mental vision, except in a concealed manner, in the hidden depth, in the manner of the splendor and radiance of that which is comprehended in the concealment and rotation [of the eye]. When the eye is closed and rolls around, a concealed splendor is seen momentarily, for it does not settle down to be seen [in a fixed way]. So it is by the supernal creatures—they are the splendor of the speculum that shines, which does not settle down to be seen, but rather "runs to and fro," as the revolving of the water in a plate when placed against the light of the sun. The flame of the sun sparkles in [the manner of] "running and returning," but does not settle down in one place. So it is with respect to those creatures, as we have said.[202]

[197] *Zohar* 1:97a–b (*Sitre Torah*).

[198] On the possible Christian influence of this passage, see Jellinek, "Christlicher Einfluss auf die Kabbalah"; Liebes, "Christian Influences in the Zohar," pp. 44–50 (English trans., pp. 140–145).

[199] *Zohar* 2:43b.

[200] See MS Munich 47, fol. 380a (discussed by Scholem in "Eine unbekannte mystische Schrift des Mose de Leon," pp. 118–119 n. 5); *Sheqel ha-Qodesh,* p. 113; *Sha'ar Yesod ha-Merkavah,* MS Vatican 283, fols. 167a–b; *Zohar Ḥadash* 39d. A similar technique is mentioned by de León's contemporary, Joseph Gikatilla, in his commentary on Ezekiel's chariot vision. Cf. MS New York–JTSA Mic. 2156, fol. 2b: "Set your eyes and contemplate, and see the vessel full of water placed in the courtyard. And you see within it all the upper forms." On the close resemblance between the commentaries on Ezekiel's chariot by Gikatilla, Moses de León, and the *Zohar,* see Farber, "Traces of the *Zohar* in the Writings of R. Joseph Gikatilla." For a similar technique in the German Pietists, see chapter 5, nn. 334–335. See also Idel in *Kabbalah: New Perspectives,* p. 140, where he discusses some of the relevant texts from de León's Hebrew works and the *Zohar,* and notes similar ideas in the German Pietists and Gikatilla.

[201] *Zohar Ḥadash* 39d.

[202] MS Vatican 283, fol. 170a. Cf. *Sheqel ha-Qodesh,* p. 123, where *Binah* is described as the

In another context the technique of rolling the closed eye is offered as a means of enabling the mystic to experience the vision of the glory seen by Ezekiel:

> These are the colors that are seen in that image [of the glory]: white, red, and green. "Such was the appearance of the surrounding radiance" (Ezek. 1:28): the light that is hidden in the rotation of the vision of the eye. "That was the appearance of the semblance of the Presence of the Lord" (ibid.): the colors that are united in the lower unity according to the unity that is united in the upper unity. [The words] "YHWH, our God, is YHWH" (Deut. 6:4) [designate] the hidden colors that are not seen and that are bound to one place, one unity above. The colors in the rainbow below that are united in it, white, red, and green, are like the hidden colors. They constitute another unity, the secret of "and His name is one" (Zech. 14:9), "Blessed be the name of His glorious kingdom," the unity below. The upper unity: "Hear, O Israel, YHWH, our God, YHWH is one" (Deut. 6:4), one parallels the other.[203]

The paradox of the vision through a closed eye is highlighted in another zoharic passage, describing the voice that emerges from the letter *bet,* which comes forth from the striking and engraving that occurs within the spark of the upper recesses of the Godhead:[204] "That voice goes out from one end of the world to the other, it ascends and descends, it goes and stands, no eye has the power to see it. When it is hidden it is revealed, and when it is revealed it is hidden. By means of the closing of the eyes it is seen, and through the closing of the ears it is heard. It is not known until it is summoned to the table of the truly righteous to be eaten."[205] Affirmed in this passage is the possibility of some kind of union between the mystic and the divine potency, here symbolized as the voice that comes out of the letter *bet,* which most likely represents the second hypostasis or Wisdom. The unitive experience is alluded to in the concluding statement that the truly righteous (a cipher for the theosophic kabbalists) consume this voice at their table. In any number of zoharic passages the voice corresponds to the sixth gradation, the masculine *Tif'eret,* but it is possible that in this context the voice that derives from Wisdom signifies the femi-

---

"concealed and hidden light that rotates the light of the true splendor in the rotation of the light of the closed eye."

[203] *Zohar* 1:18b. Cf. *Zohar Ḥadash* 63b: "YH"W, the hidden faces that no eye can endure to see. Yet it says here 'I have seen [the creatures]' (Ezek. 1:15). Rather he contemplated through the light that does not shine, like one who sees through crystal with closed eyes when the [lights] sparkle in that crystal."

[204] Regarding this spark, sometimes referred to as the "spark of darkness" (*boṣina' de-qadrinuta'*) or the "hardened spark" (*boṣina' de-qardinuta'*), see Tishby, *Wisdom of the Zohar,* pp. 276–277; Liebes, *Sections of the Zohar Lexicon,* pp. 145–151, 161–164; Matt, *Zohar,* pp. 207–208. I alluded to the phallic nature of this spark in "Letter Symbolism and Merkavah Imagery," p. 233 n. 140, and have further elaborated on this point in two studies, "Woman—The Feminine as Other in Theosophic Kabbalah" and "Erasing the Erasure."

[205] *Zohar Ḥadash* 122a.

nine Presence, which is the object of the visual and auditory revelation. Implicit here as well is some form of intersensory transfer, for the voice is both seen and heard, although it is seen only when the eye is closed and heard only when the ear is closed. The paradox of the mystical experience reaches its climax with the utterance that the voice is revealed when it is concealed and concealed when it is revealed.

Hermeneutics as a Visionary Mode

Despite the presence of these visualization techniques in the zoharic corpus, it can be shown that the main vehicle for achieving revelatory experience of a primarily visual sort is hermeneutics, the mystical interpretation of Torah, which is the corporeal form of God. That the mystic visionary is the theosophic hermeneut is substantiated further by three interpretations of the verse "And the enlightened will shine like the splendor of the sky and those who turn the many to righteousness will be like the stars forever" (Dan. 12:3):

> The enlightened (*maskilim*) are those who contemplate (*mistakkele*) the secret of Wisdom. "Will shine," for they are illuminated and shine with the splendor of supernal wisdom. "Like the splendor," the light and spark of the river that comes forth from Eden, and this is the hidden secret, which is called the firmament, in which are found the stars, constellations, sun and moon, and all the flames of light.[206]

> Who are the enlightened? Those who know how to contemplate (*le'istakkala'*) the glory of their Master and know the secret of Wisdom, to enter without shame into the world-to-come. These shine like the upper splendor. And it says "the enlightened" (*ha-maskilim*) rather than "the knowers" (*ha-yodeʿim*) for verily these are they who contemplate (*mistakla'an*) the inner, hidden secrets that are not disclosed or transmitted to every person. He who is worthy of contemplating them with his understanding is illuminated and shines with the crown of the splendor that is supernal to all. There is no splendor that shines like this, there is no splendor that shines upon this world like that splendor. This is the splendor of Torah, the splendor of the masters of wisdom who inherit this world over everything. They exit and enter into all the treasures of their Master and there is no one to prevent them.[207]

> "The enlightened will shine." These are the ones who contemplate (*mistakkelei*) the secret of Wisdom in the mysteries of the secrets of Torah, the righteous ones who fulfill the will of their Master and are engaged in Torah day and night. All who are engaged in the [study of] Torah are called *maskilim*, [for] with wisdom they contemplate (*mistakkelan*) the secret of the upper Wisdom.[208]

[206] *Zohar* 2:2a.
[207] *Zohar Ḥadash* 105a (*Matnitin*).
[208] Ibid., 106b.

From these passages it is clear that mystic contemplation, interpretative in nature, is a visual sort of comprehension.[209] The emphasis on the visual over other epistemic modes, including especially the auditory, is underscored by the zoharic description of the mystics as "masters of the eyes who know and contemplate the wisdom of their Master by means of understanding."[210] The enlightened kabbalist is one who gazes on the glory of God and thereby contemplates "the mystery of Wisdom" that is embodied in "the secret mysteries of the Torah." The one "engaged" in the study of Torah, moreover, is "enlightened," for only such a person contemplates the upper Wisdom inherent in Torah. Clearly, then, it would seem that the revelatory and midrashic modes converge, for visualization of the divine is engendered by the hermeneutic relation one has to the received text. Indeed, for the authorship of the *Zohar,* the perception of the sefirotic lights is best attained through a mystically intuitive grasp and exposition of Scripture. Although the technique of midrash was part of the kabbalistic mind-set from the beginnings of theosophic speculation in Europe, it is in the *Zohar* especially that the task of interpretation becomes the sine qua non of mystical praxis. The goal of kabbalistic exposition, however, is not hearing the word of God as related in the text, but rather seeing the hidden mysteries—that is, the divine light—concealed in the letters and words of that text. So central is the visionary element to mystical hermeneutics that the *Zohar* emphasizes that the kabbalist, the one who contemplates the mysteries of the Torah, is called by Scripture the "enlightened one" and not simply "one who knows," for the word *maskil* derives from the root *skhl,* which connotes comprehension through seeing. The enlightened are further described as being crowned with the crown of the supernal splendor, a term associated in the *Zohar,* as I have already noted, with mystical comprehension.

The meeting of the visionary and hermeneutical modes in the *Zohar* is brought out in a discourse of the Old Man, the mysterious sage who imparts esoteric wisdom to the mystical comrades through parables, concerning the nature of interpretation and the inner layers of the Torah:

> The Holy One, blessed be He, enters all the hidden things that He has made into the holy Torah, and everything is found in the Torah. The Torah reveals that hidden thing and then it is immediately clothed in another garment, where it is hidden and not revealed. And even though that thing is hidden in its garment the sages, who

[209] See Tishby, *Wisdom of the Zohar,* p. 146. Cf. Gikatilla, *Sha'are 'Orah* 1:148. Also relevant here is another motif expressed in zoharic literature that links the combination of letters and the visual revelation of secrets. See *Zohar* 2:179b. See also the lengthy discussion on letter-combination in *Zohar* 3:2a–3b.

[210] *Zohar* 2:235b; see also 232a (*Tosefta*). For a similar expression, "masters of the eyes" (*ba'ale ha-'einayim*), applied to the enlightened who look upon the golden apples encased in silver (following Maimonides' application of Prov. 25:11 to the dual levels of meaning in the biblical text)—i.e., who contemplate the inner meaning of Scripture—see R. Jonathan, *'Or ha-Sekhel,* MS New York–JTSA Mic. 1831, fol. 6a. Cf. Judah ben Samuel Campanton, *Leqaḥ Ṭov,* MS Oxford-Bodleian 1642, fol. 3b, where the wise are referred to as "masters of the eyes" (*ba'ale 'einayim*). See idem, *'Arba'ah Qinyanim,* MS New York–JTSA Mic. 2532, fol. 23a.

> are full of eyes, see it from within its garment. When that thing is revealed, before it enters into a garment, they cast an open eye upon it, and even though [the thing] is immediately concealed, it does not depart from their eyes.[211]

In this text the *Zohar* repeatedly employs metaphors derived from the phenomenon of sight. God is said to hide secret matters within the Torah and clothe them in a garment, the removal of which allows them to be seen by the sage. Hence, the mystic is called the "wise one full of eyes,"[212] a term that echoes another expression of the mystics, "masters of the eyes," which was referred to above. In contrast to the Torah, which is symbolically depicted as the beautiful maiden without eyes,[213] the mystic is described as the sage filled with eyes. Elsewhere in the *Zohar* the kabbalists are referred to as "masters of understanding, those of opened eyes, masters of faith."[214] The force of this designation is certainly that the mystic possesses a distinctive gnosis of God that is of a visionary quality. It is evident, moreover, as I have already noted, that this insight is textually mediated, so that the open eye of the mystic visionary is cast upon the Torah, and through that glance he imparts meaning to the text, just as the masculine attribute of *Yesod* pours forth onto the feminine Presence.[215] Furthermore, perhaps borrowing from Maimonides' description of truth in the introduction to the *Guide of the Perplexed,*[216] the zoharic authorship here describes the concealed truth of Torah as that which momentarily flashes out from behind its hiding place only to quickly disappear into another one.

In the continuation of this passage the *Zohar* presents the oft-cited parable of the beautiful princess secluded in her palace, hinting to her lover to approach, and ultimately uniting with him in matrimony. On the allegorical level, the princess in her castle symbolizes the Torah, which is hidden behind several layers of meaning. The lover is the mystic who must be gradually led to the deepest level of hermeneutic experience, knowledge of the esoteric layer of the

[211] *Zohar* 2:98b.

[212] This image may have been derived from Ezek. 10:12, where the wheels of the chariot are described as being "covered all over with eyes." See chapter 3, n. 85. I am unaware of any previous rabbinic source that applies this image to describe the sage. See, however, Philo, *Quaestiones et Solutiones in Exodum* III.43 (in Loeb ed., p. 236) where it is said that it is necessary for the soul "to be all eyes" so that it may "receive lightning flashes [of illumination], having God as its teacher and leader in obtaining knowledge of things and attaining to their causes." This text is related to a theme that Philo develops in a number of contexts concerning God's implanting (*enommatoo*) eyes in an individual so that he will be able to see God. See the sources cited and discussed in Delling, "The 'One Who Sees God' in Philo," pp. 33–34. See also the tradition recorded in the anonymous kabbalistic work, *Sefer ha-Ne*ʿ*elam,* MS Paris–BN 817, fol. 55b, to the effect that seventy aspects of Torah are filled with eyes. The text goes on to say that the seventy eyes are "made like a circle," for "they all hide the wisdom and illuminate the eyes and are concealed from the opening of the eyes."

[213] Cf. *Zohar* 2:95a.

[214] *Zohar* 2:74a (*Matnitin*). See also 1:232a.

[215] See Wolfson, "Beautiful Maiden without Eyes," pp. 169–170, 185–186.

[216] As noted already by Tishby in *Wisdom of the Zohar,* p. 1114 n. 49; see also Matt, *Zohar,* pp. 30–31.

text.[217] Although in this case the *Zohar* does employ acoustic language to describe the process of disclosure, it is nevertheless clear that the main mode of revelation is visual. Hence, the word of Torah, like the princess, appears in sight and then quickly vanishes. The mystic interpreter, like the lover, alone can see his beloved. It may be suggested, moreover, that in terms of kabbalistic theosophy the princess functions as a symbol for the *Shekhinah,* the feminine potency of God, which is also the divine gradation that corresponds to the Oral Torah.[218] Indeed, the four stages of the relationship between princess and lover represent four levels of meaning: *peshaṭ* (literal or contextual), *derashah* (homiletical), *haggadah* (allegorical), and *sod* (mystical or esoteric). (Only the former three are explicitly named; the fourth is implied.) From the perspective of the kabbalist, these four levels—including the literal or contextual sense—comprise four distinct hermeneutical postures that collectively make up the Oral Torah. On the symbolic plane, therefore, the parable is alluding to the mystic's relationship to the Written Torah as mediated through four aspects of the Oral Torah.

Textual interpretation, for the author of the *Zohar,* thus involves an intimate relation between the mystic and *Shekhinah;* indeed, as I have already noted, the kabbalist who is engaged or occupied with study of Torah is said to be united with the *Shekhinah.* That the model in this case as well was the Sinaitic revelation can be adduced by an analysis of the passage that directly precedes the parable, wherein the Old Man sets out to interpret Exodus 24:18, "Moses went inside the cloud and ascended the mountain": "What was that cloud? It is as it is written, 'And My bow I placed in the cloud' (Gen. 9:13). It has been taught that the rainbow removed its garments and gave them to Moses and with that garment Moses ascended to the mountain. And from it [the garment] he saw what he saw and he delighted in all."[219] The prototype of the mystics, Moses, must receive the garment of the rainbow before he ascends to the mountain to receive the Torah. In this context the rainbow is a symbol for *Yesod,*[220] and the cloud a symbol for the *Shekhinah.* Moses must put on the garment of

[217] The imagery is based, no doubt, on *Midrash Tanḥuma,* Pequdei, 4, where the Torah is parabolically compared to a king's daughter hidden behind seven chambers in a palace. See Talmage, "Apples of Gold," pp. 316–318. See also *Sefer ha-Bahir,* § 196 (cf. Scholem, *Origins,* pp. 170–171), as well as the suggestive characterization of the Torah in *Zohar* 3:35b–36a: "When a person comes to be united with the Torah she is open to receive him and to join him. But when a person closes his eyes from her and goes another way, she is closed from another side." See Tishby, *Wisdom of the Zohar,* pp. 1084–1085; Idel, *Kabbalah: New Perspectives,* pp. 227–229; Wolfson, "Female Imaging," pp. 295–297.

[218] By contrast, Liebes, in *Sections of the Zohar Lexicon,* p. 190 n. 78, cites this interpretation as that of later kabbalists but rejects it as the intended or contextual meaning of the *Zohar.*

[219] *Zohar* 2:99a; cf. 1:66a.

[220] See Idel, *Kabbalah: New Perspectives,* p. 227. Tishby, however, in *Wisdom of the Zohar,* p. 196 n. 408, explains that the rainbow in this zoharic context is a symbol for *Shekhinah,* and the cloud a symbol for the garment in which she is clothed. Matt, *Zohar,* p. 251, and Cohen-Alloro, *Secret of the Garment,* p. 77, follow this line of interpretation. Both symbolic interpretations of the rainbow are based on earlier sources; see above, nn. 30, 40.

Yesod before entering into the cloud, *Shekhinah,* and ascending farther to receive the Torah.[221] By adorning himself with the cloak of the rainbow in order to enter into the cloud, Moses emulates the theosophic process by means of which the phallic *Yesod* enters into the feminine *Shekhinah*.[222] In another sense, by this act Moses symbolically enacts the unification of the Oral Torah and the Written Torah, which, kabbalistically, correspond to *Shekhinah* and *Tif'eret*. That is, by entry into the one, the feminine Oral Torah, Moses can gain access to the other, the masculine Written Torah.[223]

The hermeneutic process follows the same pattern, for by means of interpretation a bridge is established between masculine and feminine, written and oral, and the mystical exegete, like Moses, stands in the position of *Yesod,* the conduit or channel connecting the two. Although this view is implied in any number of zoharic contexts, it is stated with particular clarity in the following passage:

> Come and see the secret of the matter. The Community of Israel [*Shekhinah*] does not stand before the King [*Tif'eret*] except by means of the Torah. Whenever earthly Israel are engaged in [the study of] Torah the Community of Israel dwells with them. . . . Thus, when the Community of Israel is aroused before the King by means of Torah, her forces are strengthened and the Holy King is glad to receive her. However, when the Community of Israel comes before the King and Torah is not found with her, her strength, as it were, is weakened.[224]

Those who study Torah strengthen the *Shekhinah* in order to enable her to unite with her masculine consort, the Holy King. The mystics engaged in Torah-study, therefore, fulfill the function of *Yesod,* the gradation that unifies the feminine and masculine potencies of God.[225]

[221] Cf. *Zohar* 2:229a, and see Naḥmanides' commentary on Exod. 24:1, ed. Chavel, 1:448. In several places in the *Zohar* the garment represents the means through which the soul cleaves to and comprehends God; see 1:38b, 75b–76a; 2:55a; 3:69a, 214a; also Cohen-Alloro, *Secret of the Garment,* pp. 68–74. The zoharic idea is based on earlier kabbalistic texts. Cf. MS Oxford-Bodleian 1938, fols. 6a–b: "The explanation [of] 'Moses went inside the cloud' (Exod. 24:28) is that he was clothed in the garment of the supernal realities and all the senses were nullified, that is, all the desires, and that cloud . . . is the cloud of the Presence that went before them constantly." See as well MS Paris–BN 824, fols. 114b–115a. Another related idea in the *Zohar* is that the righteous one below who performs certain divine commandments is clothed in the garment of the *Shekhinah;* see Tishby, *Wisdom of the Zohar,* p. 1164.

[222] In *Mishkan ha-ʿEdut,* MS Vatican 283, fol. 36a, de León notes just the opposite: as the righteous one approaches the *Shekhinah* she is the one that puts on a garment. See Cohen-Alloro, *Secret of the Garment,* p. 16 n. 1.

[223] The phallic role of Moses as uniting the Oral Torah and Written Torah at Sinai is emphasized in other zoharic contexts as well. See, e.g., *Zohar Ḥadash* 42a, 72d–73a.

[224] *Zohar* 3:22a.

[225] See also *Zohar* 1:4a, where those who study Torah the night of Pentecost are said to prepare the *Shekhinah* for her wedding to *Tif'eret,* i.e., the Oral Torah and the Written Torah. In this respect, too, the one who studies Torah is in the posture of *Yesod,* inasmuch as he acts as a conduit connecting the masculine and feminine potencies of the divine. On this passage, see Liebes, "Messiah," pp. 92–93 (English trans., p. 5).

It is surely not insignificant that in the context of unfolding the nature of mystical hermeneutics the *Zohar* interprets a biblical verse connected to the Sinaitic event. Underlying this strategy is the assumed identification between the modalities of revelation and interpretation. The mystic, like Moses, is capable of achieving union with *Shekhinah,* a union that bears the fruit of theosophic speculation and exegesis.[226] It is, moreover, the medium of visionary experience, for through the light of the *Shekhinah* the kabbalist can penetrate into the hidden depths of the text and thereby contemplate the upper secrets of the divine realm. Hence, at the end of the parable, when the lover (the mystic) finally sees the princess (the Torah) face-to-face and learns of her secret ways, the *Zohar* calls him "husband of Torah, master of the house." The same appellation, "master of the house" (*ma'rei de-veita'*), is applied elsewhere in the *Zohar* to Moses[227] and to the *ṣaddiq,* the righteous one who is the mundane correlate to *Yesod* above.[228] Similarly, the phrase "husband of Torah" is reminiscent of another phrase used in connection with Moses in the *Zohar,* "husband of Elohim."[229] Both of these expressions point to the fact that Moses had achieved union with the *Shekhinah* (referred to symbolically as "house" and as Elohim).[230] Here the two expressions are applied to the mystic who masters the secrets of Torah. Again we see the intricate and essential correlation that the author of the *Zohar* establishes between the mystic exegete and Moses and, by implication, between the processes of interpretation and revelation.

From the point of view of the *Zohar,* then, the kabbalists are linked specifically to *Yesod,* the splendor with which they are illuminated and by means of which they interpret the text of Scripture. Indeed, this correlation is essential to the spiritual worldview of the *Zohar* (including mystical, theurgical, and messianic elements), which is completely dominated by the phallocentric correspondence of the kabbalist below and the *Ṣaddiq* above. Given this ontic position the kabbalist has the task of uniting the masculine and feminine poles of the divine, which are both located in the phallus. To put the matter differently, the

226 That *Shekhinah* is the locus of exegetical activity is emphasized in *Tiqqune Zohar* (cf. *Zohar Ḥadash* 102d) by the claim that *Shekhinah* is called *pardes de-'oraita',* "the orchard of Torah," for this gradation comprises four levels of interpretation: *peshaṭ, re'iyah, derashah,* and *sod.* See Tishby, *Wisdom of the Zohar,* p. 1090; Scholem, *On the Kabbalah,* p. 58. See above n. 174.

227 See *Zohar* 1:236b; 2:22b, 238b. In 1:138b, the term is applied to Jacob, who symbolically corresponds to the same gradation as Moses, namely, *Tif'eret,* the consort of *Shekhinah.* On the difference between the level of Moses and that of Jacob, see *Zohar* 1:21b, and the Hebrew parallel in a text of Moses de León extant in MS Munich 47, fols. 336a–b.

228 Cf. *Zohar* 1:70b–71a; 2:134b.

229 See *Zohar* 1:6b; 2:238b. This is based on the biblical appellation *'ish 'elohim,* which is applied to Moses; see, e.g., Deut. 33:1. For the other biblical personalities so named, see *Sifre on Deuteronomy* 342, p. 393; *'Avot de-R. Natan,* version B, chap. 37, pp. 95–96; Ginzberg, *Legends* 6:167 n. 965. The kabbalistic interpretation of the expression is alluded to in Naḥmanides' commentary to Deut. 33:1, ed. Chavel, 2:491. See Idel, "Sexual Metaphors and Praxis," p. 206. On the attribution of the appellation to Moses and the level of prophecy implied thereby, see the tradition of R. Moses of Burgos cited in Isaac of Acre, *Me'irat 'Einayim,* p. 55.

230 On the zoharic conception of Moses' mythical unification with the *Shekhinah,* see the sources cited and discussed by Liebes in *Sections of the Zohar Lexicon,* pp. 182–184.

kabbalist must reconstitute the androgynous nature of the phallus by assuming the position of that aspect of the Godhead. This, too, is placed in a visionary context in this passage from a section in the zoharic anthology called *Sitre Torah* ("Mysteries of Torah"):[231]

> "And the enlightened will shine like the splendor of the sky" (Daniel 12:3). *Zohar*—the splendor of splendors that illuminates in its elevation.[232] *Zohar*—that which shines, glows, and flashes in several directions. *Zohar*—it rises and descends. *Zohar*—it shines to every side. *Zohar*—it flows and goes out. *Zohar*—that which never stops. *Zohar*—that which produces offspring. *Zohar*—hidden and concealed. The spark of all sparks and gradations[233] is in it; it goes out and is hidden, concealed and revealed, seen and not seen. *Zohar*—the lip of the root[234] is the spring of the well, it goes forth in the day and is hidden in the night, it delights at midnight with the offspring that it produces. *Zohar*—that which shines and illuminates everything, the totality of Torah. This is the splendor of the sky, the sky in which are dependent the sun, moon, stars, and constellations. This is called the splendor of the speculum that shines, of which no human merited except the shepherd who is trusted throughout the household.[235] . . . The splendor of the sky, the upper concealed one that shines but is not known, glows but is not seen, and he who takes does not know from whom he takes. Its concealment is hidden and concealed, the staff of Joseph the Righteous is hidden in four colors.

The traditional commentaries on the *Zohar* explain in various ways the ten references to the word *zohar* (splendor) in this passage, but it seems to me that it refers to one particular gradation in the pleroma that is characterized in ten different ways, namely, *Yesod*, the divine phallus that is the "all," for it comprises within itself the totality of the divine energies. The *maskilim* are illuminated by that particular grade.[236] The play of esotericism in the *Zohar* (as for other theosophic kabbalists) is linked specifically to the phallus: just as that

231 I will cite the text according to the version that appears in *Zohar Ḥadash* 104b–c, referring to significant variants from *Zohar* 1:100a–b in the following notes.

232 בסליקו זוהרא; see, however, the reading in a parallel text in *Zohar* 1:100a, בדליקו זהרא, which would translate "illuminates by flashing."

233 דרגין; the reading in *Zohar* 1:100a is שרגין, "lights."

234 סיפתא בעיקורא; the reading in *Zohar* 1:100a is ספרא דא, "this book." Interestingly, these words are lacking in the Cremona edition of the *Zohar*, 66b.

235 That is, Moses; cf. Num. 12:7.

236 On the identification of the word *maskil* as a symbolic reference to the divine phallus, *Yesod*, see *Zohar* 2:110a–b. It is of interest to note that in that context a distinction is made between the upper *maskil* (related exegetically to Ps. 89:1, *maskil le-'etan ha-'ezraḥi*) and the lower *maskil* (related to Ps. 142:1, *maskil le-david*). From that context it appears that just as the latter refers to the divine phallus below that overflows to the Presence, so, too, the former designates the upper phallus that is operative in the supernal brain (*moḥa' 'ila'ah*), perhaps to be identified as *Ḥokhmah*. This notion is doubtless related to the Galenic view widespread in kabbalistic sources regarding the origin of the semen in the brain. See *Gershom Scholem's Annotated Zohar* (Jerusalem, 1992), p. 1512. The idea of the upper phallus corresponding to the lower phallus underlies the application of Dan. 12:3 in zoharic literature to the *boṣina' de-qardinuta'* (see above, n. 204), the hard flame, and *Yesod*. Cf. *Zohar* 1:15a and 2:2a.

grade is characterized by a dialectic of concealment and disclosure, so, too, the one who knows the secrets conceals what is revealed and reveals what is concealed, that is, reveals in what he conceals and conceals in what he reveals.

In sum, then, mystical gnosis for the *Zohar* is primarily visual and not auditory. The mystic, like the prophet—indeed, like the greatest of prophets, Moses—can have a visual experience of God. Although the *Zohar* does specify some rather simple techniques for visualization of colors that symbolically depict aspects of the divine, for the most part the seeing of the sefirotic entities is decidedly text-oriented, that is, through midrashic activity the mystic can attain a revelation of the divine. The point is underscored particularly well in the following passage:

> "And the enlightened will shine like the splendor of the sky." This refers to those who are engaged in [the study of] Torah and contemplate words of Torah with intention and meditation of the heart. The enlightened contemplate [words of Torah] but they do not contemplate the word alone. Rather, they contemplate the place on which the word is dependent, for there is no word that is not dependent on another supernal mystery. He finds in this word another matter of the supernal mystery. From the speculum that does not shine a person can find and see the secret of the speculum that shines. . . . This is [the import of] "like the splendor of the sky": it is the sky that is known [that stands] upon the creatures below, for from within that sky one can contemplate the splendor that shines, the splendor of the supernal splendors, the splendor that comes forth from the supernal point, shining and sparkling with the radiance of the other lights on every side.[237]

The goal of the enlightened mystic, therefore, is to visualize the radiant and shining splendor (*Yesod*) through the sky (*Shekhinah*), but this is brought about through contemplative study of the words of Scripture. The iconic visualization of God is attained through a double reflection: the words of Scripture reflect the *Shekhinah,* which, in turn, reflects *Yesod.* The only access to the veiled phallus is through the disrobing of Scripture. This conviction was certainly held by the authorship of the *Zohar,* who construed the task of the kabbalist as imparting a new-old revelation by means of textual interpretation. Just as the kabbalist could reach the level of Moses by studying the Mosaic text, so, too, others studying the zoharic document could in turn share in the dynamic and shine with the splendor of Moses' gradation. This implicit assumption, which colors the entire literary effort of the main body of the *Zohar,* was stated succinctly by the anonymous author of *Tiqqunei Zohar:* "In that time 'the enlightened will shine like the splendor of the sky.' What is the 'splendor'? The gradation of Moses, our rabbi, the 'Central Pillar' [*Tif'eret*], because of whom this work is called the 'Book of Splendor' (*Sefer ha-Zohar*)."[238]

How well this kabbalist has captured the tacit assumption that bound together the circle responsible for the production of the *Zohar!* This classic of

[237] *Zohar Ḥadash* 105c.

[238] *Zohar Ḥadash* 94b (*Tiqqunim*). See also 96b.

Jewish mysticism conveys in so many different ways the presumption that its authorial voice (R. Simeon bar Yoḥai) had reached the symbolic level of Moses in the divine world and had thus identified with the historical Moses. By interpreting the Torah that the ancient Moses had revealed, this new Moses was in effect revealing a new Torah. His interpretation was concomitantly a revelation. The ecstatic nature of the literary activity of the mystical fraternity responsible for the *Zohar,* and specifically R. Simeon, who stands in the position of Moses—indeed, is Moses *redivivus*—is also duly appreciated by the anonymous kabbalist who emulated the zoharic style and thereby extended the historical circle cloaked in the personae of the mythical drama. The splendor by means of which the enlightened kabbalist is illuminated is no longer simply the ontic grade of *Yesod;* it is the literary composition that derives from that particular grade, that is, the "Book of Splendor," which corresponds to Moses: "The enlightened will shine in this composition of yours, which is *Sefer ha-Zohar,* from the splendor of the supernal Mother, *Teshuvah* (Repentance)."[239] "The enlightened will comprehend, those are the masters of kabbalah, concerning whom it is written, 'And the enlightened will shine like the splendor of the sky,' these are the ones who are occupied with this splendor that is called *Sefer ha-Zohar,* which is like the ark of Noah, for gathered into it are two from a city and seven from the kingdom, and occasionally one from a city and two from the family."[240]

In the introduction to *Tiqqune Zohar* the issue is expressed in this way: "'And the enlightened will shine like the splendor of the sky.' The enlightened are R. Simeon and his colleagues; they will shine when they gather to produce this composition. Permission is given to them and to Elijah, who is with them, and to all the souls of the [celestial] academy to descend among them, and to all the angels." The author of *Tiqqune Zohar* precisely understood that the kabbalists responsible for the literary composition of this anthology "shine in this composition, they are illuminated by its words and in its writing, in this book [they shine] like the splendor of the sky, according to its name it is called *Sefer ha-Zohar,* in the image of the central pillar, which is a book (*sefer*). Its splendor is from the Supernal Mother . . . and it is the splendor that shines in the heart of the Faithful Shepherd."[241]

Modern scholars of the *Zohar* have much to learn from this anonymous kabbalist, in terms of appreciating both the group activity that was behind the creation of this work and the state of mystical illumination that characterized the study meetings of the circle. From the vantage point of the zoharic worldview there is no real gap between prophetic inspiration and interpretation; on the contrary, homiletical prowess is an expression of an ecstatic and transformative experience. The nature of that ecstasy involved the ontic assimilation of the kabbalist (both as individual mystic and as part of a collective fellowship)

[239] *Zohar* 3:124b; cf. *Zohar Ḥadash* 103b.

[240] *Zohar* 3:153b.

[241] *Zohar Ḥadash* 103d.

into the divine phallus. As I have shown, moreover, the experience underlying that ontic assimilation is expressed in sundry ways in the zoharic corpus, including the images of crowning, illumination, and contemplative visualization. Common to the various expressions of this core experience is the convergence of the ontological and phenomenological poles: the vision of the *Shekhinah* results in the crowning of the mystic, which signifies his metamorphosis into the corona of the divine phallus. Seeing and being seen are unified in the ecstatic vision that is predicated on the uncovering of the concealed phallus. For the zoharic authorship, this unveiling is achieved primarily through hermeneutical engagement with Scripture. Facing the text, therefore, affords the kabbalist the opportunity not only to see the face of God but to become that very face in the visual confrontation. The constitution of the divine face is attained by the group of mystics who assemble together to expose the inner meaning hidden beneath the garments of Torah. The extraordinary power the *Zohar* had in subsequent generations of Jewish history must be seen against this background. The identification of midrash and visionary experience opened the door for others to similarly have visions of God by studying the letters of the sacred text. In its turn, the *Zohar* itself became a hermeneutical basis for revelatory experience.

Conclusion

IN THIS BOOK I have set out to explore the problem of iconic visualization of the divine in Jewish mystical sources from the Hekhalot compositions to the *Zohar.* I have sought to bridge the methodological gap of the phenomenological and historical approaches by studying the phenomenology of visionary experience in different historical settings. Thus on several occasions along the way I have emphasized the necessity of analyzing the warp and woof of any given religious experience in light of its lived historical context, at least as it may be reconstructed within the margins of textuality. The contextualist orientation I have adopted does not, however, presume that Jewish mysticism in its various manifestations is first and foremost a historical phenomenon. I would argue, on the contrary, that Jewish mysticism, as is the case with mysticism in other world religions, is a religious *mentalité* that has expressed itself in distinctive ways in different periods of Jewish history.

To recognize the religious character of mysticism is not to deny its historicity. The methodological issue at stake, however, is a historicist reductionism that would claim that authentic scholarship must be subservient to an empiricist notion of history: what is historical is something novel. Without denying the novelty of human history, one must seriously weigh the appropriateness of this methodology when examining mystical literature. It is much more germane to isolate through phenomenological sophistication the myths, symbols, and deep structures that have informed the life experiences of Jewish mystics through the ages. My approach, too, reflects an appreciation of the historical aspects of Jewish mysticism, but I would categorically reject the reduction of this polymorphous phenomenon to a time-bound historical construction. By doing so, one is tempted to identify Jewish mysticism as an event (or series of events) that can be charted on some chronological and geographical grid. The superficial mapping of Jewish mysticism lures one into losing sight of the common motifs and images that recur in different literary settings. These structural components are far more significant in determining the parameters of Jewish mysticism than in locating specific historical novelties. Sensitivity to historical conditions and developments is an integral part of the phenomenological enterprise, but it is a fallacy of misplaced concreteness to regard Jewish mysticism as a historical truth that can be uncovered or reconstructed solely and exclusively on the basis of the historicist approach.

My study of vision and imagination presents one test case to demonstrate this methodological point. Without attempting to impose a taxonomy of Jewish mysticism, I have sketched several persistent notions in a vast body of mystical literature written at different historical junctures. I have privileged the use of visionary experience as providing a speculum through which the scholar can gaze upon the religious texture of the various currents of Jewish mysticism. While I make no claim that the problem of visionary experience is the defining element of Jewish mysticism, this book has offered a reconfiguration of this phenomenon in the spiritual economy of Judaism. The tension between aniconism, on the one hand, and visualizing the deity, on the other, is an essential component of the relevant varieties of Jewish mystical speculation. Despite the significant historical differences that separate the anonymous mystics of the Hekhalot literature, the Rhineland Jewish Pietists, and the enlightened kabbalists of thirteenth-century Castile, they shared a common biblical heritage that concomitantly affirmed the possibility of God assuming visible form and denied that the God of Israel could be iconically represented.

In great measure the history of theosophical speculation and mystical practice in Judaism has been driven by a hermeneutical effort to resolve this fundamental tension. Whatever other religious influences have been operative in the various trends of Jewish mysticism, it is evident that the Jewish mystics are primarily interpreters of Scripture. The preoccupation with visualizing the divine stems directly from the anxiety of influence of biblical theophanies. No experience is without context, and no context in Judaism is without Scripture. Without denying the uniqueness of the visionary experience, I have argued that the fabric of that experience, not only the report of it, is shaped by traditional beliefs. It is clear that in all the bodies of mystical literature studied in this book—Merkavah mysticism, German Pietism, and Provençal-Spanish theosophic kabbalah—the mystical vision is portrayed as being phenomenologically equivalent to prophecy. Indeed, for these mystics the visual dimension of biblical prophecy dominates their religious mentality. The anthropomorphic form assumed by God in some of the prophetic accounts is applied to specific mystical practices that typically involve prayer and Torah-study.

It is through the imagination that the different Jewish mystics conjured an image of God, believing all the while that this was precisely the mechanics of prophetic vision, as represented by the verse in Hosea, "through the prophets I was imaged." Time and again this verse is cited in critical spots in Jewish mystical literature to justify the iconic depiction of God as an anthropos. The role of imagination as the locus of the theophanic image allowed the mystics to represent God iconically in a tradition informed by an essential aniconism. By locating the image of God in the imagination, the mystics were able to appropriate the epiphanic tendencies of Scripture without overstepping the boundary drawn by traditional authority. This should not be viewed as political acquiescence, reflecting rather a deep-seated tension in classical expressions of Judaism. The effort of scholars to portray Judaism as exclusively aniconic and auditory is indicative of a particular cultural bias rather than a sustained engagement with the relevant sources. The ocularcentrism in some currents of Judaism is as striking as the emphasis on hearing in other currents. All attempts on this score to contrast Judaism with Western culture in general or Christianity in particular are grossly overstated.

While practitioners of Judaism in its various historical manifestations have not adopted a theology of incarnation along the lines of Christianity, they have nonetheless struggled to uphold the scriptural evidence that God does appear to human beings in different forms, including most importantly that of an anthropos, without lapsing into a crude anthropomorphism. The commonplace view (greatly enhanced by the medieval philosophical reinterpretations of Israelite religion and rabbinic Judaism) that sharply contrasts Judaism and Christianity should not mislead us into thinking that within Judaism there has not been a tendency toward an incarnational theology. On the contrary, fragmentary theological pronouncements in classical rabbinic literature, building on the morphological evidence in the biblical canon, stand as testimony that a central component in the religious phenomenology of the rabbis was the belief that God did appear in the image of an anthropos at specific moments in Israel's sacred history. Moreover, it is evident that in some of their own aggadic reflections the rabbis imaged God in characteristics based on their own existential situation. The enframing of God in human images, so central to the aggadic enterprise, is, I submit, related to this larger question regarding a theory of incarnation. I have referred to this orientation in rabbinic teaching as docetic, inasmuch as the iconic representation is located in the imagination. Much of the history of Jewish mysticism evolved as an elaboration and further development of this doceticism. The mystics circumscribed the iconic tendency of Judaism within the intentionality of the religious imagination. Going beyond the explicit claims of the rabbis, as may be deduced from the literary evidence, the mystics cultivated visionary practices to see the imaginal body of the divine.

As I have suggested, moreover, a distinctive feature of the ocularcentrism in medieval Jewish mysticism is a phallocentrism. That is, common to the visionary accounts in the different mystical sources I examined in this work—the writings of the Hekhalot mystics, German Pietists, and theosophic kabbalists—is the notion that the object of the mystical vision is the male deity and, more specifically, the phallus. The specularized figure that provides the foundational condition for the visionary experience is the disclosure of the phallus. This disclosure is represented in the Hekhalot and Pietistic texts by a series of displacements, such as, the crown on the head of the enthroned glory, the cloak full of eyes adorning the body of the glory, the iconic visage of Jacob engraved on the throne, the fiery *ḥashmal* encased in a radiant glow like the appearance of the rainbow in the clouds. In the highly sexualized myth of theosophic kabbalah the divine phallus is still represented symbolically, but it is also explicitly identified. The development of Jewish mysticism, therefore, can be seen as the move from an implicit to an explicit phallocentrism. The transition from esotericism to exotericism is related to the visual representations of the divine phallus. The central position occupied by the phallus is evident in the earliest sources of Jewish mysticism; what is new in theosophic kabbalah is not the attribution of a phallus to the divine but rather the overt willingness to discourse about that which by its nature is concealed. In all of the mystical sources dealt with in this study there is a tension between disclosure and concealment of the divine form. This tension, I believe, is related to the fact that the ultimate object of vision is the phallus that must be hidden. The unveiling of the veiled phallus in the visionary encounter necessitates language that is paradoxical and contradictory.

The seeing of God in Jewish mysticism is intensely eroticized. This eroticism is expressed in the Hekhalot literature and the writings of the German Pietists in terms of the image of enthronement. Inasmuch as the glorious body is masculine and the throne is a feminine hypostasis, it follows that the enthronement itself is a form of sacred union. It is precisely this moment that is at the center of the mystic's vision: he alone is granted permission to witness what is concealed from the sight of all other human and angelic creatures. In the theosophic kabbalah the image of enthronement as a *hieros gamos* is maintained, but a host of additional images are employed to depict the union above, between the male and female potencies of the Godhead. The mythic structures of theosophic kabbalah greatly intensified the connection between eros and vision.

The striking fact is that in the Jewish mystical texts it is always the male mystic visually confronting the male deity. I have argued that this is so even in the case of theosophic kabbalah, inasmuch as the feminine potency of the divine, the *Shekhinah,* is localized as part of the phallus. Seeing the face of the *Shekhinah* is, in the final analysis, gazing on the exposed corona of the phallus. There are, to be sure, a significant number of passages that describe the vision of God as a beholding of the sacred union above. It is obvious from these settings as well that the ejaculated phallus is the object of vision. I have argued, moreover, that even in those texts that speak of God as male and female it is necessary to understand the use of gender imagery in its proper cultural context; when that is done it becomes clear that the woman is part of the man. The most intense descriptions of sexual copulation in kabbalistic literature are predicated on the ontological reintegration of the feminine in the masculine. That is, heterosexuality is transformed by kabbalistic symbolism into a homoeroticism: the union of male and female is a reconstitution of the male. The female is accorded contradictory roles: on the one hand, it is the task of the female to conceal the male organ, but on the other, when the male organ protrudes it is the female aspect of the phallus that is visually present and apprehended by the ocular gaze of the mystic.

The question of homoeroticism is central to understanding the phenomenological structure underlying the mystical vision of God in the kabbalistic sources. This vision is predicated on a structural homology between the mystic and the divine: by being integrated into the phallus—a process I referred to as the constitution of the divine face—the kabbalist sees that which is cloaked in utter secrecy. The ecstasy underlying this ontic integration is experienced in different ways by the mystic. One of the most important modes of experience is that of the crown. The crown is, simultaneously, the ontological referent of the vision, that is, the *Shekhinah* or the corona of the phallus, and the phenomenal datum of the experience. The crowning must be understood as the figural assimilation of the kabbalist into the divine phallus. By seeing the crown the kabbalist becomes the crown and thereby facilitates the reconstitution of the androgynous phallus. In structure, therefore, mystical vision parallels the rite of circumcision.

The wheel of exegesis makes its widest turn in zoharic literature, wherein the Torah itself is identified as the anthropomorphic form of God that is visualized in the imagination. This identification provides the conceptual background for the mystical praxis of seeing God in the text. The iconic/visual dimension of the prophetic tradition is here placed within a distinctively hermeneutical framework. The convergence of the revelatory and interpretative modes collapses any historical divide separating prophet and exegete. Indeed, the task of exegesis is thoroughly prophetic. I have shown, moreover, that in the relevant zoharic passages textual study is presented as an intensively erotic experience. The exegete stands in the position of the phallic *Yesod* and the text corresponds to the feminine *Shekhinah*. But here again it is necessary to point out that the feminine is localized as part of the phallus. When one appreciates this transmutation of gender symbols, it becomes evident that through textual study the kabbalist is visually contemplating the divine phallus. Reading is a double mirroring: the words of Scripture are a reflex of the *Shekhinah* which, in turn, is a reflex of *Yesod*. The hermeneutical task is thus to penetrate beneath the textual surface so that one beholds the phallus of God, the ontic source of secret gnosis. That which is hidden from sight comes into view for the kabbalist who has been transformed by visually contemplating the theophanic image of God reflected in Scripture through the mechanism of the phallic imagination. The hermeneutical circle is inscribed in the biblical verse "From my flesh I will see God," that is, from the sign of the covenant engraved on the penis the mystic can imaginatively visualize the divine phallus. The movement of the imagination is from the human body to God and from God back to the human body again.

Thus my path returns to Blake:

> The Eternal Body of Man is The Imagination.
>   God Himself
> that is
>   The Divine Body . . .

• APPENDIX •

MANUSCRIPTS CITED

Bar Ilan, University Library. 47.
Berlin, Staatsbibliothek. Or. Quat. 833, 942.
Budapest, Kaufmann collection, Rabbinerseminar. 238.
Cambridge, University Library. Heb. Add. 405, 671.
Florence, Biblioteca Medicea-Laurenziana. 44.13.
Jerusalem, Jewish National and University Library (JNUL). Hebrew 8°397.
Jerusalem, Sassoon collection. 290.
Jerusalem, Schocken Library. 6, 14.
London, British Museum. 737, 27,000.
Milan, Biblioteca Ambrosiana. 62, 70.
Moscow, Guenzberg collection, Russian State Library. 90, 131, 366, 775.
Munich, Bayerische Staatsbibliothek. 22, 40, 47, 54, 56, 92, 215, 221, 357, 408.
New York, Columbia University, Butler Library. X893 Ab92.
New York, Jewish Theological Seminary of America (JTSA). ENA 3021; Mic. 1370, 1609, 1690, 1727, 1731, 1737, 1777, 1786, 1801, 1805, 1815, 1822, 1831, 1842, 1869, 1878, 1885, 1887, 1892, 1897, 1915, 2156, 2194, 2206, 2325, 2411, 2430, 2469, 2532, 8115, 8122, 8128, 8558.
Oxford, Bodleian Library. Neubauer 352, 1097, 1102, 1204, 1206, 1208, 1531, 1551, 1565, 1566, 1567, 1568, 1580, 1582, 1597, 1598, 1610, 1626, 1628, 1630, 1637, 1638, 1642, 1645, 1791, 1925, 1938, 1945, 1947, 1953, 1954, 1960, 2256, 2257, 2286, 2396, 2456, 2575; Opp. Add. 4° 183.
Paris, Bibliothèque Nationale (BN). Héb. 188, 680, 772, 774, 817, 824, 825, 839, 843, 850, 1408.
Parma, Biblioteca Palatina. 2784 (De Rossi 1390), 3531.
Philadelphia, Dropsie University. 436.
Rome, Biblioteca Angelica. 46.
Vatican, Biblioteca Apostolica. Ebr. 171, 209, 211, 228, 231, 236, 283, 291, 295, 300, 428, 431, 441, 460.

• SELECT BIBLIOGRAPHY •

PRIMARY SOURCES CITED

The basic classics of pre-modern Jewish literature, such as the Bible, Mishnah, Tosefta, Babylonian and Palestinian Talmuds, have been omitted from this list. Titles of Hebrew editions with English-language title pages are given in English.

Abraham bar Azriel. *ʿArugat ha-Bosem.* Edited by Ephraim E. Urbach. 4 vols. Jerusalem: Mekize Nirdamim, 1939–63.

Abraham bar Ḥiyya. *Megillat ha-Megalleh.* Edited by Adolf Posnanski, annotated and expanded by Julius Guttmann. Berlin, 1924.

Abraham ben Eliezer Halevi. *Hor'ah ʿal She'elat ha-Mal'akhim.* Printed by G. Falk. *Kerem Ḥemed* 9 (1856): 141–148.

———. *Masoret ha-Ḥokhmah.* MSS New York–JTSA Mic. 1737, Vatican 431.

Abulafia, Abraham. *Ḥayye ha-Nefesh.* MS Munich 408.

———. *Ḥayye ha-ʿOlam ha-Ba'.* MS Oxford-Bodleian 1582.

———. *Mafteaḥ ha-Shemot.* MS New York–JTSA 1897.

———. *'Oṣar ʿEden Ganuz.* MS Oxford-Bodleian 1580.

———. *Sefer ha-Ḥesheq.* MS New York–JTSA Mic. 1801.

———. *Sefer ha-Melammed.* MS Paris–BN 680.

———. *Sitre Torah.* MS Paris–BN 774.

———. *We-Zot li-Yehudah.* In *Auswahl Kabbalistischen Mystik,* edited by Adolf Jellinek, pt. 1. Leipzig, 1853.

Abulafia, Ṭodros. *'Oṣar ha-Kavod ha-Shalem.* Warsaw, 1897. Reprint, Jerusalem: Maqor, 1970.

———. *Shaʿar ha-Razim.* Edited by Michal Kushnir-Oron. Jerusalem: Bialik Institute, 1989.

'Aggadat Bereshit. Edited by Solomon Buber. Cracow, 1903.

Albo, Joseph. *Sefer ha-ʿIqqarim.* Warsaw, 1877.

Alemanno, Yoḥanan. *Shir ha-Ma'alot li-Shelomo.* Published as *Shaʿar ha-Ḥesheq.* Livorno, 1790. Reprint, Halberstadt, 1862. Critical edition by Arthur M. Lesley, "*The Song of Solomon's Ascents* by Yohanan Alemanno: Love and Human Perfection According to a Jewish Colleague of Giovanni Pico della Mirandola." Ph.D. diss., University of California, Berkeley, 1976.

Angeleṭ, Joseph. *Kaf-dalet Sodot.* MSS Oxford-Bodleian 1630, New York–JTSA Mic. 1915.

———. *Livnat ha-Sappir.* MS British Museum 27,000.

Asher ben David. *Perush Shem ha-Meforash.* Edited by M. Ḥasidah. *Ha-Segullah* 1 no. 2 (1934): 1–15.

'Avot de-Rabbi Natan. Edited by Solomon Schechter. Vienna, 1887.

Azikri, Eleazar ben Moses. *Milei di-Shemaya.* Edited by Mordechai Pachter. Tel-Aviv, 1991.

———. *Sefer Ḥaredim.* Jerusalem, 1966.

Azriel ben Menaḥem of Gerona. *Perush ha-'Aggadot le-Rabbi 'Azri'el*. Edited by Isaiah Tishby. Jerusalem: Mekize Nirdamim, 1945.

———. *Perush le-Sefer Yeṣirah*. In *Kitve Ramban*, edited by Ḥayyim Chavel, vol. 2. Jerusalem: Mosad ha-Rav Kook, 1967.

———. "Seridim ḥadashim mi-kitve R. 'Azri'el mi-Gerona." Edited by Gershom Scholem. In *Sefer Zikkaron le-'Asher Gulak we-li-Shemu'el Klein*. Jerusalem, 1942.

———. *Sha'ar ha-Sho'el: Perush 'Eser Sefirot 'al Derekh She'elah u-Teshuvah*. Printed in Meir ibn Gabbai, *Derekh 'Emunah*.

Azulai, Abraham. *Ḥesed le-'Avraham*. Vilna, 1877.

Bachrach, Naftali. *'Emeq ha-Melekh*. Amsterdam, 1648.

Baḥya ben Asher. *Be'ur 'al ha-Torah*. Edited by Ḥayyim Chavel. 5th ed. 3 vols. Jerusalem: Mosad ha-Rav Kook, 1981.

Batte Midrashot. Edited by Solomon A. Wertheimer. New ed. with additions and corrections by Abraham Wertheimer. 2 vols. Jerusalem: Ketav wa-Sefer, 1980.

Benjamin ben Abraham. *Perush 'al Midrash 'Otiyyot de-R. 'Aqiva'*. MS Vatican 291.

Campanton, Judah ben Samuel. *'Arba'ah Qinyanim*. MS New York–JTSA Mic. 2532.

———. *Leqaḥ Ṭov*. MS Oxford-Bodleian 1642.

Cordovero, Moses. *Pardes Rimmonim*. Munkacz, 1906. Reprint, Jerusalem, 1962.

David ben Aaron Ḥazzan. *'Iggeret 'Aseret Monim*. MS Oxford-Bodleian 1637.

David ben Isaac. *Migdal David*. MS Jerusalem-JNUL Heb. 8°397.

Donnolo, Shabbetai. *Sefer Ḥakhmoni*. In *Il Commento di Sabbatai Donnolo sul Libro della Creazione*, edited by David Castelli. Florence, 1880.

Eleazar ben Judah of Worms. *Hilkhot ha-Kavod*. MS Oxford-Bodleian 2575.

———. *Ḥokhmat ha-Nefesh*. Bene-Beraq, 1987.

———. *Perush ha-Merkavah*. MS Paris–BN 850.

———. *Perush Sefer Yeṣirah le-Rabbi 'Ele'azar mi-Worms*. Przemysl, 1883.

———. *Perush Sodot ha-Tefillah*, MSS Paris–BN 772, Oxford-Bodleian 1204.

———. *Sefer ha-Ḥokhmah*. MS Oxford-Bodleian 1568.

———. *Sefer ha-Roqeaḥ*. Jerusalem, 1967.

———. *Sefer ha-Shem*. MSS British Museum 737, New York–JTSA Mic. 1885, Oxford-Bodleian 1638.

———. *Sha'are ha-Sod ha-Yiḥud we-ha-'Emunah*. Edited by Joseph Dan. In *Temirin: Texts and Studies in Kabbalah and Hasidism*, edited by Israel Weinstock, vol. 1. Jerusalem: Mosad ha-Rav Kook, 1972.

———. *Shirat ha-Roke'aḥ: The Poems of Rabbi Eleazar ben Yehudah of Worms*. Edited by Isaac Meiseles. Jerusalem, 1993 (in Hebrew).

———. *Sod 'Eser Hawwayot*. MSS Paris–BN 825, Munich 92.

———. *Sode Razayya*. Edited by Israel Kamelhar. Bilgoraj, 1936.

———. *Sode Razayya*. Edited by Shalom Weiss. Jerusalem: Shaarey Ziv Institute, 1991.

———, wrongly attributed. *Perush ha-Roqeaḥ 'al ha-Torah*. Edited by Chaim Konyevsky. 2nd rev. ed. 3 vols. Bene-Beraq: Yeshivat Ohel Yosef, 1986.

Eleazar ben Moses ha-Darshan. *Sefer ha-Gimaṭri'ot*. MS Munich 221.

Eleazar ha-Bavli. *Dīwān*. Edited by Ḥayyim Brody. Jerusalem, 1935.

Elḥanan ben Yaqar. *Sod ha-Sodot*. In *Texts in the Theology of German Pietism*, edited by Joseph Dan. Jerusalem: Akadamon, 1977 (in Hebrew).

Elijah ben Solomon Zalman. *Be'ur ha-Gera le-Sifra di-Ṣeni'uta*. Vilna, 1882.

Ephraim ben Shimshon. *Perush Rabbenu 'Efrayim 'al ha-Torah*. Edited by Ezra Korach and Zvi Leitner, with Chaim Konyevsky. Jerusalem, 1992.

Ezra ben Solomon of Gerona. *Perush ha-'Aggadot*. MSS Vatican 295, 441. Partially printed in *Liqquṭe Shikheḥah u-Fe'ah*. Ferrara, 1556.

———. *Perush le-Shir ha-Shirim*. In *Kitve Ramban,* edited by Ḥayyim Chavel, vol. 2. Jerusalem, Mosad ha-Rav Kook, 1967.

Gikatilla, Joseph. *Perush ha-Merkavah*. MS New York–JTSA Mic. 2156.

———. *Sha'are 'Orah*. Edited by Joseph Ben-Shlomo. 2 vols. Jerusalem: Bialik Institute, 1981.

———. *Sod ha-Ḥashmal*. Printed in *Arze ha-Levanon*. Venice, 1601.

Habermann, Abraham M., ed. *Ḥadashim Gam Yeshanim: Texts Old and New Collected from Various Manuscripts*. Jerusalem: Rubin Mass, 1975.

———, ed. *Shire ha-Yiḥud we-ha-Kavod*. Jerusalem, 1948.

Halevi, Judah. *Dīwān des Abu-l-Hasān Jehuda ha-Levi*. Edited by Ḥayyim Brody. 4 vols. Westmead, England: Gregg, 1971.

———. *Kitāb al-Radd wa-'l-Dalīl fī'l-Dīn al-Dhalīl*. Edited by David H. Baneth and Ḥaggai Ben-Shammai. Jerusalem: Magnes, 1977.

———. *Sefer ha-Kuzari*. Translated by Yehuda Even-Shmuel. Tel-Aviv: Dvir, 1972.

———. *Sefer ha-Kuzari*. Translated by Yehuda ibn Tibbon. Warsaw: Goldman, 1880.

Hamon, Obadiah. *Sefer Levush Malkhut*. MS Oxford-Bodleian 1597.

Ḥayyat, Judah. *Minḥat Yehudah,* commentary to *Ma'arekhet ha-'Elohut*. Mantua, 1558. Reprint, Jerusalem: Maqor, 1963.

Ḥayyim ben Benjamin of Genazzano. *'Iggeret Ḥamudot*. Edited by A. W. Greenup. London, 1912.

Ḥayyim ha-Kohen of Nikolsburg. *'Avodat Kehunah*. Jerusalem, 1965.

Hekhalot Zuṭarti. Edited by Rachel Elior. *Jerusalem Studies in Jewish Thought,* Supplement 1. Jerusalem, 1982.

Horowitz, Isaiah. *Shene Luḥot ha-Berit*. Amsterdam, 1598.

Horowitz, Pineḥas Eliyahu. *Sefer ha-Berit ha-Shalem*. Jerusalem, 1990.

Ibn Ezra, Abraham. *Abraham ibn Ezra's Two Commentaries on the Minor Prophets*. Vol. 1, Hosea, Joel, Amos. Edited by Uriel Simon. Ramat-Gan: Bar-Ilan University Press, 1989 (in Hebrew).

———. *Iggeret Ḥay ben Mekitz*. Edited by Israel Levin. Tel-Aviv, 1983.

———. *Perushe ha-Torah le-Rabbenu 'Avraham 'ibn 'Ezra*. Edited by Asher Weiser. 2d ed. 3 vols. Jerusalem: Mosad ha-Rav Kook, 1977.

———. *The Religious Poems of Abraham ibn Ezra*. Edited by Israel Levin. 2 vols. Jerusalem: Israel Academy of Sciences and Humanities, 1975–80 (in Hebrew).

———. "Ten Poems of Rabbi Abraham ibn Ezra." Edited by A. M. Habermann. In *Sefer Ḥayyim Schirmann,* edited by Shraga Abramson and Aaron Mirsky. Jerusalem, 1970 (in Hebrew).

———. *Sefer ha-Shem*. Edited by G. H. Lippmann. Fürth, 1834.

———. *Sefer Ṣaḥot*. Fürth, 1827.

Ibn Ezra, Moses. *Shire ha-Ḥol*. 2 vols. Edited by Ḥayyim Brody. Berlin, 1934.

Ibn Gabbai, Meir. *'Avodat ha-Qodesh*. 2 vols. Jerusalem, 1992.

———. *Derekh 'Emunah*. Warsaw, 1890. Reprint, Jerusalem, 1967.

Ibn Gabirol, Solomon. *Liqquṭim mi-Sefer Meqor Ḥayyim*. Translated by Shem Ṭov ibn Falaquera. Published by Salomon Munk in *Mélanges de philosophie juive et arabe*. Bilingual ed., Hebrew and Arabic. Paris, 1859.

———. *The Liturgical Poetry of Rabbi Solomon ibn Gabirol*. Edited by Dov Jarden. 2d ed. 2 vols. Jerusalem, 1977–79 (in Hebrew).

———. *Meqor Ḥayyim*. Translated by Jacob Blubstein. Edited by Abraham Zifroni. Jerusalem, 1926.

Ibn Gaon, Shem Ṭov ben Abraham. *Badde ha-'Aron u-Migdal Ḥananel*. Facsimile edition, based on MS Paris–BN, 840. Jerusalem, 1977.

Ibn Ghayyat, Isaac. *The Poems of Isaac Ibn Ghayyat*. Edited by Yonah David. Jerusalem, 1987 (in Hebrew).

Ibn Paquda, Baḥya. *Sefer Torat Hovot ha-Levatot / Kitāb al-Hidāya ilā Farā'id al-Qulūb*. Translated by Joseph Kafiḥ. Bilingual ed. Jerusalem, 1973.

———, formerly attributed. *Sefer Torot ha-Nefesh*. Translated and edited by Isaac Broydé. Paris: Levinsohn-Kilemnik, 1896.

Ibn Sahula, Isaac. *Commentary on Canticles*. Edited by Arthur Green. *Jerusalem Studies in Jewish Thought* 6 no. 3–4 (1987): 393–491 (in Hebrew).

Ibn Sahula, Meir ben Solomon, wrongly attributed (now attributed to Joshua ibn Shuʿeib). *Be'ur le-Ferush ha-Ramban*. Vilna, 1927.

Ibn Tamim, Dunash. *Sefer Yeṣirah with Commentary by Dunash ben Tamim*. Edited by Menasseh Greenberg. London, 1902 (in Hebrew).

'Iggeret ha-Qodesh. In *Kitve Ramban,* edited by Ḥayyim Chavel, vol. 2. Jerusalem, Mosad ha-Rav Kook, 1967.

Isaac ben Judah ha-Levi. *Paʿaneaḥ Raza'*. Warsaw, 1860. Reprint, Jerusalem, 1980.

Isaac ben Samuel of Acre. "The Commentary of R. Isaac of Acre to the First Chapter of *Sefer Yeṣirah*." Edited by Gershom Scholem. *Qiryat Sefer* 31 (1955–56): 379–396 (in Hebrew).

———. *'Oṣar Ḥayyim*. MS Moscow-Guenzberg 775.

———. *Sefer Me'irat ʿEinayim*. Critical edition, by Amos Goldreich. Jerusalem: Akadamon, 1981.

Isaac ben Ṭodros. *Perush ha-Maḥzor*. MS Paris–BN 839.

Isaac the Blind. *Perush Sefer Yeṣirah*. Appendix to Gershom Scholem, *The Kabbalah in Provence,* edited by Rivka Schatz. Jerusalem: Akadamon, 1970 (in Hebrew). Additional MSS consulted: Berlin Or. 942, New York–JTSA Mic. 2325.

Isaiah ben Joseph. *Ḥayye Nefesh*. MS New York–JTSA Mic. 1842.

Jacob ben Jacob ha-Kohen. "The Commentary on Ezekiel's Chariot by R. Jacob ben Jacob ha-Kohen of Castile." Edited by Asi Farber. Master's thesis, Hebrew University, 1978 (in Hebrew).

———. *Perush ha-'Otiyyot*. Edited by Gershom Scholem. In "The Traditions of R. Jacob and R. Isaac ben Jacob ha-Kohen," *Maddaʿe ha-Yahadut* 2 (1927): 201–219.

———. *Sefer ha-'Orah,* MSS Milan-Ambrosiana 62, Schocken 14, MS Florence Medicea-Laurenziana 44.14, New York–JTSA Mic. 1869, Bar Ilan 47, Vatican 428.

Jacob ben Sheshet. *Sefer ha-'Emunah we-ha-Biṭṭaḥon*. In *Kitve Ramban,* edited by Ḥayyim Chavel, vol. 2. Jerusalem: Mosad ha-Rav Kook, 1967.

———. *Sefer Meshiv Devarim Nekhoḥim*. Edited by Georges Vajda. Jerusalem: Israel Academy of Sciences and Humanities, 1968.

Jellinek, Adolf, ed. *Bet ha-Midrash*. 3d ed. 6 vols. Jerusalem: Wahrmann, 1967.

Jonathan. *'Or ha-Sekhel*. MS New York–JTSA Mic. 1831.

Joseph ben Shalom Ashkenazi. *A Kabbalistic Commentary of Rabbi Yoseph ben Shalom Ashkenazi on Genesis Rabbah*. Edited by Moshe Hallamish. Jerusalem: Magnes, 1984 (in Hebrew).

———. *Perush Sefer Yeṣirah* (attributed in this edition to Abraham ben David). In *Sefer Yeṣirah*. Jerusalem, 1962.

Joseph of Hamadan. "A Critical Edition of the *Sefer Ṭaʿamey ha-Miẓwoth* ('Book of Reasons of the Commandments') Attributed to Isaac ibn Farhi / Section I—Positive Commandments." Edited by Menachem Meier. Ph.D. diss., Brandeis University, 1974.

———. "Joseph of Hamadan's *Sefer Tashak:* Critical Text Edition with Introduction." Edited by Jeremy Zwelling. Ph.D. diss., Brandeis University, 1975.

Judah ben Barzillai al-Barceloni. *Perush Sefer Yeṣirah.* Edited by Solomon J. Halberstam. Berlin: Mekize Nirdamim, 1885. Reprint, Jerusalem: Maqor, 1970.

Judah ben Samuel he-Ḥasid. "The Book of Angels of Rabbi Judah the Pious." Edited by Joseph Dan. *Daʿat* 2–3 (1978–79): 99–120 (in Hebrew).

———. *Sefer Ḥasidim.* Edited by Jehuda Wistinetzki, with additions by Jacob Freimann. Frankfurt am Main, 1924.

Judah ben Yaqar. *Perush ha-Tefillot we-ha-Berakhot.* Edited by Shmuel Yerushalmi. 2d ed. Jerusalem: Me'ore Yisra'el, 1979.

Koriat, Judah. *Ma'or wa-Shemesh.* Livorno, 1839.

Maʿarekhet ha-'Elohut. Mantua, 1558. Reprint, Jerusalem: Maqor, 1963.

Maimonides. *See* Moses ben Maimon.

Maḥzor la-Yamim ha-Nora'im. Edited by Ernst Daniel Goldschmidt. 2 vols. Jerusalem, 1970.

Maḥzor Romania. Constantinople, 1574.

Megillat 'Aḥimaʿaṣ. Edited by Benjamin Klar. Jerusalem: Sifre Tarshish, 1974.

Mekhilta de-Rabbi Ishmael. Edited by Ḥayyim S. Horovitz and Israel A. Rabin. Jerusalem: Wahrmann, 1970.

Mekhilta de-Rabbi Shimʿon bar Yoḥai. Edited by Jacob N. Epstein and Ezra Z. Melamed. Jerualem, 1955.

Menaḥem Azariah of Fano. *Kanfe Yonah.* Koretz, 1776.

Midrash 'Aggadah. Edited by Solomon Buber. Vienna, 1884.

Midrash Bereshit Rabbah. Edited by Julius Theodor and Chanoch Albeck. 2d ed. 3 vols. Jerusalem: Wahrmann, 1965.

Midrash 'Eikhah Rabbah. Edited by Solomon Buber. Vilna: Rom, 1899.

Midrash ha-Gadol on Genesis. Edited by Mordecai Margulies. Jerusalem: Mosad ha-Rav Kook, 1975.

Midrash ha-Gadol on Leviticus. Edited by Adin Steinsaltz. Jerusalem: Mosad ha-Rav Kook, 1976.

Midrash Mishle, Edited by Buron L. Visotzky. New York: Jewish Theological Seminary of America, 1990.

Midrash Rabbah Shir ha-Shirim. Edited by Shimshon Dunanski. Jerusalem & Tel Aviv: Dvir, 1980.

Midrash Rabbi Shimʿon ha-Ṣaddiq. MSS Munich 215, Oxford-Bodleian 1960. Printed in Moses Boṭarel's commentary on *Sefer Yeṣirah.*

Midrash Samuel. Edited by Solomon Buber. Cracow, 1893.

Midrash Tanḥuma. Jerusalem: Lewin-Epstein, 1965.

Midrash Tanḥuma. Edited by Solomon Buber. 2 vols. New York: Sefer, 1946.

Midrash Tehillim. Edited by Solomon Buber. Vilna, 1891. Reprint, Jerusalem, 1966.

Midrash Wayyikra Rabbah. Edited by Mordecai Margulies. New York: Jewish Theological Seminary of America, 1993.

Midrash Zuṭa ʿal Shir ha-Shirim, Rut, 'Eikhah we-Qohelet. Edited by Solomon Buber. Vilna: Rom, 1925.

Moses ben Eleazar ha-Darshan. *Sefer ha-Qomah*. MSS Rome-Angelica 46, Milan-Ambrosiana 70.

Moses ben Maimon (Maimonides). *The Guide of the Perplexed*. Translated by Shlomo Pines. Chicago: University of Chicago Press, 1963. Hebrew translation by Samuel ibn Tibbon, *Moreh Nevukhim*. Jerusalem: Monzon, 1960.

———. *Introduction to Logic in the Hebrew Version of Moses ibn Tibbon*. Edited by Leon Roth, collated with the manuscript fragments of the Arabic original by David H. Baneth. Jerusalem, 1965 (in Hebrew).

———. *Mishneh Torah*. New York: Schlusinger, 1947.

———, formerly attributed. *De Beatitudine capita duo R. Mosi ben Maimon Adscripta*. Edited and translated by H. S. Davidowitz, with additional notes by David H. Baneth. Jerusalem: Mekize Nirdamim, 1939.

Moses ben Naḥman (Naḥmanides). *Kitve Ramban*. Edited by Ḥayyim Chavel. 2 vols. Jerusalem: Mosad ha-Rav Kook, 1967.

———. *Perushe ha-Torah le-R. Mosheh ben Naḥman*. Edited by Ḥayyim Chavel. 2 vols. Jerusalem: Mosad ha-Rav Kook, 1959–60.

Moses ben Shem Tov de León. *The Book of the Pomegranate: Moses de León's Sefer ha-Rimmon*. Edited by Elliot R. Wolfson. Brown Judaic Studies, no. 144. Atlanta: Scholars Press, 1988 (in Hebrew with English introduction).

———. Fragment of an untitled work. MS Munich 47.

———. *Mishkan ha-ʿEdut*. MS Berlin Or. Quat. 833.

———. "*Sefer ha-Mishkal:* Text and Study." Edited by Jochanan H. A. Wijnhoven. Ph.D. diss., Brandeis University, 1964.

———. *Shaʿar Yesod ha-Merkavah*. MSS New York–JTSA 1805, Vatican 283. Printed in Meir ibn Gabbai, *ʿAvodat ha-Qodesh*.

———. *Sheqel ha-Qodesh*. Edited by A. W. Greenup. London, 1911.

———. *Shushan ʿEdut*. Edited by Gershom Scholem. *Qoveṣ ʿal Yad*, n.s., 8 (1976): 325–370.

———. *Sod ʿEser Sefirot Belimah*. Edited by Gershom Scholem. *Qoveṣ ʿal Yad*, n.s., 8 (1976): 371–384.

Moses of Burgos. *Perush Shem Mem-Bet*. MS Oxford-Bodleian 1565. Printed in *Liqquṭim me-Rav Hai Gaon*. Warsaw, 1798.

Moses of Kiev. *Shoshan Sodot*. Koretz, 1784.

Naḥmanides. *See* Moses ben Naḥman.

ʿObadyah Maimonides. *The Treatise of the Pool* (*Al-Maqāla al-Ḥawḍiyya*). Edited and translated by Paul Fenton. London: Ocatgon, 1981.

Otzar ha-Geonim. Edited by Benjamin M. Lewin. 13 vols. Jerusalem, 1928–62.

Perush ʾAshkenazi li-Tehillim. MS Oxford-Bodleian 1551.

Perush ʿEser Sefirot. MS Milan-Ambrosiana 62.

Perush ʿEser Sefirot. MS Oxford-Bodleian 1598.

Perush ʿEser Sefirot. MS Oxford-Bodleian 1628.

Perush ha-ʾAderet we-ha-ʾEmunah. MS Vatican 228.

Perush Hafṭarah. MS Berlin Or. 942.

Perush ha-Merkavah. MS Oxford-Bodleian 1938.

Perush ha-Tefillot. MSS Berlin Or. Quat. 942, Oxford-Bodleian 1925, Paris–BN 188.

Perush Lamed-Bet Netivot Ḥokhmah. MS New York–JTSA 8558.

Perush Sefer Yeṣirah. MS Paris–BN 680.

Perush Shem ʿAyin-Bet. MSS New York–JTSA Mic. 8115, Cambridge Heb. Add. 671, Oxford-Bodleian 1938.

Perush Shem ha-Meforash. MSS New York–JTSA Mic. 1805, 1731, 2194.

Pesiqta de-Rav Kahana. Edited by Bernard Mandelbaum. 2 vols. New York: Jewish Theological Seminary of America, 1962.

Pesiqta Rabbati. Edited by Meir Friedmann. Vienna: Kaiser, 1880. Reprint, Tel-Aviv, 1963.

Pirqe Rabbi 'Eli'ezer. Edited by David Luria. Warsaw, 1852. Reprint, New York: Om, 1946.

Recanaṭi, Menaḥem. *Perush 'al ha-Torah.* Jerusalem, 1961.

———. *Sefer Ṭa'ame ha-Miṣwot.* MS Vatican 209.

Re'uyot Yeḥezqel. Edited by Ithamar Gruenwald, "The Visions of Ezekiel: Critical Text and Commentary." In *Temirin: Texts and Studies in Kabbala and Hasidism,* edited by Israel Weinstock, vol. 1. Jerusalem: Mosad ha-Rav Kook, 1972 (in Hebrew).

Saadiah ben Joseph Gaon. *Perushe Rabbenu Se'adyah Ga'on 'al-ha-Torah.* Edited by Joseph Kafiḥ. Jerusalem: Mosad ha-Rav Kook, 1963.

———. *Sefer ha-'Emunot we-ha-De'ot (Kitāb al-Amānāt wa'l-I'tiqādāt).* Edited by Joseph Kafiḥ. Jerusalem, 1970.

———. *Sefer Yeṣirah (Kitāb al-Mabādi) 'im Perush R. Se'adyah bar Yosef Fayyumi.* Edited by Joseph Kafiḥ. Jerusalem, 1970.

———. *Siddur R. Saadja Gaon: Kitāb Gāmi' Aṣ-ṣalawā Wat-Tasābīh.* Edited by Israel Davidson, Simha Assaf, and Issachar Joel. 5th ed. Jerusalem: Mekize Nirdamim, 1985.

Schirmann, Jefim (Ḥayyim), ed. *Hebrew Poetry in Spain and Provence.* 2 vols. Jerusalem: Bialik Institute, 1956 (in Hebrew).

———, ed. *New Hebrew Poems from the Genizah.* Jerusalem: Israel Academy of Sciences and Humanities, 1965 (in Hebrew).

Seder 'Avodat Yisra'el. Edited by Seligman Baer. Berlin, 1937.

Seder 'Eliyahu Rabbah we-Seder 'Eliyahu Zuṭa. Edited by Meir Friedmann. Vienna: Achiasaf, 1902.

Sefer ha-Bahir. Edited by Reuven Margaliot. 2d ed. Jerusalem: Mosad ha-Rav Kook, 1978.

Sefer ha-Ḥayyim. In *Texts in the Theology of German Pietism,* edited by Joseph Dan. Jerusalem: Akadamon, 1977 (in Hebrew).

Sefer ha-Ḥesheq. Lemberg, 1865 = Ashkenazi Commentary on the names of Meṭaṭron extant in MSS Cambridge Heb. Add. 405; Oxford-Bodleian 2286; Moscow-Guenzberg 90; New York–JTSA 2206.

Sefer ha-Malbush. MS Oxford-Bodleian 1960.

Sefer ha-Malkhut. Casablanca, 1930.

Sefer ha-Ne'elam. MS Paris–BN 817.

Sefer ha-Temunah. Lemberg, 1892.

Sefer ha-Yiḥud (Iyyun circle). MSS Paris–BN 825, Vatican 211.

Sefer ha-Yiḥud. MS Vatican 236.

Sefer ha-Yiḥud ha-'Amiti. MS New York–JTSA Mic. 1822.

Sefer Josippon. Edited by David Flusser. 2 vols. Jerusalem: Bialik Institute, 1980–81.

Sefer Razi'el. Amsterdam, 1701.

Sefer Tagi. MS Oxford-Bodleian 1566.

Sefer Yeṣirah. Edited by Ithamar Gruenwald, "A Preliminary Critical Edition of *Sefer Yeẓira.*" *Israel Oriental Studies* 1 (1971): 132–177.

Shir ha-Yiḥud: The Hymn of Unity with the Kabbalistic Commentary of R. Yom Ṭov

Lipmann Muelhausen. Thiengen, 1560. Facsimile reprint, Jerusalem: Magnes, 1981 (in Hebrew).

Siddur of Rabbi Solomon ben Samson of Garmaise, including the Siddur of the Ḥaside Ashkenaz. Edited by Moshe Hershler. Jerusalem, 1971 (in Hebrew).

Sifra on Leviticus. Edited by Louis Finkelstein. 5 vols. New York: Jewish Theological Seminary of America, 1983–91.

Sifre on Deuteronomy. Edited by Louis Finkelstein. New York: Jewish Theological Seminary of America, 1969.

Sifre on Numbers. Edited by Ḥayyim S. Horovitz. Jerusalem: Wahrmann, 1966.

Simeon bar Samuel. *'Adam Sikhli*. Thiengen, 1560.

Sod 'Eser Sefirot we-Sod ha-Gewanim. MS Vatican 171.

Sod ha-Qeshet. MS New York–JTSA Mic. 1887.

Sod 'Ilan ha-'Aṣilut le-R. Yiṣḥaq: Qunṭres mi-Masoret shel Sefer ha-Temunah. Edited by Gershom Scholem. *Qoveṣ 'al Yad*, n.s., 5 (1951): 64–102.

Sod we-Yesod ha-Qadmoni. MS Munich 54.

Sod Yedi'at ha-Meṣi'ut. MS Jerusalem-Schocken, Kabbalah 6.

Taku, Moses. *Ketav Tamim*. Edited by Raphael Kirchheim. *'Oṣar Neḥmad* 3 (1860): 54–99. Facsimile edition of MS Paris H711, with introduction by Joseph Dan. Jerusalem: Dinur Center, 1984.

3 Enoch, or the Hebrew Book of Enoch. Translated and edited by Hugo Odeberg. Cambridge, 1928. Reprint with prolegomenon by Jonas C. Greenfield, New York: Ktav, 1973.

3 (Hebrew Apocalypse of) Enoch. Translated by Philip S. Alexander. In *The Old Testament Pseudepigrapha*, edited by James H. Charlesworth, vol. 1. Garden City, N.Y.: Doubleday, 1983.

Tiqqune Zohar. Edited by Reuven Margaliot. 2d ed. Jerusalem: Mosad ha-Rav Kook, 1978.

Ṭobiah bar Eliezer, *Midrash Leqaḥ Ṭov*. Edited by Solomon Buber. 2 vols. Lemberg, 1888.

Toledot ha-Ari. Edited by Meir Benayahu. Jerusalem: Makhon Ben-Zevi, 1967.

Tosafot ha-Shalem: Commentary on the Bible. Edited by Jacob Gellis. 8 vols. Jerusalem: Mifal Tosafot Hashalem, 1982–89 (in Hebrew).

Treves, Naftali Herz. *Siddur Mal'ah ha-'Areṣ De'ah*. Thiengen, 1560.

Vital, Ḥayyim. *'Eṣ Ḥayyim*. Jerusalem, 1910.

———. *Ketavim Ḥadashim le-Rabbenu Ḥayyim Vital*. Jerusalem: Ahavat Shalom, 1988.

———. *'Olat Tamid*. Jerusalem, 1907.

———. *Sefer ha-Ḥezyonot*. Edited by Aaron Aescoli. Jerusalem: Mosad ha-Rav Kook, 1954.

———. *Sha'ar ha-Kawwanot*. Jerusalem, 1902.

———. *Sha'ar Ruaḥ ha-Qodesh*. Jerusalem, 1879. Reprint, Jerusalem, 1976.

———. *Sha'are Qedushah*. Jerusalem, 1983.

Zohar. Edited by Reuven Margaliot. 6th ed. 3 vols. Jerusalem: Mosad ha-Rav Kook, 1984.

Zohar Ḥadash. Edited by Reuven Margaliot. 2d ed. Jerusalem: Mosad ha-Rav Kook, 1978.

SECONDARY SOURCES CITED

Aalen, Sverre. *Die Begriffe 'Licht' und 'Finsternis' im Alten Testament, im Spätjudentum und im Rabbinismus*. Oslo: Kommisgon Hos Dybwad, 1951.

Aaron, David. "Polemics and Mythology: A Commentary on Chapters 1 and 8 of Bereshit Rabba." Ph.D. diss., Brandeis University, 1991.

Abelson, Joshua. *The Immanence of God in Rabbinical Literature*. London: Macmillan, 1912.

Alexander, Philip S. "The Historical Setting of the Hebrew Book of Enoch." *Journal of Jewish Studies* 28 (1977): 173–180.

Alexander-Frizer, Tamar. *The Pious Sinner: Ethics and Aesthetics in the Medieval Hasidic Narrative*. Tubingen: Mohr, 1991.

Allen, Terry. "Aniconism and Figural Representation in Islamic Art." In *Five Essays on Islamic Art*. Sebastopol, Calif.: Solipsist, 1988.

Allony, Nehemiah. "The Anagramic Orientation of the Hebrew Lexicography in *Sefer Yeṣirah*," in *Temirin: Texts and Studies in Kabbala and Hasidism*, edited by Israel Weinstock, vol. 1. Jerusalem: Mosad ha-Rav Kook, 1972 (in Hebrew).

———. "The Time of Composition of *Sefer Yeṣirah*." In *Temirin* (see above), vol. 2. Jerusalem: Mosad ha-Rav Kook, 1981.

Almond, Philip. *Mystical Experience and Religious Doctrine: An Investigation of the Study of Mysticism in World Religions*. Berlin & New York: Mouton, 1982.

Altmann, Alexander. "*Homo Imago Dei* in Jewish and Christian Theology." *Journal of Religion* 48 (1968): 235–259.

———. *Essays in Jewish Intellectual History*. Hanover: University Press of New England, 1981.

———. "Gnostic Themes in Rabbinic Cosmology." In *Essays in Honour of the Very Rev. Dr. J. H. Hertz, Chief Rabbi . . . on the Occasion of His Seventieth Birthday*, edited by I. Epstein, E. Levine, and C. Roth. London, n.d.

———. "Isaac Israeli's 'Chapter on the Elements' (MS Mantua)." *Journal of Jewish Studies* 7 (1956): 31–57.

———. *Studies in Religious Philosophy and Mysticism*. Ithaca: Cornell University Press, 1969.

Altmann, Alexander, and Samuel Stern. *Isaac Israeli: A Neoplatonic Philosopher of the Early Tenth Century*. Oxford: Clarendon Press, 1958.

Arbman, Ernst. *Ecstasy or Religious Trance: In the Experience of the Ecstatics and from the Psychological Point of View*. 3 vols. Uppsala: Appelberg, 1963–70.

Ariel, David S. "'The Eastern Dawn of Wisdom': The Problem of the Relation between Islamic and Jewish Mysticism." In *Approaches to Judaism in Medieval Times*, edited by David R. Blumenthal, vol. 2. Chico, Calif.: Scholars Press, 1985.

Atkinson, Clarissa W. *Mystic and Pilgrim: The Book and the World of Margery Kempe*. Ithaca: Cornell University Press, 1983.

Atlan, Henri. "Niveaux de signification et athéisme de l'écriture." In *La Bible au présent: Actes du XXIIe Colloque des intellectuels juifs de langue francaise*. Paris: Gallimard, 1982.

Auerbach, Elias. *Mimesis: The Representation of Reality in Western Literature.* Princeton: Princeton University Press, 1953.

Baer, Yitzhak. "The Hebrew Book of Josippon." In *Sefer Dinaburg,* edited by Yitzhak Baer, Julius Guttmann, and Moshe Shovah. Jerusalem: Kiryat Sefer, 1949 (in Hebrew).

———. "The Socioreligious Orientation of 'Sefer Ḥasidim.'" Translated by Jonathan Chipman in *Binah: Studies in Jewish Thought,* edited by Joseph Dan. New York: Praeger, 1989.

Baneth, D. H. "Rabbi Judah Halevi and al-Ghazzālī." *Kenesset* 2 (1942): 311–329 (in Hebrew). Translated in *Studies in Jewish Thought: An Anthology of German Jewish Scholarship,* edited by Alfred Jospe. Detroit: Wayne State University Press, 1981.

Barasch, Moshe. *Icon: Studies in the History of an Idea.* New York: New York University Press, 1992.

Bargebuhr, Frederick P. *Salomo Ibn Gabirol. Ostwestliches Dichtertum.* Wiesbaden: Harrassowitz, 1976.

Barr, James. "The Image of God in the Book of Genesis—A Study of Terminology." *Bulletin of the John Rylands Library* 51 (1968–69): 11–26.

———. "Theophany and Anthropomorphism in the Old Testament." *Supplements to Vetus Testamentum* 7 (1960): 31–38.

Baruzi, Jean. "Introduction à des recherches sur le langage mystique." *Recherches Philosophiques* 1 (1931–32): 66–82.

Bataille, Georges. *Death and Sensuality: A Study of Eroticism and the Taboo.* Translated by Mary Dalwood. New York: Walker, 1962.

Baudissin, Wolf. "'Gott schauen' in der alttestamentlichen Religion." *Archiv für Religionswissenschaft* 18 (1915): 173–239.

Bautier, Anne Marie. "Phantasia-imaginatio: De l'image à l'imaginaire dans les textes du haut Moyen Age." In *Phantasia-Imaginatio: V° Colloquio Internazionale, Roma 9–11 gennaio 1986,* edited by Marta Fattori and Massimo Bianchi. Rome: Edizioni dell'Ateneo, 1988.

Baynes, Norman H. "Idolatry and the Early Church." In *Byzantine Studies and Other Essays.* London: Athlone, 1955.

Beale, Gregory. *The Use of Daniel in Jewish Apocalyptic Literature and in the Revelation of St. John.* Lanham, Md.: University Press of America, 1984.

Benamozegh, Elijah. *Israël et l'humanité: Etude sur le problème de la religion universelle et sa solution.* Paris, 1914.

Benin, Stephen D. *The Footprints of God: Divine Accommodation in Jewish and Christian Thought.* Albany: State University of New York Press, 1993.

———. "The Mutability of an Immutable God: Exegesis and Individual Capacity in the Zohar and Several Christian Sources." *Jerusalem Studies in Jewish Thought* 8 (1989): 67–86 (English section).

Ben-Shammai, Haggai. "Saadya's Goal in His *Commentary on Sefer Yeẓira.*" In *A Straight Path—Studies in Medieval Philosophy and Culture: Essays in Honor of Arthur Hyman,* edited by R. Link-Salinger. Washington, D.C.: Catholic University of America Press, 1988.

Benz, Ernst. *Die Vision Erfahrungsformen und Bilderwelt.* Stuttgart: Klett, 1969.

Betz, Hans D. "Fragments from a Catabasis Ritual in a Greek Magical Papyrus." *History of Religions* 19 (1980): 287–295.

Betz, Otto. "Die Vision des Paulus im Tempel von Jerusalem. APg 22.17–21 als Beitrag zur Deutung des Damaskuserlebnisses." In *Verborum Veritas: Festschrift für Gustav*

Stählin zum 70. Geburtstag, edited by Otto Böchler and Klaus Haacker. Wuppertal: Theologischer Verl. Brockhaus, 1970.

Bevan, Edwyn R. *Holy Images: An Inquiry into Idolatry and Image-Worship in Ancient Paganism and in Christianity.* London: Allen & Unwin, 1940.

Biale, David. *Eros and the Jews: From Biblical Israel to Contemporary America.* New York: Basic Books, 1992.

———. *Gershom Scholem: Kabbalah and Counter-History.* Cambridge, Mass.: Harvard University Press, 1979.

———. "Gershom Scholem's Ten Unhistorical Aphorisms on Kabbalah: Text and Commentary." *Modern Judaism* 5 (1985): 67–93. Reprinted in *Gershom Scholem,* edited by Harold Bloom. New York: Chelsea House, 1987.

Bianchi, Ugo. "Docetism: A Peculiar Theory about the Ambivalence of the Presence of the Divine." In *Selected Essays on Gnosticism, Dualism, and Mysteriosophy.* Leiden: Brill, 1978.

Black, Matthew. "The Throne-Theophany Prophetic Commission and the 'Son of Man': A Study in Tradition-History." In *Jews, Greeks, and Christians—Religious Cultures in Late Antiquity: Essays in Honor of W. D. Davies,* edited by Robert Hamerton-Kelly. Leiden: Brill, 1976.

Bloch, Phillip. "Die *Yorde Merkavah,* die Mystiker der Gaonenzeit und ihr Einfluss auf die Liturgie." *Monatsschrift für Geschichte und Wissenschaft des Judentums* 37 (1893): 18–25, 69–74, 257–266, 305–311.

Bloch, Renée. "Midrash." Translated by Mary Howard Callaway in *Approaches to Ancient Judaism: Theory and Practice,* edited by William S. Green. Missoula, Mont.: Scholars Press, 1978.

Block, Daniel I. "Text and Emotion: A Study in the 'Corruptions' in Ezekiel's Inaugural Vision (Ezekiel 1:4–28)." *Catholic Biblical Quarterly* 50 (1988): 418–442.

Bloom, Harold. "Scholem: Unhistorical or Jewish Gnosticism." In *Gershom Scholem,* edited by Harold Bloom. New York: Chelsea House, 1987.

Bokser, Baruch. "Approaching Sacred Space." *Harvard Theological Review* 78 (1985): 279–299.

Boman, Thorlief. *Hebrew Thought Compared with Greek.* Translated by Jules L. Moreau. Philadelphia: Westminster, 1960.

Böwering, Gerhard. *The Mystical Vision of Existence in Classical Islam: The Qur'ānic Hermeneutics of the Sūfi Sahl At-Tustarī (d. 283/896).* Berlin & New York: de Gruyter, 1980.

Boyarin, Daniel. *Carnal Israel: Reading Sex in Talmudic Culture.* Berkeley and Los Angeles: University of California Press, 1993.

———. "The Eye in the Torah: Ocular Desire in the Midrashic Hermeneutic." *Critical Inquiry* 16 (1990): 532–550.

———. *Intertextuality and the Reading of Midrash.* Bloomington: Indiana University Press, 1990.

———. "'This We Know to Be the Carnal Israel': Circumcision and the Erotic Life of God and Israel." *Critical Inquiry* 18 (1992): 474–505.

Brentjes, Sonja. "Die erste Risala der Rasa'il Ihwan as-Safa' über elementare Zahlentheorie: Ihr mathematischer Gehalt und ihr Beziehungen zu spantantiken arithmetischen Schriften." *Janus* 71 (1984): 181–274.

Breslauer, S. Daniel. "Philosophy and Imagination: The Politics of Prophecy in the View of Maimonides." *Jewish Quarterly Review* 70 (1979–80): 153–171.

Brody, Seth L. "Human Hands Dwell in Heavenly Heights: Contemplative Ascent and

Theurgic Power in Thirteenth Century Kabbalah." In *Mystics of the Book: Themes, Topics, and Typologies*. Edited by Robert A. Herrera. New York: Peter Lang, 1993.

Bruns, Gerald. *Hermeneutics Ancient and Modern*. New Haven: Yale University Press, 1992.

———. "Midrash and Allegory." In *The Literary Guide to the Bible,* edited by Robert Alter and Frank Kermode. Cambridge, Mass.: Belknap Press of Harvard University Press, 1986.

———. "The Problem of Figuration in Antiquity." In *Hermeneutics: Questions and Prospects,* edited by Gary Shapiro and Alan Sica. Amherst: University of Massachusetts Press, 1984.

Bubacz, Bruce. *St. Augustine's Theory of Knowledge: A Contemporary Analysis*. New York: Mellen, 1981.

Bundy, Murray Wright. "The Theory of Imagination in Classical and Mediaeval Thought." *University of Illinois Studies in Language and Literature* 12 (1927): 1–289.

Buren, D. van. "The Salmê in Mesopotamia in Art and Religion." *Orientalia,* n.s., 10 (1941): 65–92.

Butler, Edward C. *Western Mysticism: The Teaching of Augustine, Gregory, and Bernard on Contemplation and the Contemplative Life*. 2d ed. New York: Harper & Row, 1966.

Bynum, Caroline Walker. *Holy Feast and Holy Fast: The Religious Significance of Food to Medieval Women*. Berkeley & Los Angeles: University of California Press, 1987.

Camassa, Giorgio. "Phantasia de Platone ai Neoplatonici." In *Phantasia Imaginatio: V° Colloquio Internazionale, Roma 9–11 gennaio 1986,* edited by Marta Fattori and Massimo Bianchi. Rome: Edizioni dell'Ateneo, 1988.

Caponigri, Aloysius R. "Icon and Theon: The Role of Imagination and Symbol in the Apprehension of Transcendence." In *Naming God,* edited by Robert P. Scharlemann. New York: Paragon, 1985.

Caquot, Andre. "Les danses sacrées en Israel et à l'entour." *Sources orientales* 6 (1963): 121–143.

Carr, Wesley. *Angels and Principalities: The Background, Meaning, and Development of the Pauline Phrase hai archai kai hai exousiai*. Cambridge & New York: Cambridge University Press, 1981.

Casey, Edward S. *Imagining: A Phenomenological Study.* Bloomington: Indiana University Press, 1976.

Cassin, Elena. *La splendeur divine*. The Hague: Mounton, 1968.

Castelli, David. *Il commento di Sabbatai Donnolo sul Libro della Creazione*. Florence, 1880.

Chenu, Marie D. *Nature, Man, and Society in the Twelfth Century.* Edited and translated by J. Taylor and L. K. Little. Chicago: University of Chicago Press, 1968.

Cherbonnier E. LaB. "The Logic of Biblical Anthropomorphism." *Harvard Theological Review* 55 (1962): 187–206.

Chernus, Ira. *Mysticism in Rabbinic Judaism*. Berlin & New York: de Gruyter, 1982.

———. "The Pilgrimage to the Merkavah: An Interpretation of Early Jewish Mysticism." *Jerusalem Studies in Jewish Thought* 6:1–2 (1987): 1–36 (English section).

———. "Visions of God in Merkabah Literature." *Journal for the Study of Judaism* 13 (1982): 123–146.

Chidester, David. "Word against Light: Perception and the Conflict of Symbols." *Journal of Religion* 65 (1985): 46–62.

———. *Word and Light: Seeing, Hearing, and Religious Discourse.* Urbana: University of Illinois Press, 1992.

Childs, Brevard. *The Book of Exodus.* Philadelphia: Westminster, 1974.

Chittick, William C. *Faith and Practice of Islam: Three Thirteenth Century Sufi Texts.* Albany: State University of New York Press, 1992.

———. *The Sufi Path of Knowledge: Ibn al-ʿArabi's Metaphysics of Imagination.* Albany: State University of New York Press, 1989.

———. *The Sufi Path of Love: The Spiritual Teachings of Rumi.* Albany: State University of New York Press, 1983.

Clerc, Charly. *Les théories relatives au culte des images chez les auteurs grecs du IIe siècle après J.-C.* Paris, 1915.

Cleve, Gunnel. "Semantic Dimensions in Margery Kempe's Whyght Clothys." *Mystics Quarterly* 12 (1986): 162–170.

Cocking, J. M. *Imagination: A Study in the History of Ideas.* Edited by Penelope Murray. London & New York: Routledge, 1991.

Coe, George A. "The Sources of the Mystical Revelation." *Hibbert Journal* 6 (1907–8): 359–372.

Cohen, Martin S. *The Shiʿur Qomah: Liturgy and Theurgy in Pre-Kabbalistic Jewish Mysticism.* Lanham, Md.: University Press of America, 1983.

———. *The Shiʿur Qomah: Texts and Recensions.* Tübingen: Mohr, 1985.

Cohen-Alloro, Dorit. *The Secret of the Garment in the Zohar.* Jerusalem: Akadamon, 1987 (in Hebrew).

Collins, John J. *The Apocalyptic Vision of the Book of Daniel.* Harvard Semitic Monographs, no. 16. Missoula, Mont.: Scholars Press, 1977.

———. "The Genre Apocalypse in Hellenistic Judaism." In *Apocalypticism in the Mediterranean World and the Near East: Proceedings of the International Colloquium on Apocalypticism. Uppsala, August 12–17, 1979,* Edited by David Hellholm. 2d ed. Tübingen: Mohr, 1989.

———. "Introduction: Towards The Morphology of a Genre." *Semeia* 14 (1979), special issue, *Apocalypse: the Morphology of a Genre,* 1–20.

Corbin, Henry. *Creative Imagination in the Sūfism of Ibn ʿArabī.* Translated by Ralph Manheim. Princeton: Princeton University Press, 1969.

———. "Et son trône était porté sur l'eau." In *In Principo: Interprétations des premiers versets de la Génèse.* Paris: Études augustiniennes, 1973.

———. *Spiritual Body and Celestial Earth: From Mazdean Iran to Shīʿite Iran.* Translated by Nancy Pearson. Princeton: Princeton University Press, 1977.

Crapanzano, Vincent. *Hermes' Dilemma and Hamlet's Desire: On the Epistemology of Interpretation.* Cambridge, Mass.: Harvard University Press, 1992.

Culianu (Couliano), Ioan P. *Eros and Magic in the Renaissance.* Translated by Margaret Cook. Chicago & London: University of Chicago Press, 1987.

———. *Expériences de l'extase: Extase, ascension et récit visionaire de l'hellenism au moyen âge.* Paris; Payot, 1984.

———. *Out of This World: Otherworldly Journeys from Gilgamesh to Albert Einstein.* Boston, Shambhala, 1991.

———. *Psychanodia I: A Survey of the Evidence of the Ascension of the Soul and Its Relevance.* Leiden: Brill, 1983.

———. *The Tree of Gnosis: Gnostic Mythology from Early Christianity to Modern Nihilism*. New York & San Francisco: Harper & Row, 1992.

Daiches, Samuel. *Babylonian Oil Magic in the Talmud and in Later Jewish Literature*. London: Hart, 1913.

Dan, Joseph. "Anafiel, Meṭaṭron, and the Creator." *Tarbiz* 52 (1982–83): 447–457 (in Hebrew).

———. *The Ancient Jewish Mysticism*. Tel-Aviv: Ministry of Defence, 1989 (in Hebrew).

———. "Ashkenazi Ḥasidic Commentaries in the Hymn *Ha-'Aderet we-ha-'Emunah*." *Tarbiz* 50 (1981): 396–404 (in Hebrew).

———. "The Ashkenazi Ḥasidic 'Gates of Wisdom.'" In *Hommage à Georges Vajda: Études d'histoire et de pensée juives*, edited by Gérard Nahon and Charles Toutai. Louvain: Peeters, 1980.

———. "The Beginnings of Hebrew Hagiographic Literature." *Jerusalem Studies in Jewish Folklore* 1 (1981): 82–101 (in Hebrew).

———. "Beyond the Kabbalistic Symbol." *Jerusalem Studies in Jewish Thought* 5 (1986): 363–385 (in Hebrew).

———. "The Chambers of the Chariot." *Tarbiz* 47 (1978): 49–55 (in Hebrew).

———. "The Commentary on the Torah of R. Eleazar of Worms." *Qiryat Sefer* 59 (1984): 644 (in Hebrew).

———. "The Concept of Knowledge in the *Shi'ur Qomah*." In *Studies in Jewish Religious and Intellectual History Presented to Alexander Altmann on the Occasion of His Seventieth Birthday*, edited by Siegfried Stein and Raphael Loewe. University, Ala.: University of Alabama Press, 1979.

———. "The Emergence of Mystical Prayer." In *Studies in Jewish Mysticism*, edited by Joseph Dan and Frank Talmage. Cambridge, Mass.: Association for Jewish Studies, 1982.

———. *The Esoteric Theology of Ashkenazi Ḥasidism*. Jerusalem: Bialik Institute, 1968 (in Hebrew).

———. "Gershom Scholem: Between History and Historiosophy." *Jerusalem Studies in Jewish Thought* 3 (1983–84): 427–475 (in Hebrew). Translated by Roberta Bell-Kliger and Priscilla Fishman in *Binah: Studies in Jewish Thought*, edited by Joseph Dan. New York: Praeger, 1989.

———. *Gershom Scholem: The Mystical Dimension of Jewish History*. New York: New York University Press, 1985.

———. *The Hebrew Story in the Middle Ages*. Jerusalem: Keter, 1974 (in Hebrew).

———. "*Ḥokhmath ha-Egoz:* Its Origin and Development." *Journal of Jewish Studies* 17 (1967): 73–83.

———. "The Intention of Prayer from the Tradition of R. Judah the Pious." *Da'at* 10 (1983): 47–56 (in Hebrew).

———. *Jewish Mysticism and Jewish Ethics*. Seattle: University of Washington Press, 1986.

———. "Kavod Nistar." In *Religion and Language: Philosophical Essays*, edited by Moshe Ḥallamish and Asa Kasher. Tel-Aviv: University Publishing Projects, 1984 (in Hebrew).

———. "Midrash and the Dawn of Kabalah." In *Midrash and Literature*, edited by Geoffrey Hartman and Sanford Budick. New Haven: Yale University Press, 1986.

———. "On the History of the Text of *Ḥokhmat ha-Egoz*." *Alei Sefer* 5 (1978): 49–53 (in Hebrew).

———. "Pesaq ha-Yirah veha-Emunah and the Intention of Prayer in Ashkenazi Hasidic Esotericism." *Frankfurter Judaistische Beiträge* 19 (1991–92): 185–215.

———. "Prayer as Text and Prayer as Mystical Experience." in *Torah and Wisdom—Studies in Jewish Philosophy, Kabbalah, and Halacha: Essays in Honor of Arthur Hyman,* edited by Ruth Link-Salinger. New York: Shengold, 1992.

———. "A Re-evaluation of the 'Ashkenazi Kabbalah.'" *Jerusalem Studies in Jewish Thought* 6:3–4 (1986): 125–139 (in Hebrew).

———. "The Religious Experience of the *Merkavah*." In *Jewish Spirituality: From the Bible through the Middle Ages,* edited by Arthur Green. New York: Crossroad, 1987.

———. "The Seventy Names of Meṭaṭron." *Proceedings of the Eighth World Congress of Jewish Studies—Division C* (1982): 19–23.

———. *Studies in Ashkenazi Ḥasidic Literature.* Ramat-Gan: Masadah, 1975 (in Hebrew).

———. *Three Types of Ancient Jewish Mysticism.* Seventh Annual Rabbi Louis Feinberg Memorial Lecture in Judaic Studies. Cincinnati: University of Cincinnati, 1984.

———. "The Vicissitudes of the Esoterism of the German Ḥasidim." In *Studies in Mysticism and Religion Presented to Gershom G. Scholem.* Jerusalem: Magnes, 1967 (in Hebrew).

Daniélou, Jean. "Trinité et angélologie dans la théologue judéo-chrétienne." *Recherches Science Religieuse* 45 (1957): 5–41.

Davidson, Herbert. "The Active Intellect in the Cuzari and Hallevi's Theory of Causality." *Revue des Études Juives* 131 (1972): 351–396.

Davies, John G. "The Origins of Docetism." *Studia Patristica* 6 (1962): 13–35.

Delling, Gerhard. "The 'One Who Sees God' in Philo." In *Nourished with Peace: Studies in Hellenistic Judaism in Memory of Samuel Sandmel,* edited by Frederick E. Greenspahn, Earle Hilgert, and Burton L. Mack. Chico, Calif.: Scholars Press, 1984.

Derrida, Jacques. *The Archeology of the Frivolous: Reading Cordillac.* Translated by John P. Leavey, Jr. Lincoln: University of Nebraska Press, 1987.

———. *Speech and Phenomena.* Evanston, Ill.: Northwestern University Press, 1973.

Dornseiff, Franz. *Das Alphabet in Mystik und Magie.* Leipzig: Teubner, 1925.

Dronke, Peter. *Fabula: Explorations into the Uses of Myth in Medieval Platonism.* Leiden: Brill, 1974.

Dubois, Claude G. *L'imaginaire de la renaissance.* Paris: Presses universitaires de France, 1985.

DuBois, Page. *Sowing the Body: Psychoanalysis and Ancient Representations of Women.* Chicago: University of Chicago Press, 1988.

Dufrene, Mikel. *In the Presence of the Sensuous: Essays in Aesthetics,* edited and translated by Mark S. Roberts and Dennis Gallagher. Atlantic Highlands, N.J.: Humanities Press International, 1987.

Dupré, Louis. *The Common Life: The Origins of Trinitarian Mysticism and Its Development by Jan Ruusbrueck.* New York: Crossroad, 1984.

Durand, Gilbert. *L'imagination symbolique.* Paris: Presses universitaires de France, 1964.

———. *Les structures anthropologiques de l'imaginaire.* Paris: Bardas, 1969.

Eco, Umberto. *Art and Beauty in the Middle Ages.* Translated by Hugh Bedin. New Haven: Yale University Press, 1986.

Efros, Israel. "Saʿadia's General Ethical Theory and Its Relation to Sufism." In *Seventy-fifth Anniversary Volume of the Jewish Quarterly Review,* edited by Abraham A. Neuman and Solomon Zeitlin. Philadelphia: Jewish Quarterly Review, 1967.

———. *Studies in Medieval Jewish Philosophy.* New York: Columbia University Press, 1974.

Eichrodt, Walter. *Theology of the Old Testament.* 2 vols. Philadelphia: Westminster Press, 1967.

Eilberg-Schwartz, Howard. "The Problem of the Body for the People of the Book." In *People of the Body: Jews and Judaism from an Embodied Perspective,* edited by Howard Eilberg-Schwartz. Albany: State University of New York Press, 1992.

El-Azma, Nazeer. "Some Notes on the Impact of the Story of the Miʿrāj on Sufi Literature." *The Muslim World* 63 (1973): 93–104.

Eliade, Mircea. *Myths, Dreams, and Mysteries: The Encounter between Contemporary Faiths and Archaic Realities.* Translated by Philip Mairet. New York: Harper & Row, 1960.

———. *The Two and the One.* Translated by J. M. Cohen. Chicago: University of Chicago Press, 1965.

Elior, Rachel. "The Concept of God in Hekhalot Mysticism." *Jerusalem Studies in Jewish Thought* 6:1–2 (1987): 13–58 (in Hebrew). Translated by Dena Ordan in *Binah: Studies in Jewish Thought,* edited by Joseph Dan. New York: Praeger, 1989.

Evans, Donald. "Can Philosophers Limit What Mystics Can Do? A Critique of Steven Katz." *Religious Studies* 25 (1989): 53–60.

Everson, A. J. "Ezekiel and the Glory of the Lord Tradition." In *Sin, Salvation, and the Spirit,* edited by D. Durken, Collegeville: University of Minnesota Press, 1979.

Évrard, Étienne. "Φαντασια chez Proclus." In *Phantasia-Imaginatio: V° Colloquio Internazionale, Roma 9–11 gennaio 1986,* edited by Marta Fattori and Massimo Bianchi. Rome: Edizioni dell'Ateneo, 1988.

Farber, Asi. "The Concept of the Merkabah in Thirteenth-Century Jewish Esotericism: Sod ha-'Egoz and Its Development." Ph.D. diss., Hebrew University, 1986 (in Hebrew).

———. "On the Sources of Rabbi Moses de Leon's Early Kabbalistic System." In *Studies in Philosophy, Mysticism, and Ethical Literature Presented to Isaiah Tishby on His Seventy-fifth Birthday,* edited by Joseph Dan and Joseph Hacker. Jerusalem: Magnes, 1986 (in Hebrew).

———. "Traces of the *Zohar* in the Writings of R. Joseph Gikatilla." *ʿAlei Sefer* 9 (1981): 70–83 (in Hebrew).

Faur, José. *Golden Doves with Silver Dots: Semiotics and Textuality in Rabbinic Tradition.* Bloomington: Indiana University Press, 1986.

Fauth, Wolfgang. "Tatrosjah-Totrosjah und Meṭaṭron in der judischen Merkabah-Mystik." *Journal for the Study of Judaism* 22 (1991): 40–87.

Fenton, Paul. *Deux traités de mystique juive.* Paris: Verdier, 1987.

———. "La 'Tête Entre Les Genoux': Contribution à l'étude d'une posture méditative dans la mystique juive et islamique." *Revue d'Histoire et de Philosophie Religieuses* 72 (1992): 413–426.

Feuchtwanger, Naomi. "The Coronation of the Virgin and of the Bride." In *Jewish Art,* edited by Aliza Cohen-Mushlin, vol. 12–13. Jerusalem: Center for Jewish Art of the Hebrew University, 1987.

Filoramo, Giovanni. *A History of Gnosticism.* Translated by Anthony Alcock. Oxford: Blackwell, 1990.

Fine, Lawrence. "The Art of Metoposcopy: A Study in Isaac Luria's Charismatic Knowledge." *Association for Jewish Studies Review* 11 (1986): 79–101.

Finke, Laurie,. "Mystical Bodies and the Dialogics of Vision," *Philological Quarterly* 67 (1988): 439–460.

Fishbane, Michael A. *Biblical Interpretation in Ancient Israel.* Oxford: Clarendon Press, 1985.

———. *The Garments of Torah: Essays in Biblical Hermeneutics.* Bloomington: Indiana University Press, 1989.

———. *The Kiss of God: Spiritual and Mystical Death in Judaism.* Seattle & London: University of Washington Press, 1994.

———. "The 'Measures' of God's Glory in the Ancient Midrash." In *Messiah and Christos: Studies in the Jewish Origins of Christianity Presented to David Flusser,* edited by Ithamar Gruenwald, Shaul Shaked, and Gedaliahu G. Stroumsa. Tübingen: Mohr, 1992.

———. "Some Forms of Divine Appearance in Ancient Jewish Thought." In *From Ancient Israel to Modern Judaism—Intellect in Quest of Understanding: Essays in Honor of Marvin Fox,* edited by Jacob Neusner, Ernst S. Frerichs, and Nahum M. Sarna, vol. 2. Atlanta: Scholars Press, 1989.

———. "The Well of Living Water: A Biblical Motif and Its Ancient Transformations." In *Sha'arei Talmon: Studies in the Bible, Qumran, and the Ancient Near East Presented to Shemaryahu Talmon,* edited by Michael Fishbane and Emmanuel Tov, with Weston W. Fields. Winona Lake, Ind.: Eisenbrauns, 1992.

Fleischer, Ezra. "Reflections on the Religious Poetry of Rabbi Yehudah Halevi." In *Yehuda Halevi: A Selection of Critical Essays on His Poetry.* Edited by Aviva Doron. Tel Aviv: Hakibbutz Hameuchad, 1988.

Flusser, David. *Judaism and the Origins of Christianity.* Jerusalem: Magnes, 1988.

Forgie, J. William. "Hyper-Kantianism in Recent Discussions of Mystical Experience." *Religious Studies* 21 (1985): 205–218.

Fossum, Jarl E. "Jewish Christian Christology and Jewish Mysticism." *Vigiliae Christianae* 37 (1983): 260–287.

———. *The Name of God and the Angel of the Lord.* Tübingen: Mohr, 1985.

Fox, Robin Lane. *Pagans and Christians.* New York: Knopf, 1986.

Fraade, Steven D. *From Tradition to Commentary: Torah and Its Interpretation in the Midrash Sifre to Deuteronomy.* Albany: State University of New York Press, 1991.

Freedberg, David. *The Power of Images: Studies in the History and Theory of Response.* Chicago: University of Chicago Press, 1989.

Funkenstein, Amos. "Naḥmanides' Symbolical Reading of History." In *Studies in Jewish Mysticism,* edited by Joseph Dan and Frank Talmage. Cambridge, Mass.: Association for Jewish Studies, 1982.

———. *Perceptions of Jewish History.* Berkeley & Los Angeles: University of California Press, 1993.

Galambush, Julie. *Jerusalem in the Book of Ezekiel: The City as Yahweh's Wife.* SBL Dissertation Series, no. 130. Atlanta: Scholars Press, 1992.

Garside, Bruce. "Language and the Interpretation of Mystical Experience." *International Journal for Philosophy of Religion* 3 (1972): 93–102.

Gaster, Moses. "Das Schiur Komah." In *Studies and Texts in Folklore, Magic, Medieval Romance, Hebrew Apocrypha, and Samaritan Archaeology,* vol. 2. 1928. Reprint, New York: Ktav Publishing House, 1971.

Gätje, Helmut. *The Qur'an and Its Exegesis: Selected Texts with Classical and Modern Muslim Interpretations.* Translated and edited by Alford T. Welch. Berkeley & Los Angeles: University of California Press, 1976.

Gershenzon, Rosalie, and Elieser Slomovic. "A Second Century Jewish-Gnostic Debate: Rabbi Jose ben Ḥalafta and the Maṭrona." *Journal for the Study of Judaism* 16 (1985): 1–41.

Giller, Pinchas. *The Enlightened Will Shine: Symbolization and Theurgy in the Later Strata of the Zohar.* Albany: State University of New York Press, 1993.

Ginsburg, Elliot K. "The *Havdalah* Ceremony in Zoharic Kabbalah." *Jerusalem Studies in Jewish Thought* 8 (1989): 183–216 (in Hebrew).

———. *The Sabbath in the Classical Kabbalah.* Albany: State University of New York Press, 1989.

———. *Sod ha-Shabbat: The Mystery of the Sabbath.* Albany: State University of New York Press, 1989.

Ginsburger, Moses. *Die Anthropomorphismen in den Thargumim.* Braunschweig: Appelhans & Pfenningstorff, 1891.

Ginzberg, Louis. *The Legends of the Jews.* 7 vols. Philadelphia: Jewish Publication Society of America, 1968.

Gnuse, Robert K. "The Temple Experience of Jaddus in the *Antiquities* of Josephus: A Report of Jewish Dream Incubation." *Jewish Quarterly Review* 83 (1993): 349–368.

Goetschel, Roland. "The Conception of Prophecy in the Works of R. Moses de León and R. Joseph Gikatilla." *Jerusalem Studies in Jewish Thought* 8 (1989): 217–237 (in Hebrew).

Goldberg, Arnold. "Rabban Yoḥanans Traum: Der Sinai in der frühen Merkavamystok." *Frankfurter judaistische Beitrage* 3 (1975): 1–27.

———. *Untersuchungen über die Vorstellung von der Schekhinah in der frühen rabbinischen Literatur.* Berlin: de Gruyter, 1969.

Goldin, Judah. *The Song at the Sea.* New Haven: Yale University Press, 1971.

———. *Studies in Midrash and Related Literature.* Edited by Barry L. Eichler and Jeffrey H. Tigay. Philadelphia: Jewish Publication Society of America, 1988.

Goldziher, Ignaz. "Le *Amr ilahi* (*ha-ʿinyan ha-ʾelohi*) chez Juda Halévi." *Revue des Études Juives* 50 (1905): 32–41.

———. "Fragment de l'original arabe du commentaire sur le Sefer Yeçirah par Isak Israéli." *Revue des Études Juives* 52 (1906): 187–190.

Goodenough, Erwin R. *Jewish Symbols in Greco-Roman Times.* 13 vols. Bollingen Series. New York: Pantheon, 1953–68.

Gottlieb, Ephraim. *Studies in the Kabbala Literature.* Edited by Joseph Hacker. Tel-Aviv: Tel-Aviv University Press, 1976 (in Hebrew).

Grabar, André. *Christian Iconography: A Study of Its Origins.* Bollinger Series xxxv.10. Princeton: Princeton University Press, 1968.

———. *L'iconoclasme byzantine.* Paris, 1957.

Graetz, Heinrich. *Gnostizismus und Judentum.* Krotoschin: Monasch, 1846.

———. "Die mystische Literatur in der gaonischen Epoche." *Monatsschrift für Geschichte und Wissenschaft des Judentums* 8 (1859): 115–118, 140–144.

———. *The Structure of Jewish History and Other Essays.* Translated and edited by Ismar Schorsch. New York: Jewish Theological Society of America, 1975.

Grant, Patrick. *Literature of Mysticism in Western Tradition.* London: Macmillan, 1983.

Grant, Robert M. "The Mystery of Marriage in the Gospel of Philip." *Vigiliae Christianae* 15 (1961): 129–140.

Green, Arthur. "Bride, Spouse, Daughter: Images of the Feminine in Classical Jewish Sources." In *On Being a Jewish Feminist: A Reader,* edited by Susannah Heschel. New York: Schocken, 1983.

———. "The Children in Egypt and the Theophany at the Sea." *Judaism* 24 (1975): 446–456.

———. *Tormented Master: A Life of Rabbi Nahman of Bratslav.* University, Ala.: University of Alabama Press, 1979.

Greenberg, Moshe. "Ezekiel's Vision: Literary and Iconographic Aspects." In *History, Historiography, and Interpretation: Studies in Biblical and Cuneiform Literatures,* edited by Haim Tadmor and Moshe Weinfeld. Jerusalem: Magnes, 1983.

Gries, Zev. *Conduct Literature (Regimen Vitae): Its History and Place in the Life of Beshtian Ḥasidism.* Jerusalem: Bialik Institute, 1989 (in Hebrew).

Grigg, Robert. "Constantine the Great and the Cult without Images." *Viator* 8 (1977): 1–32.

Grözinger, Karl E. "Der Mensch als Ebenbild Gottes—im Wandel der jüdischen Tradition." *Sätryck från Nodisk Judaistik* 10 (1989): 63–74.

———. "The Names of God and the Celestial Powers: Their Function and Meaning in the Hekhalot Literature." *Jerusalem Studies in Jewish Thought* 6:1–2 (1987): 53–70 (English section).

Gruenwald, Ithamar. *Apocalyptic and Merkavah Mysticism.* Leiden: Brill, 1980.

———. *From Apocalypticism to Gnosticism.* Frankfurt am Main: Lang, 1988.

———. "Further Jewish Physiognomic and Chiromantic Fragments." *Tarbiz* 40 (1971): 301–319 (in Hebrew).

———. "The Impact of Priestly Traditions on the Creation of Merkabah Mysticism and the Shiur Komah." *Jerusalem Studies in Jewish Thought* 6:1–2 (1987): 65–120 (in Hebrew).

———. "Jewish Apocalyptic Literature." *Aufstieg und Niedergang der Römischen Welt* II.19.1 (1979): 89–118.

———. "Midrash and the 'Midrashic Condition': Preliminary Considerations." In *The Midrashic Imagination,* edited by Michael Fishbane. Albany: State University of New York Press, 1993.

———. "The Midrashic Condition: From Talmudic to Zoharic Hermeneutics." *Jerusalem Studies in Jewish Thought* 8 (1989): 255–298 (in Hebrew).

———. "New Passages from Hekhalot Literature." *Tarbiz* 38 (1968–69): 354–372 (in Hebrew).

———. "Some Critical Notes on the First Part of Sefer Yeẓira," *Revue des Études Juives* 132 (1973): 475–512.

Gunkel, Hermann. *Die Psalmen: Götinger Handkommentar zum alten Testament.* Götingen: Vandenhoeck & Ruprecht, 1926.

Gutmann, Joseph. "Deuteronomy: Religious Reformation or Iconoclastic Revolution?" In *The Image and the Word: Confrontations in Judaism, Christianity, and Islam,* edited by Joseph Gutmann. Missoula, Mont.: Scholars Press, 1977.

———. "The 'Second Commandment' and the Image in Judaism." *Hebrew Union College Annual* 32 (1961): 161–174.

Guttmann, Julius. "Religion and Knowldege in Medieval Thought and the Modern Period." In *Religion and Knowledge.* Jerusalem: Magnes, 1955 (in Hebrew).

Halbertal, Moshe, and Avishai Margalit. *Idolatry.* Translated by Naomi Goldblum. Cambridge, Mass.: Harvard University Press, 1992.

Halivni, David Weiss, *Midrash, Mishna, Gemara: The Jewish Predilection for Justified Law.* Cambridge, Mass.: Harvard University Press, 1986.

Halperin, David J. "Ascension or Invasion: Implications of the Heavenly Journey in Ancient Judaism." *Religion* 18 (1988): 47–67.

———. *The Faces of the Chariot: Early Jewish Responses to Ezekiel's Vision.* Tübingen: Mohr, 1988.

———. *The Merkabah in Rabbinic Literature.* New Haven: American Oriental Society, 1980.

———. "Origen, Ezekiel's Merkabah, and the Ascension of Moses." *Church History* 50 (1981): 261–275.

———. "A Sexual Image in Hekhalot Rabbati and Its Implications." *Jerusalem Studies in Jewish Thought* 6:1–2 (1987): 117–132 (English section).

Hamerton-Kelly, Robert G. "The Temple and the Origins of Jewish Apocalyptic." *Vetus Testamentum* 20 (1970): 1–15.

Hamesse, Jacqueline. "Imaginatio et phantasia chez les auteurs philosophiques du 12ᵉ et du 13ᵉ siècle." In *Phantasia-Imaginatio: V° Colloquio Internazionale, Roma 9–11 gennaio 1986,* edited by Marta Fattori and Massimo Bianchi. Rome: Edizioni dell'Ateneo, 1988.

Handelman, Susan A. *Fragments of Redemption: Jewish Thought and Literary Theory in Benjamin, Scholem, and Levinas.* Bloomington: Indiana University Press, 1991.

———. *The Slayers of Moses: The Emergence of Rabbinic Interpretation in Modern Literary Theory.* Albany: State University of New York Press, 1982.

Haran, Menahem. "The Ark and the Cherubim: Their Symbolic Significance in Biblical Ritual," *Israel Exploration Journal* 9 (1959): 30–38, 89–94.

———. "The Divine Presence in the Israelite Cult and the Cultic Institutions." *Biblica* 50 (1969): 251–267.

———. *Temples and Temple-Service in Ancient Israel.* Oxford: Clarendon Press, 1978.

Hartman, Lars. "Survey of the Problem of Apocalyptic Genre." In *Apocalypticism in the Mediterranean World and the Near East. Proceedings of the International Colloquium on Apocalypticism, Uppsala, August 12–17, 1979,* Edited by David Hellholm. 2d ed. Tübingen: Mohr, 1989.

Hay, David M. *Glory at the Right Hand: Psalm 110 in Early Christianity.* Nashville: Abingdon, 1973.

Hayman, Allison P. "*Sefer Yeṣirah* and the Hekhalot Literature." *Jerusalem Studies in Jewish Thought* 6:1–2 (1987): 71–85 (English section).

Hayward, Robert. *Divine Name and Presence: The Memra.* Totowa, N.J.: Allanheld, Osmun, for Oxford Centre for Postgraduate Hebrew Studies, 1981.

Ḥazan, Ephraim. *The Poetics of the Sephardi Piyyuṭ According to the Liturgical Poetry of Yehuda Halevi.* Jerusalem: Magnes, 1986 (in Hebrew).

Heelan, Patrick A. "Perception as a Hermeneutical Act." In *Hermeneutics and Deconstruction,* edited by Hugh J. Silverman and Don Ihde. Albany: State University of New York Press, 1985.

Heide, Albert van der. "Pardes: Methodological Reflections on the Theory of the Four Senses." *Journal of Jewish Studies* 34 (1983): 147–159.

Hendel, Ronald. "The Social Origins of the Aniconic Tradition in Early Israel." *Classical Biblical Quarterly* 50 (1988): 365–382.

Herman, Emily. *The Meaning and Value of Mysticism.* London: Clark, 1922.

Herrin, Judith. *The Formation of Christendom.* Princeton: Princeton University Press, 1987.

Herrmann, Klaus, and Claudia Rohrbacher-Sticker. "Magische Traditionen der New Yorker Hekhalot-Handschrift JTSA Mic. 8128 im Kontext ihrer Gesamtredaktion." *Frankfurter Judaistische Beiträge* 17 (1989): 101–149.

Heschel, Abraham J. "On the Holy Spirit in the Middle Ages" (in Hebrew). In *Alexander Marx Festschrift.* New York: Jewish Theological Seminary of America, 1950.

Himmelfarb, Martha. *Ascent to Heaven in Jewish and Christian Apocalypses.* New York & Oxford: Oxford University Press, 1993.

———. "From Prophecy to Apocalypse: The *Book of Watchers* and Tours of Heaven." In *Jewish Spirituality: From the Bible through the Middle Ages,* edited by Arthur Green. New York: Crossroad, 1987.

———. "Heavenly Ascent and the Relationship of the Apocalypses and the Hekhalot Literature." *Hebrew Union College Annual* 59 (1988): 73–100.

Hirth, V. *Gottes Boten im Alten Testament.* Berlin: Evangelische Verlagsanstalt, 1975.

Horovitz, Jakob. "Muhammeds Himmelfahrt." *Der Islam* 9 (1919): 159–183.

Howe, Elizabeth T. *Mystical Imagery: Santa Teresa de Jesús and San Juan de la Cruz.* New York: Lang, 1988.

Hügel, Baron Friedrich von. *The Mystical Element of Religion as Studied in Saint Catherine of Genoa and Her Friends.* 2 vols. London, 1923. Reprint, London: Clarke & Dent, 1961.

Hunt, Clive. *Images of Flight.* Berkeley & Los Angeles: University of California Press, 1988.

Husserl, Edmund. *The Idea of Phenomenology.* Translated by William P. Alston and George Nakhnikian. The Hague: Nijhoff, 1973.

———. *Ideas Pertaining to a Pure Phenomenology and to a Phenomenological Philosophy. Second Book.* Translated by Richard Rojcewicz and André Schuwer. Dordrecht, Boston & London: Kluwer, 1989.

Idel, Moshe. "Additional Fragments from the Writings of R. Joseph of Hamadan," *Daʿat* 21 (1988): 47–55 (in Hebrew).

———. "The Concept of Torah in Hekhalot Literature and Its Metamorphosis in Kabbalah." In *Jerusalem Studies in Jewish Thought* 1 (1981): 23–84 (in Hebrew).

———. "Defining Kabbalah: The Kabbalah of the Divine Names." In *Mystics of the Book: Topics, Themes, and Typologies,* edited by Robert A. Herrera. New York: Lang, 1993.

———. "Enoch is Meṭaṭron." *Jerusalem Studies in Jewish Thought* 6:1–2 (1987): 151–170 (in Hebrew). French translation by Charles Mopsik, appendix to *Le livre hébreu d'hénoch ou livre des palais.* Paris: Verdier, 1989.

———. *Golem: Jewish Magical and Mystical Traditions on the Artificial Anthropoid.* Albany: State University of New York Press, 1990.

———. "*Hitbodedut* as Concentration in Ecstatic Kabbalah." *Daʿat* 14 (1985): 35–82; 15 (1986): 117–120 (in Hebrew). English trans. in *Studies in Ecstatic Kabbalah* (see below).

———. "*Hitbodedut* as Concentration in Jewish Philosophy." *Jerusalem Studies in Jewish Thought* 7 (1988): 39–60 (in Hebrew).

———. "The Image of Adam above the Sefirot." *Daʿat* 4 (1980): 41–55 (in Hebrew).

———. "Infinities of Torah in Kabbalah." In *Midrash and Literature,* edited by Geoffrey Hartman and Sanford Budick. New Haven: Yale University Press, 1986.

———. "Inquiries into the Doctrine of *Sefer ha-Meshiv.*" *Sefunot* 17 (1983): 185–266 (in Hebrew).

———. "Intention and Colors: A Forgotten Kabbalistic Responsum." In *Tribute to Sara: Studies in Jewish Philosophy and Kabbala Presented to Sara O. Heller Wilensky,* edited by Moshe Idel, Devorah Dimant, and Shalom Rosenberg. Jerusalem: Magnes, 1994 (in Hebrew).

———. "Intention in Prayer in the Beginning of Kabbalah: Between Germany and Provence." In *Porat Yosef: Studies Presented to Rabbi Dr. Joseph Safran,* edited by Bezalel and Eliyahu Safran. Hoboken: Ktav, 1992 (in Hebrew).

———. "Jewish Kabbalah and Platonism in the Middle Ages and Renaissance." In *Neoplatonism and Jewish Thought,* edited by Lenn E. Goodman. Albany: State University of New York Press, 1992.

———. *Kabbalah: New Perspectives*. New Haven: Yale University Press, 1988.
———. "Kabbalistic Material from the School of R. David ben Judah he-Ḥasid." *Jerusalem Studies in Jewish Thought* 2 (1983): 170–193 (in Hebrew).
———. "Kabbalistic Prayer and Colors." In *Approaches to Judaism in Medieval Times*, edited by David R. Blumenthal, vol. 3. Atlanta: Scholars Press, 1988.
———. *Language, Torah, and Hermeneutics in Abraham Abulafia*. Translated by Menahem Kallus. Albany: State University of New York Press, 1989.
———. "Maimonides and the Kabbalah." In *Studies in Maimonides*, edited by Isadore Twersky. Cambridge, Mass.: Harvard University Press, 1990.
———. "Mundus Imaginalis and Likkute HaRan." In *Studies in Ecstatic Kabbalah* (see below).
———. *The Mystical Experience in Abraham Abulafia*. Translated by Jonathan Chipman. Albany: State University of New York Press, 1988.
———. "On the Metamorphosis of an Ancient Technique of Prophetic Vision in the Middle Ages." *Sinai* 86 (1979): 1–7 (in Hebrew).
———. "R. Yehudah Hallewa and His 'Ẓafenat Paʿaneaḥ.'" *Shalem: Studies in the History of the Jews in Eretz-Israel* 4 (1984): 119–148 (in Hebrew).
———. "The Sefirot above the Sefirot." *Tarbiz* 51 (1982): 239–280 (in Hebrew).
———. "Sexual Metaphors and Praxis in the Kabbalah." In *The Jewish Family: Metaphor and Memory*. Edited by David Kraemer. New York & Oxford: Oxford University Press, 1989. Translated by Charles Mopsik as appendix to *Lettre sur la sainteté: Le secret de la relation entre l'homme et la femme dans la cabale*. Paris: Verdier, 1986.
———. *Studies in Ecstatic Kabbalah*. Albany: State University of New York Press, 1988.
———. "Types of Redemptive Activity in the Middle Ages." In *Messianism and Eschatology*, edited by Zvi Baras. Jerusalem: Merkaz Zalman Shazar, 1984 (in Hebrew).
———. "Universalization and Integration: Two Conceptions of Mystical Union in Jewish Mysticism." In *Mystical Union and Monotheistic Faith: An Ecumenical Dialogue*, edited by Moshe Idel and Bernard McGinn. New York: Macmillan, 1989.
———. "The World of Angels in Human Form," in *Studies in Philosophy, Mysticism, and Ethical Literature Presented to Isaiah Tishby on his Seventy-fifth Birthday*, edited by Joseph Dan and Joseph Hacker. Jerusalem: Magnes, 1986.
———. "The Writings of R. Abraham Abulafia and His Teaching." Ph.D. diss., Hebrew University, 1986 (in Hebrew).
Irigaray, Luce. *Speculum of the Other Woman*. Translated by Gillian C. Hill. Ithaca: Cornell University Press, 1985.
———. *This Sex Which Is Not One*. Translated by Catherine Porter with Carolyn Burke. Ithaca: Cornell University Press, 1985.
Ivry, Alfred. *Al-Kindi's Metaphysics*. Albany: State University of New York Press, 1974.
———. "The Philosophical and Religious Arguments in Rabbi Yehuda Halevy's Thought." In *Thought and Action: Essays in Memory of Simon Rawidowicz on the Twenth-fifth Anniversary of His Death*, edited by Alfred Avraham Greenbaum and Alfred Ivry. Tel-Aviv: Tcherikover, 1983 (in Hebrew).
Jacobson, Howard. *The Exagoge of Ezekiel*. Cambridge: Cambridge University Press, 1983.
———. "Mysticism and Apocalyptic in Ezekiel the Tragedian." *Illinois Classical Studies* 6 (1981): 272–293.
Janowitz, Naomi. *The Poetics of Ascent: Theories of Language in a Rabbinic Ascent Text*. Albany: State University of New York Press, 1989.

Jantzen, Grace M. "Mysticism and Experience." *Religious Studies* 25 (1989): 295–315.
Jay, Martin. *Downcast Eyes: The Denigration of Vision in Twentieth-Century French Thought.* Berkeley & Los Angeles: University of California Press, 1993.
Jellinek, Adolph. *Beitrage zur Geschichte der Kabbala.* Leipzig: Fritzsche, 1852.
———. "Christlicher Einfluss auf die Kabbalah." *Der Orient* 12 (1851): 580–583.
———. *Philosophie und Kabbala.* Leipzig: Hunger, 1854.
Jervell, Jacob. *Imago Dei: Gen. 1.26f. im Spatjudentum, in der Gnosis und in den paulinischen Briefen.* Göttingen: Vandenhoeck & Ruprecht, 1960.
Jonas, Hans. "Myth and Mysticism: A Study of Objectification and Interiorization in Religious Thought." *Journal of Religion* 49 (1969): 315–329.
———. "The Nobility of Sight: A Study in the Phenomenology of the Senses." In *The Phenomenon of Life: Toward a Philosophical Biology.* New York: Harper & Row, 1966.
Jospe, Raphael. "Early Philosophical Commentaries on the Sefer Yeẓirah: Some Comments." *Revue des Études Juives* 149 (1990): 369–415.
Kadushin, Max. *The Rabbinic Mind.* New York: Jewish Theological Seminary of America, 1952.
Kamin, Sara. "'*Dugma*' in Rashi's Commentary on Song of Songs" (in Hebrew). In *Jews and Christians Interpret the Bible.* Jerusalem: Magnes, 1991.
Katz, Sarah. *Openwork, Intaglios, and Filigrees: Studies and Research on Shlomo Ibn Gabirol's Work.* Jerusalem: Mosad ha-Rav Kook, 1992 (in Hebrew).
Katz, Steven T. "The Conservative Character of Mystical Experience." In *Mysticism and Religious Traditions,* edited by Steven T. Katz. New York: Oxford University Press, 1983.
———. "Language, Epistemology, and Mysticism." In *Mysticism and Philosophical Analysis,* edited by Steven T. Katz. New York: Oxford University Press, 1978.
———. "Models, Modeling, and Mystical Training." *Religion* 12 (1982): 247–275.
Kaufmann, David. *Gesammelte Schriften.* 3 vols. Frankfurt am Main: Kaufmann, 1908–10.
———. *Geschichte der Attributenlehre in der jüdischen Religionsphilosophie von Saadia bis Maimuni.* Gotha: Perthes, 1877.
———. "Notes et mélanges: La discussion sur les phylactéres." *Revue des Études Juives* 5 (1882): 273–277.
———. *Die Sinne: Beiträge zur Geschichte der Physiologie und Psychologie im Mittelalter aus hebraïschen und arabischen Quellen.* Budapest: Kön. ungar. Universitäts-Buchdruckerei, 1884.
———. *Studien über Salomon ibn Gabirol.* Budapest: Alkalay, 1899.
———. *Studies in Hebrew Literature of the Middle Ages.* Jerusalem: Mosad ha-Rav Kook, 1965 (in Hebrew).
Kearney, Richard. *Poetics of Imagining: From Husserl to Lyotard.* London: Harper Collins Academic, 1991.
———. *The Wake of Imagination.* Minneapolis: Minnesota University Press, 1988.
Keel, Othmar. *Jahwe-Visionen und Siegelkunst.* Stuttgart, 1977.
Kiener, Ronald. "The Hebrew Paraphrase of Saadiah Gaon's *Kitāb al-Amānāt wa'l-I'tiqādāt.*" *Association for Jewish Studies Review* 11 (1986): 1–25.
———. "The Image of Islam in the Zohar." *Jerusalem Studies in Jewish Thought* 8 (1989): 43–65 (English section).
———. "The Status of Astrology in the Early Kabbalah." *Jerusalem Studies in Jewish Thought* 6:3–4 (1987): 1–42 (English section).

Kirk, Kenneth E. *The Vision of God: The Christian Doctrine of the Summum Bonum.* London: Longmans, Green, 1931.

Koester, Helmut. *Introduction to the New Testament.* Vol. 1, *History, Culture and Religion of the Hellenistic Age;* vol. 2, *History and Literature of Early Christianity.* New York & Berlin: de Gruyter, 1982.

Komem, Aharon. "Between Poetry and Prophecy: Studies in the Poetry of Judah Halevi." *Molad* 2 (1969): 676–698 (in Hebrew).

Kugel, James L. *In Potiphar's House: The Interpretive Life of Biblical Texts.* New York: Harper & Row, 1990.

Kuyt, Annelies. "Once Again: Yarad in Hekhalot Literature." *Frankfurter Judaistische Beiträge* 18 (1990): 45–69.

Lagorio, Valerie M. "The Medieval Continental Women Mystics: An Introduction." In *An Introduction to the Medieval Mystics of Europe,* edited by Paul Szarmach. Albany: State University of New York Press, 1984.

Landersdorfer, P. S. *Baal Tetramorphos und die Kerube des Ezechiel.* Paderborn, 1958.

Laqueur, Thomas. *Making Sex: Body and Gender from the Greeks to Freud.* Cambridge, Mass.: Harvard University Press, 1990.

Lauterbach, Jacob Z. "Substitutes for the Tetragrammaton." *Proceedings of the American Academy of Jewish Research* 2 (1930–31): 39–67.

Leaman, Oliver. "Maimonides, Imagination, and the Objectivity of Prophecy." *Religion* 18 (1988): 69–80.

Leeuw, Gerardus van der. *Religion in Essence and Manifestation.* Translated by J. E. Turner, with appendices incorporating the additions to the second German ed. by Hans H. Penner. Princeton: Princeton University Press, 1986.

Leiter, Samuel. "Worthiness, Acclamation, and Appointment: Some Rabbinic Terms." *Proceedings of the American Academy of Jewish Research* 41–42 (1973–74): 137–168.

Leupin, Alexandre. *Barbarolexis: Medieval Writing and Sexuality.* Cambridge, Mass. & London: Harvard University Press, 1989.

Levenson, Jon D. "The Jerusalem Temple in Devotional and Visionary Experience." In *Jewish Spirituality: From the Bible through the Middle Ages,* edited by Arthur Green. New York: Crossroad, 1987.

Levin, David M., ed. *Modernity and the Hegemony of Vision.* Berkeley & Los Angeles: University of California Press, 1993.

Levin, Israel. *Mystical Trends in the Poetry of Solomon ibn Gabirol.* Lod, 1986 (in Hebrew).

Levine, Baruch A. *In the Presence of the Lord.* Leiden: Brill, 1974.

Levine, Etan. *The Aramaic Version of the Bible.* Berlin & New York: de Gruyter, 1988.

Levy, Jacob. "Remainders of Greek Phrases and Nouns in 'Hechaloth Rabbati'." In *Studies in Jewish Hellenism.* Jerusalem: Magnes, 1969 (in Hebrew).

Lichtmann, Maria R. "Complete Mysticism: Does Ruysbroeck Transcend Eckhart?" *Mystics Quarterly* 12 (1986) 179–187.

Lieb, Michael. *The Visionary Mode: Biblical Prophecy, Hermeneutics, and Cultural Change.* Ithaca: Cornell University Press, 1991.

Lieberman, Saul. "How Much Greek in Jewish Palestine?" In *Biblical and Other Studies,* edited by Alexander Altmann. Cambridge, Mass.: Harvard University Press, 1963.

———. "Mishnath Shir ha-Shirim." Appendix to Gershom Scholem, *Jewish Gnosti-*

cism, Merkabah Mysticism and Talmudic Tradition, New York: Jewish Theological Seminary of America, 1965.
———. *Shkiin.* Jerusalem: Wahrmann, 1970 (in Hebrew).
Liebes, Yehuda. "The Angels of the Shofar and the Yeshua Sar ha-Panim." *Jerusalem Studies in Jewish Thought* 6:1–2 (1987): 171–195 (in Hebrew).
———. "Christian Influences on the *Zohar.*" In *Jerusalem Studies in Jewish Thought* 2 (1983): 43–74 (in Hebrew). English translation in *Studies in the Zohar* (see below).
———. "How the Zohar Was Written." *Jerusalem Studies in Jewish Thought* 8 (1989): 1–71 (in Hebrew). English translation in *Studies in the Zohar* (see below).
———. "Hymns for the Sabbath Meals Composed by the Holy Ari." *Molad,* n.s., 4 (1972): 540–555 (in Hebrew).
———. "The Kabbalistic Myth of Orpheus." *Jerusalem Studies in Jewish Thought* 7 (1988): 425–459 (in Hebrew). English translation in *Studies in Jewish Myth and Jewish Messianism* (see below).
———. "The Messiah of the Zohar" (in Hebrew). In *The Messianic Idea in Jewish Thought: A Study Conference in Honour of the Eightieth Birthday of Gershom Scholem.* Jerusalem: Israel Academy of Sciences and Humanities, 1982 (in Hebrew). English translation in *Studies in the Zohar* (see below).
———. "Rabbi Solomon Ibn Gabirol's Use of the *Sefer Yeṣira* and a Commentary on the Poem 'I Love Thee.'" *Jerusalem Studies in Jewish Thought* 6:3–4 (1987): 73–123 (in Hebrew).
———. *Sections of the Zohar Lexicon.* Jerusalem: Akadamon, 1976 (in Hebrew).
———. *The Sin of Elisha: The Four Who Entered Paradise and the Nature of Talmudic Mysticism.* 2d ed. Jerusalem: Akadamon, 1990 (in Hebrew).
———. *Studies in Jewish Myth and Jewish Messianism.* Translated by Batya Stein. Albany: State University of New York Press, 1993.
———. *Studies in the Zohar.* Translated by Arnold Schwartz, Stephanie Nakache, and Penina Peli. Albany: State University of New York Press, 1993.
———. "'Tsaddiq Yesod Olam'—A Sabbatian Myth." *Da'at* 1 (1978): 73–120 (in Hebrew).
Lindblom, Johannes. "Theophanies in Holy Places in Hebrew Religion." *Hebrew Union College Annual* 32 (1961): 91–106.
Lipiner, Elias. *The Metaphysics of the Hebrew Alphabet.* Jerusalem: Magnes, 1989 (in Hebrew).
L'Orange, Hans Peter. *Studies on the Iconography of Cosmic Kingship in the Ancient World.* Oslo: Instituttet für Sammenlignende Kulturforskning, 1953.
MacDonald, Dennis R. "Corinthian Veils and Gnostic Androgynes." In *Images of the Feminine in Gnosticism,* edited by Karen L. King. Philadelphia: Fortress, 1988.
Mach, Michael. *Entwicklungsstadien des jüdischen Engelglaubens in vorrabbinischer Zeit.* Tübingen: Mohr, 1992.
MacKinnon, Donald M. "Some Epistemological Reflections on Mystical Experience." In *Mysticism and Philosophical Analysis,* edited by Steven T. Katz. New York: Oxford University Press, 1978.
Maier, Johann. "Das Gefährdungsmotiv bei der Himmelsreise in der jüdischen Apokalyptik und Gnosis." *Kairos* 5 (1963): 18–40.
———. *Vom Kultus zur Gnosis.* Salzburg: Mueller, 1964.
Mallory, Marilyn May. *Christian Mysticism—Transcending Techniques: A Theological Reflection on the Empirical Techniques of the Teaching of St. John of the Cross.* Assen: Van Gorcum, 1977.

Mann, Jacob. *Texts and Studies in Jewish History and Literature*. 2 vols. Philadelphia: Jewish Publication Society of America, 1935.

Marcovich, Miroslav. "The Wedding Hymn of Acta Thomae." *Illinois Classical Studies* 6 (1981): 367–385.

Marcus, Ivan. *Piety and Society: The Jewish Pietists of Medieval Germany*. Leiden: Brill, 1981.

Marmorstein, Arthur. *The Old Rabbinic Idea of God*. Vol. 2, *Essays in Anthropomorphism*. London, 1927–37. Reprint, New York: Ktav, 1968.

Marmura, Michael E. "Avicenna's Psychological Proof of Prophecy." *Journal of Near Eastern Studies* 29 (1963): 49–56.

Matt, Daniel C. "Ayin: The Concept of Nothingness in Jewish Mysticism." In *The Problem of Pure Consciousness: Mysticism and Philosophy*, edited by Robert K. C. Forman. New York: Oxford University Press, 1990.

———. "'New-Ancient Words': The Aura of Secrecy in the Zohar." In *Gershom Scholem's Major Trends in Jewish Mysticism 50 Years After: Proceedings of the Sixth International Conference on the History of Jewish Mysticism*, edited by Peter Schäfer and Joseph Dan. Tübingen: Mohr, 1993.

———. *Zohar: The Book of Enlightenment*. New York: Paulist Press, 1983.

McGinn, Bernard. *The Foundations of Mysticism*. Vol. 1 of *The Presence of God: A History of Western Christian Mysticism*. New York: Crossroad, 1991.

McNamara, Martin. *Targum and Testament: Aramaic Paraphrases of the Hebrew Bible: a Light on the New Testament*. Shannon: Irish University Press, 1972.

Meier, Franz. "Der Derwischtanz." *Asiatische Studien* 8 (1954): 107–136.

Merkur, Dan. *Gnosis: An Esoteric Tradition of Mystical Visions and Unions*. Albany: State University of New York Press, 1993.

———. "The Visionary Practices of Jewish Apocalyptists." *Psychoanalytic Study of Society* 14 (1989): 119–148.

Meroz, Ronit. "Aspects of the Lurianic Teaching on Prophecy." Master's thesis, Hebrew University, 1980 (in Hebrew).

Mettinger, Tryggve N. D. *The Dethronement of Sabaoth: Studies in the Shem and Kabod Theologies*. Lund: Gleerup. 1982.

Miles, Margaret R. *Image as Insight: Visual Understanding in Western Christianity and Secular Culture*. Boston: Beacon, 1984.

Milik, Jozef T. *The Books of Enoch: Aramaic Fragments of Qumrân Cave 4*. Oxford: Oxford University Press, 1976.

Miller, J. Maxwell. "In the 'Image' and 'Likeness' of God." *Journal of Biblical Literature* 91 (1972): 289–304.

Mirsky, Aaron. *From Duties of the Heart to Songs of the Heart: Jewish Philosophy and Ethics and Their Influence on Hebrew Poetry in Medieval Spain*. Jerusalem: Magnes, 1992 (in Hebrew).

Molé, Marijan. "La dance exstatique en Islam." *Sources Orientales* 6 (1963): 145–280.

Moore, Albert C. "Prophetic Iconoclasm: Judaism and Islam." In *Iconography of Religions: An Introduction*. London: SCM Press, 1977.

Moore, George F. "Intermediaries in Jewish Theology: Memra, Shekinah, Metatron." *Harvard Theological Review* 15 (1922): 41–85.

Moore, Peter. "Mystical Experience, Mystical Doctrine, Mystical Technique." In *Mysticism and Philosophical Analysis*, edited by Steven T. Katz. New York: Oxford University Press, 1978.

Mopsik, Charles. *Lettre sur la sainteté: Le secret de la relation entre l'homme et la femme dans la cabale*. Paris: Verdier, 1986.

———. *Le livre hébreu d'Hénoch ou livre des palais*. Paris: Verdier, 1989.

Morray-Jones, C. R. A. "Transformational Mysticism in the Apocalyptic-Merkabah Tradition." *Journal of Jewish Studies* 43 (1992): 1–31.

Moutsopoulos, E. A. *Le problème de l'imaginaire chez Plotin*. Athens, 1980.

———. *Les structures de l'imaginaire dans la philosophie de Proclus*. Paris: Belles Lettres, 1985.

Nasr, Seyyed Hossein. *An Introduction to Islamic Cosmological Doctrines*. Boulder: Shambala, 1978.

Neher, André. "Le voyage mystique des quatre." *Revue de l'Histoire des Religions* 140 (1951): 59–82.

Nemoy, Leon. "Al-Qirqisani's Account of the Jewish Sects and Christianity." *Hebrew Union College Annual* 7 (1930): 317–397.

Neumann, Erich. *The Origins and History of Consciousness*. Princeton: Princeton University Press, 1973.

Neumark, David. *History of Jewish Philosophy,* 2 vols. New York: Stybel, 1921 (in Hebrew).

Neusner, Jacob. "The Development of the Merkavah Tradition." *Journal for the Study of Judaism* 2 (1971): 149–160.

———. *The Incarnation of God: The Character of Divinity in Formative Judaism*. Philadelphia: Fortress, 1988.

———. *Symbol and Theology in Early Judaism*. Minneapolis: Fortress, 1991.

Newby, Gordon D. *A History of the Jews of Arabia from Ancient Times to Their Eclipse under Islam*. Columbia, South Carolina: University of Carolina Press, 1988.

Newson, Carol. "'He Has Established for Himself Priests': Human and Angelic Priesthood in the Qumran Sabbath Shirot." In *Archaeology and History in the Dead Sea Scrolls: The New York University Conference in Memory of Yigael Yadin,* edited by Lawrence H. Schiffman. Sheffield: JSOT Press, 1990.

———. *Songs of the Sabbath Sacrifice: A Critical Edition*. Harvard Semitic Studies, no. 27. Atlanta: Scholars Press, 1985.

Nicholson, Ernest W. "The Antiquity of the Tradition in Exodus XXIV 9–11." *Vetus Testamentum* 25 (1975): 69–79.

———. "The Interpretation of Exodus XXIV 9–11." *Vetus Testamentum* 24 (1974): 77–97.

Nicholson, Graeme. *Seeing and Reading*. Atlantic Highlands, N.J.: Humanities Press, 1984.

———. "Seeing and Reading: Aspects of Their Connection." In *Hermeneutics and Deconstruction,* edited by Hugh J. Silverman and Don Ihde. Albany, State University of New York Press, 1985.

Nicholson, Reynold A. *Studies in Islamic Mysticism*. Cambridge: Cambridge University Press, 1967.

Nickelsburg, George W. E. "Enoch, Levi, and Peter: Recipients of Revelation in Upper Galilee." *Journal of Biblical Literature* 100 (1981): 575–600.

Niditch, Susan. "The Visionary." In *Ideal Figures in Ancient Judaism,* edited by George W. E. Nickelsburg and John J. Collins. Chico, Calif.: Scholars Press, 1980.

Olyan, Saul M. *A Thousand Thousands Served Him: Exegesis and the Naming of Angels in Ancient Judaism*. Tübingen: Mohr, 1993.

Ong, Walter. *The Presence of the Word*. Minneapolis: Minnesota University Press, 1967.

Orfali, Moises. "Anthropomorphism in the Christian Reproach of the Jews in Spain (12th–15th Century)." *Immanuel* 19 (1984–85): 60–73.

Oron, Michal. "Dream, Vision, and Reality in Ḥaim Vital's *Sefer ha-Ḥezyonot*." *Jerusalem Studies in Jewish Thought* 10 (1992): 299–310 (in Hebrew).
Pagis, Dan. "The Poet as Prophet in Medieval Hebrew Literature." In *Poetry and Prophecy,* edited by James L. Kugel. Ithaca: Cornell University Press, 1990.
Parnes, A. "The Mentioning of the Name in the Poetry of Solomon ibn Gabirol." *Kenesset* 7 (1942): 280–293 (in Hebrew).
Patai, Raphael. *Water: Research into the Knowledge of the Palestinian Land and Folklore in the Biblical and Mishnaic Periods.* Tel-Aviv, 1936 (in Hebrew).
Patte, Daniel. *Early Jewish Hermeneutic in Palestine.* SBL Dissertation Series, no. 22. Missoula, Mont.: Scholars Press, 1975.
Pedaya, Ḥaviva. "'Flaw' and 'Correction' in the Concept of the Godhead in the Teachings of Rabbi Isaac the Blind." *Jerusalem Studies in Jewish Thought* 6:3–4 (1987): 157–220 (in Hebrew).
———. "The Provençal Stratum in the Redaction of *Sefer ha-Bahir,*" *Jerusalem Studies in Jewish Thought* 9 (1990): 139–164 (in Hebrew).
———. "The Spiritual vs. the Concrete Land of Israel in the Geronese School of Kabbalah." In *The Land of Israel in Medieval Jewish Thought,* edited by Moshe Hallamish and Aviezer Ravitzky. Jerusalem: Yad Izhak Ben-Zvi, 1991 (in Hebrew).
Pelikan, Jaroslav. *Imago Dei: The Byzantine Apologia for Icons.* Bollingen Series xxxv.36. Princeton: Princeton University Press, 1990.
Pespres, D. "Franciscan Spirituality: Margery Kempe and Visual Meditation." *Mystics Quarterly* 11 (1984): 12–18.
Pines, Shlomo. "God, the Divine Glory, and the Angels According to a Second-Century Theology." *Jerusalem Studies in Jewish Thought* 6:1–2 (1987): 1–14 (in Hebrew).
———. "'He Called Forth to the Nothing and It Split': Research on the *Keter Malkhut* of Solomon ibn Gabirol." *Tarbiz* 50 (1982): 339–347 (in Hebrew).
———. "La longue recension de la Théologie d'Aristotle dans ses rapports avec la doctrine ismaélienne." *Revue des Études Islamiques* (1955): 7–20.
———. "On the Term *Ruḥaniyyot* and Its Origin and on Judah Halevi's Doctrine," *Tarbiz* 57 (1988): 511–540 (in Hebrew).
———. "Points of Similarity between the Exposition of the Doctrine of the Sefirot in the Sefer Yeẓira and a Text of the Pseudo-Clementine Homilies." *Proceedings of the Israeli Academy of Sciences and Humanities* 7 (1989): 63–142.
———. "Shiʿite Terms and Conceptions in Judah Halevi's *Kuzari*." *Jerusalem Studies in Arabic and Islam* 2 (1980): 165–251.
———. "A Tenth Century Philosophical Correspondence." *Proceedings of the American Academy of Jewish Research* 24 (1955): 103–136.
Porton, Gary. "Midrash: Palestinian Jews and the Hebrew Bible in the Greco-Roman Period." In *Aufstieg und Niedergang der Römischen Welt* II.19.2 (1979): 104–138.
Prigent, Pierre. *Le Judaïsme et l'image.* Tübingen: Mohr, 1990.
Quispel, Gilles. "The Demiurge in the Apocryphon of John." In *Nag Hammadi and Gnosis,* edited by R. McL. Wilson. Leiden: Brill, 1978.
———. "The Discussion of Judaic Christianity." In *Gnostic Studies,* vol. 2. Istanbul: Nederlands Historisch-Archaologisch Instituut in het Nabije Oosten, 1975.
———. "Gnosticism and the New Testament." In *The Bible and Modern Scholarship,* edited by J. P. Hyatt. Nashville: Abingdon, 1965.
———. "Judaism, Judaic Christianity, and Gnosis." In *The New Testament and Gnosis: Essays in Honour of Robert McL. Wilson,* edited by A. H. B. Logan and A. J. M. Wedderburn. Edinburgh: Clark, 1983.

———. "The Origins of the Gnostic Demiurge." In *Kyriakon: Festschrift Johannes Quaesten,* edited by P. Granfield and J. A. Jungman. Münster: Aschendorff, 1970.
Rad, Gerhard von. *Genesis: A Commentary.* Philadelphia: Westminster, 1973.
———. *Old Testament Theology.* Vol. 1, *The Theology of Israel's Historical Traditions.* Translated by D. M. G. Stalker. New York: Harper & Row, 1962.
Rahman, Fazlur. *Prophecy in Islam: Philosophy and Orthodoxy.* London: Allen & Unwin, 1958.
Raschke, Carl, and Donna Gregory. "Revelation, the Poetic Imagination, and the Archaeology of the Feminine." In *The Archaeology of the Imagination,* edited by Charles E. Winquist. Special issue of *Journal of the American Academy of Religion Thematic Studies* 48/2, 1981.
Razhabi, Yehuda. "Borrowed Elements in the Poems of Yehudah Halevi from Arabic Poetry and Philosophy." *Molad* 5 (1975): 165–175 (in Hebrew).
Reisel, M. *The Mysterious Name of Y.H.W.H.* Assen: Van Gorcum, 1957.
Renwick, David A. *Paul, the Temple, and the Presence of God.* Atlanta: Scholars Press, 1991.
Ricoeur, Paul. *Hermeneutics and Human Sciences.* Cambridge: Cambridge University Press, 1981.
———. "L'imagination dans le discours et dans l'action." In *Du texte à l'action.* Paris: Editions du Seuil, 1986.
Rohrbacher-Sticker, Claudia. "Die Namen Gottes und die Namen Meṭaṭrons: Zwei Geniza-Fragmente zur Hekhalot-Literatur." *Franfurter Judaistische Beiträge* 19 (1991–92): 95–168.
Rolfson, H. "Images of God in the Mystics." *Mystics Quarterly* 14 (1988): 123–134.
Rosenstreich, Nathan. "Symbolism and Transcendence: On Some Philosophical Aspects of Gershom Scholem's Opus." *Review of Metaphysics* (1977): 604–614.
Rosenthal, Franz. *Knowledge Triumphant: The Concept of Knowledge in Medieval Islam.* Leiden: Brill, 1970.
———. "Some Pythagorean Documents Transmitted in Arabic." *Orientalia* 10 (1941): 104–115.
Ross-Bryant, Lynn. "Imagination and the Re-Valorization of the Feminine." In *The Archaeology of the Imagination,* edited by Charles E. Winquist. Special issue of *Journal of the American Academy of Religion Thematic Studies* 48/2, 1981.
Röttger, H. *Mal'ak Jahwe—Bote von Gott.* Frankfurt am Main, 1978.
Rowland, Christopher. *The Open Heaven: A Study of Apocalyptic in Judaism and Early Christianity.* New York: Crossroad, 1982.
———. "The Visions of God in Apocalyptic Literature." *Journal for the Study of Judaism* 10 (1979): 137–154.
———. "The Vision of the Risen Christ in Rev. 1:13ff.: The Debt of Early Christology to an Aspect of Jewish Angelology." *Journal of Theological Studies* 31 (1980): 1–11.
Ruderman, David B. *A Valley of Vision: The Heavenly Journey of Abraham ben Hananiah Yagel.* Philadelphia: University of Pennsylvania Press, 1990.
Russell, David S. *The Method and Message of Jewish Apocalyptic.* Philadelphia: Westminster, 1964.
Sanders, E. P. "The Genre of Palestinian Jewish Apocalypses." In *Apocalypticism in the Mediterranean World and the Near East: Proceedings of the International Colloquium on Apocalypticism. Uppsala, August 12–17, 1979.* Edited by David Hellholm. 2d ed. Tübinger: Mohr, 1989.

Sawyer, John F. A. "The Meaning of 'In the Image of God' in Genesis I–XI." *Journal of Theological Studies* 25 (1974): 418–426.

Schäfer, Peter, ed. *Geniza-Fragmente zur Hekhalot-Literatur.* Tübingen: Mohr, 1984.

———. *Hekhalot-Studien.* Tübingen: Mohr, 1988.

———. *The Hidden and Manifest God: Some Major Themes in Early Jewish Mysticism.* Translated by Aubrey Pomerance. Albany: State University of New York Press, 1992.

———. "The Ideal of Piety of the Ashkenazi Hasidim and Its Root in Jewish Tradition." *Jewish History* 4 (1990): 9–23.

———. "Jewish Magic Literature in Late Antiquity and Early Middle Ages." *Journal of Jewish Studies* 41 (1990): 75–91.

———. "The Problem of the Redactionist Identity of 'Hekhalot Rabbati.'" *Jerusalem Studies in Jewish Thought* 6:1–2 (1987): 1–12 (in Hebrew).

———. "Research on Hekhalot Literature: Where Do We Stand Now?" in *Rashi, 1040–1990: Hommage à Ephraïm E. Urbach,* ed. Gabrielle Sed-Ranja. Paris: Cerf, 1993.

——— et al., eds. *Synopse zur Hekhalot-Literatur.* Tübingen: Mohr, 1981.

——— et al., trans. *Übersetzung der Hekhalot-Literatur.* vol. 3. Tübingen: Mohr, 1989.

Scheindlin, Raymond P. *The Gazelle: Medieval Hebrew Poems on God, Israel, and the Soul.* Philadelphia: Jewish Publication Society of America, 1991.

———. "Redemption of the Soul in Golden Age Religious Poetry." *Prooftexts* 10 (1990): 49–67.

Schiffman, Lawrence H. *The Eschatological Community of the Dead Sea Scrolls.* Atlanta: Scholars Press, 1989.

———. "The Recall of Rabbi Neḥuniah ben ha-Qanah from Ecstasy in the *Hekhalot Rabbati.*" *Association for Jewish Studies Review* 1 (1976): 269–281.

———. *Sectarian Law in the Dead Sea Scroll: Courts, Testimony and the Penal Code.* Chico, Calif.: Scholars Press, 1983.

Schimmel, Annemarie. *Mystical Dimensions of Islam.* Chapel Hill: University of North Carolina Press, 1975.

Schofield, Malcolm. "Aristotle on the Imagination." In *Aristotle on Mind and the Senses,* edited by G. E. R. Loyd and G. E. I. Owen. Cambridge & New York: Cambridge University Press, 1978.

Scholem, Gershom. "Cheiromancy in the Zohar." *The Quest* 17 (1926): 255–256.

———. "Colours and Their Symbolism in Jewish Tradition and Mysticism." *Diogenes* 108 (1979): 84–111; 109 (1980): 64–76.

———. "The Concept of Kavvanah in the Early Kabbalah." In *Studies in Jewish Thought: An Anthology of German Jewish Scholarship,* edited by Alfred Jospe. Detroit: Wayne State University Press, 1981.

———. *The Dreams of R. Mordecai Ashkenazi, A follower of Shabbetai Zevi.* Jerusalem: Schocken, 1938 (in Hebrew).

———. *Elements of the Kabbalah and Its Symbolism.* Translated by Joseph Ben-Shlomo. Jerusalem: Bialik Institute, 1976 (in Hebrew).

———. "Ein Fragment zur Physiognomik und Chiromantik aus der Tradition der spätantiken jüdischen Esoterik." In *Liber amicorum: Studies in Honor of Professor Dr. C. J. Bleeker.* Leiden: Brill, 1969.

———. *Explications and Implications: Writings on Jewish Heritage and Renaissance,* edited by Avraham Shapira, vol. 2. Tel-Aviv: Am Oved, 1989 (in Hebrew).

———. "Index to the Commentaries on the Ten *Sefirot*." *Qiryat Sefer* 10 (1933–34): 498–515 (in Hebrew).
———. *Jewish Gnosticism, Merkabah Mysticism, and Talmudic Tradition*. New York: Jewish Theological Seminary of America, 1965.
———. *Kabbalah*. Jerusalem: Keter, 1974.
———. *Le-Ḥeqer Qabbalat R. Yiṣḥaq ben Ya'aqov ha-Kohen*. Jerusalem, 1934.
———. "La lutte entre le Dieu de Plotin et la Bible dans la Kabbale Ancienne." In *Le nom de dieu et les symbols de Dieu dans la mystique juive*, translated by Maurice Hayoun and George Vajda. Paris: Verdier, 1983.
———. *Major Trends in Jewish Mysticism*. New York: Schocken, 1956.
———. "The Name of God and the Linguistic Theory of the Kabbalah." *Diogenes* 79 (1972): 59–80; 80 (1972): 164–194.
———. *On Jews and Judaism in Crisis*. Edited by Werner J. Dannhauser. New York: Schocken, 1976.
———. *On the Kabbalah and Its Symbolism*. Translated by Ralph Manheim. New York: Schocken, 1969.
———. *On the Mystical Shape of the Godhead: Basic Concepts in the Kabbalah*. Translated by Joachim Neugroschel, edited by Jonathan Chipman. New York: Schocken, 1991.
———. *Origins of the Kabbalah*. Translated by Allan Arkush, edited by R. J. Zwi Werblowsky. Princeton: Princeton University Press, 1987.
———. *Reshit ha-Qabbalah*. Jersualem & Tel-Aviv: Schocken, 1948.
———. "Reste neuplatonischer Spekulation in der Mystik der deutschen Chassidim und ihre Vermittlung durch Abraham bar Chija." *Monatsschrift für Geschichte und Wissenschaft des Judentums* 75 (1931): 172–191.
———. "Schöpfung aus Nichts und Selbstverschränkung Gottes." In *Über einige Grundbegriffe des Judentums*. Frankfurt am Main, 1970.
———. "Traces of Gabirol in the Kabbalah." *Me'assef Sofre 'Ereṣ Yisra'el*. Jerusalem, 1940 (in Hebrew).
———. "The Traditions of R. Jacob and R. Isaac ben Jacob ha-Kohen." *Madda'e ha-Yahadut* 2 (1927): 165–293 (in Hebrew).
———. "Eine unbekannte mystische Schrift des Mose de Leon." *Monatsschrift für Geschichte und Wissenschaft des Judentums* 71 (1927): 109–123.
Schubert, Kurt. "Jewish Pictorial Traditions in Early Christian Art." In *Jewish Historiography and Iconography in Early and Medieval Christianity*, edited by Heinz Schreckenberg and Kurt Schubert. Flusser Compendia Rerum Iudaicarum ad Novum Testamentum. Assen & Maastricht: Van Gorcum, 1992.
Schülter, Margaret. "Die Erzählung von der Rückholung des R. Neḥunya ben Haqana aus der Merkava-Schau in ihrem redaktionellen Rahmen." *Frankfurter Judaistische Beiträge* 10 (1982): 65–109.
Schüssler Fiorenza, Elisabeth. "The Phenomenon of Early Christian Apocalyptic: Some Reflections on Method." In *Apocalypticism in the Mediterranean World and the Near East: Proceedings of the International Colloquium on Apocalypticism. Uppsala, August 12–17, 1979*, Edited by David Hellholm. 2d ed. Tübingen: Mohr, 1989.
Schweid, Eliezer. *Judaism and Mysticism According to Gershom Scholem: A Criticial Analysis and Programmatic Discussion*. Translated with introduction by David A. Weiner. Atlanta: Scholars Press, 1985.
Séd Nicolas. "Les traditions secrètes et les disciples de Rabbanan Yoḥanan ben Zakkai." *Revue de l'Histoire des Religions* 184 (1973): 49–66.

———. "Le Sefer Yeṣira: L'édition critique, le texte primitif, la grammaire, et la métaphysique," *Revue des Études Juives* 132 (1973): 513–528.

Sed-Rajna, Gabrielle. "L'influence de Jean Scot sur la doctrine du kabbaliste Azriel de Gérone." In *Jean Scot Érigène et l'histoire de la philosophie: ⟨Colloque⟩ Laon, 7–12 juillet 1975*. Paris: Centre national de la recherche scientifique, 1977.

Segal, Alan. "Heavenly Ascent in Hellenistic Judaism, Early Christianity, and Their Environment." *Aufstieg und Niedergang der Römischen Welt* II.23.2 (1980): 1333–1394.

———. *Rebecca's Children: Judaism and Christianity in the Roman World*. Cambridge, Mass.: Harvard University Press, 1986.

———. *Two Powers in Heaven: Early Rabbinic Reports about Christianity and Gnosticism*. Leiden: Brill, 1977.

Sells, Michael. "Apophasis in Plotinus: A Critical Approach." *Harvard Theological Review* 78 (1985): 47–65.

———. "Bewildered Tongue: The Semantics of Mystical Union in Islam." In *Mystical Union and Monotheistic Faith: An Ecumenical Dialogue,* edited by Moshe Idel and Bernard McGinn. New York: Macmillan, 1989.

Septimus, Bernard. *Hispano-Jewish Culture in Transition*. Cambridge, Mass.: Harvard University Press, 1982.

Sermoneta, Giuseppe. "La fantasia e l'attività fantastica nei testi filosofici della Maimonide." In *Phantasia-Imaginatio: V° Colloqui Internazionale, Rome 9–11 gennaio 1986*, edited by Marta Fattori and Massimo Bianchi. Rome: Edizioni dell'Ateneo, 1986.

Sevrin, J.-M. "Les noces spirituelles dans l'Evangile selon Philippe." *Le Muséon* 87 (1974): 143–193.

Sharf, Andrew, *Byzantine Jewry from Justinian to the Fourth Crusade,* London: Routledge & Kegan Paul, 1971.

———. *The Universe of Shabbetai Donnolo*. New York: Ktav, 1976.

Sherif, Mohamed A. *Ghazali's Theory of Virtue*. Albany: Sate University of New York Press, 1975.

Shokek, Shimon. "The Affinity of Sefer ha-Yashar to the Circle of Geronese Kabbalists." *Jerusalem Studies in Jewish Thought* 6:3–4 (1987): 337–366 (in Hebrew).

Silman, Yoḥanan. *Thinker and Seer: The Development of the Thought of R. Yehuda Halevi in the Kuzari*. Bar-Ilan: Bar-Ilan University Press, 1985 (in Hebrew).

Sirat, Collette. *A History of Jewish Philosophy in the Middle Ages*. Cambridge & New York: Cambridge University Press, 1985.

———. *La lettre hébraïque et sa signification*. Published with Leila Avrin, *Micrography as Art*. Paris: Centre national de la recherche scientifique; Jerusalem: Israel Museum, Department of Judaica, 1981.

———. "Le manuscrit hébreu n⁰ 1408 de la bibliothèque nationale de Paris." *Revue des Études Juives* 123 (1964): 335–358.

———. *Les theóries des visions surnaturelles dans la pensée juive du moyen âge*. Leiden: Brill, 1969.

Sister, Mosheh. "Die Typen der prophetischen Visionen in der Bibel," *Monatsschrift für Geschichte und Wissenschaft des Judentums* 78 (1934): 399–430.

Smith, Jonathan Z. "The Prayer of Joseph." In *Religions in Antiquity: Essays in Memory of Erwin Ramsdell Goodenough,* edited by J. Neusner. Leiden: Brill, 1970.

Smith, Mark A. "'Seeing God' in the Psalms: The Background to the Beatific Vision in the Hebrew Bible." *Catholic Biblical Quarterly* 50 (1988): 171–183.

Smith, Morton. "Ascent to the Heavens and Deification in 4QM." In *Archaeology and History in the Dead Sea Scrolls: The New York University Conference in Memory of Yigael Yadin,* edited by Lawrence H. Schiffman. Sheffield: JSOT Press, 1990.

———. "Ascent to the Heavens and the Beginning of Christianity." *Eranosjahrbuch* 50 (1981): 403–429.

———. "The Image of God." *Bulletin of the John Rylands Library* 40 (1957–58): 474–481.

———. "Observations on *Hekhalot Rabbati.*" In *Biblical and Other Studies,* edited by Alexander Altmann. Cambridge, Mass.: Harvard University Press, 1963.

———. "Two Ascended to Heaven—Jesus and the Author of 4Q491." In *Jesus and the Dead Sea Scrolls,* edited by James H. Charlesworth. New York: Doubleday, 1992.

Stace, Walter T. *Mysticism and Philosophy.* New York: Macmillan, 1960.

Starr, Joshua. *The Jews in the Byzantine Empire.* Athens, 1939.

Stern, David M. "*Imitatio Hominis:* Anthropomorphism and the Character(s) of God in Rabbinic Literature." *Prooftexts* 12 (1992): 151–174.

———. *Parables in Midrash: Narrative and Exegesis in Rabbinic Literature.* Cambridge, Mass.: Harvard University Press, 1991.

Stier, F. *Gott und sein Engel im Alten Testament.* Münster, 1934.

Stone, Michael E. "Apocalyptic Literature." In *Jewish Writings of the Second Temple Period: Apocrypha. Pseudepigrapha, Qumran Sectarian Writings, Philo, Josephus,* edited by Michael E. Stone. Compendia Rerum Iudaicarum ad Novum Testamentum. Assen: Van Gorcum, 1984.

———. "The Armenian Vision of Ezekiel." *Harvard Theological Review* 79 (1986): 261–269.

———. "The Book of Enoch and Judaism in the Third Century, B.C.E." *Catholic Biblical Quarterly* 40 (1978): 479–492.

———. "Lists of Revealed Things in the Apocalyptic Literature." In *Magnalia Dei—The Mighty Acts of God: Essays on the Bible and Archaeology in Memory of G. Ernest Wright,* edited by Frank M. Cross, Werner E. Lemke, and Patrick D. Miller. Garden City, N.Y.: Doubleday, 1976.

Stroumsa, Gedaliahu G. "Form(s) of God: Some Notes on Meṭaṭron and Christ." *Harvard Theological Review* 76 (1983): 269–288.

———. "Polymorphie divine et transformations d'un mythologème: L'apocryphon de Jean et ses sources." *Vigiliae Christianae* 35 (1981): 412–434.

———. Review of I. Gruenwald. *Apocalyptic and Merkavah Mysticism. Numen* 28 (1981): 108–109.

Swartz, Michael. *Mystical Prayer in Ancient Judaism: An Analysis of Maʿaseh Merkavah.* Tübingen: Mohr, 1991.

Tabor, James D. *Things Unutterable: Paul's Ascent to Paradise in its Greco-Roman, Judaic, and Early Christian Contexts.* Lanham, Md.: University Press of America, 1986.

Talmage, Frank. "Apples of Gold: The Inner Meaning of Sacred Texts in Medieval Judaism." In *Jewish Spirituality: From the Bible through the Middle Ages,* edited by Arthur Green, New York: Crossroad, 1987.

Tamar, David. "Messianic Dreams and Visions of R. Ḥayyim Vital." *Shalem: Studies in the History of the Jews in Eretz-Israel* 4 (1984): 211–229 (in Hebrew).

Tanenbaum, Adena. "Beholding the Splendor of the Creator: Philosophical Conceptions of the Soul in the Poetry of Abraham Ibn Ezra." In *Abraham Ibn Ezra and His Age:*

Proceedings of the International Symposium, Madrid, Tudela, Toledo, 1–8 February 1989, edited by Fernando Díaz Esteban. Madrid: Asociación Espanola sw Orientalistas, 1990.

Tarragen, J.-M. de. "La Kapporet est-elle une fiction ou un élément du culte tardif?" *Revue Biblique* 88 (1981): 5–12.

Ta-Shema, Israel. "The Library of the Ashkenazi Sages in the Eleventh and Twelfth Centuries." *Tarbiz* 40 (1985): 298–309 (in Hebrew).

———. "On the Commentary of the Aramaic Piyyuṭim in the Maḥzor Vitry." *Qiryat Sefer* 57 (1982): 707–708 (in Hebrew).

Temple, Richard. *Icons and the Mystical Origins of Christianity.* Shaftesbury, Dorset: Element, 1990.

Terrien, Samuel. *The Elusive Presence: Toward a New Biblical Theology.* New York: Harper & Row, 1978.

Tishby, Isaiah. "The Experiential and Visionary Notations of Rabbi Moses David Valle." *Jerusalem Studies in Jewish Thought* 9 (1990): 441–472 (in Hebrew).

———. *The Wisdom of the Zohar.* Translated by David Goldstein. Oxford: Oxford University Press, 1989.

Trachtenberg, Joshua. *Jewish Magic and Superstition.* New York: Atheneum, 1939.

Uchelen, Nicholus A. van. "Maʿaseh Merkabah in *Sefer Ḥasidim.*" *Jerusalem Studies in Jewish Thought* 6:3–4 (1987): 43–52 (English section).

———. "Tosephta Megillah III, 28: a Tannaitic Text with a Mystic Connotation?" *Jerusalem Studies in Jewish Thought* 6:1–2 (1987): 87–94 (English section).

Uffenheimer, Benjamin. "The Consecration of Isaiah in Rabbinic Exegesis." *Scripta Hierosolymitana* 22 (1971): 233–246.

———. *Prophecy in Ancient Israel.* Jerusalem: Magnes, 1984 (in Hebrew).

———. "The Religious Experience of the Psalmists and the Prophetic Mind." *Immanuel* 21 (1987): 21–23.

Underhill, Evelyn. *Mysticism: A Study in the Nature and Development of Man's Spiritual Consciousness.* London: Methuen, 1930.

Urbach, Ephraim E. "The Homiletical Interpretations of the Sages and the Expositions of Origen on Canticles, and the Jewish-Christian Dispuation." *Scripta Hierosolymitana* 22 (1971): 247–275.

———. *The Sages: Their Concepts and Beliefs.* Jerusalem: Magnes, 1969 (in Hebrew).

———. "The Traditions about Merkabah Mysticism in the Tannaitic Period." In *Studies in Mysticism and Religion Presented to Gershom G. Scholem* (Hebrew section). Jerusalem: Magnes, 1967.

Ur-Rahman, Mutazid Waliur. "Al-Farabi and His Theory of Dreams." *Islamic Culture* 41 (1967): 137–151.

Vajda, Georges. "Le commentaire de Saadia sur le Sefer Yeçira." *Revue des Études Juives* 106 (1941): 64–86.

———. "Le commentaire kairouanais sur le 'Livre de la Création." *Revue des Études Juives* 107 (1946–47): 99–156.

———. "De quelques vestiges du néoplatonisme dans la kabbale archaïque et mystique juive franco-germanique." In *Sages et penseurs sépharades de Bagdad à Cordoue,* edited by Jean Jolivet and Maurice R. Hayoun. Paris: Cerf, 1989.

———. "De Quelques infiltrations chrétiennes dans l'oeuvre d'un auteur Anglo-Juif de XIIIe siècle." *Archives d'Histoire Doctrinale et Litteraire du Moyen Age* 28 (1961): 15–34.

———. "Le problème de l'unité de Dieu d'après Dawud ibn Marwan al-Muqammis." In *Jewish Medieval and Renaissance Studies,* edited by Alexander Altmann. Cambridge, Mass.: Harvard University Press, 1967.

———. "Saʿadya commentateur du 'Livre de la Création." *Annuaire de l'Ecole Pratique des Hautes Études, Sciences Religieuses* (1959–60): 4–35. Reprinted in *Mélanges Georges Vajda,* edited by G. Weil. Hildesheim, 1982.

Verman, Mark. *The Books of Contemplation: Medieval Jewish Mystical Sources.* Albany: State University of New York Press, 1992.

———. "The Development of Yiḥudim in Spanish Kabbalah." *Jerusalem Studies in Jewish Thought* 8 (1989): 25–41 (English section).

Wacholder, Ben-Zion, and Steven Bowman. "Ezechielus the Dramatist and Ezekiel the Prophet: Is the Mysterious ζωον in the 'Εξαγωγη a Phoenix?" *Harvard Theological Review* 78 (1985): 253–277.

Walzer, Richard. "Al-Farabi's Theory of Prophecy and Divination." In *Greek into Arabic: Essays on Islamic Philosophy.* Oxford: Cassirer, 1962.

Warren, Edward W. "Imagination in Plotinus." *Classical Quarterly* 16 (1966): 277–285.

Wasserstrom, Steven M. "The Moving Finger Writes: Mughīra b. Saʿīd's Islamic Gnosis and the Myths of Its Rejection." *History of Religions* 25 (1985): 1–29.

———. "*Sefer Yeṣira* and Early Islam: A Reappraisal," *Journal of Jewish Thought and Philosophy* 3 (1993): 1–30.

Weinfeld, M. *Deuteronomy and the Deuteronomic School.* Oxford: Clarendon Press, 1972.

———. "God the Creator in Gen. I and in the Prophecy of Second Isaiah." *Tarbiz* 37 (1968): 105–132 (in Hebrew).

Weinstock, Israel. "A Clarification of the Version of *Sefer Yeṣirah.*" In *Temirin: Texts and Studies in Kabbala and Hasidism,* Edited by Israel Weinstock, vol. 1. Jerusalem: Mosad ha-Rav Kook, 1972 (in Hebrew).

Wensinck, Arent J. *The Muslim Creed: Its Genesis and Historical Development.* New York, 1932.

Werblowsky, R. J. Zwi. *Joseph Karo: Lawyer and Mystic.* 2d ed. Philadelphia: Jewish Publication Society of America, 1977.

———. "On the Mystical Rejection of Mystical Illumination." *Iyyun* 14–15 (1963–64): 205–212 (in Hebrew).

Wilder, Amos. *Early Christian Rhetoric: The Langauge of the Gospel.* Cambridge, Mass.: Harvard University Press, 1971.

Wilson, Robert McL. "Jewish Christianity and Gnosticism." In *Judéo-Christianisme: Recherches historiques et théologiques offertes en hommage au Cardinal Jean Daniélou.* Paris: Recherches de Science Religieuse, 1972.

Winston, David. *Logos and Mystical Theology in Philo of Alexandria.* Cincinnati: Hebrew Union College Press, 1985.

———. "Was Philo a Mystic?" In *Studies in Jewish Mysticism,* edited by Joseph Dan and Frank Talmage. Cambridge, Mass.: Association for Jewish Studies, 1982.

Wolfson, Elliot R. "Anthropomorphic Imagery and Letter Symbolism in the Zohar." *Jerusalem Studies in Jewish Thought* 8 (1990): 147–182 (in Hebrew).

———. "Beautiful Maiden without Eyes: *Peshaṭ* and *Sod* in Zoharic Hermeneutics." In *The Midrashic Imagination,* edited by Michael Fishbane. Albany: State University of New York Press, 1993.

———. "By Way of Truth: Aspects of Naḥmanides' Kabbalistic Hermeneutic." *Association for Jewish Studies Review* 14 (1989): 103–178.

———. "Circumcision and the Divine Name: A Study in the Transmission of Esoteric Doctrine." *Jewish Quarterly Review* 78 (1987): 77–112.

———. "Circumcision, Vision of God, and Textual Interpretation: From Midrashic Trope to Mystical Symbol." *History of Religions* 27 (1987): 189–215.

———. "Erasing the Erasure/Gender and the Writing of God's Body in Kabbalistic Symbolism." In *Circle in the Square: Studies in the Use of Gender in Kabbalistic Symbolism.* Albany: State University of New York Press, 1995. Abridged translation by Jean-Christophe Attias, "Effacer l'effacement/sexe et ecriture du corps divin dans le symbolisme kabbalistique." In *Transmission et passages en monde juif,* edited by Esther Benbassa. Paris: Cerf, forthcoming.

———. "Female Imaging of the Torah: From Literary Metaphor to Religious Symbol." In *From Ancient Israel to Modern Judaism—Intellect in Quest of Understanding: Essays in Honor of Marvin Fox,* edited by Jacob Neusner, Ernst S. Frerichs, and Nahum M. Sarna, vol. 2. Atlanta: Scholars Press, 1989.

———. "Forms of Visionary Ascent as Ecstatic Experience in Zoharic Literature." In *Gershom Scholem's Major Trends in Jewish Mysticism, 50 Years After: Proceedings of the Sixth International Conference on the History of Jewish Mysticism,* edited by Peter Schäfer and Joseph Dan. Tübingen: Mohr, 1993.

———. "God, the Demiurge and the Intellect: On the Usage of the Word *Kol* in Abraham ibn Ezra." *Revue des Études Juives* 149 (1990): 77–111.

———. "The Image of Jacob Engraved upon the Throne: Further Speculation on the Esoteric Doctrine of the German Pietists." In *Massu'ot: Studies in Kabbalistic Literature and Jewish Philosophy in Memory of Prof. Ephraim Gottlieb,* edited by Michal Oron and Amos Goldreich. Jerusalem: Bialik Institute, 1994 (in Hebrew). Revised, expanded English version in *Along the Path: Studies in Kabbalistic Myth, Symbolism and Hermeneutics.* Albany: State University of New York Press, 1995.

———. "Images of God's Feet: Some Observations on the Divine Body in Judaism." In *People of the Body: Jews and Judaism in Embodied Perspective,* edited by Howard Eilberg-Schwartz. Albany: State University of New York Press, 1992.

———. "Letter Symbolism and Merkavah Imagery in the Zohar." In *ʿAlei Shefer: Studies in the Literature of Jewish Thought Presented to Rabbi Dr. Alexandre Safran* (English section), edited by Moseh Ḥallamish. Ramat-Gan: Bar-Ilan University Press, 1990.

———. "Merkavah Traditions in Philosophical Garb: Judah Halevi Reconsidered." *Proceedings of the American Academy for Jewish Research* 57 (1991): 179–242.

———. "Mystical Rationalization of the Commandments in *Sefer ha-Rimmon.*" *Hebrew Union College Annual* 59 (1988): 217–251.

———. "The Mystical Significance of Torah-Study in German Pietism." *Jewish Quarterly Review* 84 (1993): 43–78.

———. "Mystical-Theurgical Dimensions of Prayer in *Sefer ha-Rimmon.*" In *Approaches to Judaism in Medieval Times,* edited by David R. Blumental, vol. 3. Atlanta: Scholars Press, 1988.

———. "Negative Theology and Positive Assertion in the Early Kabbalah." *Daʿat* 32–33 (1994): v–xxii.

———. "The Problem of Unity in the Thought of Martin Buber." *Journal of the History of Philosophy* 27 (1989): 419–439.

———. Review of David J. Halperin, *The Faces of the Chariot: Early Jewish Responses to Ezekiel's Vision. Jewish Quarterly Review* 81 (1990–91): 496–500.

———. Review of Jacob Neusner, *The Incarnation of God: The Character of Divinity in Formative Judaism. Jewish Quarterly Review* 81 (1990–91): 219–222.

———. "The Secret of the Garment in Naḥmanides." *Daʿat* 24 (1990): xxv–xlix.

———. "*Shiʿur Qomah* and Meṭaṭron in the Writings of the German Pietists." In the proceedings of the conference *Mystik, Magie und Kabbala im Aschkenasischen Judentum,* 9–11 Dec. 1991, Frankfurt am Main, Germany (forthcoming).

———. "The Theosophy of Shabbetai Donnolo, with Special Emphasis on the Doctrine of *Sefirot* in His *Sefer Ḥakhmoni.*" *Jewish History* 6 (1992): 281–316.

———. "The Tree That Is All: Jewish-Christian Roots of a Kabbalistic Symbol in *Sefer ha-Bahir.*" *Journal of Jewish Thought and Philosophy* 3 (1993): 31–76.

———. "Weeping, Death, and Spiritual Ascent in Sixteenth-Century Jewish Mysticism." In the proceedings of the conference *Death and Other-Worldly Journeys in Religious Traditions,* University of Chicago, 16–17 May 1991 (forthcoming).

———. "Woman—The Feminine as Other: Some Reflections on the Divine Androgyne in Theosophic Kabbalah." In *The Other in Jewish Thought and History: Constructions of Jewish Culture and Identity,* edited by L. Silberstein and R. Cohn. New York: New York University Press, 1994.

———. "*Yeridah la-Merkavah:* Typology of Ecstasy and Enthronement in Ancient Jewish Mysticism." In *Mystics of the Book: Themes, Topics, and Typologies,* edited by Robert A. Herrera. New York: Lang, 1993.

Wolfson, Harry A. *Crescas' Critique of Aristotle.* Cambridge, Mass.: Harvard University Press, 1929.

———. *Philo: Foundations of Religious Philosophy in Judaism, Christianity, and Islam.* 2 vols. Cambridge, Mass.: Harvard University Press, 1947.

———. "The Preexistent Angel of the Magharians and al-Nahawandi." *Jewish Quarterly Review* 51 (1960–61): 89–106.

———. *Studies in the History of Philosophy and Religion.* Edited by Isadore Twersky and George H. Williams. 2 vols. Cambridge, Mass.: Harvard University Press, 1973.

Yarian, Stanley O. "In the Eye of the Beholder: Visual Perception, Religious Experience, and Hermeneutics." In *The Seeing Eye: Hermeneutical Phenomenology in the Study of Religion,* edited by Walter L. Brenneman, Jr., and Stanley O. Yarian, with Alan M. Olson. University Park: Pennsylvania State University Press, 1982.

———. "Mircea Eliade: Creative Hermeneutics as a Spiritual Discipline." In *The Seeing Eye* (see above).

Zimmer, Eric. "Men's Headcovering: The Metamorphosis of This Practice." In *Reverence, Righteousness, and Rahamanut: Essays in Memory of Rabbi Dr. Leo Jung,* edited by Jacob J. Schachter. Northvale, N.J.: Jason Aronson, 1992.

———. "Poses and Postures during Prayer." *Sidra* 5 (1989): 89–130 (in Hebrew).

• *INDEX* •